icago

D1415013

DISCARD

As Others See Chicago

Impressions of Visitors, 1673–1933

COMPILED AND EDITED BY
BESSIE LOUISE PIERCE

WITH THE ASSISTANCE OF
JOE L. NORRIS

WITH A NEW FOREWORD BY
PERRY R. DUIS

THE UNIVERSITY OF CHICAGO PRESS
CHICAGO, ILLINOIS

The University of Chicago Press, Chicago 60637
The University of Chicago Press, Ltd., London

13 12 11 10 09 08 07 06 05 04   1 2 3 4 5

ISBN: 0-226-66821-5 (paper)

Library of Congress Cataloging-in-Publication Data

As others see Chicago : impressions of visitors, 1673–1933 / compiled and
  edited by Bessie Louise Pierce ; with the assistance of Joe L. Norris ;
  with a new foreword by Perry R. Duis.
     p. cm.
  ISBN 0-226-66821-5 (alk. paper)
     1. Chicago (Ill.)—Description and travel—Sources. 2. Chicago (Ill.)—
  Social life and customs—Sources. 3. Chicago (Ill.)—History—Sources.
  4. Visitors, Foreign—Illinois—Chicago. 5. Travelers' writings. I. Pierce,
  Bessie Louise, 1888–1974. II. Norris, Joe Lester, 1906–

  F548.3.A8 2004
  977.3′111—dc22

                                                                    2003026813

CONTENTS

CONTENTS

CONTENTS

CONTENTS

FOREWORD TO THE 2004 EDITION

TRAVELERS' accounts claim a special place among the historian's sources. The writings of strangers have often left the most vivid and offbeat impressions of America and its national personality and everyday life. Alexis de Tocqueville and Lord James Bryce were like psychologists who revealed to Americans the mysteries of their national inner selves. Less famous visitors who spent even limited amounts of time in cities and towns often made the most cogent observations because they regarded nothing that they saw as routine or expected. Like the fable of the Emperor's New Clothes, it often takes someone of innocence—in this case an outsider—to utter what should have been obvious to everyone but wasn't. The more removed from the subject the visitors are, the more insightful their comments often are. Travelers' accounts also have a certain allure because their serendipitous nature reflects the varied personalities of their writers.

VISITORS

As Others See Chicago grew from the publications of over a thousand European and American strangers who passed through the city on their way across America and then penned accounts of their visits. These were not typical tourists. Because most planned from the beginning to write about their experiences, they were especially aware of their environment. A few of the wealthiest travelers privately published their accounts for the benefit of family and friends, and some paused to record their observations while traveling primarily for some other purpose. But during the nineteenth century professional authors knew that there was always a large commercial market for travelers' accounts. Improvements in ships and railroad trains, along with the rise of the travel agent, not only made travel faster, cheaper, and more comfortable, but this easy access to tourism also enlarged the audience of armchair travelers who preferred to read about it instead.

Travelers' accounts were never complete pictures of the city, and collections of them present a view of the world that passed through several filters. The first is what the traveler saw and regarded as worth recording in diaries and notes; much of this information doubtless failed to make it to the printed word because an editor of the original publication found it extraneous or repetitive. The next filter was the editor of the travel compilation, who decided not only which visitors were worth reprinting, but also which passages of their works were most perceptive or descriptive. Sometimes such factors as the editor's ability to translate languages other than French, German, or Italian determined what the compilation reader eventually saw. In the case of *As Others See Chicago*, Bessie Louise Pierce's selections were probably longer and contained more perceptive observations than the brief descriptions of the city that were found in most other compilations.

The traveling writers' views of Chicago were also shaped by such factors as the length of the visit, the presence of celebrities, and the experience of following the usual pathways that strangers often followed through cities. Timetables invariably controlled arrival and departure, with a stay of so many days budgeted in between. The sense that a clock was ticking often affected travelers' perspectives. Their comments commonly included either the wish that they could have stayed longer or the regret that they had not departed sooner. Those on the tightest schedules tended to move along narrow travelers' paths that followed a common pattern. First came the arrival experience and the encounter with the gateway into the city, the railroad station. Unless the visitor was famous enough to warrant a greeting party, the arrival was followed by the cab trip—which was often coupled with a comment on drivers—through the public streets to the hotel. Then came the description of the accommodations and the dining experience (sometimes a nasty encounter with an inedible beefsteak swimming in fat). Brief visits were also largely confined to semipublic urban spaces. These were the privately owned but publicly accessible railroad trains, stations, theaters, hotels, and restaurants. Somewhat longer stays in town allowed time for additional accounting of the streets, parks, and major public buildings. Finally, lengthier visits often made it possible for the outsider to come in contact with Chicagoans of a similar class. This was one way the visitor could penetrate the barrier between public and private life. Wealthy, famous, or powerful travelers more quickly found themselves in the company of the local elite, and accounts of these travels frequently reflected the writers' absorption of business leaders' viewpoint about the town, including a booster's sense of predestined growth.

All of this is relevant to modern research into tourism and the postindustrial economy, especially regarding the issue of authenticity. The visitors thought that they were encountering the "real" Chicago, but were they? Because they were traveling individually instead of as part of a large group, travelers seldom altered the Chicago environment. (That happened only when someone as notable as the Prince of Wales came to town.) It is interesting that there were legends that Jenny Lind and Charles Dickens had visited Chicago, although neither had.

The short duration of most travel experiences also contributed to the creation of the urban stereotypes that were a common feature of visitors' accounts. As sociologist Anselm Strauss has noted, when humans are confronted with a complex set of often contradictory images and facts they tend to convert them into oversimplified impressions and stereotypes.[1] Thus travelers' accounts were often impressionistic because their stay was short, and this encouraged them to focus on particular things out of a bewildering maze of complex images. It is clear from several of Pierce's selections that an initial impression tended to set the tone for the entire entry.

What short-term visitors failed to notice in their haste was often as interesting as the things they described. Travelers did not have to come to grips with how to live in the city in the way that

---

[1] Anselm L. Strauss, *Images of the American City* (New York: Free Press of Glencoe, 1961).

locals did. Even immigrants passing through the city were forced
to encounter the street life and lower-class life that middle-class
travelers were able to avoid. Seasonality was also a factor; most
voluntary travel was conducted in warmer weather. And as some
of Pierce's selections reveal, the drafty rooms and impassible streets
that greeted wintertime arrivals often contributed to a very different and often more negative perspective of the city.

CHICAGO

A book of travelers' accounts is a most appropriate way to examine a city whose destiny was so dramatically shaped by the arrival
and departure of strangers, and by the receipt and shipment of
commodities. Before it was anything else, the future metropolis
of Chicago was a trading center and the Chicago River itself was
important primarily as a gateway to the water route between the
Great Lakes and the Des Plaines, Illinois, and Mississippi river
systems. Jean Baptiste Point du Sable, reputedly Chicago's first
permanent resident, was a fur trader of West Indian and African
descent who arrived in the late 1770s. His elaborate post, which
grew to over 4,000 square feet of buildings, stood for two decades
on the north side of the mouth of the Chicago River. (Coinci-
dentally, much of what we know about him comes from strangers'
descriptions.) In 1803, three years after Du Sable retired and departed, the federal government erected Fort Dearborn to protect
the strategic spot. After the Black Hawk War of 1832 cleared the
way for white settlement of the region and the rich Northern Illinois farm lands began to produce bountiful grain surpluses, it was
the concentration of hundreds of farmers and wagons at this new
trading hub that caused Americans to take notice of Chicago. The
focus of life in the town was the arrivals and departures at the
riverfront. When thirteen people decided to apply for the first
charter in 1833 they were primarily interested in dividing up the
riverfront dock space. Soon the tall grain elevators and docks to
facilitate loading lake ships bound for New York, as well as the
brick Lake House Hotel, became the dominant structures in
town.

Even though the number of people who traveled for pleasure

was in general small before the late nineteenth century, the difficulties involved in getting to Chicago further filtered out the less
hearty and determined. During the early nineteenth century descriptions of the labor involved in traveling dominated the accounts. Although Pierce edited out the repetitious observations
about the difficulties of getting to Chicago, the journey was often uncomfortable and impeded by weather and accidents. As
Pierce clearly notes, 1848 saw the first steps toward making Chicago a transportation hub. During this time, travelers tended to
follow transportation routes that were developed initially for
freight. The Illinois and Michigan Canal, the first railroad, and
the first telegraph all began operation that year. Chicago could
thus expand its exchange function to include the first stages of
industrialization. Its widening economic grip on the West allowed
it to absorb mountains of wood for millwork and lumber, as well
as live animals for meat that was preserved in salt and shipped
east. Railroads gradually displaced the water-borne commerce to
Eastern markets. The mid-nineteenth-century frenzy of rail construction placed Chicago at the center of an iron web that grew
to include some thirty interstate lines. During the Civil War, the
demand for military supplies provided the catalyst for the second,
more diversified stage of industrialization.[2]

The nature of travelers' accounts evolved with improved communications and transportation. For most, the railroad train became the predominant symbol of Chicago. Some early visitors,
however, sought travel experiences more related to the prevalent
romanticism of the day, and toured the fast-disappearing prairie
lands to the south and west of the city.

The city's emergence as the center of an economic empire meant
that most travelers to the West had to pass through town. Because visitors' guidebooks to Chicago did not appear until the later
1850s, and even then probably were not circulated much outside
of town, travelers knew relatively little about Chicago in advance
of their journeys. As a result, they were frequently taken by sur-

[2] Carl Abbott, "Civic Pride in Chicago, 1844–1860," *Journal of the Illinois State Historical Society* 4 (Winter 1970): 399–421.

prise by the city. Their reactions reflected the interests and biases
of both themselves and their times, often more openly than did
other observers. Because they were residents of either Atlantic
seaboard cities or of Europe, the initial travel direction of virtu-
ally all of the writers who came through Chicago was from East
to West. Only a few passed through Chicago on the return leg
of a circle tour. Geography—and their own social class back-
grounds—meant that they tended to approach the city by the lake
with the perspective and attitudes of the more developed, sophisticated, urban, and urbane sections of the country. And so, before
Chicago reached its own level of maturity, it was usually described
in condescending tones as perhaps more crude than it really was.[3]

The same images of backwardness that dominated the early
views of the city were a useful contrast to the levels of sophistication Chicago would eventually achieve. From the perspective of
later history, these early accounts also reveal the prevalent belief
of the time that Chicago's growth was predestined. The naysay-
ers who foresaw stagnation rather than greatness were consequently useful in rallying enthusiasm in the face of an economic
depression or the Great Fire. The stereotype of an unpolished (yet
booming) cow town was further strengthened by the fact that most
of the visitors were male. Men tended to place greater emphasis
on such attributes as "industry" and "energy," and say less about
culture and refinement. Fortunately, Pierce's feminist consciousness caused her to include a more balanced representation of female travelers, including Frederika Bremer, Harriet Martineau,
Sarah Margaret Fuller [Ossoli], Isabella Lucy Bird Bishop, and
Lady Duffus Hardy, who were among the relatively few women
who wrote in the genre.[4]

Travelers' accounts reveal other biases. Some were interested in

[3] For two excellent views of Chicago's image, see Sarah S. Marcus, "Up from the
Prairie: Images of Chicago and the Middle West in Popular Culture, 1865–1983"
(Ph.D. diss., University of Wisconsin, 2001); and Lisa Krissoff Boehm, "Infamous
City: Popular Culture and the Enduring Myth of Chicago, 1871–1968" (Ph.D. diss.,
Indiana University, 1999).

[4] On the difficulties and dangers of travel confronting racial minorities and women
in general, see Barbara Welke, "Gendered Journeys: A History of Injury, Public Transport, and American Law, 1865–1920," (Ph.D. diss., University of Chicago, 1995).

investigating specific topics, such as church populations or schools. Patrick Shirreff was attempting to bring back advice for those who might be interested in immigrating to the West. Immigrant enclaves tended to be important only when visitors from their homeland visited town. The accounts by Fredericka Bremer and Christian Jevne, for instance, included descriptions of the German and Norwegian communities, respectively. Most other visitors, who were from elite or professional classes, tended to ignore the ethnic dimension of Chicago, even though by 1850 over half of the city's population was foreign-born.

For visitors, Chicago began to assume contradictory images. On one hand, it was a unique place. The momentum of its growth was so rapid and strong that not even something as devastating as the Great Fire of 1871 could interrupt it.[5] The resulting demand for labor drew immigrants and small-town American folk by the thousands. To make room for them, the city reached out and annexed 125 square miles of suburbs and farmland in 1889, and thus became the second-largest city in America. The population exploded to a million by 1890, two million by 1909, and three by 1923. And because the city lacked much of an industrial past, it could emerge by the 1880s with the newest cutting-edge technologies and the largest factory buildings.

This was especially attractive to the late-nineteenth-century travelers whose accounts reflected a growing trend in tourism toward visiting workplaces.[6] Vacationers sought to sample the authentic life experience of their host city by visiting its major industries. In Chicago, that especially meant the Union Stock Yards, and by the 1880s the various meat-packing companies were issuing small souvenir guidebooks that described the process. These pamphlets were, in turn, illustrated with engravings of typical tourists in all their finery as they enjoyed the view.

[5] For a comparison of Chicago and a modern counterpart, see G. W. Kennedy, "Discovering Shock City: Houston and the Public Media," *Journal of Popular Culture* 15 (Spring 1982): 157–62; on the city and moral shock, see Laura Hapke, "Down There on a Visit: Late-Nineteenth Century Guidebooks to the City," *Journal of Popular Culture* 20 (Fall 1986): 41–55.

[6] Cindy Aron, *Working at Play: A History of Vacations in the United States* (New York: Oxford University Press, 1999), 146–47.

Chicago also emerged as the archetypal American city, a personification of such national characteristics as hard work, individualism, opportunity, and democratic involvement in government. Julian Ralph found its ethnic structure more cosmopolitan than Eastern cities and very representative of the predominant trend toward social fragmentation found in all industrial cities. William T. Stead thought that he could describe America by staying two weeks in Chicago instead of traveling. Like other American cities, its chaotic mixture of homes, stores, and small factories began to sort itself into enclaves based on social class, land-use, race, and nationality. Demographic and economic growth pushed everything outward, with industry stretched out along the river branches and rail lines. Superimposed over this was a pattern of neighborhood-building that vaguely resembled circular waves from a pebble dropped in a still pond. Meanwhile, an ethnic structure once dominated by Irish, German, and Scandinavian immigrants saw a new influx of diverse groups from southern and eastern Europe. Those with a little bit of money could escape the city thanks to the availability of cheap land, abundant suburban railroad service, and inexpensive balloon-frame houses. Yet the very poor remained trapped in obsolete neighborhoods encircling the downtown. They fell under the influence of politicians who rewarded political support with election-day drinks, city jobs, and other welfare-like benefits that competed with the offerings of numerous charities as well as the burgeoning settlement house movement.

In Chicago's case, the attempt to view it as typical and atypical resulted in its image as the great American exaggeration.[7] It was the extreme example of the American Everyplace. No place on earth seemed to be more determined to be largest, fastest growing, costliest, most innovative, and most violent. Such audacity

[7] Chicago's reputation at the end of the nineteenth century is expertly treated in Arnold Lewis, *An Early Encounter with Tomorrow: Europeans, Chicago's Loop, and the World's Columbian Exposition* (Urbana: University of Illinois Press, 1997); see also Catherine Cocks, *Doing the Town: The Rise of Urban Tourism in the United States, 1850–1915* (Berkeley: University of California Press, 2001), which compares Chicago with New York, San Francisco, and Washington, D.C.; and J. Philip Gruen, "The Urban Wonders: City Tourism in the Late-Nineteenth Century American West," *Journal of the West* 41 (Spring 2002): 10–19.

caused the city to find its way into conversations about almost any topic of the day. Every industrial town had smoke; Chicago's coal fires in its locomotives, ships, and furnaces produced an impenetrable pall. The pace of sidewalk traffic was faster in cities; Chicagoans tried to prove statistically that they walked faster than New Yorkers. Industrialization was the lifeblood of most cities; Chicago was the Silicon Valley of the early-twentieth century, always at the cutting edge of size and innovation. Several cities had fairs; Chicago created the World's Columbian Exposition, arguably the greatest in the nation's history. Every growing city seemed to put business and self-promotion high on its agenda; Chicago's pushiness in obtaining the 1893 fair earned it the "Windy City" moniker. It promised to "make culture hum," and in record time its Art Institute, universities, and symphony orchestra rose to unexpected levels of excellence. Crime and violence increased the risks of urban life; Chicago had more than its share of violent strikes—Haymarket and Pullman among them. In the national scramble for superlatives, Chicago always seemed to come in first.

Chicago was also the symbolic city in a land of stark contrasts that set good next to evil. Its slums included some of the worst concentrations of obsolete and dilapidated housing anywhere; one statistical study revealed congestion greater than the infamous Black Hole of Calcutta. But Chicago was also the birthplace of the skyscrapers of tomorrow, and engaged in a perpetual race with New York for the claim of the tallest building. Its city council was so corrupt that it was nicknamed "the Grey Wolves." And, of course, it had its pantheon of criminals. Yet at the same time, Chicago was home to the first juvenile court and an extraordinary concentration of seminaries. It was symbolic that for a decade Al Capone and Jane Addams lived and worked only a few miles from each other.

By the late nineteenth century a boomerang effect began to shape the city's image. The Great Fire and the Stock Yards emerged as the predominant symbols, the keys to understanding the city. Urban tourism emerged during this period, as visitors came to see the city's sights and then returned home to tell about their experiences. The appearance of mass-produced stereopticon slides as well as the boom in travel narratives also supplied images and descriptions of Chicago. As more descriptions of the city appeared in print, the world got to know it better. As a result, knowing in advance about the city tended to reduce the visitors' sense of wonder about the tall buildings and bustling street life. The World's Columbian Exposition produced such a huge number of guidebooks that were dispersed across the country that many visitors came very well equipped to take on the city as well as the fair. The exposition found that the visitors' aides it had hired had little to do. It is also worth noting that after the fair, a number of foreign writers bypassed Chicago altogether on their tour routes, largely because they would not have been able to reveal anything that potential readers did not already know.

As the years passed into the twentieth century, travelers' accounts of Chicago reflected new trends. First, traditional descriptive travelers' accounts, which attempted to divine each city's unique personality, began to decline as a genre. Writers instead attempted to use their travel experiences to assess the character of the whole nation, much as Alexis de Tocqueville had done. Works in this latter category deemphasized the uniqueness of each place in order to generalize about commonalities. Among those who did comment on Chicago specifically, there was an increasing tendency to focus on the city's personality or its "soul" instead of its physical characteristics. The prominent people who began to emerge as the symbols of the city were less often businessmen than unconventional and colorful characters: the bombastic Mayor William Hale "Big Bill" Thompson, Al Capone, Colonel Robert R. McCormick, and, later on, Sir George Solti and Michael Jordan. While Pierce's source material tended to come from travelers, most of them still foreign, the predominant image of Chicago tended to come from American writers reacting to some specific event, rather than writing as part of a general interest in the city.

Chicago remained an attraction for visitors, but the world was changing. The youthful metropolis could shrug off criticism and ignore complaints about the way it lured away industries and promising talent from other towns, but by World War I the Chamber of Commerce and Industry had begun to sense a flattening of the growth curve. When it became clear that Chicago would not become the center of the emerging automobile and aircraft industries as it had in telecommunications, local savants began to take interest in the growing importance of conventions and tourism traffic in the local economy. Visitors had always filled hotel rooms, but coming to the city to conduct business was seldom a matter of choice. However, a convention or a vacation in Chicago was another matter because there were often competing choices. Other cities had better weather, more commodious convention facilities, and better-known natural attractions. These alternative destinations, in turn, made such intangibles as the city's image and reputation much more important. This new emphasis on the importance of image could not have come at a worse time for Chicago, because image was emerging as its leading problem.

THE BIRTH OF THE BOOK

Every book has a story. It begins with an idea, passes through a research–writing–editing process, becomes a tangible product, and ends with reviews and a reputation. In a sense *As Others See Chicago* started in the background of Bessie Louise Pierce's life.[8] A permanent resident for only two years when she began the book, Pierce was ideally suited to collect travelers' accounts because she had herself first encountered Chicago as an out-of-towner. Born in Waverly, Iowa, in 1888, she was the older of two daughters of a prosperous dry goods merchant. The family soon moved to Iowa City, where both young women attended the State University of Iowa. An aunt who was a physician in Michigan provided the Pierce sisters with the inspiration to pursue professional careers instead of husbands. Ann began what would be a long career as a professor of music at the hometown university. Meanwhile, Bessie began to teach in the local schools, but soon decided to earn an advanced degree in Chicago. The big city had always fas-

---

[8] Biographical information on Pierce based on her papers in Special Collections, the University of Chicago Library. See also Perry R. Duis, "Bessie Louise Pierce: Symbol and Scholar," *Chicago History* 5 (Fall 1976): 130–40; and Duis, "Bessie Louise Pierce," in *Women Building Chicago, 1790–1990*, ed. Rima Lunin Schultz and Adele Hast (Bloomington: Indiana University Press, 2001), 607–99.

cinated her. She had grown up hearing stories from Iowans who had attended the World's Columbian Exposition, and she had visited the city several times as a youth.[9] Moreover, she was one of the targeted categories of students that the University of Chicago was trying to recruit: small-town teachers who could keep their jobs and still earn a master's degree by attending three of four summer terms. The quarter system, which the university promoted, helped by making the summer session coequal to the other quarters, rather than a lesser variable as it had been in the semester system. This academic installment plan was part of the original concept of William Rainey Harper, the university's first president, to entwine the institution itself in the culture of the Midwest and its thousands of small towns and cities. Extension courses, traveling lectures by faculty, and a correspondence school would make the Hyde Park campus the intellectual capital of the region.[10]

Bessie Pierce fell in love with Chicago during the summers of 1913–1916, but when she decided to pursue a doctorate, her employment circumstances dictated that she be at home at the State University of Iowa. She was one of the first graduate students of Arthur Schlesinger, who would be a lasting influence in her life, as well as one of the nation's most distinguished historians. He encouraged scholars to study social rather than traditional political history, and emphasized the influence of such heretofore ignored factors as women and cities in the American past. Pierce blended her practical experience in education with her interests in social movements to write a dissertation on the history of non-educational influences on school systems. Her 1923 Ph.D. degree also enabled her to join the university's education school. She gained tenure, produced two other books and numerous articles during the next decade, and was well on her way to distinction in the education field.[11]

---

[9] Ann Moss, "Chicago's Boswell," *Chicago Tribune*, June 15, 1958.

[10] Richard J. Storr, *Harper's University: The Beginnings* (Chicago: University of Chicago Press, 1966), 19–26, 196–209. Harper's background in the Chautauqua movement increased his awareness of the need to bring culture to small towns.

[11] Bessie Louise Pierce, *Public Opinion and the Teaching of History in the United States* (New York: A. A. Knopf, 1926); *Civic Attitudes in American School Textbooks*

Then in 1929 Pierce received a letter that would change her life. It was from Charles Merriam, a political scientist from whom she had taken summer courses at the University of Chicago. He extended an invitation to her to join the Division of Social Science and take charge of a project to collect historical information about Chicago. At first she wavered because of the abruptness of such a large career change and the fact that it made no promise of tenure, but an exchange of letters with Schlesinger finally convinced her to take the job. "I arrived in Chicago with the [1929 Stock Market] Crash," she would later remember.[12]

Clearly another factor in Pierce's hesitation involved the nature of the Chicago history project. The university's sociology department had pioneered in the study of cities, and what they really wanted was a historical dimension to their data. Some years earlier they had already sent a graduate student named Vivien Palmer to collect interviews and other historical information about several of the individual neighborhoods.[13] Pierce's job would be to take that research to a larger citywide level. But the Iowan had other ideas, and she quickly eased herself away from the sociologists. Instead her vision was for a detailed multivolume general history of the entire city. And so, in the fall of 1929 the History of Chicago Project was born.

Bessie Pierce's arrival in Chicago would add a new chapter to the saga of who would control the city's past and for what purposes. The story had started ninety years earlier with nonacademic historians who had used Chicago's history primarily for financial reasons. Joseph Balestier's 1840 effort, the first history of the city, was a rallying call for citizens not to give up on Chicago during a severe depression.[14] By the 1850s the remarkable eco-

---

(Chicago: University of Chicago Press, 1930); and *Citizens' Organizations and the Civic Training of Youth* (New York: C. Scribner's Sons, 1933).

[12] Conversation with Perry R. Duis, who was her research assistant from 1966 to 1968.

[13] Vivien M. Palmer, *Documents: History of . . . Communit[ies], Chicago,* 6 vols. (Chicago: Chicago Historical Society, 1925–30). These compilations cover twenty-one communities. There is a copy at the Chicago Historical Society.

[14] Joseph Balestier, *Annals of Chicago,* Fergus' Historical Series, no. 1 (Chicago: Fergus Printing Co., 1876).

nomic rise of the city became the bedrock for booster claims of further growth.[15] After the 1871 Great Fire popular historians, mainly journalists, again used that same pre-Fire optimism to bolster morale and cheerfully reassure everyone that Chicago would be reborn from the ashes.[16] The 1880s brought the most detailed and influential history with the publication of A. T. Andreas's three-volume set. Primarily an atlas publisher, the profit-motivated Andreas loaded his books with biographical sketches, so that their subjects would then eagerly purchase the sets. He applied the same profitable formula to numerous atlases of midwestern counties.[17] The impending World's Columbian Exposition occasioned another round of such vanity histories.[18]

The second decade of the new century saw a new division of local history into scholarly and popular directions. On one hand there was the work of Milo M. Quaife, whose *Chicago and the Old Northwest* (1913) was the first thoroughly researched academic study of the early years of the region. Quaife was careful to produce a balanced and unromanticized view of conflict between native and European cultures.[19] During the early decades of the century the Illinois and Wisconsin state historical journals began to publish a stream of footnoted articles, many of them about Chi-

[15] This is the theme of William Cronon, *Nature's Metropolis: Chicago and the Great West* (New York: W. W. Norton, 1991).

[16] Elias Colbert and Everett Chamberlin, *Chicago and the Great Conflagration* (Cincinnati: C. F. Vent, 1871); James W. Sheahan and George P. Upton, *The Great Conflagration: Chicago: Its Past, Present and Future: Embracing a Detailed Narrative of the Great Conflagration in the North, South and West Divisions* (Philadelphia: Union Publishing Co., 1871).

[17] A. T. Andreas, *History of Chicago*, 3 vols. (Chicago: A. T. Andreas, 1884–86). On Andreas's career, see Michael P. Conzen, "Maps for the Masses: Alfred T. Andreas and the Midwestern County Atlas Map Trade," *Chicago History* 13 (Spring 1984): 47–63.

[18] Joseph Kirkland, *The Story of Chicago*, 2 vols. (Chicago: Dibble Publishing House, 1892–94); *Biographical Dictionary and Portrait Gallery of Representative Men of Chicago and the World's Columbian Exposition* (Chicago: American Biographical Publishing Co., 1892); and John J. Flinn, *Handbook of Chicago Biography* (Chicago: Standard Guide Co., 1893).

[19] Milo M. Quaife, *Chicago and the Old Northwest, 1673–1835* (Chicago: University of Chicago Press, 1913; reprint, Urbana: University of Illinois Press, 2001). For information on Quaife and the place of the book in historiography, see Perry R. Duis's "Introduction" in reprint edition, vii–xviii.

cago. The multivolume *Centennial History of Illinois* (1918) was of similarly high intellectual quality.[20] But most of these books were bought by serious scholars and few general readers encountered them outside of libraries.

The other direction of Chicago historical writing was aimed at a decidedly more casual reading audience. Lloyd Lewis and Henry Justin Smith were journalists with access to the newspaper morgues. Their books, though well-researched, were more market-driven. *Chicago: A History of Its Reputation* (1925) explored the question of what America thought of the city, but in doing so the authors sometimes tended to emphasize events that were bizarre rather than representative, and personalities that were colorful rather than truly important in the city's history.[21] Superlatives reigned. Crooked bosses became lovable scoundrels. Robber barons were depicted as cold and calculating, but readers could never get enough details of their private lives. The more atypical the violence was, the more pages of coverage it demanded. Capone, who would not go to prison until 1931, was still very much a Chicago presence.

While historians fed the popular appetite for sensationalism during the 1920s, local business leaders publicly wrung their hands over how the popular press marketed and sold Al Capone. The civic elite complained that gangster-worship was a serious impediment to the city's economic development, and a few of them formed the Secret Six in order to help finance the federal investigation that would eventually lead to Capone's downfall.[22] By 1926 local boosters had already begun to talk about countering the gangster image by hosting another world's fair. Their efforts culminated in the Century of Progress Exposition. Another fair would not only allow the city to retell the story of its growth, but

[20] Clarence W. Alvord, ed., *Centennial History of Illinois*, 6 vols. (Springfield: Illinois Centennial Commission, 1917–1920).

[21] Lloyd Lewis and Henry Justin Smith, *Chicago: The History of Its Reputation* (New York: Harcourt, Brace and Co., 1929).

[22] More perceptive on the topic than the numerous Capone biographies is David E. Ruth, *Inventing the Public Enemy: The Gangster in American Culture, 1918–1934* (Chicago: University of Chicago Press, 1996).

also use the occasion to cleanse its reputation. Indirectly *As Others See Chicago*, a book about the city's image, was a product of that same civic soul-searching.[23]

In this literary milieu Bessie Pierce was asked to write a volume of travelers' accounts. The city was making plans for the Century of Progress Exposition, and the University of Chicago Press wanted to mark the occasion with books that might have a chance of selling. Pierce was deep into work on her first volume, which would cover the years before 1848, but it was only half-finished and would not ultimately appear until 1937. Milo Quaife received the contract for a very brief general history of the early region and produced *Checagou*. This allowed him to emphasize and interpret information he had recently unearthed about Jean Baptiste Point du Sable, the region's first permanent resident.[24] Finally, a young economist named Homer Hoyt published a history of the city's physical development under the unfortunate title of *One Hundred Years of Land Values in Chicago*.[25]

Pierce was given the contract for a volume of travelers' accounts. With her long-time research assistant, Joe L. Norris, she began poring over the shelves of visitors' writings in the Harper Library stacks. The task was made somewhat easier by Solon Buck's massive state bibliography, which contained over seven hundred travelers' accounts published before 1865.[26] It was more of a challenge to find postbellum accounts that met her standards for substance. Visitors had produced many dozens of accounts that recounted how difficult it was to travel and described the arrival-departure process in detail, but few said anything perceptive about the city.

[23] Dennis E. Hoffman, *Scarface Al and the Crime Crusaders: Chicago's Private War Against Capone* (Carbondale: Southern Illinois University Press, 1993).

[24] Milo M. Quaife, "Documents: Property of Jean Baptiste Point Sable," *Mississippi Valley Historical Review* 15 (June 1928): 89–92; *Checagou: From Indian Wigwam to Modern City, 1673–1835* (Chicago: University of Chicago Press, 1933).

[25] Homer Hoyt, *One Hundred Years of Land Values in Chicago: The Relationship of the Growth of Chicago to the Rise in Its Land Values, 1830–1933* (Chicago: University of Chicago Press, 1933).

[26] Solon Justus Buck, *Travel and Description, 1765–1865*, vol. IX, *Illinois Historical Collections* (Springfield: Illinois State Historical Library, 1914); this work was later supplemented by Robert R. Hubach, *Early Midwestern Travel Narratives: An Annotated Bibliography, 1634–1850* (Detroit: Wayne State University Press, 1961).

Pierce decided that the source category "foreign travelers" was too confining so she chose "visitors" in order to include American strangers. After making selections, she and Norris then had to research the authenticity of each piece and the background of each contributor. The account by Frank Norris, for instance, finally made the cut after extensive correspondence that verified the writer's presence in Chicago at the time it was written.[27] Pierce then divided the accounts into the eras similar to those of her larger history and produced chapter introductions that remain miniature masterpieces of summary.

It was perhaps ironic that a book that chronicled visitors' impressions of a supremely self-confident city hit the bookstores in the spring of 1933 during its darkest hour. The hard times of the early 1930s diminished the city's population by an estimated 140,000, as thousands of unemployed Chicagoans gave up their houses, apartments, and rooms to return home to farms and small towns. Even the devastation of the Great Fire had not been able to destroy the city's sense of efficacy because the task of rebuilding was entirely in the hands of Chicagoans. The Great Depression was different. It was an international crisis over which local leadership had no control, a particularly frustrating situation for the headstrong city by the lake. As unemployment reached nearly fifty percent, officials were unable to count, let alone feed, the hungry. Tens of thousands of adults and children, forced to roam the nation in search of work, got off the freight trains at America's rail hub. The spring of 1933 also saw bank runs by panicky depositors, which shook the financial system to its foundation, and led the newly inaugurated Franklin D. Roosevelt to declare a bank holiday.[28]

While Chicagoans joined the rest of the nation in placing their hope in the new president, their local leadership was in turmoil. On February 15, 1933, Mayor Anton Cermak, who had gone to Miami Beach, Florida, to meet with president-elect Roosevelt, was

[27] Elmer Geertz to Joe L. Norris, 14 Oct. 1931, Bessie L. Pierce Papers, Box 25, Special Collections, University of Chicago Library.

[28] Roger Biles, *Big City Boss in Depression and War: Mayor Edward J. Kelly of Chicago* (DeKalb: Northern Illinois University Press, 1984), describes the tumultuous times.

shot in the stomach by Gueseppi Zangara. Chicago's only immigrant mayor lingered until March 6th before succumbing to peritonitis.[29] Soon after "Anton the Martyr" was laid to rest, local politicians selected Alderman Frank J. Corr as acting mayor while the state legislature enacted special legislation to allow the Chicago City Council to install a nonmember to finish Cermak's term. The new mayor, Edward J. Kelly, former head of the Sanitary District, took office on April 13th. Despite the turmoil, there was no sense of permanent decline. Rather, there was a grim sort of self-confidence that the noise and industrial smoke of prosperity would eventually return.

A product of its times, there is almost a sense of nervous boosterism about the concluding section of *As Others See Chicago* previously absent from Pierce's other works about the city. Perhaps she was unsure about how to structure a time period that had not yet ended, particularly when so many of the major characters were still alive. Her introduction made some broad references to recent corruption and crime, but she generally let her visitors describe contemporary topics that she may have been reluctant to discuss.

As Others See Chicago appeared amidst a spate of books celebrating A Century of Progress. By this time the exposition had reinvented its purpose. The bright colors of its art deco design and the theme of technology leading the way out of economic depression became more important than boosterism and correcting Chicago's gangster image. The fair, which was extended a second year, recorded a total of 39,052,236 paid admissions—most of them out-of-towners—before the gates closed for good.[30] The popular authors of the 1920s reworked their stories into shorter and more optimistic volumes with such titles as *Chicago's Progress* and *Chicago's Great Century, 1833–1933*, the latter designated as the of-

[29] Alex Gottfried, *Boss Cermak of Chicago: A Study of Political Leadership* (Seattle: University of Washington Press, 1962), 366–73. Mayor Joseph Medill (1871–73) was born in Canada and brought to the United States as an infant, but never regarded himself as an immigrant. Cermak was only a year old when his parents emigrated from Kladno, Czechoslovakia, but he used his immigrant background to appeal to ethnic voters in creating the Democratic machine.

[30] Lenox R. Lohr, *Fair Management: The Story of the Century of Progress* (Chicago: The Cuneo Press, 1952), 48–49. Lohr was the general manager of the exposition.

ficial history by the exposition corporation.[31] Competition and hard times caused Pierce's volume to pass rather quickly into history. In January 1936, the University of Chicago Press allowed it to go out of print.[32] It soon became a favorite of Chicagoiana collectors, commanding high prices.

Bessie Louise Pierce moved on to other projects. Although she never finished her massive *History of Chicago*, she did publish three volumes (1937, 1940, 1957) that took the story up to the time of the World's Columbian Exposition. Even though her work is regarded as the first scholarly history of a major American city, she continued to maintain a visitor's perspective of the city. "For a person not a Chicagoan, I'm the greatest booster that ever was . . . I liked the city from the start and have become more enthralled as the years (29 of them) have whizzed by," she admitted in a 1958 interview.[33] In 1972 Pierce moved back to Iowa City, where she had continued to maintain the family home. She died there on October 4, 1974.

Perry R. Duis
The University of Illinois at Chicago

[31] Henry Justin Smith, *Chicago's Great Century, 1833–1933* (Chicago: Consolidated Publishers Inc., 1933); Glenn A. Bishop and Paul T. Gilbert, *Chicago's Progress: A Review of the World's Fair City* (Chicago: Bishop Publishing Co., 1933).

[32] Rollin Hemens to Bessie Louise Pierce, 31 Jan. 1936, Pierce Papers, Box 16, Special Collections, University of Chicago Library.

[33] Ann Moss, "Chicago's Boswell," *Chicago Tribune,* June 15, 1958.

PREFACE

A T A TIME when the city of Chicago at its Century of Progress Fair will be visited by many citizens of the United States and of the rest of the world, it seems especially appropriate to assemble some of the impressions of visitors who have come in the past. Not all the accounts reproduced in this volume are easily accessible to the general reader; all are intended to be suggestive, rather than exhaustive, of the impressions of travelers who have come to Chicago during different periods of the city's development. Some are written after only a brief sojourn and, to the reader who has lived here, may appear shallow, crude, unfair, even unkind in the analysis of life observed. Others are the impressions of those who saw the city more than once or who may have passed some time in studying the characteristics later portrayed. On the whole, Chicago has been treated kindly by the stranger within her gates; yet the descriptions set forth in the following pages run the whole gamut of pleasing eulogy to relentless disapproval, although there is mirrored little of the malicious.

In selecting these accounts, there has been kept constantly in mind the desirability of obtaining a variety of impressions not only of fellow-Americans but of travelers from other nations. Therefore, there are English, French, Scotch, Swedish, Norwegian, Italian, Brahmin, German, and Hungarian narratives, besides those of Americans. Of travelers from abroad the English are the most frequent visitors to chronicle their reactions, especially before the present century.

Many of the characteristics observed are not indigenous in Chicagoans alone but are those attributed to Americans in general. Toward all Americans and all American cities have been directed the praise and censure of foreign critics, particularly by visitors to the United States before 1900. Often the folk who came wondered what kind of character would evolve from the amalgamation of so many diverse nationalities, each with its own peculiar characteristics, transplanted in a country the success of whose government, even to the end of the nineteenth century, was a source of conjecture to commentators whose own was not in the hands of the common people. The absence of widespread class consciousness, general education of the masses, the power of public opinion, deference to women, hurry and energy, unremitting search for business opportunities and wealth, high standards of personal morality, spoiled children, boastfulness, and crudity in the arts and in social amenities, where convention played only a small part, were subjects of frequent comment. Although accounts of conditions observed in their American sojourn at times reflect a prejudice which colored reactions, none the less the reader many times finds the germ of truth imbedded in what at first appears superficial and caustic. On the other hand, praise of American practices excessively indulged in evoked a skepticism as to the validity and truthfulness of the remarks of those who attempted to paint the picture in too vivid colors. Whereas the traveler of the early nineteenth century noted local differences in the character of the people and in the customs of living seen in different parts of the country, he of the twentieth century observed these differences had apparently capitulated to uniformity and a homogeneity of outlook and practice. Yet foreign travelers were not alone in their criticism of things American, for even among our own citizens such comment was not unknown. Many of the qualities pilloried by the foreigner received less generous treatment by Americans themselves. American critics of politics, business, and society can be found who, at close range, weighed American civilization in the balance and found it wanting.

In editing the following selections, spelling and punctuation of the original, as far as possible, have been retained. In most cases topic headings used do not appear in the original but have been coined by the editor. Preceding each selection is a brief sketch of the author's life which endeavors to set forth salient features of his career. The accounts have been grouped under well-defined periods of Chicago's history, briefly described in order to give perspective to the reader not familiar with the annals of the city, and so written as to furnish a historical background for the accompanying selections.

An acknowledgment of all the courtesies received from those who have aided in the preparation of this volume would be extensive. Mention of only a few can be made. I am under special obligation to publishers and authors for permission to quote from their publications and writings, as indicated in connection with the excerpts reprinted. Mr. Guy Parsloe, of the Institute of Historical Research of the University of London, graciously helped in obtaining permission to use some of the British accounts. Throughout the preparation of the volume, Professors Edith Abbott, E. W. Burgess, Avery Craven, Charles E. Merriam, Donald Slesinger, Leonard D. White, and Chester W. Wright, of the University of Chicago, have co-operated with advice and assistance. Professor W. L. Bullock, of the University of Chicago, generously helped in obtaining a suitable account by an Italian observer, and Dr. T. C. Blegen, of the State Historical Society of Minnesota, in like manner, aided in the quest of a chronicle by a Norwegian.

For assistance in the collection of data contained in the introductory notes for the period 1871–93, I am indebted to Mr. Wood Gray, of the University of Chicago research staff. To Mr. Joe L. Norris, of the research staff, I am particularly obligated for help in the preparation of the biographical sketches and in all other phases of the book. Translations from French and Italian writers were rendered by Misses Lelah Belle Davis and Irene Bassett. Misses Muriel Bernitt, Helen Cavanaugh, and Mary Kennedy assisted in proofreading the manuscript.

BESSIE LOUISE PIERCE

PART I

THE BEGINNING OF A CITY

-»»-«««-

INTRODUCTION

A THOUGH Chicago was not incorporated as a town until 1833, her history stretches back to the days of the intrepid French explorer and the gay and courageous *voyageur* of the seventeenth and eighteenth centuries, whose insatiable curiosity and unbounded zeal lured them into unfrequented paths. Long before the establishment of Fort Dearborn in 1803, these dauntless and adventurous spirits knew the present site of Chicago as a place of portage on the route to the Mississippi, since the English on the eastern seaboard of North America and the Spanish in the Southwest made it necessary that the St. Lawrence and the Great Lakes be the French highways into the interior of the new country.

The first white men known to have used the Chicago Portage were Jolliet and Marquette, although before them other Frenchmen may have traversed it.[1] In May of 1673, with five companions they left Sault Ste. Marie bent on the discovery and exploration of a great river which, by the Indians, was called the Mississippi. Returning in the autumn, they crossed over the Chicago Portage. In the country through which they journeyed they met prairies and woods, small lakes and rivers, cattle and wild beasts; and the fertility of the soil evoked prophecies of abundant stores for the future. At "a village of Illinois called

[1] The nearness of the French to Chicago makes possible the previous knowledge of this portage. Father Claude Allouez, Jesuit missionary in the Northwest, knew of it in 1670 (letter from Father Allouez to the Father Superior in Louise P. Kellogg, *Early Narratives of the Northwest* [New York: Charles Scribner's Sons, 1917], p. 152). Miss Kellogg also suggests that the route recommended by the Indians to Nicolet in 1634 might have been the Chicago Portage (Kellogg, *The French Régime in Wisconsin and the Northwest* [Madison: State Historical Society of Wisconsin, 1925], p. 82). It is also believed by some that La Salle used the Chicago Portage on a western trip in 1670 (Milo M. Quaife, *Chicago and the Old Northwest* [Chicago: University of Chicago Press, 1913], pp. 21–22). Cf. Francis Borgia Steck, *The Jolliet-Marquette Expedition, 1673* (Washington: Catholic University of America, 1927), pp. 122–23; 130–33; 146, n. 16. Also Isaac Joslin Cox, *The Journeys of Réné Robert Cavelier Sieur de la Salle* . . . . (2 vols.; New York: A. S. Barnes & Co., 1905), I, xii.

3

Kaskaskia, consisting of 74 cabins,"[2] a cordial reception impelled Marquette to promise that he would come back and preach the Gospel. Poor health forced his return to Green Bay, but in late autumn, 1674, he set out for the Illinois country. Ice and snow and other hardships of travel compelled him to winter at Chicago, where, through the offices of La Toupine, a famous French trader, he was able to obtain subsistence.

Then for several years Chicago again slipped into obscurity, until the western endeavors of La Salle, beginning in 1679, made it an important post of western trade, whose portage was destined to know traders, soldiers, missionaries, and adventurers.

But commercial enterprise was not to continue uninterrupted and untroubled, for the Jesuits, seeking control of the western country to set up a theocratic state, obtained a royal edict in 1696 which recalled all traders and soldiers in the Northwest. Thus the commercial post became the center of missionary endeavor under the auspices of Father Pinet,[3] who opened the mission of the Guardian Angel, destined to be closed in 1697 for one year by Frontenac, then governor of Canada, whose imperialistic leaning craved sole control of the new country. The following year, however, the mission was reopened, carrying on its religious activities among the Indians so successfully that St. Cosme, a Seminary priest visiting Chicago in 1699, noted that God blessed "the labors and zeal of this holy missionary."[4]

[2] According to Louise P. Kellogg (*Early Narratives of the Northwest*, p. 257, n. 2), this village was located near the present village of Utica, La Salle County, Illinois. It was later removed to its present site in southern Illinois. See the same work for an account of the journey.

[3] Father Pinet was born at Perigueux (Limoges), France, November 11, 1660 (O.S.). He entered the Jesuit novitiate at Bordeaux, August 29, 1682. From 1684 to 1690 he was an instructor at Tulle, Perigueux, and Pau. In 1694 he went to Canada, where he was sent to Michillimackinac. Two years later he established the mission of the Guardian Angel at Chicago. Early in 1700 Pinet was sent to the Tamarois Indians on the Mississippi in the region of what is today Cahokia. He remained here until 1702, when he went to the Kaskaskias. According to Shea (*Early Voyages up and down the Mississippi* [Albany: Joel Munsell, 1861], p. 53, n. 21), he died at Cahokia; but the list of missionaries compiled by Arthur Edward Jones (Thwaites, *Jesuit Relations*, LXXI, 158) says he died at Chicago, July 16, 1704. Father Gilbert J. Garraghan (*The Catholic Church in Chicago, 1673-1871* [Chicago: Loyola University Press, 1921], p. 21, n.15) sets aside both Jones and Shea and claims Pinet died among the Kaskaskias, August 1, 1702.

[4] See p. 20.

During the first half of the eighteenth century Chicago was heard of occasionally as a military base, an Indian village, a council point, and a trade center;[5] but the Fox wars made the old routes by way of Green Bay and Chicago dangerous, and trade shifted to the Wabash-Maumee valleys. It was not until the close of the Revolutionary War that it again assumed importance, as goods from Michillimackinac for Spanish traders on the Mississippi passed over the portage,[6] and another people found habitat here.

On August 3, 1795, the United States, following the defeat of the western Indians by General Anthony Wayne, gained control over land six miles square at the mouth of the Chicago River. Immediately the news of plans to establish a fort and an Indian agency prompted William Burnett, a St. Joseph merchant, to obtain a house at Chicago in order to lay in a store of goods and liquor.

But the garrison did not arrive at once. In 1803, however, Captain John Whistler came with a small body of troops with orders to construct and occupy a fort, christened Fort Dearborn, one of the great chain of posts which marked the western march of the new American nation. To the newcomers, the flat, swampy land presented a monotonous and barren scene, broken only by four rude huts or traders' cabins,[7] a little community typical of other outlying posts of its day. When the War of 1812 broke, the United States proposed to use it as one of the bases from which to launch a flank attack upon the English in Canada, but this plan proved unsuccessful. Thereupon General William Hull, in command of the Northwest, apprehensive lest the whole section fall into the hands of the English, ordered the evacuation of Fort Dearborn.

[5] Kellogg, *The French Régime in Wisconsin*, pp. 283-84. *New York Colonial Documents*, IX, 890. Lignery to De Siette, June 19, 1726, in Wisconsin State Historical Society, *Collections*, III, 155. *Calendar of State Papers, America and West Indies, 1700*, No. 523, inclosure liv. Journal of Captain Harry Gordon in Newton D. Mereness, *Travels in the American Colonies* (New York: Macmillan Co., 1916), p. 476.

[6] Wayne Edson Stevens, *The Northwest Fur Trade, 1763-1800* (University of Illinois, "Studies in the Social Sciences," Vol. XIV, No. 3, Urbana, 1928), pp. 110, 111.

[7] John Wentworth, *Early Chicago—Fort Dearborn* in "Fergus Historical Series" (Chicago: Fergus Printing Co., 1881), No. 16, p. 13.

To abandon the fort was no easy task. To some, such as John
Kinzie, the trader, it meant financial ruin; and to members of
the garrison it proclaimed the loss of home and imminent danger
for their families. Escorted by Captain William Wells and some
friendly Miami, Captain Nathan Heald and those who had
shared his lot at the fort, filed out of its gates on August 15,
1812, bound for Fort Wayne. Although warned of an impending
attack by the Indians by Black Partridge, a friendly Pottawattomie chief, it was too late to change plans. They had gone only a
short distance from the fort when many were struck down by
the relentless tomahawks of Indians disappointed at the disposal
of the stores and liquor of the fort, while others were taken captive with a ransom of one hundred dollars put upon their heads.
The Kinzies escaped to Detroit; Captain Heald and his wife
sought refuge with the British and were later paroled; while a
few others escaped or were released. In 1816 the fort was rebuilt; and, although not the most remote American outpost in
the Northwest, it still retained all the characteristics of the frontier settlement. Again it became a point of trade and an Indian
agency, to which had returned John Kinzie and other survivors
of the Fort Dearborn massacre.[8]

To the visitor who, at this time, came to the future Chicago,
it presented, on the one hand, "a summer climate of delightful
serenity," natural meadows with "all the advantages for raising
stock, of the most favored part of the valley of the Mississippi,"
and the possibilities of a great depot of inland commerce between the North and the South, "a great thoroughfare for
strangers, merchants, and travellers."[9] To another, sterility of
soil, monotonous scenery, inhospitable climate, and an unpromising future bulked large in prophecies of the future.[10] At any
rate, when Gurdon S. Hubbard, an employee of the American
Fur Company, visited Chicago in 1818, he found, in addition to

[8] M. M. Quaife, *Chicago and the Old Northwest*, treats of these events. Accounts of
the massacre are reproduced in the Appendixes.

[9] Henry R. Schoolcraft, *Narrative Journal of Travels through the Northwestern Regions of the United States* (Albany: E. & E. Hosford, 1821), pp. 383-85. See also Samuel
A. Storrow's description, pp. 23-26.

[10] See Keating's description, pp. 31-39.

the buildings of Fort Dearborn, only a storehouse of his company, the residence of the factor, a log cabin at "Hardscrabble,"
and the cabins of Antoine Ouilmette and John Kinzie.[11] Three
years later, John Tipton, visiting this section, discovered only
nine or ten families in what was soon to be a town of many times
that number;[12] and John H. Fonda, bound for Solomon Juneau's
trading post at Milwaukee in 1825, found merely an Indian
agency with about fourteen houses.[13]

Although the decade from 1820 to 1830 foreshadowed in no
way the transformation and changes to take place during the
lifetime of those then living, it witnessed the gradual seizure of
Indian lands by the whites,[14] the evacuation of the fort in 1823,
to be reoccupied again because of the Winnebago War in 1827,
abandoned in 1831, to be regarrisoned the following year, and
the appointment of a Canal Commission by the state legislature
in 1829.

This last event proved of no mean importance in the future
annals of the city, for the commissioners proceeded to lay out at
either end of the proposed route the towns of Chicago and Ottawa. In the summer of 1830, the first town lots of Chicago,
80×180 feet, were sold at public auction at prices ranging from
forty to sixty dollars.[15] The year before, the commissioners of
Peoria County granted Archibald Caldwell the first license to
keep tavern; and in March, 1831, J. N. Bailey was appointed
first postmaster of Chicago. The building of the first lighthouse,
the designation of Chicago as county seat of Cook County, and
the establishment of a school, all pointed toward a realization of
that permanency which the little village sought.

In this modest community, life mirrored all the characteris-

[11] G. S. Hubbard, *Autobiography* (Chicago: Lakeside Press, 1911), p. 39.

[12] John Tipton, Journal, 1821 (John Tipton Papers, Indiana State Library, Indianapolis).

[13] John H. Fonda, "Early Reminiscences of Wisconsin" in Wisconsin State Historical
Society, *Collections*, V (1867–69), 216–17.

[14] In 1821 the Ottawas and Pottawattomies signed a treaty at Chicago ceding land to
the encroaching whites.

[15] James Nevin Hyde, *Early Medical Chicago* in "Fergus Historical Series" (Chicago:
Fergus Printing Co., 1879), No. 11, p. 21.

tics common to the frontier settlement. Anything which broke the regular monotony of daily toil was considered amusement: the weekly prayer meeting, the dances at Mark Beaubien's, horse-racing, wolf hunts, and the debating society. Not until 1838 was there a permanent theater, when The Rialto in its quarters on the upper floor of an old wooden building on Dearborn Street sought to serve the lighter fancies of Chicago's populace.

In 1832 the Blackhawk War broke the serenity which, for a brief moment, had embraced the little band of settlers. Refugees, fleeing from fear of possible Indian attacks, flooded Chicago. Companies of volunteers were organized throughout the state. In this, the last Indian war for Illinois, the threat and character of the struggle brought military assistance not only from nearby Michigan but also from the nation's government at Washington. The federal troops, coming from the East, infected with Asiatic cholera, carried with them sickness and death. Toward midsummer the plague abated somewhat, and in September the Blackhawk War came to an end. The following year Chicago was incorporated as a town, although still on the fringe of the frontier. Stark and sparsely tenanted, stretched a wilderness between Detroit and the little village. To reach it the traveler by land must follow an old Indian trail to the southwest from Detroit to Ypsilanti, through South Bend, La Porte, and Michigan City, for there were no railways and few well-worn paths.

But the spring of 1833 saw a rush of immigrants to the country recently freed from danger of the Indian. Soon many in quest of fortune were passing through Chicago en route to the new West. Since Chicago was unprepared to care for the great number of newcomers, many had to set up living-quarters in their covered wagons.[16] Some of the wayfarers elected to remain. Houses were constructed in an incredibly brief time.[17] By the end of 1833 four establishments bore the name of hotel: the Old Wolf Point Tavern, rechristened The Travelers Home; The

[16] See Charles Butler's description, pp. 40-53.   [17] *Ibid.*

Sauganash; The Green Tree Tavern; and the Mansion House.[18] Chicago's population soon doubled. At the beginning of 1833 about two hundred and fifty souls could be classed as inhabitants; but by the middle of the following year, the number had jumped to approximately eight hundred. But this rapid growth in population can be accounted for to some extent by the qualifications imposed, for mere payment of board by the week constituted residence. To hang out a sign indicative of a profession or a trade proved equally effective.[19]

With its growth in numbers, Chicago acquired the earmarks of an established society. The *Chicago Democrat,* under the editorship of John Calhoun, appeared on November 26, 1833. On January 1, 1834, Dr. John T. Temple opened the first mail route to Ottawa, although not a letter was sent on the initial trip. In addition to a public school, several private institutions afforded opportunities for the "young idea to shoot." As the thirties advanced, the services of physicians, dentists, lawyers, and other professional men became more and more available. A medical college was approved as early as 1837, but obstacles prevented its inception until 1843.

Nor were the religious interests of the struggling and rapidly solidifying village neglected. By 1833, four churches were caring for the religious and social development of their particular memberships. Before many years had passed, the number of churches increased so rapidly that there came to be second and even third congregations of the same denomination.

Located as it was, and in the days before the railroad had reached Illinois, Chicago based the hope of a glorious future on the development of water transportation. On March 2, 1833, Congress bowed to persistent pleading and appropriated $25,000 for the improvement of the Chicago harbor. Work began the following July and one year later had progressed to the point where the schooner "Illinois," with a capacity of one hundred tons, entered the river. Trade immediately increased. By the

[18] A. T. Andreas, *History of Chicago* (3 vols.; Chicago: A. T. Andreas Co., 1886), I, 132.

[19] *Ibid.*, pp. 122, 128.

close of the year 1835 it mounted to approximately one million dollars.[20] In July, 1836, ground was broken for a canal; and twelve years later the "General Frye," the first boat to be locked through the canal, floated into Lake Michigan through the Illinois-Michigan Canal.

Real estate prices reached high peaks. In 1833 Captain Luther Nichols refused to give Jean Beaubien forty cords of wood, worth $1.25 a cord, for the Tremont House lot. In 1835 this same piece of ground sold for $500, and in only two years more it was valued at ten times that amount.[21] On May 28, 1835, the government opened its land sale, drawing large numbers of adventurers and speculators to the city. By September 30, $459,958 worth of land had been disposed of. Undiscriminating purchasers and unscrupulous sellers bargained in the practice of the time in a newly organized and undeveloped section of the country. When William B. Ogden, later to be mayor of Chicago, came to the city to superintend the sale of 182 acres belonging to Charles Butler, his brother-in-law, he thought $100,000, the price paid for the land, far too high. When one-third of Butler's tract sold for as much as the total purchase price, he was fully convinced that the people had become unbalanced.

This fever of speculation carried in its wake "wildcat" currency, which by 1837 brought ruin to many in the general suspension of specie payment. Schools and other cultural enterprises received a setback, many commercial projects were blighted, and the town in general was in the throes of financial distress. In 1836, William B. Ogden and J. Y. Scammon, among others, had received a charter for the Galena and Chicago Union Railroad; but it was necessary to abandon work, along with other undertakings, until the Panic of 1837 had spent its course.

On March 4, 1837, the state legislature granted Chicago a new charter, which incorporated it into a city (May 2), thereby making it easier to obtain loans. On June 1, the city council issued $5,000 in city scrip carrying interest at 1 per cent monthly and receivable for taxes.

[20] *Ibid.*, p. 143.　　　　　　　　　[21] *Ibid.*, p. 137.

For Chicago, as well as the nation in general, the later thirties were filled with misfortune. In addition to financial ills, common to all sections, the city was scourged with an epidemic similar to Asiatic cholera in the summer of 1838, which forced the stoppage of work on the Canal. A drought set in during July with no relief until November. Streams dried up, the water became brackish, and malaria broke out. On October 27, 1839, Chicago suffered its first big fire, in which the Tremont House and seventeen other buildings were destroyed, at an estimated loss of sixty to seventy-five thousand dollars.

But Chicago was not made of the stuff to be crushed by adversity. By 1844 prosperity was on the upgrade. Roads leading into the city improved, building increased, interest in education was rekindled, and scientific advance was reflected in the establishment of Rush Medical School and the equipment of a general hospital.

Visitors to the city during the forties mirrored different reactions. Some, like Friedrich von Raumer, who came in 1844, saw little but a town situated "in a country even more level than that around Berlin," a village which, "like all the towns in the West," had "grown out of nothing in a short space of time."[22] To travelers like Raumer there was nothing even vaguely portentous of what the coming years were to bring. But among those who came were some who envisaged a great future for the struggling and ambitious community on the shores of Lake Michigan, and who agreed with its most enthusiastic citizens as to a greatness in store. Of these was Thurlow Weed, who in 1847 attended the River and Harbor Convention, and predicted that in "ten years, Chicago will contain more inhabitants than Albany."[23] He saw "broad avenues," a residence section "thickly planted with trees," "four admirably-conducted public-schools" much larger than those in Albany and "filled with children," and large houses of public worship. He rode a few

[22] Friedrich von Raumer, *America and the American People* (New York: J. and H. G. Langley, 1846), p. 451.

[23] Thurlow Weed, "Report of the River and Harbor Convention" (from the *Albany Evening Journal*, July 14, 1847). Reprinted in the "Fergus Historical Series" (Chicago: Fergus Printing Co., 1882), No. 18, pp. 153–54.

miles out of the city "to get a glimpse of the prairies" and noted that

. . . . we found the road all the way occupied with an almost unbroken line of wagons, drawn generally by two yokes of oxen, bringing wheat to the City. These teams are called 'prairie schooners.' That eccentric member of Congress from Alabama, Felix Grundy McConnell, among his last acts, asked the House of Representatives to 'Resolve, That this is a great country, and constantly increasing.' One needs to visit Chicago to realize and confess that the proposition is one of undeniable truth.[24]

Weed also found all Chicagoans "looking forward anxiously to the completion of the [Illinois and Michigan] Canal," at which the River and Harbor Convention delegates had cast prophetic eyes, seeing in it another agency in promoting the "magic-like growth" of the city. In April, 1848, this dream came true after sixteen years of spasmodic labor, and a new channel of trade was open, contributing its share to multiplying the city's population more than six times in a decade.

The year 1848 was destined to witness the beginning of other undertakings which would bring about, in a brief space of time, an evolution from a frontier town serving only the home market to the metropolitan center of a growing trade with a rich and rapidly expanding hinterland. On October 25, the Galena and Chicago Union Railroad sent out a locomotive with a tender and two cars, which made its first run, a distance of five miles. It was during this year also that the electric telegraph was installed and Chicago was provided with a means of rapid communication with the world outside. An Era of Expansion had begun.

[24] *Ibid.*

FATHER JACQUES MARQUETTE[1]

FATHER JACQUES MARQUETTE, missionary, was born at Laon, France, in 1637. At the age of seventeen he entered the Society of Jesus, and was ordained as priest in 1666. This same year he sailed for Canada, arriving at Quebec in September. After a few weeks here he went to Three Rivers, where he studied the Indian languages. He began his missionary work in 1668 among the Nez-Perces. In 1673 Governor Frontenac ordered him to accompany the explorer, Jolliet, on his expedition down the Mississippi River. The party set out from Green Bay in May, 1673, and on the return in the early fall they passed through the Chicago Portage.

Father Marquette had promised to return to the Illinois country the following year and preach the gospel to the Indians; but poor health, resulting from the hardships of the previous voyage, detained him at Green Bay until October, 1674. In this month, however, be began his return to Kaskaskia. Because of his illness, progress was slow and the little party did not reach Chicago until December. Here he wintered until March, 1675, leaving at that time for Kaskaskia, where he arrived in April. After preaching to the Indians for a few weeks, his health demanded his return to Canada. He grew steadily worse and finally died May 18, 1675, near the Marquette River in Michigan.

⇥⇥⇥ ⇤⇤⇤

A WINTER AT CHICAGO

December 14 [*1674*]. Having encamped near the portage, 2 leagues up the river, we resolved to winter there, as it was impossible to go farther, since we were too much hindered and my ailment did not permit me to give myself much fatigue. Several Ilinois passed yesterday, on their way to carry their furs to nawaskingwe; we gave them one of the cattle and one of the deer that Jacque[2] had killed on the previous day. I do not think that I have ever seen any savages more eager for French tobacco than they. They came and threw beaver-skins at our feet, to get some pieces of it; but we returned these, giving them some pipefuls of

[1] Reuben Gold Thwaites (ed.), *The Jesuit Relations and Allied Documents* (73 vols.; Cleveland: Burrows Bros. Co., 1896–1901), LIX, 173–83. Reprinted by permission of Burrows Bros. Co.

[2] This was probably Jacques Largilliers, a Jesuit *donné*, in the service of the mission at Green Bay.

13

the tobacco because we had not yet decided whether we would go farther.

December 15. Chachagwessiou and the other Ilinois left us, to go and join their people and give them the goods that they had brought, in order to obtain their robes. In this they act like the traders, and give hardly any more than do the French. I instructed them before their departure, deferring the holding of a council until the spring, when I should be in their village. They traded us 3 fine robes of ox-skins for a cubit of tobacco; these were very useful to us during the winter. Being thus rid of them, we said The mass of the Conception. After the 14th, my disease turned into a bloody flux.

December 30. Jacque arrived from the Ilinois village, which is only six leagues from here; there they were suffering from hunger, because the cold and snow prevented them from hunting. Some of them notified la Toupine[3] and the surgeon that we were here; and, as they could not leave their cabin, they had so frightened the savages, believing that we would suffer from hunger if we remained here, that Jacque had much difficulty in preventing 15 young men from coming to carry away all our belongings.

January 16, 1675. As soon as the 2 frenchmen learned that my illness prevented me from going to them, the surgeon came here with a savage, to bring us some blueberries and corn. They are only 18 leagues from here, in a fine place for hunting cattle, deer, and turkeys, which are excellent there. They had also collected provisions while waiting for us; and had given the savages to understand that their cabin belonged to the black gown; and it may be said that they have done and said all that could be expected from them. After the surgeon had spent some time here, in order to perform his devotions, I sent Jacque with

---

[3] Pierre Moreau, whose surname was La Toupine. He was born near Xaintes, France, in 1639. In the *procès-verbal* drawn up by St. Lusson at Sault Ste. Marie in 1671 he is described as "a soldier in the garrison of the castle of Quebec." He became a noted fur-trader, and it is claimed that as a friend of Frontenac the latter protected him in illegal trading. He died at Quebec in 1727. It is also supposed that he was with Marquette and Jolliet on their expedition to the Mississippi River in 1673 (Steck, *op. cit.*, p. 150).

him to tell the Ilinois near that place that my illness prevented me from going to see them; and that I would even have some difficulty in going there in the spring, if it continued.

December 24. Jacque returned with a sack of corn and other delicacies, which the French had given him for me. He also brought the tongues and flesh of two cattle, which a savage and he had killed near here. But all the animals feel the bad weather.

December 26. 3 Ilinois brought us, on behalf of the elders, 2 sacks of corn, some dried meat, pumpkins, and 12 beaver-skins: 1st, to make me a mat; 2nd, to ask me for powder; 3rd, that we might not be hungry; 4th, to obtain a few goods. I replied: 1st, that I had come to instruct them, by speaking to them of prayer, etc.; 2nd, that I would give them no powder, because we sought to restore peace everywhere, and I did not wish them to begin war with the muiamis; 3rd, that we feared not hunger; 4th, that I would encourage the french to bring them goods, and that they must give satisfaction to those who were among them for the beads which they had taken as soon as the surgeon started to come here. As they had come a distance of 20 leagues, I gave them, in order to reward them for their trouble and for what they had brought me, a hatchet, 2 knives, 3 clasp-knives, 10 brasses of glass beads, and 2 double mirrors, telling them that I would endeavor to go to the village,—for a few days only, if my illness continued. They told me to take courage, and to remain and die in their country; and that they had been informed that I would remain there for a long time.

February 9. Since we addressed ourselves to the blessed Virgin Immaculate, and commenced a novena with a mass,— at which Pierre[4] and Jacque, who do everything they can to relieve me, received communion,—to ask God to restore my health, my bloody flux has left me, and all that remains is a weakness of the stomach. I am beginning to feel much better, and to regain my strength. Out of a cabin of Ilinois, who encamped near us for a

---

[4] Pierre Porteret, another Jesuit *donné*, who accompanied Marquette. Porteret is also supposed to have been a member of the Jolliet-Marquette Expedition of 1673 (Steck, *op. cit.*, p. 150).

month, a portion have again taken the road to the Poutewata-
mis, and some are still on the lake-shore, where they wait until
navigation is open. They bear letters for our Fathers of st.
François.

February 20. We have had opportunity to observe the tides
coming in from the lake, which rise and fall several times a day;
and, although there seems to be no shelter in the lake, we have
seen the ice going against the wind. These tides made the water
good or bad, because that which flows from above comes from
prairies and small streams. The deer, which are plentiful near
the lake-shore, are so lean that we had to abandon some of those
which we had killed.

March 23. We killed several partridges, only the males of
which had ruffs on the neck, the females not having any. These
partridges are very good, but not like those of france.

March 30. The north wind delayed the thaw until the 25th of
March, when it set in with a south wind. On the very next day,
game began to make its appearance. We killed 30 pigeons,
which I found better than those down the great river; but they
are smaller, both old and young. On the 28th, the ice broke up,
and stopped above us. On the 29th, the waters rose so high that
we had barely time to decamp as fast as possible, putting our
goods in the trees, and trying to sleep on a hillock. The water
gained on us nearly all night, but there was a slight freeze, and
the water fell a little, while we were near our packages. The
barrier has just broken, the ice has drifted away; and, because
the water is already rising, we are about to embark to continue
our journey.

The blessed Virgin Immaculate has taken such care of us during our wintering that we have not lacked provisions, and have
still remaining a large sack of corn, with some meat and fat. We
also lived very pleasantly for my illness did not prevent me from
saying holy mass every day. We were unable to keep Lent, except on Fridays and saturdays.

March 31. We started yesterday and traveled 3 leagues up
the river without finding any portage. We hauled our goods
probably about half an arpent. Besides this discharge, the river

has another one by which we are to go down. The very high lands alone are not flooded. At the place where we are, the water has risen more than 12 feet. This is where we began our portage 18 months Ago. Bustards and ducks pass continually; we contented ourselves with 7. The ice, which is still drifting down, keeps us here, as we do not know in what condition the lower part of the river is.

JOHN FRANCIS BUISSON de ST.COSME[1]

JOHN FRANCIS BUISSON DE ST. COSME, missionary, was born in New France, January 30, 1667, and was ordained as priest in 1690. In the summer of 1698, Francis Laval, Bishop of Canada, sent three Seminary priests into the Southwest to establish missions among the unconverted Indians of that region: Francis Jolliet de Montigny, Antoine Davion, and St. Cosme. They were accompanied by several other Canadians, *voyageurs*, and *engagés*.

At Michillimackinac the party met with Henri de Tonty, friend of La Salle and commandant in Illinois, who accompanied them into the latter country. Unable to make a portage from the Root River to the Fox, they proceeded to Chicago, where they arrived in October. From there they went on to their various stations, St. Cosme going to the Natchez Indians.

He became very popular among these people but was not successful in converting them to Christianity. In 1707 he found it necessary to visit Mobile, and set out with a few Frenchmen for that place. When they had almost reached their destination, the party was massacred by some hostile Indians. The Natchez, however, avenged his death by exterminating the tribe which committed the murders, and gave his name to the chief's younger son.

The following account is part of a letter written by St. Cosme from the Arkansas country, January 2, 1699, to the Bishop of Quebec. The original manuscript is in the University of Laval, Quebec.

➤➤ ◄◄◄

THE MISSION OF THE GUARDIAN ANGEL

On the 10th of October, having left Meliwarik[2] early in the morning, we arrived in good season at Kipikawi,[3] which is about eight leagues from it. There we parted with Mr. de Vincennes's party,[4] who continued their course towards the Miamis. Some Indians had led us to suppose that we might ascend by this river, and that after making a portage of about nine leagues, we could

---

[1] John Gilmary Shea (ed.), *Early Voyages up and down the Mississippi by Cavelier, St. Cosme, Le Sueur, Gravier, and Guignas* (Albany: Joel Munsell, 1861), pp. 50–56.

[2] Milwaukee.

[3] Racine, Wisconsin.

[4] This is one of the earliest references to Jean Baptiste Bissot, sieur de Vincennes. He founded a French post among the Miami Indians, and died at what is now Fort Wayne, Indiana, in 1719. It was his nephew who founded Vincennes, Indiana.

18

descend by another river called Pistrui,[5] which empties into the River of the Illinois about twenty-five or thirty leagues from Chikagu. We avoided this river, which is about twenty leagues in length up to the portage. It passes through quite pleasant prairies, but as there was no water in it, we judged sagely too that there would not be in the Bestikwi,[6] and that instead of shortening our way, we should have had to make nearly forty leagues of the way as a portage. This obliged us to take the route of Chicagu, which is about twenty-five leagues from it. We remained five days at Kipikuskwi.[7]

We left it on the 17th, and after having been detained by wind the 18th and 19th, we cabined on the 20th five leagues from the Chicaqw. We should have reached it early on the 21st, but the wind, which suddenly sprung up from the lake, obliged us to land half a league from Apkaw.[8] We had considerable difficulty in getting ashore and saving our canoes. We had to throw everything into the water. This is a thing which you must take good care of along the lakes, and especially on [Lake] Missigan, (the shores of which are very flat) to land soon where the water swells from the lake, for the breakers get so large in a short time that the canoes are in risk of going to pieces and losing all on board; several travellers have already been wrecked there. We went by land, Mr. de Montigny,[9] Davion and myself, to the

[5] Fox River.

[6] Another name for the Fox River.

[7] Racine, Wisconsin.

[8] Chicago. In editing this account, Shea had recourse to a transcript made for Francis Parkman. The copyist was unable to make out correctly some of St. Cosme's handwriting, and "Apkaw" is undoubtedly meant to be "Chicago."

[9] "Rev. Francis Jolliet de Montigny, the leader of the party whose journey is here described, was born at Paris, but ordained at Quebec, March 8, 1693. After being Curé of St. Ange Gardien and Director of the Ursulines, he set out to found a mission of the Seminary of Quebec on the Mississippi. He bore the appointment of Vicar General of the Bishop of Quebec, and was attended, as we here see, by Messrs. Davion and St. Cosme. The outfit of this mission is said to have cost 10,800 livres. They founded a mission at Tamarois, of which the Jesuits complained; and after considerable altercation Mr. de Montigny in 1700 retired, and going to France, refused to return to America. He was then sent to China where he labored with great zeal and, becoming Secretary to Cardinal de Tournon shared his exile and attended him on his death-bed in prison at Macao. Mr. de Montigny then returned to Paris and there became Director of the Foreign Missions, and died in 1725 at the age of 64" (note by John G. Shea).

house of the Reverend Jesuit Fathers, our people staying with the baggage. We found there Rev. Father Pinet and Rev. Father Buinateau,[10] who had recently come in from the Illinois and were slightly sick.

I cannot explain to you, Monseigneur, with what cordiality and marks of esteem these reverend Jesuit Fathers received and caressed us during the time that we had the consolation of staying with them. Their house is built on the banks of the small lake, having the lake on one side and a fine large prairie on the other. The Indian village is of over 150 cabins, and one league on the river there is another village almost as large. They are both of the Miamis. Rev. Father Pinet makes it his ordinary residence except in winter, when the Indians all go hunting, and which he goes and spends at the Illinois. We saw no Indians there, they had already started for their hunt. If we may judge of the future by the little while that Father Pinet has been on this mission, we may say that God blesses the labors and zeal of this holy missionary. There will be a great number of good and fervent Christians there. It is true that little fruit is produced there in those who have grown up and hardened in debauchery, but the children are baptized and even the medicine men, most opposed to Christianity, allow their children to be baptized. They are even very glad to have them instructed. Many girls already grown up and many young boys are being instructed, so that it may be hoped that when the old stock dies off there will be a new Christian people.

On the 24th of October, the wind having fallen, we made our canoes come with all our baggage, and perceiving that the waters were extremely low we made a *cache* on the shore and took only what was absolutely necessary for our voyage, reserving till spring to send for the rest, and we left in charge of it Brother Alexander, who consented to remain there with Father Pinet's man, and we started from Chicaqw on the 29th and put up for the night about two leagues off, in the little river which is then

---

[10] "Father Julian Binnateau was a missionary in Maine in 1693, and died of a fever brought on by his labors soon after this visit of St. Cosme, as Father Gravier in 1700 does not refer to him" (note by John G. Shea).

lost in the prairies. The next day we began the portage, which is about three leagues long when the water is low, and only a quarter of a league in the spring, for you embark on a little lake that empties into a branch of the river of the Illinois,[11] and when the waters are low you have to make a portage to that branch. We made half our portage that day, and we should have made some progress further, when we perceived that a little boy whom we had received from Mr. de Muys,[12] having started on alone, although he had been told to wait, had got lost without any one paying attention to it, all hands being engaged. We were obliged to stop and look for him. All set out, we fired several guns, but could not find him. It was a very unfortunate mishap, we were pressed by the season and the waters being very low, we saw well that being obliged to carry our effects and our canoe it would take a great while to reach the Illinois. This made us part company, Mr. Montigny, de Tonty and Davion,[13] continued the portage next day, and I with four other men returned to look for this little boy, and on my way back I met Fathers Pinet and Buinateau who were going with two Frenchmen and one Indian to the Illinois. We looked for him again all that day without being able to find him. As next day was the feast of All Saints this obliged me to go and pass the night at Chikagou with our people, who having heard mass and performed their devotions early, we spent all that day too in looking for that little boy without being able to get the least trace. It was very difficult to find him in the tall grass, for the whole country is prairies; you meet only some clumps of woods. As the grass was high we durst not set fire to

[11] Mud Lake.

[12] "M. de Muys. An officer of this name figures several times in the French reports of the west (O'Callaghan's New York Col. Doc., ix), and is apparently the one appointed governor of Louisiana in 1707; a lieutenant of the same name was at Fort Le Boeuf in October, 1753" (note by John G. Shea).

[13] "Rev. Anthony Davion began a mission among the Tonicas, but labored almost in vain. On the murder of Rev. Mr. Foucault he retired to Mobile, but returned to his post in 1704, and remained for over twelve years till in fact, the incorrigible tribe drove him out. He retired to New Orleans about 1722, and died in France about 1727. He is said to have been a native of Normandy and to have arrived at Quebec in 1690" (note by John G. Shea).

it for fear of burning him. Mr. de Montigny had told me not to stay over a day, because the cold was becoming severe; this obliged me to start after giving Brother Alexander directions to look for him and to take some of the French who were at Chicagou.[14]

[14] This little boy returned to the mission thirteen days later, exhausted and out of his mind.

SAMUEL A. STORROW[1]

A FEW scattered facts are all that are known of Samuel A. Storrow. He was born in New Hampshire, but he probably lived most of his life in Massachusetts. In 1815 he was acting judge advocate in the United States Army and was judge advocate in 1816. He resigned his commission February 5, 1820.

In the late summer of 1817 he trekked west, at the request of Major General Jacob Brown, to make a critical report to the general on the military posts in the Northwest and the general condition of the country. On August 17, 1817, Storrow left Detroit for Fort Gratiot and arrived there on the evening of August 19. After reporting upon the desirability of the location as a protective outpost for Detroit, he left on a small vessel for Michillimackinac on August 22. About twenty-four hours later a severe tempest forced the boat into the strait, where it was kept until the twenty-fifth, not reaching Michillimackinac until the morning of the twenty-eighth.

On September 1, he left for the Falls of St. Mary's, where he found an establishment of the North-West Fur Company. St. Mary's was more strategically located than Michillimackinac, and he recommended the transfer of the post at the latter place to St. Mary's. In a birch canoe manned by Canadian *voyageurs* he returned to Michillimackinac on September 7. A couple of days later he embarked in an open boat for Green Bay. The frequent storms on the lake often required travel overland, and Storrow remarked that the scene of the soldiers, who accompanied him carrying their baggage, resembled Africa more than America. The party arrived at the fort of Green Bay on the nineteenth.

His remarks on the journey from there to Chicago are similar to those he made on other parts of his trip. He talked of the climate, soils, geological formation, Indians, trade routes, and the military advantages.

A five days' journey, after leaving Chicago on October 4, put him in Fort Wayne. The ease of the voyage and the natural highways impressed him. With prophetic eye he envisaged a canal to be cut between the Chicago and Des Plaines rivers, using Fort Wayne as an entrepôt for the collection of the products of Ohio and Indiana, thus making Chicago an important gateway to the Mississippi Valley.

From Fort Wayne he returned to Detroit on October 16. From there he traveled through upper Canada to Fort George, then to Niagara, to Brownsville, New York, where he joined General Brown.

[1] Samuel A. Storrow, "The North-West in 1817," in Wisconsin State Historical Society, *Collections*, VI (1869–72), 169–81. Reprinted by permission of the State Historical Society of Wisconsin.

THE SOIL OF CHICAGO

After a short stay at Green Bay, I made arrangements with a Fals Avoine chief to conduct me as a guide to the Winnebago Lake; from whence it was my determination to proceed on foot, through the wilderness, to Chicago. At mid-day of the 22d of September, I took leave of Maj. Taylor[2] and the officers of the 3d Regiment, who had most kindly entertained me. I likewise took a reluctant leave of my excellent companion, Mr. Pierce.[3] For the residue of the day my course lay on the left bank of the river, through good lands and a growth of oak. I passed two springs strongly impregnated with sulphur, and at night stopped at a rapid of the river called Kakalin, being the last house and the last whites I expected to see for the distance of 250 miles. . . . .

On the 2d of October, after walking for three or four hours, I reached the river Chicago, and, after crossing it, entered Fort Dearborn, where I was kindly entertained by Major Baker[4] and the officers of the garrison, who received me as one arrived from the moon. At Chicago I perceived I was in a better country. It had become so by gradual melioration. That which I had left was of a character far above mediocrity, but labors under the permanent defects of coldness of soil and want of moisture. The native strength of it is indicated by the growth of timber, which is almost entirely of white oak and beech, without pine, chestnut, maple, ash, or any kind which denotes warmth. The country suffers at the same time from water and from the want of it.

[2] Zachary Taylor, later president of the United States.

[3] Lieutenant John Sullivan Pierce, artillery, stationed at Michillimackinac, accompanied Storrow from that place to the Falls of St. Mary's, and then on to Green Bay. Lieutenant Pierce was born in New Hampshire. He was commissioned third lieutenant in the third artillery, April 5, 1814, and was promoted to second lieutenant May 1 of this same year and to first lieutenant April 20, 1818. He resigned February 1, 1823, and died in 1825.

[4] Major Daniel Baker, born in New Hampshire, was commissioned ensign January 8, 1799. Honorably discharged June 15, 1800, he re-enlisted and was commissioned second lieutenant February 16, 1801; a first lieutenant August 11, 1806; captain March 12, 1812; breveted major April 15, 1814, but retained as captain; major, June 1, 1819; lieutenant colonel, May 1, 1829. Major Baker was distinguished for services and bravery at the battle of Maguago and the affair at Lyon's Creek in the War of 1812, and at the Battle of Bad Axe in 1832, when he commanded a regiment. Major Baker died October 10, 1836.

The deficiency of circulation, not of water itself, produces this contradiction. It is not sufficiently uneven to form brooks to lead off its redundant rains and form a deposit for mid-summer. The snows of winter dissolve and remain on the ground until exhaled by the sun at a late period of spring. In prairies that are entirely level this produces a cold which is scarcely dissipated by the heat of summer; in such as are undulated, it renders one-half (that on which the water rests) useless, or of inferior value. It must be remembered, moreover, that this region is not to undergo the changes incident to new countries generally, from the thinning of forests and exposure of the soil. It is already on the footing of the oldest, and has received for the lapse of ages all the heat it is ever to derive from the sun alone. At some remotely future period, when a dense population enables the husbandman to apply artificial warmth to his grounds, means of life may be extracted from this soil which are latent at present. It requires industry, and is capable of repaying it.

THE CHICAGO RIVER

The river Chicago (or, in English, Wild Onion river) is deep and about forty yards in width, before it enters the Lake, its two branches unite—the one proceeding from the north, the other from the west, where it takes its rise in the fountain of the De Plein, or Illinois, which flows in an opposite direction. The source of these two rivers illustrates the geographical phenomenon of a reservoir on the very summit of a dividing ridge. In the autumn, they are both without any apparent fountain, but are formed within a mile and a half of each other by some imperceptible undulations of the prairie, which drain it and lead to different directions. But in the spring, the space between the two is a single sheet of water, the common reservoir of both, in the centre of which there is no current towards either of the opposite streams. This circumstance creates the singular fact of the insulation of all the United States excepting Louisiana, making the circumnavigation of them practicable, from the Gulf of St. Lawrence to that of Mexico, with the single hindrance of the Falls of Niagara.

The Chicago forms a third partition of the great country I had passed. The Ouisconsin and Fox Rivers make a water communication between the Mississippi and Michigan, with the exception of four miles. The Millewackie and *River a la Roche* the same, with half the exception. The Chicago and De Plein make, in the manner I have described, the communication entire. The ground between the two is without rocks, and, with little labor, would admit of a permanent connection between the waters of the Illinois and Michigan.

The site and relations of Fort Dearborn I have already explained. It has no advantage of harbor, the river itself being always choked, and frequently barred, from the same causes that I have imputed to the other streams of this country. In the rear of the fort is a prairie of the most complete flatness, no sign of elevation being within the range of the eye. The soil and climate are both excellent. Traces yet remain of the devastation and massacre committed by the savages in 1812. I saw one of the principal perpetrators, (Nes-cot-no-meg.)[5]

[5] Nuscotnemeg ("Mad Sturgeon"), a Pottawattomie chief, was one of the bitterest enemies of the white man. By 1812 he had achieved renown by his list of white murders. Engaged in a horse-stealing expedition in 1810, he and his band murdered four white men near Portage des Sioux. With one other Indian he made his escape and took refuge with the Prophet. Governor Edwards and Governor Harrison made demands for Nuscotnemeg's return, but without success. In the massacre of Fort Dearborn he was one of the prominent chiefs of the hostile Indians.

—»» «««—

JOHN TIPTON[1]

JOHN TIPTON was born in Sevier County, Tennessee, August 14, 1786. Seven years later his father, Joshua, who had emigrated from Maryland, was killed by the Indians. In 1807 Tipton moved his family to Brinkley's Ferry, Harrison County, Indiana. In two years he became a member of Captain Spier Spencer's Yellow Jackets, later reaching the rank of ensign, serving in the Indian campaigns which ended in the Battle of Tippecanoe. At this time the death of his captain and both lieutenants left him in command of the company.

His activities next led him into the realm of politics. Harrison County elected him sheriff in 1815, to which office he was re-elected through 1819. He then became a member of the legislature, and in the following year he was on the commission which selected the site of the new state capital, Indianapolis. In 1821 he was chosen chairman of a commission of the legislature to confer with one from Illinois for the surveying of the boundary line between the two states. The survey was begun at Vincennes early in the summer of 1821, and the line marked to Lake Michigan. Two years later Tipton was appointed government Indian agent for the Pottawattomie and Miami Indians. In January, 1831, Indiana's first senator, James Noble, died and to John Tipton fell the duty of filling the vacancy. He was elected to serve a full term in the senate in 1832. April 5, 1839, he died.

Trained on the frontier, Tipton, although without education, was a keen observer; and his journal of the Battle of Tippecanoe is one of the valuable source accounts of that memorable campaign. His literary knowledge grew with the years, as shown by the various notices he inserted in Corydon newspapers asking the return of certain of his library books.

As the author of the journal in many instances never troubled himself with terminal punctuation, the editor has taken the liberty to supply periods and capitalize the beginning of many sentences. Likewise, the editor has supplied the words in brackets in order to make clear the meaning.

—»» «««—

FORT DEARBORN AND CHICAGO

Satureday, 30th June 1821, par[t] of this day we spent in examining Chicago, the Lake, Shore, River, &c.

Fort Dearborn stands on the western Shoar of Lake Michigan [on the] south side of the mouth of [the] Chicago River, in Lati-

[1] John Tipton, Journal, "Surveying line between Indiana and Illinois, 1821," MS. Tipton Collection, Indiana State Library, Indianapolis. Printed by permission of the Indiana State Library.

tude 42 degrees 9 minute[s] north, [and] about 210 miles north
& 8 west from vincennes. [It] is about 50 yds square with one
Blockhouse in the south west corner, one six pounder in a Bastion [in the] south E corner on the Lake, & one in the north west.
[There is] no Bastion in the north east [corner] on the Lake &
mouth of the River. [There are] comfortable Barracks and
Rooms for soldiers & officers, a good Brick magazene, the latter
Built Before this place fell into the hands of the Indians in 1812
& would not Burn when the oald Fort was Destroyed. [The
fort] is now under the command of Major Cremmis[2] of the 3d
US Regt & Capt Bradly[3] with about 140 fine healthy soldiers.

The Grarison [garrison] cultivates an excellent Gueardion
[garden and] has a fine large field of good wheat which Just Be-
gining to head. At 12 oclock attended an inspection of Arms.

The village of Chicago consist[s] of about 9 or 10 houses &
families mostly French Trader[s] without any kind of civil government. The village [is] situate[d] on Boath Side [s] of the
mouth of [the] Chicago River. The Prairie here [is] high, Dry,
Sandy Soil ellivated about 15 feet above the levil of the water of
the Lake. Chicago River at is [its] mouth [is] about 3 or 4 chain
wide. [It] puts in from west to east through the Prairie with a
small grove on its S Bank & one on the north, neither of which
continues down to the Lake Shoar. A high narrow Sod Barr
puts out from the front of Land on the north Side of Chicago
River [and] Runs parrellell with the Lake *Shore* about 40 chain.
The River passes between this Barr and the main land below
the village & its mouth [is] constantly chocked up with Sand,
affording not more than 2 feet of water at the mouth while the
common depth of the River from this Barr to the fork, the dis-

---

[2] There appears to have been no Major Cremmis in the United States Army. Major
Daniel Baker was the commanding major at this time. Tipton may have meant Major
Alexander Cummings, who preceded Baker.

[3] Captain Hezekiah Bradly, born in Virginia, was commissioned ensign of the Second
Regiment of Infantry, December 12, 1808; second lieutenant, January 1, 1810; first
lieutenant, August 15, 1812; and captain, April 19, 1814. May 17, 1815 he was trans-
ferred to the Third Regiment of Infantry. He was sent to re-establish and command
Fort Dearborn in 1816. He was breveted Major, April 19, 1824. Bradly died March 18,
1826.

tance of half a mile, is 16 feet. (Through the Barr the soldiers have cut a pass for the water of the River opiset its mouth.) The north fork runs parrellell with the Lake *Shore* for some distance, then runs more west and extends 25 mile[s] in the country. The South fork Rises in a pond 5 mile west of the mouth in a levil prairie, through which pond there is nine mile of a portage to the Le Plein River, a Branch of Illinois. We are told in high time of water it flows out of this Pond into Boath River and that cannoes can pass [from] it out of one River into the other.

A communication can easily be opened between them. The Greatest difficulty seems to be that of the water beeing 5 or 6 feet higher in the Le Plein River than the levil of the Lake.

The Le Plein River has some falls of small manitude [magnitude] for some distance down it, and is intersected by the Kankekee River at the distance of 60 miles from Chicago which then forms the Illinois River. Throughout the whole country [there] seems to be a grate wont of Timber & what *few* groves we have seen is low scrubby Trees mostly oak and fiew of sufficient lenght to afford more than one rail lenght, an[d] many not so long. Grate part of the Prairie [is] low and wet, and the dry land [is] very sandy on the margin of the lake. Half mile south of Chicago are some hills of white sand that appeare to have been formed by the Beating of the waves and wind, [and are] ellivated some ten or 12 feet above the levil of the Prairie, and near 30 above the Lake on which grows a small grove of low pine. Near this grove, on the edge of the Prairie, [we] saw the bones of the men killed at the time Ft Dearborn was evacuated in 1812 in attempt to effect their retreat to Ft Wayn under William Wells.

This evening we spent with Doctr Walcott[4] Indian agent at

[4] Dr. Alexander Wolcott, physician and Indian agent, was born in Windsor, Connecticut, February 14, 1790, son of Alexander Wolcott and Frances Burbank. Dr. Wolcott graduated from Yale University in 1809; but as that University had no medical school until 1814, he received his medical training elsewhere. In 1820 he was appointed United States Indian agent at Chicago, succeeding Charles Jewett (or Jouett). In the same year Dr. Wolcott married Ellen Marion Kinzie, daughter of John Kinzie. Miss Kinzie is said to have been the first white child born in Chicago. She was born in December, 1804. Dr. Wolcott served as Indian agent until his death in 1830. He also acted as surgeon for the garrison at various times.

this place who invited Mrss McClintoc, mcdonald,[5] & myself to his house where we had a verry pleasant evening, had wine &c &c &c. From the Doctor we obtained much satisfactory information Relative to the Lake, Rivers, country, &c.

Sunday, the first of July.
We left Chicago early having procured from Capt Bradly, of the Army, Pork & Flour for our Return.

[5] John McDonald, Knox County, Indiana, was the surveyor and was paid $4.50 per mile.
  Samuel McClintock was the Illinois commissioner.

WILLIAM H. KEATING[1]

WILLIAM H. KEATING (August 11, 1799—May 17, 1840), geologist and historian of Long's Expedition, was a descendant of Irish emigrants who fled to France to escape religious persecution. At the outbreak of the French Revolution, his father, Baron John Keating, a colonel in the French army stationed in the West Indies, resigned his commission and moved to Delaware, where William was born.

Graduated from the University of Pennsylvania in 1816, Keating was sent abroad and studied in the polytechnic and mining schools of France and Switzerland. On his return to this country he served as professor of chemistry at his Alma Mater from 1822 to 1827. In 1823, as geologist and historian, he accompanied Long's Expedition to discover the extent of the fur trade carried on by the American and British companies in the upper Mississippi and Red River valleys, and to make geological studies of the country along the 49th Parallel of North Latitude.

The party traveled by light carriages from Philadelphia to Wheeling, and from there on by horseback, making topographical and geological studies of the country; finding the latitude and longitude of all "the remarkable points"; describing the animals, vegetation, climate, and the Indians and their customs. Keating was interested in the expedition not only for these purposes but also because it gave him an opportunity to compare the value of various makes of scientific tools and to discover the advantages of materials and workmanship for reliability and accuracy.

In 1822 he was elected a member of the American Philosophical Society. The year following the Long Expedition, he was influential in establishing the Franklin Institute, Philadelphia, and became professor of chemistry there. He later studied law and was admitted to the Philadelphia bar, building up a lucrative law practice. At the time of his death, he was in London negotiating a first-mortgage loan for the Reading Railroad Company.

Little did the geologist dream that Chicago, a village which presented "no cheering prospect," consisting "of but a few huts,"and "inhabited by a race of miserable men," where "it was impossible for the garrison, consisting of from seventy to ninety men, to subsist upon the grain raised in the country," and where the provisions for the garrison had to be brought from Mackinaw or St. Louis, would, within a hundred years, become the greatest grain center of the world and the second city in the United States.

[1] William H. Keating, *Narrative of an Expedition to the Source of St. Peter's River* (2 vols.; London: George B. Whittaker, 1825), I, 162–75.

31

THE NATURAL HISTORY, INDIANS, AND DISADVANTAGES
OF CHICAGO

In the afternoon of the fifth of June [1823], we reached Fort
Dearborn (Chicago), having been engaged eight days in travelling a distance of two hundred and sixteen miles, making an average, of twenty-seven miles per day. Our estimate of the distance
exceeds the usual allowance by sixteen miles, on account of the
circuitous route which we took to avoid crossing the Elkheart.
At Fort Dearborn we stopped for a few days, with a view to examine the country and make further preparations for the journey to the Mississippi. . . . .

Fort Dearborn is situated in the State of Illinois, on the south
bank, and near to the mouth of the Chicago river; the boundary
line between this state and that of Indiana strikes the western
shore of Lake Michigan ten miles north of its southernmost extremity, and then continues along the shore of the lake until it
reaches the forty-second and a half degree of north latitude,
along which it extends to the Mississippi. The post at Chicago
was abandoned a few months after the party visited it. Its establishment had been found necessary to intimidate the hostile
and still very powerful tribes of Indians that inhabit this part
of the country; but the rapid extension of the white population
to the west, the establishment along the Mississippi of a chain
of military posts which encloses them, and at the same time
convinces them of the vigilance of the government, and of the inevitable destruction which they would bring upon themselves by
the most trifling act of hostility on their part, have, it is thought,
rendered the continuance of a military force at this place unnecessary. An Indian agent remains there,[2] in order to keep up
amicable relations with them, and to attend to their wants,
which are daily becoming greater, owing to the increasing scarcity of game in the country.

We were much disappointed at the appearance of Chicago and
its vicinity. We found in it nothing to justify the great eulogium
lavished upon this place by a late traveller, who observes that

[2] Dr. Alexander Wolcott.

"it is the most fertile and beautiful that can be imagined." "As a farming country," says he, "it unites the fertile soil of the finest lowland prairies with an elevation which exempts it from the influence of stagnant waters, and a summer climate of delightful serenity."[3] The best comment upon this description of the climate and soil is the fact that, with the most active vigilance on the part of the officers, it was impossible for the garrison, consisting of from seventy to ninety men, to subsist upon the grain raised in the country, although much of their time was devoted to agricultural pursuits. The difficulties which the agriculturist meets with here are numerous; they arise from the shallowness of the soil, from its humidity, and from its exposure to the cold and damp winds which blow from the lake with great force during most part of the year. The grain is frequently destroyed by swarms of insects. There are also a number of destructive birds of which it was impossible for the garrison to avoid the baneful influence, except by keeping, as was practiced at Fort Dearborn, a party of soldiers constantly engaged in shooting at the crows and blackbirds that committed depredations upon the corn planted by them. But, even with all these exertions the maize seldom has time to ripen, owing to the shortness and coldness of the season. The provisions for the garrison were, for the most part, conveyed from Mackinaw in a schooner, and sometimes they were brought from St. Louis, a distance of three hundred and eighty-six miles up the Illinois and Des Plaines rivers.

The appearance of the country near Chicago offers but few features upon which the eye of the traveller can dwell with pleasure. There is too much uniformity in the scenery; the extensive water prospect is a waste uncheckered by islands, unenlivened by the spreading canvass, and the fatiguing monotony of which is increased by the equally undiversified prospect of the land scenery, which affords no relief to the sight, as it consists merely of a plain, in which but few patches of thin and scrubby woods are observed scattered here and there.

The village presents no cheering prospect, as, notwithstand-

[3] Henry R. Schoolcraft, *Narrative Journal of Travels through the Northwestern Regions of the United States* (Albany: E. & E. Hosford, 1821), p. 384.

ing its antiquity, it consists of but few huts, inhabited by a miserable race of men, scarcely equal to the Indians from whom they are descended. Their log or bark-houses are low, filthy and disgusting, displaying not the least trace of comfort. Chicago is, perhaps, one of the oldest settlements in the Indian country; its name, derived from the Potawatomi language, signifies either a skunk, or wild onion; and each of these significations has been occasionally given for it. . . . The number of trails centering all at this spot, and their apparent antiquity, indicate that this was probably for a long while the site of a large Indian village. As a place of business, it offers no inducement to the settler; for the whole annual amount of trade on the lake did not exceed the cargo of five or six schooners, even at the time when the garrison received its supplies from Mackinaw. It is not impossible that at some distant day, when the banks of the Illinois shall have been covered with a dense population, and when the low prairies which extend between that river and Fort Wayne, shall have acquired a population proportionate to the produce which they can yield, that Chicago may become one of the points in the direct line of communication between the northern lakes and the Mississippi; but even the intercourse which will be carried on through this communication, will, we think, at all times be a limited one; the dangers attending the navigation of the lake, and the scarcity of harbours along the shore, must ever prove a serious obstacle to the increase of the commercial importance of Chicago. The extent of the sand banks which are formed on the eastern and southern shore, by the prevailing north and north-westerly winds, will likewise prevent any important works from being undertaken to improve the post of Chicago.

The south fork of Chicago river takes its rise, about six miles from the fort, in a swamp which communicates also with the Des Plaines, one of the head branches of the Illinois. Having been informed that this route was frequently travelled by traders, and that it had been used by one of the officers of the garrison, who returned with provisions from St. Louis a few days previous to our arrival at the fort, we determined to ascend the Chicago river in order to observe this interesting division of waters.

We accordingly left the fort on the 7th of June, in a boat, which after having ascended the river about four miles, we exchanged for a narrow pirogue that drew less water; the stream we were ascending was very narrow, rapid, and crooked, presenting a great fall; it continued so for about three miles, when we reached a sort of swamp designated by the Canadian voyagers under the name of *le petit lac*. Our course through this swamp, which extended for three miles, was very much impeded by the high grass, weeds, &c. through which our pirogue passed with difficulty. Observing that our progress through the fen was very slow, and the day being considerably advanced, we landed on the north bank, and continued our course along the edge of the swamp for about three miles, until we reached the place where the old portage road meets the current, which was here very distinct towards the south. We were delighted at beholding for the first time, a feature so interesting in itself, but which we had afterwards an opportunity of observing frequently on the route, *viz.*: the division of waters starting from the same source, and running in two different directions, so as to become the feeders of streams that discharge themselves into the ocean at immense distances apart. Although at the time we visited it, there was scarcely water enough to permit our pirogue to pass, we could not doubt, that in the spring of the year, the route must be a very eligible one. Lieut. Hopson,[4] who accompanied us to the Des Plaines, told us that he had travelled it with ease, in a boat loaded with lead and flour. The distance from the fort to the intersection of the Portage road and Des Plaines, is supposed to be about twelve or thirteen miles; the elevation of the feeding lake above Chicago river was estimated at five or six feet; and, it is probable, that the descent to the Des Plaines is less considerable. The Portage road is about eleven miles long; the usual distance travelled by land seldom however exceeds from four to nine miles; in very dry seasons it has been said to amount to thirty miles, as the portage then extends to Mount Juliet, near the confluence of the

4 Lieutenant John D. Hopson was born in Vermont and entered West Point September 24, 1818. He stood thirtieth in his graduating class; and on graduation, July 1, 1822, he was commissioned second lieutenant of the Third Infantry. He was promoted to first lieutenant September 23, 1827, and died February 17, 1829.

Kankakee. When we consider the facts above stated, we are irresistibly led to the conclusion, that an elevation of the lake of a few feet (not exceeding ten or twelve), above their present level, would cause them to discharge their waters, partly at least, into the Gulf of Mexico; that such a discharge has at one time existed, every one conversant with the nature of the country must admit; and it is equally apparent that an expenditure, trifling in comparison to the importance of the object, would again render Lake Michigan a tributary of the Mexican gulf. Impressed with the importance of this object, the legislature of Illinois has already caused some observations to be made upon the possibility of establishing this communication; the commissioners appointed to that effect, visited Chicago after we left it, and we know not what results they obtained, as their report has not reached us; but we have been informed that they had considered the elevation of the *petit lac* above Chicago to be somewhat greater than we had estimated it. It is the opinion of those best acquainted with the nature of the country, that the easiest communication would be between the Little Calamick and some point of the Des Plaines, probably below the Portage road; between these two points there is, in wet seasons, we understand, a water communication of ten or twelve miles. Of the practicability of the work, and of the sufficiency of a supply of water no doubt can exist. The only difficulty will, we apprehend, be in keeping the communication open after it is once made, as the soil is swampy, and probably will require particular care to oppose the return of the soft mud into the excavations.

In the immediate vicinity of Chicago, a secondary limestone is found, disposed in horizontal strata; it contains many organic remains. This limestone appears to us to be very similar in its geological as well as mineralogical aspect, to that observed above the coal formation on the Miami; but no superposition being visible, it is impossible for us to determine at present its relative age; we, however, incline to the opinion, that it is one of the late secondary limestones. We have to regret that the specimens which were obtained of the same have been lost, and that we are

deprived of the opportunity of comparing them with those collected in other parts of our route. This limestone, which lies
exposed to view in some places, is for the most part covered
with an alluvial deposit consisting of the detritus of primitive
rocks. . . . .

Although the quantity of game in this part of the country is
diminishing very rapidly, and although it is barely sufficient for
the support of the Indians, still there is enough, and particularly
of the smaller kind, to offer occupation to the amateur sports-
man. There are many different kinds of aquatic birds, which
feed upon the wild rice (Zizania aquatica), and other plants
that thrive in the swamps which cover the country. Mr. Say observed, among others, the mallard (Anas boschas), shoveller-
duck (A. clypeata), blue winged teal (A. discors), common mer-
ganser (Mergus serrator), common coot (Fulica americana),
stellate heron or Indian hen (Ardea minor), &c. &c. In the lake
there is also a great quantity of fish, but none appears to be of a
very superior quality; the white fish (Coregonus albus, Lesueur),
which is the greatest delicacy found in the lakes, is not caught
at Chicago, but sometimes twenty or thirty miles north of it. . . . .

During our short residence at Chicago, we were, by the favour
of Dr. Wolcott, the Indian agent, furnished with much information concerning the Indians of this vicinity, through his interpreter, Alexander Robinson, a half-breed Chippewa, who informed
us that the Indians who frequent this part of the country are
very much intermixed, belonging principally to the Potawatomis, Ottawas, and Chippewas, (onchepewag,) from which circumstance a great admixture of the three languages prevails
here. The vicinity of the Miamis has also, in his opinion, tended
to adulterate the language of the Potawatomis in the neighbourhood of Fort Wayne; and it is believed that this language is
spoken in the greatest purity, only along the banks of the St.
Joseph of Lake Michigan. Robinson did not suppose the Potawatomis to exceed two thousand five hundred souls; but it is
probable that their number must be greater, especially as they
are united with the Kickapoos, whose population amounts to

six hundred in the State of Illinois. According to his observations, the Potawatomis believe that they come from the vicinity of the Sault de Ste. Marie, where they presume that they were created. A singular belief, which they entertain, is, that the souls of the departed have, on their way to the great prairie, to cross a large stream, over which a log is placed as a bridge; but that this is in such constant agitation, that none but the spirits of good men can pass over it in safety, while those of the bad slip from the log into the water, and are never after heard of. This information they pretend to have had revealed to them by one of their ancestors, who, being dead, travelled to the edge of the stream, but not liking to venture on the log, determined to return to the land of the living, which purpose he effected, having been seen once more among his friends, two days after his reputed death. He informed them of what he had observed, and further told them, that while on the verge of the stream, he had heard the sounds of the drum, to the beat of which the blessed were dancing on the opposite prairie. This story they firmly believe.

With the view to collect as much information as possible on the subject of Indian antiquities, we inquired of Robinson whether any traditions on this subject were current among the Indians. He observed, that their ancient fortifications were a frequent subject of conversation; and especially those in the nature of excavations made in the ground. He had heard of one, made by the Kickapoos and Fox Indians, on the Sangamo river, a stream running into the Illinois. This fortification is distinguished by the name of Etnataek. It is known to have served as an intrenchment to the Kickapoos and Foxes, who were met there and defeated by the Potawatomis, the Ottawas, and the Chippewas. No date was assigned to this transaction. We understand that the Etnataek was near the Kickapoo village on the Sangamo.

The hunting grounds of the Potawatomis appear to be bounded on the north by the St. Joseph (which on the east side of Lake Michigan separates them from the Ottawas) and the Milwacke, which on the west side of the lake, divides them from the Menomones. They spread to the south along the Illinois river about two hundred miles; to the west their grounds extend as far as Rock river, and the Mequin or Spoon river of the Illinois: to the east they probably seldom pass beyond the Wabash. . . . .

Having spent a few days in Chicago, the party left that post on Wednesday, June 11th.

CHARLES BUTLER[1]

CHARLES BUTLER, financier, real estate broker, and railroad promoter, was born at Kinderhook Landing, New York, January 15, 1802, one of the twelve children of Medad and Hannah (Tylee) Butler. At the age of seventeen he entered the law office of Martin Van Buren as a clerk at the salary of $100 per year. In 1822 he served as deputy clerk of the state senate, and two years later was admitted to the New York bar and began practice in Geneva. In 1825, he married Eliza A. Ogden, the sister of William B. Ogden, Chicago's first mayor.

At an early stage of his career, Butler assumed a dual rôle of real estate promoter and lawyer. As the former he early drifted into financing farmers in western New York, and as a lawyer he first gained repute by conducting the prosecution against the kidnappers of William Morgan, the Freemason.

The Black Hawk War aroused Butler's curiosity in the West. In 1833, with Arthur Bronson of New York City, also a financier and real estate broker, he came to Chicago. The future possibilities for investment in Ohio, Indiana, and Chicago stimulated Butler's interest and imagination, leading him to become a prominent eastern promoter of western railroads. Returning to New York, financial offices were opened in Wall Street; and his brother-in-law, William B. Ogden, was sent to Chicago to take care of interests there. The Panic of 1837 left most of the western states financially ruined. The desire of many legislatures to repudiate their bonded indebtedness is a well-known story. As agent for foreign and domestic bondholders of Michigan and Indiana, the situation necessitated a trip to the West; and after a long fight with unruly legislators of both states he succeeded in having the debts refunded, the bondholders losing nothing.

Butler was a man of wide and varied interests. While in Chicago, he aided Reverend Jeremiah Porter in the organization of the First Presbyterian Church and its Sunday School, to which he later gave a library of two hundred volumes, the first library in the city which could well be called "public." He was one of the founders of Hobart College, Geneva, New York, and also of the Union Theological Seminary in New York City. Of the latter, he was president of the Board of Directors from 1870 until his death on December 13, 1897. He was also made a member of the Council of the College of the City of New York in 1836.

The following impressions of Butler, penned in 1881, were based upon several letters and a diary written at the time of his visit to Chicago in 1833. For this reason, the account here used, although composed nearly fifty years later, preserves much contemporary flavor. It is used in preference to the papers

[1] Charles Butler to Chicago Historical Society, December 17, 1881. *Autograph Letters* (Chicago Historical Society), Vol. XXXI. Reprinted by permission of the Chicago Historical Society and the Library of Congress, Manuscript Division.

from which it was taken, because of better literary form. Where additional information is found in the letters and diary, it has been included in footnotes to this account.

→»» «««

CHICAGO IN 1833 IN THE EYES OF AN INVESTOR

From Michigan City[2] to Chicago, a distance of about sixty miles, the journey was performed by me on horseback. There was but one stopping place on the way and that was the house of a Frenchman named Bayeaux who had married an Indian woman.[3] At Calumet River, which was crossed on a float, there was an encampment of Pottawattamie Indians. There were some trees on the westerly bank of the river and in some of these the Indians had hammocks. In making the journey from Michigan City to Chicago I followed the shore of the Lake nearly the whole distance.[4]

I approached Chicago in the afternoon of a beautiful day, the 2d of August [1833]; the Sun setting in a cloudless sky. On my left lay the Prairie bounded only by the distant horizon like a vast expanse of ocean; on my right in the Summer stillness lay Lake Michigan. I had never seen anything more beautiful or captivating in nature. There was an entire absence of animal

[2] Charles Butler to his wife, Eliza, Chicago, Illinois, August 4, 1833: "We left Niles on Thursday morning & rode about 45 miles to *Michigan City!* at the south east corner of Lake Michigan where we lodged at what may be called the city Hotel viz a small log house, with a single room, which answered the purpose of drawing room, sitting room, eating room, and sleeping room. in this room some 11 or 12 persons lodged in beds and on the floor, including of course our host & his wife; the fact is that we have become accustomed & familiarized to scenes, & things which we never dreamed of before leaving home, and which we then should have revolted at; but necessity knows of no laws, & we have been obliged to accommodate ourselves to the custom of the country."

The originals of the 1833 letters and diary are in the Charles Butler Collection, Manuscript Division, Library of Congress.

[3] Charles Butler, Diary, entry of August 2, 1833: "We have now rode 16 miles along the beach & have stopped to feed & refresh. We had provided ourselves with sundry things, crackers, dried beef, port wine &c at Detroit which now come in use."

[4] *Ibid.*: "Passed 'Grand Calimick creek or river' which empties into the Lake Michigan in Indiana rode to Mann's at little Calimick river which empties into the Lake in Illinois about 3 miles west of the line—country for some Distance back has been low & marshy except occasional oak land. Mann's is 12 miles from Chicago never did poor pilgrims more earnestly long to get to a resting place. . . . . Have seen today a great many Indians, Pottawattimies, wretched looking beings *naked*—saw two gran[d] seignors playing cards."

life, nothing visible in the way of human habitation or to indicate the presence of man, and yet it was a scene full of life, for there, spread out before me in every direction, as far as the eye could reach were the germs of life in earth, air and water. I approached Chicago in these closing hours of day, "So calm, so clear, so bright,"—and this was the realization of the objective point of my journey— —

But what was the condition of this objective point, this Chicago of which I was in pursuit, to which I had come? A small settlement, a few hundred people all told, who had come together mostly within the last year or two. The houses, with one or two exceptions, were of the cheapest and most primitive character for human habitation, suggestive of the haste with which they had been put up. A string of these buildings had been erected without much regard to lines on the south side of the Chicago River [South Water Street and Wacker Drive]. On the west side of the South branch, near the junction, a tavern had been improvised for the entertainment of travellers, erected by James Kinzie, but kept by a Mr. Clock, and there we found lodgings.[5] On the north side of the Chicago River at that time, there was but a single building, known as the Block House. I crossed the river in a dug out canoe about opposite to it; my recollection is that the house which had once been occupied by Mr. Kinzie the Indian agent, on the north side near the lake shore had been previously destroyed by fire. The Government had just entered upon the Harbor improvement of the Chicago River; the work was under the charge of Major Bender.[6] Fort Dearborn was a military establishment and just at this time there was a transfer of a company of United States troops from Green Bay or Sault Ste. Marie to Fort Dearborn under the command, I think, of Major Wilcox accompanied by the Rev.

[5] David Clock, proprietor of the Green Tree Tavern.

[6] Butler, Diary, entry of August 3, 1833: "dined with Majr. Geo Bender at the Fort: Lieut. Smith, & Capt. Wilcox: the two last members of the Temperance society & did not drink wine. Capt Wilcox pious & asked a blessing. Majr Bender *almost* a temperance & pious man. He is a gentleman of accomplished mind & manners & an ornament to his profession: There are a great many of the officers & soldiers in the army pious & the temperance reform has elevated the standard of character in the army."

Jeremiah Porter,[7] as Chaplain, to whom I had a letter of introduction. On the morning after my arrival in walking out, I met
a gentleman from whom I enquired where he could be found,
and on exhibiting my letter, he said he was the person and that
he was then on his way to attend the funeral of a child, and he
asked me if I would accompany him as it was nearby, which I
did. On going to the house, which was one of the kind I have
described, new and cheap, we found the father and mother; the
dead child lay in a rude coffin. There was no one else present,
except the parents, Mr. John Wright, Dr. Kimball,[8] Mr. Porter
and myself and it became a question how the remains of the
child should be conveyed to the Cemetery which was on the
west side of the north branch of the river. I recollect that while
we were attending this simple service, we were interrupted by
the noise of the hammer of a workman outside who was engaged
in putting up a shanty for some new comers, and Mr. Porter
went out and secured the assistance of this workman. We acted
as bearers in conveying the remains of this poor child from the
house to the grave and assisted in burying it.[9]

Emigrants were coming in almost every day in wagons of
various forms and in many instances families were living in their
covered wagons while arrangements were made for putting up
shelter for them. It was no uncommon thing for a house such
as would answer the purpose for the time being to be put up in
a few days. Mr. Bronson[10] himself made a contract for a house
to be put up and finished in a week. There were perhaps from
two to three hundred people in Chicago at that time, mostly

[7] Reverend Jeremiah Porter, pastor of the First Presbyterian Church. Also chaplain
of the Fort Dearborn garrison.

[8] John Wright was a storekeeper. His son, John S. Wright, was a real estate and railroad promoter and editor of *Prairie Farmer* and author of *Chicago: Past, Present, and
Future*. Dr. Kimball may be E. S. Kimberly, an early physician.

[9] Butler, Diary, entry of August 3, 1833: "It seemed to me unfeeling in the neighbors
not to come in at least at the funeral & exhibit some interest in the afflictions of a fellow
creature: the family have recently come here as have nearly all the other families in the
place . . . . the people are so much engaged, every family with its own peculiar engagements, that they have no feeling in common with each other's afflictions—a state of feeling & society incident & natural to a *new* place—this is the reason why no one attended
the funeral of this little girl."

[10] Arthur Bronson of New York City.

strangers to each other. In the tavern[11] at which we staid the partitions were chiefly upright studs with sheets attached to them. The house was crowded with people—emigrants and travellers—many of them could only find a sleeping place on the floor, which was covered with weary men at night.

The east window of my bedroom looked out upon Lake Michigan in the distance; Fort Dearborn lying near the margin of the lake, and at this time there was nothing or very little to obstruct the view between the inn and the lake, the Fort and the buildings connected with it being the principal objects and those buildings were very low structures and I could from my window follow the course of the river, the water of which was as pure as that of the Lake, from the point of junction to its entrance into the lake. . . . .[12]

It was on this visit to Chicago with Mr. Bronson, that we spent some time and made the acquaintance of the principal men of the place. Among these, as I now remember, were Mr. Richard J. Hamilton, the Kinzies (John H. and his brother Robert A.) and James Kinzie (the latter a half brother of the former), Mr. John Wright, Dr. Temple, Gurdon S. Hubbard, Col. Owen, and George W. Dole.[13]

[11] Green Tree Tavern. Butler, Diary, entry of August 2, 1833: "Our Tavern presents a fair sample of the state of things at Chicago. It is new & unfinished. The partition walls not lathed & plastered & of course free communication between all the rooms. Mr. B[ronson] & I are accommodated with a *private room!*"

[12] Butler, Diary, entry of August 3, 1833: "The south west window of my room looks off on the prairie, which is boundless to the sight & the sun setting in it is very beautiful. The land around Chicago is not in [the] market. It is uncultivated. Hard clay & limestone bottom."

[13] Colonel Richard Jones Hamilton (1799–1860), lawyer; school teacher; soldier; witness to Indian Treaty of 1833; president of Board of School Trustees; commissioner of school lands of Cook County; judge probate; recorder of deeds; and other public offices.

John H. Kinzie (1803–65), employee of American Fur Company; Indian agent; registrar of public lands; a paymaster in the Union army during the Civil War.

Robert A. Kinzie (1810–73), brother of John H., fur-trader; early Chicago hardware merchant; paymaster in Union army during Civil War with rank of major. He remained in the army until his death.

James Kinzie (1793–1866), half-brother to John H. and Robert A. Kinzie. Fur-trader; first sheriff of Cook County appointed by the governor. In 1835 he removed to Racine, Wisconsin, where he spent the rest of his life.

Dr. John T. Temple (1804–77), physician; credited with having made first autopsy in Chicago; third or fourth civil practitioner in Chicago; received the contract for the

The present condition and prospects of Chicago and its future and that of the country around it, was of course, the subject of constant and exciting discussion. At this time the vast country lying between Lake Michigan and the Mississippi River, (which then seemed to be the natural boundary of the west) and the country lying northwest of it, which now includes Wisconsin, Minnesota and Iowa, lay in one great unoccupied expanse of beautiful land, covered with the most luxuriant vegetation—a vast flower garden—beautiful to look at in its virgin state and ready for the plough of the Farmer. One could not fail to be greatly impressed with this scene, so new and extraordinary and to see there the germ of that future, when these vast plains would be occupied and cultivated, yielding their abundant products of human food and sustaining millions of population. Lake Michigan lay there 420 miles in length north and south, and it was clear to my mind that the productions of that vast country lying west and north west of it on their way to the Eastern market, the great Atlantic seaboard—would necessarily be tributary to Chicago, in the site of which even at this early day the experienced observer saw the germ of a city, destined from its peculiar position near the head of the Lake and its remarkable harbor formed by the river, to become the largest inland commercial Emporium in the United States. . . . .[14]

first mail route from Chicago to Ottawa, Illinois (1834); one of the founders of Rush Medical School; erected the Temple Building. Later he became a convert to the Homeopathic School and moved to St. Louis, where he died.

Gurdon S. Hubbard (1802–86), fur-trader; employee of American Fur Company; soldier; early meat-packer in Chicago; forwarding and commission merchant; member of the first board of canal commissioners; real estate broker; 1868 his packing-house was destroyed by fire; the great fire of 1871 seriously crippled him financially and he retired into private life.

Colonel Thomas J. V. Owen (1801–35), Indian agent at Chicago (1831–33), succeeding Dr. Alexander Wolcott; president of first Board of Town Trustees (1833).

George W. Dole (1800–1860) came to Chicago in 1831; soldier in Black Hawk War; grain-dealer; town trustee and treasurer (1833); member of firm of Newberry and Dole, which later became Dole, Rumsey and Company, forwarding and commission merchants. Dole is said to have been the first meat-packer in Chicago and to have shipped the first grain from Chicago (1839).

[14] Butler, Diary, entry of August 3, 1833: "The prairie extends upwards of 300 miles from Chicago. The country northwest from C. very fine. I learn the Govt. is constructing a harbor at this point & there is no reason why C. should not become a very large city. It is at the head of navigation—it enjoys commercial advantages equal to Buffalo, & in

With this feeling of inspiration with regard to the future of Chicago which pervaded in common the leading spirits of the place, we entered into plans to promote its future development, and among these the most important which was at that time discussed was a project for the construction of a canal or railway to connect Lake Michigan at Chicago with the Illinois River at Ottawa or Peru a distance of about 80 or 100 miles. A grant had been made by Congress to the Territory or State of Illinois at an early day of each alternate section of land in aid of the construction of a canal between Lake Michigan at Chicago and the Illinois River, but no steps had been taken to avail of this grant.

New Orleans at this time was regarded as a market for the valley of the Mississippi as it could be reached by the Mississippi River and its tributaries, so the construction of such a canal between Lake Michigan and the Illinois River would secure to Chicago the benefit of this western outlet to market by a continuous water communication and this was regarded as an object of great importance for the future development of the country. The leading men of Chicago were anxious that we should interest ourselves in the prosecution of this work and so enthusiastic had we become in our views of the future of this region of country and of Chicago as its commercial centre, that we entered into their views and it was agreed that an application should be made to the Legislature to incorporate a company for the construction of a Canal or a Railroad between Chicago and the Illinois River to which company the State should convey its land grant, coupled with conditions for the construction of either a canal or a railway within a certain time and upon such conditions as might be imposed by the Legislature, and that certain

---

addition to this it has the finest back country in the world. It is on the great western thoroughfare to St. Louis on the Mississippi. A line of steam Boats will be established next year between this point & the mouth of the St. Joseph's which will there be connected with a line of stages to Detroit & thus the hardest part of the route (round the head of the Lake) will be saved."

Similar descriptions of the advantages of Chicago can be found in Butler's letter to his wife, Eliza, dated Chicago, August 4, 1833; his letter to Bowen Whitney, dated Chicago, August 7, 1833; and his letter to the editors of the *Albany Argus*, entitled "The Far West—Internal Improvement—Trade and Intercourse with the State of New York," dated Detroit, August, 1833.

persons who were then present at Chicago of whom Mr. Lucius
Lyon (afterwards the first Senator in Congress from the State
of Michigan), Mr. Hamilton, Mr. Kinzie and Dr. Temple, I
think, as a Committee were to take charge of this memorial and
submit it at the next session of the Legislature of the State of
Illinois. A memorial to the Legislature and a letter of instructions to the committee were carefully prepared by Mr. Bronson
and myself embodying our views and suggesting the terms and
conditions upon which the Company should be incorporated.

The Committee were to proceed to Jacksonville with the
Memorial at the next session of the Legislature. Whether this
proposition was ever formally submitted to that body or not I
am not able to state, but it is certain that the discussion caused
by it had the effect to stimulate the Legislature at the session of
1834-35, to avail of the liberal and yet dormant grant made by
Congress for the purpose, and a bill was passed at that session
authorizing a loan for the construction of the Canal as a State
work; and the work was soon after commenced and though retarded by embarrasments which overtook the State and for a
time prostrated its credit, it was finally completed and remains
to this day a monument not only of the enterprise of the State,
but its integrity in the fulfillment of its pecuniary obligations to
its creditors.

Sunday morning, 4th Augt.[15]

rose at ½ p. 6. Endeavored to cultivate a sense of the divine
presence & the Lord's day. Devotion languid. . . . . Attended
sunday School with Mr Porter in the Garrison's small school.
About 8 teachers. Mr. [Philo] Carpenter superintendent. . . . .
Was informed by Mr Porter that several of the officers & soldiers
were pious. The soldiers were drawn up, inspected & drilled
which seems to me to be unnecessary on the Sabbath. . . . .

They have no place of worship yet. By permission of the officers they have been permitted to occupy a room in the Garrison
which must now be given up. In a new place like this the set-

---

[15] The following extracts through Friday, August 9, 1833, are taken from Butler's
Diary. The letter of 1881 has omitted the information in the foregoing, and it is included
here as a part of the account.

tlers must submit to a great many privations embarrassments & inconveniences but God has blessed this place abundantly & in a few years, we can anticipate that here the institutions of religion & education will be planted, & will grow luxuriantly. Mr Porter said he found it impossible to get accomodations for himself & consequently he was obliged to take a room in the upper part of a store

The school house is a wretched old log house.

This is *the most important point* in the great west for missionary effort: it is a concentrating & diffusive point: it is at the head of navigation & of course a great commercial point. It has a very extensive back country extending to the Mississippi & rich beyond calculation. . . . . There should be here a Bible, Tract, & Sunday School depository forthwith. A moral influence should be diffused in the beginning to give character to the society which is growing up here. . . . .

Sunday P. M. Service in school house. . . . . Prayer meeting in the Garrison at 6 P.M. Attended it. Heard a soldier pray! Capt. Wilcox & wife & Lieut. S[mith] & a number of the soldiers pious the Garrison in a good state. How consistent & beautiful that a soldier who fights the battles of his country should enlist in the service of the redeemer. . . . .

Monday, 5th Aug.

Spent the day viewing the place. . . . .

Spent evening at the monthly concert which was interesting. . . . .

Tuesday, 6th Augt.

. . . . Spent day in visiting, reading & writing. . . . .

Tea with Capt. Wilcox & Lady, a very genteel woman & spent the evening there with Mr. Porter & Majr. Bender. Spent some time with Dr. Temple & conversed on the subject of the country & its advantages.

Dr. Maxwell says that Chicago is as healthy a place as Sacketts Harbor. My inquiries respecting the health of the place have confirmed me in this opinion. It is a healthy point.

Peaches cannot be raised here. The exposure is too great. There is no fruit in the country. . . . .

Thursday, 8th Augt.

. . . . Spent evening with Rev. Mr. Porter: Suggested to him the importance of Chicago as a tract, bible & sunday School depository & engaged to interest myself in it.

Friday, 9th Augt.

Rose at 10 m past 3: mounted horse with saddle bags & left for Detroit at 4.0 Clock. . . . .

LAND SPECULATION[16]

While at Chicago our attention was directed to the property which Mr. Robert A. Kinzie had offered us, viz:—his quarter interest as one of the heirs at law of his father, in the north fractional half of Section 10. This purchase was declined after a careful reconnoissance of the land by me in person, accompanied by a surveyor, mainly because the remaining 3-4 being owned by other persons their co-operation in the disposition of the property would be essential to a satisfactory management. It was ascertained that Major General Hunter,[17] then and now in the United States Army, had become the owner of one half interest in the same property and that he also owned 80 acres in the adjoining section No. 9, that is to say, the East half of the North East 1-4 of Section 9, now known as Wolcott's Addition, and as the result of our consideration on the subject we concluded to open a negotiation with him for the purchase of his entire interest in Chicago. This negotiation was begun by correspondence with him. His engagement in the service of the country at remote military stations rendered communication with him difficult and slow and the negotiation with him, though commenced in the Fall of 1833, was not consummated until late in

[16] Letter of 1881 starts again at this point.

[17] Major General David Hunter entered West Point from Illinois, September 14, 1818. He stood twenty-fifth in his graduating class. In 1833 he was captain of the First Dragoons. He was made major general of the Volunteers during the Civil War. He died February 2, 1886.

the Summer of 1834, when a proposition was received from him offering the property, viz: the half of Kinzie's Addition and the whole of Wolcott's Addition and Block No. 1 in the Town of Chicago, lying on the north side of the river for the price of Twenty thousand Dollars, at which sum it was purchased by my friend Mr. Arthur Bronson and his associates in the Fall of 1834, and the title to it was taken in the name of his brother, Mr. Frederic Bronson. For private reasons I took no interest in the purchase, although the negotiations up to the final offer of Major Hunter had been conducted in accordance with the original suggestion for our joint account and interest. In the month of May following I purchased of Mr. Bronson the same property for the consideration of One hundred thousand Dollars. While the title was in Mr. Bronson, arrangements had been made for an auction sale of the property in the month of June, following simultaneously with the Government sale of lands which had been advertised to take place at Chicago in May 1835; the first of the kind in that portion of the United States, the surveys for which had been completed and the Indian title to which had been extinguished. It was expected that this would attract a very large concourse of people to Chicago, as it did, for it brought into notice and offered for sale lands in the most attractive and fertile portion of the United States. The sale of the lots in the property, which I had acquired by purchase from Mr. Bronson was to follow after the sale of public lands; all the preliminary steps to effect it had been taken, and Mr. Frederic Bronson was then on his way to Chicago to superintend the Sale. Of course all these proceedings were now subject to my control and the disposition to be made by me in regard to it was under consideration. In making the purchase I had contemplated this condition and had in view my brother-in-law, Mr. William B. Ogden, as the best person to take charge of the whole business. He was then a member of the Legislature of this State, from the County of Delaware, during the memorable session of 1835. I wrote to him requesting that he would terminate his labor there at the earliest possible moment and go to Chicago to take charge of this property. This he consented to do and in May, 1835 he went to Chicago and there met Mr. Frederic Bronson who turned the property over to him as my agent. This was Mr. Ogden's introduction to Chicago, and his first visit to the country west of Niagara. He had been born at Walton on the Delaware River in Delaware County, and had lived there up to this period of his life. His father who had been a successful business man engaged in manufacturing industry and in the lumber trade, had been stricken down by paralysis and disabled from active business when William his eldest son was about seventeen years of age and in consequence the responsibilities of the family and the conduct of business had devolved mainly on him.

It was in May 1835, that Mr. Ogden went to Chicago for the purpose above stated. The Spring had been one of unusual wetness and on his arrival at Chicago to take charge of the property committed to his care, his first impressions were not at all favorable. The property lay there on the north side of the river an unbroken field covered with a coarse growth of oak and underbrush, wet and marshy, and muddy from the recent heavy rains. Nothing could be more unattractive, not to say repulsive in its surface appearance. It had neither form nor comeliness, and he could not at first sight in looking at the property, in its then primitive condition, see it as possessing any value or offering any advantages to justify the extraordinary price for which it had been bought, and he could not but feel that I had been guilty of an act of great folly in making the purchase and it was a cause of sad disappointment and of great depression. To him it was a new experience; it was novel and different from anything that he had ever been engaged in. But Mr. Ogden had gone there for a purpose and to execute an important trust. A great deal of work had to be done to prepare this wilderness field for the coming auction. It had to be laid out and opened up by streets and avenues into blocks and lots, the boundaries of which must be carefully defined, maps and plans must be made, surveys perfected and land-marks established. Mr. Ogden addressed himself to this work with energy and brought to it his extraordinary ability in the handling of all material interests. The work that he accomplished on this property in a short time under circumstances discouraging and depressing was wonderfully effective. He conceived what would be required in order to attract the attention of purchasers so that by the time the auction sale approached he could exhibit it in business form. It will be remembered that the tract covered 131 acres exclusive of the half belonging to the Kinzies which lay in mass with it, say 51 acres, which added to my purchase represented by Mr. Ogden made a tract of 182 acres. The Government sale of lands had brought together a large collection of people from all parts of the country, particularly from the East and Southeast and these were there when Mr. Ogden offered the property on the north side. The result of the auction was a surprise to him, for the sales amounted to more than a Hundred thousand Dollars, and included about one-third of the property. This result, although it was astonishing to him, seemed yet to fail of making the impression on his mind of the future of the town which was to become the scene of his after life and in the development and growth of which he himself was to become an active and most important factor.

As he expressed himself to me in giving an account of the transaction, he could not see where the value lay nor what it was that justified the payment of such prices. He thought the people were crazy and visionary. Having completed the sales, he left Chicago in the Summer and did not return there until the Summer following (1836). But he was not long after this experience in grasping the idea of the future of that portion of the United States and of the natural advantages which Chicago offered as the site of a commercial town, which in the future growth of the country would become so important. As the result of this agency and the care of this large property interest regarding it as an occupation, he gave his mind to the consideration of the whole subject, and it determined him in the end to make his home in the West and identify himself with the fortunes of Chicago. It was a field suited to his taste and to his habits, and for which his previous life and experience in his native Country had trained him, although that life and experience had up to this time been narrow as was the boundary of the

Delaware River on which he had been reared. Now, his mind and his energies were directed to the development of the vast and boundless prairies of the West. He had been reared in a country of dense forests and surrounded on every side by mountain scenery, and now, he was in a field where there were no forests and no mountains.

It was not long before Mr. Ogden became imbued with an enthusiastic appreciation of the capabilities and attractions of this new Country. His descriptions of it were poetic and inimitable.

And from this time onward up to the close of his life he gave to Chicago the full benefit of his rare talents and ability. And he has left in the City of his adoption the distinctive marks of his life work, as well as through the West and Northwest, where the great railways which he projected and promoted to completion will remain ever as monuments of his genius and his enterprise. No man exercised a more magical influence in stimulating all around him to acts of usefulness and improvement in the interest of intellectual, social and material progress, and the development of the country; and few men were capable of accomplishing so much useful work in so short a time. He was comprehensive and broad in his views as the country in which he lived. The later years of his life were devoted largely to the extension of lines of railway to the Pacific coast, and especially the Northern Pacific, which is now approaching completion. Mr. Ogden had always regarded this route as one of the most important and the country which it traversed—and which by its completion would be opened to settlement—as one of the most attractive and richest in its soil productions of any of the projected lines connecting the Atlantic with the Pacific coast.

-»»·«««-

CHARLES JOSEPH LATROBE[1]

C HARLES JOSEPH LATROBE was one of the most famous English travelers to America from 1820 to 1840. He was born in London, March 20, 1801, the son of the Reverend Christian Ignatius Latrobe. Young Latrobe was educated for the Moravian ministry, a profession he abandoned to travel. From 1824 to 1826 he made his first journey to Switzerland, and while there gained repute as an Alpine climber of no little courage. In 1830, he took a long walking trip in the Tyrol.

Two years later Latrobe was seized with a desire to visit the United States, which at that time was becoming popular among English tourists. In March, 1832, therefore, he left London for Paris, where he met his traveling companion, Count Albert Pourtales. The second week of April they sailed for New York in the company of Washington Irving.

The first part of the summer was spent in Philadelphia, Baltimore, and Washington. Later, with Washington Irving as guide, they went to Boston, via the Connecticut Valley. At the conclusion of this Boston visit, Latrobe returned to the Ohio River and followed it down to the Mississippi and then up that river to St. Louis, stopping at various towns along the way. The following year (1833) he saw Chicago, and after a short stay continued across the state to St. Louis again. From there he visited part of the Northwest and then went to New Orleans.

His account of this American journey is told in *The Rambler in North America*. He wrote with the attitude, however, of a gay and sophisticated young man; but on the whole the account is impartial and his observations interesting, interpolated in several instances by various philosophic reflections. Before he left a friend wrote to him:

"We have had plenty of descriptions of the American House of Representatives, the President's Levee. Tell me how the poor are provided for. . . . . Is there any remnant of a religious establishment? Railways, are they increasing? Do they pay or not? . . . . let your letters, in short, be about men, and not about mountains, and let them inform me of what I have never heard, not what has been presented to the world a hundred times before."

But Latrobe was avowedly not interested in economic conditions. He did, however, make a feeble attempt to please his friend by asking in one city what provision was made for the poor. "The poor? We have no poor!" was the answer; and with that, inquiry ceased. At the time of the publication of *The Rambler in North America*, he wrote another friend of what he might not expect to see in the account:

"You must not expect pages of statistical information . . . . and taproom

---

[1] Charles Joseph Latrobe, *The Rambler in North America* (2d ed.; 2 vols.; London: R. B. Seeley & W. Burnside, 1836), II, 202–16

54

colloquies with Captain *This* or Judge *That* . . . . much less, sly peeps into the interior of families who may have exercised the rites of hospitality towards the stranger."

In 1834, Latrobe accompanied Washington Irving on a trip to Mexico. Three years later he was commissioned by the English government to visit the West Indian Islands and report on the workings of the educational fund provided for negroes there. In 1839, he was appointed superintendent of Port Phillip district of New South Wales, and with the reorganization of the Australian government in 1851 he was made lieutenant-governor of Victoria. Shortly after this, came the gold rush; and his administration was sorely tried by the turbulence coming with the movement into the new country. However, Latrobe proved himself capable and generally popular. In May, 1854, he was retired and returned to England, where he was made a Companion of the Bath in 1858. He died December 2, 1875.

Among books of travel Latrobe's were always considered as "best-sellers," and reviews for the most part were very favorable. The list of his works include: *The Alpenstock* (London, 1829); *The Pedestrian* (London, 1832); *The Rambler in North America* (2 vols.; London, 1835, and reprinted in New York); *The Rambler in Mexico* (London, 1836); *The Solace of Song* (poems, London, 1837). He also translated Hallbeck's *Narrative of a Visit* . . . . *to the New Missionary Settlement of the United Brethren.*

-»» ««-

THE POTTAWATTOMIE TREATY

I have been in many odd assemblages of my species, but in few, if any, of an equally singular character as with that in the midst of which we spent a week at Chicago. . . . .

We found the village on our arrival crowded to excess, and we procured with great difficulty a small apartment; comfortless, and noisy from its close proximity to others, but quite as good as we could have hoped for.

The Pottawattomies were encamped on all sides,— on the wide level prairie beyond the scattered village, beneath the shelter of the low woods which chequered them, on the side of the small river, or to the leeward of the sand hills near the beach of the lake. They consisted of three principal tribes with certain adjuncts from smaller tribes. The main divisions are, the Pottawattomies of the Prairie and those of the Forest, and these are subdivided into distinct villages under their several chiefs.

The General Government of the United States, in pursuance of the scheme of removing the whole Indian population westward of the Mississippi, had empowered certain gentlemen[2] to frame a Treaty with these tribes, to settle the terms upon which the cession of their Reservations in these States should be made.

A preliminary council had been held with the chiefs some days before our arrival. The principal Commissioner[3] had opened it, as we learnt, by stating, that, 'as their Great Father in Washington had heard that they wished to sell their land, he had sent Commissioners to treat with them.' The Indians promptly answered by their organ, 'that their Great Father in Washington must have seen a bad bird which had told him a lie, for that far from wishing to sell their land, they wished to keep it.' The Commissioner, nothing daunted, replied: 'that nevertheless, as they had come together for a Council, they must take the matter into consideration.' He then explained to them promptly the wishes and intentions of their Great Father, and asked their opinion thereon. Thus pressed, they looked at the sky, saw a few wandering clouds, and straightway adjourned *sine die*, as the weather is not clear enough for so solemn a council.

However, as the Treaty had been opened, provision was supplied to them by regular rations; and the same night they had had great rejoicings,—danced the war-dance, and kept the eyes and ears of all open by running howling about the village.

Such was the state of affairs on our arrival. Companies of old warriors might be seen sitting smoking under every bush; arguing, palavering, or 'pow-wowing,' with great earnestness; but there seemed no possibility of bringing them to another Council in a hurry.

Meanwhile the village and its occupants presented a most motley scene.

FORT DEARBORN AND CHICAGO

The fort contained within its palisades by far the most enlightened residents, in the little knot of officers attached to the slender garrison. The quarters here consequently were too confined to afford place of residence for the Government Commis-

---

[2] Governor George B. Porter, of Michigan; Thomas J. V. Owen, Indian agent at Chicago; William Weatherford.

[3] Governor George B. Porter.

sioners, for whom and a crowd of dependents, a temporary set of plank huts were erected on the north side of the river. To the latter gentlemen we, as the only idle lookers on, were indebted for much friendly attention; and in the frank and hospitable treatment we received from the inhabitants of Fort Dearborn, we had a foretaste of that which we subsequently met with everywhere under like circumstances, during our autumnal wanderings over the Frontier. The officers of the United States Army have perhaps less opportunities of becoming refined than those of the Navy. They are often, from the moment of their receiving commissions, after the termination of their Cadetship at West Point, and at an age when good society is of the utmost consequence to the young and ardent, exiled for long years to the posts on the Northern or Western frontier, far removed from cultivated female society, and in daily contact with the refuse of the human race. And this is their misfortune—not their fault;— but wherever we have met with them, and been thrown as strangers upon their good offices, we have found them the same good friends and good company.

But I was going to give you an inventory of the contents of Chicago, when the recollection of the warm-hearted intercourse we had enjoyed with many fine fellows whom probably we shall neither see nor hear of again, drew me aside.

Next in rank to the Officers and Commissioners, may be noticed certain store-keepers and merchants resident here; looking either to the influx of new settlers establishing themselves in the neighbourhood, or those passing yet farther to the westward, for custom and profit; not to forget the chance of extraordinary occasions like the present. Add to these a doctor or two, two or three lawyers, a land-agent, and five or six hotel-keepers. They may be considered as stationary, and proprietors of the half a hundred clapboard houses around you.

Then for the birds of passage, exclusive of the Pottawattomies of whom more anon—and emigrants and land-speculators as numerous as the sand. You will find horse-dealers, and horse-stealers,—rogues of every description, white, black, brown, and red—half-breeds, quarter-breeds, and men of no breed at all;—

dealers in pigs, poultry, and potatoes;—men pursuing Indian claims, some for tracts of land, others, like our friend Snipe,[4] for pigs which the wolves had eaten;—creditors of the tribes, or of particular Indians, who know that they have no chance of getting their money, if they do not get it from the Government agents;—sharpers of every degree; peddlars, grog-sellers; Indian agents and Indian traders of every description, and Contractors to supply the Pottawattomies with food. The little village was in an uproar from morning to night, and from night to morning; for, during the hours of darkness, when the housed portion of the population of Chicago strove to obtain repose in the crowded plank edifices of the village, the Indians howled, sang, wept, yelled, and whooped in their various encampments. With all this, the whites seemed to me to be more pagan than the red men.

You will have understood, that the large body of Indians, collected in the vicinity, consisted not merely of chiefs and warriors, but that in fact the greater part of the whole tribe were present. For where the warrior was invited to feast at the expense of Government, the squaw took care to accompany him; and where the squaw went, the children or pappooses, the ponies, and the innumerable dogs followed;—and here they all were living merrily at the cost of the Government.

THE POTTAWATTOMIE INDIANS

The features of the Pottawattomies are generally broad and coarse; their heads large, and their limbs fuller than the Osages. Among their warriors you rarely see one with the head shaved, retaining nothing but the scalp-lock. On the contrary, they wear it bushy and long, frequently plaited into long tails, sometimes hanging back in the nape of the neck, and at others over the face in front. Their sculls are remarkably flat behind.

[4] Snipe was one of the men Latrobe met on his trip to Chicago. He was a "backsettler, as good-natured as it is possible for a man to be, but a bore in every sense of the word. His name I cannot record, but he went among us by the sobriquet of 'Snipe,' from the peculiar form of his nose, and the manner in which he would push it forward into every conversation. He was on his way to Chicago, to be present at the impending Treaty, with a view to prefer certain claims to the Government Commissioner for the loss of hogs, which, doubtless, the wolves had eaten; but which, no matter, the Indians might be made to pay for." (Quoted from *The Rambler in North America*, II, 188–89.)

Of their dress, made up as it is of a thousand varieties of apparel, but little general idea can be given. There is nothing among them that can be called a national costume. That has apparently long been done away with, or at least so far cloaked under their European ornaments, blankets, and finery, as to be scarcely distinguishable. Each seemed to clothe him or herself as best suited their individual means or taste. Those who possessed the means, were generally attired in the most fantastic manner, and the most gaudy colours. A blanket and breechcloth was possessed with very few exceptions by the poorest among the males. Most added leggings, more or less ornamented, made of blue, scarlet, green, or brown broad-cloth; and surcoats of every colour and every material; together with rich sashes, and gaudy shawl or handkerchief-turbans.

All these diverse articles of clothing, with the embroidered petticoats and shawls of the richer squaws and the complicated head-dress, were covered with innumerable trinkets of all descriptions, thin plates of silver, beads, mirrors, and embroidery. On their faces, the black and vermillion paint was disposed a thousand ways, more or less fanciful and horrible. Comparatively speaking, the women were seldom seen gaily drest, and dandyism seemed to be more particularly the prerogative of the males, many of whom spent hours at the morning toilet. I remember seeing one old fool, who, lacking other means of adornment and distinction, had chalked the whole of his face and bare limbs white.

All, with very few exceptions, seemed sunk into the lowest state of degradation, though some missionary efforts have been made among them also, by the American Societies. The Pottawattomie language is emphatic; but we had no means of becoming acquainted with its distinctive character, or learning to what class of Indian tongues it belonged.

All was bustle and tumult, especially at the hour set apart for the distribution of the rations.

CHICAGO

Many were the scenes which here presented themselves, pourtraying the habits of both the red men and the demi-civilized beings around them. The interior of the village was one chaos of mud, rubbish, and confusion. Frame and clapboard houses were springing up daily under the active axes and hammers of the speculators, and piles of lumber announced the preparation for yet other edifices of an equally light character. Races occurred frequently on a piece of level sward without the village, on which temporary booths afforded the motley multitude the means of 'stimulating;' and betting and gambling were the order of the day. Within the vile two-storied barrack, which, dignified as usual by the title of Hotel,[5] afforded us quarters, all was in a state of most appalling confusion, filth, and racket. The public table was such a scene of confusion, that we avoided it from necessity. The French landlord[6] was a sporting character, and every thing was left to chance, who, in the shape of a fat housekeeper, fumed and toiled round the premises from morning to night.

Within, there was neither peace nor comfort, and we spent much of our time in the open air. A visit to the gentlemen at the fort, a morning's grouse-shooting, or a gallop on the broad surface of the prairie, filled up the intervals in our perturbed attempts at reading or writing in doors, while awaiting the progress of the treaty.

I loved to stroll out towards sun-set across the river, and gaze upon the level horizon, stretching to the north-west over the surface of the Prairie, dotted with innumerable objects far and near. Not far from the river lay many groups of tents constructed of coarse canvass, blankets, and mats, and surmounted by poles, supporting meat, mocassins, and rags. Their vicinity was always enlivened by various painted Indian figures, dressed in the most gaudy attire. The interior of the hovels generally displayed a confined area, perhaps covered with a few half-rotten mats or shavings, upon which men, women, children, and baggage were heaped pell-mell.

Far and wide the grassy Prairie teemed with figures; warriors mounted or on foot, squaws, and horses. Here a race between three or four Indian ponies, each carrying a double rider, whooping and yelling like fiends. There a solitary horseman with a long

<hr>

[5] Sauganash Hotel.   [6] Mark Beaubien.

spear, turbaned like an Arab, scouring along at full speed;—groups of hobbled horses; Indian dogs and children, or a grave conclave of grey chiefs seated on the grass in consultation.

It was amusing to wind silently from group to group—here noting the raised knife, the sudden drunken brawl, quashed by the good-natured and even playful interference of the neighbours; there a party breaking up their encampment, and falling with their little train of loaded ponies, and wolfish dogs, into the deep black narrow trail running to the north. You peep into a wig-wam, and see a domestic feud; the chief sitting in dogged silence on the mat, while the women, of which there were commonly two or three in every dwelling, and who appeared every evening even more elevated with the fumes of whiskey than the males, read him a lecture. From another tent a constant voice of wrangling and weeping would proceed, when suddenly an offended fair one would draw the mat aside, and taking a youth standing without by the hand lead him apart, and sitting down on the grass, set up the most indescribable whine as she told her grief. Then forward comes an Indian, staggering with his chum from a debauch; he is met by his squaw, with her child dangling in a fold of her blanket behind, and the sobbing and weeping which accompanies her whining appeal to him, as she hangs to his hand, would melt your heart, if you did not see that she was quite as tipsy as himself.

Here sitting apart and solitary, an Indian expends the exuberance of his intoxicated spirits in the most ludicrous singing and gesticulation; and there squat a circle of unruly topers indulging themselves in the most unphilosophic and excessive peals of laughter.

It is a grievous thing that Government is not stronghanded enough to put a stop to the shameful and scandalous sale of whiskey to these poor miserable wretches. But here lie casks of it for sale under the very eye of the Commissioners, met together for purposes, which demand that sobriety should be maintained, were it only that no one should be able to lay at their door an accusation of unfair dealing, and of having taken advantage of the helpless Indian in a bargain, whereby the people of the United States were to be so greatly the gainers. And such was the state of things day by day. However anxious I and others might be to exculpate the United States Government from the charge of cold and selfish policy toward the remnant of the Indian tribes, and from that of resorting to unworthy and diabolical means in attaining possession of their lands,—as long as it can be said with truth, that drunkenness was not guarded against, and that the means were furnished at the very time of the Treaty, and under the very nose of the Commissioners,—how can it be expected but a stigma will attend every transaction of this kind. The sin may lie at the door of the individuals more immediately in contact with them; but for the character of the people as a nation, it should be guarded against, beyond a possibility of transgression. Who will believe that any act, however formally executed by the chiefs, is valid, as long as it is known that whiskey was one of the parties to the Treaty.

THE TREATY

'But how sped the Treaty?' you will ask.

Day after day passed. It was in vain that the signal-gun from the fort gave notice of an assemblage of chiefs at the council fire. Reasons were always found for its delay. One day an influential chief was not in the way; another, the sky looked cloudy, and the Indian never performs any important business except the sky be clear. At length, on the 21st of September, the Pottawattomies resolved to meet the Commissioners. We were politely invited to be present.

The Council-fire was lighted under a spacious open shed on the green meadow, on the opposite side of the river from that on which the Fort stood. From the difficulty of getting all together, it was late in the afternoon when they assembled. There might be twenty or thirty chiefs present, seated at the lower end of the enclosure; while the Commissioners, Interpreters, &c. were at the upper. The palaver was opened by the principal Commissioner. He requested to know why he and his colleagues were called to the council? An old warrior arose, and in short sentences, generally of five syllables, delivered with monotonous intonation, and rapid utterance, gave answer. His gesticulation was appropriate, but rather violent. Rice, the half-breed Interpreter, explained the signification from time to time to the audience; and it was seen that the old chief, who had got his lesson, answered one question by proposing another, the sum and substance of his oration being—'that the assembled chiefs wished to know what was the object of their Great Father at Washington in calling his Red Children together at Chicago!'

This was amusing enough after the full explanation given a week before at the opening session; and, particularly when it was recollected that they had feasted sumptuously during the interval at the expense of their Great Father, was not making very encouraging progress. A young chief rose and spoke vehemently to the same purpose. Hereupon the Commissioner made them a forcible Jacksonian discourse, wherein a good deal which was a-kin to threat, was mingled with exhortations not to play with their Great Father, but to come to an early determination, whether they would or would not sell and exchange their territory: and this done, the council was dissolved. One or two tipsy old chiefs raised an occasional disturbance, else matters were conducted with due gravity.

The relative positions of the Commissioner and the whites before the Council-fire, and that of the Red Children of the Forest and Prairie, were to me strikingly impressive. The glorious light of the setting sun streaming in under the low roof of the Council-House, fell full on the countenances of the former as they faced the West—while the pale light of the East, hardly lighted up the dark and painted lineaments of the poor Indians, whose souls evidently clave to their birth-right in that quarter. Even though convinced of the necessity of their removal, my heart bled for them in their desolation and decline. Ignorant and degraded as they may have been in their original state, their degradation is now ten-fold, after years of intercourse with the whites; and their speedy disappearance from the earth appears as certain as though it were already sealed and accomplished.

Your own reflection will lead you to form the conclusion, and it will be a just one,—that even if he had the will, the power would be wanting, for the Indian to keep his territory; and that the business of arranging the terms of an Indian Treaty, whatever it might have been two hundred years ago, while the Indian tribes had not, as now, thrown aside the rude but vigorous intellectual character which distinguished many among them, now lies chiefly between the various traders, agents, creditors, and half-breeds of the tribes, on whom custom and necessity have made the degraded chiefs dependant, and the Government Agents. When the former have seen matters so far arranged that their self-interest, and various schemes and claims are likely to be fulfilled and allowed to their hearts' content,—the silent acquiescence of the Indian follows of course; and till this is the case, the Treaty can never be amicably effected. In fine, before we quitted Chicago on the 25th, three or four days later, the Treaty with the Pottawattomies was concluded,—the Commissioners putting their hands, and the assembled chiefs their paws to the same.

By it, an apparently advantageous 'swop' was made for both parties;—the main conditions of which, if the information we received was correct, were,—that the Indians should remove from the territory they now occupied, within three years time— being conveyed at Government expense across the Mississippi, and over the State of Missouri, to the western boundary of the latter, where five millions of acres of rich and fine land were to be set apart for them;—and that they were to be supported for one year after their arrival in their new possession. Moreover, the Government bound itself to pay them over and above, a million of dollars; part of this sum being set aside for the payment of the debts of the tribe—part for a permanent school-fund—and part for agricultural purposes, presents, and so forth.

PATRICK SHIRREFF[1]

P
ATRICK SHIRREFF, an East Lothian farmer and prominent Scotch agriculturist, visited the United States and Canada in 1833. His purpose, he explained, was to explore the country in order to give advice to a younger brother who was planning on settling somewhere in the United States or Canada, preferably in the Illinois country. Shirreff, therefore, was primarily interested in agriculture; and, although he took note of political forms and non-agricultural aspects of American life, his main interest lay in the American farmer.

Shirreff left Mungoswells, April 20, 1833, traveling by stage and train to Liverpool, from where he sailed, April 24, on the packet ship "Napoleon." His boat reached New York May 30; and after a short visit, in which he described the hotels, customs, theaters, and the effects of Mrs. Trollope's criticism of American manners, he journeyed to Philadelphia. From there he returned to New York and then proceeded to Albany and Boston, next visiting Canada and reaching Detroit, where he prepared for the trip to the Illinois country.

Among those who left Detroit for Chicago with Shirreff was Latrobe,[2] who describes the farmer as a "heavy Pennsylvanian farmer, on a land-hunting expedition; a man of few words and apparently few ideas, for the only speech of his which is on record, was uttered about noon on the second day's journey, when he suddenly asked, 'Does cattle in this country die o' the morran, sir?' and he was instantly set a-musing for the rest of the journey by the answer, 'No!' which was promptly returned by his neighbor." Shirreff, on the other hand, was in the same degree lacking enthusiasm for some of his fellow-passengers, including Pourtales, Latrobe's French traveling companion, whom he described as, "Mr. D——, a young gentleman, who, from his pronunciation of the English language, I imagined from Germany." While Latrobe found Major W——, another companion on the boat, a very interesting and fine gentleman, Shirreff thought the army man carried the whole weight and dignity of the nation on his shoulders, and that he was "repulsive . . . . to his countrymen."

In detail Shirreff describes the journey from Detroit to Chicago—the inns, storms, his "botanizing," methods of travel, and the typical meals of "flapcakes, bacon, and fried potatoes"—for he was a careful observer. His account is valuable, particularly in the parts regarding American agriculture. Besides many interesting and amusing incidents, he gives a good description of the agri-

---

[1] Patrick Shirreff, *A Tour through North America; Together with a Comprehensive View of the Canadas and United States as Adapted for Agricultural Emigration* (Edinburgh: Oliver & Boyd, 1835), pp. 219–30.

[2] See pp. 54–64 for Latrobe's description.

cultural possibilities of both Canada and the United States, of American farming methods, produce and production, public lands, agricultural finance, and
emigrant information.

-»» «««-

TRADE AND HOTELS IN 1833

At Niles we changed our stage-coach for an open waggon
drawn by four horses, which was the first time a regular stage
had passed from Niles to Chicago, the mail having hitherto been
carried on horseback. The waggon and horses were to carry us
through all the way, as proper posts and relays had not been established on the road. We breakfasted before setting out, and a
guide was sent with our driver. . . . .

Chicago consists of about 150 wood houses, placed irregularly
on both sides of the river, over which there is a bridge. This is
already a place of considerable trade, supplying salt, tea, coffee,
sugar, and clothing to a large tract of country to the south and
west; and when connected with the navigable point of the river
Illinois, by a canal or railway, cannot fail of rising to importance.
Almost every person I met regarded Chicago as the germ of an
immense city, and speculators have already bought up, at high
prices, all the building-ground in the neighbourhood. Chicago
will, in all probability, attain considerable size, but its situation
is not so favourable to growth as many other places in the Union.
The country south and west of Chicago has a channel of trade to
the south by New Orleans; and the navigation from Buffalo by
Lake Huron is of such length, that perhaps the produce of the
country to the south of Chicago will find an outlet to Lake Erie
by the waters of the rivers Wabash and Mamee. A canal has
been in progress for three years, connecting the Wabash and
Mamee, which flows into the west end of Lake Erie; and there
can be little difficulty in connecting the Wabash with the Illinois,
which, if effected, will materially check the rise of Chicago.

At the time of visiting Chicago, there was a treaty in progress
with the Pottowatamy Indians, and it was supposed nearly 8000
Indians, of all ages, belonging to different tribes, were assembled
on the occasion, a treaty being considered a kind of general
merry-making, which lasts several weeks; and animal food,

on the present occasion, was served out by the States government. . . . .

Besides the assemblage of Indians, there seemed to be a general fair at Chicago. Large waggons drawn by six or eight oxen, and heavily laden with merchandise, were arriving from, and departing to, distant parts of the country. There was also a kind of horse-market, and I had much conversation with a dealer from the State of New York, having serious intentions of purchasing a horse to carry me to the banks of the Mississippi, if one could have been got suitable for the journey. The dealers attempted to palm colts on me for aged horses, and seemed versed in all the trickery which is practised by their profession in Britain.

A person showed me a model of a threshing-machine[3] and a churn, for which he was taking orders, and said he furnished the former at $30, or £.6, 10s. sterling. There were a number of French descendants, who are engaged in the fur-trade, met in Chicago, for the purpose of settling accounts with the Indians. They were dressed in broadcloths and boots, and boarded in the hotels. They are a swarthy scowling race, evidently tinged with Indian blood, speaking the French and English languages fluently, and much addicted to swearing and whiskey.

The hotel at which our party was set down, was so disagreeably crowded, that the landlord could not positively promise beds, although he would do every thing in his power to accommodate us.[4] The house was dirty in the extreme, and confusion reigned throughout, which the extraordinary circumstances of the village went far to extenuate. I contrived, however, to get on pretty well, having by this time learned to serve myself in many things, carrying water for washing, drying my shirt, wetted by the rain of the preceding evening, and brushing my shoes. The table was amply stored with substantial provisions, to which justice was done by the guests, although indifferently cooked, and still more so served up.

[3] Some years previous a relative, John Shirreff, had invented a threshing machine operated by the wind, which he was unsuccessful in getting the East Lothian farmers to accept.
[4] Sauganash Hotel.

When bed-time arrived, the landlord showed me to an apartment about ten feet square, in which there were two small beds already occupied, assigning me in a corner a dirty pallet, which had evidently been recently used, and was lying in a state of confusion. Undressing for the night had become a simple proceeding, and consisted in throwing off shoes, neck-cloth, coat, and vest, the two latter being invariably used to aid the pillow, and I had long dispensed with a nightcap. I was awoke from a sound sleep towards morning, by an angry voice uttering horrid imprecations, accompanied by a demand for the bed I occupied. A lighted candle, which the individual held in his hand, showed him to be a French trader, accompanied by a friend, and as I looked on them for some time in silence, their audacity and brutality of speech increased. At length I lifted my head from the pillow, leant on my elbow, and with a steady gaze, and the calmest tone of voice, said,—

'Who are you that address me in such language?' The countenance of the angry individual fell, and he subduedly asked to share my bed. Wishing to put him to a farther trial, I again replied,—'If you will ask the favour in a proper manner, I shall give you an answer.' He was now either ashamed of himself, or felt his pride hurt, and both left the room without uttering a word. Next morning, the individuals who slept in the apartment with me, discovered that the intruders had acted most improperly towards them, and the most noisy of the two entered familiarly into conversation with me during breakfast, without alluding to the occurrence of the preceding evening.

On arriving at Chicago, I learned there was a mail-waggon which passed down the Illinois river once a-week, and had set off a few hours before, and was the only conveyance in that direction. I could not think of remaining a week waiting for the waggon, and not finding a suitable horse to purchase, I determined on walking. The passengers who had travelled together from Niles lodged at the same hotel, with exception of the Major, who perhaps found shelter in the fort. The old soldier seemed to have commenced a regular fuddling fit; and his wife, who was a prudent sensible person, was in great distress, being thirty miles from the residence of her son, and her husband quite un-controllable.[5] Finding the destination of the old lady lay no great way out of my route, I hired a waggon to take the old people and myself there next morning, the soldier having been easily coaxed into the arrangement, and for which his wife ex-pressed thankfulness. On the waggon reaching the door of the hotel, its owner, who was of French descent, insisted that he had only bargained to convey two, and that unless he received $2 from me, I must remain behind. After a noisy altercation on both sides, he offered to accept of $1 extra, but feeling indignant at his attempt at imposition, I shouldered my knapsack, and trudged off on foot. I have often looked back with regret on this pro-ceeding, as it was improper to leave the old lady without seeing her fairly on her journey, and silly to have exchanged high words with an individual who would altogether disregard them. This was the only instance which occurred to me in the States, of ex-periencing an attempt at imposition, or which was calculated to ruffle my temper.

[5] Among the party from Detroit to Chicago was an old Revolutionary War soldier, known as Captain Cook, and his wife, who were on the way to the home of their son in Illinois. Captain Cook had a weakness for strong liquor and President Jackson, and whenever he could he imbibed freely of whiskey and extolled the praises of Jackson and the great American democracy.

CHARLES FENNO HOFFMAN[1]

CHARLES FENNO HOFFMAN (1806–84) was the son of Judge Josiah Ogden Hoffman, of New York. At the age of nine he was sent to an academy at Poughkeepsie, but after a short residence there he ran away to escape harsh treatment. He was then placed under the tutelage of a Scotch clergyman in New Jersey. In 1817 Hoffman had his leg crushed in a ferryboat accident in New York City, and the leg had to be amputated. Notwithstanding this handicap, he became proficient in athletics. He entered Columbia University, leaving before graduation, and began the study of law in the office of Harmanus Bleecker in Albany; and at the age of twenty-one he was admitted to the bar. Later Columbia conferred upon him an honorary degree of Master of Arts.

While he was studying law, Hoffman contributed many articles to newspapers. After three years of law practice he decided to transfer his efforts to literature and joined Charles King in the editorship of the *New York American*. In 1833, he established the *Knickerbocker Magazine* but, after a few numbers, turned it over to Timothy Flint. After leaving the *Knickerbocker*, Hoffman bought the *American Monthly Magazine*, and was its editor for a number of years. He also edited the *New York Mirror* for a year, and in 1846 he began the editorship of the *Literary World*. Relinquishing the editorship in a year and a half, he assumed the relationship of contributor, writing the "Sketches of Society," a series of essays of which the most popular were "The Man in the Reservoir" and "The Man in the Boiler."

In 1848 Hoffman received an appointment to the civil service in Washington but was prevented from accepting it by the attack of a mental disorder the following year, from which he never fully recovered. He died June 7, 1884.

His trip to Chicago was taken in 1833–34 for his health. The account of this visit to the West was published in 1835 (London) under the title of *A Winter in the Far West* and was his first book. Other writings, chiefly poetry, followed. Among his best-known poems was "Monterey," a favorite of General U. S. Grant. Accused of plagiarizing Thomas Moore by the *Quarterly Review* in 1844, Hoffman published a new edition of his poems under the title of *The Echo, or Borrowed Notes for Home Circulation*. He was also the author of "Jacob Leisler" in Spark's *American Biography*.

Although Hoffman kept close to the facts in his *A Winter in the Far West*, the account is replete with literary embellishments. Many interesting comments on food, Indians, mode of travel, and the country through which he traveled precede the description of Chicago given here.

[1] Charles Fenno Hoffman, *A Winter in the Far West* (1st ed.; 2 vols.; London: Richard Bentley, 1835), I, 224–53. Reprinted as *A Winter in the West* in "Fergus Historical Series" (Chicago: Fergus Printing Co., 1882), No. 20, pp. 10–31.

Chicago, Jan. 1, 1834.

We left the prairie on the east, after passing through "the door" and entering a forest, where the enormous black-walnut and sycamore trees cumbered the soil with trunks from which a comfortable dwelling might be excavated. The road was about as bad as could be imagined; and after riding so long over prairies as smooth as a turn-pike, the stumps and fallen trees over which we were compelled to drive, with the deep mud-holes into which our horses continually plunged, were anything but agreeable. Still, the stupendous vegetation of the forest interested me sufficiently to make the time, otherwise enlivened by good company, pass with sufficient fleetness, though we made hardly more than two miles an hour throughout the stage. . . . . Our route was still along the shore; and after passing round the end of the lake and taking a northwardly direction, the way in which the icy blast would come down the bleak shore of the lake "was a caution." We galloped at full speed, every man choosing his own route along the beach, our horses' hoofs ringing the while as if it were a pavement of flint beneath them. The rough ice piled up on the coast prevented us from watering our beasts; and we did not draw a rein till the rushing current of the Calaminc, which debouches into Lake Michigan some ten miles from Chicago, stayed our course. A cabin on the bank gave us a moment's opportunity to warm, and then, being ferried over the wintry stream, we started with fresh vigour, and crossing about a mile of prairie in the neighbourhood of Chicago, reached here in time for an early dinner. Our horses this morning seemed none the worse for this furious riding; their escape from ill consequences being readily attributable to the excellence of the road, and the extreme coldness of the weather while travelling it. For my own part, I never felt better than after this violent burst of exercise.

We had not been here an hour before an invitation to a public ball was courteously sent to us by the managers; and though my soiled and travel-worn riding-dress was not exactly the thing to present one's self in before ladies of an evening, yet, in my earnestness to see life on the frontier, I easily allowed all objections to be overruled by my companions, and we accordingly drove to the house in which the ball was given. It was a frame-building, one of the few as yet to be found in Chicago; which, although one of the most ancient French trading-posts on the Lakes, can only date its growth as a village since the Indian war, eighteen months since. When I add that the population has *quintupled* last summer, and that but few mechanics have come in with the prodigious increase of residents, you can readily imagine that the influx of strangers far exceeds the means of accomodation; while scarcely a house in the place, however comfortable-looking outside, contains more than two or three finished rooms. In the present instance, we were ushered into a tolerably-sized dancing room, occupying the second story of the house, and having its unfinished walls so ingeniously covered with pine-branches and flags borrowed from the garrison, that, with the whitewashed ceiling above, it presented a very complete and quite pretty appearance. It was not so warm, however, that the fires of cheerful hickory, which roared at either end, could have been readily dispensed with. An orchestra of unplaned boards was raised against the wall in the centre of the room; the band consisted of a dandy negro with his violin, a fine military-looking bass drummer from the fort, and a volunteer citizen, who alternately played an accompaniment upon the flute and triangle. Blackee, who flourished about with a great many airs and graces, was decidedly the king of the company; and it was amusing, while his head followed the direction of his fiddle-bow with pertinacious fidelity, to see the Captain Manual-like precision with which the soldier dressed to the front on one side, and the nonchalant air of importance which the cit [*sic*] attempted to preserve on the other.

As for the company, it was such a complete medley of all ranks, ages, professions, trades, and occupations, brought together from all parts of the world, and now for the first time brought together, that it was amazing to witness the decorum with which they commingled on this festive occasion. The managers (among whom were some officers of the garrison) must certainly be *au fait* at dressing a lobster and mixing regent's punch, in order to have produced a harmonious compound from such a collection of contrarieties. The gayest figure that was ever called by quadrille-playing Benoit never afforded me half the amusement that did these Chicago cotillons. Here you might see a veteran officer in full uniform balancing to a trades-man's daughter still in her short frock and trowsers, while there the golden aiguillette of a handsome surgeon[2] flapped in unison with the glass beads upon a scrawney neck of fifty. In one quar-ter, the high-placed buttons of a linsey-woolsey coat would be *dos à dos* to the elegantly turned shoulders of a delicate-looking southern girl; and in another, a pair of Cinderella-like slippers would *chassez* cross with a brace of thick-soled broghans, in mak-ing which, one of the lost feet of the Colossus of Rhodes may have served for a last. Those raven locks, dressed *à la Madonne*, over eyes of jet, and touching a cheek where blood of a deeper hue mingles with the less glowing current from European veins, tell of a lineage drawn from the original owners of the soil; while these golden tresses, floating away from eyes of heaven's own colour over a neck of alabaster, recall the Gothic ancestry of some of "England's born." How piquantly do these trim and beaded *leggins* peep from under that simple dress of black, as its tall nut-brown wearer moves, as if unconsciously, through the graceful mazes of the dance. How divertingly do those inflated gigots, rising like windsails from that little Dutch-built hull, jar against those tall plumes which impend over them like a commodore's pennant on the same vessel.

[2] Dr. Philip Maxwell, physician, was born at Guilford, Windham County, Ver-mont, April 3, 1799. He studied medicine with Dr. Knott of New York City, but he took his degree from one of the medical schools of his native state.

Dr. Maxwell began his practice in Sackett's Harbor, New York, but left it tem-porarily when he was elected to the state legislature. In 1832 he was appointed an assistant surgeon in the United States Army and assigned to duty at Green Bay, Wis-consin. February 3, 1833, he was ordered to Fort Dearborn and arrived there March 15. He remained here until the discontinuance of the post, December 28, 1836. July 7, 1838, he was promoted to surgeon and served with General Taylor at Baton Rouge and on the St. John's River in Florida.

After his discharge from the army, September 23, 1842, he began a civil practice in Chicago, and from 1845 to 1855 he was the partner of Dr. Brockholst McVickar.

Dr. Maxwell died November 5, 1859.

But what boots all these incongruities, when a spirit of festive good-humour animates every one present? "It takes all kinds of people to make a world," (as I hear it judiciously observed this side the mountains;) and why should not all these kinds of people be represented as well in a ballroom as in a legislature? At all events, if I wished to give an intelligent foreigner a favourable opinion of the manners and deportment of my countrymen in the aggregate, I should not wish a better opportunity, after explaining to him the materials of which it was composed, and the mode in which they were brought together from every section of the Union, than was afforded by this very ball. "This is a scene of enchantment to me, sir," observed an officer to me, recently exchanged to this post, and formerly stationed here. "There were but a few traders around the fort when I last visited Chicago; and now I can't contrive where the devil all these well-dressed people have come from!" I referred him to an old resident of three months standing, to whom I had just been introduced, but he could throw no light upon the subject; and we left the matter of peopling Chicago in the same place where philosophers have put the question of the original peopling of the continent. I made several new acquaintances at this new-year's ball, and particularly with the officers of the garrison, from whose society I promise myself much pleasure during my stay. . . . . .

THE WEATHER

Chicago, Illinois, Jan. 10, 1834.

It has been so cold, indeed, as almost to render writing impracticable in a place so comfortless. The houses were built with such rapidity, during the summer, as to be mere shells; and the thermometer having ranged as low as 28 below zero during several days, it has been almost impossible, notwithstanding the large fires kept up by an attentive landlord, to prevent the ink from freezing while using it, and one's fingers become so numb in a very few moments when thus exercised, that after vainly trying to write in gloves, I have thrown by my pen, and joined the group, composed of all the household, around the bar-room fire. This room, which is an old log-cabin aside of the main house, is one of the most comfortable places in town, and is, of course, much frequented; business being, so far as one can judge from the concourse that throng it, nearly at a stand-still. Several persons have been severely frost-bitten in passing from door to door; and not to mention the quantity of poultry and pigs that have been frozen, an ox, I am told, has perished from cold in the streets at noonday. An occasional Indian, wrapped in his blanket, and dodging about from store to store after a dram of whiskey; or a muffled-up Frenchman, driving furiously in his cariole on the river, are almost the only human beings abroad; while the wolves, driven in by the deep snows which preceded this severe weather, troop through the town after nightfall, and may be heard howling continually in the midst of it. . . . .

A HORSE RACE AND A WOLF HUNT

January 13.

I had got thus far in a letter to you, when several officers of the garrison, to whom I am indebted for much hospitable attention and many agreeable hours, stopped opposite the door with a train of carioles, in one of which I was offered a seat to witness a pacing-match on the ice. There were several ladies with gentlemen in attendance already on the river, all muffled up, after the Canadian fashion, in fur robes, whose gay trimmings presented a rich as well as most comfortable appearance. The horses, from which the most sport was expected, were a black pony bred in the country, and a tall roan nag from the lower Mississippi. They paced at the rate of a mile in something less than three minutes. I rode behind the winning horse one heat, and the velocity with which he made our cariole fly over the smooth ice was almost startling. The southern horse won the race; but I was told that in nine cases out of ten, the nags from his part of the country could not stand against a French pony.

In the middle of the chase, a wolf, probably roused by the sleigh-bells from his lair on the river's bank, trotted along the prairie above, within gun-shot, calmly surveying the sport. The uninvited presence of this long-haired amateur at once suggested a hunt for the morrow; and arrangements were accordingly made by the several gentlemen present for that most exciting of sports, a wolf-chase on horseback.

It was a fine bracing morning, with the sun shining cheerily through the still cold atmosphere far over the snow-covered prairie, when the party assembled in front of my lodgings, to the number of ten horsemen, all well mounted and eager for the sport. The hunt was divided into two squads; one of which was to follow the windings of the river on the ice, and the other to make circuit on the prairie. A pack of dogs, consisting of a greyhound or two for running the game, with several of a heavier and fiercer breed for pulling it down, accompanied each party. I was attached to that which took the river; and it was a beautiful sight, as our friends trotted off in the prairie, to see their different-colored capotes and gaily equipped horses contrasted with the bright carpet of spotless white over which they rode; while the sound of their voices was soon lost to our ears, as we descended to the channel of the river, and their lessening figures were hid from our view of the low brush which in some places skirted its banks. The brisk trot in which we now broke, brought us rapidly to the place of meeting, where, to the disappointment of each party, it was found that neither had started any game. We now spread ourselves into a broad line, about gun-shot apart from each other, and began thus advancing into the prairie. We had not swept it thus more than a mile, when a shout on the extreme left, with the accelerated pace of the two furthermost riders in that direction, told that they had roused a wolf. "The devil take the hindermost," was now the motto of the company, and each one spurred for the spot with all eagerness. Unhappily however, the land along the bank of the river, on the right, was so broken by ravines choked up with snow, that it was impossible for us, who were half a-mile from the game when started, to come up at all with the two or three horsemen who led the pursuit. Our horses sunk to their cruppers in the deep snow-drift. Some were repeatedly thrown; and one or two breaking their saddle-girths, from the desperate struggles their horses made in the snow-banks, were compelled to abandon the chase entirely.

My stout roan carried me bravely through all; but when I emerged from the last ravine on the open plain, the horsemen who led the chase, from some inequality in the surface of the prairie, were not visible; while a fleet rider, whose tall figure and Indian head-dress had hitherto guided me, had been just unhorsed, and, abandoning the game afoot, was now wheeling off apparently with some other object in view. Following on the same course, we soon encountered a couple of officers in a train, who were just coming from a mission of charity in visiting the half-starved orphans of a poor woman, who was frozen to death on the prairie a day or two since—the wolves having already picked her bones before her fate became known.[3] One by one the whole squad to which I belonged collected around to make inquiries about the poor children; and then, as our horses generally were yet in good condition, we scattered once more over the prairie, with the hope of rousing more game.

Not ten minutes elapsed before a wolf, breaking from the dead weeds which, shooting eight or ten feet above the level of the snow, indicated the banks of a deep ravine, dashed off into the prairie, pursued by a horseman on the right. He made instantly for the deep banks of the river, one of whose windings was within a few hundred yards. He had a bold rider behind him, however, in the gentleman who led the chase (a young educated half-blood, well connected at Chicago).[4] The precipitous banks of the stream did not retard this hunter for a moment; but, dashing down to the bed of the river, he was hard upon the wolf before he could ascend the elevation on the opposite side. Our whole squad reached the open prairie beyond in time to take part in the chase. Nothing could be more beautiful. There was not an obstacle to oppose us in the open plain; and all our dogs having followed the other division of our company, nothing re-

---

[3] "Mrs. Smith, wife of a Mr. Smith residing at Blue Island who left this place 2d of January (which was the coldest day we have experienced this winter) for her home, and when within a mile and a half of her dwelling, she sank benumbed and exhausted to rise no more. When found, she was dreadfully mangled and torn to pieces by the wolves. She has left a husband and five children to mourn her untimely end." (*Chicago Democrat*, January 28, 1834.)

[4] Madore Benjamin Beaubien.

mained but to drive the wolf to death on horseback. Away, then, we went, shouting on his track; the hotly-pursued beast gaining on us whenever the crust of a deep snow-drift gave him an advantage over the horse, and we in our turn nearly riding over him when we came to ground comparatively bare. The sagacious animal became at last aware that his course would soon be up at this rate, and turning rapidly in his tracks as we were scattered over the prairie, he passed through our line, and made at once again for the river. He was cut off and turned in a moment by a horseman on the left, who happened to be a little behind the rest; and now came the keenest part of the sport. The wolf would double every moment upon his tracks, while each horseman in succession would make a dash at and turn him in a different direction. Twice I was near enough to strike him with a horsewhip, and once he was under my horse's feet; while so furiously did each rider push at him, that as we brushed by each other and confronted horse to horse, while riding from different quarters at full speed, it required one somewhat used "to turn and wind a fiery Pegasus" to maintain his seat at all. The rascal, who would now and then look over his shoulder and gnash his teeth, seemed at last as if he was about to succumb; when, after running a few hundred yards in an oblique direction from the river, he suddenly veered his course, at a moment when every one thought his strength was spent, and gaining the bank before he could be turned, he disappeared in an instant. The rider nearest to his heels became entangled in the low boughs of a tree which grew near the spot; while I, who followed next, was thrown out sufficiently to give the wolf time to get out of view by my horse bolting as he reached the sudden edge of the river. The rest of the hunt were consequently at fault when they came up to us; and after trying in vain to track our lost quarry over the smooth ice for half an hour, we were most vexatiously compelled to abandon the pursuit as fruitless, and proceed to join the other squad of our party, who could now be seen at some distance, apparently making for the same point to which our route was leading. A thicket on the bank soon hid them from our view; and we then moved more leisurely along in order to breathe our horses. But suddenly the distant cry of hounds gave intimation that new game was a-foot; and, on topping a slight elevation, we discerned a party of horsemen far away, with three wolves running apparently about a pistol-shot a-head of them. Our squad was dispersed in an instant. Some struck off at once in the prairie, in a direct line for their object, and were soon brought to in the deep snow-banks; others, taking a more circuitous course, proceeded to double the ravines that were filled with the treacherous drift; and some, more fortunate, took to the frozen river, where the clatter of their hoofs on the hard ice seemed to inspirit their horses anew. I chanced to be one of the latter, and was moreover the first to catch sight again of one of the animals we were pursuing, and find myself nearer to him than any of our party. The wolf was of the large grey kind. But one of the hunters had been able to keep up with him; and him I could distinguish far off in the prairie, turning and winding his foaming horse as the wolf would double every moment upon his tracks, while half-a-dozen dogs, embarrassed in the deep snow, were slowly coming up. I reached the spot just as the wolf first stood at bay. His bristling back, glaring eyes, and ferociously distended jaws might have appalled the dogs for a moment; when an impetuous greyhound, who had been for some time pushing through the snow-drifts with unabated industry, having now attained a comparatively clear spot of ground, leaped with such force against the flank of the wolf as to upset him in an instant, while the greyhound shot far a-head of the quarry. He recovered himself instantly, but not before a fierce, powerful hound, whose thick neck and broad muzzle indicated a cross of the bull-dog blood with that of a nobler strain, had struck him first upon the haunch, and was now trying to grapple him by the throat. Down again he went, rolling over and over in the deep snow, while the *clicking* of his jaws, as he snapped eagerly at each member of the pack that by turns beset him, was distinctly audible. The powerful dog, already mentioned, secured him at last by fixing his muzzle deeply into the breast of the prostrate animal. This, however, did not prevent the wolf giving some fearful wounds to the other dogs which beset him; and, accordingly, with the permission of the gentleman who had led the chase, I threw myself from my horse, and gave the game the *coup de grace* with a dirk-knife which I had about me. Two of our party soon after joined us, each with a prairie wolf hanging to his saddle-bow; and the others gradually collecting, we returned to Chicago, contented at last with the result of our morning's sport.

It was with no enviable feelings, I assure you, that, on making my arrangements an hour ago to start in the new line of stage-coaches which has just been established between this point and St. Louis, I found myself compelled to part with the friend to whom I was chiefly indebted for my share in the glorious sports I have just attempted to describe to you—the four-footed companion of my last six weeks' rambles. . . . . It is no little consolation to me that I leave my Bucephalus in excellent hands; nor does this necessary separation so engross my sympathies that I have none to spare for other partings. Upon these however, I shall not dilate here; though you must not be surprised to find me returning more than once hereafter to characters, scenes, and incidents at Chicago, which I have hitherto left untouched.

→》《←

HARRIET MARTINEAU[1]

H ARRIET MARTINEAU (1802–76) was the third daughter and the sixth of eight children of Thomas Martineau and Elizabeth (Rankin) Martineau.

As a child, her health was not good, and when young she became very deaf. Her father, a manufacturer of camlet and bombazine at Norwich, gave his children a good classical education, believing it an insurance against poverty, a belief justified later when Miss Martineau was forced to earn her own living because of business reverses.

At first she became a seamstress, which provided a certain livelihood for her; but even then she engaged in some writing. Her first literary productions were religious in character and were published in a Unitarian magazine, *The Monthly Repository*. Her first article brought success, and she decided to devote the rest of her life to literature. Articles and books followed. At one time *The Monthly Repository* conducted a contest for the best articles for the conversion of Jews, Catholics, and Mohammedans; and Miss Martineau carried off the prizes. She became a friend of the Wordsworths and of Carlyle, whose lecture trip in 1839 she managed.

A study of economics led her into the realm of living conditions affecting the masses, and she gave voice to pleas for higher standards of living for the poor. An espousal of the law of Malthus caused reviewers to assail her bitterly as an old maid "Malthusian" who thought bearing children was something of an evil and a nuisance and who was "innocent" of questions "she should have asked her mamma."

In 1834, she came to the United States. Because of her writings she was fairly well known before her arrival. Newspapers boomed her popularity, and she became the lioness of the hour. But the hour was not long. Although she found Abolitionists in Boston in disfavor, she attended one of their meetings and allowed herself to address it. Immediately she found herself cut off from certain circles. Indeed, a voyage down the Ohio had to be postponed because of the extreme prejudice against her owing to her views on slavery. In 1836, however, she made a trip to the Northwest, at which time she visited Chicago.

It was natural that a book should come out of the experiences of her visit here, and this country eagerly looked forward to it. When *Society in America* was published in 1837, her uncomplimentary remarks regarding the American people and customs provoked in some a feeling of wounded vanity. They charged her with ingratitude of the basest sort. "She has ate of our bread," wrote one woman, "and drunk of our cup; and she calls dear, delightful, intellectual Boston pedantic!" But another American with a sense of humor asked,

[1] Harriet Martineau, *Society in America* (3 vols.; London: Saunders & Otley, 1837), I, 348–55.

"Did you expect to bribe her with a cup of tea?" The *North American Review* said of her book: "America her theme, satire was to be her song." On the other hand, she received the commendation of no less a person than James Freeman Clark, although even his praise was not unadulterated.

However, many of her comments were apt, and, as such, were accepted by many Americans. Her chief criticisms arose, not because the United States was different from England, but because she held America inconsistent in the application of political doctrines set forth in the Declaration of Independence and other charters of Americanism. To her, aristocracy, slavery, and mob-law were not true republican principles.

Her other book on the United States, *A Retrospect of Western Travel*, is less philosophical than *Society in America* and, therefore, to some readers offers greater appeal, for it deals more with personal incidents and events than with her reaction to American political conditions.

-»» «««-

HOUSES, HOTELS, AND PEOPLE

On our road to Chicago, the next day,—a road winding in and out among the sand-hills, we were called to alight, and run up a bank to see a wreck. It was the wreck of the Delaware;—the steamer in which it had been a question whether we should not proceed from Niles to Chicago. She had a singular twist in her middle, where she was nearly broken in two. Her passengers stood up to the neck in water, for twenty-four hours before they were taken off; a worse inconvenience than any that we had suffered by coming the other way. The first thing the passengers from the Delaware did, when they had dried and warmed themselves on shore, was to sign a letter to the captain, which appeared in all the neighbouring newspapers, thanking him for the great comfort they had enjoyed on board his vessel. It is to be presumed that they meant previously to their having to stand up to their necks in water.

In the wood which borders the prairie on which Chicago stands, we saw an encampment of United States' troops. Since the rising of the Creeks in Georgia, some months before, there had been apprehensions of an Indian war along the whole frontier. It was believed that a correspondence had taken place among all the tribes, from the Cumanches, who were engaged to fight for the Mexicans in Texas, up to the northern tribes among whom we were going. It was believed that the war-belt was circulating among the Winnebagoes, the warlike tribe who inhabit the western shores of Lake Michigan; and the government had sent troops to Chicago, to keep them in awe. It was of some consequence to us to ascertain the real state of the case; and we were glad to find that alarm was subsiding so fast, that the troops were soon allowed to go where they were more wanted. As soon as they had recovered from the storm which seemed to have incommoded everybody, they broke up their encampment and departed.

Chicago looks raw and bare, standing on the high prairie above the lake-shore. The houses appear all insignificant, and run up in various directions, without any principle at all. A friend of mine who resides there had told me that we should find the inns intolerable, at the period of the great land sales, which bring a concourse of speculators to the place. It was even so. The very sight of them was intolerable; and there was not room for our party among them all. I do not know what we should have done, (unless to betake ourselves to the vessels in the harbor,) if our coming had not been foreknown, and most kindly provided for. We were divided between three families, who had the art of removing all our scruples about intruding on perfect strangers. None of us will lose the lively and pleasant associations with the place, which were caused by the hospitalities of its inhabitants.

I never saw a busier place than Chicago was at the time of our arrival. The streets were crowded with land speculators, hurrying from one sale to another. A negro, dressed up in scarlet, bearing a scarlet flag, and riding a white horse with housings of scarlet, announced the times of sale. At every street-corner where he stopped, the crowd flocked round him; and it seemed as if some prevalent mania infected the whole people. The rage for speculation might fairly be so regarded. As the gentlemen of our party walked the streets, storekeepers hailed them from their doors, with offers of farms, and all manner of land-lots, advising them to speculate before the price of land rose higher. A young lawyer, of my acquaintance there,[2] had realized five hun-

[2] Joseph N. Balestier, who later moved to Brattleboro, Vermont.

dred dollars per day the five preceding days, by merely making out titles to land. Another friend had realized, in two years, ten times as much money as he had before fixed upon as a competence for life. Of course, this rapid money-making is a merely temporary evil. A bursting of the bubble must come soon. The absurdity of the speculation is so striking, that the wonder is that the fever should have attained such a height as I witnessed. The immediate occasion of the bustle which prevailed, the week we were at Chicago, was the sale of lots, to the value of two millions of dollars, along the course of a projected canal; and of another set, immediately behind these. Persons not intending to game, and not infected with mania, would endeavor to form some reasonable conjecture as to the ultimate value of the lots, by calculating the cost of the canal, the risks from accident, from the possible competition from other places, &c., and, finally, the possible profits, under the most favorable circumstances, within so many years' purchase. Such a calculation would serve as some sort of guide as to the amount of purchase-money to be risked. Whereas, wild land on the banks of a canal, not yet even marked out, was selling at Chicago for more than rich land, well improved, in the finest part of the valley of the Mohawk, on the banks of a canal which is already the medium of an almost inestimable amount of traffic. If sharpers and gamblers were to be the sufferers by the impending crash at Chicago, no one would feel much concerned; but they, unfortunately, are the people who encourage the delusion, in order to profit by it. Many a high-spirited, but inexperienced, young man; many a simple settler, will be ruined for the advantage of knaves.

Others, besides lawyers and speculators by trade, make a fortune in such extraordinary times. A poor man at Chicago had a pre-emption right to some land, for which he paid in the morning one hundred and fifty dollars. In the afternoon, he sold it to a friend of mine for five thousand dollars. A poor Frenchman,[3] married to a squaw, had a suit pending, when I was there, which he was likely to gain, for the right of purchasing some land by

_____
[3] John B. Beaubien.

the lake for one hundred dollars, which would immediately become worth one million dollars.

There was much gaiety going on at Chicago, as well as business. On the evening of our arrival a fancy fair took place. As I was too much fatigued to go, the ladies sent me a bouquet of prairie flowers. There is some allowable pride in the place about its society. It is a remarkable thing to meet such an assemblage of educated, refined, and wealthy persons as may be found there, living in small, inconvenient houses on the edge of a wild prairie. There is a mixture, of course. I heard of a family of half-breeds[4] setting up a carriage, and wearing fine jewellery. When the present intoxication of prosperity passes away, some of the inhabitants will go back to the eastward; there will be an accession of settlers from the mechanic classes; good houses will have been built for the richer families, and the singularity of the place will subside. It will be like all the other new and thriving lake and river ports of America. Meantime, I am glad to have seen it in its strange early days.

We dined one day with a gentleman[5] who had been Indian agent among the Winnebagoes for some years. He and his lady seem to have had the art of making themselves as absolutely Indian in their sympathies and manners as the welfare of the savages among whom they lived required. They were the only persons I met with who, really knowing the Indians, had any regard for them. The testimony was universal to the good faith, and other virtues of savage life of the unsophisticated Indians; but they were spoken of in a tone of dislike, as well as pity, by all but this family; and they certainly had studied their Indian neighbours very thoroughly. . . . .

We had the fearful pleasure of seeing various savage dances performed by the Indian agent and his brother,[6] with the accompaniments of complete costume, barbaric music, and whooping. The most intelligible to us was the Discovery Dance, a highly descriptive pantomine. We saw the Indian go out armed for

[4] The Beaubien family.

[5] John H. Kinzie.   [6] John H. Kinzie and his brother Robert A.

war. We saw him reconnoitre, make signs to his comrades, sleep, warm himself, load his rifle, sharpen his scalping-knife, steal through the grass within rifle shot of his foes, fire, scalp one of them, and dance, whooping, and triumphing. There was a dreadful truth about the whole, and it made our blood run cold. It realised hatred and horror as effectually as Taglioni does love and grace.

We were unexpectedly detained over the Sunday at Chicago; and Dr. F.[7] was requested to preach. Though only two hours' notice was given, a respectable congregation was assembled in the large room of the Lake House; a new hotel then building. Our seats were a few chairs and benches, and planks laid on trestles. The preacher stood behind a rough pine-table, on which a large Bible was placed. I was never present at a more interesting service; and I know that there were others who felt with me.

[7] Rev. Dr. Charles Follen, pastor of the First Unitarian Church of Chicago.

-》》 《《-

JAMES SILK BUCKINGHAM[1]

JAMES SILK BUCKINGHAM (1786–1855) was born at Flushing near Falmouth, and at the age of ten he began the life of a sailor. On his third voyage, he was taken prisoner by the French and kept as a prisoner of war at Corunna. Upon his release he gave up life on the sea, and in 1818 he established the *Calcutta Journal.* His outspoken criticism and attacks on the abuses in the Indian government brought him into conflict with the government and the East India Company, and in April, 1823, his newspaper was suspended and he was expelled from India. He suffered heavy pecuniary loss from this and appealed to Parliament. A select committee recommended redress, but it was not until a good many years later that the East India Company acknowledged the injury and granted him a pension of £200 a year.

In 1824 he established the *Oriental Herald and Colonial Review* but ceased publication in December, 1829. January 20, 1830, he published the first issue of the *Oriental Quarterly Review*, which he intended to take the place of the *Oriental Herald.* But after two issues he discontinued it. In 1827, he started the *Sphynx*, a weekly journal of politics, literature, and news; but this lived less than two years. For a short time in 1828 he edited the *Athenaeum* but sold his interest in the same year to John Sterling. From 1832 to 1837 he served as a member of Parliament from Sheffield. He took special interest in reform of social conditions—the abolition of flogging in the army and navy, of the impressment of seamen, and the promotion of temperance. He was one of the founders of the British and Foreign Institute in 1843, which drew a great deal of satire from *Punch*. In 1851 he was elected president of the London Temperance League.

Although Buckingham was a voluminous writer, he was better known to his contemporaries as a lecturer. After leaving Parliament, he came to America, where he spent almost four years. Three books were the result of his visit to the United States: *America, Historical, Statistic, and Descriptive* (3 vols.); *Eastern and Western States of America* (3 vols.); and *Slave States* (2 vols.). *Eastern and Western States* covers his journeys through Maine, New Hampshire, Massachusetts, Connecticut, Ohio, Kentucky, Indiana, Illinois, Missouri, Iowa, Wisconsin, and Michigan; and the book is filled "with ample details of History, Topography, Productions, Statistics, Cities, Towns, Rivers, Institutions, and Manners and Customs of each." Buckingham is one of the more favorable commentators on the United States and is as interested in telling previous history as in what he observed.

[1] J. S. Buckingham, *The Eastern and Western States of America* (3 vols.; London: Fisher, Son, & Co., n.d.), III, 255–68; 282–83.

CHICAGO IN 1840

When daylight opened upon us, we obtained a distant sight of the white houses of Chicago a long way off, on the plain; but, distant as they still seemed, never did weary mariner hail the first opening of the harbour, into which he was running to escape shipwreck or storm, with more joy than did we welcome these first tokens of our approach to a place of rest. It was past sunrise before we reached the town, having been 6 hours coming the last 12 miles, and 40 hours performing the whole journey of 96 miles. But we found delightful quarters in the excellent hotel of the Lake House, and what was still better, the cordial greetings and welcome of former friends, whom we had known at Baltimore and Washington, and we felt ourselves, therefore, by the contrast, in Elysium.

We remained at Chicago about a week, and passed it most agreeably; the comforts of the Hotel being equal to that of any house we had met with since leaving Baltimore, and superior to most of those in the West; and the society being the most hospitable and polished that we had for a long time mixed with. . . . .

The original enclosure of the old Fort Dearborn still remains on the shore of the lake, and just opposite to the hotel in which we resided, with its high and pointed stockades for defence, its interior lawn or square, and the barracks opening inwards towards it, forming a venerable relic of the comparatively olden time, in this otherwise entirely new town of Chicago. . . . .

The site of Chicago is perfectly level, being the continuation of the green prairie, which extends westward of the town much farther than the eye can reach. On the east, it has the Lake Michigan, close to the beach of which it begins, and the inlet called the river Chicago, which gives name to the town, divides it into about two equal parts. It is not a river, as it has no source or spring, and no current or flow; but it extends for some miles into the level plain, and is not more than 50 yards broad, but sufficiently deep for large vessels, so that it forms an excellent and safe harbour for all ships and boats frequenting it. A small lighthouse affords a beacon-light to approaching navigators; and a double pier, in parallel lines, jutting out a considerable distance from the beach, forms a safe and easy channel of entrance and exit to and from the creek, so that it is accessible at all hours of the day or night.

The town is planned with the usual symmetry, and the streets are of ample width, being mostly lined with rows of trees separating the side-walks from the main centre. None of the streets are yet paved; indeed, many of them have still the green turf of the prairie grass in their centre, while the only side-walks yet made are of planks of wood, except a small piece of flag-stone pavement round the Lake House hotel, which, from the scarcity of stone and high price of labour, cost 900 dollars to lay down. Most of the stores are capacious and substantial, many of them being built of brick; and the main-street of business presents as bustling an aspect as any street in Cincinnati or St. Louis. There are four hotels, all good, and the Lake House is very superior, being the property of a gentleman who resides in it with his numerous family, and kept by an English landlord, Mr. Shelley; and as both of these like comforts themselves, they provide them amply for their guests and visitors.

The private residences are mostly pretty villas, some of them large and elegant, built with great taste, and surrounded with well-planted gardens. These are mostly on the north side of the river, where the more opulent families reside, and on this side the Lake House is situated. This is called the fashionable quarter, as the business streets and business transactions are chiefly on the other side. The communication is by horse and a foot ferry-boat, drawn across the river by a rope, and passing and repassing every five minutes, maintained by subscription among the inhabitants, and therefore charging no fee for crossing. There is said to be a strong feeling of rivalry between the dwellers on the opposite sides of the river, as at Providence, in Rhode Island; the people on the one side not patronizing anything originating or carrying on upon the other, with as much zeal as if it began and was conducted in their own quarter.

Of churches, there are but three Protestant—the Episcopal, Baptist, and Methodist; and two Catholic. The Unitarians have a congregation, but these worship in a large saloon, built for a lecture-room, or place of public meeting, capable originally of holding 1000 persons, but now divided off into two rooms, each furnishing comfortable space for 500. Considerable excitement was occasioned during our stay here, by an expected riot among the Irish Catholics, on behalf of a priest who was a great favourite with them. It appears that this reverend father had in some manner caused the church of which he was pastor, and certain lands, house, and furniture attached to it, to be made, by legal instrument, his own individual and exclusive property; and deeming himself thus in secure and immoveable possession, he defied all his ecclesiastical superiors. He had been for some time habitually intemperate, and it was alleged that he had also committed extensive frauds. This is certain, that the Catholic Bishop of the Diocese, and the Vicar-General from St. Louis, had come on to Chicago from the south, for the purpose of forcing the priest to surrender the property which he unlawfully held, and then publicly excommunicating him. The expectation of this ceremony drew crowds of Protestants together on the Sunday morning it was appointed to take place; and the sympathy felt by the Irish labourers on the canal, here pretty numerous, for one of their own priests, who freely drank whisky with them, was such, that they had declared they would clear the church, if any attempt were made to excommunicate their favourite. The Bishop and Vicar-General hearing this, went among these men, and addressed them on the subject, reminding them of their allegiance to the church, and their duty of obedience to its decrees; told them they knew no distinction of nation or habit among Catholics, but that the only distinction which must be maintained, was between the worthy and the unworthy, the faithful and unfaithful sons of the church; and concluding by warning them that if they offered the slightest resistance to any public ceremony enjoined by the church, they would themselves incur the guilt of sacrilege, and be accordingly subjected to the very pains and penalties of excommunication which they wished to avert from another. This had the effect of calming them into submission, and the priest learning this, consented to assign over to his superiors the property of the church which he had unlawfully withheld from it, and to leave the town on the following day, so that all further proceedings were stayed against him.

The population of Chicago is estimated at about 6,000 persons, the greater number of whom are actively engaged in trade; but there is a larger proportion of retired families, army officers, and persons living on incomes derived from land and funds, and therefore not engaged in commerce, than is generally found in towns of so small a size. These constitute a circle of most agreeable society; and with them we enjoyed several pleasant walks, morning visits, and evening parties.

So extravagant were the expectations or pretensions of the speculators who founded this town here, that they mapped it out on paper to extend more than four miles inland from the Lake, along which its broadest front would of course be; and a gentleman stated to us that he had purchased some land adjoining the outer edge of the thus extended town on paper, for 1,000 dollars an acre, for which he could not realize 100 dollars now, and might possibly never be able to get 50 dollars.

The climate of Chicago is very agreeable in summer. From the bright blue Lake of Michigan, which forms so prominent an object in the picture from every part of the town, and which contrasts so strikingly with the boundless green prairie in the opposite quarter of the horizon, there blows, during almost every hour of the day, a cool and refreshing breeze, which greatly tempers the solar heat, and makes the climate delicious. But this fine weather is confined to the months of June, July, and August; for in May it is chilly, and in September stormy; and all the rest of the year it is bitterly cold, the thermometer being as often below zero as above it during the three coldest months of winter. It is, however, extremely healthy during all the year.

When the canal is completed to unite the waters of Lake Michigan with those of the Illinois and Mississippi, Chicago cannot fail to become a large city; but the difficulty of obtaining the 5,000,000 dollars still necessary for that purpose, is very great, in the present low condition of the American State credit. A railroad might have been constructed at one-tenth of the expense, as the whole way is perfectly level. Indeed, there are certain periods of the year, when the waters are high, in which boats have been known to pass from the Illinois into the Fox river, and thence into the Chicago creek, and so perform their transit by water all the way; but this is only at distant intervals of time, though it shows the perfectly level nature of the tract between.

While at Chicago, I was waited upon by some Englishmen, who were anxious to know whether I was the same Mr. Buckingham who had taken so much pains to rouse the people of England against the further continuance of the East India Monopoly; and this question being answered in the affirmative, the parties said they had not come to reproach me for what I had done, as they had no doubt I was actuated by good motives, and that the granting of an equally free trade to all the nation, was for the public benefit. But they added, that they were persons who were in the Company's service in London, attached to their warehouses and other commercial establishments, and that being thrown out of employment by this breaking up of their monopoly, they had been induced to come out to America to better their condition. They had heard of the rising prospects of Chicago, and had been tempted in an evil hour to come thus far; but having been among the unfortunate buyers of land-lots, who could not realize their purchases, they had lost everything they had saved in their former service and brought out with them, and were now struggling up in the world as well as they could. They possessed at present the means of earning their subsistence, but little more; yet seeing that others were in a similar condition, having lost all their capital, and being obliged, like themselves, to begin the world again, they endeavoured to be content. They intended to remain here, as they felt assured that the chances of getting forward in this country, for persons in their situation, was much greater than in England, to which, therefore, strongly as they desired to see it again, they had no thought of returning, until they had earned sufficient to enable them to do so in comfort and independence.

During our stay at Chicago, we saw some of the largest and finest steamboats that exist in the United States. These are employed in the navigation of the Lakes from hence to Buffalo, a distance of nearly 1,000 miles, and a great portion of the way out of sight of land. They are accordingly built of large size, from 600 to 800 tons, of great solidity, equal to that of ships navigating the ocean, with their engines, some few of high, but the greater number of low pressure, of the best construction, and all their interior arrangement of sleeping-berths, staterooms, cabins, and saloons, excellent. The Illinois takes the first rank, perhaps, in her united attractions, being large, strong, safe, fast, and peculiarly elegant. She is built after the fashion of the Eastern boats, such as go between New York and Providence or Boston, but much more elegant than any of these. The Illinois, indeed, may be called a floating palace, the most costly decorations being everywhere lavished on her, as may be judged of from the fact of her costing 130,000 dollars from the builder's hands. The Great Western is another splendid boat, still larger than the Illinois, and almost as richly ornamented, but built on the plan of the Mississippi boats, with a double deck of cabins, so as to accommodate about 500 passengers, with high-pressure engines, but combining also speed, safety, and comfort, in an unusual degree. The Buffalo, the Erie, and the Cleveland, are all fine boats, in the same line, and all have their equipments in officers, servants, and table, on the most liberal scale. . . . .

We left Chicago on the morning of Thursday, the 2nd of July, in one of the largest and finest of the Lake steamboats, the Erie. Though we had been there only five days, our parting was as if from friends of much longer standing; we were accompanied to the boat by several friends, and the parting adieus on the deck were of the most affectionate kind; while the terraced-roof of the Lake House was crowded by the younger members of the families living there, who greeted us, as we stood out into the Lake, with waving of hats and handkerchiefs, hoisting the American flag, and then lowering it half-mast as if in mourning—giving, in short, evidences and tokens of stronger feelings than we had witnessed for some time, and reminding us more vividly of home and its endearments, and those from whom we received similar adieus when we parted from them. It should be added, that these families were from Baltimore, Florida, and Virginia, where warmth, cordiality, and generosity are more frequently met with than among the people of the Northern States, whose sense of decorum would perhaps have repressed the exhibition even of the little feeling they might have experienced in similar circumstances.

-》》-《《-

SARAH MARGARET FULLER[1]

SARAH MARGARET FULLER, Marchioness Ossoli, was born in Cambridgeport, Massachusetts, May 23, 1810. She was the eldest of the eight children of Timothy Fuller, a prominent Massachusetts politician. She received a classical education and, after the death of her father in 1835, became the head and chief support of the family. For the next eight years writing, teaching, and traveling absorbed her time. In the summer of 1843 she toured the Great Lakes and visited Chicago. *Summer on the Lakes* recorded impressions gained on this trip.

As a friend of Emerson, Hawthorne, Ripley, Channing, J. F. Clarke, and Hedge, she was associated with intellectual enterprises far more than most women of her day. In December, 1844, she accepted a position from Horace Greeley as literary critic of the *Tribune*, writing articles which dealt chiefly with philanthropy, literature, and art.

In 1846, at the invitation of some friends, she went to Europe, where she spent a year touring the Continent. On her second return to Rome, 1847, she married Giovanni Angelo, Marquis Ossoli. She took an active interest in the Italian struggle for independence in 1849, and when the French took Rome that year she and her family fled to Florence. On May 17, 1850, she, with her husband and baby sailed for America. The voyage seemed to be ill-fated from the start. Smallpox broke out; the captain died and was buried at sea; strong head-winds detained them at Gibraltar while the smallpox was at its height; and the baby was taken seriously ill. On July 16, as the boat was nearing home, it was wrecked off of Fire Island, and the Marquis and Marchioness with their baby were lost.

At the time of Margaret Fuller's visit to Chicago, the town had a population of over seven thousand. As a type of mid-western life, with its Hoosier wagons, its growing trade and shipping, and its constantly changing faces, it offered to her interesting and novel situations. But to an Easterner who had lived among the mountains, that great "sea of land," the prairie, proved the most impressive of all sights: limitless, dull and monotonous, with its "encircling vastness" and its peculiar beauty.

-》》-《《-

THE PRAIRIE

Chicago, June 20, [1843]

There can be no two places in the world more completely thoroughfares than this place and Buffalo. They are the two

[1] S. M. Fuller, *Summer on the Lakes in 1843* (New York: Charles C. Little & James Brown, 1844), pp. 30, 33-35, 70, 80.

correspondent valves that open and shut all the time, as the life-blood rushes from east to west, and back again from west to east.

Since it is their office thus to be the doors, and let in and out, it would be unfair to expect from them much character of their own. To make the best provisions for the transmission of produce is their office, and the people who live there are such as are suited for this; active, complaisant, inventive, business people. There are no provisions for the student or idler; to know what the place can give, you should be at work with the rest, the mere traveller will not find it profitable to loiter there as I did. . . . .

In Chicago I first saw the beautiful prairie flowers. They were in their glory the first ten days we were there—

"The golden and the flame-like flowers."

The flame-like flower I was taught afterwards, by an Indian girl, to call "Wickapee;" and she told me, too, that its splendors had a useful side, for it was used by the Indians as a remedy for an illness to which they were subject.

Beside these brilliant flowers, which gemmed and gilt the grass in a sunny afternoon's drive near the blue lake, between the low oakwood and the narrow beach, stimulated, whether sensuously by the optic nerve, unused to so much gold and crimson with such tender green, or symbolically through some meaning dimly seen in the flowers, I enjoyed a sort of fairyland exultation never felt before, and the first drive amid the flowers gave me anticipation of the beauty of the prairies.

At first, the prairie seemed to speak of the very desolation of dullness. After sweeping over the vast monotony of the lakes to come to this monotony of land, with all around a limitless horizon,—to walk, and walk, and run, but never climb, oh! it was too dreary for any but a Hollander to bear. How the eye greeted the approach of a sail, or the smoke of a steamboat; it seemed that any thing so animated must come from a better land, where mountains gave religion to the scene.

The only thing I liked at first to do, was to trace with slow and unexpecting step the narrow margin of the lake. Sometimes a heavy swell gave it expression; at others, only its varied coloring, which I found more admirable every day, and which gave it an air of mirage instead of the vastness of ocean. Then there was a grandeur in the feeling that I might continue that walk, if I had any seven-leagued mode of conveyance to save fatigue, for hundreds of miles without an obstacle and without a change.

But after I had rode out, and seen the flowers and seen the sun set with that calmness seen only in the prairies, and the cattle winding slowly home to their homes in the "island groves" peacefullest of sights—I began to love because I began to know the scene, and shrank no longer from "the encircling vastness."

It is always thus with the new form of life; we must learn to look at it by its own standard. At first, no doubt my accustomed eye kept saying, if the mind did not, What! no distant mountains? what, no valleys? But after a while I would ascend the roof of the house where we lived, and pass many hours, needing no sight but the moon reigning in the heavens, or starlight falling upon the lake, till all the lights were out in the island grove of men beneath my feet, and felt nearer heaven that there was nothing but this lovely, still reception on the earth; no towering mountains, no deep tree-shadows, nothing but plain earth and water bathed in light.

Sunset, as seen from that place, presented most generally, low-lying, flaky clouds, of the softest serenity, "like," said S., "the Buddhist tracts."

One night a star shot madly from its sphere, and it had a fair chance to be seen, but that serenity could not be astonished.

Yes! it was a peculiar beauty of those sunsets and moonlights on the levels of Chicago which Chamouny or the Trosachs could not make me forget. . . . .

THE LAKE

Chicago Again

Chicago had become interesting to me now, that I knew it as the portal to so fair a scene. I had become interested in the land, in the people, and looked sorrowfully on the lake on which I must soon embark, to leave behind what I had just begun to enjoy.

Now was the time to see the lake. The July moon was near its full, and night after night it rose in a cloudless sky above this majestic sea. The heat was excessive, so that there was no enjoyment of life, except in the night, but then the air was of that delicious temperature, worthy of orange groves. However, they were not wanted;—nothing was, as that full light fell on the faintly rippling waters which then seemed boundless. . . . .

The most picturesque objects to be seen from Chicago on the inland side were the lines of Hoosier wagons. These rude farmers, the large first product of the soil, travel leisurely along, sleeping in their wagons by night, eating only what they bring with them. In the town they observe the same plan, and trouble no luxurious hotel for board and lodging. In the town they look like foreign peasantry, and contrast well with the many Germans, Dutch, and Irish. In the country it is very pretty to see them prepared to "camp out" at night, their horses taken out of harness, and they lounging under the trees, enjoying the evening meal.

On the lake side it is fine to see the great boats come panting in from their rapid and marvellous journey. Especially at night the motion of their lights is very majestic.

When the favorite boats, the Great Western and Illinois, are going out, the town is thronged with people from the south and farther west, to go in them. These moonlight nights I would hear the French rippling and fluttering familiarly amid the rude ups and downs of the Hoosier dialect.

At the hotel table were daily to be seen new faces, and new stories to be learned. And any one who has a large acquaintance may be pretty sure of meeting some of them here in the course of a few days.

JOHN LEWIS PEYTON[1]

JOHN LEWIS PEYTON (1824–96), author, was the son of John Howe Peyton, a Virginia lawyer. He graduated from the law school of the University of Virginia in 1845. Poor health, however, made a change necessary; and in 1848 he took a six months' trip in the West, visiting Wisconsin, Missouri, Illinois, Michigan, and West Canada.

A trip to Europe followed; and a few years after he first visited Chicago, he returned, intending to settle there. But ill health and homesickness sent him back to the South after about two years' residence. Through the influence of Stephen A. Douglas, President Pierce offered Peyton the office of United States District Attorney for the Territory of Utah; but as he had no particular desire to clash with Brigham Young, he declined. He was then offered a federal judgeship in one of the territories, and finally the secretaryship of the legation to Sardinia. These, he also declined.

In 1861 he was appointed as one of the European agents for the Confederacy and was successful in running the blockade at Charleston. After the war, he remained in Europe and engaged in literary pursuits. The Reform Club of London elected him an honorary member, and he became a Fellow of the Royal Geographic Society of London and of the Society of Americanists of Luxembourg. He returned to the United States in 1876.

SEEING CHICAGO FROM A "TRAP"

The morning after my arrival in Chicago (November 22nd.) the weather had moderated, and the snow was rapidly disappearing, in the course of two days none remained upon the ground. To my surprise, I found my friend, Mr. Morris[2] a boarder in the American Hotel, and he now informed me of the cause, namely, the death of his wife early the past summer. Since then he had given up his house and lived in the hotel—his two little daughters having been placed at a boarding school in the city. . . . .

In the afternoon Mr. Shirley[3] called with his "trap" and a pair

[1] John Lewis Peyton, *Over the Alleghanies and across the Prairies. Personal Recollections of the Far West One and Twenty Years Ago* [1848] (2d ed.; London: Simpkin, Marshall & Co., 1870), pp. 323–53.

[2] Buckner S. Morris, Chicago lawyer and judge.

[3] Thomas Shirley, a Virginian who came to Chicago to practice law. He was noted for his great height and handsomeness. His original name was Thomas Fleishman, but he changed it to that of his grandfather—Shirley.

of Morgan horses to drive me about the city and point out the sights of Chicago. The city is situated on both sides of the Chicago River, a sluggish, slimy stream, too lazy to clean itself, and on both sides of its north and south branches, upon a level piece of ground, half dry and half wet, resembling a salt marsh, and contained a population of 20,000. There was no pavement, no macadamized streets, no drainage, and the three thousand houses in which the people lived, were almost entirely small timber buildings, painted white, and this white much defaced by mud. I now recall but a single exception to this rule, in a red brick, two story residence in the north division, surrounded by turf, and the grounds ornamented with trees and shrubbery which was built and occupied by J. B. Russell, formerly an officer in the army. . . . . The city was not yet lighted with gas, and the gardens were open fields where I often saw horses, cows and animals of inferior dignity, sunning themselves, instead of what I expected to see, shrubs and flowers. To render the streets and side walks passable, they were covered with deal boards from house to house, the boards resting upon cross sills of heavy timber. This kind of track is called "the plank road." Under these planks the water was standing on the surface over three-fourths of the city, and as the sewers from the houses were emptied under them, a frightful odour was emitted in summer, causing fevers and other diseases, foreign to the climate. This was notably the case during the summer of 1854, when the cholera visited the place, destroying the population at the rate of one hundred and fifty a day. It not unfrequently happened that from the settling or rolling of a sleeper, that a loose plank would give way under the weight of a passing cab, when the foul water would spurt into the air high as the windows.[4]

[4] "To correct this state of affairs, the authorities have since, at an enormous cost, covered the entire city, four feet deep with sand, thus driving out the water and making a dry spot of what was once a swamp. They have also constructed fine stone drains, leading into the country south of the city, and thence communicating with the waters of the Illinois river, by which they are borne south to the Mississippi. At this moment, I believe, they are cutting a canal to convey through the city the waters of the lake—the lake being higher than the bed of the Illinois river—and thus, while making a canal connecting Lake Michigan and the Mississippi, they will provide the means of thoroughly draining the city, and keeping it clean by this rapid current of pure water. Chicago has thus been turned into a healthy spot." (Note by J. L. Peyton.)

On the outskirts of the town where this kind of road terminated, the highways were impassable, except in winter when frozen, or in summer when dry and pulverized into the finest and
most penetrating of dust. At all other seasons they were little
less than quagmires. As may be imagined, the communication
with the interior was principally carried on in canoes and batteaux. Of architectural display there was none. The houses
were built hurriedly to accommodate a considerable trade centering here, and were devoid of both comforts and conveniences.
Every one in the place seemed in a hurry, and a kind of restless
activity prevailed which I had seen no where else in the West,
except in Cincinnati. A central point in the western route of
emigrants, it was even at this inclement season animated by
passing parties. In summer, I understood emigrant parties went
through daily. Those whom I now saw, were wild, rough, almost
savage looking men from North Germany, Denmark and Sweden—their faces covered with grizzly beards, and their teeth
clenched upon a pipe stem. They were followed by stout, well-
formed, able-bodied wives and healthy children. Neither cold
nor storm stopped them in their journey to the promised land,
on the frontiers of which they had now arrived. In most instances they followed friends who had prepared a resting place
for them.

BUSINESS IN CHICAGO

Chicago was already becoming a place of considerable importance for manufacturers. Steam mills were busy in every part of
the city preparing lumber for buildings which were contracted
to be erected by the thousand the next season. Large establishments were engaged in manufacturing agricultural implements
of every description for the farmers who flocked to the country
every spring. A single establishment, that of McCormick, employed several hundred hands, and during each season completed from fifteen hundred to two thousand grain-reapers and grass-
mowers. Blacksmith, wagon and coachmaker's shops were busy
preparing for a spring demand, which, with all their energy, they
could not supply. Brickmakers had discovered on the lake shore,

near the city and a short distance in the interior, excellent beds of clay, and were manufacturing, even at this time, millions of brick by a patent process, which the frost did not hinder, or delay. Hundreds of workmen were also engaged in quarrying stone and marble on the banks of the projected canal; and the Illinois Central Railway employed large bodies of men in driving piles, and constructing a track and depôt on the beach. Real estate agents were mapping out the surrounding territory for ten and fifteen miles in the interior, giving fancy names to the future avenues, streets, squares and parks. A brisk traffic existed in the sale of corner lots, and men with nothing but their wits, had been known to succeed in a single season in making a fortune—sometimes, certainly, it was only on paper.

This process was somewhat in this wise—A. sells a lot to B. for 10,000 dollars, B. sells to C. for 20,000 dollars, no money passing, C. writes to his friend D. in New York of the rapid rise in the price. The property had gone in a very short time from 10,000 dollars to 20,000 dollars and would double within ninety days, such was the *rush* of capitalists to the West, and the peculiar situation of this property, adjoining the Depôt, (on paper) of the "North Bend and Southern Turn Great Central Railway and Trans-Continental Transportation Company." D. immediately takes the property at 25,000 dollars, and writes to his friend E. in Boston concerning that wonderful Western place Chicago, relating how property has risen in value and regretting that he is not able to hold on to a very desirable and highly valuable piece of real estate he owns in that city worth 50,000 dollars, but for which he is willing to take 40,000 dollars, to such extremities is he brought by his necessities. Now E. who is a live Yankee, up alike to business and snuff, sees through the matter, "smells a rat" and of course holds back. The whole affair is about to collapse and result in the bankruptcy of A. B. C. and D.; but D. who is an irrepressible New Yorker, fertile in expedients and full of resources, knows that Southerners "bleed freely," and accordingly before consenting to "go under" determines to try an expedient, and drops a note to his Virginian friend Mr. Old Porte giving him the same story. The old Virginian, Mr.

Porte, who has lived in the country on his hereditary acres, like the patriarchs of old, surrounded by his family, bond and free, and his flocks of cattle and sheep, as did Father Abraham, is immediately penetrated with gratitude at the great generosity and kindness of his friend, that absent but ever faithful friend D., who is willing on the score of ancient friendship to make a sacrifice of 10,000 and to accept on his account 40,000 dollars for a property low at 50,000 dollars, and Mr. Old Porte comprehending how advantageous it will be to his children, of whom, as is somewhat common in the Old Dominion, he has a good round baker's dozen, immediately writes to express his gratitude and to accept the property on the proposed terms. Exit Mr. Old Porte on his way rejoicing. He reaches his banker to make arrangements to meet the payments, after having cogitated somewhat as follows:—

"Egad, those New Yorkers are capital fellows, no Yankee about them, descended from the Old Dutch settlers, fine race the Knickerbockers. Why cannot the North and South understand each other better? we might live together like brothers. D——n it I don't think the Yankees quite so bad as people represent. Allowances must be made for the way they are brought up, the devil's not so black as he is painted, we must not forget that they are brothers, must try to eradicate prejudice and get up a national feeling."

Arrived at the Bank he completes the transaction, and encloses to Mr. D. one-fourth of 40,000 dollars which being divided between A. B. C. and D. sets up these enterprising gentlemen, who starting a "wild cat" bank, soon come to the enjoyment of things hoped for.

The probable sequel of such a transaction may be stated in a few words. Mr. Old Porte punctually meets his payments as they fall due, and is constantly kept under the impression that any small extravagance he may indulge among his fellow Virginians, keeping up social life after the style of his ancestors, is a bagatelle to be a hundred-fold made up to his family by the rapid enhancement in the value of his Chicago property. In a few years, Mr. Old Porte is in the course of nature gathered to his fathers, and his estate put in process of settlement. Among other assets to be reduced to cash, are his Chicago 'lots,' which disposed of at auction fetch in round numbers, we will suppose seven thousand dollars, which "outsiders" think a wonderful evidence of the progress of the city. Mr. X. Y. Z—having bought the same five years previously for five hundred dollars and sold it for six hundred dollars. The outside Yankees hearing the estate of the late Mr. Old Porte of Virginia derives the benefit of the rise, will probably say,

"What humbugs those Virginians are, they are always talking about Yankee greed, yet they come all the way to the north-west in search of plunder, hunting for opportunities to make money by gambling speculations. A tree is known by its fruit. Let F. F. V.'s talk as they please of us as a money grubbing race, we know what they are. Let us thank God, we are not as they."

Now this little imaginary transaction is but the truth and substance as to thousands of real transactions which were then, and have been constantly since taking place in Chicago, making the fortunes of some and ruining the estates of others.

WILDCAT BANKING

Wishing to change a few American (gold) eagles, for I had provided myself with this kind of solid currency for my Western tour, my friend Shirley accompanied me to a timbershed, or shanty, bespattered with mud and defaced by the sun and storm, where the great banking establishment of those days was conducted by George Smith and Co. When there, placing my eagles upon the counter, Mr. Willard, the manager, a lean, yellow, thick-skinned, but shrewd man of business from the East, though I hardly think he could be classed among the wise men, returned me notes of the denomination of one, two, three, and four dollars, which read as follows:

"The Bank of Atlanta, Georgia, promises to pay the bearer on demand, one dollar, when five is presented at their banking-house at Atlanta.

GEORGE SMITH, President.
"WILLARD, Cashier."

I objected most decidedly to receiving this currency, because Atlanta was by the usual route of travel nearly two thousand miles distant; because when the notes were presented, the bank of Atlanta might pay them in the currency of another 'wild cat' bank, probably conducted by Tom Mackenzie in Texas or New Mexico, and because they would only pay them in particular amounts of five dollars, a sum, I said ironically, which a judicious man was not likely to accumulate in his hands of this kind of currency. Stating these objections, both Messrs. Willard and Shirley smiled at my ignorance and inexperience, my "old fogyism," and explained that these notes were as current in Chicago and the state of Illinois as gold; and much more plentiful, thought I to myself. Nevertheless, on their assurances I accepted them, with a mental reservation, however, that I would divest myself of the trash before my departure.

We now left the bank for a ramble about the "Garden City," as Chicago was then and is now called, from the fact that the houses were very small and the gardens enormous. The gardens in the west division in fact having no enclosures, might be supposed to extend indefinitely westward, as Judge Douglas wished, with regard to the Missouri compromise line to the Pacific. Returning to the hotel, Mr. Rossiter[5] informed me that my bank notes (and my pocket was stuffed with them) were called "wild cat money," and such institutions as that at Atlanta "Wild Cat Banks;" but he said the circulating medium of the United States was so far below the actual wants of the people, that they were compelled to resort to such systems of credit to get on rapidly and improve the country, and as long as farmers would take the money (as they now did) there would be no difficulty.

"Why, sir," said Mr. Rossiter, looking around his establishment with pride, "this hotel was built with that kind of stuff, and what is true of 'The American' is very nearly true of every other house in Chicago. I will take 'wild cats' for your bill, my butcher takes them of me, and the farmer from him, and so we go, making it pleasant all round. I only take care," continued

5 Asher Rossiter. He built the American Temperance House, and in 1852 he took over the proprietorship and changed the name to American House.

Mr. Rossiter, "to invest what I may have at the end of a given time in corner lots. Then I'll be prepared, I guess, for the deluge or crash, when it comes, and sooner or later it must come, as sure as the light of day. Mr. Smith has already in circulation six millions of his wild cat currency, and in order to be prepared for contingencies—to be out of the way of a hempen collar and Chicago lamp-post, when people are ruined by his financiering devices—he remains in New York and carries on his operations through Mr. Willard and his 'lambs,' as the clerks are called. On this kind of worthless currency, based on Mr. Smith's supposed wealth and our wants, we are creating a great city, building up all kinds of industrial establishments, and covering the lake with vessels—so that suffer who may when the inevitable hour of reckoning comes, the country will be the gainer. Jack Rossiter will try, when this day of reckoning comes, to have 'clean hands' and a fair record, and I would advise you, on leaving Illinois, to do likewise—wash your hands of Smith and Co. A man who meddles, my dear sir, with wild cat banks is on a slippery spot, and that spot the edge of a precipice."

It required no persuasion to make me follow the sensible advice of my host, and when I afterwards stepped on the steamer which was to bear me across the lake on my return, I divested myself of the last note—which had come into my possession in the way of change—a note of small denomination, by presenting it to the hotel-porter as a gratuity for what one was not then likely to get from Western 'helps,' a little common civility. Pat was delighted to receive the shin plaster, and gave 'yer 'onour' many thanks.[6]

While Mr. Rossiter was holding forth upon the delicate nature of Western credit, two gentlemen were announced, my host disappeared, and upon being introduced, I found the gentlemen were Mr. William B. Ogden, one of the earliest settlers in Chicago, and now one of the solid men, having through his industry, enterprise and good judgment, amassed a fortune of several millions. A solid fortune with none of the *fera natura*, or wild

[6] "In justice to Mr. Smith, who is now one of the wealthiest New Yorkers, I must say that he honourably redeemed all of his paper circulation and that no one has occasion to regret his financial operations." (Note by J. L. Peyton.)

cat genus about it; but the whole represented by real estate in Chicago and Cook County. His friend, whom he introduced was the Honourable Stephen A. Douglas, a distinguished senator from Illinois, whose fame was every day rising, but who had not reached the point attained by Mr. Clay, Mr. Crittenden, or General Cass.

A DINNER AT CHICAGO

I was much struck with the personal appearance, the manners and conversation of Judge Douglas, and shall have more to say of him hereafter. Mr. Ogden informed me that he had heard of my proposed visit to Chicago from Hon. James B. Murray, formerly mayor of New York City, and of my arrival from Mr. Scammon of Chicago, and had called to ask me to join a party at dinner the next day, an invitation which I had much pleasure in accepting. The day following, upon arriving at Mr. Ogden's fine frame and timber building in the north division of the city, I found that he was a bachelor living in a sumptuous establishment, and entertaining *en prince*. The dinner party consisted of Judge Douglas, Mr. Morris, Colonels E. D. Taylor, J. B. Russell and R. J. Hamilton, Mr. Mahlon D. Ogden, brother of the host, Honourable N. B. Judd, Mr. MacCogg,[7] Mr. Shirley, Mr. Hammond,[8] Mr. Lisle Smith, Mr. Butterfield of the General Land Office,[9] Mr. Stephenson, an English gentleman of fortune, who had purchased an estate in Illinois, and become a naturalized citizen, Mr. Elston, subsequently Her Britannic Majesty's Consul-General for Illinois, and Captain Williams, formerly of the British Army, who had retired from the service, purchased an estate of twelve hundred acres on the Rock River, and was now successfully applying science to practical agriculture on the prairie of Illinois. During and after the dinner much interesting conversation took place. . . . .

DRAINAGE OF LAND

During the conversation which took place at Mr. Ogden's I incidently expressed a wish to see a portion of the country on

[7] Ezra B. McCagg.

[8] Charles G. Hammond.   [9] Justin Butterfield.

the lake shore south of the city, and extending as far as Michigan City in Indiana. A section which, as I understood from Mr. Morris, presented some singular physical peculiarities. At this time having been accustomed to using the level and of examining lands with reference to drainage, &c., I was of the opinion that an inspection of the section referred to without the level would enable me to determine the question of the feasibility of draining it, and of course of its value. When the party was over, Judge Douglas invited Mr. Shirley and myself to take seats in his carriage, as he should drive home by way of "The American." We accepted the offer, and Mr. Shirley's conveyance, in which I had gone to the dinner, returned empty. During this drive Judge Douglas referred to the particular section which I had expressed a desire to see, and the question of the drainage, and said if my time would admit of it, he should be glad to take me on a visit to it, and have my opinion on the practicability of turning it into dry land. It gave me pleasure to accept his invitation and offer my services to solve if possible the question which possessed so much interest to him, and I said there could be no better opportunity than the present for making the examination, as the country being frozen we could traverse the swamp on foot. Accordingly, therefore, arrangements were made by Judge Douglas to leave with me early the next morning. About ten o'clock next day he called, and we drove to his cottage in the suburbs of the southern division of the city. Here we stopped for a short time, and he produced a decanter of capital sherry and some biscuits, whereupon we talked away as if we had been friends for a half century. Two men in the employment of the Judge joined us at the cottage, and we drove in his trap to a point about twelve miles south of the city and five into the interior. Here we were upon a frozen lake or swamp, with alternate ridges of sand, this was the section to which he referred. It was not supposed possible to drain this swamp, and consequently the land was considered valueless. We spent the residue of the day making our *reconnaissance*, and ascertained that while, apparently, a dead level and a hopeless swamp, it was in reality an inclined plain, with its lower sections, on the sandy bluffs of Lake Michigan, susceptible, at an inconsiderable cost comparatively, of being thoroughly drained. This concluded, we returned to the Judge's cottage, where we spent the night. Next morning Judge Douglas informed me of his purpose to purchase a large portion of this apparent waste. By draining it, he believed it would yield a fortune to himself and children. At the same time he offered me a share in the enterprise, which I declined, while warmly thanking him for his great liberality. . . . .

A VISIT TO THE THEATER

This evening I dined with Dr. Brainard, a professor in Rush Medical College, Chicago, and among those whom I had not previously met, there were present Dr. J. Hermann Byrd, Dr. Davis,[10] also a professor in Rush College, Colonel William H. Davis, Thomas Hayne, Francis Clark, and J. W. Waughop, formerly of Virginia, but now a prosperous lawyer who was *bona fide* making the fortune which Mr. Old Porte so long supposed he was laying up for his children. From the conversation of these gentlemen I acquired much information, and became more and more alive to the wonderful energy of the people, many of whom were New Englanders. They seemed determined to build here, where one was so much required for the purposes of trade, the finest City of the West. The obstacles to their enterprise presented by the nature of the soil, by the insignificant character of the river, which is small, tortuous in its course and obstructed by shoals and sand bars; by the want of any other harbour than the mouth of this miserable stream, and the further obstacle presented by the severity of the climate, they were determined to overcome and found a city which should become famous not only throughout the West, but the world.

From Dr. Brainard's Mr. Shirley drove me to the Chicago Theatre, where Hamlet was played that night—a promising young Western actor, named Perry, taking the principal part. The Theatre was then owned by the manager, Mr. Rice,[11] who was a good actor and a pleasant man. The house was well at-

[10] Dr. Nathan S. Davis.

[11] John B. Rice, founder of the Rice Theaters in Chicago.

tended, and the play a decided success. During the performance Mr. Shirley conducted me to the green-room where we spent a short time with Mr. Rice, Mrs. Rice, Miss Hart and Miss Mitchell—one of the most admired of the Western stars. After the performance, we accepted an invitation and went to Mr. Rice's residence in Wabash Avenue, where a number of his friends and some of the principal members of the company were assembled for supper. Here the evening passed rapidly amidst the sparkle of wit, humour and champagne. Among the striking gentlemen present was Mr. George M——[12]. . . . .

A WINTER MORNING

The morning following my attendance at the theatre from Dr. Brainard's, I found Chicago covered with snow two feet deep on a level, and at places where it was drifted from thirty to forty feet deep! The population was stirring, however, like a hive of bees to open a pathway, by throwing it from the trottoirs into the streets before it became so frozen as to be immovable, except with enormous labour. By mid-day the pavements were tolerably comfortable, but we seemed to be moving in a trench—the shops on one side and the snow upon the other. The snow thrown into the streets raised their level about four feet, so that we walked on the side-walk, the feet of the horses pulling the sleighs were almost even with our shoulders. Becoming as the season advances more and more firmly frozen and compactly beat down, the streets are smooth and slippery to a degree, forming admirable roads for sleighs, in which everyone not on foot moves about, and they furnish delightful means of locomotion. Coach bodies are placed upon sleds, and ladies go to make morning calls in them as also to parties and picnics.

AMUSEMENTS

Picnicking was by the by one of the Chicago winter amusements, and they are sometimes very amusing. They are organized somewhat after this fashion. A hotel from ten to fifteen miles in the country is secured for a particular evening and din-

[12] This may refer to George W. Meeker.

ner prepared for six or seven o'clock, as the case may be. By this hour sleighs arrive from Chicago, driven by the beaux and freighted with the belles and their chaperons nestling under buffalo robes and other furs. After dinner, dancing commences, the services of one of the numerous German bands in Chicago having been previously secured. Dancing is usually kept up till eleven when the sleighs reappear and taking up their 'freight,' one by one disappear in the night. I had the good fortune to attend one of these midnight picnics as they were called to which my friend S[hirley] secured me an invitation. . . . .

From our dinner table, the day following the pic-nic, we adjourned to the Tremont House, to a ball given by the bachelors. These balls occurred once a week during the winter, and were called the "Bachelors' Assembly Balls," and were intended as a return by the *brave garçons* of Chicago to the community, for the lavish hospitalities bestowed upon them by managing mammas. The rooms were large, handsomely decorated, brilliantly lighted and enlivened, and embellished by a dashing company. The music was all that could be desired, and the supper beyond praise.

Everything passed off the evening of my attendance agreeably, and as this was usually the case, these assemblies were decidedly popular. In the company there were many young married ladies, and even those who could lay claims to being "fair, fat and forty." I soon discovered that Chicago society in its freedom from restraint and easy sociability was more French than English, and more American than either. Many of the handsomest, gayest and most desirable-looking ladies were mothers, and in the same room mothers and daughters were often "tripping the light fantastic toe." This I thought entirely as it should be, and admirable evidence of the healthfulness of the northwestern climate. It was also a refutation, complete and perfect of the common error—I might almost say popular superstition in England—that American ladies fade at forty and go off at fifty. Frail creatures, they are not quite so frail and fleeting in their charms as their British sisters imagine, certainly not in Chicago. . . . .

It cannot be denied that life in the "garden city" was pleasant, most pleasant. Business, however, before pleasure, was a
maxim early impressed upon my mind, and business now called
me south. My preparations to be off were accordingly made,
and a P.P.C. left upon my numerous newly-made and highly-
valued friends and acquaintances. Other preliminaries settled,
I availed myself of a mild spell of weather to cross the lake to
St. Joseph's in Michigan. During the summer regularly, and
when the weather permitted in winter, a steam packet plied
between the two points. . . . .

PART II

AN ERA OF EXPANSION

INTRODUCTION

T HE traveler who visited Chicago from 1848 up to the time of the Great Fire in 1871 came to a city which was developing and expanding in all aspects of human interest and endeavor. In 1848 the Illinois and Michigan Canal was completed, bringing promise of rich and vast tonnage in foodstuffs from neighbors living to the Southwest. At the same time other man-made devices in transportation were adding their contributions to the upbuilding of a city destined, within the memory of those now living, to become the world's greatest distributor of grain, live stock, and lumber and to become one of the world's leading cities in the wholesale trade of clothing and shoes, hardware, and groceries.

Over plank roads rumbled wagons laden with the produce of the region near by on the average of two hundred a day during 1848. By 1850, these highways of trade ran southwest from Chicago sixteen miles and northwest eighteen miles. Soon, however, competition from water carriers and from railroads reduced the market offerings of the plank roads. By 1850, forty-two miles of the Galena and Chicago Railroad linked Chicago and Elgin, and in two years more the Illinois Central was building its way into the little city. In the next two decades tentacles of steel reaching north, south, east, and west clutched at the produce of all America, even of the world, and made Chicago, with its ten thousand miles of track, the distributing center of the Middle West.

Into this busy community poured groups of immigrants and native Americans, all seeking the betterment of their earthly lot. In 1850, Chicago housed 28,269 persons, of whom 6,096 were Irish, 5,094 were Germans, 1,883 Welsh and English, 610 Scotch, and 240 Southern Europeans. Ten years later the foreign group had grown to 54,624 out of a total population of 109,206. The march forward was steady and uninterrupted. When the Great Fire came, it found a city of 298,977, of which 144,557 were born in foreign countries. Of this latter group during the war between the states, a liberal proportion shouldered arms, a fact noted by the famous London *Times* correspondent, William Howard Russell, although his statement is somewhat exaggerated:

Nearly one half of the various companies enrolled in this district are Germans, or are the descendants of German parents and speak only the language of the old country; two-thirds of the remainder are Irish, or of immediate Irish descent; but it is said that a grand reserve of American born lies behind this *avant garde*, who will come into the battle should there ever be need for their services.[1]

A natural concomitant of an increasing populace here was, as is usually the case, the construction of dwelling houses and other buildings. Although opinion among travelers was not unanimous, most of them agreed that cheap workmanship and materials and uninteresting design made an "unusual uniformity about the buildings, from the fact that they have all been built almost at the same time."[2] On the other hand, some visitors spoke with enthusiasm of "beautiful villa-residences" of great variety which were met in sight-seeing,[3] and of some of the public edifices and business buildings.[4] By 1856 the total volume of building reached $5,709,000; but the panic the following year served as a deterrent, although in the sixties construction was resumed on a large scale. Yet, in a community absorbed in the daily struggle for trade and whose rawness was that of youth, it is not strange that little time or attention was focused upon beautifying its environs. Rather, it was necessary to direct all energies to the acquisition of daily necessities and the mundane quest of business supremacy.

But beautiful trees lined Chicago's streets and furnished cause

[1] William Howard Russell, *My Diary North and South* (Boston: T. O. H. P. Burnham, 1863), p. 358.

[2] Edward Dicey, *Six Months in the Federal States* (2 vols.; London: Macmillan Co., 1863), I, 151.

[3] See, for example, Mrs. C. M. Kirkland's description in her "Illinois in Spring-time: With a Look at Chicago," *Atlantic Monthly*, II (September, 1858), 486–88.

[4] *Chicago Daily Tribune*, January 1, 1863.

for calling her "the Garden City." Long rows of dwellings found often in the East were not reproduced here, perhaps accounting for the complimentary tone of some visitors. On the whole, however, this new town on the squat, uninteresting prairie at that time appeared to the traveler "one of the most miserable and ugly cities" in America, sitting on the shore of the lake "in wretched dishabille," resembling "rather a huckstress than a queen."[5]

Added to the plainness and monotony of some of its buildings was the appearance of the streets. Muddy thoroughfares and the uneven street grading and paving of the city were common topics of discussion among visitors of the early fifties in particular. In 1855, however, a new regrading of the streets attempted to rescue Chicago from the mud which, at times, nearly engulfed pedestrians and vehicles. The new level necessitated the elevation of buildings, which, in some cases, were raised only for the owners to be confronted with a still higher grade requirement in 1857. During this time Chicago was a city of "ups and downs," as described by James Stirling, an English visitor in 1856:

> When you walk along even the principal streets, you pass perhaps a block of fine stone-built stores, with splendid plate-glass windows (finer than any in New York), with a good granite pavement in front: a few steps on you descend by three or four wooden steps to the old level of the street, and find a wooden pavement in front of low, shabby-looking wooden houses. The opposite side of the street presents probably the reverse. In some places the wooden causeway of the street may be raised, while the foot pavement is low; or the granite pavement may be raised to the new level while the middle of the street is still the old plankroad, two or three feet below. At the Tremont House both are on the old low level, and only the high granite curb-stone, over which you have to clamber, reminds you of the reform yet to come.[6]

Further discomfort and inconvenience in going from one part of the city to another were found in the pivot or swinging bridges "so constructed that all vessels are permitted to go through them"[7] which frequently prevented pedestrians and others from

---

[5] See Fredrika Bremer's description reproduced, in part, pp. 125–32.

[6] James Stirling, *Letters from the Slave States* (London: John W. Barker & Son, 1857), pp. 2–3.

[7] John Reynolds, *Sketches of the Country on the Northern Route from Belleville, Illinois to the City of New York, and Back by the Ohio Valley* (Belleville: J. A. Willis, 1854), p. 128.

keeping appointments as scheduled while boats made their way up and down the river.

Until within the sixties, Chicago was chiefly the great exchange center of the great Middle Valley and the far-reaching Northwest, buying and selling in large quantities but manufacturing in a less degree. As early as 1854 she was the world's greatest grain center, with Archangel the nearest rival, acclaimed by the English novelist Anthony Trollope as "the favorite city haunt of the American Ceres," seated amidst "the dust of her full barns."[8]

As early as 1851, Daniel S. Curtiss in his *Western Portraiture and Emigrant's Guide* painted a picture of the rapid development of economic forces destined to attain still greater heights in the years to come:

> The leading articles of export from this city are wheat, flour, pork, beef, cattle, horses, wool, lard, etc., eastward by steamboat and sail vessels; lumber, merchandise, ironware, wood and iron machinery, farming utensils, etc., southward by canal, and westward by railroad. . . . . The slaughtering business has been more extensively carried on during the present year than ever before in Chicago. There is perhaps no other Western city that slaughters the number of cattle which Chicago does. The whole number of cattle slaughtered, during the season, was 27,500; and the amount of capital invested about three fourths of a million of dollars. In addition, about 10,000 sheep have been slaughtered within two months. . . . . Some idea of the labor and productiveness of the farming region which seeks Chicago as its transportation depot, may be formed from the fact, that in a single year the value of exports from that place has been between two and three millions of dollars; besides its vast lumber trade, of nearly two hundred million feet, distributed in all directions, to supply the wants of a vast country, so rapidly being settled and ornamented with fine buildings, fences, etc.[9]

Visiting Chicago in 1854, John Reynolds, a native of the state of Pennsylvania and one-time governor of Illinois, recorded that "the manufactories of Chicago are advancing with astonishing rapidity,"[10] and recounted, as among the leading factories, those producing locomotives, steam engines, railroad cars,

[8] Anthony Trollope, *North America* (New York: Harper & Bros., 1862), p. 156. Quoted by permission of Harper & Bros.

[9] Daniel S. Curtiss, *Western Portraiture and Emigrant's Guide* (New York: J. H. Colton, 1852), pp. 45, 51, 58.

[10] Reynolds, *op. cit.*, p. 136.

truss bridges, white limestone and bricks, coaches, carriages, wagons, furniture, agricultural implements, linseed oil, soap and candles, and leather.

By 1867, James Parton, the biographer of Andrew Jackson, Aaron Burr, and other famous Americans, when he visited Chicago, expressed satisfaction with the strides taken in manufacture:

At first Chicago began to make on a small scale the rough and heavy implements of husbandry. That great factory, for example, which now produces an excellent farm-wagon every seven minutes of every working day, was founded twenty-three years ago by its proprietor investing all his capital in the slow construction of one wagon. At the present time, almost every article of much bulk used upon railroads, in farming, in warming houses, in building houses, or in cooking, is made in Chicago. Three thousand persons are now employed there in manufacturing coarse boots and shoes. The prairie world is mowed and reaped by machines made in Chicago, whose people are feeling their way, too, into making woollen and cotton goods. Four or five miles out on the prairie, where until last May the ground had never been broken since the creation, there stands now the village of Austin, which consists of three large factory buildings, forty or fifty nice cottages for workmen, and two thousand young trees. This is the seat of the Chicago Clock Factory, ... The machinery now in operation can produce one hundred thousand clocks a year; and the proprietors had received orders for eight months' product before they had finished one clock. . . . . A few miles farther back on the prairies, at Elgin, there is the establishment of the National Watch Company, which expects soon to produce fifty watches a day, ... They are beginning to make pianos at Chicago, besides selling a hundred a week of those made in the East; and the great music house of Root and Cady are now engraving and printing all the music they publish. Melodeons are made in Chicago on a great scale.[11]

While Chicago was striding toward economic leadership in the Middle West, she was not neglecting things of the spirit. Reynolds, in 1854, mentioned "upwards of sixty christian churches and one Jewish synogogue," many of whose "church edifices are beautiful and splendid, and all are convenient and comfortable."[12] A little over a decade later Parton observed:

We abhor superlatives, but we must claim the privilege of asserting that, in the construction of buildings, designed for the assembling together of many people, Chicago surpasses the rest of the world. There are, positively, no churches anywhere else in which elegance and convenience are so perfectly combined as in the newer churches of Chicago.[13]

[11] James Parton, "Chicago," *Atlantic Monthly*, XIX (March, 1867), 325–45. Quoted by permission of *Atlantic Monthly*.

[12] Reynolds, *op. cit.*, p. 135.   [13] Parton, *op. cit.*, p. 343.

No less a matter of observation was the sanctity with which the Sunday was clothed in Chicago:

The traveller who stays over a Sunday in Chicago witnesses as complete a suspension of labor as in Boston or Philadelphia. A great majority of the eager and busy population on that day resigns itself to the influence of its instructors; and the hundred and fifty churches are well filled with attentive people.[14]

Art and music likewise had their patrons. Parton commented on "a surprising taste for decoration," and added that "it is more common to see good engravings and tolerable paintings in the residences of Chicago than in those of New York."[15] By 1850 a philharmonic society under Julius Dyhrenfurth attempted a series of concerts, which received poor support. This group was followed by other philharmonic societies formed in 1852 and in 1860. Organizations of German musicians, the Music Union of Vocal and Instrumental Music, and the Mendelssohn Society, followed by the Oratorio Society, were further evidence of an interest in the finer things of life. Foreign and American musicians visiting the city were received with enthusiasm; and an orchestra under the direction of Theodore Thomas, later a resident of the city, attested further to the interest of Chicagoans in worth-while music.

The drama also attained greater artistry in its productions, being aided by the adoption of suitable scenery and the installation of necessary mechanical devices in the Rice Theatre opened first in 1847, destroyed by fire in 1850, but rebuilt immediately. In 1857, McVicker's Theatre was constructed, and Crosby's Opera House opened in 1865.

The reading tastes of the populace also received favorable comment from the city's many visitors: "The book-stores, the shelves of which are crowded with the best literature, are not exotic," declared Parton.

All our leading publishing houses have their lists of publications completely represented, and Chicago itself is rapidly becoming second only to New York as a distributing point. The demand for foreign books, for costly books, for valuable books is very great. . . . . Allied to the book business is the news

[14] *Ibid.*, p. 344. See also Moses Armstrong's remarks in his *The Early Empire Builders of the Great West* (St. Paul: E. W. Porter, 1901), pp. 182–85.

[15] Parton, *loc. cit.*

business, which is not the least among the noteworthy things of this city. The business is an outgrowth of the express business. . . . . The express has opened in almost every town, certainly in almost every réspectable village, a newsstand; and the influence of these cheap establishments in the diffusion of intelligence, as well as this other function, the provision of a peculiar class of cheap literature, it will be the duty of some future historian to determine.

The railroads running out from Chicago have given every facility to the development of the news business, and accordingly there has grown up in the city a very large and most admirably conducted establishment,—the Western News Company, under the management of its founder, Mr. John R. Walsh. It is, we believe, less than ten years since this establishment was started, in a small way, Mr. Walsh, then a young man with very limited capital. It is now one of the institutions of Chicago and transacts a business of three quarters of a million dollars a year. Hardly one of those trains that leave the city every fifteen minutes but takes out to other places some of its parcels. Hardly a cabin in the Northwest that is beyond the reach of its influence. Hardly a family that is not indebted to it for a cheerful visit during the week or month.

The truth is, that much of the best young brain, taste, and civilization of the country has gone to the Northwest, and Chicago, besides supplying it with an annual fifty millions of dollars' worth of dry goods, and no end of boards, has to minister to its woolen needs, and distribute over the country five millions of dollars worth of books. At Chicago the other day, fifty graduates of Yale, all residents of the city, were gathered about one table.[16]

By 1853 Chicago sustained over thirty newspapers, credited by one visitor with having a large part in making Chicago economically successful.[17] The later sixties found Chicago with newspapers "conducted with vigor, enterprise, and liberality of expenditure," with correspondents in New York, London, Paris, Washington, and other cities.[18] By 1860 twenty-seven literary periodicals had been established; and for children, there were fifteen juvenile journals circulating by 1871.

Chicago's school system elicited much and favorable comment from her visitors, even from those who found the city ugly and unattractive. In general, the school buildings were said to be well ventilated and lighted, large and convenient. Instruction embraced pupils from the elementary grades through those of mature years, adults having a chance to attend school in the evening as early as 1856. By 1857 three industrial schools were established and commercial colleges flourished. As early as 1850,

[16] *Ibid.*

[17] Reynolds, *op. cit.*, p. 118.   [18] Parton, *op. cit.*, p. 342.

weekly teachers' institutes were held, and by 1856 a teachers' training department offered opportunity for practice to prospective teachers. Nor was higher training neglected. Northwestern University was established in 1853, the first University of Chicago in 1857, and St. Ignatius College, later Loyola University, in 1869.

In the twenty years preceding the Fire, private academies and professional schools thrived, as well as those which provided training in medicine, law, and pharmacy. The Garrett Biblical Institute was founded in 1856, the Chicago Theological Seminary in 1858, the Presbyterian Theology Seminary was moved from New Albany, Indiana, in 1859, and the Baptist Theological Seminary opened in 1867, affording training to ministers of the gospel of various denominations.

In 1856 the Chicago Historical Society was founded, followed the next year by the Chicago Academy of Sciences and in six years by the Chicago Astronomical Society. During the 1850's the Mechanics Institute flourished; and the Young Men's Association, becoming the Chicago Library Association, was active until 1871. In 1852 the Young Men's Christian Association was organized; but its greatest vigor appeared after 1858 under D. L. Moody, its function being chiefly the religious development of young men of the community.

Manifold and complicated were the problems of governing a community into which had come some for the sole purpose of becoming rich and among whom were many foreigners ignorant of American customs and practices. Crime and vice were not absent, and the city's governing forces were sometimes charged with disloyalty to their pledges.[19] But confidence in their ability to conquer difficulties affecting both the spiritual and the physical was never lacking in Chicago's citizenry, and was so sincere and apparent that it frequently provided a similar conviction for observers from abroad. Indomitable courage and ceaseless energy, intentness of purpose and boundless faith in their city's future, led visitors frequently to comment with enthusiasm up-

[19] See Fredrika Bremer's description, p. 131.

on the character of the populace and the city's prospects. Heralded as "a stupendous monument of the enterprise and energy
of man,"[20] this "wonderful city"[21] was one of superlatives in many
avenues of endeavor, and thus characterized by Anthony Trollope:

At Chicago the hotel was bigger than other hotels, and grander. There were
pipes without end for cold water which ran hot, and for hot water which would
not run at all. The post-office also was grander and bigger than other post-
offices—though the postmaster confessed to me that the matter of the delivery
of letters was one which could not be compassed. Just at that moment it was
being done as a private speculation; but it did not pay, and would be discontinued. The theatre too was large, handsome, and convenient; but on the
night of my attendance it seemed to lack an audience.
Men in those regions do not mind failures, and when they have failed, instantly begin again. They make their plans on a large scale, and they who
come after them fill up what has been wanting at first. Those taps of hot and
cold water will be made to run by the next owner of the hotel, if not by the
present owner. In another ten years the letters, I do not doubt, will all be delivered. Long before that time the theatre will probably be full.[22]

In common with others, James Stirling, coming from England
in 1856, reflected the attitude of many of his time:

Ever since I came into the States, I have been hearing of Chicago, as the
great feature of the new Western World, and was therefore prepared for a
wonderful city. But the reality exceeded my expectations. It is a city, not in
growth, but in revolution; growth is much too slow a word for the transformation of a hamlet of log-huts into a western New York, in the space of a few
years.[23]

"No man has seen the West who has not seen Chicago," declared Henry Ward Beecher in 1856;[24] and Lillian Foster, visiting here a few years later, assured the readers of her book, *Way-
Side Glimpses*, that this city was "more astonishing than the
wildest visions of the most vagrant imagination."[25]

[20] James William Massie, *America: The Origin of Her Present Conflict, Her Prospect
for the Slave, and Her Claim for Anti-Slavery Sympathy* (London: John Snow, 1864), p.
249.
[21] Sir S. Morton Peto, Bart., *The Resources and Prospects of America Ascertained during a Visit to the States in the Autumn of 1865* (New York: Alexander Strahan, 1866),
p. 92.
[22] Trollope, *op. cit.*, pp. 156–57.   [23] Stirling, *op. cit.*, p. 1.
[24] See Henry Ward Beecher's description of Chicago in his *Eyes and Ears* (Boston:
Ticknor & Fields, 1862), pp. 96–101.
[25] Lillian Foster, *Way-Side Glimpses* (New York: Rudd & Carleton, 1860), p. 70.

The year 1871, however, brought to an end an epoch in which the crudity of a new and growing community was ever evident, although its energy was tireless and its citizens possessed of an unquenchable thirst for the better things of life. On the night of October 7, 1871, a fire started in a West Side boiler factory but was finally extinguished. The next night another fire broke out in the barn of Mrs. Patrick O'Leary on the West Side. Fanned by a stiff wind, the flames soon spread; and not until they had wrought ruin as far as Lincoln Park on the North Side were they stopped. This was not Chicago's first great fire, for, in October, 1857, one had wrecked a half-million dollars' worth of property and destroyed the lives of twenty-three persons, which led to the creation of a salvage corps by the insurance companies, in turn superseded by a paid fire company in 1858.

The exact cause of the Great Fire of 1871 will probably never be known. A long and continuous drought during the autumn had made the wooden buildings, streets, and fences dry as tinder. Facilities for fire protection were inadequate. It was estimated that 2,600 acres of buildings were destroyed and 92,000 people left homeless. The total loss was said to range from $186,000,000 to $500,000,000. Relief from all over the world poured into the stricken community. A new Chicago soon arose from the ashes.

FREDRIKA BREMER[1]

FREDRIKA BREMER, a prolific Swedish writer, reached the United States in 1849 when she was forty-eight years of age. She had begun to write verses at the age of eight, and in 1828 came her first fame as a writer in the publication of *Teckningar ur Hvardagslifet*, followed rapidly by further successes. Miss Bremer traveled extensively and wrote voluminously, gaining fame abroad after 1839; when some of her books were translated in Germany and England. Excellent translations of her works by Mary Howitt also increased to a great degree her reputation as an able and interesting writer. In her later books Miss Bremer set forth her attitude on the emancipation of women. Her writings also express honest and thoughtful impressions of family life in the old and new worlds. *The Homes of the New World* (1853) and *Life in the Old World* (1862) are the result of researches of this nature. Critics accord highest praise to *The Neighbors* (1837).

Miss Bremer died in 1865.

-»» «««-

PRAIRIES

On the morning of the 13th of September, I saw the sun shine over Chicago. I expected to have been met at Chicago by some friends, who were to take me to their house. But none came; and on inquiring, I learned that they were not now there. Nor was this to be wondered at, as I was two months after the appointed time. I now, therefore, found myself quite alone in that great unknown West. And two little misadventures occurring just now with my luggage made it still less agreeable. But precisely at the moment when I stood quite alone on the deck—for my kind new acquaintance had left the steamer somewhat earlier— my gladness returned to me, and I felt that I was not alone; I felt vigorous, both body and mind. The sun was there too; and such a heartfelt rejoicing filled my whole being, in its Lord and in my Father, and the Father of all, that I esteemed myself fortunate that I could shut myself up in a little solitary room at an hotel in the city, and thus be still more alone with my joy.

[1] Fredrika Bremer, *The Homes of the New World* (2 vols.; New York: Harper & Bros., 1853), I, 601–6, 610–12. Reprinted by permission of Harper & Bros.

But my solitude was not of long continuance. Handsome, kind people gathered round me, offered me house, and home, and friendship, and every good thing, and all in Chicago became sunshine to me.

In the evening I found myself in that pretty villa, where I am now writing to you, and in the beautiful night a serenade was given in the moonlight gardens, in which was heard the familiar

Einsam bin ich nicht allein.

It was a salutation from the Germans of the city.

September 17*th.* Prairies! A sight which I shall never forget.

Chicago is situated on the edge of the prairie-land. The whole State of Illinois is one vast rolling prairie (that is to say, a plain of low, wave-like hills); but the prairie proper does not commence until about eighteen miles from the city. My new friends wished me to pass a day of prairie-life. We drove out early in the morning, three families in four carriages. Our pioneer, a dark, handsome hunter, drove first with his dogs, and shot when we halted by the way, now and then, a prairie hen (grouse) on the wing. The day was glorious; the sky of the brightest blue, the sun of the purest gold, and the air full of vitality, but calm; and there, in that brilliant light, stretched itself far, far out into the infinite, as far as the eye could discern an ocean-like extent, the waves of which were sunflowers, asters, and gentians. The plain was splendid with them, especially with the sunflowers, which were frequently four yards high, and stood far above the head of our tallest gentleman.

We ate our dinner in a little wood, which lay like a green shrub upon that treeless, flowery plain. It was an elevation, and from this point the prairie stretched onward its softly waving extent to the horizon. Here and there, amid this vast stretch, arose small log-houses, which resembled little birds' nests floating upon the ocean. Here and there, also, were people making hay; it looked like some child's attempt, like child's play. The sun-bright soil remained here still in its primeval greatness and magnificence, unchecked by human hands, covered with its flowers, protected and watched alone by the eye of the sun.

And the bright sunflowers nodded and beckoned in the wind, as if inviting millions of beings to the festival set out on the rich table of the earth. To me it was a festival of light. It was a really great and glorious sight; to my feeling less common and grander even than Niagara itself.

The dark hunter, a man of few words but evidently of strong feelings, leaned upon his gun and said softly, "Here I often stand for hours and gaze on creation!"

And well he might That sight resembled an ecstasy in the life of nature. It was bathed in light; it reposed blissfully in the bosom of light. The sunflowers sang praises to the sun.

I wandered about in the wood and gathered flowers. The asters grew above my head. Nearly all the flowers which now cover the prairies are of the .class Syngenesia, and of these the Solidago and Helianthus predominate. The prairies are covered each different month with a different class of flowers; in spring white, then blue, then purple, and now mostly of a golden yellow.

In the course of the day we visited one of the log-houses on the plain. A nice old woman was at home. The men were out getting in the hay. The house was one year old, and tolerably open to the weather, but clean and orderly within, as are houses generally in which live American women. I asked the good woman how the solitude of this great prairie agreed with her. She was tired of it, "it was so monotonous," she said. Yes, yes, there is a difference between seeing this sight of heaven and earth for one day and for a whole year! Nevertheless, I would try it for a year.

We did not see a cloud during the whole of this day, nor yet perceive a breath of air; yet still the atmosphere was as fresh as it was delicious. The Indian summer will soon begin. The whole of that little prairie-festival was cloudless, excepting that the hunter's gun went off and shot one of our horses in the ear, and that a carriage broke down; but it was near the end of the journey and was taken all in good part, and thus was of no consequence.

Chicago, September 27th.

I have heard a great deal about the Indians from Mr. and Mrs. K.,[2] in whose extremely agreeable family I have now my home. Mr. K. is the government agent in all transactions with the Indian tribes in these Northwestern States, and he and his family were among the earliest settlers in the wilderness there. Mrs. K., who writes with facility and extremely well, has preserved in manuscript many incidents in the lives of the first colonists, and of their contests with the Indians, and among these many which occurred in her own family. The reading of these narratives is one of the greatest pleasures of the evenings; some are interesting in a high degree; some are full of cruel and horrible scenes, others also touchingly beautiful, and others, again, very comic.

There is material for the most beautiful drama in the history of the captivity of Mrs. K.'s mother and her free restoration. I know nothing more dramatic than the first terrible scene of the carrying off of the little girl; then the attachment of the Indian chief to the child, the affection which grew up in his heart for her as she grew up in his tent, and was called by the savage tribe "the White Lily;" the episode of the attempt to murder her by the jealous wife of the chief; and, lastly, the moment when the chief, after having for several years rejected all offers of negotiation and gifts, both on the part of the parents and the government, for the restoration of the child, yielded at length to prayers, and consented to a meeting of the mother and daughter, but on the express condition that she should not seek to retain her; and then, when arrived at the appointed place of meeting, with all his warriors in their complete array, he rode alone—spite of all their remonstrances—across the little brook which separated the camp of the whites from that of the Indians, and saw the young girl and her mother throw themselves into each other's arms with tears of joy, he stood overpowered by the sight and exclaimed, "The mother must have her child!" turned his horse, recrossed the brook, and rejoined his own people without a glance

[2] The Kinzie family.

at the darling of his heart, "the White Lily," who now, in the fifteenth year of her age, returned to her family! What an excellent subject for dramatic treatment! I hope that Mrs. K. will some day publish this beautiful narrative, together with several others which I heard during these evenings.

The massacre of Chicago belongs to the unpleasing portion of the chronicle, and Chicago still retains fresh traces of this event. Yet even that is ennobled by beautiful human actions.

The wooing of my noble and gentlemanly host by the Indian chief Fourlegs for his daughter, and the arrival of the fat Miss Fourlegs on her buffalo hides in the city, where she met with a refusal, belong to the comic portion of the chronicle, and very much amused me. For the rest, the gentle and refined Mr. K., like many others who have lived much among the Indians, has a real attachment to them, and seems to have an eye rather for the virtues than the failings which are peculiar to this remarkable people. The K.'s resided long in Minnesota, and only within the last few years at Chicago (Illinois), where they have a handsome house with a large garden.

Chicago is one of the most miserable and ugly cities which I have yet seen in America, and is very little deserving of its name, "Queen of the Lake;" for, sitting there on the shore of the lake in wretched dishabille, she resembles rather a huckstress than a queen. Certainly, the city seems for the most part to consist of shops. One sees scarcely any pretty country houses, with their gardens, either within or without the city—which is so generally the case in American towns—and in the streets the houses are principally of wood, the streets formed with wood, or, if without, broad and sandy. And it seems as if, on all hands, people came here merely to trade, to make money, and not to live. Nevertheless, I have, here in Chicago, become acquainted with some of the most agreeable and delightful people that I ever met with any where; good people, handsome and intellectual; people to live with, people to talk with, people to like and to grow fond of, both men and women; people who do not ask the stranger a hundred questions, but who give him an opportunity of seeing and learning in the most agreeable manner which he can desire;

rare people! And besides that, people who are not horribly pleased with themselves and their world, and their city, and their country, as is so often the case in small towns, but who see deficiencies and can speak of them properly, and can bear to hear others speak of them also.

To-day and last evening also, a hot wind has been blowing here, which I imagine must be like the Italian sirocco. One becomes quite enervated by it; and the air of Chicago is a cloud of dust.

September 23d. But in the evening, when the sun descends, and the wind subsides, I go to some higher part of the city, to see the sun set over the prairie land, for it is very beautiful; and, beholding this magnificent spectacle, melancholy thoughts arise. I see in this sun-bright western land thousands of shops and thousands of traders, but no Temple of the Sun, and only few worshipers of the sun and of eternal beauty. Were the Peruvians of a nobler intellectual culture than this people? Had they a loftier turn of mind? Were they the children of the light in a higher degree than the present race who colonize the western land of the New World? . . . .

GERMANS IN CHICAGO

There are a great number of Germans in Chicago, especially among the tradespeople and handcraftsmen. The city is only twenty years old, and it has increased in that time to a population of twenty-five thousand souls. A genuine "baby" of the Great West! but, as I have already said, somewhat unkemmed as yet. There is, however, here a street, or, more properly speaking, a row of houses or small villas along the shore of the lake, standing on elevated ground, which has in its situation a character of high life, and which will possess it in all respects some day, for there are already people here from different parts of the globe who will constitute the sound kernel of a healthy aristocracy.

Chicago bears on its arms the name of "the City in the Garden;" and when the prairie land around it becomes garden, there will be reason for its poetical appellation.

I have seen here, also, light and lofty school-rooms, and have heard the scholars in them, under the direction of an excellent master, sing quartettes in such a manner as affected me to tears. And the children, how eager, how glad to learn they were! Hurra! The West builds light school-rooms where the young may learn joyfully, and sing correctly and sweetly! The West must progress nobly. The building of the Temple of the Sun has already commenced.

My friends here deplored the chaotic state, and the want of integrity which prevails in political affairs, and which may be principally attributed to the vast emigration of the rudest class of the European population, and the facility with which every civil right is obtained in the state. A year's residence in the state gives the immigrant the right of a citizen, and he has a vote in the election of the governors both of the city and the state. Unprincipled political agitators avail themselves of the ignorance of immigrants, and inveigle them by fine speeches to vote for the candidate whom they laud, and who sometimes betrays them. The better and more noble-minded men of the state are unable to compete with these schemers, and therefore do not offer themselves; hence it most frequently happens that they are not the best men who govern the state. Bold and ambitious fortune-hunters most easily get into office; and once in office, they endeavor to maintain their place by every kind of scheme and trick, as well as by flattering the masses of the people to preserve their popularity. The ignorant people of Europe, who believe that kings and great lords are the cause of *all* the evils in the world, vote for that man who speaks loudest against the powerful, and who declares himself to be a friend of the people.

I also heard it lamented that the Scandinavian immigrants not unfrequently come hither with the belief that the State Church and religion are one and the same thing, and when they have left behind them the former, they will have nothing to do with the latter. Long compulsion of mind has destroyed, to that degree, their powers of mind; and they come into the West very frequently, in the first instance, as rejectors of all church communion and every higher law. And this is natural enough for people not accustomed to think greatly; but is a moment of transition which can not last very long in any sound mind, and in a hemisphere where the glance is so clear and alive to every thing which contributes to the higher life of man or of society.

Illinois is a youthful state, with a million inhabitants, but is able with her rich soil, to support at least ten millions. The climate, however, is not favorable to immigrants from Europe, who during the first few years suffer from fever and other climatic diseases.

In the morning I leave Chicago and cross Lake Michigan to Milwaukee, in Wisconsin. An agreeable young man came last evening to fetch me there.

I have been merely a few days in Chicago, and yet I have seen people there with whom I should like to live all my days.

But these feelings for amiable people whom I meet with now and then during my pilgrimage are to me as "a tent of one night", under which I repose thankfully. I would fain linger yet longer; but I must the next morning remove my tent and proceed still further—and I do so with a sigh.

Farewell, ye charming people in that ugly city! Receive my thanks, warm hearts of Chicago!

J. J. AMPÈRE[1]

J. J. AMPÈRE (1800–1864) was the only son of André Marie Ampère, the great French scientist who gave his name to one of the measurements of electricity. He early became interested in folk songs and poetry. During his travels in Northern Europe he studied those of the Scandinavian people, and upon his return to France in 1830 he delivered a series of lectures on these and early German poetry at the Athenaeum at Marseilles. The first of these was printed as *De l'histoire de la Poésie* (1830) and was practically the first introduction of the French public to the Scandinavian and German epics. He later became professor of the history of French literature at the Collège de France. A journey to Northern Africa in 1841 was followed by a tour through Greece and Italy in company with Prosper Mérimée and others. In 1848 he was elected a member of the French Academy, and in 1851 he visited America.

The result of the voyage was the publication of his two-volume work, *Promenade en Amérique*. In the Foreword he ascribed his first interest in the United States to M. Alexis de Tocqueville's work *La démocratie en Amérique* and expressed concurrence in De Tocqueville's observations. His trip to America was also prompted by a desire to investigate the New World after his study of the old countries of Europe, and by the hope that the tour would prove the inspiration for imaginative and creative work. He realized the difficulty in attempting to understand a nation so young and to determine what she might become some day.

Ampère in his descriptions showed himself a good observer, more concerned with intellectual and social approach to an understanding of the American people than with the economic or political. He was curious about Harvard University; he knew Jared Sparks and Edward Everett; and he became interested in Unitarianism. With Charles Sumner he discussed the slavery question, and he turned his attention to the poetry of Longfellow.

As he traveled westward through Canada to Chicago, he took stock of the different groups of people whom he saw. In Chicago his observant faculties were reflected in the wide range of subjects he discussed; among other things: the physical setting of the city, the commercial benefits to be derived from the location, the sale of public lands, the great importance of the invention of the McCormick reaper to the development of the grain industry, amusements and the religious bent of the inhabitants.

On the whole, the book is written with the zest and style of a true scholar genuinely interested in portraying a literary picture of what he has seen.

---

[1] J. J. Ampère, *Promenade en Amérique: États-Unis, Cuba, Mexique* (2 vols.; Paris: Michel Lévy Frères, 1860; translated by Irene Bassett), I, 182–88, 191–94, 198–203. Reprinted by permission of Colmann-Lévy, Éditeurs.

THE PHYSICAL SETTING OF CHICAGO

People had especially urged me to go to Chicago. Chicago is a city situated on the shores of Lake Michigan, at the beginning of the "prairies," that is to say, of those great steppes which extend westward to the Mississippi and beyond: virgin lands toward which flow streams of emigrants, and which, in their hands, change rapidly to cultivated fields whose products return to the east; the granary of the United States and a resource for Europe in her bad years. . . . .

Chicago is today what Cincinnati was thirty years ago, the last sentinel of the civilization of this side of the Mississippi; for beyond is St. Louis, the real outpost of the western movement, the vanguard of this army of clearers of the forest, whom the great river does not stop, and who will venture clear to the sandy plains which stretch to the foothills of the Rocky Mountains. . . . .

Chicago is not a great city like St. Louis, but it was pointed out to me as very curious in the rapidity of its progress, and its situation on the border, so to speak, of civilization, at least in this region. A railroad[2] leads right to Lake Michigan; this road traverses great forests cut up by ponds and little rivers. You arrive in the evening at the edge of the lake,[3] you cross it on a steamboat during the night, and the next morning you find yourself in Chicago. One must not trust the forecasts and predictions in regard to the future growth of American cities. They wanted to create a capital at Washington, and the vast space that was prepared for the fancied destinies of the city has remained in large measure almost empty. On the other hand, Mr. Keating, who in 1823 accompanied Major Long on his expedition, and traversed with him the lands of the Potwanies [sic] and Chippewas then occupying the country that I am visiting by railway, wrote: "The dangers of navigation on Lake Michigan and the small number of ports which its shore offers will always be a serious obstacle to the population of Chicago." Now the population of this city which fifteen years ago did not even exist, is today 34,000 souls.

---

[2] Michigan Central Railroad.   [3] Michigan City, Indiana.

A few leagues from Chicago, in a region not at all hilly and very little above sea level, is found the divide of the waters which flow into the St. Lawrence or into the Mississippi. Here the two basins touch, are almost on the same level, and even communicate by a canal in the rainy season. A slight unevenness of the soil determines whether a drop of water shall go to lose itself in Hudson Bay or in the Gulf of Mexico. Are there not, in the lives of individuals and peoples, moments which resemble that place?

The hotel[4] to which I went is one of the largest and best in the United States; they tell me that the proprietor[5] was, a few years ago, a tailor in the backwoods; he went bankrupt and came to Chicago, where, with his brother,[6] he sold trousers at fifty cents a pair; now he has built the magnificent hotel which one is quite astonished to find here by Lake Michigan. The aspect of this lake is as wild as its name: at least that is what I found while walking on the outskirts of the city along a somber sandy beach. I saw nothing but an expanse of green water tossed by a hard cold wind; I heard nothing but the gasping cough of a steam engine, and the intermittent grinding of a saw, mingled with the noise of the waves. Before me there extended into the lake a long wooden pier; the planks and the joists are half broken; there remains just what is necessary, nothing more. The city lies there like a boat stranded on a shore. Nearby is the suburb which is inhabited by the well-to-do citizens of Chicago. Here there are beautiful walks and frame houses with white columns, and elegant porticoes, all surrounded by gardens full of flowers. One of these houses is at the center of a veritable park. I see beautiful conservatories. Am I still beside Lake Michigan?

HOUSES, CHURCHES, AND SCHOOLS

Another house is that of Mr. Ogden, to whom I have been referred. No one can better inform me concerning Chicago than Mr. Ogden; no one is better acquainted with the city; he saw its birth and helped to make it. . . . . As we were walking in his garden, he showed me a tree, a survivor of the primitive forests,

---

[4] Tremont House.   [5] Ira Couch.   [6] James Couch.

and he told me: "Fifteen years ago I came here; I tied my horse to this tree, which was in the depths of a forest." This place now resembles the primitive forests as much as the most charming cottage in the suburbs of London or on the heights of Passy.[7]

Mr. Ogden presented me to a French lady of Chicago,[8] perfectly French in language and manners, and whose father was an Indian chief. . . . .

There are thirty-six churches in Chicago. They belong to various Christian denominations. I hear it said, and not for the first time: We like a diversity of sects; we see in that a guarantee against the preponderance of any one of them. This is indeed the democratic spirit that eyes with suspicion anything in society which might exercise under one name or another too much influence and too much authority; but is this so much the religious spirit, that spirit which appears moreover to be so powerful in America? The sentiments of the Americans in the matter of religion are for me an enigma which in some respects I still do not understand. If one really admits some kind of profession of faith, it is impossible that one should consider as equally in possession of the truth, various sects which are divided on very important points and which often anathematize each other. Perhaps in the United States the great number are more convinced of the excellence and moral usefulness of religion than of the truth of such and such a dogma. Perhaps as men of action rather than reflection, and very much in a hurry, their will adheres strongly to beliefs which they have neither the taste nor the time to examine. I know many Americans like that in Paris.

While following with Mr. Ogden a beautiful walk which extends along the shore of the lake, I perceive a pretty little frame house; it is that of the Catholic bishop who is highly esteemed.[9] I ask if there are many Protestants who embrace Catholicism; I

[7] "I have had the pleasure of seeing Mr. Ogden again in Rome. 'What was the population of Chicago,' he asked me, 'when you came there three years ago?' . . . . '34,000 persons.' . . . . 'Chicago now contains 65,000.' 'How many railroads were there?' . . . . 'Only one.' . . . . 'There are eleven.' " (Note by J. J. Ampère.)

[8] Catherine Chevalier, wife of Alexander Robinson.

[9] Rt. Rev. James Oliver Van Velde, S.J.

am told, as I have been several times before, that such cases are rare and exceptional. The Catholic population is increasing considerably through emigration, which is largely Catholic, being composed mostly of Irish, and of Germans who come principally from the parts of Germany where Catholicism reigns; but almost no conversions are mentioned except those of a few persons who have travelled in Europe, or of children who have been sent to Catholic schools. On the other hand they tell me that the Irish children who attend the city schools often become Protestants. In the United States, Catholicism is not the object of any malevolent prejudice; but I do not believe that the majority would be disposed to embrace it.

There are a great number of Baptists here. Like the Anabaptists of bloody memory, whom, however, they are far from resembling, they admit only baptism by immersion; their belief is based on a passage of the Epistles of Saint Paul, where it is said that he who is baptized is as if plunged into the tomb to be born again into a new life. Taking these passages literally, the Baptists believe that one should be plunged as if buried beneath the waters. For that, complete immersion is necessary; thus in Chicago in the winter one often sees Baptist ministers breaking the ice of the lake and entering the water waist-high, in order to immerse the adult neophytes whom they hold in their arms. . . . .

But let us return to Chicago. After the churches, the first thing one thinks about in building a city is the schools. There are six public schools in Chicago, in which are instructed three thousand children. The schools have a thirty-sixth of the lands to be sold of which the state has the disposal, and proceeds of a local tax, which amounts here to 30,000 francs. The teachers receive about 1200 francs, which is considered insufficient. They are helped by assistants, who teach the little boys and girls to read. In the United States many women are employed in the elementary teaching of the two sexes, and this proves very satisfactory. They have the patience and the gentleness necessary for this painful instruction. Too many other careers are open to the activities of men for them to be long content with teaching children to read. A society has been formed in New England for the purpose of sending women teachers into the west. They render the greatest service there, and contribute effectually to the culture of the rude people who inhabit these new regions. At the same time it often happens that these young women marry advantageously with the settlers who have begun to grow rich. Thus the situation works out to the profit of every one, the children, the settlers, and the teachers.

THE REAPER

Two months ago I was in England. An agricultural gathering had brought me to within some twenty leagues of London. I was to see a reaper in operation. Quite a number of country gentlemen and farmers had assembled with the same intention. A horizontal saw put in motion by the movement of the machine cut with great rapidity a considerable quantity of stalks of wheat at a time. This machine, drawn by a horse, circled the field, cutting at each round a strip of grain several feet wide. A farmer on the machine threw back the cut grain as the action of the saw piled it up. This was the only intervention of man in the operation. It seems to me that it would not be impossible to have the bundles thrown off by the machine itself.[10] Such as it is, it had the greatest success, in the eyes of the experts present at the experiment. What recalls this machine to me today is that we read on one side of it: Chicago. It is indeed an inhabitant of this city, Mr. Mac-Cormick [sic], who invented it. It is from the shores of Lake Michigan, from the prairie regions, from this city born yesterday, that comes a discovery which is arousing the interest of the farmers of England, and which in several agricultural contests was victorious over rival machines. If Mr. Mac-Cormick's [sic] reaper was successful in England, where they admire finish and perfection in agriculture as in everything, where land is high, and cultivation very careful, one can see how it would succeed even better in America where land can be had for almost nothing, and where it is a question not of doing well but of doing rapidly and much, and where it does not matter if one leaves a

[10] "I have read in an English newspaper that the improvement which I predicted at that time has since been realized." (Note by J. J. Ampère.)

little grain, if only one can quickly gather the harvest from an immense field. Farewell to the reapers of Theocritus and Virgil, and the patriarch Boaz ordering his men to leave some grain in the furrow so that Ruth might glean after them! Another complaint of poetry against machinery which has done it so much injury; but let these grievances not stop, which themselves have a certain poetry, at least a grandeur, since they represent the power and the triumph of man over nature.

RECREATION

In this far-away country where they can make machines that Europe admires, they cannot produce vaudevilles, for this evening they are playing a vaudeville of M. Scribe, whose spirit is so French and whose successes so cosmopolitan; they are also playing *La Bohémienne*. This Bohemian girl is the Esméralda of M. Victor Hugo: the characters of *Notre-Dame de Paris* have penetrated this far. I did not go to the theater, since I was invited to a subscription concert where I heard a good pianist and a rather good violinist. The latter, they tell me, is a bankrupt merchant. The orchestra was composed of German amateurs; afterwards there was dancing and waltzing much as in Paris, except that those around me were not well acquainted with this new society, which tomorrow may be somewhere else. The American does not attach himself willingly to the soil, and nevertheless he has a very strong national feeling. His country is for him first of all the whole Union, and second the locality where he is living, but only as long as he remains there; for he knows the "patriotism of his own church steeple" only he willingly changes steeples.

THE PRAIRIE

Before leaving Chicago I wanted at least a glimpse of the prairie. To this end I took a train which traverses it for a certain distance. I got off at a station in the midst of a deserted region. There is no postoffice there, as one can imagine; there is not a house, not a tree. Away over there I see a little red cabin: it seems to be the last habitation in sight; beyond there is nothing but plains without end. Not a noise, not a movement; the sky seems, as on the ocean, to plunge down behind the horizon. It is of these plains that Mr. Bryant, the American poet, said: "They extend so far that it is a boldness of the gaze to plunge to their limit." I recall the beautiful lines where he sang of the interior of these immense steppes of which I am walking on only the edges, but where I at least can cry with him:

"And I am in the wilderness alone."

After having passed two hours in the heart of this empty and limitless space, I hear the distant noise of a train, I see the smoke rise and flow across the solitude; then I notice the electric telegraph wire which crosses it; I no longer see how I can have felt myself so distant, so alone, and I come back to Chicago, where I arrive in time to pass a very agreeable evening listening to music and having ices in the charming home of Mr. Ogden.

ISABELLA LUCY BISHOP[1]

MRS. ISABELLA LUCY (BIRD) BISHOP, traveler, missionary, and writer, was the daughter of an English minister. In 1847, at the age of sixteen, she was launched on a literary career by composing an essay on fiscal protection, later privately published. The greater number of her writings discussed her experiences and impressions as an extensive traveler, before and after her marriage to Dr. John Bishop, a medical missionary. As a missionary she lived in Ireland, India, Tibet, Persia, Palestine, China, and Japan. The story of her sojourn in these countries is chronicled in a number of books. She was also a contributor to the *Sunday Magazine* and *Leisure Hour*. October 7, 1904, she died.

Her first visit to the United States was in 1854, in a search for better health. Seven months were spent in this country and Canada, and her impressions are recorded in *The Englishwoman in America*. In 1857–58 she came again, studying especially the current religious revival which she found swaying the American populace. Her reactions were published first as a series of letters in *The Patriot*. In 1859 they appeared in book form under the title *The Aspects of Religion in the United States of America*.

Again in 1871, seeking improved health, she returned to America; and the following year she journeyed to Australia and New Zealand. In 1873, in the United States once more, she spent the autumn months gathering experiences in the Rocky Mountains, which resulted in *A Lady's Life in the Rocky Mountains*, first published as articles in *Leisure Hour* but appearing in book form in 1879.

Before her first visit to the United States, Mrs. Bishop testifies that she thought of this country, as did many others of her time, as a land conspicuous for "smoking, spitting, 'gouging,' and bowie-knives—for monster hotels, steamboat explosions, railway collisions, and repudiated debts . . . . for keeping three millions of Africans in slavery—for wooden nutmegs, paper money, and 'fillibuster' expeditions. . . . . " Although coming with the prejudices which foreigners sometimes held, such predispositions gradually disappeared as she came to know Americans. Her books picture many American characteristics and customs as worthy of commendation and even of imitation, although she found Americans nationally sensitive and the lower classes in some instances living sordidly. The description of her experience as a guest in a cheap hotel in Chicago is unusual, since most foreign visitors were in contact only with the best available accommodations.

[1] [Isabella Lucy (Bird) Bishop], *The Englishwoman in America* (London: John Murray, 1856), pp. 146–51, 153–54, 155–58. Reprinted by permission of John Murray.

141

AN ADVERTISING HOUSE

During the morning we crossed some prairie-country, and stopped at several stations, patches of successful cultivation showing that there must be cultivators, though I rarely saw their habitations. The cars still continued so full that my friends could not join me, and I began to be seriously anxious about the fate of my luggage. At mid-day, spires and trees, and lofty blocks of building, rising from a grass-prairie on one side, and from the blue waters of Lake Michigan on the other, showed that we were approaching Chicago. Along beaten tracks through the grass, waggons with white tilts drawn by oxen were proceeding west, sometimes accompanied by armed horsemen.

With a whoop like an Indian war-whoop the cars ran into a shed—they stopped. . . . .

Meaning to stay all night at Chicago, we drove to the two best hotels, but, finding them full, were induced to betake ourselves to an advertising house, the name of which it is unnecessary to give, though it will never be effaced from my memory. The charge advertised was a dollar a day, and for this every comfort and advantage were promised.

The inn was a large brick building at the corner of a street, with nothing very unprepossessing in its external appearance. The wooden stairs were dirty enough, and, on ascending them to the so-called "ladies' parlour," I found a large, meanly-furnished apartment, garnished with six spittoons, which, however, to my disgust, did not prevent the floor from receiving a large quantity of tobacco-juice.

There were two rifles, a pistol, and a powder-flask on the table; two Irish emigrant women were seated on the floor (which swarmed with black beetles and ants), undressing a screaming child; a woman evidently in a fever was tossing restlessly on the sofa; two females in tarnished Bloomer habiliments were looking out of the window; and other extraordinary-looking human beings filled the room. I asked for accommodation for the night, hoping that I should find a room where I could sit quietly. A dirty chambermaid took me to a room or dormitory containing four beds. In one part of it three women were affectionately and assiduously nursing a sick child; in another, two were combing tangled black hair; upon which I declared that I must have a room to myself.

The chambermaid then took me down a long, darkish passage, and showed me a small room without a fireplace, and only lighted by a pane of glass in the door; consequently, it was nearly dark. There was a small bed with a dirty buffalo-skin upon it; I took it up, and swarms of living creatures fell out of it, and the floor was literally alive with them. The sight of such a room made me feel quite ill, and it was with the greatest reluctance that I deposited my bonnet and shawl in it.

Outside the door were some medicine-bottles and other suspicious signs of illness, and, after making some cautious inquiries, we found that there was a case of typhus fever in the house, also one of Asiatic cholera, and three of ague! My friends were extremely shocked with the aspect of affairs. I believe that they were annoyed that I should see such a specimen of an hotel in their country, and they decided, that, as I could not possibly remain there for the night, I should go on to Detroit alone, as they were detained at Chicago on business. Though I certainly felt rather out of my element in this place, I was not at all sorry for the opportunity, thus accidentally given me of seeing something of American society in its lowest grade.

We went down to dinner, and only the fact of not having tasted food for many hours could have made me touch it in such a room. We were in a long apartment, with one table down the middle, with plates laid for one hundred people. Every seat was occupied, these seats being benches of somewhat uncouth workmanship. The floor had recently been washed, and emitted a damp fetid odour. At one side was a large fireplace, where, in spite of the heat of the day, sundry manipulations were going on, coming under the general name of cookery. At the end of the room was a long leaden trough or sink, where three greasy scullery-boys without shoes, were perpetually engaged in washing plates, which they wiped upon their aprons. The plates, however, were not washed, only superficially rinsed. There were four

brigand-looking waiters with prodigious beards and mous-
tachios.

There was no great variety at table. There were eight boiled
legs of mutton, nearly raw; six antiquated fowls, whose legs were
of the consistence of guitar-strings; baked pork with "onion fix-
ings," the meat swimming in grease; and for vegetables, yams,
corncobs, and squash. A cup of stewed tea, sweetened with mo-
lasses, stood by each plate, and no fermented liquor of any description was consumed by the company. There were no carving-
knives, so each person *hacked* the joints with his own, and some
of those present carved them dexterously with bowie-knives
taken out of their belts. Neither were there salt-spoons so everybody dipped his greasy knife into the little pewter pot containing salt. Dinner began, and after satisfying my own hunger
with the least objectionable dish, namely "pork with onion fix-
ings," I had leisure to look around me.

Every quarter of the globe had contributed to swell that motley array, even China. Motives of interest or adventure had
drawn them all together to this extraordinary outpost of civilisation, and soon would disperse them among lands where civilisation is unknown.

As far as I could judge, we were the only representatives of
England. There were Scots, for Scots are always to be found
where there is any hope of honest gain—there were Irish emigrants, speaking with a rich brogue—French traders from St.
Louis—Mexicans from Santa Fé—Californians fitting out, and
Californians coming home with fortunes made—keen-eyed
speculators from New England—packmen from Canada—
"Prairie-men," trappers, hunters, and adventurers of all descriptions. Many of these wore bowie-knives or pistols in their
belts. The costumes were very varied and picturesque. Two
Bloomers in very poor green habiliments sat opposite to me, and
did not appear to attract any attention, though Bloomerism is
happily defunct in the States.

There had been three duels at Chicago in the morning, and
one of the duellists, a swarthy, dark-browed villain, sat next but
one to me. The quarrel originated in a gambling-house, and this

Mexican's opponent was mortally wounded, and there he sat, with the guilt of human blood upon his hands, describing to his *vis-à-vis* the way in which he had taken aim at his adversary, and no one seemed to think anything about it. From what I heard, I fear duelling must have become very common in the West, and no wonder, from the number of lawless spirits who congregate where they can be comparatively unfettered.

The second course consisted exclusively of pumpkin-pies; but when the waiters changed the plates, their way of cleaning the knives and forks was so peculiarly disgusting, that I did not attempt to eat anything. But I must remark that in this motley assembly there was nothing of coarseness, and not a word of bad language—indeed, nothing which could offend the most fastidious ears. I must in this respect bear very favourable testimony to the Americans; for, in the course of my somewhat extensive travels in the United States, and mixing as I did very frequently with the lower classes, I never heard any of that language which so frequently offends the ear in England.[2] . . . .

PHYSICAL SETTING

After dinner, being only too glad to escape from a house where pestilence was rife, we went out into Chicago. It is a wonderful place, and tells more forcibly of the astonishing energy and progress of the Americans than anything I saw. Forty years ago the whole ground on which the town stands could have been bought for six hundred dollars; now, a person would give ten thousand for the site of a single store. It is built on a level prairie, only slightly elevated above the lake surface.

It lies on both sides of the Chicago river, about a mile above its entrance into Lake Michigan. By the construction of piers, a large artificial harbour has been made at the mouth of this river. . . . .

Chicago is connected with the western rivers by a sloop canal —one of the most magnificent works ever undertaken. It is also

[2] "I must not be misunderstood here. Profane language is only too notoriously common in the States, but custom, which in America is frequently stronger than law, totally prohibits its use before ladies." (Note by I. L. Bishop.)

connected with the Mississippi at several points by railroad. It is regularly laid out with wide airy streets, much more cleanly than those of Cincinnati. The wooden houses are fast giving place to lofty substantial structures of brick, or a stone similar in appearance to white marble, and are often six stories high. These houses, as in all business streets in the American cities, are disfigured, up to the third story, by large glaring sign-boards containing the names and occupations of their residents. The side walks are of wood, and, wherever they are made of this unsubstantial material, one frequently finds oneself stepping into a hole, or upon the end of a board which tilts up under one's feet. The houses are always let in flats, so that there are generally three stores one above another. These stores are very handsome, those of the outfitters particularly so, though the quantity of goods displayed in the streets gives them rather a barbaric appearance. The side walks are literally encumbered with bales of scarlet flannel, and every other article of an emigrant's outfit. At the outfitters' stores you can buy anything, from a cartnail to a revolver; from a suit of oilskin to a paper of needles. The streets present an extraordinary spectacle. Everything reminds that one is standing on the very verge of western civilisation.

The roads are crowded to an inconvenient extent with carriages of curious construction, waggons, carts, and men on horseback, and the sidewalks with eager foot-passengers. By the side of a carriage drawn by two or three handsome horses, a creaking waggon with a white tilt, drawn by four heavy oxen, may be seen—Mexicans and hunters dash down the crowded streets at full gallop on mettlesome steeds, with bits so powerful as to throw their horses on their haunches when they meet with any obstacle. They ride animals that look too proud to touch the earth, on high-peaked saddles, with pistols in the holsters, short stirrups, and long, cruel-looking Spanish spurs. They wear scarlet caps or palmetto hats, and high jack-boots. Knives are stuck into their belts, and light rifles are slung behind them. These picturesque beings—the bullock-waggons setting out for the Far West—the medley of different nations and costumes in the streets—make the city a spectacle of great interest.

The deep hollow roar of the locomotive, and the shrill scream from the steamboat, are heard here all day; a continuous stream of life ever bustles through the city, and, standing as it does on the very verge of western civilisation, Chicago is a vast emporium of the trade of the districts east and west of the Mississippi. . . . .

We returned to tea at the hotel, and found our viands and companions just the same as at dinner. It is impossible to give an idea of the "western men" to any one who has not seen one at least as a specimen. They are the men before whom the Indians melt away as grass before the scythe. They shoot them down on the smallest provocation, and speak of "head of Indian," as we do in England of head of game. Their bearing is bold, reckless, and independent in the extreme; they are as ready to fight a foe as to wait upon women and children with tender assiduity; their very appearance says to you, "Stranger, I belong to the greatest, most enlightened, and most progressive nation on earth; I may be the President or a *millionaire* next year; I don't care a straw for you or any one else." . . . .

At seven o'clock, with a feeling of great relief, mingled with thankfulness at having escaped untouched by the terrible pestilence which had ravaged Chicago, I left the hotel, more appropriately termed a *"caravanserai,"* and my friends placed me in the "Lightning Express," warranted to go sixty-seven miles an hour.

Unless it may be St. Louis, I fancy that Chicago is more worth a visit than any other of the western cities. Even one day at it was worth a voyage across the Atlantic, and a land-journey of eighteen hundred miles.

WILLIAM FERGUSON[1]

WILLIAM FERGUSON, Scotch scientist and author, was born in 1823. Although he was a noted scientist and was an honorary fellow of the Linnean Society, the Royal Society of Edinburgh, and the Geological Society, his books are not on scientific subjects, but include *America by River and Rail* (1856); *Addresses Delivered to the Christian Conference at Perth* (1871); and *The Great North of Scotland Railway: a Guide* (1881).

Ferguson visited the United States in the early summer of 1855, and during his tour kept a journal, which he published the following year as *America by River and Rail*. He was interested in collecting the opinions of all persons he met, and included them in his book with strict impartiality. His first impression of Americans was gained from those he met in hotels and on the trains, whom he considered frivolous dollar-chasers, not a type to make America great. But upon contact with Americans in their homes he changed his appraisal, for he found the great middle-class possessing a spiritual righteousness which he believed presaged no limit to the future greatness of the United States. Successively he visited Boston, New York, Philadelphia, and the southern states. His attention was especially caught in a trip to the sea islands off Charleston by a colored church and school he found there. Returning north, he stopped in the anthracite coal region, and then passed through Ohio to Illinois. The latter state he reached in June and traveled extensively through it by rail and other methods of transportation. Six chapters of his book are devoted to observations on the state and its people. At this time he saw Chicago. He next crossed the Mississippi and went as far as Iowa. His return was by way of Detroit and Buffalo into Canada, where he completed his tour.

⇢⇻⇻⇺

STREETS, BUILDINGS, WATERWAYS, AND RAILWAYS

We reached Chicago about half-past nine. A cloud of hotel bills was scattered throughout the cars. I counted those of eight different houses; and when we arrived, it was no easy matter to get the ladies to the omnibus through the crowd of touters, or runners, as they are called here. However, all was managed safely, and we rattled away over the wooden streets of Chicago, to the Tremont-house. The bustle of this house is wonderful. Rooms had been secured for us all some days before, else we

---

[1] William Ferguson, *America by River and Rail* (London: James Nisbet & Co., 1856), pp. 362–64, 369–70, 424–25.

148

would have no chance of getting any, as the place is always full,
—such multitudes of people are passing to and fro.

Friday, *June* 1.—There has been much rain and storm which
is not the kind of weather to see Chicago in. It is an immense
place, covering a vast area of level ground, only a few feet raised
above the level of the lake. The streets are laid with deals,
which in many places are loose; and, as there is no fall to drain
the water off, the streets are deep with mud, till such time as the
the water has sunk through the sand. In wet weather, all is mud,
which the vehicles, rattling over the loose planks, splash up on
the passers-by plentifully; and in dry weather, all is sand, which
the gusts from the lake blow into eyes, and mouth, and ears in
a provoking way.

The town has little character, so far as the laying-out of the
streets and buildings is concerned. The streets are laid out rec-
tangularly, and the city is cut up into three divisions by the
branches of the Chicago river. This runs up into the city at
right angles to the lake, and divides—one branch going northwest, and the other south and south-west. The business division
of the town is the south-east, and the aristocratic residences are
in the north-east quarter. In this division there are some fine
houses, though nearly all of wood. They stand apart, and are
buried among trees. In the business part of the town, the houses
are continuous, and mostly of brick, without any pretensions to
taste. The branching of the river is very confusing and inconvenient, in one sense, from its separating the different parts of
the town, but it is very important to trade, as it gives a great
deal of river frontage. The traffic across the bridges is very
great. It has just been counted for one day, when it was found
that 44,000 people, and 1900 teams crossed by Clerk [*sic*] Street
bridge. It is proposed to form a tunnel under the river.

This evening we went out to see the lake, which was very
rough. Once the shore had almost a straight line, but the projection of a pier at the mouth of the river, turned the current of
the waves from the lake upon the shore, south of the river, and
they have washed out a deep bay. In consideration of certain

rights granted to them by the City of Chicago, the Illinois Central Railway Company have built an extensive breakwater, to stop this encroachment of the lake; and between this breakwater and the shore, their railway is built on piles, for a considerable distance. There is a bar at the mouth of the harbour, so that vessels require to beat up from the south to avoid it. To-night, the waves were breaking upon and beating in spray over the pier, and several timber ships were attempting to beat over the bar. They looked hard put to sometimes, but they succeeded in getting over, and came up the river. . . . .

There are completed, and in operation, 1628½ miles of railway, radiating north, south, and west from Chicago; and if we add the Michigan Southern and Northern Indiana, the Michigan Central, and the New Albany and Salem railways, arriving from the east, the mileage open at the end of 1854 was 2436½ miles. There are now in course of speedy formation lines which, in a very few years, will swell the above figures to 6738 miles; and as 5075 miles of these lines pour western and north and south-western produce into Chicago, and 1663 miles communicate with the east and south-east, partially bringing produce, but chiefly carrying it away, it is fairly evident that the business centring [sic] at Chicago must increase still more rapidly than it has hitherto done. . . . .

Now that I am about to leave Chicago, I find that I do so without regret, though I leave behind in it some whom I could have wished to see more of—people thoroughly worthy of esteem. Of Chicago itself, what can I say? It seems mad after money. It is an extraordinary fact. It is the entrepôt of the west, and must continue to increase. Of its inner life I saw but little; for its outward is all-absorbing, and carried me away. Yet I had glimpses of such inner life, and feel assured that there are there those who are the "salt." Let us trust they will not only preserve, but leaven it also; otherwise, the future of this west is very dark and perilous.

-»» «««-

ANONYMOUS[1]

T HE following article was printed anonymously. A search through guides and indexes failed to reveal the name of the author. Nor did a letter addressed to the publishers elicit the desired information.

-»» «««-

CHICAGO IN THE FIFTIES

Chicago is what Mr. Ralph Waldo Emerson would call a representative town.

It is the type of that class of American towns which have made themselves conspicuous, and almost ridiculous, by their rapid growth.

In 1850, it had a population of twenty-six thousand. In 1856, it claims to be—the first grain-market in the world—the first lumber-market in the world—the third city in the Union in post-office revenues. That it has the best back country in the world—the best rail-road communication with that back country—that its population is over ninety thousand—that "its motto is still 'ONWARD,' and its destinies among the stars."

I would remark, for the benefit of any intelligent English person who may peruse this article, that the last statement is not to be regarded as strictly official. It was not voted by the common council, nor signed by the mayor; but it is merely an humble effort of my own to give expression, in language adapted to the occasion, to what I conceive to be the prevailing sentiment of the place. I do not propose to verify, or to impeach, by statistics or otherwise, any of the foregoing propositions; but I hold these truths to be self-evident—that Chicago is a large town—and that people in that neighborhood are generally aware of the fact.

Business has called me thither several times during the past

[1] "Chicago in 1856," *Putnam's Monthly Magazine*, VII (June, 1856), 606–13. Reprinted by permission of the *Atlantic Monthly*.

year, both in the busy season of navigation and in the comparatively dull period of the winter months, and the results of my observations, during these visits, I propose to give below.

Before visiting Chicago, I had a curiosity to know how such a town, grown up, so to speak, in a night, but without, probably, all that artistic finish which Aladdin was able to command, would appear to a stranger unacquainted with western life. What was its situation and surroundings? How its streets looked, and the people in its streets? Having been there, I now know, and thinking that others, who might not be compelled to go there (as I was), might have the same curiosity, while looking for myself, I also endeavored to look for them, with the benevolent intention of conveying to them my ideas of its appearance; and to these external and casual phenomena I shall mainly confine myself. . . . .

THE CHICAGO RIVER

The harbor of Chicago is the river, and nothing more. It is a short, deep, sluggish stream, creeping through the black, fat mud of the prairie, and in some places would hardly be thought worthy of a name; but it makes itself wonderfully useful here. Outside of its mouth a vessel has no protection, nor are there any piers or wharves. The mouth of the river has been docked and dredged out, to afford a more easy entrance; but, after you are once in, it narrows to a mere canal, from fifty to seventy-five yards in width. The general course of the river, for about three-fourths of a mile, is at right angles with the lake shore, and this portion is what is known as *the* Chicago River. It here divides, or, more properly, two branches unite to form it, coming from opposite directions, and at nearly right angles to the main stream. These are called, respectively, the "North Branch" and the "South Branch," and are each navigable for some four miles, giving, in the aggregate, a river front of some fifteen or sixteen miles, capable of being increased by canals and slips, some of which have already been constructed. Into the "South Branch" comes the Illinois Canal, extending from this point one hundred miles to Lasalle, on the Illinois River, forming water communication between the Lakes and the Mississippi. For the want of a map, take the letter H; call the upright column on the right hand the lake shore; let the crossbar represent the Chicago River, the left hand column will stand for the two branches, and you have a plan of the water lines of the city of Chicago, which will answer very well for all purposes of general description. The three divisions thus formed are called, respectively, "North Side," "South Side," "West Side."

In this narrow, muddy river lies the heart and strength of Chicago. Dry this up, and Chicago would dry up with it, mean and dirty as it looks. From the mouth of the St. Joseph River, in Michigan, round to Milwaukie [*sic*], in the state of Wisconsin, a distance by the lake shore of more than two hundred and fifty miles, Chicago is the only place where twenty vessels can be loaded or unloaded, or find shelter in a storm. A glance at the map, then, will show that it is the only accessible port—and hence the commercial centre—of a vast territory, measuring thousands of square miles of the richest agricultural country in the world.

On this fact, and not on the present actual value, are really based those fabulous prices of corner lots and wharf improvements, which have sometimes provoked the sneers of the skeptic; but who shall say that the basis is not a sound one?

In these lots and wharves (I regret to say it) I have no interest, and, therefore, cannot dwell upon their future glory further with pleasure to myself; but I wish it distinctly understood, that I would not *swop* my home-lot (bleak hillside as it is), with its one cow, three apple-trees, and two great rocks, for all the swampy corner lots in Chicago. Thus, having hurled my defiance, I return to my subject, which is bridges.

STREETS AND BRIDGES

The streets, which are of handsome width, say sixty feet, are laid out at right angles, forming about sixteen blocks to the mile. It will be seen, then, that all the streets, running east and west, cross one of the "Branches," and likewise that each of the Branches, all the streets running north and south cross the main Chicago River. The level of the streets is not more than three or four feet above the level of the river; the river being navigable, of course all bridges must be draw-bridges. There is a bridge every third, fourth, or fifth street, more or less. During the winter, when the river is frozen fast, the bridges assume that staid and respectable air of permanency which characterizes well-regulated bridges everywhere. But, when once navigation is opened, there is an end to all stability. These bridges, as is scandalously asserted of certain ladies' tongues, are hung in the middle, and play at both ends. Policemen are stationed on either side, to prevent persons from driving, jumping, or being pushed into the water, and the motive power (two men with a cross-bar, standing in the middle of the bridge) keeps up, like Mr. Mantilini at the mangle, a perpetual "grind." People jump on and jump off as long as the policemen will let them; those that are on, horse and foot, quietly stand still, and are ground round to the other side; only the luckless driver of a vehicle finds himself wrong end first, and must wait for an additional turn to set him right. He does not wait long.

A bridge, however, cannot be turned in a minute (I think it usually takes about two), and, while the process is going on, a row of vehicles and impatience frequently accumulates that is quite terrific. I have seen a closely-packed column a quarter of a mile in length, every individual driver looking as if he thought he could have turned that bridge sixteen times, while he had been waiting. There is a great deal of scolding on such occasions, and—alas for human nature!—sometimes, I fear, a slight degree of profanity; but they ought to know that it does not do any good. Nobody wants to drive into the river, and the police would not let them, if they did.

THE BRIDGE IN FICTITIOUS LITERATURE

In the future fictitious literature of Chicago, the "Bridge," I think, must be, as it now is in real life, the turning point. The work of the western Ingraham rises before me:

SUCCESS TRIUMPHANT
or,
The Lover at Clark Street Bridge;

Chap. I. A young gentleman on the south side loved a young lady on the north side, and was engaged to be married to her at ten o'clock.

Chap. II. He had a rival living on the west side, whom the young lady, being naturally very amiable, had also engaged to marry at the same time.

Chap. III. Having, through extreme agitation, cut himself badly in shaving, the south-side lover did not leave home until 9.45, rail-road time. The Clark-street bridge was open. Heavens! what *could* be done. He looked up stream: Wells street bridge was open, too. But—did his eyes deceive him? no—the Fates were still propitious—there stood his rival at the Wells street bridge, having come over from the west side to cross that way.

Fool! muttered South-side between his teeth; why didn't he cross North Branch? I'll beat him yet. But suppose Wells street bridge should shut!! His heart died within him at the thought— great drops of perspiration stood on his livid brow. He looked down stream to the Lake-house ferry; but the rope was down. He beat his clenched hands with despair.

Chap. IV. The plot thickens. Something must be done. He makes a stern resolve. One steam-tug, the Fairy Belle, is coming up stream, another, the Zekel Barnes, is going down. He seizes the auspicious moment; he leaps for his life. He only knows that he leaps for a wife. With one bound he is on the Fairy Belle, with another on the bridge now swinging in the middle of the stream; again he leaps, and scarce touching the Zekel Barnes, a fourth bound lands him on the north side. With a shout of defiance to his despairing rival, he rushes forward, while boat-men and bridge-tenders suspend their labors, and stand transfixed with breathless astonishment at the surpassing feat.

Chapter V. He won his bride. Her father was rich. And now in a six-story house, built of best yellow stone, on a quarter-section lot, in a green old age, he relates to a numerous and still increasing family, the fearful legend of the Clark Street Bridge. —FINIS.

If those bridges were permanent and could be built of stone, Chicago, with her growing wealth, would some day rival Venice in this department of magnificence. But, unless I misjudge the Anglo-saxo-yankee, this necessity will become the mother of some great invention in the matter of the movable bridge. Already tunnels are talked of, and will, doubtless, be built; but Chicago must ever remain "THE CITY OF BRIDGES."

BUILDINGS

With material for building Chicago is well supplied. The ground on which the city stands, yields, at the depth of a few feet, a fair quality of clay. The dirt that a man digs out of his cellar he can bake into bricks to build his house. The lake shore supplies him with sand. The native brick is of a dirty yellow or pale red, and not handsome, nor of the best quality; but at a reasonable price can be obtained the drab-colored Milwaukie brick, which, in beauty and durability, yields to no others. Already, notwithstanding the expense of transportation, they have been introduced into our eastern cities. The block on Broadway, New York, known as "Trinity Building," is of this material.

The Court-house, in Chicago, a very creditable building, of the Doric order, though without columns, and standing in the center of a handsome square, inclosed by a substantial iron paling, on a marble foot, is built of blue lime-stone, brought from Lockport, in the state of New York. But a much more elegant material has since been discovered in great abundance, about twenty miles from the city, on the line of the Illinois Canal. It is a compact lime-stone of a pale yellow shade, somewhat lighter than the Caen stone now so fashionable in New York. The grain is so fine that the fracture, or cut surface, resembles that of chalk in texture. It is durable, is easily wrought, and the color is peculiarly pleasing and grateful to the eye. There is another stone of similar texture, of the color of freshly-fractured slate, or of the mark made on a slate by a pencil; but it is not so beautiful as the kind before mentioned. It soils readily, and had at a short distance the effect of a dirty white. There are also other architectural stones in considerable abundance and variety; but none of great beauty or importance have come under my observation. The Presbyterian Church on Wabash avenue is built of a blue, bituminous lime-stone, the pitchy matter of which has exuded and run down the sides, giving the building the appearance of having a partial coat of tar. The general impression it produces is that of great antiquity; and if this idea could be preserved and harmonized by the early-pointed Gothic, and a good growth of ivy, the effect would be very fine.

Michigan avenue, the favorite street for private dwellings, on the south side, runs directly on the lake shore on a sort of bluff formed by the action of the winds and waves. It is something more than a mile in length, and has an elevation of twelve or fourteen feet above the water. The houses are built only on the west side, leaving the view of the lake entirely unobstructed. There are many fine private residences on this street, and one, belonging to the Roman Catholic bishop of the diocese, might, both in size and style, be fairly ranked as a palace. On the north side, which, toward the lake shore, is rather more quiet and retired, are many fine cottages of the best suburban styles, adorned with conservatories and gardens, and embowered in groves of locust, ash, and oak.

THOROUGHFARES

Both carriage-way and sidewalks are planked—stone being as yet too expensive a material, and too slowly laid for this new and fast metropolis. In the spring of the year, the ground asserts its original character of swamp. The planks actually float, and, as the heavy wagons pass along, ornamental jets of muddy water play on every side.

The sidewalks of Chicago are as remarkable, in their way, as the bridges. With almost every block of buildings there is a change of grade, sometimes of one foot, sometimes of three feet, sometimes of five. These ascents or descents are made by steps, or by short, steep, inclined planes of boards, with or without cleats or cross-pieces, to prevent slipping, according to the fancy of the adjoining proprietor who erects them. The profile of a Chicago sidewalk would resemble the profile of the Erie Canal where the locks are most plenty. It is one continual succession of ups and downs. The reason of this diversity is, that it was found necessary, at an early period in the history of the place, to raise the grade of the streets. It was afterward found necessary to raise the grade still higher, and again still higher—as each building is erected, its foundation and the sidewalk adjoining have been made to correspond to the grade then last established, and so it will not happen until the city is entirely rebuilt, that the proper grade will be uniformly attained. In the meantime, the present state of things will repress undue curiosity in the streets, and keep fire-engines off the sidewalks, which is a great point gained.

DRESS OF CHICAGOANS

In the winter season, the dress of the people, as well as the mercury in the thermometer, indicates a severe climate. Across the prairie and the lake, the wind sweeps with unbroken violence. People drive in from the country with large hoods, made from the cape of the cloak, drawn over their heads. Fur overcoats are much worn; the legs are wrapped in woolen leggins; fur tippets stand up high around the face, and the feet are covered with large shoes made of buffalo hide, with the hair turned in. The fashionable head-gear of the young gentlemen is a cap without a visor, looking like a lady's muff cut in two in the middle, and stuck on the head of her beau. To my eye they are not elegant.

There is an abundance of omnibuses, public carriages, and hacks. The wheeled vehicles seen in the streets, are mostly of eastern style and manufacture; but the sleighs are, to a great extent, domestic. The sleighing, until the last two years, has been slight, and not much provision was made for it. Now everybody sleighs, but it is mostly on sawed board runners with the box of a wagon or buggy placed upon them; and if a coat of blue paint is added to the runners, the establishment is quite complete.

In the principal streets, the motion of teams, carriages, and foot-passengers, is equal to that in the great avenues of New York, Broadway excepted. Water street, parallel with the river, on the south side, is the street for heavy trade. Lake street, next south, is the principal dry goods and retail shopping mart. But business is by no means confined to a narrow locality. Over a space of from one to two miles in each direction, every avenue is alive with the stir and bustle of an active, enterprising population.

At intervals, along the river, rising above surrounding objects, are large, irregular structures, five or six stories in height, surmounted by square turretlike attics, rising twenty or thirty feet more. These are the grain warehouses and elevators for unloading, cleaning, storing, weighing, and reshipping the wheat which comes in by the cars and is to go out in the vessels. The grain is raised from the cars by buckets on an endless belt, like those in an ordinary mill, only containing about a peck each. It is thus carried up into the turrets, being fanned and screened by the way, where it falls into a hopper, is weighed and runs through a trough down into the hold of a vessel lying along-side to receive it.

From the top of these elevators, though by no means a clean and comfortable place to reach, one can get a fine view of—all that he can see. Chicago stands, as everything else does in Illinois, on a prairie, which may be described as *a country having a face but no features*. On the east lies the lake, with its ever-rolling surface of bluish green; on all other sides, the prairie, unbroken in its level, save by the structures of man. A low line of trees in the west, however, some seven miles distant from the city, marks the course of the river Desplaines, one of the main feeders of the Illinois. For sunrises and sunsets this country ought to be unsurpassed.

FORT DEARBORN

In a back yard on one of the narrow streets, near the great dépôt of the Illinois central road, stands a small log building, not more than sixteen feet square, and about the same height, with a projection at the top; the whole structure resembling a good sized Virginia smoke-house. This is the fortification which figures in our history as Fort Dearborn; nor have I, in the least, exaggerated its insignificance. It is what is called a block-house, and the projection at the top has a slit, some six feet long and three inches wide, for musketry, and a large square hole for a small piece of artillery. Near by are the Barracks, two long two-story buildings, built of logs and brick, with projecting eaves and stairs, and galleries on the outside—looking like the farm-house to which the smoke-house belonged. I would like to know how many thousand dollars were appropriated by Congress to build that fort. The United States still own the fort and ground, and have erected near by a commodious and elegant marine hospital, built of Milwaukie brick. I regret to hear that the fort and barracks are to be torn away during the coming summer; they ought to have been preserved, with sufficient ground to form a public park.

On the opposite side of the street from the fort, in another yard and still further from the lake, surrounded by buildings higher than itself, stands a substantial stone light-house. It once did duty nearer the lake shore; but, having long been a faithful public servant, it has retired in a green old age to spend the remainder of its years in an unostentatious privacy; not that it has itself moved, but, like those venerable men in knee-breeches, it has stood still while the lake shore and the rest of the world have pushed far out beyond it, and its duty is now performed by a young upstart of a light-house, standing on the pier at the mouth of the river.

"Hic in obscuritate lucet,
Quae in auctoritate stetit."

THE WATER SUPPLY

Water is supplied to the city, pumped up from the lake into a reservoir, and distributed by pipes. A small portion of the lake is fenced off by a pier of piles and earth; a pipe is laid from the pond thus formed to a tank or well a few rods distant; over the tank is placed the engine-house and pumps, and the thing is done. No further filtration is deemed necessary; the water is abundant and good. The ice obtained here, I have never seen equaled. It would do Dr. Kane good to see it. Huge blocks of it, eight feet high and two feet square, have been standing about on the sidewalks this winter as samples, and through the thickest of these I have read with ease the smallest type of the New York daily papers.

HOTELS AND HOTEL FOOD

On this topic, so interesting to the traveler, I ought to be full and satisfactory; but I can only say that at the Briggs House, where I spent some weeks, I did not enter my name with any title, either civil, military, or medical, I did not report myself as a member of the press, a public lecturer, or an actor, nor did I intimate that I expected to publish an article on Chicago, nevertheless, I was civilly treated, provided with a comfortable room, and plenty to eat, and paid my bill of $2.50 per day at the end of the time, satisfied that the same comfort was not to be had for less money, anywhere in Chicago. Higher praise for a hotel, I think, cannot well be imagined. To hotel-keepers in Chicago there is no rest, and but a limited supply to lodgers. All night long, some of the one hundred trains, that daily arrive and depart, is either arriving or departing. It is either "3 o'clock, sir," or "4 o'clock, sir" or "5 o'clock, sir" as you are constantly informed during the night, by somebody pounding at your neighbor's door or your own. But breakfast lasts until 10 o'clock, and when everybody has got up, then there are a few quiet hours during which the *rest* can sleep, and they are generally well improved.

When you travel, says Bayard Taylor, dress and eat as far as possible in accordance with the tastes and habits of the people you are among. At the Briggs House, therefore, I scanned the bill of fare with great attention, to detect any new and curious dishes, and finally brought off a copy in my pocket, as a subject for future reflection. I make a note of the characteristic dishes only—

Fish.
Baked White Fish. Boiled Trout.
Baked Pickerel.
Roast.
Prairie Chicken. Wild Goose. Venison.
Confectionery.
Glass E. Jenny Lind.

This latter is probably to be ranked as novelty in orthography rather than in confectionery, as I suspect the same thing exists elsewhere, as Glace Jenny Lind. The first mode of spelling is more phonographic, Websterian, and independent.

The white fish and trout of the upper lakes, I heard so highly commended, that I had made up my palate for a delicacy, which proved to be figuratively, as well as literally, a scaly one. They are, both of them, a rank, coarse fish, entirely inferior to our cod, bass, fresh mackerel, or blue fish, and not to be spoken of in connection with Connecticut river shad. I have tried them at divers places, and cooked in various ways, still my experience is the same. Perhaps the white fish is equal in flavor to the halibut, certainly not superior.

A gentleman, who was not fond of fish, told me that he thought I might get better at Mackinaw; but as these came fresh from Green Bay, I saw no reason to think so. The pickerel I preferred to the trout and white fish. I have, on one occasion only, eaten the fish called muskalonge, boiled; this was at Cleveland, and I then considered it very fine; but whether it was owing to the quality of the fish or my appetite, I cannot now say.

Prairie chickens and venison are so common in the eastern markets, that they hardly deserve notice. The prairie chicken is about the size of the domestic bantams, and in color and flavor resembles the pigeon. The wild goose I forgot to taste. The advertisement for North's Circus, and Mr. Neafie's appearance in Jack Cade, are at the bottom of the bill.

Chicago already requires a directory of two hundred and fifty pages, solid matter, without the advertisements; and from this work I learn that there are *nine* omnibus routes, *thirteen* railroad lines, converging here, *sixteen* newspapers, of which *six* are published daily, *sixty* clergymen, and *two hundred and twenty* lawyers.

I occasionally spent an hour in some of the courts; but as the bar is composed mainly of men not very long from the East, there is little to strike an eastern man as peculiar. There is rather more freedom in illustration, and more frequent use of phrases which, of themselves, mean little or nothing, but as delivered with a tone and manner implying great import. There is also a much more frequent reference to general principles, and to organic laws, than in those states where precedents are more abundant. This feature, when able counsel are employed, frequently gives to the argument a breadth and scope which render the proceedings more attractive to a casual spectator than the dry citation of authorities, usually heard in our eastern courts. I was quite interested, on one occasion, by hearing a lawyer, who was himself an old settler residing in one of the country towns, and was trying to make good his client's pre-emption title, against a more recent claimant, under a tax sale, or some other hocus-pocus procedure, describe with no little eloquence how his client and his neighbors had fought and suffered in defense of that land in the days of the Black Hawk War. But the law was on the other side; the jury were proof against prejudice, though the point was ingeniously presented, and the fighter of Indians lost his case. Perhaps poetical justice to the Indians was thus preserved, and perhaps not. I have not a very high respect for Indians, and prefer *plain white* to any other color, both for men and women.

The judges, jury, and lawyers patronize the apple-boys rather more freely than would be considered proper in some places; and one occasion, when a military company passed in the street, lawyers, sheriff, jury, and spectators, in fact, everybody, except the judge, made a general stampede to the windows to see them go by. I went with the rest.

MONEY

The federal currency is assuming the ascendant throughout the West, and dimes and half dimes are driving sixpences and shillings to the wall. As a natural consequence, one pays in most cases ten cents for what used to cost six. A tribute to patriotism. I noticed at the bar, however, that drinks are but a *dime*. I suppose, in this case, the other party can afford to pay the tribute.

Sunday in Chicago, though not observed as it is in New England, is, I think, more respected than in any town of 20,000 inhabitants, or upwards, south of Philadelphia. Some few stores are seen open, but not of a prominent class. The movement of the people is generally churchward, and the churches are well filled. The streets are quiet; and, though I have no doubt that, in a place of such varying population, where people of all grades of character are congregated, without the restraints of home to the well-disposed, and of an efficient police to the vicious, crime and immorality exist to an alarming extent; yet the Puritan element so far predominates in the population of the place, that wickedness is neither popular nor respectable.

Speculation, too great eagerness to get rich on the part of men who have nothing to lose, and a lack of those healthful restraints which exist in an older community, have, undoubtedly, combined to weaken and lower the moral sense of the people, in regard to business transactions. There is a leniency exhibited towards sharp bargains, over-reaching, undue coloring, and actual misrepresentation (doubtless, more apparent to a stranger than to a resident, and for that reason just so much the more dangerous), which, if allowed to go unchecked, will, by degrees, destroy that vital morality which is indispensable to the prosperity of a commercial state. This is not a peculiar fault of Chicago, but of the whole West; and as men grow more independent in their resources, and temptations for speculation decrease, the evil may abate; but it deserves notice, and demands vigilance.

In one of the most conspicuous corners in Chicago is a large six-story building, which deserves a passing notice. It was built (so I was told) by a clerk in the city, with funds purloined from his employer. When detection became unavoidable, he left town, and sent back an agent to negotiate. The matter was finally arranged by the employer taking the building, and paying the thief *ten thousand dollars;* and it was remarked, so great had been the rise in the value of the property, that even then the employer had *altogether the best of the bargain.* I ought to add, that I do not think that this was regarded as a legitimate business transaction.

Such was Chicago, as I saw it, looking at the outside of things, in the fall and winter of 1855–6. What it will be next year at this time—ten years hence—fifty years hence—those who live shall see. If any one wishes to *guess*, an opportunity is now offered.

EDWARD L. PECKHAM[1]

ON THURSDAY, June 4, 1857, in possession of a through ticket to Iowa City, Iowa, costing $30.55, Edward L. Peckham, botanist, left Providence, Rhode Island, for the West. The story of this experience is set down in a journal, replete with an easterner's reflections on western life and culture. His trip brought him to the Middle West by way of Chicago, whence he went to Iowa City, Iowa, then the "westernmost point accessible by railroad." Here he took the stage to Des Moines. From this latter point he proceeded by stage to Council Bluffs, through alternate seas of mud and beauty. He found travel impossible except by foot or horseback, and, after a short stay, he began his return home. As was sometimes the case with travelers from the East, Peckham was not favorably impressed with this new and raw section of the country. Hot, tiresome railroads, uncomfortable stages, poor hotel accommodations, constant reminders of a western optimism, and a steady diet of "fried veal, fried ham, fried and mashed potatoes, eggs, bread, poor coffee, and suspicious looking dishes of preserves" aroused his irritability. To him, in contrast, Rhode Island appeared an Elysium, to which he gladly returned.

-»» «««-

CHICAGO—A MEAN SPOT

Saturday, June 6, 1857. At 8 a.m., in Chicago, at Briggs', and while waiting in the office among piles of trunks and valises, for a room—who should walk in but Tower and Vaughan,[2] all three were pleasantly surprised, but soon parted to meet again bye and bye. They to walk and myself to my room to wash, shave, etc., for I needed both. After doing which, I sallied forth. Chicago, the world renowned Chicago, is as mean a spot as I ever was in, yet. It is situated on the west side of the southern extremity of Lake Michigan, and built a few feet above the lake, on an extensive and level marsh. The streets are laid out in

[1] E. L. Peckham, "My Journey Out West," *Journal of American History*, XVII (3d quarter, No. 3, 1923), 227–30. Reprinted by permission of the *Journal of American History*, published by National Historical Society, New York.

[2] John C. Vaughan, editor of the Chicago *Tribune*. He had been associated with Joseph Medill on the Cleveland *Leader*, and joined Medill on the *Tribune* in 1855. Vaughan withdrew from the paper in March, 1857. The editor was unable to find any information concerning Mr. Tower.

squares and are in miserable condition of soft clay mud, which in many places, shakes and trembles as it is passed over. The side walks are very uneven, up hill and down, the buildings put up before the streets were graded and filled in, being the lowest from 3 to 8 feet below the foundation of houses raised upon the new grade, the ascent and descent being made by very steep steps to save room. How persons can navigate this dirty city in a dark night without a broken arm or neck is a mystery to me. Chicago river runs through the center of the city, the south side occupied by the wealthy and enterprising, the north by Germans and Irish and other foreigners. Miserable hovels are mixed up with the most beautiful and costly stores and edifices, such as I never saw in any other place. Truly, there is but one Chicago. Michigan avenue is the only street where one can walk in safety, and in [is] the avenue of the city. It is wide and runs parallel with the shore of the lake. It is adorned by many beautiful private residences, and commands a grand view of the ocean-like waters, with its numerous steam and sail vessels moving hither and thither. Some near enough to hear the cry of the sailors, others hardly discernable on the distant verge. I strolled down to the shore (which is composed of a fine glass house land) and with my leather drinking cup, imbibed freely from the huge Michigan bowl, and also thoroughly washed my linen gloves. Land on this street is selling at $5.00 per square foot, an unheard of price, but then, only rich people can live here. Indeed it is the only street fit to live in.

The only objection to this place, by some, is the Michigan Railroad which is built on spiles, immediately in front, about 200 or 300 feet from the shore and on a line with it. Nothing in Chicago costs less than 10 cents, called a dime, 5's and 3's used only to make change, and no cents to be seen. Soda, ale and even papers of tobacco all cost a dime. Money letting here from 20 to 50 per cent on Real Estate security. Some fear a general crash, others scout the idea as impossible. Some predict to it the fate of Buffalo. Others say there is no resemblance between the two, but all go ahead and speculate.

Sunday, June 7, 1857. A very warm sultry day, with a warm

wind blowing from the west, which raised clouds of dust. Keeping comfortable was impossible. How I missed the southwest chamber of my mother's house! How I longed after the shady trees and rocks of New England! I walked to Michigan avenue, but the wind was off shore, and a bright sun pouring down its hot rays. I returned to the hotel. Never before in my whole life was I so situated, but that my legs could find some cool place of retreat, if not in town, why then out of town, and as soon as my room was put in order, I went to it, and taking off all superfluous clothing, amused myself in reading my newspaper. I should have avoided dinner, but a craving appetite forced me to the table, where I was seated between two men, who ate with their elbows so extended that they resembled birds on the wing, and I expected every moment to see them start up and alight on the other side. It was not without some danger that I managed to get the food to my mouth, and in doing so, had several narrow escapes from their huge beams which were playing about my head and which I dodged as well as I could. After dinner I sought my room again, where, about 4, I was joined by Tower and Vaughn. They had been invited to church somewhere, and were cursing the heat and Chicago and almost everything else. About 6, at Dan's suggestion, we took a walk on the north side of the river, which is crossed by large swinging bridges after this fashion. In the center of the river and parallel with it, is built a narrow strip of earth and stone as long as the river is wide. The bridge is then built and by machinery is made to swing around on its center bearing all the while upon the artificial pier, or whatever they may call it, and finally covering it until the vessels pass through, when the bridge is swung or twisted back.

The north side of Chicago river is inhabited mostly by Germans and contrasts very unfavorably with the south side. Although it was Sunday, the shops were all open, and everywhere seen groups of Germans, smoking, jabbering and drinking Lauger beer to their hearts' content. Here also, were numerous children of all ages and sexes, gathered about the doors and in the streets, who are never seen on the south side. We walked leisurely along through miserable Irish shanties till we reached the lake, there, at the mouth of the river, is built a pier or break-water some one-fourth of a mile long, extending into the lake, on the end of which is a lighthouse. Vaughn wanted to go out to it, but as the clouds to the southwest looked rather threatening, we went only sufficiently far to receive the breeze, which was a great relief. Crowds of men and boys, chiefly Irish, lined the pier, all engaged in fishing or looking on. The north side of the pier the water was smooth and pleasant, but the south being exposed to the southwest wind, which was very fresh, the water was very turbulent and wishy washy, with no regularity at all to the seas. A schooner was coming up at a rapid and beautiful rate, rounded to, opposite us, and mistayed. The waves washed over her, and she was forced to "put to sea" again. The scene was very excit-ing, and the wind so strong that with difficulty I kept my hat on. At length we left and took to our dusty and heated quarters, paid our bills, mine being $4.50 for four meals and one night's rest, had our trunks brought down, ready to leave. The weather began to cool very fast as the sun went down, and I was very comfortable when seated on the balcony in front. I was intro-duced to Mr. Walker,[3] the heaviest dealer in grain in Illinois. He is very wealthy, owns an estate on the avenue, and is president of some prominent railroad. I was told also of a Mr. Peek,[4]

[3] Charles Walker (February 2, 1802—June 28, 1869) was born in Plainfield, New York, the son of William W. and Lucretia Walker. He attended and taught school at Unadilla Forks, and later engaged in business at the same place. In 1824 he moved to Burlington Flats and gradually added a grist mill, potash factory, and tannery to his business. Soon he had established branches in various places over the state of New York and began to engage in the grain business. The damage at sea in 1828 of a cargo of dairy products which he was shipping to the South swept away his savings, but he rebuilt his business and in 1834 he sent his brother Almond to Chicago with a large sup-ply of leather goods. He came to Chicago in the spring of 1835 and was so impressed with the future possibilities of the city that he invested in some real estate. By 1845 his business had so increased that he removed to Chicago permanently. He began extensive dealings in grain, and by 1851 through his connections with associated houses in Peoria and Buffalo he became one of the largest grain-dealers in the United States. About 1851, after a severe attack of cholera, he was forced to withdraw from the active management of his business; and his eldest son, C. H. Walker, became manager. In 1847 he was elected one of the directors of the Galena and Chicago Union Railroad, and in 1856 be-came president of the Chicago, Iowa and Nebraska Railroad, which was designed to be a continuation of the Galena and Chicago. He served as vice-president of the Chicago Board of Trade in 1848 and as president in 1850 and 1851.

[4] This was probably Philip F. W. Peck. He was born in Providence, Rhode Island, in 1809. He came to Chicago in 1831 and established the Peck Company, a merchandising firm. He later dealt in real estate and grain and practiced law. He died in 1871.

formerly of Providence who is worth $3,000,000, brother of Benj. Church's wife.

At 9 p.m. we walked down to the depot, and after some delay, by the absence of the check master, got our duds (or I did mine) checked to Iowa City. They have a rule here that no baggage will be checked unless a ticket is shown by the owner. As I passed out, a stranger, who had no ticket and who was very anxious to get checks, asked me to lend him the ticket I had just shown. On the spur of the moment I did so, but instantly regretted it, for he might run off with it. Fool, that I am, muttered I; am I caught at last! but I kept good watch upon him, and he soon returned me my ticket, thanked me heartily, and hurried off to join some ladies who were awaiting him. Well, thought I, I have done a good deed, but a dangerous one, and will not soon repeat it. We left at 10. p.m. in the dark.

WILLIAM HOWARD RUSSELL[1]

W ILLIAM HOWARD RUSSELL was born near Dublin in 1821 and died in 1907. His education was acquired at Trinity College and Cambridge. At first he chose a legal career, but soon turned his talents to the press.

As correspondent for the London *Times* Russell was sent into many countries, and he reported many important events such as the Danish-Prussian War, the Crimean War, and the Sepoy Mutiny in India. In 1860 he became publisher and editor of the *Army and Navy Gazette*, but returned to the services of the *Times* in order to report the War between the States in America, where, he declared, it had been his fate to see Americans "under their most unfavorable aspect; with all their national feelings, as well as the vices of our common humanity, exaggerated and developed by the terrible agonies of a civil war, and the throes of political revolution."[2]

Following his sojourn in America, he was sent to describe the Franco-Prussian War. During the 1870's he visited India with the Prince of Wales and was with Lord Wolseley in the Zulu War. Later he was with the latter in Egypt.

In 1881 Russell again visited the United States and also traveled through Canada. *Hesperothen* is the result of this visit.

The extract which follows is taken from *My Diary North and South*, written from his diaries and notebooks which he declared he "assiduously kept" while in the United States. Although the account here given is not in complete conformance with the real situation, it proves interesting in the light of a Britisher's impressions of Chicago during the war.

⇶⇷

THE SETTING OF CHICAGO

The scene now began to change gradually as we approached Chicago, the prairie subsided into swampy land, and thick belts of trees fringed the horizon; on our right glimpses of the sea could be caught through openings in the wood—the inland sea on which stands the Queen of the Lakes. Michigan looks broad and blue as the Mediterranean. Large farmhouses stud the country, and houses which must be the retreat of merchants and citizens of means; and when the train, leaving the land alto-

[1] William Howard Russell, *My Diary North and South* (Boston: T. O. H. P. Burnham, 1863), pp. 352–53, 356–59.

[2] *Ibid.*, Introductory, p. x.

gether, dashes out on a pier and causeway built along the borders of the lake, we see lines of noble houses, a fine boulevard, a forest of masts, huge isolated piles of masonry, the famed grain elevators by which so many have been hoisted to fortune, churches and public edifices, and the apparatus of a great city; and just at nine o'clock the train gives its last steam shout and comes to a standstill in the spacious station of the Central Illinois Company, and in half-an-hour more I am in comfortable quarters at the Richmond House, where I find letters waiting for me, by which it appears that the necessity for my being in Washington in all haste, no longer exists. The wary General who commands the army is aware that the advance to Richmond, for which so many journals are clamoring, would be attended with serious risk at present, and the politicians must be content to wait a little longer. . . . .

CHICAGO IN THE CIVIL WAR

I have already seen so many statements respecting my sayings, my doings, and my opinions, in the American papers, that I have resolved to follow a general rule, with few exceptions indeed, which prescribes as the best course to pursue, not so much an indifference to these remarks as a fixed purpose to abstain from the hopeless task of correcting them. The "Quicklys" of the press are incorrigible. Commerce may well be proud of Chicago. I am not going to reiterate what every Crispinus from the old country has said again and again concerning this wonderful place—not one word of statistics, of corn elevators, of shipping, or of the piles of buildings raised from the foundation by ingenious applications of screws. Nor am I going to enlarge on the splendid future of that which has so much present prosperity, or on the benefits to mankind opened up by the Illinois Central Railway. It is enough to say that by the borders of this lake there has sprung up in thirty years a wonderful city of fine streets, luxurious hotels, handsome shops, magnificent stores, great warehouses, extensive quays, capacious docks; and that as long as corn holds its own, and the mouths of Europe are open, and her hands full, Chicago will acquire greater importance, size, and wealth with every year. The only drawback, perhaps, to the comfort of the money-making inhabitants, and of the stranger within the gates, is to be found in the clouds of dust and in the unpaved streets and thoroughfares, which give anguish to horse and man.

I spent three days here writing my letters and repairing the wear and tear of my Southern expedition; and although it was hot enough, the breeze from the lake carried health and vigor to the frame, enervated by the sun of Louisiana and Mississippi. No need now to wipe the large drops of moisture from the languid brow lest they blind the eyes, nor to sit in a state of semi-clothing, worn out and exhausted, and tracing with moist hand imperfect characters on the paper.

I could not satisfy myself whether there was, as I have been told, a peculiar state of feeling in Chicago, which induced many people to support the Government of Mr. Lincoln because they believed it necessary for their own interest to obtain decided advantages over the South in the field, whilst they were opposed *totis viribus* to the genius of emancipation and to the views of the Black Republicans. But the genius and eloquence of the Little Giant have left their impress on the facile mould of democratic thought; and he who argued with such acuteness and ability last March in Washington, in his own study, against the possibility, or at least the constitutional legality, of using the national forces, and the militia and volunteers of the Northern States, to subjugate the Southern people, carried away by the great bore which rushed through the placid North when Sumter fell, or perceiving his inability to resist its force, sprung to the crest of the wave, and carried to excess the violence of the Union reaction.

Whilst I was in the South I had seen his name in Northern papers with sensation headings and descriptions of his magnificent crusade for the Union in the West. I had heard his name reviled by those who had once been his warm political allies, and his untimely death did not seem to satisfy their hatred. His old foes in the North admired and applauded the sudden apostasy of their eloquent opponent, and were loud in lamentations over his loss. Imagine, then, how I felt when visiting his grave at Chicago, seeing his bust in many houses, or his portrait in all the shop-windows, I was told that the enormously wealthy community of which he was the idol were permitting his widow to live in a state not far removed from penury.

"Senator Douglas, sir," observed one of his friends to me, "died of bad whiskey. He killed himself with it while he was stumping for the Union all over the country." "Well," I said, "I suppose, sir, the abstraction called the Union, for which by your own account he killed himself, will give a pension to his widow." Virtue is its own reward, and so is patriotism, unless it takes the form of contracts. . . . .

If a native of the British Isles, of the natural ignorance of his own imperfections which should characterize him, desires to be subjected to a series of moral shower-baths, douches, and shampooing with a rough glove, let him come to the United States. In Chicago he will be told that the English people are fed by the beneficence of the United States, and that all the trade and commerce of England are simply directed to the one end of obtaining gold enough to pay the Western States for the breadstuffs exported for our population. We know what the South think of our dependence on cotton. The people of the East think they are striking a great blow at their enemy by the Morrill tariff and I was told by a patriot in North Carolina, "Why creation! if you let the Yankees shut up our ports, the whole of your darned ships will go to rot. Where will you get your naval stores from? Why, I guess in a year you could not scrape up enough of tarpentine [sic] in the whole of your country for Queen Victoria to paint her nursery-door with."

Nearly one half of the various companies enrolled in this district are Germans, or are the descendants of German parents, and speak only the language of the old country; two-thirds of the remainder are Irish, or of immediate Irish descent; but it is said that a grand reserve of Americans [sic] born lies behind this avant garde, who will come into the battle should there ever be need for their services.

Indeed so long as the Northern people furnish the means of

paying and equipping armies perfectly competent to do their work, and equal in numbers to any demands made for men, they may rest satisfied with the accomplishment of that duty, and with contributing from their ranks the great majority of the superior and even of the subaltern officers; but with the South it is far different. Their institutions have repelled immigration; the black slave has barred the door to the white free settler. Only on the seaboard and in the large cities are German and Irish to be found, and they to a man have come forward to fight for the South; but the proportion they bear to the native-born Americans who have rushed to arms in defence of their menaced borders, is of course far less than it is as yet to the number of Americans in the Northern States who have volunteered to fight for the Union.

I was invited before I left to visit the camp of a Colonel Turchin, who was described to me as a Russian officer of great ability and experience in European warfare, in command of a regiment consisting of Poles, Hungarians, and Germans, who were about to start for the seat of war; but I was only able to walk through his tents, where I was astonished at the amalgam of nations that constituted his battalion; though, on inspection, I am bound to say there proved to be an American element in the ranks which did not appear to have coalesced with the bulk of the rude, and, I fear, predatory Cossacks of the Union. Many young men of good position have gone to the wars, although there was no complaint, as in Southern cities, that merchants' offices have been deserted, and great establishments left destitute of clerks and working hands. In warlike operations, however, Chicago, with its communication open to the sea, its access to the head waters of the Mississippi, its intercourse with the marts of commerce and of manufacture, may be considered to possess greater belligerent power and strength than the great city of New Orleans; and there is much greater probability of Chicago sending its contingent to attack the Crescent City than there is of the latter being able to despatch a soldier within five hundred miles of its streets.

-»»-«««-

CHRISTIAN H. JEVNE[1]

CHRISTIAN H. JEVNE (September 13, 1839—March 17, 1898) was a native of Norway who came to the United States in the year 1864. Landing in New York, he proceeded directly to Chicago, where his uncle, Otto Jevne, obtained for him a position with the firm of Knowles, Cloyes and Company, coffee and spice merchants. Having been trained in the tenets of trade in his youthful days after finishing public school in his native land, Christian Jevne showed an aptitude for commercial enterprise. In 1865 he formed a partnership with Henry Parker, a brother-in-law of Knowles, his former employer, embarking into the wholesale and retail trade in groceries, teas, coffees, wines, and fruits. The following year his two brothers, Hans and Carl, arrived in America; and with them he bought out his partner, Henry Parker, and continued the business. Although the fire of 1871 laid his business in ruins, he was able to rebuild; and soon his enterprise became one of the most flourishing in Chicago. To him is accorded the distinction of having the first electric light in the city installed in his store in 1880 and operating the coffee roaster and mill by electricity. In 1870 Jevne married Clara Kluge.

The following letter is reproduced to show the reaction of this Norwegian immigrant to the city of Chicago into which he came with little money, but where he became a prosperous wholesale and retail merchant.

-»»-«««-

A NORWEGIAN IMMIGRANT IN CHICAGO IN THE 1860's

Chicago, December 10th, 1864

Dear Parents!

As I had already begun to fear, that my letter had not come through,[2] I was just in the act of writing to you, when Uncle[3] on the 5. Nov. brought me a letter from O. Kolberg which destroyed my doubt, it had worried me a great deal that you perhaps

---

[1] Christian H. Jevne, "An Immigrant in Chicago, 1864," Norwegian-American Historical Association, *Studies and Records* (Northfield, Minnesota, 1928), III, 67–72. Translated by Brynjolf J. Hovde. Reprinted by permission of the Norwegian-American Historical Association.

[2] "The translator has endeavored to preserve, as far as possible, all the peculiarities of composition and punctuation that appear in the original; Mr. Jevne appears to have been a trifle weak in punctuation. But the letter is an interesting human document, simple, straightforward, and unpretending." (Note by Brynjolf J. Hovde.)

[3] Otto Jevne, senior member of the firm of Jevne and Almini, fresco-painters and dealers in artists' and painters' materials.

remained uncertain whether I had reached my destination or not, and I knew that that would have caused you great uneasiness, which was unnecessary, as I not only am safely arrived, but also have been well the whole while, and am getting along in every way as well as one could wish, considering that I am in a strange land, and among strange people, and a strange language, for I can not get these cussed[4] Yankees to speak Norwegian, I therefore have to jabber English all day long, it is far from being of the best, but that makes no difference, because they are used to broken English. My word![5] How the English language is mutilated here, Frenchmen and Italians especially deal with it in a barbarous manner.

Never a day passes in which I do not send a thought over to dear Norway, in recollection of you my precious parents, and of relatives and friends as well. Oh, what a joyous day it will be for me when I once again set foot on the cliffs of Norway. (They are quite as dependable as America's stoneless, sandy soil.) and that the great happiness, might be vouchsafed me, to see you once again. I am coming home some time, provided God will let me live and keep my health. You may be sure I had a good many moments of hesitation before I could make up my mind to undertake so long and uncertain a journey, and to leave the Wignes [sic] which has become so dear to me it was absolutely one of the hardest days I have experienced, when I left Wignes and when I left you, my dear parents, weeping on the dock, not knowing whether I should be able to see you again or not, but all things pass, the farther I got along on the way the better it became, because then I had to think about finding my way through to my destination, although I wished in a small way that I could have turned back, but when one is aboard the train one must travel with it. Perhaps it was as wise as it was bad for me that I got the impulse to come here, for I must admit, in or-

[4] "*Disse hersens Yankeir*. The word *hersens* is untranslatable; it is slang in Norwegian, and perhaps the nearest approximation to it in English slang is 'cussed,' or 'darned,' or 'blamed'; it is too mild for 'damned.' " (Note by Brynjolf J. Hovde.)

[5] "The Norwegian has *Hutetu*, an untranslatable expletive." (Note by Brynjolf J. Hovde.)

der not to be unfair to this country, that there are better and more numerous chances[6] for young men here than in Norway, when they once become familiar with conditions here, but when one arrives and gets off at the railway station, comes out upon the street, and does not know which way to turn, and besides cannot speak with people, then one is likely to wish he were back home, and that he never had seen America, but it would not go any better with an American if he should come to Norway under the same circumstances. Very likely there are many who set out in the belief that they will find here both wealth and ideal conditions,[7] but alas, how bitterly are they disappointed in their expectations, here one must work, for here nothing may be had for nothing.

There are many here, perhaps the greater number, who waste what they earn, by frequenting the dance halls and the saloons, there are any number of such delights.

I am still with the same man,[8] and we get along pretty well, at first it was somewhat difficult, to be sure, as I had to stand there like a Hottentot able to do only what they pointed to, but now I can dispatch every customer that enters just as efficiently as a Yankee, and it is all about the same sort of thing as standing behind the counter at Wignes, except that I am occupied all the time, and must be in the store from 7 o'clock to 6:30 in the evening. I attend school in the evenings from 7 to 9, namely at a commercial institute, in order to learn English, bookkeeping, banking, and brokerage, this course costs 65 dollars, in greenbacks, (because here one gets $2\frac{1}{2}$ dollars in paper for 1 dollar in gold). On Sundays I go up to my uncle's place to pass the time in his company and to chatter English with my small cousins, for they cannot speak Norwegian, although, they understand it when it is spoken to them, but always answer in English. Uncle's family consists of his wife three boys and one girl, his wife's

[6] "The writer uses the Norwegianized form of the English word 'chances,' thus, *chancer*." (Note by Brynjolf J. Hovde.)

[7] "The original reads *baade Guld og grønne Skove*, literally 'both gold and green forests,' an idiom which connotes riches and pleasures." (Note by Brynjolf J. Hovde.)

[8] The name of this firm was Knowles, Cloyes & Company.

mother is also here now, whereas she usually stays with her son out in the country The daughter of Almini is also staying with Uncle, because Almini's wife is dead leaving only this one child. Uncle and Almini do a good business, and they have a very good reputation here in Chicago, and in many of the larger cities hereabouts. The Yankees tell me that Uncle is one of the foremost fresco-painters here. I have promised many, who desired to journey hither, that I would write to them about this country, but I shrink from fulfilling these promises, partly because I do not know of anything to say about the land or the agriculture, for I have not been outside the city limits since I came here, and partly because I certainly do not want to advise anyone to leave, if they want to leave then let them start off at once, that is what I did. I wish Hans would exert himself to learn English, for I might perhaps desire to have him here after a while; I could wish that you were all here, but that is out of the question, because it is much too long and difficult a journey for old people.

It might perhaps be interesting to you to hear a little something about this city, which is not more than thirty years old and now numbers about 200,000 inhabitants. Chicago is situated as you know on the shores of Lake Michigan, from which a stream or river leads into the city and branches off in two directions, on this river there pass the whole day long, hundreds of steam and sail ships, and at points where the streets cross the river there have been constructed swinging bridges, which are swung about by two men when the ships pass. The streets are very wide and long. Some over one Norwegian mile,[9] the sidewalks of which are made of slabs of white stone in the best part of the city elsewhere of planks. In most of the streets there have been laid rails, on which very handsome cars are operated, quite similar to railway coaches, which are drawn by two horses, it costs five cents to travel upon them either for a short or a long distance. There are about seventy churches here, of which three Norwegian two Swedish, and a great number German, for about half of the population here are Germans, as far as that goes there

[9] "A Norwegian mile is equivalent to about seven English miles." (Note by Brynjolf J. Hovde.)

are all nationalities here, and therefore also all religions, such as Jesuits, Mormons, Methodists and also a great multitude of Catholics, who make an awful noise. I have been in both Norwegian Swedish and English churches, in the latter they sing most beautifully. The churches are prettily painted, and equipped with stoves, so that one does not have to freeze there The houses are mostly of stone, (white), 4 to 7 stories high. There is a hotel in the same street as I live, which is 7 stories, has 220 windows facing the street, and about 400 rooms Uncle did the decorating of the best rooms in this hotel.

About the war it can hardly be of any use to speak, inasmuch as you are quite as well informed about it as I, suffice to say, they are fighting as usual, and the Union army has now been quite successful of late. People have been greatly wrought up now for a while over the presidential election, for here all people are politicians (mostly political boilersmiths).[10] Some Democratic, who wanted McClellan for President, others Republicans who voted for Lincoln, who furthermore was reëlected. You may greet Bookbinder Magnussen[11] and tell him that I have met his brother-in-law, and delivered the pictures, which they were very happy to receive They asked me to send their greetings when I wrote home. I should also have written to my sisters Anne and Agnethe, but I suppose you can send them this, and I would further ask you to give my regards to Madam Hoff, and to Holmens, also to my good friend Holdtfodt, and tell him further that he must not go to America, he would only suffer hardship in his old age.

I shall now close my letter,[12] with the request that you will greet all acquaintances and friends from me, and if opportunity affords also those up north in Wignes. If anyone whom you

[10] "The original reads *Politiske Kandestøbere*. Ludvig Holberg satirized the petty politician in a play called *Den politiske Kandestøber;* Mr. Jevne here succumbs to the temptation to make a clever allusion." (Note by Brynjolf J. Hovde.)

[11] "In Norway the word denoting a person's occupation is used in connection with his name, whether it be an exalted or a very humble occupation, as a title both of honor and of identification." (Note by Brynjolf J. Hovde.)

[12] "The original has the quaint archaic *Jeg vil nu slutte min Skrivelse*, 'I will now conclude my writing.' " (Note by Brynjolf J. Hovde.)

know sets forth to come over here then by all means[13] ask them to look me up, if they come to Chicago, something which is usual. They can inquire for Jevne and Almini No. 101 Washington Street. Last summer when I arrived it was so warm here that I did not know what to do with myself, and now it is just as cold as in Norway, if not colder. I regret that I did not manage to bring with me one of Tante Kolberg's feather comforters, for here they use nothing more than blankets on the beds. Now it is not long till Christmas, so my letter will reach you too late to wish you a Merry Christmas, for which reason I shall have to be content merely to wish you a Happy New Year, and I hope God will permit you to experience many joyful and happy days still. I wish I might be in Norway during the Christmas holidays. Space permits no more, therefore I will close with a heartfelt greeting from your forever devoted son.

Christian H. Jevne. (So long.)

Some time I am going to send a newspaper home, it costs no more than 4 cents. If you see that it comes through all right, then I wish you would send me a copy of *Morgenbladet*,[14] if it is not too expensive. It must be sent in a newspaper wrapper. You can write your name on that.

Christian.

One thing I had almost forgotten, namely, to greet you from Uncle and family.

My address is Christian H. Jevne,

Chicago
P. O. Box 1175.

Kindly send the enclosed little message to M. O. Glemmestad Vignes.[15]

---

[13] "The text has *saa kjaere bed dem opsøge mig*; the word *kjaere*, 'my dear,' is used here in a sense that renders it impossible of literal translation; it indicates deep desire." (Note by Brynjolf J. Hovde.)

[14] "The newspaper *Morgenbladet*, then as now the most important in Norway, published at Oslo." (Note by Brynjolf J. Hovde.)

[15] "According to Mr. Carl Jevne's statement, the writer here means M. O. Glemmestad in Vigness. Everywhere else in the letter the name of the town of Vigness is spelled with a W." (Note by Brynjolf J. Hovde.)

F. BARHAM ZINCKE[1]

F. BARHAM ZINCKE, clergyman of the Church of England, was born in 1817 and died in 1893. He obtained his professional training at Wadham College, Oxford, graduating in 1839. The next year he was ordained to the curacy of Andover, Hampshire, and remained there for one year. From 1841 to 1847 he served as curate of Wherstead and thereafter as vicar. In addition to this post, he was appointed chaplain-in-ordinary to the queen.

During all of his life Reverend Zincke had an interest in all humanity, particularly its education and religion. He wrote several books on what now could be called "mass education." Throughout all his travels he observed the customs, social and economic conditions of mankind. A list of his publications include *Some Thoughts about the School of the Future; On the Duty and the Discipline of Extemporary Preaching; Egypt of the Pharaohs and the Kedive; A Month in Switzerland; Swiss Allmends; Walk in the Grisons; and The Plough and the Dollar.*

During the winter of 1867–68 Zincke toured the United States, spending a good deal of his time in the southern and southwestern sections of the country. In his visit to Chicago, the schools and churches as examples of education and religion in general in the United States especially appealed to him. The physical appearance of the city also elicited remarks; but he did not appear interested in the slums or wickedness, both of which caused comment from some observers.

The result of this visit to America was *Last Winter in the United States* (1863). In the South he was interested in cotton culture and the remnants of *ante-bellum* social life. Zincke also made note of the character of American hotels, the size of American families, the scenery, and American speech. He was amazed at what he called the "purity" of the English spoken by the American people and attributed it to our public school system and the omnivorous reading done by Americans. As to the "development of the faculties," Zincke believed the United States had little which was original, for he believed America too busy with the more practical side of life, in "bringing a new world into subjection to man."

-»»-«««-

CHICAGO'S BUILDINGS

On arriving at Chicago, my first thought was to see the Lake, one of the great fresh-water seas I had been reading of, since I

---

[1] F. Barham Zincke, *Last Winter in the United States* (London: John Murray, 1868), pp. 183–97. Reprinted by permission of John Murray.

was a boy. I was now within a few paces of it, and was only prevented by the houses from looking upon it. I had driven to the Sherman House, a large hotel on one side of the square in the centre of which stands the City Hall; and I had been told that the only good view of the city, and of the Lake, was to be had from the gallery round the top of the dome of this building. It was not long before I ascended the stairs that led to it; and as I stepped out on the balcony, the boundless blue water, reflecting the undimmed hazeless sky, and washing up almost to the foot of the building, and stretching away beyond the horizon, suddenly burst on the view. It was Lake Michigan. Imagination does much on such occasions. I felt satisfied. It was not only worth seeing, but it was worth coming to see.

Here, in these vast reservoirs, is Nature carrying on some of her hydraulic operations upon the grandest scale in the world. Here, too, at this very spot, at its southern point, the countless buffalo used to drink the water of the Lake, and here it was that the red man was waiting to welcome him; and now the white man is ploughing, and harvesting, and building cities all around its shores, and its waters are wafting to this great central depôt the produce of his labours, and then bearing it away again, to feed the millions of New England and of the distant seaboard cities, and even to aid the deficient supplies of Old England and France.

Chicago well deserves its reputation. Its stores, and private houses and churches, are good, and would be so considered in any city. Its stores are in buildings, two floors higher than the shops of Oxford or Regent Street, as is generally the case in all the large American cities. They have an air of solidity, and are not entirely devoid of external decoration. There are suburbs containing many good private residences, the best of which are to be seen in Michigan Avenue, along the shores of the Lake. These are built of a cream-coloured stone, and many of them give one a favourable idea of the architectural taste, as well as of the wealth, of their inhabitants. From the gallery of the City Hall I counted twenty-three towers and spires; but this is very far from giving the number of churches, as perhaps the majority of them still being incomplete, or only temporary structures, are without these embellishments. In the central parts of the city, where all the buildings are good and massive, and the smoke—for here they burn bituminous coal—has put a complexion upon them something like that of London, you could never guess that you were standing in a city so young, that many of its inhabitants, still young themselves, remember the erection of the first brick house in the place; you would be more likely to suppose that you were surrounded by the evidences and appliances of the commercial prosperity of many generations.

On my mentioning to a 'citizen' of Chicago the number of churches I had counted from the top of the City Hall, 'Yes,' he replied, 'we are a religious people outwardly.'

CITY ORDINANCES

In this, one of the youngest cities in the world, I observed some regulations that would be worthy of adoption elsewhere. For instance, wherever in the city a case of small-pox occurs, a large yellow sheet is pasted to the door of the house, announcing in conspicuous letters, 'Small-pox here.' I could not but compare this wise regulation with our carelessness on the same subject at home. This very disease of small-pox, or scarlet fever, or any other infectious disease, may have struck down many of the inmates of a house; yet, according to our custom, it is allowable for the occupiers of the house, if they keep a shop, to invite customers to enter, and to sell them articles of dress, or of food which in some way or other may become vehicles of infection.

Another very useful arrangement I found in operation here, is that by which the whole city is instantly informed of the existence of a fire, and of the locality in which it has burst out. The city is, for this purpose, divided into districts, each district being known by its number. In some central and conspicuous place in each, is a box containing an apparatus by which a bell may be rung in a room at the City Hall. In this room there are men constantly watching the bells. As soon as the bell of any district is rung, the watchers reply with a hurried kind of chime on the large bell of the City Hall, which can be heard in every part of the city. This is to announce that there is a fire. There is then a pause of half a minute, after which the number of the district is struck on the bell. This informs everyone of the exact locality of the fire. The policeman on duty in each district is the person whose business it is to go to the box and ring the bell. In order, however, to save time, it is competent for any respectable citizen to do this; for the place where the key of the box is kept is always mentioned on the outside of the box, and the keeper of the key is ordered to give it up to any respectable applicant. I was surprised to find how often during the night announcements of fire were made from the City Hall.

A few days before my arrival at Chicago there had been, in the best part of the city, one of those monster fires which are of such frequent occurrence in American towns. A fine hall belonging to the Young Men's Christian Association, and many of the largest stores in the city, had been completely destroyed. This gave the merchants of the place an opportunity for exercising the liberality which is one of the characteristics of America, and in no part of America exists in a higher degree than in Chicago. In a few hours after the occurrence, before the embers had ceased to smoulder, enough had been subscribed to rebuild the hall of the Young Men's Christian Association on a larger scale than that of the one that had been destroyed; and the merchants of the place had met, and had put down their names for considerable sums, to form a fund upon which their brother merchants who had been burnt out by the great fire, and lost their stock in trade, might draw for as much as was needed for rebuilding, and re-establishing themselves in business. Repayment was not to be thought of till the recovery of their affairs conveniently admitted of it. . . . .

TRINITY CHURCH

On Sunday evening I attended a service at Trinity Church, having been attracted by the exterior of the building, which is a conspicuous object from some points in Michigan Avenue. I mention this because I observed a peculiarity in the means used for lighting it, which might occasionally be adopted with advantage in London, and large cities where sites are costly. I suppose the space was so confined by dwelling houses on the north and south sides, that windows in the walls of the aisles were inadmissible. This difficulty had been met boldly by enlarging the clerestory windows, and adding in the roof rows of quatrefoil skylights, filled with very dark stained glass. I should have been glad to have seen the effect of this by daylight. Nine tenths of the congregation I saw in this church that evening were gentlemen, from which I inferred that the service was intended mainly for the rougher sex.

What is conventionally regarded by us as the American type of features is not uncommon on the Eastern seaboard, but is seldom seen in the West. The clergyman[2] whom I saw officiating in Trinity Church might have sat for the bust of a Greek philosopher. He had a massive head, with much refinement about it; a lofty forehead, a straight nose, and a magnificent beard. He spoke in a manly and soldierly way of what he had witnessed on the battlefields of the late war. . . . .

SECULAR AND RELIGIOUS SCHOOLS

I was taken over some of the schools of Chicago by the Superintendent of Schools for the city. Those I saw were chiefly used by the children of German and Irish parents. They did not appear so quick as the children of native Americans: the variety, also, of feature, and more general fulness of face observable among them, indicated their foreign extraction. Americanization in these particulars takes place in the second or third generation. They were cleanly and orderly, and looked well clothed and well fed. In the Illinois system there are ten grades; the tenth is the lowest in the Primary School, and the first the highest in the Grammar School. No copy slips are used in these schools. They write at first from something set before them on the black board as I noticed was done at Cincinnati. When sufficiently advanced, they write each day from memory something they were taught on the previous day. In Chicago the number of children attending school is very much below the number of those who are of an age to attend. This is what might have been

[2] Rev. R. J. Keeling.

expected in a town that has grown to such dimensions in a single generation. Great efforts, however, are being made to overtake the work. The difficulty just at present is to get school-buildings quickly enough. It is certain that neither the city itself, nor their zealous and able superintendent, will fall short of the occasion. . . . .

On a Sunday, while I was at Chicago, the gentleman who had given up to me his berth in the sleeping-car to Cincinnati, took me to see one of the large Sunday-schools, which have been organized on a very extensive scale in this great Western city, and from which great results are expected. The one I went to see is held in a Congregationalist church. It is customary at the end of the meeting to give out the number of those who are present, as everybody is supposed to be interested in the maintenance and spread of the movement. At the meeting I witnessed there were 998 persons present, of whom 84 were teachers. They now have in the city 75 of these schools; of these, however, only five are organized on the scale of the one I am speaking of. One of the five is held in an Episcopal church, I believe that of the Holy Trinity. The pupils in these Sunday-schools are not confined to one class in society, or to children, or to the members of any particular communion. All classes attend them; so do many grown-up persons, and all religious denominations, except the Roman Catholics, are to be found among the taught and the teachers.

The work of the day commenced by singing three hymns, which were evidently intended to excite religious emotions of a highly enthusiastic kind. The leading manager then recited the Commandments, all present repeating, after each commandment, the petition of our Ante-Communion service. To this was added what follows the commandments in the American Episcopal service. 'Hear also what the Lord Jesus Christ says: "Thou shalt love the Lord thy God with all thy heart, and with all thy soul, and with all thy mind. This is the first and great commandment. And the second is like unto it, Thou shalt love thy neighbour as thyself. On these two commandments hang all the law and the prophets."' The last chapter in St. Mark's Gospel was then read, the chief manager reading the first verse, and all present simultaneously reading the second, and so on throughout the chapter. The object of their reading it in this alternate method is to prevent monotony, and to keep up attention. The pupils had been requested to commit five verses of this chapter to memory. These verses were now repeated simultaneously. This was all that was learnt by heart; and even the learning of this was left entirely to the discretion of each pupil. A prayer was then offered; but, as a preliminary to it, the subjects it was proposed to make mention of in the prayer were announced, with a few brief and pointed comments. The whole assemblage was now divided into classes of fourteen in each, with a separate teacher for each. This was done without a single person leaving his seat, by the simple process of reversing the back of every alternate seat; so that, where before there were a hundred pews holding seven persons each, there were now fifty holding fourteen each. The change was effected in a few seconds. Each teacher now commented on, and expounded to his class, the five verses that had been committed to memory. Then followed another hymn, and another short prayer, being founded entirely on the five verses which had formed the subject for the day's instruction. The whole was concluded with the singing of the Doxology.

This Sunday-school was divided into three grades. First came the infants. They were placed in a large room behind the west-end gallery, and over the porch. None of them could read. Nothing was attempted in this department except awakening the moral sentiments, and teaching a few facts of Christian history, and if possible a little Christian doctrine. This was done by telling the children little stories. Three of these I heard. My friend, who was the chief doer of all that was done and taught on the occasion of my visit, told these infants, in a very effective manner, well adapted to their little understandings, how he had spent on himself, after a long and uncertain struggle (which he minutely described to them), the first ten cents he had ever possessed; and how ashamed he afterwards felt of himself.

As soon as they can read, they are promoted in to the second grade, which has its place in the gallery. After a time they are passed on to the third or highest grade, which has its place in the body of the church.

It is believed that this Sunday-school organisation has already effected a great deal of good, by bringing all classes together, and by influencing, in a way nothing else could, the destitute, the ignorant, and the reckless. And still more abundant fruit is expected from it in the future.

Who is there but will entertain bright hopes for America, where among the rural population the moral tone is sound and healthy, and in the cities there is so much zeal for doing good?

CHICAGO'S DRINKING WATER

From the time I left New York till I reached Chicago, I had nowhere seen in the towns clear drinking water. At New Orleans it was of the colour of a mulatto, at Cincinnati of a mestizo, and at the intermediate places of the intermediate shades. At Richmond it had a kind of ochreous tint. The reason is the same everywhere. The rivers, with the water of which the towns are supplied, all run through a yellowish or reddish loamy soil—sometimes sandy, sometimes clayey; this is easily worn away, and carried off in suspension by the stream, and is largely added to, after rains, by the surface-washing of the country. At Chicago, by a boldly-conceived and most successfully carried-out plan, the whole city is supplied with the purest water. A tunnel, large enough for two mules to work abreast in it, was carried out for a distance of two miles beneath the lake. At this point they had reached water which is perfectly free from all the impurities of the shore; and here it is admitted into the tunnel in sufficient volume to supply all the wants of a population of about 280,000 souls. It is calculated that this tunnel will be ample for all that 100,000 more inhabitants will require. When the population has grown to this extent, a second tunnel will have to be constructed. The water is pumped up from the level of the tunnel to reservoirs that are above the level of the city: which latter is not the original level of the prairie, but considerably above it; for it having been found, after a great part of the city was built, that it was subject to being occasionally flooded, they raised the ground several feet. In doing this they did not pull down or bury any part of the streets and blocks of houses that were already completed, but lifted them up to the desired height by hydraulic machinery. In this way the Sherman House, one of the large American hotels (I stayed in it while at Chicago) was elevated to the level of the raised street, without a guest leaving it, or any interruption of its business.

ALEXANDER FREAR[1]

ALEXANDER FREAR, politician, was born in Poughkeepsie, New York, in 1820. While still a young man, he came to New York City and engaged in the cloth business. Early in life he entered politics, and in 1858 served as councilman for the seventh district and in 1860–61 as alderman for the eleventh district. In 1866 he went to the state assembly at Albany, where he remained until 1872. At Albany, in the capacity of Boss Tweed's spokesman on the floor of the assembly, he became the father of what was known as the Frear Charter for the city of New York, a Tweed measure. His political activities also led him into the office of Commissioner of Emigration and Commissioner of Public Charities for the city of New York in 1871. He died May 22, 1882.

THE GREAT FIRE OF 1871

On Sunday night, October 8, I was at the Sherman House. I went there at the request of my sister, to see if some of her friends who were expected from Milwaukee had arrived. I had promised to attend to the matter on Saturday, but was prevented by unexpected business. There was a large crowd of strangers and business men of the city at the hotel. The corridor and parlors were full of idlers, much as usual. While looking over the register some one said, "There go the fire-bells again"; and the remark was made jocosely, "They'll burn the city down if they keep on." I paid little attention to the conversation, which did not interest me, and having ascertained that the names that I wanted were not on the register, I sauntered in the corridor a while, and meeting Mr. Nixon, the upholsterer on Lake street, I sat down a moment. . . . . Mr. Nixon made the mistake of pointing out to me a person whom I knew very well by sight, and who lived in Chicago, insisting that it was George Francis Train. And while we were disputing about it my nephew, a young man of 18, came up and I appealed to him to identify the person. He

[1] Alexander Frear, "Chicago; The Full Story of the Great Fire: Narrative of an Eye Witness," *New York World*, October 15, 1871. Reprinted by permission of the Press Publishing Company.

then told us that a big fire was burning on the west side. I asked him if he would mind walking to Ewing street, where my sister was stopping, and letting her know that her friends were not in town; but he replied that I had better go myself, because the fire was in that vicinity, and he had a friend waiting for him up stairs. When I came down the wind was blowing fiercely through Clark street to the river, and I had some difficulty in getting across the Court-house square. It could not have been 10 o'clock, for they were singing in the Methodist church as I passed Follansbe's bank. I noticed the glare of the fire on the west side as I came along, but thought nothing of it. There were very few people out, and I did not meet with a policeman until I reached Monroe street. He was walking rapidly towards me, and I asked him if he knew anything about the fire. He looked at me but made no reply, and kept hurrying on. There was a small party of men on the corner of Adams street. I asked them the same question, and one of them said, "It must be a damn'd big fire this time; you can't put out a high wind with water." The rest of them said nothing, but I thought they looked a little scared. While I stood there a policeman came up Adams street on horseback and turned into Clark street. Some of them hallooed to him, but he paid no attention. I kept on, but before I had reached the next street the cinders began to fall thick all around me and it was growing lighter all the time. A great many people were looking out of their windows, and the streets seemed to get full of people suddenly. They were not excited. They stood about in groups listening to the wind that was making a noise very much like the lake on a stormy night. I went into a Dutch beer saloon to get a cigar, seeing the door half open. The gas was burning, but the persons who kept the place were all in the street. I helped myself to a cigar from an open box that stood on the counter and left a stamp for it; lighting it at the gas-burner, I went out without being questioned. When I was holding it up to the jet I noticed for the first time that I was considerably excited myself; my hand shook and I could hear my heart beat. I don't think I was two minutes in the place, but when I came out the cinders were falling like snow flakes in every direction and

lit the street, and there was a great hubbub of men and vehicles.
I started to run toward Van Buren street, but the walks were so
crowded with people and the cinders were blown so thickly and
fast that I found it was impossible. Besides the wind blew my
hat off twice. I took to the middle of the street and found that
the crowd coming in the opposite direction was increasing. But
it was difficult to see anything clearly on account of the cinders.
Somewhere between Van Buren and Polk streets I found the
crowd jammed into the thoroughfare solidly. There was a four-
story brick house on the east side that overlooked the others all
around it. A man on top seemed to be gesticulating and shouting to the crowd, but whatever he said was lost in the wind. It
was some time before I made out that he was shouting to some
one in a window below, and the man below repeated it to the
crowd. All I could distinctly hear was, "burning on both sides
of the river," and just then there was a great pressure in the
crowd of the people and a man on horseback forced his way
through. He seemed to be a gentleman, and I thought an insurance officer. He had in his hand one of the little red flags that
switchmen use, which he waved on either side. What he said I
could not hear, but it had the effect of producing a panic in the
throng. No sooner did I understand that it was impossible and
dangerous to proceed further, and had turned round with the
purpose of running to the first bridge, than I saw the light of the
fire extending far back in the direction I had come, the flames
lighting the houses on the east side of Clark street as far as I
could see. I ran as fast as I could to the Adams street bridge.
Vehicles and people were streaming in from all the streets to the
west. I paid little attention to anything, my anxiety to reach
my sister's house being very great. With difficulty I got to the
bridge, which was beset by teams desiring to cross, and tugs
screaming in the stream to get through. There was much confusion, and suddenly a rush of people was made toward me as
the bridge began to swing, and I ran to get over. A woman carrying a bureau drawer, and blinded by the sparks, in her desper-
ation struck me with her burden in the breast, breaking the
crystal of my watch and stunning me for a moment. It was 1:30

o'clock. While I held the watch in my hand a live coal fell on it as large as a silver half-dollar.

All of Adams street, reaching to Des Plaines on the west side was choked with people. But they were free from the terrible rain of cinders, the wind carrying them in a northeasterly direction across the river. Des Plaines street was comparatively clear; and on turning into it I lost my hat. Without attempting to recover it I ran as fast as I could in the direction of Ewing street. My sister's house was out of the line of the fire, but there was no telling at what moment the wind would veer. My brother, who is a lumber merchant, was absent in Sheboygan. The house was occupied by his family, consisting of Mrs. Frear and three children (two girls and a boy, all of them under fifteen years of age, the youngest, Johnny, a cripple with rheumatism), and a lodger who was employed as a clerk in Mr. Frear's office. The family were in great consternation. I told Mrs. Frear that I thought there was no present danger as the fire was not burning this side of Jefferson street, but was being blown swiftly to the east. We were within a block, however, of Jefferson street, and the heat was intense, and the excitement of the neighbors was very great. I found that she had her clothing and valuables all packed in trunks, which were pulled into the hallway, and she told me that Mr. Wood (the clerk) had gone to get one of Mr. Farwell's trucks to take her things to the warehouse on Wabash avenue. I tried to dissuade her in vain, and finally, finding she was resolute, I consented to get a coach and take the children to Mrs. Kimball's on Wabash avenue, she saying she would remain and look after the house until the danger was over.

Fortunately there was not much trouble in getting a coach, and I started as soon after as possible with the three children. The Kimballs were all abed, and I was some time ringing at the door (holding Johnny wrapped in my arms in a rug) before I roused them.

The driver of the coach put his horses to their utmost speed in returning. When we reached the vicinity of Madison street bridge he threw the door open and said we couldn't get across. The noise of men and vehicles was so great that he had to shout at the top of his voice. We then drove up to Randolph street, and here we were stopped again, the bridge being open. It seemed that the string of vessels passing through was endless. We were an hour and a half in getting back, I think. The whole of Ewing street was barricaded with vehicles and household effects. Mrs. Frear was much cooler now that her children were safe. Most of her valuables had been got off, and as it was no longer possible to get a dray up to the house the heavy furniture had to remain. While we were talking Mr. Wood burst into the room and said that the fire had reached Wabash avenue and was sweeping all before it. His appearance as well as his language was terrifying. Nearly blinded by the flying embers, he had dashed water on his head and face, and his matted hair and be-grimed skin added to his frightened looks, made him seem like another person.

I begged Mrs. Frear not to alarm herself, and ran up to the roof. The house was a two-story and a half frame building, but it joined another which was an addition to a planing-mill. I clambered to the roof of the latter, and was nearly swept off by the wind. As near as I could make out Wood was right. . . . . Wherever I could see at all the wind blew the burning houses into a mass of live coals that was dazzling. When I returned I found Mrs. Frear had her water-proof cloak on, and had put her jewelry and money into a satchel and was ready to start. I begged of her to remain, saying that I would see to the safety of the children, but she only answered: "My poor Johnny; my poor, sick Johnny." Mr. Wood and myself then endeavored to get another conveyance. The front steps and the sidewalks were thronged with terror-stricken women, and the street was en-cumbered with luggage. The three of us fought our way through . . . . till we reached Mr. McGowan's in Halsted street, and here we were fortunate enough to get a cab. Wood then went back to the house, and we started for Wabash avenue, Mr. McGowan driving us himself. I afterwards found out that he had to take us all the way round to Clark street, on the north side, to get over the river. But at the time I did not notice our direction until we had crossed the river, being occupied in trying to pacify Mrs. Frear. We got as far as Washington street in the avenue when the horse was stopped and McGowan got into an altercation with an officer. I sprang out, and was told that it was useless to go any further, for the whole of the avenue was on fire. The roadway was full of people, and the din of voices and the *mêlée* of horses rendered unmanageable by the falling embers was terrible. In the confusion it was difficult to get any information; but I was told that the block in which the Kimballs lived [the refuge of Mrs. Frear's children] was burning, and that the people were all out. To add to my distress Mrs. Frear jumped out of the vehicle and started to run in the direction of the fire. Nothing, I am satisfied, saved her from being crushed to death in a mad attempt to find her children but the providential appearance of an acquaintance, who told her that the children were all safe at the St. James Hotel. When we reached the hotel I found it impossible to get her through the crowd without trouble, and so I took her into Soldon & Ward's hair dressing-room in the basement, and went up stairs to look for the children alone. There was a great deal of excitement in the house, but there seemed to be no apprehension of danger from the fire at that distance. The guests and servants of the house were nearly all at the windows or down in the doorways. I found that Mrs. Frear's acquaintance had either intentionally or unintentionally deceived her. The children were not in the house. When I informed her of it she fainted. When she was being taken up-stairs to the parlor I found she had lost her satchel. Whether it was left in the cab when she jumped out or was stolen in the house I cannot say. It contained two gold watches, several pins and drops of value, a cameo presented to her by Mrs. Stephen A. Douglas, a medal of honor belonging to her husband (who was an officer in the First Wisconsin Volunteers during the War) and about $200 in bills and currency stamps, besides several trinkets of trifling value. Leaving her in the care of some ladies I then started for John F. V. Farwell's stores, on Wabash avenue, thinking it possible the children were sent there, where their mother's property was. When I came into Wabash avenue the full extent of the fire and its danger to the city became for the first time apparent to my mind. I saw the flames distinctly, and, remembering that they were two miles distant when I first saw them, I began to realize the awful nature of the calamity. I spoke to several persons on the street. They seemed to think the flames would be stayed when they reached the durable and massive structures, and that it was only the wooden buildings that caused such a furious burning. The Farwell stores were all closed. The watchman said there had been no goods much less children brought there. I then ran as fast as I could through Randolf street to the Sherman House, thinking we might have mistaken the hotel. They had the hose laid on and a party of men were on the roof putting out the cinders. I was told that the place had already been ignited twice. The corridor was a scene of intense excitement. The guests of the house were running about wildly, some of them dragging their trunks to the stairway. Everything was in confusion, and my heart sank within me as I saw that the panic was spreading among those who were the best protected. I looked out of one of the south windows of the house and shall never forget the terribly magnificent sight I saw. The Court-house Park was filled with people who appeared to be huddled together in a solid mass, helpless and astounded. The whole air was filled with the falling cinders, and it looked like a snow-storm lit by colored fire. The weird effect of the glare and the scintillating light upon this vast silent concourse was almost frightful. While in the corridor of the Sherman House I encountered my nephew, and he asked me if I wanted to see the fire, saying he had one of George Garrison's horses and only wanted a rubber blanket to throw over him to protect him from the sparks. I told him about Mrs. Frear, but he thought there was no reason to worry. He got a blanket somewhere and we started off in a light wagon for Wabash avenue, stopping at Wright's, under the Opera House, to get a drink of coffee, which I needed very much. There were several of the firemen of the Little Giant[2] in there. One of them was bathing his head with whiskey from a flask. They declared that

[2] This fire company (John Campion, captain) was said to be the first engine company to throw a stream of water on the fire at Mrs. O'Leary's barn.

the entire department had given up, overworked, and that they could do nothing more. While we stood there an Irish girl was brought in with her dress nearly all burnt from her person. It had caught on the Court-house steps from a cinder. When we went out a man in his coat-sleeves was unhitching the horse; and when we came up he sprung into the wagon, and would have driven off in spite of us if I had not caught the horse by the head. He then sprang out and struck my nephew in the face and ran toward State street. We drove as rapidly as we could into Wabash avenue— the wind sweeping the embers after us in furious waves. We passed a broken-down steamer in the middle of the roadway. The avenue was a scene of desolation. The storm of falling fire seemed to increase every second, and it was as much as we could do to protect ourselves from the burning rain and guide the horse through the flying people and hurrying vehicles. Looking back through Washington street, towards the Opera House, I saw the smoke and flames pouring out of State street, from the very point we had just left, and the intervening space was filled with the whirling embers that beat against the houses and covered the roofs and window-sills. It seemed like a tornado of fire. To add to the terrors the animals, burnt and infuriated by the cinders, darted through the streets regardless of all human obstacles. Wabash avenue was burning as far down as Adams street. The flames from the houses on the west side reached in a diagonal arch quite across the street, and occasionally the wind would lift the great body of flame, detach it entirely from the burning buildings, and hurl it with terrific force far ahead. All the mansions were being emptied with the greatest disorder and the greatest excitement. Nobody endeavored to stay the flames now. A mob of men and women, all screaming and shouting, ran about wildly, crossing each other's paths and intercepting each other as if deranged. We tried to force our way along the avenue, which was already littered with costly furniture, some of it burning in the streets under the falling sparks, but it was next to impossible. Twice we were accosted by gentlemen with pocket-books in their hands, and asked to carry away to a place of safety some valuable property. Much as we may have desired to assist them, it was out of our power. Women came and threw packages into the vehicle, and one man with a boy hanging to him caught the horse and tried to throw us out. I finally got out and endeavored to lead the animal out of the terrible scenes. When we had gone about a block I saw the Court-house was on fire, and almost at the same moment some one said the St. James had caught on the roof. I was struck on the arm by a bird-cage flung from an upper window, and the moment I released the horse he shied and ran into a burning dray-load of furniture, smashing the wheel of the wagon and throwing my companion out on his shoulder. Fortunately he was only bruised. But the horse, already terrified, started immediately, and I saw him disappear with a leap like that of a panther. We then hurried on toward the St. James Hotel, passing through some of the strangest and saddest scenes it has ever been my misfortune to witness. I saw a woman kneeling in the street with a crucifix held up before her and the skirt of her dress burning while she prayed. We had barely passed her before a runaway truck dashed her to the ground. Loads of goods passed us repeatedly that were burning on the trucks, and my nephew says that he distinctly saw one man go up to a pile of costly furniture lying in front of an elegant residence and deliberately hold a piece of burning packing board under it until the pile was lit. When we reached the wholesale stores north of Madison street the confusion was even worse. These stores were packed full of the most costly merchandise, and to save it at the rate the fire was advancing was plainly impossible. There was no police, and no effort was made to keep off the rabble. A few of the porters and draymen employed by these stores were working manfully, but there were costermongers' wagons, dirt carts, and even coaches backed up and receiving the goods and a villanous [sic] crowd of men and boys chaffing each other and tearing open parcels to discover the nature of their contents. I reached the St. James between 2 and 3 o'clock on Monday morning. It was reported to be on fire, but I did not see the flames then. Mrs. Frear had been removed in an insensible state to the house of a friend on the north side. I could learn no other particulars.

The house was in a dreadful state of disorder. Women and children were screaming in every direction and baggage being thrown about in the most reckless manner. I now concluded that Mrs. Frear's children had been lost. It was reported that hundreds of people had perished in the flames.

There was a crowd of men and women at the hotel from one of the large boarding-houses in the neighborhood of State and Adams street, and they said they barely escaped with their lives, leaving everything behind. At this time it seemed to me that the fire would leave nothing. People coming in said the Sherman House was going, and that the Opera House had caught. Finally word was brought that the bridges were burning, and all escape was cut off to the north and west. Then ensued a scene which was beyond description. Men shouted the news and added to the panic. Women, half-dressed and many of them with screaming children, fled out of the building. There was a jam in the doorway and they struck and clawed each other as if in self-defence. I lost sight of my nephew at this time. Getting out with the crowd I started and ran round toward the Tremont House. Reaching Dearborn street the gust of fire was so strong that I could hardly keep my feet. I ran on down toward the Tremont. Here the same scene was being enacted with tenfold violence. The elevator had got jammed, and the screams of the women on the upper floors were heart rending. I forced my way upstairs, seeing no fire, and looked into all the open rooms, calling aloud the names of Mrs. Frear's daughters. Women were swarming in the parlors; invalids, brought there for safety, were lying upon the floor. Others were running distracted about, calling upon their husbands. Men, pale and awe-struck and silent, looked on without any means of averting the mischief. All this time the upper part of the house was on fire. The street was choked with people, yelling and moaning with excitement and fright. I looked down upon them from an upper window a moment, and saw far up Dearborn street the huge flames pouring in from the side streets I had traversed but an hour ago, and it appeared to me that they were impelled with the force of a tremendous blow-pipe. Everything that they touched melted.

Presently the smoke began to roll down the stairways, and almost immediately after the men who had been at work on the roof came running down. They made no outcry, but hurried from the house as if for their lives. I went up to the fourth story, looking into every room, and kicking open those that were locked. There were several other men searching in the same manner, but I did not notice them. While up here I obtained a view of the conflagration. It was advancing steadily upon the hotel from two or three points. There was very little smoke; it burned too rapidly, or what there was must have been carried away on the wind. The whole was accompanied by a crackling noise as of an enormous bundle of dry twigs burning, and by explosions that followed each other in quick succession on all sides. When I was going down I found one of the men dragging an insensible woman downstairs by her shoulders. She was an unusually large woman, and had on a striped satin dress and a great quantity of jewelry, which I supposed she had put upon her person for safety. I assisted him to carry her down, and when she reached the lower story to my surprise she suddenly recovered her consciousness and ran away followed by the man. From the street entrance I could see up Dearborn street as far as the Portland Block and it was full of people all the distance, swaying and surging under the rain of fire. Around on Lake street the tumult was worse. Here for the first time I beheld scenes of violence that made my blood boil. In front of Shay's magnificent dry goods store a man loaded a store truck with silks in defiance of the employes of the place. When he had piled all he could upon the truck some one with a revolver shouted to him not to drive away or he would fire at him, to which he replied "Fire and be damned!" and the man put the pistol in his pocket again. Just east of this store there was at least a ton of fancy goods thrown into the street, over which the people and vehicles passed with utter indifference, until they took fire. I saw myself a ragamuffin on the Clark street bridge, who had been killed by a marble slab thrown from a window, who had white kid gloves on his hands, and whose pockets were stuffed with gold-plated sleeve-buttons, and on that same bridge I saw an Irish woman leading a goat that was big with young by one arm, while under the other she carried a piece of silk.

Lake street was rich with treasure, and hordes of thieves forced their way into the stores and flung out the merchandise to their fellows in the street, who received it without disgrace, and fought over it openly. I went through the street to Wabash avenue, and here the thoroughfare was utterly choked with all manner of goods and people. Everybody that had been forced from the other end of the town by the advancing fire had brought some article with him, and, as further progress was delayed, if not completely stopped by the river, the bridges of which were also choked, most of them, in their panic, abandoned their burdens, so that the street and sidewalks presented the most astonishing wreck. Valuable oil paintings, books, pet animals, musical instruments, toys, mirrors, and bedding were trampled under foot. Added to this the goods from the stores had been hauled out and had taken fire, and the crowd breaking into a liquor establishment were yelling with the fury of demons as they brandished champagne and brandy bottles. The brutality and horror of the scene made it sickening. A fellow standing on a piano declared that the fire was the friend of the poor man. He wanted everybody to help himself to the best liquor he could get, and continued to yell from the piano until some one as drunk as himself flung a bottle at him and knocked him off it. In this chaos were hundreds of children wailing and crying for their parents. One little girl in particular I saw whose golden hair was loose down her back and caught fire. She ran screaming past me and somebody threw a glass of liquor upon her which flared up and covered her with a blue flame. It was impossible to get through to the bridge and I was forced to go back toward Randolf street. There was a strange and new fascination in the scenes that I could not resist. It was now daylight and the fire was raging closely all about me. The Court-house, the Sherman House, the Tremont House, and the wholesale stores on Wabash avenue, and the retail stores on Lake street were burning. The cries of the multitude on the latter streets had now risen into a terrible roar, for the flames were breaking into the

river streets. I saw the stores of Mr. Drake, Hamlin, and Farwell burn. They ignited suddenly all over in a manner entirely
new to me, just as I have seen paper do that is held to the fire
until it is scorched and breaks out in flame. The crowds who
were watching them greeted the combustion with terrible yells.
In one of the stores—I think it was Hamlin's—there were a
number of men at the time on the several floors passing out
goods, and when the flames blown over against it enveloped the
building, they were lost to sight entirely; nor did I see any effort
whatever made to save them, for the heat was so intense that
everybody was driven as before a tornado from the vicinity of
the buildings. I now found myself carried by the throng back
to near Lake street, and determined if possible, to get over the
river. I managed to accomplish this after a severe struggle and
at the risk of my life. The rail of the bridge was broken away,
and a number of small boats loaded with goods were passing
down the stream. How many people were pushed over the
bridge into the water I cannot tell. I saw one man stumble under
a load of clothing and disappear, nor did the occupants of the
boats pay the slightest attention to him nor to the crowd overhead, except to guard against anybody falling into their vessels.
Once over the river I felt safe. It seemed to me highly improb-
able that the fire would leap the stream, which at this point is
the widest. Alas, those who were there told me that the flames
of the burning storehouses on Water street were blown into the
windows on the other side, and that before the houses that line
the south side were half consumed those on the other were crackling and flaming with intensity. I went through North Water
street, meeting with a frantic multitude teeming from each of
the bridges, and by a tiresome detour got round to the West side.
When I arrived at my sister's house I found my nephew there,
who informed me that Mrs. Frear had been taken to a private
house in Huron street, and was perfectly safe and well cared for.
I was wet and scorched and bedraggled. My clothes were burnt
full of holes on my arms and shoulders and back. I asked Wood
to make some coffee, which he promised to do, and I fell down
in the hallway and went to sleep. I could not have lain there

half an hour when Wood awoke me, saying the fire was sweeping everything before it in the direction of Lincoln Park, and that Mrs. Frear must be moved again. We both started out then and walked and ran as fast as we could in the direction of the north side. It was about 8:30 o'clock. We could see across the river at the cross streets that where yesterday was a populous city was now a mass of smoking ruins. All the way round we encountered thousands of people, but the excitement had given way to a terrible grief and scenes of desolation. Des Plaines and the northern part of Jefferson street were piled up twelve and fifteen feet high with goods. Luckily Wood knew where to find Mrs. Frear, and he arrived at the house just in time to get her into a baker's wagon, which Wood and I pulled for half a mile. She was in a terrible condition, being hysterical, and when we were in Des Plaines street again there came an omnibus, loaded with frightened children, through Lake street. They were crying and screaming, and Mrs. Frear heard them and began to screech at the top of her voice. The man who was driving the omnibus stopped and yelled after us to know where we were taking that woman. It was impossible to get the wagon through the street on account of the goods, and so we were forced to go half a mile farther out of our way. Once at home a number of her neighbors came to her assistance, and about 4 o'clock in the afternoon word came from the Kimballs that the children were all safe out at Riverside. I spent the greater part of the day in searching for her property without avail. I have lost nothing myself by the fire but what I can recover, but on Monday afternoon I went to bed with a sick headache and a fever, which were the result of mental excitement rather than physical exposure.

PART III

THE RISE OF A MODERN CITY

INTRODUCTION

I N SPITE of the losses and the hardships of seventy-one, Chicago still possessed a location which could tap the reservoirs of grain, live stock, lumber, coal, copper, iron, and building-stone of Middle and Northwest America. Her lake frontage and river wharfage and her eighteen great trunk lines of railway connections remained, and about three hundred thousand people were left to start life anew. Soon the manufacturing establishments which were a natural complement of railway and lake commerce were rebuilt, but only after the immediate and pressing needs of a homeless and destitute populace had been met. In this, other cities of America and foreign countries contributed generously, sending almost five million dollars worth of food, clothing, and other necessities. Eastern capital again assisted in the upbuilding of the community, and seaboard holders of mortgages felt constrained to aid in resuscitation in order that their original investments might be safeguarded. Spokesmen of faith in Chicago's ultimate supremacy, such as William Bross of the *Chicago Tribune,* sounded a clarion call for help in the extension of credit, promising bounteous return for such investments. About one-half of the eighty-eight millions of insurance coverage, especially that held by British agencies, was collected, serving as a bulwark in the rehabilitation program.

Soon after the Fire, farmers' teams and wagons for miles around were enlisted in the work of removing débris, which was utilized in building out the shore line between the Illinois Central Railroad tracks and the breakwater. Titles were generally proved in courts of equity, the written records having been destroyed; resultant high prices of labor and material were in one way or another met. As immediate gloom gave way to hope, original plans for hasty and cheap rebuilding were replaced by intentions to construct buildings larger, more permanent, and more pleasing to the eye than their predecessors. In a municipal election held a month after the conflagration Joseph Medill was elected mayor on a "fireproof" ticket. An ordinance to lessen the danger from fire was passed which prohibited wooden structures. Within fixed limits architects took added care to protect exposed materials with fire clay. Unfortunately, many evaded the restrictions, and enforcement was not always apt. But within three years hardly an evidence of the burning remained visible. In 1874, a new fire found materials for destruction of over eighteen squares in the heart of the city, occasioning a loss of four million dollars.

But the growth of the Northwest took Chicago along with it in spite of handicaps and disasters. In 1872, alone, half as many miles of railway were laid in the section as in the ten years preceding. Over these rails, in 1873, came 50 per cent more grain than in 1869, although the panic of that year served to retard normal business development. Fifteen warehouses, with a capacity of 14,100,000 bushels, served in 1874 to care for the grain until such time as it should be moved to some point outside of Chicago. The Union Stock Yards took twice as many hogs in 1872 as had arrived in 1870. By 1874, into the city came 843,966 cattle, 333,655 sheep, and 4,758,379 hogs, and by 1884, 1,817,697 cattle, 801,630 sheep, and 5,351,967 hogs.

Three years after the Fire, 10,827 vessels arrived in the port of Chicago and 12,312 cleared it. The early eighties witnessed continued growth and expansion in the number and size of these commercial carriers, reaching 13,351 arrivals in 1882 and 13,626 clearances. Sales in the wholesale drygoods trade alone in 1874 attained $50,000,000 and in boots and shoes $11,500,000. In the next decade both showed steady gains, mounting in the case of the former to $57,000,000, and in the latter to $17,000,000. At the end of 1872, twenty-one national banks, eight state, and eighteen savings banks reported a total of $38,129,134 in deposits. Twenty years later the number of national banks had increased by three, with total deposits of $122,354,131.71 and capital listed at $21,300,000, approximately twice as much as in the year after the Fire.

No less important than the industrial recovery was the restoration of municipal and county functions. The Fire not only
had leveled buildings in its path but had destroyed sidewalks
and streets, largely made of wooden planks and blocks, water
mains, sewers, gas mains, and bridges. The police and fire departments had been temporarily disorganized. The legislature
of the state appropriated $2,955,340, in the form of repayment
of the city's expenditures on the canal, for the rebuilding of
bridges and public works, the payment of interest on bonded
debts, and the maintenance of the fire and police departments.
For a time the La Salle Street tunnel remained the sole means
of communication with the North Side. Notable reorganization
took place in the police department, as well as a considerable increase in the extent and efficiency of its services. Within thirteen years it grew from 425 to 924 men. In 1875 the direction of
the department was removed from a board of commissioners and
placed in the hands of a superintendent. In 1873 the detective
force was reorganized, with Samuel A. Ellis as its head. Seven
years later Captain W. J. McGarigle introduced a new police
telephone and signal system, which, in connection with a body
of patrol wagons, made the force more mobile and effective in the
preservation of order. At the same time, the fire force was more
than doubled in numbers and its system of fire-alarm telegraph
improved and extended.

Although the loss to the city in public works, including the
burning of the City Hall, water works, water mains, and meters,
gas mains, sewage works, bridges, sidewalks and pavements,
tunnels, lamp posts, and in removing river obstructions, reached
the sum of $2,220,250.90, by 1874 twice as many improved
streets as before the Fire were found, 111 miles of street pavements being laid. The need for a City Hall was met by the erection of a temporary structure at Adams and La Salle streets
opened in January, 1872. A permanent and appropriate building,
the combined City Hall and County Building, long in use, was not
completed until 1885. The county in addition constructed the
Cook County Hospital, an infirmary, and an asylum. The federal agencies were housed in a new structure completed in 1880.

Within two weeks after the Fire educational facilities of some sort were available for young learners, and by June, 1873, five schools were rebuilt. But the rapid increase in the numbers of pupils constantly pressed the authorities hard to provide adequate accommodations. Changes in educational practices were indicated by the discontinuance, in 1875, of reading of the Scriptures and of the repeating of the Lord's Prayer and, in 1885, the dropping of Greek from the curriculum. Acceptance of educational theories of the time was evinced further in the establishment, in 1884, of the Chicago Manual Training School, supported by the Chicago Commercial Club.

Intra-city transportation, during the seventies, in large measure was furnished to the public by horse cars; but in 1881 the Chicago City Railway ventured to replace the horse-drawn vehicles with cable cars, the motive power being furnished by stationary steam engines in a central plant. The startling speed of eight or nine miles an hour made by these cars excited the admiration of visitors to the city and evoked protests from Chicago citizens because of numerous accidents. Omnibuses and cars provided the chief means for a constantly growing populace to reach their business location from outlying districts which were rapidly being transformed from farm land into suburban residences for the city's workers.

In the twenty years following the Fire, the scope and scale of building reconstruction, evidence of the expanding life of the community, brought colorful observations from visitors. Costs of down-town real estate mounted. A general increase in the height of structures, with the inclusion of elevator service, although not as frequently found then as now, gave cause for comment. The magnificence with which the leading hotels had been rebuilt kindled enthusiasm in their guests, who observed that the word "hotel" in the United States meant more than food and lodging, for it included many of the benefits of a public club.[1] At the time of the Fire the new Grand Pacific had just been opened; and the third Palmer House, in which was located the famous William S. Eaton barber shop, in which "the floor

---

[1] See Leng's description, pp. 221–22.

is beautifully inlaid with tiles and *real silver dollar* pieces,"[2] was in the process of construction. With the Sherman House and the Tremont these hotels called forth the plaudits of visitors to the city, who marveled at the luxuriousness and unrivaled character of their service.

In 1869, following an enactment of the legislature, Governor Palmer had appointed members of the South, West, and Lincoln Park commissions. The construction of an extensive and pretentious park system encircling the city was then begun on a scale fitted to future needs, to be maintained by public taxation and affording recreational opportunities for the city's populace. Care for necessities directly following the Fire retarded the immediate fruition of the plan; but by 1880, although still in embryo, it was reported as "growing rapidly."[3]

Thus, on all hands were seen indications of an approaching maturity in the life of the city. Numerous and pervasive social and cultural aspirations bore witness to a development of things of the spirit. Club life had had a promising inception as early as 1861 with the Dearborn Club, reorganized in 1868 as the Chicago Club. In 1876 it opened an impressive new building, where visiting notables frequently were received by the city's leaders. In 1869, a Jewish organization, the Standard Club, had taken form. Ten years later another social body, the Calumet Club, appeared. Along with groups of a social bent came the Commercial Club, representing definitely the economic interests of the city, and the Union League and the Iroquois Club, personating the political affiliations of their members. At the same time women began to associate themselves in groups, later to play a large part in shaping the civic and philanthropic, as well as the social, character of Chicago's urban development. From the foreign aid received in the wake of the Fire a consignment of eight thousand books from England, for which Thomas Hughes, author of *Tom Brown at Rugby*, was largely responsible and to which Browning, Tennyson, Darwin, Kingsley, and other liter-

[2] Archibald Porteous, *A Scamper through Some Cities of America* (Glasgow: David Bryce & Son, 1890), p. 62. Italics in the original.

[3] See Lady Hardy's remarks, p. 2.9.

ary notables contributed, formed a nucleus for the Chicago Public Library organized in 1872. In the promotion of this project Joseph Medill took a leading part, and William F. Poole, formerly librarian of the Boston Athenaeum, was put in charge. In 1877 the Chicago Historical Society found new quarters and within a few years entered upon a period of uninterrupted activity and growth. Art received an impetus by the opening of private galleries and the establishment in 1882 of the Art Institute of Chicago as the successor of the older Academy of Design and Chicago Academy of Fine Arts. It was fitting that the more practical industrial arts should receive recognition in instituting the annual Inter-State Industrial Exposition in the Exposition Art Hall.

In the rapid growth and development, material and cultural, of Chicago after the Fire, interest in musical appreciation likewise was promoted by such groups as the Apollo Musical Club and the Beethoven Society, organized in 1872 and 1874, respectively, and by Theodore Thomas and his symphony orchestra. During these years opera continued to be given by traveling companies. With the arrival of Colonel J. H. Mapleson's Italian Company from Her Majesty's Theatre, London, in 1879, music of this type entered upon a period of greater popularity and patronage. Seven years later the season was made memorable by the visit of Adelina Patti. Light operas abounded.

Through legacies in the wills of some of the early economic leaders of the community, such as Walter L. Newberry, John Crerar, Philip D. Armour, and William B. Ogden, philanthropic and learned undertakings were given momentum. Both the American and the foreign language press were accorded encomiums by critics of the day, and periodical literature of excellent character abounded. Guests of literary and dramatic authority, including Oscar Wilde, Henry Irving, and Ellen Terry, were received with enthusiastic acclaim, invoking the appreciation and praise of these distinguished visitors.

During the later years of the nineteenth century in Chicago, as elsewhere, exponents of Puritanism endeavored to mold the entire community according to their pattern. Strict observance of the Sabbath they held a *sine qua non* of respectability; they frowned upon players and playgoing and the lighter fancies of the day. In particular, they objected to the open saloon on Sunday, and through groups such as the Law and Order League endeavored to enforce their convictions. Crusading evangels, including groups of women, invaded places in question and, frequently, by emotional appeals, attempted to get stubborn adversaries to recant. In 1874, women opponents of the saloon and the sale of liquor joined in a protest against the intemperance of the day by organizing the Woman's Christian Temperance Union, with Frances E. Willard as a guiding spirit. Such issues were, at times, the battleground of political antagonists whose campaigns were waged on "open" and "closed" Sundays and similar planks in their platforms.

By 1873 Chicago had over two hundred and twelve churches, representing Protestants, Jews, and Catholics. Five Unitarian churches offered refuge to nonconformists of the orthodox Protestant faith, and residents of Scandinavian and German birth found denominational groups worshiping in their native tongue. Two African churches cared for the negro whose trek northward had already begun. A writer in *Scribner's Monthly* for September, 1875, declared:

Chicago is no place for weakness. Nor can mediocrity in the scholastic attainments of clergymen find much favor here. Chicago pays good salaries for teachers of Divine truths, and is able to command them. The poor preacher, that is, the man who preaches poorly can hardly find much comfort here. He must soon become conscious that he is not up to the Chicago standard. . . . . The apostle of to-day is a scholar and an orator, a man of intellectual ability, and qualified in all respects to minister to the spiritual wants of a metropolitan flock.[4]

Increasing leisure and a growing monotony of urban life brought, in Chicago, as in other parts of America, a stimulation of organized exercise and recreation. In 1871, the Chicago "White Stockings" participated in the formation of the National Professional Base-Ball Association and five years later in the organization of the National Base-Ball League. The opening of the Washington Park Club for horse racing and the formation

[4] J. W. Sheahan, "Chicago," *Scribner's Monthly*, X (September, 1875), 547.

of the Farragut Boat Club and the Chicago Bicycle Club give further evidence of an increased interest in sport of various sorts.

As the years advanced and Chicago moved forward with a faith consistent with her past achievements, the number of her citizens and residents increased in the two decades following the Fire to 1,099,850. Nearly 41 per cent of these were aliens, of whom 167,082 were Germans, 72,954 Scandinavians, and 70,028 Irish. Added to these came representatives from nearly all other countries of the world, creating problems of Americanization not always easily soluble, but providing Chicago and the surrounding area with sturdy laborers and skilful artisans.

Woven into the warp and woof of Chicago's growing urbanization, and touching all aspects of her life, was a constantly pulsating and expanding industry, based on the two solid foundations of agriculture and transportation. As the new economic era dawned, there passed from the scene some of the early leaders of commercial and civic life: John Wentworth, Gurdon S. Hubbard, Cyrus H. McCormick, William Bross, and Colonel William Hale Thompson. Immensity and complexity superseded the relative simplicity of earlier days; and such business organizations as the meat packing industry and the Pullman Car Plant, in particular, called forth the admiration of Chicago's visitors, who saw in them characteristics of modern economic America. Late in 1865 the Union Stock Yards had opened, and had escaped the Fire. In 1875 Philip D. Armour came to Chicago and, with his brother, slaughtered beeves and hogs and sent salted, smoked, and pickled meats all over the world. Fresh meat was supplied to the city by Nelson Morris; while Gustavus Swift, after unremitting and arduous endeavor, finally succeeded in opening an eastern market for Chicago's fresh-dressed beef. Swift and Armour, pioneers in the development of the refrigerator car, with the earlier firm of Libby, McNeill, and Libby, were dominant factors in Chicago meat packing. The rapidity and division of labor of the slaughtering and packing processes and the perfect use of by-products fascinated and astounded both foreign and domestic visitors.

No less admired was the "model city" of Pullman, with shops and parks and comfortable homes for those engaged in turning out the "Palace Car." As "the extension of the broadest philanthropy to the working man, based on business principles," it appealed to the visitor as a real "development of an idea."[5]

One side of the industrial development, however, bore characteristics less palatable. Some of the men who contributed the labor, as distinguished from the management and capital of these and other business activities, felt the returns sadly incommensurate with their contributions. The Panic of 1873, begotten by overspeculation in enterprises of the growing Northwest, devastation caused by the War between the States, and reactions from European financial disasters, gripped in a gradually widening circle many of the laborers who had flocked in to work on the reconstruction of the city, depriving thousands of them of a means of livelihood. Even though Chicago, with her economic welfare resting at that time primarily on a firm foundation of grain and meats, weathered the depression better than many eastern cities, there was intense suffering. In this fertile soil labor leaders of Marxian leanings began to get a hearing. In 1877, largely as a result of disagreements between labor and railroad companies, a paralyzing transportation strike moved on Chicago from the East. Railway employees struck for an eight-hour day and a 20 per cent increase in wages. For three days riots and armed conflicts took place between strikers, strike sympathizers, and other discontented elements (including criminals) on the one hand, and the police, special peace officers, and militia on the other. In all, ten strikers were killed and forty-five strikers and nineteen policemen injured. The strike was forcibly broken.

From these outbreaks sprang a growing bitterness among the laboring elements toward those controlling capital, which bore fruit in tragedy eight years later. One small group found leaders and spokesmen of idealism and violence among both the native and foreign-born who vaguely claimed adherence to the principles of anarchism. Throughout 1884, 1885, and into 1886 there

[5] See the description taken from *The* (London) *Times*, pp. 244–49.

were murmurs of trouble in strikes in the McCormick works, on the street-car lines, and in other industries. Clashes with the police and with Pinkerton detectives employed by the owners were frequent. In February, at an encounter outside the McCormick plant, six men died under the fire of the police. A great mass meeting of protest was called to meet the next evening in the Haymarket, on Randolph Street between Desplaines and Halsted. Mayor Carter Harrison and the chief of police attended and found the meeting peaceable except for the impassioned addresses of some of the anarchist radical labor leaders. They ordered the police reserves home and left the scene. Some time later, however, a subordinate police official, angered by the speeches, marched upon the meeting with a large force and ordered it to disperse. Instantly a bomb was thrown, killing seven police and injuring many others. On orders, the remaining police fired repeatedly into the assembled audience.

The unprecedented throwing of a bomb, coming on a long period of strife and uneasiness, caused panic and fear among the public. Under an excited public pressure the anarchist leaders were indicted, tried, and found guilty. In spite of the fact that the actual thrower was never produced. The death penalty was imposed upon seven and life imprisonment upon the eighth, a verdict upheld by the higher courts. Four of them were eventually hanged, one avoided the death penalty by committing suicide, and two had their sentences eventually commuted to life imprisonment. One result of the bomb-throwing and the outcome of the trial was the setting-back of the legitimate labor movements. These, represented largely in the Knights of Labor and the American Federation of Labor, were working for an eight-hour day, better wages, and better living and working conditions. The latter organization can be said to have found its beginning in Chicago in 1885.

From these troublous happenings was born an awakened public conscience as to the conditions surrounding the so-called "submerged classes," expressing itself in organized effort toward a betterment of conditions. For example, the Civic Federation, with Lyman Gage as president, became a free-speech open forum where social problems were discussed and social theories freely offered. The Eli Bates settlement was known as early as 1876; and in 1889 Jane Addams opened Hull House, in the very center of a benighted district of the city. Chicago, with all its faults, had a conscience; and, although likened to a boy whose growth keeps him in advance of the dimension of his garments, the late nineteenth century found the second city of the United States endeavoring to solve the many problems implicit in a growing urbanization. Never did Chicagoans doubt their capacity to solve these problems; never did they doubt the ultimate success of their city. Travelers, although commenting favorably on "the genial, polished, and well read" society they encountered in which were found "more warmth and much less constraint than in the East,"[6] a "New York with the heart left in,"[7] nevertheless noted the naïve confidence Chicagoans universally reflected.

> Grace Greenwood once told me [wrote Emily Faithfull] that the genuine Chicagoan had not only learned the Scotchman's prayer, "Lord, gie us a gude conceit o' oorsels," but had it abundantly answered! Thus it is alleged that when a true-spirited citizen from Chicago first visits New York, he exclaims, "It isn't much of a city after all." When he drinks New York whisky he complains it isn't half as good as he gets at home, for it only burns "half-way down!" The Sunday newspapers can't compare with his; and as for the feet to be seen on Fifth Avenue, he contemptuously remarks, "Call that a foot!— our girls have them twice the size!"[8]

However, the tireless and unceasing energy and industry of Chicago, called, by Max O'Rell her "go-aheadism,"[9] coupled with her much discussed civic pride, gained, against the invitations of other cities, the privilege of housing the celebration of the fourth centennial of the discovery of America. A sandy, undeveloped tract along the lake shore about seven miles south of the center of the city was chosen as the site, and Daniel A. Burnham was placed in charge of the planning and construction. He gathered about him a notable group of architects, among

---

[6] See Max O'Rell, *Jonathan and His Continent* (*Rambles through American Society*) (Madame Paul Blouët, trans.; New York: Cassell & Co., 1889), pp. 44–45.

[7] Emily Faithfull quoting Grace Greenwood. See Emily Faithfull, *Three Visits to America* (Edinburgh: David Douglas, 1884), p. 52.

[8] *Ibid.*   [9] O'Rell, *op. cit.*, p. 43.

whom Charles B. Atwood, designer of the Art Building (today's Museum of Science and Industry), particularly made his reputation in this enterprise. Augustus St. Gaudens led the contingent of sculptors and Frank D. Millet the painters. Working against time, the plans were formulated and the buildings erected. On the twenty-first day of October, 1892, before a vast crowd the half-finished structures were dedicated by Vice-President Levi P. Morton.

Fittingly the buoyant city chose Carter Harrison, who had served previously to guide the city's destinies, to be its World's Fair mayor. On May 1, 1893, President Cleveland, in person, headed a great delegation of notables to the opening of the Exposition and pressed the key that unfurled the flags, loosened the waters of its fountains, set the machinery turning, and unveiled the Liberty Statue, amid salutes of heavy guns of warships off shore. In spite of disagreements in the Fair management, financial stringencies resulting from the Panic of 1893, and other troubles, crowds in increasing numbers entered the Exposition grounds, until on October 9, Chicago Day, over 700,000 paid admissions were recorded. From all over the country came many whose horizon had heretofore been delimited by the boundaries of town, county, or state. Beautiful architectural effects, classic paintings, and music were only a few of the agencies which opened broader and more satisfying vistas for many of the Fair's visitors. Many, like Arthur Sherburne Hardy, must have felt "admiration for the conception of the Fair, ... amazement at its realization." For, said he, "Our western city has given the fragile beauty of a perfect flower, but has also wrought into it the strength and vigor of its virgin soil. . . . . We *see* the past there, but we *feel* the future."[10]

[10] Arthur Sherburne Hardy, "Last Impressions," *Cosmopolitan*, XVI (December, 1893), 200.

SIR JOHN LENG[1]

SIR JOHN LENG was born at Hull, England, in 1828. He was educated at the Hull grammar school, and at the age of nineteen he became the sub-editor of the *Hull Advertiser*. In 1851 he accepted the position of editor of the bi-weekly *Dundee Advertiser*, and in this capacity he soon became one of Scotland's outstanding journalists. His knowledge of newspaper organization, his literary tastes, and his promptness in adopting modern methods of reporting and printing enabled him to raise the *Dundee Advertiser* from a backward, little-known paper to one of the leading dailies of Great Britain. He established a half-penny daily and two popular weeklies, one devoted largely to things literary.

Leng was a pioneer in the use of stereotyping processes and in introducing illustrations in the daily papers. He was also the first editor to establish an office in Fleet Street, London, with direct telegraphic communication to the home office.

As a member of the radical wing of Parliament, 1889–1905, he was prominent in introducing and supporting measures for home rule, employers' liability, and labor needs. In 1904, he received an LL.D. from St. Andrews in recognition of his work.

Leng traveled widely, visiting continental Europe, India, Ceylon, the Near East, and America. He made three trips to this country; on his third in 1906 he was taken ill, and died at Delmonte, California. During his lifetime he published five books dealing with his travels. A sixth, treating of his last, was published posthumously by his wife. Those books relating to America are *America in 1876*, *Letters from the United States and Canada*, and *Through Canada to California*. In addition to travel books he published numerous pamphlets on socialism, free trade, and economic subjects in general. He also contributed heavily to the Leng Trust for the encouragement of the study of Scotch literature and music.

-》》-《《-

FIVE YEARS AFTER THE FIRE

The story of the rapid rise and progress of Chicago has often been told. The thrilling narratives of its Great Fire, and the wonderful energy of its people in rebuilding the city, were read over the whole world. One's first impression on seeing the Chicago of to-day is that it is scarcely possible the magnificent business streets we see extending over a vast area can all have

[1] John Leng, *America in 1876* (Dundee: Dundee Advertiser Office, 1877), pp. 73–83.

been rebuilt in so short a time. The fire in October 1871 spread over nearly four square miles—some 2100 acres—and destroyed over $240,000,000 worth of property, of which only $40,000,000 were recovered from the Insurance Offices; and yet here in September, 1876 the business part of the city probably surpasses in the even regularity and magnificence of its shops, stores, and warehouses any other in the world. Conceive a city all whose principal streets correspond to Victoria Street in London, or the most central parts of Glasgow and Manchester, and you will understand the style of the Chicago of to-day. There are miles of streets consisting of blocks five, six, seven, and eight storeys high. The thoroughfares are crowded, busy, and bustling; and abounding signs of life and energy in the people and their modes of trading are everywhere apparent. Imagine a city of which all the principal public buildings—the Custom-House, Post-Office, Court-House, Exchange, railway stations, banks, hotels, newspaper offices, warehouses, and shops—were completely burnt down in a conflagration that raged for three days and nights over four square miles of ground, and imagine all these replaced, in the course of five years, by much finer and more costly buildings, and you are enabled to form some idea of the wonderful activity that characterises the Chicago people. I wish I had time to reproduce some of the stories I heard of what occurred during the fire, and how men, after realising their losses, set themselves to re-establish themselves almost before the fire was extinguished. With some remarks made by a Chicago citizen I was much impressed. He said, "I think our fire led to the grandest display of true Christian feeling the world ever saw. Here we were, hundreds of thousands of people—houseless, homeless, without food or shelter; and first from all parts of the United States, and then from every country and city in the civilised world money came pouring in till in less than a fortnight we had to telegraph them to stop—that they were sending too much. As it is, we have 500,000 dollars unspent, and if we had not telegraphed there would have been 5,000,000. The telegraph for days and weeks was chiefly employed in bringing us news of help. The first thing we did was to send off our wives and families into the country, and then set to work to relieve those who could not help themselves. I never had my clothes off or slept in a bed till after the tenth day. That was when we knew the water supply was on again, which took off the tension, as we were all afraid the fire might break out again. There were thousands like myself. It was not a time for sleep but for work, and men worked then as they had never done before, giving their first attention to others rather than themselves." Four thousand houses were built by the Relief Committees and furnished with all absolute requirements within a month. The public Boards met and resolved to maintain public credit. The number of firms not able to meet their engagements was comparatively small. The Banks, although almost all their safes were destroyed, stood firm; the State forwarded a large sum in cash to the Municipality, and confidence was promptly restored. Then the rebuilding of the city commenced at such a rate as has perhaps never been equalled. Architects, builders, and workmen came from all parts of the States. Buildings worth between £7,000,000 and £8,000,-000 sterling were completed within the first year. One architect alone had £1,200,000 worth in hand. The rate of restoration was marvellous, and the general style of the work excellent.

BUILDINGS

More than any other I have yet visited, Chicago is the city of great hotels. With the exception of the Palace Hotel at San Francisco, the Palmer House is the most costly on the American Continent. It is most ornate in its decorations, and most luxurious in its furniture, but is not so spacious and airy as the Grand Pacific, which is "run" by Mr. Drake,[2] who has the reputation

[2] John B. Drake, pioneer hotel-operator. He became a partner of the Gage brothers in 1855, operating the Tremont House. Drake bought complete control in 1868 and continued to operate the hotel until the fire of 1871. When he found that the Tremont was doomed, he purchased the Michigan Avenue Hotel while the fire was raging across the street, taking a chance the hotel would be saved. Fortunately, it escaped the flames; and Drake operated it as the Tremont House until 1873. Late in 1874 he purchased the lease and furnishings of the Grand Pacific Hotel. Drake was also interested in other enterprises. He was one of the founders in 1865 of the Union Stock Yards. Upon the organization of the Illinois Trust and Savings Bank, in 1873, he was made second vice-president, and in 1878 became first vice-president. He was one of the founders of the Chicago Commercial Club and the Presbyterian Hospital. He served as one of the Fire Commissioners under Mayor H. D. Colvin (1873–75) and as a director of the Chicago and Alton Railroad. He was among the first in 1881 to adopt the use of electric lights, and popularized his hotel by doing so.

of being the most skilful hotelkeeper in the United States—a perfect master of the business. He took me through the wonderful subterranean regions of the Grand Pacific, and showed me how they "run" these monstrous hotels in all their details. In addition to the Palmer House and Grand Pacific there are also the Sherman and Tremont Hotels, very large and first-class houses. I was also introduced by a Chicago gentleman to the new Club House,[3] which has just been opened, and which is most tastefully decorated and furnished in the early English style advocated by Westlake. There are now in course of erection splendid County and City buildings, a new Post Office and Custom House, &c. The warehouse blocks are of great extent, and no little sensation had been caused in Chicago just before I arrived by the goliath Stewart dry goods firm of New York having leased two of these blocks. It was rumoured that Claflin and others of the New York houses were about to follow, having discovered that the course of trade, like that of Empire, is tending westward. The dry goods business is said to be gradually centring in Chicago, and leaving New York to be the financial centre. Judging from its growth in the past, he would be a bold man who would venture to prognosticate the limits of Chicago in the future. Its situation at the head of lake and river navigation, and on the direct highways from all parts of the North and West of the American Continent to the seaboard, eminently favours the development of an enormous commercial business. The Lake and the Chicago River generally standing about the same height there is no trouble from the rise and fall of the tides, while the elevators and warehouses give greater facilities for handling grain, provisions, and lumber than are now possessed in any other place. I went through and up to the top of the largest and highest elevator in Chicago and the world. It has twenty-three elevating shafts, on the same principle as a dredging machine, ten of which work direct out of the cars. It will empty 500 cars of 200,000 bushels a day, and will load a vessel with 60,000 bushels in two or three hours. The main body of the interior is a labyrinth of bins and spouts—the corn, wheat,

[3] Dearborn Club.

barley, and oats being chiefly stored at the top ready to run down the spouts into the vessels on one side, after being elevated from the trains on the other. This B Central Elevator,[4] as it is called, is worked by a splendid steam engine of 500 H.-P., which drives all the shafting by an india-rubber belt 4 feet wide, 315 feet long, and weighing 3600 lbs. Paper cores are used here for the belts to run upon with great success. From the highest storey of this elevator we have a panoramic view of the city, the commercial advantages of whose position are very conspicuous.

The risk of another vast conflagration is greatly diminished by the erection of stone and brick edifices—the building of wooden frame houses being now interdicted. But the greatest security is in the abundant water supply. The pumping system at Ottawa is the finest I have seen driven by water power, and that at Chicago the finest by steam power. The City has determined that if another fire occurs there shall be no lack of water to extinguish it—the whole of Lake Michigan—to which the Loch of Lintrathen would literally be only a drop in a bucket—having to be pumped out before the supply would be exhausted. A subaqueous tunnel draws in the water from a great depth two miles out in what is called "the Crib" in the Lake, and a gang of enormous engines pumps the water with such force as will reach the tops of the highest buildings in quantities sufficient to flood out any fire. For drinking purposes the water is now excellent in quality, and remarkably cool even in the height of summer. The tunnel from the lake is large enough to supply a million of people with 57 gallons each per day; while the pumping power at present is equal to 120,000,000 gallons during the same period.

THE STOCKYARDS

Next to the Elevators and Water Works the great sight in Chicago is the Stockyards, where hogs, cattle, and horses are brought in by thousands and hundreds of thousands to be sold— the cattle to be shipped, and the hogs to be slaughtered. The afternoon I visited the Stockyards was rather too hot for com-

---

[4] Built by the Illinois Central Railroad. J. and E. Buckingham, proprietors. Total capacity 1,500,000 bushels.

fortable observation of wholesale hog-butchery. We saw for some time hogs having their throats cut at the rate of eight every minute, or nearly 500 an hour, at an establishment which in the ensuing winter will kill, cut up, cure, and pack at the rate of 6000 a day. We followed the butchered pigs till they were hung up, ready to be sent to the ice-chambers below, where they remain 48 hours, when they are cut up and salted, preparatory to being packed. The scale on which everything is conducted is astonishing.

THE BOARD OF TRADE

Commercially one of the most interesting sights in Chicago is the Board of Trade, a large room in which great and sometimes enormous transactions are carried on daily in a manner quite unintelligible to the uninitiated, who hear nothing but apparently frantic and delirious shouts, howls, and screams. Everywhere else in Chicago people seem to be lively but sensible; here they seem to be maniacs, ejaculating and gesticulating in ways suggesting the immediate issue of a Commission *de lunatico inquirendo*. In course of time it will probably occur to the Board that some method may be devised for conducting its business in a quieter and more orderly and rational manner. Sensible men could surely effect their purchases and sales without such a confusion of tongues.

"THE SITUATION OF CHICAGO," WATERWORKS AND PARKS

The only defect in the situation of Chicago is its flatness. It is built on a dead level, very slightly above that of the Lake, and from this cause great difficulty was for long experienced with the drainage, which went into the Chicago River, and made it one of the foulest streams in the world. Very remarkably, however, the watershed between North and South is only about twelve miles from Chicago on the Alton Road, and it was ascertained that by cutting down the Illinois and Michigan Canal a depth of about $8\frac{1}{2}$ feet for twenty-six miles a current of water could be carried from Lake Michigan which would ultimately flow into the Mississippi. The cutting, having to be made to a great extent through rock, was of great difficulty, and the people of Chicago had almost despaired of success, when unexpectedly one fine morning the inky river was seen to flow with clear water from the Lake—the deepening of the Canal had been completed, and Chicago was being drained into the Gulf of Mexico! So far as water supply and drainage are concerned, Chicago has achieved wonders, and she is now carrying out some splendid conceptions in the way of Boulevards and Parks. The whole city will soon be environed by Parks of great extent and beauty, approached by Boulevards from all parts of the town. The growth of the trees is so rapid that already these are making considerable appearance. Mr. L. B. Sidway, a member of the South Park Commission, drove us through the South Park,[5] and it was surprising to see what has been accomplished—the extent and variety of the plantations, and the fine specimens of shrubs and flowers. The Managers of Kew Gardens have sent for a large number of seeds out of 2800 varieties already supplied by this Park, of which Professor Babcock[6] is the very able Superintendent.

I attended the First and Second Presbyterian Churches and visited Mr. Moody's Tabernacle during the Sunday I spent in Chicago; and I was specially impressed by the instant readiness, not merely of gentlemen with leisure, but of active business men, to give themselves great trouble in showing whatever the city contains, and furnishing whatever information can be procured respecting it.

[5] South Park was created in 1869. It is now a part of Washington Park.

[6] Professor H. H. Babcock, prominent botanist and member of the Chicago Academy of Science. He served as president of the Academy 1880–81.

LADY DUFFUS HARDY[1]

LADY DUFFUS HARDY (née Mary Anne MacDowell), only and posthumous child of T. Charles MacDowell of Fitzroy, was born in London, February 19, 1824. In January, 1850, she was married to Thomas Duffus Hardy, who was knighted in 1869. Before she was thirty years of age, Lady Hardy published her first novel, *Savile House*, in two volumes. In 1857 she brought out her second, *The Artist's Family*. Both of these were printed under the pseudonym of Addlestone Hill. She continued publishing at intervals of a few years, most of her novels running into many pages. She was the author of *The Two Catherines* (anonymous), *A Casual Acquaintance*, *A Hero's Work*, *Paul Wynter's Sacrifice*, *Daisy Nichol*, *A Woman's Triumph*, *Lizzie*, *Madge*, *Beryl Fortescue*, *In Sight of Land*, *A Dangerous Experiment*, *A Buried Sin*, *War Notes from the Crimea*, *The Unknown God*, and many short stories and articles written for various English magazines. A civil pension of £100 was granted her in 1879 and another of £55 in 1881.

Lady Hardy traveled extensively. In 1879–80 she came to the United States and published two books about her American tour: *Through Cities and Prairie Lands* (1881) and *Down South* (1883). She visited nearly every state of the Union, going west by the northern route through the Mormon settlement to San Francisco. After spending many weeks in California, she returned through the Southwest to Kansas and St. Louis, finishing her trip in Washington, Baltimore, and New York. The romantic West of the late seventies and early eighties appealed to her, and most of *Through Cities and Prairie Lands* relates to that section rather than to the eastern part of the United States. Her death occurred in London, May 19, 1891.

-»-«-

GRAND AND STATELY CHICAGO

We reached Chicago that evening, and were most kindly received at the Palmer House, a palatial hotel built by Mr. Potter Palmer[2] for the luxurious entertainment of the travelling public.

[1] Lady Duffus Hardy, *Through Cities and Prairie Lands* (New York: R. Worthington, 1881), pp. 75–79. Reprinted by permission of Chapman and Hall, Ltd. (successors of R. Worthington).

[2] Potter Palmer was born in Albany County, New York, in 1826. In 1852 he visited Chicago and was so impressed with the future possibilities of the city that he sold his store in Lockport, New York, and made Chicago his home. He established a retail merchandise store in his new home, and by the time he was forty he was world-famous and one of the richest men in the West. In the sixties his health broke, and he sold his

It is more like an elegantly appointed home than a mere resting-place for such birds of passage as ourselves. Each suite of apartments is perfect in itself, with a bath-room and every convenience attached, richly curtained and carpeted, with luxurious lounges and the easiest of easy-chairs; once settled in their soft embrace it is difficult to tear one's self from their downy arms. Being cosily installed beneath this hospitable roof, one feels, like "poor *Joe*," disinclined to "move on." The spacious halls and corridors are furnished in accord with other portions of the house. The walls are lined with *fauteuils*, sofas, and all the appointments of a handsome drawing-room.

As soon as we had enjoyed the luxury of a bath (and after two days' dusty travel, what a luxury that is!), we went to the dining saloon in search of our dinner, and found an unusually good one, excellently served and abundantly supplied. If we had staid for a month and eaten *pro rata* as at our first meal, we should have ruined our digestive organs and rejoiced in internal discords for ever afterwards. Our *ménu* was illustrated. On one side was depicted a pigstye and a hovel—"Chicago forty years ago." On the other was a wonderful city—"The Chicago of to-day."

Knowing of the fiery scourge which a few years ago had marred and scarred the beauty of that fair city, we expected to find traces of ugliness and deformity everywhere, crippled buildings, and lame, limping streets running along in a forlorn crooked condition, waiting for time to restore their old vigour and build up their beauty anew. But, Phoenixlike, the city has risen up out of its own ashes, grander and statelier than ever. On the outskirts the line of fire can still be traced; gaunt skeletons of houses still remain to point the way it took, and more than one ruined church, stripped of its altar and regal signs of grace, stands blind and helpless in the sunshine; while in the suburbs picturesque shells of once beautiful homes greet us here and there. But once

---

interests to Marshall Field and Levi Z. Leiter. He spent the next few years in Europe On his return to Chicago he entered the real estate field. The fire of 1871 destroyed thirty-two of his buildings, but it laid the foundation of a new fortune. He developed State Street and made it the present street of department stores. The first Palmer House was built in 1869–70. It was destroyed by the Fire, and he opened the second Palmer House on the same location in 1873. Potter Palmer died in 1902.

within the boundaries of the city we lose all traces of the conflagration. The business streets are lined with handsome massive houses, some six or seven stories high, substantially built,
sometimes of red brick with stone copings and elaborate carving, while others are built of that creamy stone which reminds
one of the Paris boulevards. No wooden buildings are allowed
to be erected within a certain distance of the city. The fashionable trading localities are State and Clark streets, though there
are several others which are well patronized by a less fashionable
multitude. On either side are large handsome drygoods, millinery, and other stores of all possible descriptions, the windows
being arranged with a tasteful elaboration that might stand side
by side with our fashionable establishments at home, and lose
nothing by the comparison. The different banks, churches, and
municipal buildings which had been destroyed by the great fire-
fiend are all re-erected in a substantial style, though with varying degrees of eccentric architecture. The new water-works,
situated at the northern end of the city, are the most beautiful
illustrations of the vagaries of the architectural brain. It must
have wandered into dreamland and caught up its prevailing
idea, for never were so many cupolas and buttresses, pinnacles
and towers, grouped together on one spot; none but a true artist
could have arranged them into so harmonious a whole, and produced from a combination of such opposite forms so imposing
an effect.

A painter may indulge in all the eccentricities of his genius,
may derive his inspiration from what source he will, there is no
restriction to the realms of his art. He may choose his subject,
and illustrate it according to his own fancy; he may wander far
from the realms of art, and give to the wood a "harmony in blue
and gold," or a "study in brass and impudence," and his productions are called "original." But if an architect outruns the
bounds prescribed by the five orders of architecture, and dares
to give play to his fancy, his work is stigmatized as "bastard
art," and he is considered a fit subject for a lunatic asylum. On
our drives through and about the city we were struck by the
dearth of trees. There were no signs of pleasant green shade any

where; they had all been destroyed by the great fire. Streets and avenues had been rebuilt, and they were replanting as fast as they could; but nature will not be hurried in her work, her children must have time to grow, and though her fairest fruits are sometimes forced into an unnatural growth, she revenges herself by robbing them of their sweetest flavour.

Along the shore road we drove to the park at the northern end of the city,[3] which gives promise of being a delightful promenade and recreation ground; but it is at present only a park in embryo, though it is growing rapidly. Flowers and shrubs are being planted, grassy knolls built up, and paths and winding ways cut and gravelled. In the course of a few years it will have outgrown its present ragged state, and have bloomed into a delightful pleasure-ground, with the whispering waves of that inland sea, Lake Michigan, kissing with soft foam lips its grassy slopes, while great ships go sailing and steamers ride royally on the breast of the wide waters on one side, and the great city, with its hubbub, bustle and roar, lies upon the other. Chicago is indeed a great city, full of energy and enterprise. Signs of its hidden strength and powers of progress greet us everywhere; but at present it appears to be wholly devoted to money-making. Art, science (except such science as serves its purpose), and literature are in a languishing state. But it is young yet. Perhaps when it is fully developed, and grown strong in muscle, and bone, and brain, the soul may be born to glorify the commonplace, and stir the latent genius of this city into life and beauty.

With some regret we sit down to our last dinner in this bright, bustling city, and go to bed to dream of tomorrow, for in the morning we begin our journey west, and the magnet which has drawn us across the sea lies at the Golden Gate.

3 Lincoln Park, laid out in 1865 and officially created by act of legislature in 1869.

-»»-«««-

ANONYMOUS[1]

THE following two articles appeared in a series of descriptions of the United States in *The* (London) *Times* under the title of "A Visit to the States." They were published anonymously, probably written by a correspondent traveling in this country. The first of the articles—dealing with New York—was in the issue of August 29, 1887. Other sketches came at various intervals during the rest of the year and part of the following. The second selection, produced in this volume, appeared as Article XXX, "A Visit to the States," October 24, 1887, beginning on page 237 of this volume.

-»»-«««-

PROMINENT CHARACTERISTICS OF CHICAGO

An overhanging pall of smoke; streets filled with busy, quick-moving people; a vast aggregation of railways, vessels, and traffic of all kinds; and a paramount devotion to the Almighty Dollar are the prominent characteristics of Chicago. The name of this wonderful city is of Indian origin, a probable corruption of "Cheecaqua," said to have been the title of a dynasty of Indian chiefs who ruled the country west and south of Lake Michigan. This was also a word applied in the Indian dialect to the wild onion that grew luxuriantly on the banks of the river; and they also gave a similar name to the thunder, which they believed to be the voice of the Great Spirit, and to the odoriferous animal that abounded in the neighbourhood which to the white man was known as the "polecat." These are seeming incongruities of use for the same word, but it has been suggested that all may be harmonized if Chicago is to be interpreted as meaning "strong." The Indians were usually not over supplied with words, and they generally selected the most prominent attribute in naming an object. All these various things in one way or another are undoubtedly "strong," and it is equally evident that a prodigious amount of strength exists in Chicago. . . . .

[1] *The* (London) *Times*, "A Visit to the States," Article XXIX (London, October 21, 1887); "A Visit to the States," Article XXX (London, October 24, 1887). Reprinted by permission of *The* (London) *Times*.

The surrounding prairie for miles is crossed in all directions by railways and a large portion of the city and its suburbs is made up of series of huge stations, car yards, elevators, cattle pens, and storehouses, that almost overwhelm the visitor with the prodigious scale of their elaborate perplexity. The profits of their traffic have piled up grand buildings on the broad streets in the business section, and the long rows of dwelling-houses are running out for miles over the prairie. Chicago is the world's greatest corn, cattle, and timber market, and this energetic and enterprising city contains probably more of the speculative, extravagant, shrewd, and reckless elements of American humanity than even New York. It has attracted people of all nationalities, and they flourish in native luxuriance. The Irish Fenian and the Continental anarchist are in full development, but are under control. Theatres and concert gardens are in successful operation on Sunday, and the necessity of the over-strained people for constant artificial stimulation is probably the reason why Chicago seems to contain a much more liberal supply of spirit and beer shops than almost any other community. Everything is allowed to go on without much hindrance and thus the place grows unstinted. Chicago also has an advantage in commanding the entrance to the great North-West, nearly all the routes to that vast region of limitless future expansion leading through Chicago, and much of its financial and business interests being controlled by the Chicagoans. The people are very proud of their city's amazing progress, but are generally so engrossed in pushing their business enterprises and in piling up fortunes that there is little time to think of much else.

A CITY REBUILT

The ruins of the great fire have been obliterated by the new and magnificent city that has risen on the shore of the lake, with better buildings, constructed of imperishable materials, replacing the original structures, largely wooden houses, which then fed the flames. Down by the lake side there now stands on guard the solid stone tower of the waterworks, rising 160 ft., at which to get the proper head of water, and over the top four enormous pumping engines force 75 millions of gallons daily. Far out on the clear green surface of the lake is seen the "Crib," with its surmounting lighthouse whence the water supply is drawn into the tunnel that feeds the pumps. From the top of this tall tower there is a grand view over lake and city, the former clear and beautiful as far as eye can see—a strong easterly wind dashing its breakers against the shore, the latter largely enshrouded by the enveloping pall of smoke and puffing steam jets that rise above the buildings. To the north, on the edge of the lake, is the distant green foliage of the Lincoln-park. This is the nearest of the extensive series of beautiful parks, with connecting boulevards, which enclose the city, stretching completely around from the shore above to the shore below. That somebody in Chicago has found time to design these parks and put such beneficent work into execution has been an admirable thing for the people. The broad expanse of prairie was low, level, and treeless originally, but art has planted abundant foliage, with little lakes and miniature hills, ornamented by beautiful flower gardens and shrubbery, large sums being spent upon their care and steady development. The Drexel Boulevard, one of the routes to the South-park, 200 ft. wide, is the finest of the connecting roadways, and is destined to be among the celebrated avenues of America. This broad parkway has a magnificent drive on either side of a central walk for pedestrians, the latter winding among picturesque gardens, and the whole well shaded, though the trees are yet young. The finest residential street of the city is Michigan-avenue. This is a boulevard bordering the lake, and fronted by a park stretching down to the water, where it has an edge of railways, with their rushing trains, like everything else here. Further south grand residences are upon both sides of this avenue, which is the popular driveway. It is the "Rotten-Row" of Chicago, where all the elaborate turnouts go for an airing.

TRADE, TRAFFIC, AND BUILDING

The river of Chicago, like its railways, testifies to the pressure of trade. A multitude of swinging bridges cross over it, and two tunnels are carried under, to accommodate the traffic. The huge grain elevators are stationed along its banks, and vessels lie alongside, with streams of corn pouring in. A few weeks ago, when the elevators were all filled and more storage room was needed, another was built in a hurry, being completed within two weeks, and big enough to hold 400,000 bushels. The wide streets, generally 80 ft., facilitate the enormous amount of moving traffic in the business section, though at times they are almost uncomfortably crowded. While the level of the surface near the lake is but 14 ft., and is in no case elsewhere higher than 30 ft., above the water, the drainage is tolerably well protected. The city has some fine suburban residential sections fronting the lake and adjacent to the parks and boulevards, and already many of the wealthy townsfolk have built themselves palaces to live in. It also has magnificent public buildings erected since the great fire for the purposes of the National and City Governments. Its grand business structures soar skyward, as in New York, and are filled to the topmost story with offices, where the trade of the town is transacted, and the hundreds of visitors and customers are swiftly carried to the upper regions by the ever-moving lifts. This trade of Chicago is something almost astonishing to contemplate. The great "North Woods" that cover Michigan, Wisconsin, and Minnesota, and spread far over the Canadian border, get most of their outlet through Chicago, and the timber yards are a considerable part of the city's surface, there appearing to be enough boards and planks piled up to supply a half-dozen States. The 25 elevators will hold as many millions of bushels of corn, and vast quantities are also stored in railway cars or aboard vessels. It is not infrequent that one-third of the entire "visible supply" of wheat and maize in the United States is stored at one time in Chicago, while the extensive western regions, which are tributary, will be ready when required to pour in as much more. . . . .

THE UNION STOCK YARDS

Vast as the breadstuffs movement may be, the trades for which Chicago is equally noted are in hogs and cattle. The hog is regarded as the most compact form in which the Indian corn crop of the States can be transported to market. Hence the corn is fed to the hog on the farm, and he is sent to Chicago as a package provided by nature for its utilization. A ride out among the rows of wooden buildings still existing by the square mile in the southern suburbs, as if to tempt another great fire, leads to the "Union Stock Yard." The extensive enclosure is entered through a modest gray sandstone, turreted gateway, surmounted by a carved bull's head, and the cattle pens stretch far away on either hand. This stock yard is a town of itself, with its own banks and hotel, "Board of Trade," post-office, town-hall, and special fire department, the latter being a necessity, as it occasionally has very destructive fires. About £400,000 has been invested in this undertaking, which covers nearly a square mile, a large part of it being cattle pens, through which lead eight miles of streets, and having sufficient capacity to accommodate 200,000 animals at one time. The scene in this place is most animated, the cattle men riding about on horseback, driving their herds, while adjacent are the immense "packing houses" that prepare the pork and beef for market. During the past twelve-month these establishments have killed and packed 4,426,000 hogs and 1,608,000 beeves, their product going to all parts of the world. This represents a very large proportion of the whole number of these animals in the States which are fatted to kill, for at the opening of this year it was estimated there were in the country, of hogs of all ages, 44 millions, and of cattle, exclusive of milch cows, 33 millions. The products of the packing reach enormous figures, being no less than 1,055 millions of pounds of pork and lard for the year and 573 millions of pounds of dressed beef. A very large proportion of the pork and lard, 810 million of pounds, were exported beyond the States, and of this 90 per cent went to the United Kingdom. The packers say their hog trade does not increase, but their beef trade grows at an extraordinary rate. The "Chicago dressed beef," sent in "refrigerator cars" all over the country, is largely supplanting the butcher's services for the dead meat markets of the States, and much of it, packed in refrigerator apartments on steamers, also goes abroad. The railways all have extensive terminals in connexion with this great stock yard and the packing houses, bringing in the live animals by hundreds of car loads and taking away the pork and lard and the dressed beef in long lines of refrigerator cars, the invention of ingenious methods for "cold storage" having been a fruitful subject of Yankee genius.

In converting the hogs and cattle into pork and beef, the chief establishment is Armour's, which does about one-fourth of this business in Chicago. The works connected with the stock yard cover about 30 acres, and of this 20 acres are used for "chill-rooms" and storage, for all the fresh meats are kept at a temperature of about 35 deg. to 40 deg., and the pork is also cooled for about 48 hours after killing before being packed. In the various buildings there are 80 acres of floor space. An army of 5,000 persons is employed in these works, which turn out all kinds of meats—green, salted, pickled, spiced, smoked, and canned. During the twelvemonth the Armour establishment slaughtered 1,113,000 hogs, 380,000 beeves, and 86,000 sheep, and the sales of their products reached over 10 millions sterling, the goods, weighing about 331 millions of pounds, being sent to market in various parts of the world. The processes of slaughtering and dressing are reduced to the most expeditious and economic principles, and in many respects have become a fine art. To kill and prepare 12 to 15 hundred beeves and eight to ten thousand hogs in one day requires a complete system. The steers are driven into long pens, and an expert rifleman, walking upon a platform over them, discharges a rifle shot into the brain just behind the horns. The killing is instantaneous, the steer, without even a groan, falling like a log. The animal is then drawn forward from the pen, the hide quickly removed, and the carcass prepared and cut up ready for storage in the "chill rooms" and subsequent shipment. These beef-killing processes are speedily performed, but the science most thoroughly developed is the hog-killing. . . . .

CHICAGO BOARD OF TRADE

For her grain and provision trades, of which Chicago is very proud, she has recently erected a grand monument and abiding

place at a cost of more than £200,000. At the head of La Salle-
street, and making a fitting close to the view along that highway
of imposing business structures stands the tall building with its
surmounting clock and spire of the Chicago "Board of Trade."
It is one of the elaborate architectural ornaments of the city;
and the animated and, at times, most exciting business done
within, marks the nervous beating of the pulse of this metropolis
of corn and meat. The interior is a magnificent hall, lighted by
high-reaching windows and surmounted by a central skylight
nearly a hundred feet above the floor. Grand columns adorn
the sides, and the elaborate frescoes above are in keeping with
the artistic decoration of the place. Upon the broad floor, between 9 and 1 o'clock each day, assemble the wheat and corn
and pork and lard and railway kings of the town, in a typical
American life scene of concentrated and boiling energy, feeding
the furnace in which Chicago's high-pressure enterprise glows
and roars. These gladiators have their respective "pits," or
amphitheatres, upon the floor, so that they gather in three great
groups, around which hundreds run and jostle, the scene from
the overlooking gallery, as the crowds sway and squirm, and
with their calls and shouting make a deafening uproar, being a
veritable Bedlam. These "pits" deal respectively in wheat,
Indian corn, and pork; while in a fourth space, with extensive
enclosed desks, a regiment of telegraph operators work with
nimble fingers to send instant reports of the doings to the outer
world. High upon the side of the grand hall, in full view of all,
are hung three huge dials, whose moving hands keep record of
the momentary changes in prices made by the noisy and excited
throngs in the "pits," thus giving notice of the ruling figures
for the next month's "options" for wheat, Indian corn, and
"short ribs," for these exciting transactions are largely speculative. A bordering fringe of tables for samples, or for writing,
and an array of large blackboards, bearing the figures of market
quotations elsewhere, enclose this animated scene. This Chicago
"Board of Trade" has witnessed some of the wildest excitements
of America, as its shouting and at times almost frenzied groups
of speculative dealers in the "pits" may make or break a "cor-

ner;" and here in fitful fever beats the pulse of the great city whose exalted province it is to feed the world.

INFLUENTIAL MEN OF CHICAGO

There is a general belief among the people of Chicago, which is shared by a large body of thoughtful Americans, that the rapidly-growing city upon the bank of Lake Michigan is destined to become ultimately the largest and most important in the States. Its unrivalled advantages and unexampled expansion would seem to foreshadow this, for it pushes ahead with boundless energy, and is having an amazing accumulation of wealth and an astonishing development in all directions. Already a movement has been started for bringing under the Chicago municipal government the various suburban towns, which will increase the population beyond one million and make it probably the second American city. The amount of business done in Chicago is second only to that of New York. It steadily attracts the shrewdest men of the great West to take part in its vast and profitable enterprises, and it is in such a complete manner the depôt and store-house for the products and the supplier for the enormous prairie region around it, and for the great North-West and the country as far out as the Rockies and the Pacific, that other Western cities cannot displace or even hope to rival it. Yet at the same time so youthful is this municipal giant and so recent has been its marvellous growth that scarcely any of the leading spirits who are making it what it is were born here. Almost all came to Chicago after attaining manhood, being attracted by its business advantages. The New England race and the New York Yankee, who is descended from New England stock, have been the chief builders and developers of Chicago, and are to-day its most prominent men in public spirit, in trade, and in wealth.

PHILIP D. ARMOUR[2]

I have already referred to the Chicago trade in meats and provisions, and in this connexion described the extensive opera-

[2] Philip D. Armour (May 16, 1832—January 6, 1901). In 1863 he went to Milwaukee and joined the firm of Plankington, Armour and Company, meat-packers and grain-

tions of the Armour packing houses. This vast establishment conducts the largest annual business among the great houses of America. Philip D. Armour, the head of this enterprise of beef and pork, is in middle life, and was of New York origin, a bluff, hearty, and vigorous, hard-headed business man. Whether it be in meats or in wheat, or in railways, or in anything else, he is fully imbued with the expansive and versatile trading spirit of Chicago, and is always ready for any operation, no matter how extensive or intricate, that presents fair opportunity for profit.

MARSHALL FIELD[3]

Chicago also possesses the greatest merchant of America. It might be supposed that New York would be the city most likely to have the largest purely mercantile establishment in the United States, and such was the case in the last generation, when Alexander T. Stewart was the leader of trade there. But changed methods have come with newer people, and the western world of America is advancing. Chicago used to be in debt to New York and dependent for supplies. Now the Lake City is not only out of debt but is herself very rich and a creditor of the country further westward. Her merchant princes long since cut themselves loose from New York intermediaries and are now buyers at first hands, while they have a boundless and rapidly-growing region to supply. The leading Chicago merchant, whose house conducts the largest purely mercantile business in the country, if not in the world, today, is Marshall Field, a modest man, of New England birth, who is also the wealthiest citizen of

dealers. In 1875 he came to Chicago to assume headship of Armour and Company, a firm dealing in meats and grain, established by his brother H. O. Armour some years before. P. D. Armour was the first packer in the modern sense of the word, and his products were known all over the world. Fresh beef was not at first a specialty of his, but he began dressing fresh beef when the use of refrigeration in transportation began to be used.

[3] Marshall Field (August 18, 1834—January 16, 1906) came to Chicago in 1856. He began work as a clerk for Cooley, Wadsworth and Company. In 1861 he was made general manager, and in 1862 he was admitted to partnership. The firm's name was now called Cooley, Farwell, and Company. In 1864, when Leiter was admitted, the name became Farwell, Field and Company. The next year Potter Palmer offered his business for sale to Field and Leiter, and they withdrew from Farwell, Field and Company, to take over the new store. In time Field developed it to the largest department store in the world. Field gave ten acres on the Midway for a campus for the new University of Chicago, and also gave several millions for the establishment of the Field Museum.

Chicago and of the entire State of Illinois, having a fortune estimated at £4,000,000, and being the head of a great dry goods and miscellaneous establishment, with annual sales exceeding £6,000,000. His extensive retail mart is in State-street, and in another part of the city an entire block is occupied by the magnificent building wherein is conducted his wholesale trade, extending to the remotest parts of the country. Marshall Field is regarded as the leading Chicago merchant of the present very active generation.

FARWELLS[4]

There are scores of other great Chicago merchants whose stores are architecturally imposing piles that cover acres, and whose wealth and trade have also made them multi-millionaires. Prominent among them are the Farwells, whose house is probably second only to that of Field. They are in the front rank of the builders and developers of the great city, and one of the brothers, Charles B. Farwell, is United States Senator from Illinois. These huge store buildings are as impressive in Chicago as they are in New York. Many blocks are occupied by them in the business section—through which runs the chief highway— State-street.

POTTER PALMER (PALMER HOUSE)

The visitor to Chicago is always impressed with this magnificent highway, 125 feet wide, lined with splendid buildings and crowded with busy people. This famous street owes much of its development to another Chicagoan, of New York birth—Potter

---

[4] John V. Farwell (July 29, 1825—August 20, 1908) came to Chicago in 1845. Five years later he was admitted into partnership in Cooley, Wadsworth and Phelps. In 1862, when Marshall Field became a partner, the name was changed to Cooley, Farwell and Company, and in 1864 to Farwell, Field and Company. After the withdrawal of Field and Leiter, the firm's name became John V. Farwell and Company. J. V. Farwell was called the "Christian storekeeper" and was a close friend of D. L. Moody. It was through the latter's influence that J. V. Farwell gave the land for the first Y.M.C.A. building in Chicago, and incidentally the first Y.M.C.A. building in the United States.

Charles B. Farwell (July 1, 1823—September 23, 1903), brother of John V., came to Chicago the year before John. He engaged in real estate and financiering. In 1849 he was corresponding clerk for the George Smith banking house. In 1864 he purchased an interest in his brother's store and became general manager. He went to Congress in 1870 and was re-elected in 1872, 1874, and, on his return to politics, again in 1880. In 1887 he was elected to the United States Senate to fill the vacancy caused by the death of John A. Logan. He was returned again in 1891.

Palmer—who originally bought a frontage of one mile upon this street, extended and widened it, embellishing it with splendid structures that made it the leading street. Palmer, who was a great sufferer by the Chicago fire, is best known to the public to-day on account of his hotel, the "Palmer House," which is said to be the most profitable hotel property in the United States, the country of big hotels, and is a remarkable type of the American caravanserai. Upon Mr. Palmer's splendid fireproof structure £500,000 has been expended in building and decoration. The word "hotel" in its broadest sense in the States includes much more than merely food and lodging. It means, in addition, a sort of public club. There are extensive parlours, reception, reading, writing, and smoking rooms, lifts constantly running, electric call bells and lights, with complete attendance and messenger service; billiards, pool room, ten-pin alley, most gorgeous bar and barber's shop, each having a fortune invested in their decoration; the eating rooms that keep going from before daylight till past midnight without interruption; the restaurant, wine, and coffee rooms; an aggregation of all kinds of shops where everything needed can be bought without going out of doors; news-stand, railway booking office, and luggage "checking" department; boots, coat and parcel rooms, hotel post-office, telegraph station, and general telephone. Then there is the hotel "office," a most surprising bureau of odds and ends, where one can get pens, ink, paper, and envelopes, cards, telegrams, and letters, cigar lights, matches, and toothpicks, can consult directories, and ask all sorts of questions about all kinds of things, and have them intelligently answered by that most omniscient being, the "hotel clerk." Telegraphic stock and market "tickers" and general news bulletins are conveniently placed to report the latest news, and particularly the speculative market quotations, to gratify the thirst the guests have for such knowledge, while a broker's office and special stock and grain exchange are invitingly open, so that an immediate "flyer" in corn or pork or stocks may be taken. The capacious hall in front of the office is a news exchange for the busy town, who bustle and talk, and give, in the swarming crowd who throng there, an active business air. Such is the generous aggregation given in a great hotel for "five dollars a day on the American plan," and the visitor surely gets his money's worth.

BANKERS

The business activity of Chicago is such that its leading bank, the "First National," at times does a larger banking movement than any of the greatest banks in New York. Another of the prominent men in moving the industries of Chicago is L. J. Gage, the banker, who manages this bank in its larger building on Dearborn-street, and has a force of 150 clerks to keep the accounts.[5] With £600,000 capital and £200,000 surplus this bank has sometimes nearly £5,000,000 deposits and will have £12,000,000 clearings in a week, besides a vast exchange business with New York and London, based upon the immense eastward movement of corn and provisions on through bills of lading. It takes a clear head and resolute will, with great banking ability, to manage the exchanges and credits of such a place as Chicago; but this bright-eyed banker inherits from his Yankee ancestry the skill that for 20 years has controlled the banking policy of the great city, and done very much to assist its marvellous growth.

GEORGE M. PULLMAN[6]

Probably the best known Chicago name throughout America, as well as abroad, is that of Pullman, which has become a word

[5] Lyman J. Gage (June 28, 1836—January 26, 1927), financier, came to Chicago in 1855 hoping to enter a banking house. His first job, however, was in a planing mill. In 1858 he got a clerkship in the Merchants' Savings Loan and Trust Company. In 1868 he was made cashier of the First National Bank of Chicago, and by 1875 was one of the foremost western bankers. In 1882 he was made vice-president and general manager and in 1891 became president. McKinley appointed him Secretary of the Treasury in 1897, and he served until 1902. He retired from active business in 1906 and moved to California.

[6] George M. Pullman (March 3, 1831—October 19, 1897), came to Chicago in 1856 and his first work consisted of raising several buildings, among them the Tremont House, to the new grade level. In 1859 he remodeled two sleeping cars; and, although they did not compare with his later palace cars, they were a big improvement over the old sleepers. He moved to Colorado on a mining venture but returned in 1863. In 1864–65 he built the first palace car. In 1867 the Pullman Palace Car Company was incorporated, and in the 1880's he built Pullman City and moved all of his shops there. He enlarged his business so as to include freight cars, street cars, and other types of cars. His was soon the largest car-building company in the country.

synonymous with all the phrases that describe the completest comfort in railway travelling. George M. Pullman came from New York, and was originally a cabinetmaker, his first services to Chicago being in devising ingenious methods for raising its buildings, some 30 years ago, when it was decided to place the city upon a higher level in order to secure drainage. He raised the buildings by putting hundreds of jackscrews under them, while trade went on without interruption during the process. In those days the appliances for securing the comfort of the railway traveller on long journeys were in their infancy, and the first rude attempts were being made to devise a sleeping coach. Mr. Pullman on one occasion went into a sleeping coach upon a night train and laid down upon the berth, but did not sleep. He was stretched out upon the vibrating couch for about two hours with eyes wide open, and in that time had struck upon a new idea. When he arose and left the train he had determined to develop from his brief experience of that inchoate sleeping berth a plan that was destined to expand into the completest and most comfortable coach for the traveller, either awake or sleeping—a home upon wheels. During several years he revolved the project in his fertile brain, and his first experiment was made in 1859, when he turned two ordinary passenger coaches into sleeping cars, and placed them upon the night trains of the Chicago and Alton Railway between Chicago and St. Louis, one running each way. He charged 2s. for a berth, and the first night his receipts were 8s. When Pullman settled in Chicago permanently and began this business, he thought himself well-to-do in the world with a capital all told of £1,600.

The development of the sleeping-car project, which is the history of a busy life, shows the possibilities of the Great West, both in the effect of the growth of a city and a business in the expansion of a man, and the influence of a man in building a city. It was not until he had run his experimental coaches for about five years that Mr. Pullman felt able to carry out his plan as he had evolved it in his brain, and he then built his ideal sleeping coach. This took a year to construct, in 1864-65, and was built in a rude shed in a railway car-yard in Chicago. He

called it the "Pioneer," and it cost £3,600, and in it he developed
his idea of harmony, which combined comfort and luxury with
attractiveness of decoration, and when finished it was regarded
as a marvel far in advance of any railway coach construction of
that day. This first coach is still doing daily and profitable duty
upon the Pullman lines. But when it was completed, although
its fame travelled far, yet it was so heavy, so wide, and so high
that no railway could undertake to run it, as it necessitated elevating bridges and cutting off station platforms. He had a
famous white elephant on his hands, but he bided his time.
Suddenly President Lincoln's assassination profoundly shocked
the country, and the funeral, with its escort of mourning states-
men, was progressing from Washington to Chicago on the way
to the grave at Lincoln's home in Springfield, the capital of
Illinois. The nation was watching its progress, and the railways
transporting the *cortège* were doing their best. The railway between Chicago and Springfield asked for the use of the "Pioneer" in the funeral train. They sent out gangs of men, and cut
off the station platforms, elevated the bridges, and took several
days to prepare the line, so that the coach could go over it, and
Pullman's dream at last was realized. His coach of the future
carried the dead president to his grave, and became known
throughout the world. A few weeks later General Grant, the
conqueror of the rebellion, had a triumphal progress from the
camp to his Illinois home. Five days were spent in clearing the
railway between Detroit and Galena, where he lived, and the
"Pioneer" carried the General over that line.

Mr. Pullman then had the future in his own hands. The public had seen his coach, and the most distinguished men had
been riding in it. They would be satisfied with nothing inferior,
and the railways began demanding the coaches. The lines leading out of Chicago used them, and before long they were put
upon the Great Pacific and the Pennsylvania lines. The result
is "Pullman's Palace Car Company," which to-day has invested
in its works and coaches nearly six millions sterling, and is besides the greatest railway car-builder in America, furnishing all
kinds of equipment to railways from Canada to Texas, and hav-

ing 1,400 of its own palace coaches running, to carry the first-class passengers upon 80,000 miles of American railways, stretching from the Atlantic to the Pacific, and from Halifax and Quebec to San Francisco and the city of Mexico, as well as much more in Europe. These coaches run into every city in the states, and cover nearly all the available mileage, the Wagner coaches upon the Vanderbilt lines being largely constructed after the Pullman style, and many of them built at the Pullman shops. So prosperous is the company that it regularly makes eight per cent. dividends, has a very large surplus, and a yearly income of about £1,200,000 from these coaches. Besides building equipment for railways amounting to £2,000,000 annually, and running its own coaches, the Pullman Company also provides for excursion parties. It often happens that a congenial party will charter a coach or a train and go about the country sight-seeing for weeks and months. They have no anxiety or trouble about their home upon wheels, the Pullman people moving them and providing for all their wants. One of the prominent excursion agents of the States who cater for the best class of sight-seeing travellers—Raymond and Whitcomb—are this year paying the Pullman Company about £16,000 rental for the use of their coaches, the hiring being at the rate of £7 a piece per day. I have already described the "Chicago Limited Express." Mr. Pullman is now preparing to equip a transcontinental train of similar character and appointments, which will be run between New York and San Francisco, a weekly train each way, reducing the time of transit across the Continent, now occupying six days, to within 100 hours. He is also preparing to place a train of the vestibule coaches upon the London, Brighton, and South Coast Railway between London and Brighton. This vestibule buffer, which has already been described, is regarded as a sure preventive of "telescoping" in cases of collision.

Another Pullman enterprise will have great interest for English readers. The company so rapidly expanded into enormous business that a few years ago it became necessary to provide permanent construction shops for its works near Chicago. The result has been the building of the model manufacturing town of

Pullman, about 10 miles south of Chicago, and practically a suburb of the great city. It has been all made within seven years, upon a tract of land that had no inhabitants as late as 1880. Lake Calumet, an oval sheet of water, about three miles long, is situated a short distance inland from Lake Michigan, and the Illinois Central Railway passes south from Chicago on its long journey to the Gulf of Mexico, a short distance to the westward. A tract of nearly 4,000 acres was acquired with this railway running down its centre, and stretching along the narrow strip between the lake and the railway is the town of Pullman, spreading for almost two miles, with its shops and parks, its ornamental grounds and comfortable homes for the operatives. Riding down the line of the Illinois Central, over the flat land and among the succession of villages which have grown up between Chicago and Pullman, the visitor alights at one of the best station buildings seen on the line, and finds the new settlement is in front of him, spreading far on either hand. There is a fine hotel, which is a model of artistic design and worthy of the largest city; and across the park, with its ornamental grounds and lake, are seen the extensive shops, with their clock spire and huge water tower rising high above. The Pullman town, like the Pullman coach, is a model of neatness and elegance. Flower beds and lawns front the shops, and the solid walls enclosing the grounds give them quite an English air. Stretching across the town from the station to Lake Calumet is a wide boulevard, shaded by rows of elms—the One Hundred and Eleventh Street in continuation of the numerical order of South Chicago—and this divides the workshops from the residential portion. Five noble avenues stretch southward from it, each appropriately named after an inventor closely identified with the varied industries of the place—Stephenson, Watt, Fulton, Morse, and Pullman—and upon these the cottages of the operatives are built.

No place in the United States has attracted more attention or been more closely watched than Pullman. Like the sleeping coach, the town is the development of an idea, worked out to harmonious and successful results by its inventor. It is the extension of the broadest philanthropy to the working man, based upon the strictest business principles. There has been £1,500,000 invested in carrying out this idea, and every penny is at the same time made to return an income. The operatives in the first instance are employed upon wages paid every fortnight, and their earnings are said to exceed those of any other community of working people in the United States, averaging per capita (exclusive of the higher pay of the general management) £118 per annum. There are some 4,000 operatives, and the pay disbursed in money every fortnight is about £20,000. The company, in order to secure the best return, seeks to provide in the completest possible way for its people. Their workshops, covering about 83 acres, are constructed in the most airy and healthful manner, and upon these about £750,000 has been expended. An equal amount has been invested in building the residential portion of the town, the public edifices, and in the public works and decoration of the place. Everything is constructed of bricks made upon the estate, and of clay taken from the bed of Lake Calumet. The first investment was in a complete sewerage system, the sewage being all pumped up and sent away by gravity to a large farm three miles off, where it is utilized, and this cost £60,000. Then a complete water-works system was devised, the pure water from Lake Michigan being brought in an elevated to the top of a huge water tower and reservoir, from which an ample supply is led into every house in the town, no matter how humble. Competent architects and landscape gardeners skilfully laid out the town and built the houses, so that it is a gem of artistic attractiveness, with lawns and shade trees upon its well-paved streets, all kept in the best order by the company. All the shops where purchases are made have been collected in an elaborate structure called the Arcade, where the people do their shopping, fully protected from the weather, and a large covered market house is also provided, with a public hall in the upper portion.

Nothing is free, however, it being recognized as a lamentable fact that benefits got for nothing are not much prized. There are nearly 1,600 cottages and tenements for the operatives, and

133 new ones are building. There is no compulsion exercised about anything, and the people may live in the town or elsewhere as they see fit, so that in practice the town contains about 3,500 operatives who work for the company and about 1,000 who labour for other industries in the town or elsewhere, while some 500 of the company's operatives live outside. The dwellings are let upon a monthly rental, £1 being charged for a flat with two rooms, and 28s. to 36s. for flats with three or four rooms. The smallest separate house complete in itself contains four rooms, and this is let for £2 8s. monthly. The best cottages occupied by the working men fetch £5, and the tenant usually gets a large part of this back by subletting rooms to working men without families, there being no restrictions in this respect. The highest-priced cottages, occupied usually by officials, are £9 to £10 monthly, and contain 10 to 11 rooms, with bath, &c. Every house has both water and gas. Compared with tenements of similar character and capacity in Chicago the rentals of the latter are usually one-third to one-fifth higher, with less advantages, while the expenses of living in Chicago are about 20 per cent higher. Pullman is surrounded by a wide expanse of agricultural land, extensively devoted to market gardens, and this, with the entire freedom given the people to buy of whom and where they please, the company having no stores for the sale of goods, makes a competition among sellers to get the cash that is in hand to be spent by the people, which cheapens all supplies. The dress goods and similar articles are sold as low as in Chicago.

The Arcade is fully rented, and the company gets £6,000 annual return from it. One of the finest theatres in the West is constructed in its upper portion, and all the travelling companies appear here. It will hold 1,000 people, and the admission prices are kept low. I attended a theatrical performance with an audience of about 700, and the house yielded £70. The company has provided for additional amusements the best athletic grounds near Chicago, for ball playing, racing, and boating. The regattas and games often attract many thousands. There is a good library maintained for a small fee, and also a bank, and in its savings fund department the operatives have deposits amounting to £45,000. There are no saloons in the town, for no one is permitted to sell liquor, and as an additional protection sufficient land is controlled around the outskirts of the town to compel the man who must have spirits or beer to go nearly a mile over the border to get it. This carefulness, combined with the excellent sanitary arrangements and the vigour of a working population largely composed of people in the prime of life, make the town an abnormally healthy place. It has for its 10,000 people only four physicians and one funeral purveyor, and they say that more could not earn a living, for the annual death rate is only eight in one thousand compared with 22 in Chicago. Yet births at the rate of 400 in a year, combined with the influx of new arrivals, show how the census will expand, for new houses are built in accordance with the general comprehensive plan as the increase in population may require. The householder has no care for streets, water, gas, drainage, garbage, or for the lawns and trees, as these are all looked after by the company, which thus stands in place of and does even more than the ordinary American town government, besides having its affairs incomparably better managed. There is throughout Pullman an air of artistic harmony and neatness that is very attractive; while the operatives and their families appear in a far better condition, and look as if they were of an improved class compared with those usually seen in factory towns. Schools and churches are provided, and one church—the Presbyterian—is an exquisitely beautiful building that fits as a gem into the picture. The various secret and charitable societies that have so generally spread over the States, such as the Odd Fellows, Knights of Pythias, and others, all flourish. If the content of the working men can be secured by good treatment and pleasant surroundings, then the inhabitants of this model town ought to be supremely happy. The great Corliss steam engine looking like two enormous Cornish pumps, which was so much admired as it moved the vast aggregation of machinery at the Philadelphia Centennial Exposition in 1876, has been transported to this place, and stands in the centre of the extensive workshops, furnishing the motive power which turns out £6,000 worth of completed work every day. The army of operatives who serve around it are in no way restricted in thought or action outside the shops, either in politics or religion, in their habits or amusements, or as to where or how they expend their earnings, which, (less their rent) are always paid every fortnight in cash. When these wonderful industrial and philanthropic results, achieved upon the bank of Lake Calumet by one of the leading men of Chicago, are considered, it seems almost a miracle that has been wrought, even in this rapidly developing Western country, in thus turning an uninhabited prairie into a populous, industrious, and attractive town within the short space of seven years.

RUDYARD KIPLING[1]

RUDYARD KIPLING, poet and novelist, was born in Bombay, India, December 30, 1865. In 1878 he entered the United Services College at Westward Ho, North Devon, where he spent the next four years. At the age of seventeen he returned to India. Through the influence of his father he obtained work on the Lahore *Civil and Military Gazette*, and in 1887 he became the assistant editor of the Allahabad *Pioneer*. In 1889 he returned to England by way of China, Japan, and America, promising to write the impressions of his trip for the *Pioneer*. By this time he was well known in India, and within the next few years his popularity spread through the English-speaking world. In 1907 he received the Nobel Prize for Literature, and in 1926 the Gold Medal of the Royal Society of Literature was presented to him.

In his travels in America, Kipling spanned the entire continent, viewing many sights—from salmon fisheries, cowboys, and the Mormon settlement at Salt Lake, to the cities of Chicago, Buffalo, and New York. His impressions, on the whole, were not pleasing and are reflected in his comments describing his observations. American speech he considered not a language but merely "dialect, slang, provincialism, accent and so forth." He did not approve of American women, American newspapers and their correspondents, American hotel clerks, or American preachers. The description of his visit is couched in interesting and colorful language. Although most American cities he visited are, in no sense, praised, Chicago was especially unappealing to him.

-》》 《《-

HOW I STRUCK CHICAGO, AND HOW CHICAGO STRUCK ME. OF RE-
LIGION, POLITICS, AND PIG-STICKING, AND THE IN-
CARNATION OF THE CITY AMONG SHAMBLES.[2]

"I know thy cunning and thy greed,
Thy hard high lust and wilful deed,
And all thy glory loves to tell
Of specious gifts material."

I have struck a city—a real city—and they call it Chicago. The other places do not count. San Francisco was a pleasure-resort as well as a city, and Salt Lake was a phenomenon. This

---

[1] Rudyard Kipling, *From Sea to Sea: Letters of Travel*, Part II (New York: Charles Scribner's Sons, 1906), pp. 230–48. Copyright 1899 and reprinted by permission of Messrs. A. P. Watt & Son and Doubleday, Doran & Co., Inc., publishers.

[2] Title as in the original.

place is the first American city I have encountered. It holds
rather more than a million people with bodies, and stands on
the same sort of soil as Calcutta. Having seen it, I urgently
desire never to see it again. It is inhabited by savages. Its water
is the water of the Hughli, and its air is dirt. Also it says that it
is the "boss" town of America.

I do not believe that it has anything to do with this country.
They told me to go to the Palmer House which is a gilded and
mirrored rabbit-warren, and there I found a huge hall of tes-
sellated marble, crammed with people talking about money and
spitting about everywhere. Other barbarians charged in and
out of this inferno with letters and telegrams in their hands, and
yet others shouted at each other. A man who had drunk quite
as much as was good for him told me that this was "the finest
hotel in the finest city on God Almighty's earth." By the way,
when an American wishes to indicate the next county or State
he says, "God A'mighty's earth." This prevents discussion and
flatters his vanity.

Then I went out into the streets, which are long and flat and
without end. And verily it is not a good thing to live in our East
for any length of time. Your ideas grow to clash with those held
by every right-thinking white man. I looked down interminable
vistas flanked with nine, ten, and fifteen storied houses, and
crowded with men and women, and the show impressed me with
a great horror. Except in London—and I have forgotten what
London is like—I had never seen so many white people together, and never such a collection of miserables. There was no
colour in the street and no beauty—only a maze of wire-ropes
overhead and dirty stone flagging underfoot. A cab-driver volunteered to show me the glory of the town for so much an hour,
and with him I wandered far. He conceived that all this turmoil and squash was a thing to be reverently admired; that it
was good to huddle men together in fifteen layers, one atop of
the other, and to dig holes in the ground for offices. He said that
Chicago was a live town, and that all the creatures hurrying by
me were engaged in business. That is to say, they were trying to
make some money, that they might not die through lack of food

to put into their bellies. He took me to canals, black as ink, and filled with untold abominations, and bade me watch the stream of traffic across the bridges. He then took me into a saloon, and, while I drank, made me note that the floor was covered with coins sunk into cement. A Hottentot would not have been guilty of this sort of barbarism. The coins made an effect pretty enough, but the man who put them there had no thought to beauty, and therefore he was a savage. Then my cab-driver showed me business blocks, gay with signs and studded with fantastic and absurd advertisements of goods, and looking down the long street so adorned it was as though each vender stood at his door howling: "For the sake of money, employ, or buy of, *me* and me only!" Have you ever seen a crowd at our famine-relief distributions? You know then how men leap into the air, stretching out their arms above the crowd in the hope of being seen; while the women dolorously slap the stomachs of their children and whimper. I had sooner watch famine relief than the white man engaged in what he calls legitimate competition. The one I understand. The other makes me ill. And the cab-man said that these things were the proof of progress; and by that I knew he had been reading his newspaper, as every intelligent American should. The papers tell their readers in language fitted to their comprehension that the snarling together of telegraph wires, the heaving up of houses, and the making of money is progress.

I spent ten hours in that huge wilderness, wandering through scores of miles of these terrible streets, and jostling some few hundred thousand of these terrible people who talked money through their noses. The cabman left me: but after a while I picked up another man who was full of figures, and into my ears he poured them as occasion required or the big blank factories suggested. Here they turned out so many hundred thousand dollars' worth of such and such an article; there so many million other things; this house was worth so many million dollars; that one so many million more or less. It was like listening to a child babbling of its hoard of shells. It was like watching a fool playing with buttons. But I was expected to do more than listen or watch. He demanded that I should admire; and the utmost that I could say was: "Are these things so? Then I am very sorry for you." That made him angry, and he said that insular envy made me unresponsive. So you see I could not make him understand.

About four and a half hours after Adam was turned out of the Garden of Eden he felt hungry, and so, bidding Eve take care that her head was not broken by the descending fruit, shinned up a cocoanut palm. That hurt his legs, cut his breast, and made him breathe heavily, and Eve was tormented with fear lest her lord should miss his footing and so bring the tragedy of this world to an end ere the curtain had fairly risen. Had I met Adam then, I should have been sorry for him. To-day I find eleven hundred thousand of his sons just as far advanced as their father in the art of getting food, and immeasurably inferior to him in that they think that their palm-trees lead straight to the skies. Consequently I am sorry in rather more than a million different ways. In our East bread comes naturally even to the poorest by a little scratching or the gift of a friend not quite so poor. In less favoured countries one is apt to forget. Then I went to bed. And that was on a Saturday night.

Sunday brought me the queerest experience of all—a revelation of barbarism complete. I found a place that was officially described as a church. It was a circus really, but that the worshippers did not know. There were flowers all about the building, which was fitted up with plush and stained oak and much luxury, including twisted brass candlesticks of severest Gothic design. To these things, and a congregation of savages, entered suddenly a wonderful man completely in the confidence of their God, whom he treated colloquially and exploited very much as a newspaper reporter would exploit a foreign potentate. But, unlike the newspaper reporter, he never allowed his listeners to forget that he and not He was the centre of attraction. With a voice of silver and with imagery borrowed from the auction-room, he built up for his hearers a heaven on the lines of the Palmer House (but with all the gilding real gold and all the plate-glass diamond) and set in the centre of it a loud-voiced, argumentative, and very shrewd creation that he called God. One sentence at this point caught my delighted ear. It was *apropos* of some question of the Judgment Day and ran: "No! I tell you God don't do business that way." He was giving them a deity whom they could comprehend, in a gold and jewel heaven in which they could take a natural interest. He interlarded his performance with the slang of the streets, the counter, and the Exchange, and he said that religion ought to enter into daily life. Consequently I presume he introduced it *as* daily life—his own and the life of his friends.

Then I escaped before the blessing, desiring no benediction at such hands. But the persons who listened seemed to enjoy themselves, and I understand that I had met with a popular preacher. Later on, when I had perused the sermons of a gentleman called Talmage and some others, I perceived that I had been listening to a very mild specimen. Yet that man, with his brutal gold and silver idols, his hands-in-pocket, cigar-in-mouth, and hat-on-the-back-of-the-head style of dealing with the sacred vessels, would count himself spiritually quite competent to send a mission to convert the Indians. All that Sunday I listened to people who said that the mere fact of spiking down strips of iron to wood and getting a steam and iron thing to run along them was progress. That the telephone was progress, and the network of wires overhead was progress. They repeated their statements again and again. One of them took me to their city hall and board of trade works and pointed it out with pride. It was very ugly, but very big, and the streets in front of it were narrow and unclean. When I saw the faces of the men who did business in that building I felt that there had been a mistake in their billeting.

By the way, 'tis a consolation to feel that I am not writing to an English audience. Then should I have to fall into feigned ecstacies over the marvelous progress of Chicago since the days of the great fire, to allude casually to the raising of the entire city so many feet above the level of the lake which it faces, and generally to grovel before the golden calf. But you, who are desperately poor, and therefore by these standards of no account, know things, and will understand when I write that they have managed to get a million of men together on flat land, and that the bulk of these men together appear to be lower than *mahajans* and not so companionable as a Punjabi *jat* after harvest. But I don't think it was the blind hurry of the people, their argot, and their grand ignorance of things beyond their immediate interests that displeased me so much as a study of the daily papers of Chicago. Imprimis, there was some sort of dispute between New York and Chicago as to which town should give an exhibition of products to be hereafter holden, and through the medium of their more dignified journals the two cities were ya-hooing and hi-yi-ing at each other like opposition newsboys. They called it humour, but it sounded like something quite different. That was only the first trouble. The second lay in the tone of the productions. Leading articles which include gems such as: "Back of such and such a place," or "We noticed, Tuesday, such an event," or "don't" for "does not" are things to be accepted with thankfulness. All that made me weep was that, in these papers, were faithfully reproduced all the war-cries and "back-talk" of the Palmer House bar, the slang of the barbers' shops, the mental elevation and integrity of the Pullman-car porter, the dignity of the Dime Museum, and the accuracy of the excited fishwife. I am sternly forbidden to believe that the paper educates the public. Then I am compelled to believe that the public educate the paper?

Just when the sense of unreality and oppression was strongest upon me, and when I most wanted help, a man sat at my side and began to talk what he called politics. I had chanced to pay about six shillings for a traveling-cap worth eighteen pence, and he made of the fact a text for a sermon. He said that this was a rich country and that the people liked to pay two hundred per cent on the value of a thing. They could afford it. He said that the Government imposed a protective duty of from ten to seventy per cent on foreign-made articles, and that the American manufacturer consequently could sell his goods for a healthy sum. Thus an imported hat would, with duty, cost two guineas. The American manufacturer would make a hat for seventeen shillings and sell it for one pound fifteen. In these things, he said, lay the greatness of America and the effeteness of England. Competition between factory and factory kept the prices down to decent limits, but I was never to forget that this people were a rich people, not like the pauper Continentals, and that they enjoyed paying duties. To my weak intellect this seemed rather like juggling with counters. Everything that I have yet purchased costs about twice as much as it would in England, and when native-made is of inferior quality. Moreover, since these lines were first thought of I have visited a gentleman who owned a factory which used to produce things. He owned the factory still. Not a man was in it, but he was drawing a handsome income from a syndicate of firms for keeping it closed in order that it might not produce things. This man said that if protection were abandoned, a tide of pauper labour would flood the country, and as I looked at his factory I thought how entirely better it was to have no labour of any kind whatever, rather than face so horrible a future. Meantime, do you remember that this peculiar country enjoys paying money for value not received. I am an alien, and for the life of me cannot see why six shillings should be paid for eighteen-penny caps, or eight shillings for half-crown cigar-cases. When the country fills up to a decently populated level a few million people who are not aliens will be smitten with the same sort of blindness.

But my friend's assertion somehow thoroughly suited the grotesque ferocity of Chicago. See now and judge! In the village of Isser Jang on the road to Montgomery there be four *changar* women who winnow corn—some seventy bushels a year. Beyond their hut lives Puran Dass, the money-lender, who on good security lends as much as five thousand rupees in a year. Jowala Singh, the *lohar*, mends the village plows—some thirty, broken at the share, in three hundred and sixty-five days; and Hukm Chund, who is letter-writer and head of the little club under the travellers' tree, generally keeps the village posted in such gossip as the barber and the midwife have not yet made public property. Chicago husks and winnows her wheat by the million bushels, a hundred banks lend hundreds of millions of dollars in the year, and scores of factories turn out plow gear and machinery by steam. Scores of daily papers do work which Hukm Chund and the barber and the midwife perform, with due regard for public opinion, in the village of Isser Jang. So far as manufactures go, the difference between Chicago on the lake and Isser Jang on the Montgomery road is one of degree only, and not of kind. So far as the understanding of the uses of life goes Isser Jang, for all its seasonal cholera, has the advantage over Chicago. Jowala Singh knows and takes care to avoid the three or four ghoul-haunted fields on the outskirts of the village; but he is not urged by millions of devils to run about all day in the sun and swear that his plowshares are the best in the Punjab; nor does Puran Dass fly forth in a cart more than once or twice a year, and he knows, on a pinch, how to use the railway and the telegraph as well as any son of Israel in Chicago. But this is absurd. The East is not the West, and these men must continue to deal with the machinery of life, and to call it progress. Their very preachers dare not rebuke them. They gloss over the hunting for money and the twice-sharpened bitterness of Adam's curse by saying that such things dower a man with a larger range of thoughts and higher aspirations. They do not say: "Free yourself from your own slavery," but rather, "If you can possibly manage it, do not set quite so much store on the things of this world." And they do not know what the things of this world are.

I went off to see cattle killed by way of clearing my head, which, as you will perceive, was getting muddled. They say every Englishman goes to the Chicago stock-yards. You shall find them about six miles from the city; and once having seen them you will never forget the sight. As far as the eye can reach stretches a township of cattle-pens, cunningly divided into blocks so that the animals of any pen can be speedily driven out close to an inclined timber path which leads to an elevated covered way straddling high above the pens. These viaducts are two-storied. On the upper storey tramp the doomed cattle, stolidly for the most part. On the lower, with a scuffling of sharp hoofs and multitudinous yells, run the pigs. The same end is appointed for each. Thus you will see the gangs of cattle waiting their turn—as they wait sometimes for days; and they need not be distressed by the sight of their fellows running about in the fear of death. All they know is that a man on horseback causes their next-door neighbours to move by means of a whip. Certain bars and fences are unshipped, and, behold, that crowd have gone up the mouth of a sloping tunnel and return no more. It is different with the pigs. They shriek back the news of the exodus to their friends, and a hundred pens skirl responsive. It was to the pigs I first addressed myself. Selecting a viaduct which was full of them, as I could hear though I could not see, I marked a sombre building whereto it ran, and went there, not unalarmed by stray cattle who had managed to escape from their proper quarters. A pleasant smell of brine warned me of what was coming. I entered the factory and found it full of pork in barrels, and on another storey more pork unbarrelled, and in a huge room the halves of swine, for whose use great lumps of ice were being pitched in at the window. That room was the mortuary chamber where the pigs lie for a little while in state ere they begin their progress through such passages as kings may sometimes travel. Turning a corner and not noting an overhead arrangement of greased rail, wheel, and pulley, I ran into the arms of four eviscerated carcasses, all pure white and of a human aspect, being pushed by a man clad in vehement red. When I leaped aside, the floor was slippery under me. There was a flavour of farmyard in my nostrils and the shouting of a multitude in my ears. But there was no joy in that shouting. Twelve men stood in two lines—six a-side. Between them and overhead ran the railway of death that had nearly shunted me through the window. Each man carried a knife, the sleeves of his shirt were cut off at the elbows, and from bosom to heel he was blood-red. The atmosphere was stifling as a night in the Rains, by reason of the steam and the crowd. I climbed to the beginning of things and, perched upon a narrow beam, overlooked very nearly all the pigs ever bred in Wisconsin. They had just been shot out of the mouth of the viaduct and huddled together in a large pen. Thence they were flicked persuasively, a few at a time, into a smaller chamber, and there a man fixed tackle on their hinder legs so that they rose in the air suspended from the railway of death. Oh! it was then they shrieked and called on their mothers and made promises of amendment, till the tackle-man punted them in their backs, and they slid head down into a brick-floored passage, very like a big kitchen sink that was blood-red. There awaited them a red man with a knife which he passed jauntily through their throats, and the full-voiced shriek be-came a sputter, and then a fall as of heavy tropical rain. The red man who was backed against the passage wall stood clear of the wildly kicking hoofs and passed his hand over his eyes, not from any feeling of compassion, but because the spurted blood was in his eyes, and he had barely time to stick the next arrival. Then that first stuck swine dropped, still kicking, into a great vat of boiling water, and spoke no more words, but wallowed in obedi-ence to some unseen machinery, and presently came forth at the lower end of the vat and was heaved on the blades of a blunt paddle-wheel-thing which said, "Hough! Hough! Hough!" and skelped all the hair off him except what little a couple of men with knives could remove. Then he was again hitched by the heels to that said railway and passed down the line of the twelve men—each man with a knife—leaving with each man a certain amount of his individuality which was taken away in a wheel-barrow, and when he reached the last man he was very beauti-ful to behold, but immensely unstuffed and limp. Preponder-ance of individuality was ever a bar to foreign travel. That pig could have been in no case to visit you in India had he not part-ed with some of his most cherished notions.

The dissecting part impressed me not so much as the slaying. They were so excessively alive, these pigs. And then they were so excessively dead, and the man in the dripping, clammy, hot passage did not seem to care, and ere the blood of such an one had ceased to foam on the floor, such another, and four friends with him, had shrieked and died. But a pig is only the Unclean animal—forbidden by the Prophet.

I was destined to make rather a queer discovery when I went over to the cattle-slaughter. All the buildings were on a much larger scale, and there was no sound of trouble, but I could smell the salt reek of blood before I set foot in the place. The cattle did not come directly through the viaduct as the pigs had done. They debouched into a yard by the hundred, and they were big red brutes carrying much flesh. In the centre of that yard stood a red Texan steer with a head-stall on his wicked head. No man controlled him. He was, so to speak, picking his teeth and whistling in an open byre of his own when the cattle arrived. As soon as the first one had fearfully quitted the viaduct, this red devil put his hands in his pockets and slouched across the yard, no man guiding him. Then he lowed something to the effect that he was the regularly appointed guide of the establishment and would show them round. They were country folk, but they knew how to behave; and so followed Judas some hundred strong, patiently, and with a look of bland wonder in their faces. I saw his broad back jogging in advance of them, up a lime-washed incline where I was forbidden to follow. Then a door shut, and in a minute back came Judas with the air of a virtuous plough-bullock and took up his place in his byre. Somebody laughed across the yard, but I heard no sound of cattle from the big brick building into which the mob had disappeared. Only Judas chewed the cud with a malignant satisfaction, and so I knew there was trouble, and ran round to the front of the factory and so entered and stood aghast.

Who takes count of the prejudices which we absorb through the skin by way of our surroundings? It was not the spectacle that impressed me. The first thought that almost spoke itself aloud was: "They are killing kine;" and it was a shock. The pigs were nobody's concern, but cattle—the brothers of the Cow, the Sacred Cow—were quite otherwise. The next time an M. P. tells me that India either Sultanises or Brahminises a man, I shall believe about half what he says. It is unpleasant to watch the slaughter of cattle when one has laughed at the notion for a few years. I could not see actually what was done in the first instance, because the row of stalls in which they lay was separated from me by fifty impassable feet of butchers and slung carcasses. All I know is that men swung open the doors of a stall as occasion required, and there lay two steers already stunned, and breathing heavily. These two they pole-axed, and half raising them by tackle they cut their throats. Two men skinned each carcass, somebody cut off the head, and in half a minute more the overhead rail carried two sides of beef to their appointed place. There was clamour enough in the operating-room, but from the waiting cattle, invisible on the other side of the line of pens, never a sound. They went to their death, trusting Judas, without a word. They were slain at the rate of five a minute, and if the pig men were spattered with blood, the cow butchers were bathed in it. The blood ran in muttering gutters. There was no place for hand or foot that was not coated with thicknesses of dried blood, and the stench of it in the nostrils bred fear.

And then the same merciful Providence that has showered good things on my path throughout sent me an embodiment of the City of Chicago, so that I might remember it for ever. Women come sometimes to see the slaughter, as they would come to see the slaughter of men. And there entered that vermilion hall a young woman of large mould, with brilliantly scarlet lips, and heavy eyebrows, and dark hair that came in a "widow's peak" on the forehead. She was well and healthy and alive, and she was dressed in flaming red and black, and her feet (know you that the feet of American women are like unto the feet of fairies?)—her feet, I say, were cased in red leather shoes. She stood in a patch of sunlight, the red blood under her shoes, the vivid carcasses tacked round her, a bullock bleeding its life away not six feet away from her, and the death factory roaring all round her. She looked curiously, with hard, bold eyes, and was not ashamed.

Then said I: "This is a special Sending. I have seen the City of Chicago!" And I went away to get peace and rest.

PAUL DE ROUSIERS[1]

P AUL DE ROUSIERS, French economist, was born in 1857. After varied experiences, including much foreign travel, he began a life-study of the modern industrial system. He became interested in many sociological questions, but he concerned himself with them only in so far as they were related to "Big Business." Of these, problems of labor occupied a good deal of his attention, his sympathies resting with the laboring classes which he believed were being pushed continuously farther down the scale of living. In 1896 he published *The Labor Question in Britain*, a work well received by the critics.

During the nineties much discussion concerning "trusts" agitated the United States. In 1898 Rousiers published *Les industries monopolisées aux États-Unis*, dealing with business combinations, based not only on study but also on personal observations made during an American tour in 1890. His *Les grandes industries modernes*, published in 1924, and considered by many as his greatest work, is the result of the study of half a lifetime. Rousiers has been interested also in the economic activities of the League of Nations, and in 1927 he submitted his manuscript on *Cartels and Trusts and Their Development* to the preparatory committee for the International Economic Conference.

In a book, *American Life*, published in 1892, and from which an extract is produced, Rousiers surveyed the history of the United States from the time of its discovery. In this he held that up to 1890 American riches were exploited by Europe but that a reversal appeared imminent. Among other things, the American protective tariff system and its effects upon the rest of the world engaged his attention. He studied the labor troubles in the anthracite region and the growth of large cities as related to industry, and in the American system of education be beheld danger of an alliance with industrialism.

To him, as to many other foreign and domestic visitors, the West was the most characteristic part of the nation, for he believed that here was everything that America professed. To him the great moving force of the United States and the outstanding characteristic of the American people was endless energy, evidence of which he found on all hands. He beheld the American cast in the mold of action and not that of enjoyment or of sorrow, trusting neither the future nor worshiping the past, but acting in the present.

[1] Paul de Rousiers, *American Life* (A. J. Herbertson, trans.; Paris: Firmin-Didot & Co., 1892), pp. 171–83. Reprinted by permission of Firmin-Didot & Co.

Go to Chicago and you will see the point, or, at least, one of the most important points, where Western farming ends; and you will also find Chicago is a manufacturing centre.

If you wish to study the history of industry, if you wish to know in what way it first developed in the States, you need not go to Eastern cities—to Boston, New York, Philadelphia or Pittsburg—but you must begin your investigation at Chicago, St. Louis, Kansas City or St. Paul, where industry is making its first appearance. For this reason we shall go to the great cities of the Mississippi Valley and begin our study of a new form of American activity—industrial labor. . . . .

Chicago, to which we must always return, as it sums up all the characteristics of a great Western city, is the capital of the railroads—the place where most of the great lines meet—and thus it is that all the produce of the country is so effectively drawn to Chicago. This enormous transport movement needs an immense rolling-stock. Hence arises an industry already highly developed, of which Chicago is naturally the centre, with all the more reason, as Illinois, Minnesota, Michigan, and above all, Wisconsin, send her the raw material—the timber.

The first great industry which is established, outside those of the packing-houses, flour-mills, and dairies, where agricultural produce is worked up, is then an industry connected with transport. It is still indirectly, yet closely, related to agriculture. It arises because cattle and grain must be sent to distant markets before being used; while it, nevertheless, arises as a separate industry, and gives a manufacturing aspect to the place where it is practised, which makes them look somewhat like Eastern cities.

For example, everybody knows that the labor question is discussed at Chicago, and that strikes often break out there. The American and even the French newspapers often announce that this or that shop has stopped working. It is one point common to West and East. It is, therefore, necessary to visit other places besides packing-houses and elevators before giving a complete account of the essential features of Chicago. The making of railroad rolling-stock must be inspected. After visiting Armour we must call on Pullman.

Mr. Pullman is the builder after whom the American *wagons de luxe*—the Pullman cars—have been called; but he does not confine his attentions to turning out palaces on wheels. Ordinary passenger and freight-cars are also needed; and, indeed, he turns out more freight-cars than anything else, for the number that are in circulation is infinitely greater than that of either sleeping or even ordinary passenger cars. An idea of the importance of his workshops can be had from the fact that a freight-car is turned out every quarter of an hour during the ten hours of each day's work. On the other hand, only three sleeping-cars can be finished in a week of sixty hours. Their cost is from $16,000 to $20,000 each.

The planning of these workshops is remarkable, and every detail seems to have been considered. To cite one point, the buildings in which freight-cars are built are a series of vast sheds as broad as the cars are long. Opposite each car a large bay opens on the iron way and a car, as soon as it is finished, runs along the rails and leaves the shop. All the timber that forms a car is cut to the required size and is got ready for fitting together in a special department, whence it is brought along the same rails to the sheds where the car is built. Tiny little locomotives are running along the lines which are built in the spaces between the various workshops. Some are hauling magnificent Pullman cars, glittering with copper and gilding; others drag trucks of planks, joists, bolts and the iron needed in car-building. Everything is done in order and with precision; one feels that each effort is calculated to yield its maximum effect, that no blow of a hammer, no turn of a wheel is made without cause. One feels that some brain of superior intelligence, backed by a long technical experience, has thought out every possible detail.

Besides the fitting-shops that deliver the finished car, there are many preparatory shops. The most important are the timber-shops, for wood is the raw material most used in the making of every kind of car; then comes the metal-works, wheel and bolt shops, forges, steel-works, etc., and then those which are more especially for passenger-cars, such as the hair-cloth factory, etc., etc.

It is easy to understand the wonderful material complexity of such an enterprise. It needs a number of different kinds of factories which must be run for the common end. From the purely industrial point of view, it is an interesting sample of the great American manufactories.

The Pullman Palace Car Company does not only make the rolling-stock, but it superintends the running of part of it over the whole surface of the States.

In fact, all the *wagons de luxe* on the American railroads belong to them, except those on the five lines owned or controlled by the Vanderbilts, where Wagner palace-cars replace them. The Wagner palace-cars bear their inventor's name. Wagner was the first man to conceive a sleeping-car. He started a factory at Buffalo, and signed a contract with Vanderbilt for the running of his cars. When Wagner died, Vanderbilt got hold of his works, and today it is his heirs who own the Wagner Palace Car Company. Naturally, they have the custom of all the Vanderbilt roads. But while Wagner was being absorbed by the powerful house of Vanderbilt, Pullman started an opposition business which soon surpassed its rival in the excellence of its work and in its better organization. That is why the Pullmans run over more than 60,000 miles of road without any legal guarantee of this monopoly, which they retain simply because of the advantages which they give.

The advantages are of more than one kind. As far as the companies are concerned, Mr. Pullman gives them a very large percentage for running his cars, and thus gets the preference; and the comfort of the Pullman cars is made still more acceptable to the public by the excellent organization of the service. For the car is not only a good carriage, but also a first-class hotel, where you can sleep, eat, bathe, and, what is so rare in America, also find an attentive and polite servant, who will blacken your boots, brush your clothes, carry your bag and receive your "tip" with a smile. He is usually a negro—or at least a mulatto—but a negro properly and carefully dressed, with some external self-respect, and all the qualities of a good servant. The European experiences a veritable pleasure in finding this worthy man after leaving an American hotel, where personal attention is not at all understood, despite the luxury they display and the machines they own. But the traveller is astonished, as well as delighted. How is it that the Pullman Company have been able to get such a body of men together in this country? How do they manage to keep it together on that vast net-work of American railroads, far from personal supervision?

This is a problem that cannot be solved, or at least the solution cannot be understood except by visiting Pullman City, the town recently founded and built by Mr. Pullman, to hold his workshops and lodge part of his workmen. In seeing what colossal difficulties have been overcome in doing this, and what results Mr. Pullman has got, it is easy to understand how he has dressed the negroes as he has done. The demonstration is one by *a fortiori*.

Mr. Pullman's endeavor has been as follows: To mould not only a body of employees, but a whole population of workmen and their families to ways of living which would raise their moral, intellectual and social level. Strongly imbued with the Anglo-Saxon idea, that exterior respectability aids true self-respect, he wished to test his theory on his workmen, and conceived the great plan which many treated as that of a madman ten years ago, and which everybody admires to-day in its realized form. This scheme was nothing less than to build a new town according to sanitary, healthy principles; to make it not only elegant, but convenient; and to transfer thither the workshops of the Pullman Car Company, and to lodge some of the workmen in it.

The plan was carried out to the letter. On May 25th, 1880, the works were begun on 4,000 acres of ground, which the Company had bought for the purpose, twelve miles north [*sic*] of Chicago, on a meadow near the shores of Lake Calumet, crossed by the Illinois Central Railroad. First of all, the future town was supplied with a complete system of sewers, designed so as to assure perfect healthiness, and then the water and gas mains were laid in every part. This underground work being completed, the superstructure was begun. Besides workshops and houses, a hotel, a church, a library and a theatre were not forgotten, and everything was arranged with the greatest taste, any monotony being avoided by diversifying the architecture and leaving wide spaces for streets between each row of houses, and by making promenades and squares, in which trees were planted.

There only remained the peopling of these pretty stone or brick-houses, so coquettishly built and so conveniently fitted up. The Company let them to its workers, and, in spite of the high rents, Pullman City soon had 8,500 inhabitants.

At Pullman City a suite of two rooms costs from $4 to $9 a month, according to its size and situation; the dearest being those in small houses, which allow the tenant more freedom, for it is a great consideration in the eyes of Americans to have a home of one's own. The workmen who wish cheap lodgings live in large blocks, which Mr. Pullman built for this purpose. Large families, who need more than two apartments, can find the three, four or five rooms they seek at from $4.60 to $15 a month. Detached cottages with five rooms rent at $16 to $20, and houses of from six to nine apartments at $23 to $100 per month. Of course these are not workmen's dwellings, but residences for the managers at the works.

I have intentionally insisted on these prices because they show two characteristic features of Mr. Pullman's creation. In the first place, they prove that it is no charitable institution. Mr. Pullman has clearly said this to those who have asked him, and he said to me, "I have not contributed fifty cents to all that you see here. I have never had any idea of giving alms to my men, and every dwelling pays the rent it ought to do in order to give the company a sufficient revenue for the money sank in building Pullman City."

In the second place their highness in price is easily explained by the conveniences of all sorts that the workman finds in these model dwellings. The housewives are especially loud in praise of the enormous simplification thus made in their daily duties: no more buckets of refuse to carry out to the pavement; no more water to carry up; for all rubbish, sweepings, filth of every sorts are at once let down into the underground sewers, which carry them to an immense reservoir. A powerful pump forces them three miles to a model farm, where Mr. Pullman has started market-gardening. Water-taps and water are abundant in every house.

A workman can set up house in Chicago for a little less than it costs him in Pullman City, but he must go to a badly-aired, unhealthy and hideous-looking district. Only men well enough off to buy a house can have a comfortable home in Chicago.

Mr. Pullman wished to prove that it was possible for everybody to have roomy apartments, supplied with every desirable modern improvement, without paying excessive rents. The quickness with which his houses have been occupied is a proof that he was right.

But Mr. Pullman aims higher than this. He is not only an intelligent and progressive builder; he is also a mindful overseer, a man truly anxious about the moral progress of his work-people. From this higher point of view Pullman City is of the greatest interest, for nowhere can one see a better example of how an American understands his duties as employer.

To prevent any misconception, I must explain that in America, as in Europe, many manufacturers do not trouble themselves about this duty, and deliberately set it aside. Mr. Pullman is thus far from representing the average type of an American employer of labor; in fact, he is a specimen of the very highest type. In stating the motives which made him build Pullman City, I am not giving the reader a sample of the ordinary relations in America between master and men; but I am showing him what a noble-minded American employer considers his duty, when he seriously thinks of it at all. If you wish to compare Pullman with some European manufacturers, you must select one who is famous for the institutions he has established for his men, and not the first great manufacturer of whom you think; and it is only by doing this that your comparison will teach you anything. This being understood, let us see how Mr. Pullman was led to carry out his schemes.

I mentioned above that he wished to raise the moral, intellectual and social level of the workingman by placing him in respectable surroundings. That is his base of operations, but it has several accessory aids. One of the first of these is the absolute prohibition of any saloon. He manages this by refusing to let any of his houses to any saloonkeeper, which he can easily do, as all belong to him; and every tenant suspected of selling liquor is purely and simply asked to find a shelter elsewhere. This is the only restrictive measure adopted by Mr. Pullman. Like many of his countrymen, he has seen the ravages produced by an abuse of alcohol in all classes of American society, and especially among workingmen. He wished to remove the temptations to drink whiskey from his workmen, and he has got a band of select men by this simple device. Indeed, drunkards, dissolutes and idlers, who are used to hanging about where the bottle is, have all fled from this temperance town, and only those of sober tendency remain. Add to this the fact that nobody is obliged to live in Pullman City, even among the workmen of the Palace Car Company, and it is evident that there is, properly-speaking, no compulsion at all. A houseowner who refuses to lease to an innkeeper has never yet been considered a tyrant.

Beside this precaution against the entrance of a disturbing element, Mr. Pullman has neglected nothing that would help his workmen to develop intellectually and socially. He has founded a public library, schools and a church. One church was not enough for the needs of a community belonging to many religious bodies, so he has favored the erection of sectarian churches. At Pullman City there is a theatre, large open spaces for the national game of base-ball, and numerous other attractions of a similar sort. There has been no wish to make a town of exaggerated austerity, but quite the opposite, as every honest means of recreation has been fostered.

These things are not given by Mr. Pullman to his men; but, let me repeat it, they are offered to them if they care to pay the prices asked. With the exception of the public-library—which is an outcome of his personal liberality—all the institutions mentioned above are founded on the principle that each must contribute to their sustenance in the measure that he makes use of them. It is very remarkable that the workmen willingly accept the bargain offered. They pay more for their houses than they would do in Chicago, because they appreciate the advantages gained by so doing. They support the churches because they think them useful, and the theatre or base-ball because they wish to amuse themselves, without any of them needing to give a cent to the church, theatre, or base-ball association if he prefer to remain sceptic or to amuse himself at home.

Mr. Pullman has thus thoroughly understood the aspirations of the men in his factory; he has not dreamt of an impossible material wellbeing, or a moral progress to which they are opposed. He has realized the practical maximum of material wellbeing that is suited to his men; he has brought to their doors every means of moral and intellectual progress, and has kept away that great danger of large cities—the saloon; and lastly he has been backed up in his work-shops. He has supplied the necessary steps for those who wish to climb higher.

That is the essential feature of the oversight exercised by Mr. Pullman; it is an oversight adapted to those who can profit by it. For French workmen there would be too much luxury in the fittings of the houses. They could not pay such rents out of their lower wages, and they would contract habits out of keeping with their means. The same drawbacks do not affect American workmen, who earn wages much higher than ours, and live a fuller life. Further, they have many chances of raising themselves to a better position; and it is not imprudent to be preparing themselves for it. Another remarkable feature is the absence of compulsion. I have already said that no worker is forced to stay in Pullman City. It is not an obligatory phalansterium; no special restrictions exist, even for those who live there, except that prohibiting saloons. A visitor to the town is at once struck by its unusual appearance, for it is not only artistically built, but its inhabitants have also an air of carefulness and a look harmonizing with the frame in which they are seen. I spent a Saturday there. After midday most of the works were stopped and the men allowed a half holiday. I met gentlemen in the streets who, I was informed, were workmen walking with their wives or sweethearts. There was not a man in shirt-sleeves, as is so commonly the case in many American cities. The habit of outside propriety and dignity is being developed here without any special prescription. It is enough to admit the workmen who wish a comfortable dwelling to live in this town, built especially to satisfy them. A set of picked families has thus been formed, and they have shown an example to the others, who have followed it.

It has become the custom to doff one's hat when waiting for Mr. Pullman in his Chicago office. That may seem a simple matter to a French reader, but an American, who is not accustomed to the habits of the place, stands stupefied when he sees all the heads uncovered. Indeed, I have seen plenty people take it more at ease when with President Harrison, and I remember one man who kept his hat on his head when speaking to the Governor of Minnesota in his private-room, without the Governor thinking of telling him of his want of good manners. The introduction of a case of simple honest manners is one good result of Mr. Pullman's action.

On entering his reception-room one is face to face with a man very properly and carefully dressed, and perfectly calm. He willingly gives details and explanations about his work in Pullman City, and seems very anxious that his purpose should not be misunderstood. "People often deceive themselves about the idea which guides me in my work," he said, "For instance, it has been compared with that which your countryman, Mr. Godin, started at Guise; but there is not any relation whatever between his plan and mine. I have no wish to mix all my workmen in a vast community, but only to prove to them that decency, propriety and good manners are not unattainable luxuries for them; that it is not necessary to be loosely or carelessly dressed in order to do good work, to save money, and to raise themselves in the social scale. I have been understood, as you can easily see; and owing to the favorable conditions of Pullman City, there is growing up a nucleus of families who are thorough believers in this idea, and who will adhere to those habits of respectability which

I have tried to make general. I have been accused of being an autocrat and of shutting up my people in a gilded cage. That is another error, and the first of them you meet can tell you that I have not tried, in the slightest way, to interfere in any of their decisions. Besides, I should not have gained my end had I forced them to fulfill it, for I wish to grow a reasoned-out conviction, and not simply to force them to this or that way of conducting themselves." "But," I said, "do you not wish to part with the ownership of these houses some day or other? Will it not be a great mistake to force your workers to be always tenants in this land where others come to have homes of their own?" "It is truly my intention," he replied, " to form another town, near this one, where each resident will build a cottage after his own inclination, suited to his own needs, and which will be his own. I have already bought a large area of unoccupied land for this purpose, but I do not think the time has yet come for beginning this enterprise. If I had sold the sites to my workmen at the beginning of the experiment, I should have run the risk of seeing families settle who are not sufficiently accustomed to the habits I wish to develop in the inhabitants of Pullman City, and all the good of my work would have been compromised by their presence. But to-day, after ten years' apprenticeship, several families have become confirmed in their habits, recognize the advantages of them, and will see that they are observed wherever they may settle. Such families form the pick, and I hope to sell the building lands near my workshops to some of them, little by little."

Such is Mr. Pullman's idea. Raise the workman wherever he shows any desire to get on, help him as much as possible, but do it in such a way as appeals to him; that is to say, back up his goodwill, strengthen his resolutions, complete his imperfect capabilities; and when he has progressed enough to be able to go alone, let him develop freely by himself, cut the leading strings that have guided him so far, but which will now hinder his onward march. It is a lofty and just ideal. Here it has taken a particular form which cannot be copied in all its details elsewhere; but, allowing for the special circumstances which accompanied the creation of Pullman City, it can safely be asserted that it is one of the best examples of true oversight that the great world of industry can exhibit.

I was in Chicago in 1890, just when the strikes had stopped the work in many factories. At Pullman City work went on actively. However, in 1885 an important strike took place there, and, after what Mr. Pullman told me himself, for ten days the men did not come to the works; but at the end of that time they were tired of this, and, seeing that the Company neither made advances nor threats, they returned to work of their own accord.

This quiet, negative way of dealing with things is part of Mr. Pullman's system. He mixes very little with his men, and never concerns himself about their private affairs. The duties of management to which he must attend leave him little time for details; and the love of independence which overpowers every other sentiment in the American, would not make the workers take kindly to such protection. When there is any ill feeling between them, he simply waits till it disappears; but he prevents it as much as possible by altering the wages according to the state of the labor-market. The excellent planning of his works enables him to pay manual labor at a high rate, and statisticians report that its price is a little higher in Mr. Pullman's than in similar workshops.

All wages are paid by piecework, and vary greatly with the skill of the worker. True artisans, too, are to be found in Pullman, men who know their trade, which is quite different from the simple handwork which is often met with in manufactories. It is said that not one of these men earns less than about $3.60 a day. This explains how they can afford to pay such rents as are quoted above.

A large proportion of the tradesmen are foreigners. Only half the population of Pullman was born in America; Sweden and Norway sent a seventh; Germany an eighth; then came in order of importance Ireland, Canada, England, Holland, Scotland, Denmark, Switzerland, France and Italy.

A word has yet to be said about the running of this large business. Mr. Pullman is the true and only master, although he does not own all the capital which is engaged. The Pullman Palace

Car Company has issued shares of $100, which are sold to-day for $200, and are on the Exchange list; but these represent only a small portion of the whole stock. The largest amount is in the hands of Mr. Pullman himself, the balance in those of two or three moneyed Chicago men, such as Armour, the great butcher, and Marshall [Field], of the great drygoods store. In spite of appearances, the Pullman Car Company is thus one of the same sort of societies we have already seen at work when discussing railroads, large ranches, packing-houses, flour-mills and elevators; it is a private undertaking, not an administrative machine, like our joint-stock companies (*sociétés d'actionnaires*). In fact one man really manages all this enormous amount of manufacture and transport, and he is the man who made the business, as he is the man who made Pullman City. . . . .

The industry formed by Mr. Pullman is a typical Western industry, and in passing through the great cities of the Mississippi Valley we come across several of the same sort—factories for making cars, wagons, street-cars, etc.; but his example of high-principled oversight is rarely followed. I know well enough that everybody has not the means of accomplishing such a feat as building a town for his workmen; but I must also remark that the industrial chiefs of the West usually concern themselves very little about their employees, and do not seem to be very anxious either for their material or moral advancement.

GUISEPPE GIACOSA[1]

G UISEPPE GIACOSA (October 21, 1847—September 2, 1906), was born at Colleretto Parella, Piedmont, Italy, the son of a distinguished magistrate. The father had planned that the son should follow in his footsteps, but an early comedy, *Una partita a scacchi* (*"A Game of Chess"*), was so successful that young Giacosa turned his attention to playwriting.

His early plays, on the whole, may be classified as comedies in verse and characterized by what has been called "healthy romanticism." In *Tristi amori* (*"Hapless Love"*), a drama of modern social realism, Giacosa abandoned verse in favor of prose as the method of conveying his thought. He now gave attention to the conflict between nineteenth-century idealism and bourgeois materialism; and Ibsen proved a great influence in shaping his social philosophy, as evidenced in *Tristi amori* and *Diritte dell'anima* (*"The Rights of the Soul"*).

The Lady of Challont, one of his early plays, was written for Sarah Bernhardt, who produced it first in the city of New York. Besides a number of plays, Giacosa wrote the *libretti* for several well-known operas, in collaboration with Luigi Illica. Among these were *La Bohême*, *Madam Butterfly*, and *Tosca*.

In 1901 he ventured into a new field of literature, establishing *La lettura*, and editing it until his death. The breadth of Giacosa's interests is discovered not only in his achievements as playwright and librettist but also in his branching out into historical works, essays, and stories. In 1898 he published *Impressioni d'America*, considered a work showing clarity of thought and keen insight into the characteristics of American life.

-»» «-

A CITY OF SMOKE

Looking forward to the great event, I spent the first days of my stay in Chicago seeing people and country escorted by some of our courteous compatriots. . . . . In the morning, I went out early, curious to visit the big city which is today the second, and will be—they say—ten years hence, the first in the United States. . . . . In Chicago, I knew that American life flourished abundantly: enormous factories, interminable streets, amazing shops, deafening sounds. . . . . And then there was the Exposition whose colossal frame must have appeared already in the

[1] Guiseppe Giacosa, "Chicago and Her Italian Colony," *Nuova Antologia*, CXXVIII (March, 1893), 16–28. Translated by Miss L. B. Davis. Reprinted by permission of *Nuova Antologia*.

midst of parks and charming gardens, bathed by that famous Lake Michigan which they boast vaster than the Adriatic, more navigable than the Mediterranean, and as calm to the view and smiling to leave behind as the lakes of upper Italy and Switzerland.

Alas, the foundations for the Exposition were scarcely started, and the boasted park and gardens seemed to me an abject and unpretentious thing. But on the plans which were given me to peruse, were sketched on those lowlands a varied undulation of hills; great valleys were etched there, promontories were thrown into the lake, breaking the monotonous shores, forming a bay between the lake and the land, marking the limits of improvised forest—in a word, those peaceful beaches were predestined to be truly an earthly cataclysm produced by measured and unfailing strength. Beautiful on the map, I thought, but the work of ten years. I perceived very soon how, in Chicago, a thing is no sooner said than done . . . . and how a fanciful mechanical power may have reduced the impracticable to mere absurd mathematics.

I had two different impressions of Chicago, one sensual and immediate, which comes from seeing persons and things. The other, intellectual and gradual, born from intelligence, induction and comparisons. To the eye, the city appears abominable. . . . . I would not want to live there for anything in the world. I think that whoever ignores it is not entirely acquainted with our century and of what it is the ultimate expression.

During my stay of one week, I did not see in Chicago anything but darkness: smoke, clouds, dirt and an extraordinary number of sad and grieved persons. Certain remote quarters are the exception, in which there breathes from little houses and tiny gardens a tranquil air of rustic habitation where a curious architecture with diverting and immature whims makes a pleasant appearance, where the houses seem to be toys for the use of the hilarious people who live there in complete repose, eating candy, swinging in their faithful little rocking chairs, and contemplating oleographs.

But with the exception of these rare cases, the rich metropolis gave me a sense of oppression so grave that I still doubt whether, beyond their factories, there exist celestial spaces. Was it a storm-cloud? I cannot say, because the covered sky spreads a light equal and diffused, which makes no shade; while here, depending on the time of day, a few thick shadows line the houses. And I can not even say that a ghost of the sun shines, because the appearance of things close up makes me always uncertain and confused. I am inclined to believe that that spacious plain, *café au lait* in colour, which stretches along the edge of the city, which appears to the eye three hundred paces wide, and which disappears in gray space, might be the lake; but I could not press close to it with security. Certainly the ships plow through a dense atmosphere rather than a watery plain.

I recall one morning when I happened to be on a high railroad viaduct. From it the city seemed to smolder a vast unyielding conflagration, so much was it wrapped in smoke. . . . . Perhaps, in Chicago, I was influenced by bad weather, by which incentive I do not affirm how things may be, but that I saw them thus, and hence was born the ill-tempered, pouting expression which I read on almost every face. It made me feel, in noting it, how I interpose in such a crowd; a few might show a little courtesy, I do not mean with hats off, but by a nod or glance of recognition. They all were running about desperately. In New York there are more people than in Chicago, and none idle; nevertheless I observe on their streets our same quick friendliness. Here, it seems to me, all might be lost, as I, without company in the formidable tumult. Or if two persons should discourse together, their speech would be in a whining tone, low and nasal, without the least variance of accent. . . . . They say that all Americans have nasal voices. That does not seem to me true of New Yorkers, or only slightly; but it could be said of Chicagoans that their voices come out of their nostrils, and that articulation is made in the pharynx. It is a positive fact that a great many noses in Chicago are in a continuous pathological condition. I have seen in many shop windows certain apparatus for covering the nose, a kind of nasal protector, or false nostrils—but without intent to deceive. I did not see any in operation, however; October, as it seems, still yields to the most delicate the use of the natural nose, but the kingdom of the artificial must be nearby, and I cannot forgive myself for having missed seeing it.

Furthermore, the mass of factories is overpowering without being imposing. That immense building, the Auditorium, where there is a hotel for more than 1,000 guests, an abundance of seats and writing desks of every kind, a conservatory of music, and on the sixth or seventh floor, I don't recall which, a theatre seating 8,000 persons; is this not marvelous to think upon? Its vastness lacks ostentation: it is a vastness of the whole, ostentation means a coordination of parts. All the immense factories of Chicago have low, squatty doors and suffocating stories which the menacing building crushes ridiculously. The two floors of the Tolomei Palace at Siena would be, in Chicago, divided into eight compartments. Certain important houses of twenty stories do not measure one and half voltas, the height of the Stozzi Palace. Surely they take care to mask the frequency of compartments by means of openings which reach from the first floor to the fourth, but to see this from the street, in the height of a single window, three men seated at three writing desks, people and furniture almost suspended in the air, and leaning against a transparent wall, gives one a feeling of irritating unrest. . . . .

The dominant characteristic of the exterior life of Chicago is violence. Everything leads you to extreme expressions: dimensions, movements, noises, rumors, window displays, spectacles, ostentation, misery, activity and alcoholic degradation.

Certain dramatic manifestations recognize in colour and grandeur . . . . the actors of a company and, in like proportions, the principal scenes of a play. A military band passes on the street, followed by a troop of generals in imposing uniforms; the flag which accompanies them announces a new grain machine. Those imperial coaches, shining white with rays of gold, which are drawn by four gigantic white horses, decked with plumes and flowers, carry slabs of meat dripping blood from the butchers' knives; "Armour and Co." I can still see, right in the middle of the sidewalk, placed somewhere on a half column, a crystal goblet which my arms could not reach around, filled to the brim with anglo-saxon teeth. "The set of twenty lower jaws, all extracted by Dr. ———," the sign said, "one visit makes a customer." Then you heard of the beautiful idea of that Chicago upholsterer: those promises to decorate with the most ornate furnishings the nuptial suite of the couple who would consent to be married in his shop window. The couple was found, the scene was made ready, a pastor happened along, and the knot was tied.

In a hairdressing shop, I counted fifty chairs opposite fifty mirrors and served by as many figaros. The day of my arrival, I saw rubbish—still smoking—from a house burned the night before. The day of my departure (and I remained but a single week) I saw on this same site, the iron framework of a new building, already erected to the height of a third story and already the scaffolding of each story completed. The removal of useless materials and the furnishing of new, followed without regard for the neighbors. Provided that the double wheel tracks of the street car may remain, the public ground belongs to the one first to occupy it. The rush of life does not permit the comforts of legal formality. On the street crossing, at the sides of the houses, are mountains of cut stone, brick, rafters and flat iron dropped there in the hurry of unloading, and left there until they are required by the gradual consumption of the neighboring factory. No one thinks of the inconvenience to the passerby, he understands . . . . by mere intuition that everyone sacrifices slight individual conveniences to the free sway of the great mechanical forces. Chicago would not be the Mushroom City, as its inhabitants boast, if—as it happens to most of us—the very small guardianships of the individual might be distracted from production and from the increase of a great part of collective activities. If the railroad stations, beyond the nucleus of the central building, might have to surround with a wall and extensive palisades the communications between the various quarters, they would not be so frequent there as the need demands. . . . . On the level open spaces, between the houses and the urban movement, a large sign with the word "Danger" warns the people to look about. Let everyone think of himself. The train rushes in, without slow-ing down, loudly ringing the bell, like a church on a fête day. Life and health are for the one who has eyes and mind.

Oh how the bells on those trains do ring! The windows in my room at the Hotel Richelieu overlook the lake, I was told; but between the hotel and the lake run twenty or thirty railroad tracks. I wanted to count the number of trains that passed in an hour, I counted thirty-eight, and all of the hours are alike, it is the same night and day, it is like a double hammer: the sound as it fades away on one side is the beginning of what increases on the other; and each bell has its own timbre and each hammer its rhythm; thus the night allows me time to meditate on my blessings. And what about the street cars? There are all kinds and I have ridden on them all; horse cars, steam cars, funiculars, trolleys drawn by air wires.

Their daily circulation is estimated at 2,000,000 passengers. Whoever crosses the principal streets, and it is in rare moments that someone is not passing, feels creak under his feet certain iron channels in the pavement, the kilometric ridges of steel that drag along from a distance. Where the street stops on the revolving bridges, over the navigable canals that connect the lake with the city, the electric street car descends, like a mole, into a deep tunnel. The descent begins far back, the middle of the street sinks between ever-increasing high walls which gradually shut out the daylight. This increasing dusk starts one to thinking: the car has no lighting facility, and you are sitting crowded against diverse and unknown men. From the front window, appears out of the very depths, the black mouth of the tunnel. Will it be closed? But at the last uncertain light of day, and at the first re-round of an approaching curve, a brightness escapes that blinds you. The trolley pole of the street car, the same one that gets its impetus from the suspended wire, induces the current from it, which causes the sparks; gradually it proceeds, ascends, and extinguishes afterward. . . . .

The extraordinary abundance and convenience of trams and busses, and also the bad pavements, are reasons why one encounters so few carriages. . . . . The small vehicles do not mix well in this enormity of rush and tear. The countless number of immovable obstructions forces them to a walk and the network of car tracks and the congestion on the streets crushes them.

Since I have mentioned vehicles I must not be silent on the subject of the hand carts . . . . destined for religious health propaganda. I say "hand" because there was no wagon tongue and it was drawn and pushed by man force, but a horse would have frothed at it. It was a kind of box without sides, placed on four little hidden wheels, which carried a rather heavy harmonium, a little music stool and five massive reading desks . . . . a prayer book and other musical instruments.

It was walking along in the dirt, and proceeded grazing the edge of the sidewalk. At first I thought it was a masquerade. In front of the cart walked a crowd, mostly negroes, dressed in dingy clothes—brown in colour—short trousers and derbies. The first two men supported a worn-out banner stretched from two poles, on which were written some verses from the Bible; others beat upon drums and sang psalms. On the wagon proper there was not a living soul; the actors of this vagabond scene were also movers.

As the procession arrived opposite a sale of liquor, or at a non-prohibition restaurant, the standard-bearers lowered the banner, the Moors formed a circle, and the six men who were standing nearby jumped up on the box. These were all white men, with suspicious looking faces and a repentant air, wearing long frock coats that had once been black, derby hats, and with hair dishevelled. One of them sat down at the harmonium, a second unwrapped the prayerbook, the others sang the plain song. First came the reading from a moral passage, then a wave of harmony, then the reading; sounds and singing vied in a strident discord, all in a low dispirited tone. The psalm-singing over, the procession set out for other places of alcoholic perdition. They preached well without an audience; the passersby did not look on or approve or laugh. The drinkers do not take offense at them, and the walking apostles do not seem to pay attention either to the indifference of the crowd or to the crowd itself. . . . . To see them so indifferent to business would make one suspect them of being paid. I was assured that they were not. . . . . I do not wish to digress here to describe the alcoholic brutality of too many Americans; I will talk of that when I speak again of New York, where I had time to observe close up and more at length, but I noted in Chicago, and a few days later in Cincinnati, a fact which seems to me deeply significant. At the exit of the theatres the men in the crowd gravitate willingly toward the Bar to drink whiskey and nibble, stimulated by a great thirst, dry crusts of bread, or sometimes hard cheese, served free to the customers. Between the acts of the play, almost all of the men, by a nod of the head, make the bartender the first, second and third of importance in the crowd. Drunkenness which is caused from *liqueurs* is not gradual as it is from wine, it does not rush resounding to the brain but strikes beyond there and strangles one. It is important to know that many bars, and not the lowest, in Chicago and Cincinnati, instead of giving to each customer who requests it a fringed napkin on which to wipe his face—such as is used by most of us, arranged a common service: . . . . Along the entire counter, from the public part to the center . . . . runs a roller towel between metallic hooks of exquisite workmanship, and there hang, from rings, more little table napkins which are replenished every day, and who knows, perhaps twice a day, but no more. On these, as is understood, the customers dry their moustaches and wipe their mouths. "A kissed mouth is renewed as the moon," said Boccacio, but a napkin so kissed is not renewed but is cast aside. The fact is that in the evening, between the colour and smell and dampness, these towels fairly speak, and to anyone who uses them, the parts of giving and possessing are equal. I believe, however, that they did not receive more than they gave. Well, I saw men in tall hats and long brown coats, trousers duly turned up *à la anglaise*, and in irreprehensible starched collars and cuffs, take those napkins by the edges as though they might have escaped from the things to be laundered.

So, from the stand-point of immediate sensations, Chicago is not pleasant, and for the person who comes directly from Europe, if the smoky fog hits him on the back as it touched me, he will find it positively abominable. But the misery which draws from it willful, intellectual and physical energies, of which man is capable; the ideas of a social order, simple and progressive; the sight of so many ways open to human industry; the sight of so many natural resources, and of its increase in work,—all these lead him to a concept of actual life so clear, so open-minded, so large and so powerful, and to a certain apprehension of the future, which make him forget quickly the disgust he suffered, which perhaps also made him blush. From the moment that I left it, Chicago became more magnificent and noble in imagination. . . . . I recall the particular discomforts and all the minute facts to which my vain criticism of refinement was put; but there remain for me no general impressions of the great city, these do not find a means of intervening. The name of Chicago does not bring them to my mind.

If classical reminiscences could apply to a population as independent of traditional inconveniences, I would say that Chicago gave me the idea of a classicality less formal than our ancient and so much larger, of how much the earth has increased from Rome, after all. Now the inhabitants have an acute civic pride and willingly would date the present era from the first origins of the city which some living witness can still recall. As Americans in general resemble each other more than do Europeans, so the inhabitants of Chicago resemble one another more than any other Americans, which fact attracts to them the antipathy of the henceforth historical city of the United States. New York covers by a mask of disdainful ostentation the unrest which her rival of the west causes her, to which disputes must finally cede the seat of the Columbian Exposition. Chicago calls attention to these restless jealousies and strives hard to deserve more. With undaunted faith in her own destiny, she draws out a feeling of civic dignity which one might say came from worldly ostentation.

I shall cite an example from an almost literary character.

Everyone remembers a rebellion of an anarchist group, several years ago. The governor of Illinois, to which state Chicago belongs, did not.go there with a light hand: for four murdered policemen, four anarchists mounted the gallows. But the punishment of the guilty is not enough, they wish to erect a monument in honor of the victims. We are always erecting statues "ad personam," and besides, we have agreed upon a kind of hierarchic statue in not an inferior grade of bronze or marble. There in Lincoln Park, where rises the statue of General Grant, was erected, a short distance from it, a memorable statue representing the lowest officials of the law: the policeman.

The pedestal records the date of the rebellion and this truly Roman inscription:

IN THE NAME OF THE PEOPLE OF ILLINOIS
I COMMAND PEACE

From what I have just said, one might infer that it is not exactly worthwhile to go to Chicago, because the sensual and immediate impressions are unpleasant, and the many books which treat it extensively ought to suffice. No one is pressing me to publish here, but everyone sees better with his own eyes than with those of others. Certainly the books which are seriously received, collect more news notices than a colony of tourists can collect; but from the stand-point of real things, everyone of us, by our uninformed process, surely draws some notions which better fit our own talent and put it in movement. The book must, of necessity, expound the facts in succession and then always in this display which better turns to the discussions of the author. Reality places it in simultaneous order and you reason for yourself.

Books have told me of many more things about Chicago than I have seen, and many marvels that I had neither the means nor will of ascertaining. I had learned from a book that the population had increased in seventy years from one hundred inhabitants to one and one-half millions; and in the fire of 1871, seven thousand houses were destroyed; that the heads of beasts slaughtered in a year's time amounted to 10,000,000; the cans of meat, to a thousand millions, without counting that shipped out in barrels; that, on an average there arrive day after day 175,000 foreigners. But when I read that the level of an entire quarter of the city was raised . . . . five, six, eight metres, the ideal con-

cept is not . . . . comparable to that which comes from the measure of lands and from the vista of factories. These were raised
by weights and held in position until the surface soil reloaded
them. And I wager that whoever reads, imagines here two story
houses, perhaps of wood—who knows. . . . .

So when the Reclus registers 471 kilometric squares of land
attributed by the laws of the state to the municipal territory of
Chicago, and adds that such immense expanse is, therefore, not
yet entirely built up, the famous plains of progress of our cities,
destined to remain dead letters in the municipal archives year
after year, are presented to the thought of the reader. But whoever crosses those bare shores, finds marked there the measure of
every single building and, plainly written on nailed sign-boards,
the name and number of each street. . . . .

Finally, we learn from books that Chicago is, from the point
of view of wealth, the greatest emporium known to the world of
natural resources, and one of the major centers of industrial productions; but whoever has not seen people and things in motion
cannot comprehend how these two elements of social prosperity
interpenetrate continuously. . . . . In other cities there are
quarters diversely marked by various functions of life. Here,
freight depots; there factories; elsewhere, banking districts or
very small parks, and restricted in certain quarters, where is reflected luxury and elegance and various means of pleasure. The
foreigner who is not interested in special curiosities remains for
the most part in these privileged and cosmopolitan quarters to
which this maxim is applicable: "The country is the whole
world." And because things do not come to him, he ignores
them, or if he seeks them, he receives as many separate acquaintances as reason can coordinate in the future, but which combine
badly in one comprehensive idea.

Moreover, in Chicago all the life and all the customs and all
the laws of life are at every moment and in every place and almost in the same measure, presented to the senses of the visitor.
It is not necessary to search, and it is impossible not to see. The
privileged—if not the most eccentric—quarters are not, as I have
pointed out before, given to reposing residences and to Sunday

leisure. Aside from these, wherever you may go, the enormous wagons that make the houses tremble, the smoke that blinds you, the smells which take your breath, the incumbrances of merchandise which block the passageways, the mountains of sacks piled up in the little court yards, the disturbance of the rubbish dumps, the violence of the porters, the whistles and bells of a hundred interminable trains, the fury of the people,— all these together command you to avoid the contemporary activity and the formidable complexity of all earthly and human forces. And while you are imagining thus what place this city, born only yesterday, holds in the life of the world, you may feel surging within you a sentiment that is stupefying not only to the sight of so much work and so many riches, but also of respect for their lawful applications and origins. . . . .

In Chicago, a business man unacquainted, as I am, with economics, dismisses from his mind the probability of riches founded on the material presence of things useful to man. He understands that human activity is entirely within one to increase the real value of things, and that individual riches come from true voluntary contributions given to universal prosperity.

JULIAN RALPH[1]

JULIAN RALPH, author and journalist, was born in New York, May 27, 1853. He received his early education in both public and private schools, and at the age of twenty-two began his life work as a journalist, joining the staff of the New York *Daily Graphic*. He soon left this paper for a place on the New York *Sun*, where he remained for twenty years.

In 1891–92, and again in 1893, Ralph made an extensive tour of the United States for *Harper's Magazine*. It was on the first tour that he wrote the account of his visit to Chicago which is reproduced here. The New York *Journal* sent him to England in 1896 to act as its London correspondent, where he remained for the rest of his journalistic career. He also served as the London correspondent for the Brooklyn *Eagle*, and in 1899 he joined the staff of the London *Daily Mail*. In addition to various magazine articles he is the author of several books, among them *On Canada's Frontier*, *Our Great West*, *Chicago and the World's Fair*, *Dixie*, and *War's Brighter Side*.

Ralph was deeply interested in the Far and Middle West. Especially did Chicago capture his fancy, for he found the city vigorous and virile, characteristics which are the dominant note of *Our Great West*, published in 1893. Previous to publication in book form, however, various chapters appeared in *Harper's Magazine* and *Harper's Weekly*. The book is not an example of exaggerated journalism; nor does it play up the trilogy of the romantic West— the Indian, the cowboy, and the buffalo. He felt no eastern superiority to the alleged crudeness of the West; but, on the other hand, he gained a sense of pride in an energetic people, populating this vast region. As he traveled through the commercial centers of Duluth, Chicago, and other western cities, Ralph talked to industrial leaders, obtaining for his book greater insight into actual conditions and a more accurate picture than he would otherwise have had. The West was not only commercial but it was also beautiful in Ralph's eyes—a reaction reflected at times in almost fulsome praise of the grandeur of Western scenery.

-»> «-

A RAPIDLY MOVING AND BUSINESS-LIKE CITY

With few exceptions, the great expositions of the world have been held in Christendom's great capitals, and the cities that have known them have been scarcely subordinate to the expositions themselves in the attractions they have offered to the masses of sight-seers who have gathered in them. Chicago lacks

[1] Julian Ralph, *Our Great West* (New York: Harper & Bros., 1893), pp. 1–23, 30–63. Reprinted by permission of Harper & Bros.

many of the qualities of the older cities that have been chosen for this purpose, but for every one that is missing she offers others fully as attractive. Those who go clear-minded, expecting to see a great city, will find one different from that which any precedent has led them to look for. Those who go to study the world's progress will not find in the Columbian Exposition, among all its marvels, any other result of human force so wonderful, extravagant, or peculiar as Chicago itself.

While investigating the management and prospects of the Columbian Exposition, I was a resident of Chicago for more than a fortnight. A born New-Yorker, the energy, roar, and bustle of the place were yet sufficient to first astonish and then to fatigue me. I was led to examine the city, and to cross-examine some of its leading men. I came away compelled to acknowledge its possession of certain forceful qualities which I never saw exhibited in the same degree anywhere else. I got a satisfactory explanation of its growth and achievements, as well as proof that it must continue to expand in population and commercial influence. Moreover, without losing a particle of pride or faith in New York—without perceiving that New York was affected by the consideration—I acquired a respect for Chicago such as it is most likely that any American who makes a similar investigation must share with me.

The city has been thought intolerant of criticism. The amount of truth there is in this is found in its supervoluminous civicism. The bravado and bunkum of the Chicago newspapers reflect this quality, but do it clumsily, because it proceeds from a sense of business policy with the editors, who laugh at it themselves. But underlying the behavior of the most able and enterprising men in the city is this motto, which they constantly quoted to me, all using the same words, "We are for Chicago first, last, and all the time." To define that sentence is, in a great measure, to account for Chicago. It explains the possession of a million inhabitants by a city that practically dates its beginning after the war of the rebellion. Its adoption by half a million men as their watchword means the forcing of trade and manufactures and wealth; the getting of the World's Fair, if you please. In order to comprehend Chicago, it is best never to lose sight of the motto of its citizens.

I have spoken of the roar and bustle and energy of Chicago. This is most noticeable in the business part of the town, where the greater number of the men are crowded together. It seems there as if the men would run over the horses if the drivers were not careful. Everybody is in such a hurry and going at such a pace that if a stranger asks his way, he is apt to have to trot along with his neighbor to gain the information, for the average Chicagoan cannot stop to talk. The whole business of life is carried on at high pressure, and the pithy part of Chicago is like three hundred acres of New York Stock Exchange when trading is active. European visitors have written that there are no such crowds anywhere as gather on Broadway, and this is true most of the time; but there is one hour on every week-day when certain streets in Chicago are so packed with people as to make Broadway look desolate and solitudinous by comparison. That is the hour between half-past five and half-past six o'clock, when the famous tall buildings of the city vomit their inhabitants upon the pavements. Photographs of the principal corners and crossings, taken at the height of the human torrent, suggest the thought that the camera must have been turned on some little-known painting by Doré. Nobody but Doré ever conceived such pictures. To those who are in the crowds, even Chicago seems small and cramped; even her street cars, running in breakneck trains, prove far too few; even her streets that connect horizon with horizon seem each night to roar at the city officials for further annexation in the morning.

We shall see these crowds simply and satisfactorily accounted for presently; but they exhibit only one phase of the high-pressure existence; they form only one feature among the many that distinguish the town. In the tall buildings are the most modern and rapid elevators, machines that fly up through the towers like glass balls from a trap at a shooting contest. The slow-going stranger, who is conscious of having been "kneaded" along the streets, like a lump of dough among a million bakers, feels himself loaded into one of those frail-looking baskets of steel netting, and the next instant the elevator-boy touches the trigger, and up goes the whole load as a feather is caught up by a gale. The descent is more simple. Something lets go, and you fall from ten to twenty stories as it happens. There is sometimes a jolt, which makes the passenger seem to feel his stomach pass into his shoes, but, as a rule, the mechanism and management both work marvellously towards ease and gentleness. These elevators are too slow for Chicago, and the managers of certain tall buildings now arrange them so that some run "express" to the seventh story without stopping, while what may be called accommodation cars halt at the lower floors, pursuing a course that may be likened to the emptying of the chambers of a revolver in the hands of a person who is "quick on the trigger." It is the same everywhere in the business district. Along Clark Street are some gorgeous underground restaurants, all marble and plated metal. Whoever is eating at one of the tables in them will see the ushers standing about like statues until a customer enters the door, when they dart forward as if the building were falling. It is only done in order to seat the visitor promptly. Being of a sympathetic and impressionable nature, I bolted along the street all the time I was there as if some one on the next block had picked my pocket.

In the Auditorium Hotel the guests communicate with the clerk by electricity, and may flash word of their thirst to the bar-tender as lightning dances from the top to the bottom of a steeple. A sort of annunciator is used, and by turning an arrow and pressing a button, a man may in half a minute order a cocktail, towels, ice-water, stationery, dinner, a bootblack, and the evening newspapers. Our horse-cars in New York move at the rate of about six miles an hour. The cable-cars of Chicago make more than nine miles an hour in town, and more than thirteen miles an hour where the population is less dense. They go in trains of two cars each, and with such a racket of gong-ringing and such a grinding and whir of grip-wheels as to make a modern vestibuled train seem a waste of the opportunities for noise. But these street cars distribute the people grandly, and while they occasionally run over a stray citizen, they far more frequently clear their way by lifting wagons and trucks bodily to one side as they whirl along. It is a rapid and a business-like city. The speed with which cattle are killed and pigs are turned into slabs of salt pork has amazed the world, but it is only the ignorant portion thereof that does not know that the celerity at the stockyards is merely an effort of the butchers to keep up with the rest of the town. The only slow things in Chicago are the steam railway trains. Further on we will discover why they are so.

CHICAGO'S BUILDINGS

I do not know how many very tall buildings Chicago contains, but they must number nearly two dozen. Some of them are artistically designed, and hide their height in well-balanced proportions. A few are mere boxes punctured with window-holes, and stand above their neighbors like great hitching-posts. The best of them are very elegantly and completely appointed, and the communities of men inside them might almost live their lives within their walls, so multifarious are the occupations and services of the tenants. The best New York office buildings are not injured by comparison with these towering structures, except that they are not so tall as the Chicago buildings, but there is not in New York any office structure that can be compared with Chicago's so-called Chamber of Commerce office building, so far as are concerned the advantages of light and air and openness and roominess which its tenants enjoy. In these respects there is only one finer building in America, and that is in Minneapolis. It is a great mistake to think that we in New York possess all the elegant, rich, and ornamental outgrowths of taste, or that we know better than the West what are the luxuries and comforts of the age. With their floors of deftly-laid mosaic-work, their walls of marble and onyx, their balustrades of copper worked into arabesquerie, their artistic lanterns, elegant electric fixtures, their costly and luxurious public rooms, these Chicago office buildings force an exclamation of praise, however unwillingly it comes.

They have adopted what they call "the Chicago method" in putting up these steepling hives. This plan is to construct the actual edifice of steel framework, to which are added thin outer walls of brick, or stone masonry, and the necessary partitions of fire-brick, and plaster laid on iron lathing. The buildings are therefore like enclosed bird-cages, and it is said that, like bird-cages, they cannot shake or tumble down. The exterior walls are mere envelopes. They are so treated that the buildings look like heaps of masonry, but that is homage paid to custom more than it is a material element of strength. These walls are to a building what an envelope is to a letter, or a postage-stamp is to that part of an envelope which it covers. The Chicago method is expeditious, economical, and in many ways advantageous. The manner in which the great weight of houses so tall as to include between sixteen and twenty-four stories is distributed upon the ground beneath them is ingenious. Wherever one of the principal upright pillars is to be set up, the builders lay a pad of steel and cement of such extent that the pads for all the pillars cover all the site. These pads are slightly pyramidal in shape, and are made by laying alternate courses of steel beams crosswise, one upon another. Each pair of courses of steel is filled in and solidified with cement, and then the next two courses are added and similarly treated. At last each pad is eighteen inches thick, and perhaps eighteen feet square; but the size is governed by the desire to distribute the weight of the building at about the average of a ton to the square foot.

This peculiar process is necessitated by the character of the land underneath Chicago. Speaking widely, the rule is to find from seven to fourteen feet of sand super-imposed upon a layer of clay between ten and forty feet in depth. It has not paid to puncture this clay with piling. The piles sink into soft and yielding substance, and the clay is not tenacious enough to hold them. Thus the Chicago Post-office was built, and it not only settles continuously, but it settles unevenly. On the other hand, the famous Rookery Building, set up on these steel and cement pads, did not sink quite an inch, though the architect's calculation was that, by squeezing the water out of the clay underneath, it would settle seven inches. Very queer and differing results have followed the construction of Chicago's biggest buildings, and without going too deep into details, it has been noticed that while some have pulled neighboring houses down a few inches, others have lifted adjoining houses, and still others have raised buildings that were at a distance from themselves. The bed of clay underneath Chicago acts when under pressure like a pan of dough, or like a blanket tautened at the edges and held clear of underneath support. Chicago's great office buildings have basements, but no cellars.

I have referred to the number of these stupendous structures. Let it be known next that they are all in a very small district, that narrow area which composes Chicago's office region, which lies between Lake Michigan and all the principal railroad districts, and at the edges of which one-twenty-fifth of all the railroad mileage of the world is said to terminate, though the district is but little more than half a mile square or 300 acres in extent. One of these buildings—and not the largest—has a population of 4000 persons. It was visited and its elevators were used on three days, when a count was kept, by 19,000, 18,000, and 20,000 persons. Last October there were 7000 offices in the tall buildings of Chicago, and 7000 more were under way in buildings then undergoing construction. The reader now understands why in the heart of Chicago every work-day evening the crowds convey the idea that our Broadway is a deserted thoroughfare as compared with, say, the corner of Clark and Jackson streets.

These tall buildings are mainly built on land obtained on 99-year leasehold. Long leases rather than outright purchases of land have long been a favorite preliminary to building in Chicago, where, for one thing, the men who owned the land have not been those with the money for building. Where very great and costly buildings are concerned, the long leases often go to corporations or syndicates, who put up the houses. It seems to many strangers who visit Chicago that it is reasonable to prophesy a speedy end to the feverish impulse to swell the number of these giant piles, either through legislative ordinance or by the fever running its course. Many prophesy that it must soon end. This idea is bred of several reasons. In the first place, the tall buildings darken the streets, and transform the lower stories of opposite houses into so many cellars or damp and dark base-ments. In the next place, the great number of tall and splendid office houses is depreciating the value of the humbler property in their neighborhoods. Four-story and five-story houses that once were attractive are no longer so, because their owners can-not afford the conveniences which distinguish the greater edifices wherein light and heat are often provided free, fire-proof safes are at the service of every tenant, janitors officer a host of serv-ants, and there are barber-shops, restaurants, cigar and news-stands, elevators, and a half-dozen other conveniences not found in smaller houses. It would seem, also, that since not all the people of Chicago spend their time in offices, there must soon come an end of the demand for these chambers. So it seems, but not to a thoroughbred Chicagoan. One of the foremost business men in the city asserts that he can perceive no reason why the entire business heart of the town—that square half-mile of which I have spoken—should not soon be all builded up of cloud-capped towers. There will be a need for them, he says, and the money to defray the cost of them will accompany the demand. The only trouble he foresees will be in the solution of the prob-lem what to do with the people who will then crowd the streets as never streets were clogged before.

METROPOLITAN AREA

This prophecy relates to a little block in the city, but the city itself contains $181\frac{1}{2}$ square miles. It has been said of the many annexations by which her present size was attained that Chicago reached out and took to herself farms, prairie land, and villages, and that of such material the great city now in part consists. This is true. In suburban trips, such as those I took to Fort Sher-idan and Fernwood, for instance, I passed great cabbage farms, groves, houseless but plotted tracts, and long reaches of the former prairie. Even yet Hyde Park is a separated settlement, and a dozen or more villages stand out as distinctly by them-selves as ever they did. If it were true, as her rivals insist, that Chicago added all this tract merely to get a high rank in the cen-sus reports of population, the folly of the action would be either ludicrous or pitiful, according to the stand-point from which it was viewed. But the true reason for her enormous extension of municipal jurisdiction is quite as peculiar. The enlargement was urged and accomplished in order to anticipate the growth and needs of the city. It was a consequence of extraordinary foresight, which recognized the necessity for a uniform system of boulevards, parks, drainage, and water provision when the city should reach limits that it was even then seen must soon bound a compact aggregation of stores, offices, factories, and dwellings. To us of the East this is surprising. It might seem incredible were there not many other evidences of the same spirit and sagacity not only in Chicago, but in the other cities of the West, especially of the Northwest. What Minneapolis, St. Paul, and Duluth are doing towards a future park system reveals the same enterprise and habit of looking far ahead. And Chicago, in her park system, makes evident her intentions. In all these cities and in a hundred ways the observant traveller notes the same forehandedness, and prepares himself to understand the temper in which the greatest of the Western capitals leaned forth and absorbed the prairie. Chicago expects to become the largest city in America—a city which, in fifty years, shall be larger than the consolidated cities that may form New York at that time.

Now on what substance does Chicago feed that she should foresee herself so great? What manner of men are those of Chicago? What are the whys and the wherefores of her growth?

A CITY OF YOUNG MEN

It seems to have ever been, as it is now, a city of young men. One Chicagoan accounts for its low death rate on the ground that not even its leading men are yet old enough to die. The young men who drifted there from the Eastern States after the close of the war all agree that the thing which most astonished them was the youthfulness of the most active business men. Marshall Field, Potter Palmer, and the rest, heading very large mercantile establishments, were young fellows. Those who came to Chicago from England fancied, as it is said that Englishmen do, that a man may not be trusted with affairs until he has lost half his hair and all his teeth. Our own Eastern men were apt to place wealth and success at the middle of the scale of life. But in Chicago men under thirty were leading in commerce and industry. The sight was a spur to all the young men who came, and they also pitched in to swell the size and successes of the young men's capital. The easy making of money by the loaning of it and by handling city realty—sources which never failed with shrewd men—not only whetted the general appetite for big and quick money-making, but they provided the means for the establishment and extension of trade in other ways and with the West at large.

It is one of the peculiarities of Chicago that one finds not only the capitalists but the storekeepers discussing the whole country with a familiarity as strange to a man from the Atlantic coast as Nebraska is strange to most Philadelphians or New-Yorkers. But the well-informed and "hustling" Chicagoan is familiar with the differing districts of the entire West, North, and South, with their crops, industries, wants, financial status, and means of intercommunication. As in London we find men whose business field is the world, so in Chicago we find the business men talking not of one section or of Europe, as is largely the case in New York, but discussing the affairs of the entire country. The figures which garnish their conversation are bewildering, but if they are analyzed, or even comprehended, they will reveal to the listener how vast and how wealthy a region acknowledges Chicago as its market and its financial and trading centre.

Without either avowing or contesting any part of the process by which Chicago men account for their city's importance or calculate its future, let me repeat a digest of what several influential men of that city said upon the subject. Chicago, then, is the centre of a circle of 1000 miles diameter. If you draw a line northward 500 miles, you find everywhere arable land and timber. The same is true with respect to a line drawn 500 miles in a northwesterly course. For 650 miles westward there is no change in the rich and alluring prospect, and so all around the circle, except where Lake Michigan interrupts it, the same conditions are found. Moreover, the lake itself is a valuable element in commerce. The rays or spokes in all these directions become materialized in the form of the tracks of 35 railways which enter the city. Twenty-two of these are great companies, and at a short distance sub-radials made by other railroads raise the number to 50 roads. As said above, in Chicago one-twenty-fifth of the railway mileage of the world terminates, and serves 30 millions of persons, who find Chicago the largest city easily accessible to them. Thus is found a vast population connected easily and directly with a common centre, to which everything they produce can be brought, and from which all that contributes to the material progress and comfort of man may be economically distributed.

A financier who is equally well known and respected in New York and Chicago put the case somewhat differently as to what he called Chicago's territory. He considered it as being 1000 miles square, and spoke of it as "the land west of the Alleghanies and south of Mason and Dixon's line." This region, the richest agricultural territory in the world, does its financiering in Chicago. The rapid increase in wealth to both the city and the tributary region is due to the fact that every year both produce more, and have more to sell and less to buy. Not long ago the rule was that a stream of goods ran eastward over the Alleghanies, and another stream of supplies came back, so that the West had little gain to show. But during the past five years this back-setting current has been a stream of money returned for the products the West has distributed. The West is now selling to the East and to Europe and getting money in return, because it is manufacturing for itself, as well as tilling the soil and mining for the rest of the world. It therefore earns money and acquires a profit instead of continuing its former process of toiling merely to obtain from the East the necessaries of life. . . . .

When we understand what are the agricultural resources of the region for which Chicago is the trading-post, we perceive how certain it was that its debt would be paid, and that great wealth would follow. The corn lands of Illinois return a profit of $15 to the acre, raising 50 to 60 bushels at $42\frac{1}{2}$ cents a bushel last year, and at a cost for cultivation of only $7 an acre. Wheat produces $22.50 an acre, costs a little less than corn, and returns a profit of from $12 to $15. Oats run 55 bushels to the acre, at 27 cents a bushel, and cost the average farmer only, say, $6 an acre, returning $8 or $9 an acre in profit. These figures will vary as to production, cost, and profit, but it is believed that they represent a fair average. This midland country, of which Chicago is the capital, produces two thousand million bushels of corn, seven hundred million bushels of oats, fifty million hogs, twenty-eight million horses, thirty million sheep, and so on, to cease before the reader is wearied; but in no single instance is the region producing within 50 per cent of what it will be made to yield before the expiration of the next twenty years. Farming there has been haphazard, rude, and wasteful; but as it begins to pay well, the methods begin to improve. Drainage will add new lands, and better methods will swell the crops, so that, for instance, where 60 bushels of corn to the acre are now grown, at least 100 bushels will be harvested. All the corn lands are now settled, but they are not improved. They will yet double in value. It is different with wheat; with that the maximum production will soon be attained.

MANUFACTURES

Such is the wealth that Chicago counts up as tributary to her. By the railroads that dissect this opulent region she is riveted to the midland, the southern, and the western country between the Rockies and the Alleghanies. She is closely allied to the South, because she is manufacturing and distributing much that the South needs, and can get most economically from her. Chicago has become the third manufacturing city in the Union, and she is drawing manufactures away from the East faster than most persons in the East imagine. To-day it is a great Troy stove-making establishment that has moved to Chicago; the week before it was a Massachusetts shoe factory that went there. Many great establishments have gone there, but more must follow, because Chicago is not only the centre of the midland region in respect of the distribution of made-up wares, but also for the concentration of raw materials. Chicago must lead in the manufacture of all goods of which wood, leather, and iron are the bases.

The revolution that took place in the meat trade when Chicago took the lead in that industry affected the whole leather and hide industry. Cattle are dropping 90,000 skins a week in Chicago, and the trade is confined to Chicago, St. Louis, Kansas City, Omaha, and St. Paul. It is idle to suppose that those skins will be sent across the Alleghanies to be turned into goods and sent back again. Wisconsin has become the great tanning State, and all over the district close around Chicago are factories and factory towns where hides are turned into leather goods. The West still gets its finer goods in the East, but it is making the coarser grades, and to such an extent as to give a touch of New England color to the towns and villages around Chicago. . . . .

Chicago has in abundance all the fuels except hard coal. She has coal, oil, stone, brick—everything that is needed for building and for living. Manufactures gravitate to such a place for economical reasons. The population of the north Atlantic division, including Pennsylvania and Massachusetts, and acknowledging New York as its centre, is 17,401,000. The population of the northern central division, trading with Chicago, is 22,362,379. Every one has seen each succeeding census shift the centre of population farther and farther West, but not every one is habituated to putting two and two together.

"Chicago is yet so young and busy," said he who is perhaps the leading banker[2] there, "she has no time for anything beyond each citizen's private affairs. It is hard to get men to serve on a committee. The only thing that saves us from being boors is our civic pride. We are fond, proud, enthusiastic in that respect. But we know that Chicago is not rich, like New York. She has no bulk of capital lying ready for investment and reinvestment; yet she is no longer poor. She has just got over her poverty, and the next stage, bringing accumulated wealth, will quickly follow. Her growth in this respect is more than paralleled by her development into an industrial centre."

So much, then, for Chicago's reasons for existence. The explanation forms not merely the history of an American town, and a town of young men, it points an old moral. It demon-

[2] Lyman J. Gage, probably.

strates anew the active truth that energy is a greater force than money. It commands money. The young founders of Chicago were backed in the East by capitalists who discounted the energy they saw them display. And now Chicago capitalists own the best street railway in St. Louis, the surface railway system of Toledo, a thousand enterprises in hundreds of Western towns.

CLUBS

Chicago has been as crude and rough as any other self-creating entity engaged in a hard struggle for a living. And latterly confidence in and exultation over the inevitable success of the battle have made her boastful, conceited, and noisy. But already one citizen has taken to building houses for rental and not for sale. He has arranged an imitation Astor estate as far ahead as the law will permit, which is to say to one generation unborn. Already, so they boast in Chicago, you may see a few tables in the Chicago Club surrounded by whist-players with gray locks and semi-spherical waistcoats *in the afternoons during business hours!*—a most surprising thing, and only possible at the Chicago Club, which is the old club of the "old rich." These partially globular old whist-players are still in business, of course, as everybody is, but they let go with one hand, as it were, in the afternoons, and only stroll around to their offices at four or five o'clock to make certain that the young members of the other clubs have not stolen their trade while they were playing cards. The other clubs of Chicago merely look like clubs, as we understand the word in New York. They are patronized as our dining-clubs are, with a rush at luncheon-time, although at both ends of the town, in the residence districts, there are clubs to which men drift on Sundays.

A DISTINCTLY AMERICAN CITY

And here one is brought to reflect that Chicago is distinctly American. I know that the Chicagoans boast that theirs is the most mixed population in the country, but the makers and movers of Chicago are Americans. The streets of the city are full of strange faces of a type to which we are not used in the

East—a dish-faced, soft-eyed, light-haired people. They are Scandinavians; but they are malleable as lead, and quickly and easily follow and adopt every Americanism. In return, they ask only to be permitted to attend a host of Lutheran churches in flocks, to work hard, live temperately, save thriftily, and to pronounce every *j* as if it were a *y*. But the dominating class is of that pure and broad American type which is not controlled by New England or any other tenets, but is somewhat loosely made up of the overflow of the New England, the Middle, and the Southern States. It is as mixed and comprehensive as the West Point school of cadets. It calls its city "She-caw-ger." It inclines to soft hats, and only once in a great while does a visitor see a Chicagoan who has the leisure or patience to carry a cane. Its signs are eloquent of its habits, especially of its habit of freedom. "Take G——'s candy to the loved ones at home," stares from hundreds of walls. "Gentlemen all chew Fraxy because it sweetens the breath after drinking," one manufacturer declares; then he adds, "Ladies who play tennis chew it because it lubricates the throat." A bottler of spring water advertises it as "God's own liver remedy." On the billboards of a theatre is the threat that "If you miss seeing Peter Peterson, half your life will be gone." In a principal street is a characteristic sign product, "My fifteen-cent meals are world-beaters;" yet there are worse terrors for Chicago diners-out, as is shown by the sign, "Business lunch—quick and cheap."

CHICAGO'S PARKS, STREETS, AND HOMES

But the visitor's heart warms to the town when he sees its parks and its homes. In them is ample assurance that not every breath is "business," and not every thought commercial. Once out of the thicket of the business and semi-business district, the dwellings of the people reach mile upon mile away along pleasant boulevards and avenues, or facing noble parks and parkways, or in a succession of villages green and gay with foliage and flowers. They are not cliff dwellings like our flats and tenements; there are no brownstone cañons like our up-town streets; there are only occasional hesitating hints there of those Philadelphian and Baltimorean mills that grind out dwellings all alike, as nature makes pease and man makes pins. There are more miles of detached villas in Chicago than a stranger can easily account for. As they are not only found on Prairie Avenue and the boulevards, but in the populous wards and semi-suburbs, where the middle folk are congregated, it is evident that the prosperous moiety of the population enjoys living better (or better living) than the same fraction in the Atlantic cities.

Land in New York has been too costly to permit of these villa-like dwellings, but that does not alter the fact that existence in a home hemmed in by other houses is at best but a crippled living. There never has been any valid excuse for the building of these compressed houses by New York millionaires. It sounds like a Celtic bull, but, in my opinion, the poorer millionaires of Prairie Avenue are better off. A peculiarity of the buildings of Chicago is in the great variety of building-stones that are employed in their construction. Where we would build two blocks of brownstone, I have counted thirteen varieties of beautiful and differing building material. Moreover, the contrasts in architectural design evidence among Chicago house-owners a complete sway of individual taste. It is in these beautiful homes that the people, who do not know what to do with their club-houses, hold their card-parties; it is to them that they bring their visitors and friends; in short, it is at home that the Chicagoan recreates and loafs.

It is said, and I have no reason to doubt it, that the clerks and small tradesmen who live in thousands of these pretty little boxes are the owners of their homes; also that the tenements of the rich display evidence of a tasteful and costly garnering of the globe for articles of luxury and *virtu*. A sneering critic, who wounded Chicago deeply, intimated that theirs must be a primitive society where the rich sit on their door-steps of an evening. That really is a habit there, and in the finer districts of all the Western cities. To enjoy themselves the more completely, the people bring out rugs and carpets, always of gay colors, and fling them on the steps—or stoops, as we Dutch legatees should say— that the ladies' dresses may not be soiled. As these step cloth-ings are as bright as the maidens' eyes and as gay as their cheeks, the effect may be imagined. For my part, I think it argues well for any society that indulges in the trick, and proves existence in such a city to be more human and hearty and far less artificial than where there is too much false pride to permit of it. In front of many of the nice hotels the boarders lug out great arm-chairs upon the portal platforms or beside the curbs. There the men sit in rows, just as I can remember seeing them do in front of the New York Hotel and the old St. Nicholas Hotel in happy days of yore, to smoke in the sunless evening air, and to exchange comments on the weather and the passers-by. If the dead do not rise until the Judgment-day, but lie less active than their dust, then old Wouter Van Twiller, Petrus Stuyvesant, and the rest of our original Knickerbockers will be sadly disappointed angels when they come to, and find that we have abandoned these practices in New York, after the good example that our first families all set us.

It is in Chicago that we find a great number of what are called boulevarded streets, at the intersections of which are signs bearing such admonitions as these: "For pleasure driving. No traffic wagons allowed;" or, "Traffic teams are not allowed on this boulevard." Any street in the residence parts of the city may be boulevarded and turned over to the care of the park commissioners of the district, provided that it does not lie next to any other such street, and provided that a certain proportion of the property-holders along it are minded to follow a simple formula to procure the improvement. Improved roadbeds are given to such streets, and they not only become neat and pretty, but enhance the value of all neighboring land. One boulevard in Chicago penetrates to the very heart of its bustling business district. By means of it men and women may drive from the southern suburbs or parks to the centre of trade, perhaps to their office doors, under the most pleasant conditions. By means of the lesser beautified avenues among the dwellings men and women may sleep of nights, and hide from the worst of the city's tumult among green lawns and flower-beds.

Chicago's park system is so truly her crown, or its diadem,

that its fame may lead to the thought that enough has been said about it. That is not the case, however, for the parks change and improve so constantly that the average Chicagoan finds some of them outgrowing his knowledge, unless he goes to them as he ought to go to his prayers. It is not in extent that the city's parks are extraordinary, for, all told, they comprise less than two thousand acres. It is the energy that has given rise to them, and the taste and enthusiasm which have been expended upon them, that cause our wonder. Sand and swamp were at the bottom of them, and if their surfaces now roll in gentle undulations, it is because the earth that was dug out for the making of ponds has been subsequently applied to the forming of hills and knolls. The people go to some of them upon the boulevards of which I have spoken, beneath trees and beside lawns and gorgeous flower-beds, having their senses sharpened in anticipation of the pleasure-grounds beyond, as the heralds in some old plays prepare us for the action that is to follow. Once the parks are reached, they are found to be literally for the use of the people who own them. I have a fancy that a people who are so largely American would not suffer them to be otherwise. There are no signs warning the public off the grass, or announcing that they "may look, but mustn't touch" whatever there is to see. The people swarm all over the grass, and yet it continues beautiful day after day and year after year. The floral displays seem unharmed; at any rate, we have none to compare with them in any Atlantic coast parks. The people even picnic on the sward, and those who can appreciate such license find, ready at hand, baskets in which to hide the litter which follows. And, O ye who manage other parks we wot of, know that these Chicago playgrounds seem as free from harm and eyesore as any in the land.

The best parks face the great lake, and get wonderous charms of dignity and beauty from it. At the North Side the Lincoln Park commissioners, at great expense, are building out into the lake, making a handsome paved beach, sea-wall, esplanade, and drive to enclose a long, broad body of the lake-water. Although the great blue lake is at the city's edge, there is little or no sailing or pleasure-boating upon it. It is too rude and treacherous.

Therefore these commissioners of the Lincoln Park are enclosing, behind their new-made land, a watercourse for sailing and
rowing, for racing, and for more indolent aquatic sport. The
Lake Shore Drive, when completed, will be three miles in length,
and will connect with yet another notable road to Fort Sheridan
twenty-five miles in length. All these beauties form part of the
main exhibit at the Columbian Exposition. Realizing this, the
municipality has not only voted $5,000,000 to the Exposition,
but has set apart $3,500,000 for beautifying and improving the
city in readiness for the Exposition and its visitors, even as a
bride bedecketh herself for her husband. That is well; but it is
not her beauty that will most interest the visitors to Chicago.

I have an idea that all this is very American; but what is to be
said of the Chicago Sunday, with its drinking shops all wide
open, and its multitudes swarming out on pleasure bent? And
what of the theatres opening to the best night's business of the
week at the hour of Sunday evening service in the churches? I
suspect that this also is American—that sort of American that
develops under Southern and Western influences not dominated
by the New England spirit. And yet the Puritan traditions are
not without honor and respect in Chicago, witness the fact that
the city spent seventeen and a quarter millions of dollars during
the past five years upon her public schools. . . . .

THE WOMEN OF CHICAGO

When I wrote my first paper upon Chicago I supposed myself
well-equipped for the task. I saw Chicago day after day, lived
in its hotels and clubs, met its leading business men and officials,
and got a great deal which was novel and striking from what I
saw around me and from what I heard of the commercial and
other secrets of its marvellous growth and sudden importance.
It is customary to ridicule the travellers who found books upon
short visits to foreign places, but the ridicule is not always deserved. If the writers are travelled and observant spectators, if
they ask the right questions of the right men, and they set down
nothing of which they are not certain, the probability is that
what they write will be more valuable in its way than a similar

work from the pen of one who is dulled to the place by familiarity. And yet I know now that my notes upon Chicago only went
half-way. They took no heed of a moiety of the population—the
women, with all that they stand for.

I saw the rushing trains of cable-cars in the streets and heard
the clang-clang of their gongs. It seemed to me then (and so it
still seems, after many another stay in the city) that the men in
the streets leap to the strokes of those bells; there is no escaping
their sharp din; it sounds incessantly in the men's ears. It seems
to joy them, to keep them rushing along, like a sort of Western
conscience, or as if it were a goad or the perpetual prod of a bayo-
net. It is as if it might be the voice of the Genius of the West,
crying "Clang-clang (hustle)—clang-clang (be lively)," and it
needs no wizard sight to note the effect upon the men as they
are kept up to their daily scramble and forge along the thoroughfares—more often talking to themselves when you pass
them than you have ever noticed that men in other cities are
given to doing. I saw all that, but how stupid it was not to notice
that the women escaped the relentless influence!

They appear not to hear the bells. The lines of the masculine
straining are not furrowed in their faces. They remain composed and unmoved; insulated, inoculated. They might be the
very same women we see in Havana or Brooklyn, so perfectly
undisturbed and at ease are they—even when they pass the
Board of Trade, which I take to be the dynamo that surcharges
the air for the men.

I went into the towering office-buildings, nerving myself for
the moment's battle at the doors against the outpouring torrent
and the missile-like office boys who shoot out as from the mouths
of cannon. I saw the flying elevators, and at every landing
heard the bankers and architects and lawyers shout "Down!" or
"Up, up!" and saw them spring almost out of their clothes, as if
each elevator was the only one ever built, and would make only
one trip before it vanished like a bubble. The office girls were as
badly stricken with this *St. Vitus hustle* as the men, which must
account for my not noticing that the main body of women—
when they came to these buildings to visit husbands or brothers

—were creatures apart from the confusion; reposeful, stylish, carefully toiletted, serene, and unruffled.

I often squeezed into the luncheon crowd at the Union League Club and got the latest wheat quotation with my roast, and the valuation of North Side lots with my dessert; but I did not then know that there was a ladies' side-entrance to the club-house, leading to parlors and dining-rooms as quiet as any in Philadelphia, where impassive maids in starched caps sat like bits of majolica-ware and the clang-clang of the car-bells sounded faintly, like the antipodean echoes in a Japanese sea-shell. I smoked at the Chicago Club with Mayor Washburne,[3] and the softening influence of women in public affairs happened not to come into our talk; with Mr. Burnham, the leading architect, and heard nothing of the buildings put up for and by women. Far less was there any hint, in the crush at that club, of the Argonauts[4]— those leisurely Chicago Club-men who haunt a separate house where they loaf in flannels and the women add the luxurious, tremulous shiver of silk to the sounds of light laughter and elegant dining.

And every evening, while that first study of the city went on, the diurnal stampede from the tall buildings and the choking of the inadequate streets around them took place. The cable-cars became loaded and incrusted with double burdens in which men clung to one another like caterpillars. Thus the crowded business district was emptied and the homes were filled. Any one could see that, and I wrote that there was more home-going and home-staying there than in any large Eastern city in this country. But who could guess what that meant? Who could know the extent of the rulership of the women at night and in the homes, or how far it went beyond those limitations? Who would dream that—in Chicago, of all places—all talk of business is tabooed in the homes, and that the men sink upon thick upholstering, in the soft, shaded light of silk-crowned lamps, amid

[3] Hempstead Washburne, mayor from 1891 to 1893. He was the son of Elihu B. Washburne.

[4] The Argonaut Club, an exclusive yacht club of Chicago. Its membership is limited to fifty-one members, the supposed number of the crew of the mythical ship "Argo."

lace-work and bric-à-brac, and in the blessed atmosphere of music and gentle voices—all so soothing and so highly esteemed that it is there the custom for the men to gather accredited strangers and guests around them at home for the enjoyment of dinner, cigars, and cards, rather than at the clubs and in the hotel lobbies. I could not know it, and so, for one reason and another, the gentle side of Chicago was left out of that article. . . . .

In whichever of our cities an Englishman stays long enough to venture an opinion of it that is what he is sure to say. It is true of all of them, and most true of Chicago. But to discover that there is a well-spring of repose there requires a longer acquaintance than to note the need of it. There is such a reservoir in Chicago. It is in the souls, the spirit of the women, and it is as notable a feature of the Chicago homes as of those of any American city. But the women contribute more than this, for, from the polish of travel and trained minds their leaders reflect those charms which find expression in good taste and manners, a love of art and literature, and in the ability to discern what is best, and to distinguish merit and good-breeding above mere wealth and pedigree.

What the leaders do the others copy, and the result is such that I do not believe that in any older American city we shall find fashionable women so anxious to be considered patrons of art and of learning, or so forward in works of public improvement and governmental reform as well as of charity. Indeed, this seems to me quite a new character for the woman of fashion, and whether I am right in crediting her with it the reader will discover before he finishes this paper. It is necessary to add that not all the modish women there belong in this category. There is a wholly gay and idle butterfly set in Chicago, but it is small, and the distinctive peculiarity of which I speak lies in the fact that in nearly all the societies and movements of which I am going to write we see the names of rich and stylish women. They entertain elegantly, are accustomed to travel, and rank with any others in the town, yet are associated with those forceful women whose astonishing activity has worked wonders in that city. . . . .

There is no gainsaying the fact that, in the main, Chicago society is crude; but I am not describing the body of its people; it is rather that reservoir from which is to spring the refinement and graces of the finished city that is to be here considered. If it is true that hospitality is a relic of barbarism, it still must be said that it flourishes in Chicago, which is almost as open-armed as one of our Southern cities. As far as the men are concerned, the hospitality is Russian; indeed, I was again and again reminded of what I have read of the peculiarities of the Russians in what I saw of the pleasures of the younger generation of wealthy men in Chicago. They attend to business with all their hearts by day, and to fun with all their might after dark. They are mainly college men and fellows of big physique, and if ever there were hearty, kindly, jolly, frank fellows in the world, these are the ones. They eat and drink like Russians, and, from their fondness for surrounding themselves with bright and elegant women, I gather that they love like Russians. In like manner do they spend their money. In New York heavy drinking in the clubs is going out of fashion, and there is less and less high play at cards; but in Chicago, as in St. Petersburg, the wine flows freely, the stakes are high. Though the pressure is thus greater than with us in New York, I saw no such effects of the use of stimulants as would follow Chicago freedom were it indulged in the metropolis. And a lady, who is familiar with the gay set, told me that the Chicago women of that circle join the men with such circumspection, when dining, that the newspaper reports of the flushed faces and noisy behavior of our own rapid set at the opera after heavy dining seem to them both shocking and incredible.

But enough of what is exceptional and unrepresentative. The Chicago men are very proud of the women, and the most extravagant comments which Max O'Rell[5] makes upon the prerogatives of American ladies seem very much less extravagant in Chicago than anywhere else. Their husbands and brothers tell me that there is a keen rivalry among the women who are well-to-do for the possession of nice houses, and for the distinction of giving good and frequent dinner-parties, and of entertaining

[5] Max O'Rell, *Jonathan and His Continent* (New York: Cassell & Co., Ltd., 1889).

well. "They spend a great deal of money in this way," I was told, "but they are not mercenary; they do not worship wealth and nag their husbands to get more and more as do the women of the newer West. Their first question about a new-comer is neither as to his wealth nor his ancestry. Even more than in Washington do the Chicago women respect talent and vie with one another to honor those who have any standing in the World of Intellect." In the last ten years the leading circles of women there have undergone a revolution. Women from the female colleges, and who have lived abroad or in the Eastern cities, have displaced the earlier leaders, have married and become the mistresses of the homes as well as the mothers of daughters for whose future social standing they are solicitous.

The noted men and women who have visited Chicago, professionally or from curiosity, in recent years, have found there the atmosphere of a true capital. They have been welcomed and honored in delightful circles of cultivated persons assembled in houses where are felt the intangible qualities that make charming the dwellings of true citizens of the world. For costliness and beauty the numerous fine residences of Chicago are celebrated. Nowhere is there seen a greater variety in the display of cultivated taste in building. In a great degree fine houses are put up in homage to women, and we shall see, if I mistake not, that these women deserve the palaces in which they rule. But, to return to the interiors of the homes, what I find to praise most highly there is the democracy of the men and women. It is genuine. The people's hearts are nearer their waistcoats and basques out there. They aren't incrusted with the sediment of a century of caste-worship and pride and distrust. They may be more new and crude—and all else that we in the East are in the habit of charging them with being—but they may thank God for some of the attributes of their newness. They are more genuine and natural and frank. They are more truly American, and if I like them, and have let that liking appear in what I have written of them, it is because their democracy is sufficient to overwhelm a myriad of their faults.

I have seen a thing in Chicago—and have seen it several more times than once—that I never heard of anywhere else, and that looked a little awkward at first, for a few moments. I refer to a peculiar freedom of intercourse between the sexes after a dinner or on a rout—a *camaraderie* and perfect accord between the men and the women. In saying this I refer to very nice matrons and maidens in very nice social circles who have nevertheless stayed after the coffee, and have taken part in the flow of fun which such a time begets, quite as if they liked it and had a right to. In one case the men had withdrawn to the library, and a noted entertainer was in the full glory of his career, reciting a poem or giving a dialect imitation of a conversation he had overheard on a street-car. The wife of the host trespassed, with a show of timidity, to say that the little girls, her daughters, were about to go to bed, and wanted the Noted Entertainer to "make a face" for them—apparently for them to dream upon.

"Why, come in," said the host.

"Oh, may we?" said his wife, very artlessly, and in came all the ladies of the party, who, it seems, had gathered in the hallway. The room was blue with smoke, but all the ladies "loved smoke," and so the evening wore on gayly. The only sign of recognition of the novelty of the situation was an occasional covert allusion to the stories that a certain shy and notedly modest man *might tell* if the ladies were not present, but all that was said or told was as pure as crystal, and the whole evening was so enjoyable that if any man missed the customary after-dinner "tang" he was disinclined to mention it. . . . .

I have been present on at least a dozen occasions and when the men smoked and drank and the women kept with them, being —otherwise than in the drinking and smoking—in perfect fellowship with them. Such conditions are Arcadian. They are part and parcel of the kinship that permits the Chicagoans to bring their rugs out and to sit on the stoops in the evenings. It will be a sad day when Chicago gets too big and too proud, and when her inhabitants grow too suspicious of one another to permit of such naturalness. . . . .

Their stylishness is the first striking characteristic of the women of Chicago. It is a Parisian quality, apparent in New

York first and in Chicago next, among all our cities. The number of women who dress well in Chicago is very remarkable, and only there and in New York do the shop-girls and working women closely follow the prevailing modes. Chicago leads New York in the employment of women in business. It is not easy to find an office or a store in which they are not at work as secretaries, accountants, cashiers, type-writers, saleswomen, or clerks. It has been explained to me that women who want to do for themselves are more favored there than anywhere else. The awful fire of twenty years ago wrecked so many families, and turned so many women from lives of comfort to paths of toil, that the business men have from that day to this shown an inclination to help every woman who wants to help herself. Women are encouraged to support themselves, honored for their efforts to do so, and gallantly assisted by all true Chicago men who have the native spirit. We shall see that great results have sprung from this necessity of one sex and encouragement by the other. But one notices the little results everywhere, every day. Observe, for instance, this sign in the cable-cars:

THE LADIES DON'T SPEAK OF IT
BUT THEY ARE AGAINST THE
SPITTING HABIT IN THE STREET CARS.
JUST ASK THEM.

The influence of the homes is felt everywhere. It is even more truly a city of homes than Brooklyn, for its flats and tenements are few. Such makeshifts are not true homes, and do not carry household pride with them in anything like the degree that it is engendered in those who live in separated houses which they own. Such, mainly, are the dwellings of Chicago. In that city there are no blocks of flats, tenements, or apartments (by whatever name those barracks may be called).

One of the famous towering office buildings of Chicago is, in the main, the result of a woman's financiering. I refer to "the Temple" of the Woman's Christian Temperance Union, an enormous and beautiful pile, which is, in a general way, like the great Mills Building in Broad Street, New York. It is thirteen stories high, it cost more than a million of dollars, and the scheme of it as well as the execution thereof, from first to last, was the work of women and children. Mrs. Matilda B. Carse,[6] who is grandiloquently spoken of in the Chicago newspapers as "the chief business woman of the continent," inspired and planned the raising of the money. For ten years she advocated the great work, and in the course of that time she formed a corporation called "The Woman's Temple Building Association," for carrying forward the project. She was elected its first president, in July, 1887, and it was capitalized at $600,000. Frances Willard, of the National organization of the Union, co-operated towards enlisting the interest and aid of the entire Temperance Union sisterhood, which adopted the building as its headquarters or "temple." Four hundred thousand dollars worth of the stock was purchased with what is referred to as "the outpouring of 100,000 penny banks," and bonds were issued for $600,000. The building is expected to yield $250,000 a year in rentals. The income is to be divided, one-half to the National organization, and the rest, *pro rata* to the various State organizations, according to the amount each subscribed to the fund. Mrs. Carse's was the mind which planned the financial operation, but the credit of carrying it out rests with Miss Willard, the several other leaders of the Union, and the good women everywhere who have faith in them.

Mrs. Carse is the woman to whom the members of the Chicago Woman's Club refer all plans for raising funds. The Chicago Woman's Club is the mother of woman's public work in that city. An explanation of what that means seems to me to rank among the most surprising of the chapters which I have had occasion to write as the result of my western studies. I know of no such undertakings or co-operation by women elsewhere in

[6] Matilda B. Carse was born near Belfast, Ireland, and came to Chicago in 1858. Her husband, Thomas Carse, a railroad manager, died in 1870. From 1878 to 1917 she was president of the Chicago Woman's Christian Temperance Union. In addition to being the founder of the Woman's Temple Building, she was also the founder of the Bethesda Day Nursery, Talcott Day Nursery of the Chicago W.C.T.U., and the Woman's Temperance Publishing Association. She was president of the latter for eighteen years. She was a member of the Board of Lady Managers of the World's Columbian Exposition and the first woman member of the Board of Education of Cook County, Illinois. Mrs. Carse died June 3, 1917.

our country. This very remarkable Woman's Club has 500 members and six great divisions called the committees on Reform, Philanthropy, Education, Home, Art and Literature, Science and Philosophy. The club has rooms in the building of the famous Art Institute. It holds literary meetings every two weeks, each committee or division furnishing two topics in a year. The members write the papers and the meetings discuss them. Each committee officers and manages its own meetings; the chairwoman of the committee being in charge, and opening as well as arranging the discussions. The Art and Literature and the Science and Philosophy committees carry on classes, open to all members of the club. They engage lecturers, and perform an educational work. Apart from these class meetings, the club-rooms are in use every day as a headquarters for women. They include a kitchen, a dining-room, and a tea-room—tea, by-the-way, being served at all the committee meetings.

The membership is made up of almost every kind of women, from the ultra-fashionable society leaders to the working women, and includes literary and other professional women, business women, and plain wives and daughters. "And," say the members, "women who never hear anything anywhere else, hear everything that is going on in the world by attending the club meetings.". . . .

Each woman on entering the club designates the division she wishes to enter. Her name is catalogued accordingly, and she works with that committee. Each committee holds periodic meetings, at which subjects are given out for papers and discussion at the next session. The Home Committee, for instance, deals with the education and rearing of children, domestic service, dress reform, decorative art, and kindred subjects. That has always been the method in the club, but a result of that and other influences has been that "Chicago ladies have been papered to death," as one of them said to me, and in the last few years the development of a higher purpose and more practical work has progressed. It began when the Reform Committee undertook earnest work, and ceased merely to hear essays and discuss prison reform, to go "slumming," and to pursue all the fads that were going. This committee began its earnest work with the County Insane Asylum, where it was found that hundreds of women were herded without proper attention, three in a bed, sometimes; with insufficient food, with only a counterpane between them and the freezing winter air at night, and no flannels by day. The root of the trouble was the old one—the root of all public evil in this country— the appointment of public servants for political reasons and purposes. The first step of the Reform Committee was to ask the county commissioners to appoint a woman physician to the asylum. Dr. Florence Hunt was so appointed, and went there at $25 a month. She found that the nurses made up narcotics by the pailful to give to the patients at night so as to stupefy them, in order that they, the nurses, might be free for a good time. The new doctor stopped that and the giving of all other drugs, except upon her order. Then she insisted upon the employment of fit nurses. She and the women doctors who followed her there suffered much petty persecution, but a complete reform was in time accomplished, and the woman physician became a recognized necessity there. To-day, as a consequence, the asylums at Kankakee, Jackson,[7] and Elgin—all Illinois institutions—have women physicians also. I am assured that no one except a physician can appreciate how great a reform it was to establish the principle that women suffering from mental diseases should be put in charge of women. Mrs. Helen S. Shedd was at the front of the asylum reform work, which is still going on.

She next led the Reform Committee into the Poorhouse, where they went, as they always do, with the plea "There are women there; we want a share in the charge of that place for the sake of our sex." They have adopted the motto, "What are you doing with the women and children?" And they find that the politicians cannot turn aside so natural and proper an inquiry. The politicians try to frighten the women. They say, "You don't want to pry into such things and places; you can't stand it." But the Chicago ladies have proven that they can stand a very great deal, as we shall see, on behalf of humanity; espe-

[7] Jacksonville.

cially feminine humanity. "You are using great sums of money for the care of the poor, the sick, the insane, and the vicious," they say. "One-half of these are women, and we, as women, insist upon knowing how you are performing your task. We do not believe you bring the motherly or the sisterly element to your aid; we know that you do not understand women's requirements." That line of argument has always proved irresistible.

While I was in Chicago in August some of the women were looking over the plans for four new police-stations. It transpired as they talked that they have succeeded in establishing a Woman's Advisory Board of the Police, consisting of ten women appointed by the Chief of Police, and in charge of the quarters of all women and children prisoners, and of the station-house matrons, two of which are appointed to each station where women are taken. Through the work of her women, Chicago led in this reform, which is now extending to the chief cities of the country. Now, all women and juveniles are separated from the men in nine of the Chicago precinct stations, to one of which every such prisoner must be taken, no matter at which time or on what charge such a person is arrested. . . . . She [the chief matron, Mrs. Jane Logan] has an office in a down-town station, where the worst prisoners are taken as well as the friendless girls and waifs who drift in at the railway stations. The waifs are all taken to her, and she never leaves them until they are on the way back to their homes, or to better guardianship. She maintains an "annex," kept clean and sweet, with homelike beds and pictures, and to this place are taken any first offenders and others, of saving whom she thinks there is a chance. Female witnesses are also kept there instead of in the prisoners' cells, and all who go to the annex are entirely secluded from reporters as well as all others. Two of the best matrons of the force are in charge day and night. All women and girl prisoners are attended at court, even the drunken women being washed and dressed and made to look respectable. Mrs. Logan always goes herself with the young girls to see that they are not approached, and in order that if it is just and advantageous that they should escape punishment she may plead with the court for their release. Formerly, every woman who was arrested was searched by men and thrown in a cell in the same jail-room with the male prisoners. Lost children, homeless girls, and abandoned women were all huddled together. The women of the city "couldn't stand it," they say. They worked eight years, led by Miss Sweet,[8] to bring about the now accomplished reform.

In all cases in which women complain of abuse or mistreatment by the police or others, Mrs. Logan sits on the Police Trial Board "to show the unfortunate woman that she has a friend." The Board is composed of five inspectors and the assistant chief of police, and the president asked her to join its sessions whenever a woman is involved in any case that comes before it. The police do not oppose the work of the women. Desperate and abandoned females used to make fearful charges against the patrolmen and others on the force under the old regime. Under the new system there is a great change in this respect. . . . .

The Protective Agency protects women and children in all their rights of property and person, gives them legal advice, recovers wages for servants, sewing-women and shop-girls who are being swindled; finds guardians for defenseless children; procures divorces for women who are abused or neglected; protects the mothers' right to their children. It has obtained heavy sentences against men in cases of outrage—so very heavy that this crime is seldom committed. In a matter akin to this, the women of this society perform what seems to me a most extraordinary work. It is a part of the belief of these ladies that all women have rights, no matter how bad or lost to decency some of them may be. Therefore, they stand united against the ancient custom, among criminal lawyers, of destroying a woman's testimony by showing her bad character. This these women call "a many-century-old trick to throw a woman out of court and deny her justice.". . . .

[8] Ada Celeste Sweet was born February 23, 1853. She became United States pension agent in Chicago on the death of her father in 1874, who was then agent; and she held this position until 1885. In 1886 she became the literary editor of the *Chicago Tribune*. She opened a United States claims office in Chicago in 1888 but retired in 1905. She then wrote editorials for the *Chicago Journal*. From 1911 to 1913 she was manager of the woman's department of the Equitable Life Assurance Society.

The Philanthropy Committee of the Woman's Club began its active work in the county jail where it found a shocking state of affairs. There was only one woman official in the jail, and at four o'clock every afternoon she locked up the women and went away. When she had gone the men were free to go in, and they did. The women of the committee demanded the appointment of a night matron, and the sheriff said he required an order from certain judges who were nominally in charge. This they obtained, and then they were told they must secure from the county an appropriation for the proposed matron's salary. The county officials granted the money conditionally upon the nomination for the place being made by the Woman's Club. The matron was appointed, the work of reform was begun, and it was as if a fresh lake breeze had blown through the unwholesome place. The men cannot intrude upon the women now, and little vagrant girls of ten to fourteen years of age are no longer locked up with hardened criminals. The children have a separate department, where toys and books and a kindly matron brighten their lives while they are awaiting trial. Still another department in the jail is a school for the boys, who are sometimes kept there three or four months before being tried. It was after this work in the jail that the Philanthropy Committee took up the police-station reforms. The first matrons who were put in charge of the stations were political appointees, except a few who were nominally recommended by the Woman's Christian Temperance Union. The whole system was a sham; the women had to have political backing; they were not in sympathy with the movement, and were not competent. They were "just poor," and had large families, and merely wanted the money. There are twenty-five satisfactory matrons now. Each appointment was first recommended after investigation by the women of the Police Advisory Board, which endeavors to secure those who have not large families or absorbing cares at home, but who have time to spare, and character, nerve, and tact.

A few years ago there was a movement among Chicago men for the foundation of an Industrial School for Homeless Boys who were not criminals. The idea was to train the boys and put them out for adoption. The plan languished and was about to be abandoned, when the Woman's Club took hold of it. A Mr. George, a farmer, had promised to give three hundred acres of land worth $40,000 if any one would raise $40,000 for the buildings. The Woman's Club rose "as one man," got the money in three months, and turned it over to the men, who then founded the Illinois Manual Training-school at Glenwood, near the city. An advisory board of women in the club attends to the raising of money, the provision of clothing, and the exercise of a general motherly interest in the institution, which is exceptionally successful.

This list of gentle reforms and revolutions is but begun. The Education Committee of this indomitable club discovered, a few years since, that the statute providing for compulsory education was not enforced. The ladies got up a tremendous agitation, and many leading men, as well as women, went to the Capitol at Springfield and secured the passage of a mandatory statute insuring the attendance at school of children of from six to fourteen years during a period of sixteen weeks in each year. Five women were appointed among the truant officers, and the law was strictly carried out. It is found that it works well to employ women in this capacity. They are invited into the houses by the mothers, who tell them, as they would not tell men, the true reasons for keeping their children from school, as, for instance, that they have but one pair of shoes for six children. A beautiful charity resulted from this work. . . . .

A very remarkable member of the Woman's Club is Jane Addams, of whose gentle character it is sufficient to say that her friends are fond of referring to her as "Saint Jane." She is not robust in health, but, after doing more than ten men would want to do, she usually explains that it is something she has found "in which an invalid can engage." She is a native of Illinois, is wealthy, and while on a visit to London, becoming interested in Toynbee Hall, evolved a theory which has brightened her own and very many other lives. It is that "the rich need the poor as much as the poor need the rich;" that there is a vast number of girls coming out of the colleges for whom there is not enough to do to interest them in life, and who grow ennuied when they might be active and happy. It is her idea that when they interest themselves in their poor brothers and sisters they find the pure gold of happiness. She asked the aid of many ladies of leisure, and went to live in one of the worst quarters of Chicago, taking with her Miss Ellen Starr, a teacher, and a niece of Eliza Allen Starr, the writer. She found an old-time mansion with a wide hall through the middle and large rooms on either side. It had been built for a man named Hull, as a residence, but it had become an auction-house, and the district around it had decayed into a quarter inhabited by poor foreigners. The woman who had fallen heir to it gave it to Miss Addams rent free until 1893. She and Miss Starr lived in it, filled it plainly but with fine taste, with pictures and ornaments as well as suitable furniture and appointments for the purposes to which it was to be put. A piano was put in the large parlor or assembly-room, which is used every morning for a kindergarten. A beautiful young girl, Miss Jennie Dow, gave the money for the kindergarten, and taught it for a year. Miss Fanny Garry [*sic*], a daughter of Judge Garry, organized a cooking-school, and, with her young friends to assist her, teaches the art of cooking to poor girls.

A great many of the best known young men and ladies in North Side circles contribute what they can to the success of this charity, now known as Hull House, and the subject of general local pride. These young persons teach Latin classes, maintain a boys' club, and instruct the lads of the neighborhood in the methods of boyish games; support a modelling class, a class in woodcarving, and another in American history. Every evening in the week some club meets in Hull House—a political economy club, a German club, or what not. Miss Addams's idea is that the poor have no social life, and few if any of the refinements which gild the intercourse that accompanies it. Therefore, on one night in each week, a girls' club meets in Hull House. The girls invite their beaus and men friends, and play games and talk and dance, refreshing themselves with lemonade and cake. The young persons who devote their spare time to the work go right in with the girls and boys, and help to make the evenings jolly; one who is spoken of as "very swell" bringing his violin to furnish the dance music. The boys' club has one of the best gymnasiums in the city. The boys prepare and read essays and stories, and engage in improving tasks. There is a *crèche* in the Hull House system, and the sick of the district all go there for relief. College extension classes are also in the scheme, and public school-teachers attend the classes with college graduates, who enlist for the purpose of teaching them.

One of the new undertakings of the Chicago women is the task set for itself by the Municipal Reform League. It was organized in March, 1892, by the ladies who were connected with World's Fair Congresses, a comprehensive work, for the description of which I have no space. A large committee was studying municipal reform when they decided to found an independent society, to endure long after the World's Fair, and to devote itself to local municipal reform, and especially to the promotion of cleanliness in the streets. . . . . Six hundred members are on the rolls, and these include one hundred men, among whom are millionaires and working-men. Money has been contributed liberally, but only the secretary received compensation. The work performed is all in the direction of forcing the public officials to do their duty. The Health Department is in charge of the alleys and the Street Department of the streets. . . . . Already many wealthy ladies drive down the alleys instead of the streets, and even walk through the byways; and so do many influential men, for the purpose of detecting negligence and reporting it. The complaints are forwarded, in the society's formal manner, to the responsible commissioners. . . . . The reformers will not stop until they have destroyed the entire contract system and have made the police do the work of inspection. Already ten policemen are detailed to this work, and eighteen more are to extend the system. An amazing and disheartening discovery attended the beginning of this undertaking. The garbage of the city was supposed to be burned as it accumulated; instead, it was being dumped in a circle of hillocks around the outskirts of the town. A plan for disposing of it by fire had failed, and the officials sat helplessly down and gave up the job. The women took up the task, and now (July, 1892) three methods are undergoing trial, and 180 tons a day are being burned. That mere incident in the history of this movement for clean streets is a grand return for the investment of interest in the project which the public has made. . . . .

These unusual activities and undertakings are but a part of what the women are doing, and are in addition to the kindly and humane efforts which the reader had doubtless expected to hear about, and which but parallel those which interest and occupy American ladies everywhere. There are proportionately as many workers in the hospitals, schools, and asylums, as many noble founders and supporters of refuges and hospitals, as many laborers in Church and mission work in Chicago as in New York or Boston. If the readers understand that those of which I have told are all added, like jewels upon a crown, to all the usual benefactions, the force of this chapter will be appreciated.

There are in Chicago, as elsewhere, Browning and Ibsen and Shakespearian circles and clubs, and if the city boasts few *littérateurs* or artists of celebrity, there is no lack of lovers and students of the work of those who live elsewhere. The Twentieth Century Club, founded, I believe, by the brilliant Mrs. George Rowswell Grant, is the most ambitious literary club, and has a large and distinguished membership. It meets in the houses of wealthy ladies, and is at times addressed by distinguished visitors whom it invites to the city. The Chicago Literary Club is another such organization, and of both these men as well as women are members. The Chicago Folk-lore Society, a new aspirant to such distinction, was organized in December, 1891. . . . . The motto of this society illumines its field of work. It is, "Whence these legends and traditions?" It has started a museum of Indian and other relics and curios, and may make an exhibition during the World's Fair. It will certainly distinguish itself during the congress of folk-lore scholars to be held in Chicago in 1893. . . . .

I had a most interesting talk with one of the women active in certain of the public works I have described, and she told me that one reason why the women succeeded so well with the officials and politicians is that they are not voters, are not in politics, and ask favors (or rights) not for themselves but for the public. That, she thought, sounded like an argument against granting the suffrage to women; but she said she would have to let it stand, whatever it sounded like. She said that the Chicago men not only spring to the help of a woman who tries to get along "but they hate to see her fail, and they won't allow her to fail if they can help it." She remarked that the reason that active Chicago women do not show the aggressive, harsh spirit and lack of graceful femininity which is often associated with women who step out of the domestic sphere, is because the Chicago women have not had to fight their way. The men have helped them. She gloried in the strides the women have made towards independence in Chicago. "A fundamental principle with us," she said, "is that a girl may be dependent, but a woman must be independent in order to perform all her functions. She must be independent in order to wisely make a choice of her career— whether she will be a wife and mother, and, if so, whose wife and mother she will be."

-»»·«««-

FRANÇOIS EDMOND BRUWAERT[1]

F RANÇOIS EDMOND BRUWAERT[2] was born in Paris September 25, 1847. He took degrees in letters, sciences, and law at the Sorbonne, and in 1870 he was admitted to the bar in Paris.

Shortly thereafter he began his career in the consular and diplomatic services of the French government as attaché of the ministry of foreign affairs. After serving in various capacities with the ministry in Paris he was made second-class consul at Chicago, where he first took up his duties in January, 1882, and became a consul of the first class in July, 1884. In June, 1885, he went to New York as acting consul general, returning to Chicago as consul general in November, 1887, after serving for a short time as consul at Melbourne. He returned to New York in 1889 as acting consul general, becoming consul general there in 1894 and remaining until 1897.

In 1893 he married Susan A. King, a daughter of Mrs. J. McGregor Adams of Chicago.

After a short period of detached service at the French embassy at Washington, M. Bruwaert was appointed minister of France to Cuba in 1902. Thereafter he served as minister to various South American nations until his retirement from the diplomatic service in 1911, when he took up his residence in Paris.

Shortly before the outbreak of the war he went with Mme. Bruwaert into Germany in search of data concerning one of the old German engravers upon whose biography he was working. They were interned, but subsequently released on the Swiss frontier, and resided in Geneva and Lausanne until M. Bruwaert's death in March, 1927.

During his consular career M. Bruwaert acted as secretary of the international postal conferences of 1879 and 1881, secretary of the conferences on the French commercial treaties with Sweden and Belgium in 1881, plenipotentiary at Pekin in 1885, and signatory of the French commercial treaty with China in 1886 and, of special interest in this connection, commissioner of France at the World's Columbian Exposition at Chicago.

M. Bruwaert held various honors and decorations at the time of his death; among others: Officer of the Legion of Honor, Chevalier of Leopold of Belgium, Commander of Charles III of Spain, and Commander of Gustav Vasa of Sweden. One of his greatest interests after his retirement was the Académie d'Éducation et d'Entr'aide Sociales, of Paris, founded by him for the dissem--

[1] M. E. Bruwaert, "Chicago et l'Exposition Universelle Colombienne," *Le tour du monde*, LXV (1893), 294–304. Translated by Irene Bassett. Reprinted by permission of *Le tour du monde*. Edited by Librarie Hachette.

[2] The biographical information here given was graciously supplied by Mr. William Burry, Sr., of Chicago.

ination of information on sociological subjects. He was also much interested in aiding the work of the Association Amicale des Fonctionnaires et Agents du Ministère des Affaires Étrangères.

→»» «««

CHICAGO AND THE WORLD'S COLUMBIAN EXPOSITION

Several routes lead to the Exposition from the center of the city: the distance is 8 to 10 kilometers, depending upon the entrance which one is trying to reach. This distance is covered in 30 minutes by the trains of the Illinois Central, which charges 23 sous for the trip one way, 25 sous for the round trip, and only 20 sous even for the round trip if one buys a twenty-five ride ticket. The cable car on Cottage Grove takes 45 minutes for the trip: their price is only 5 sous, and if one has the good fortune to occupy one of the four places at the front of the first car one can, in fine weather, have a very interesting excursion across the whole south side. In summer, during the warm weather, when the thermometer registers 33 to 35 degrees centigrade, and people yearn for some bit of coolness, nothing is so sought after as this front seat: no driver, no other seats, no horses, obstruct the view or the breeze. Small boats make the trip by water; an elevated under construction also leads in the direction of the park.

A central station is prepared to receive the visitors: the steps that one descends lead down behind the Administration Building, and the crowd of visitors surges around both sides of this building toward the court of honor. The entrance to this court will certainly be very effective: at the back is a great double colonnade between the pillars of which appear the waters of the great lake; in front of these Corinthian columns, and dominating them with its great mass, rises the immense statue of the Republic, by French, holding in its right hand the pike of the Revolution, and wearing on its head the Liberty cap. The feet of the goddess are bathed by the tranquil waters of the great basin. Nearer us, at the head of the basin, is the boat of Progress, propelled by the Sciences, graceful Parisiennes standing and bearing down with a uniform movement upon the closely-placed oars; old Time is at the helm. It is the work of Mr. Mc-Monnies, a young American of the Boulevard Montparnasse; a Parisian sculptor, M. Grandin, came over especially to set it up. Here at the left are a part of the Palace of Mines, and the façade with the great circular gallery of the Palace of Electricity. Farther away are the great outlines of the south façade of the Manufactures' Building, outlines reminding one of those of the Palais de l'Industrie on the Champs-Élysées. At the right is the Agriculture Building, surmounted at each corner by groups of Atlases, of the weaker sex, who in groups of four are supporting globes or zodiacs, works which are similar to that of Carpeaux at the Luxembourg, and which are a product of the talent of Martiny, a young Frenchman with a great future. The colored loggia of the Machinery Building attracts attention. This building and the preceding one are beyond another Corinthian colonnade, and the basin at the end of which the colonnade is located surrounds a great fountain, a tall obelisk that is guarded by the four lions of Fountain Square or Trafalgar Square. Before crossing over this basin on the balustraded bridge which leads to the Agriculture Building, one should turn to admire at this distance the Palace of Administration, a little Pantheon in classic form, and to glance at the canal. In the distance, a kilometer away, appears the Fine Arts Building charmingly surrounded by a frame of foliage somewhat nearer us; in the foreground are the elongated dome of the Illinois Pavilion, the Woman's Building and the caryatides, the columns of its roof gardens; nearer, the low dome of the great conservatories; and between the architectural lines of the Manufacturing and Electricity Buildings, graceful groups of trees do not quite conceal a Japanese village.

Beyond the lions the cloister of the south colonnade opens out on the court of the Agriculture Building: on the shore of a lagoon one discovers a French bakery, emigrated from the Quai d'Orsay: bread is almost unknown in Chicago, each family preparing its own dough and baking it more or less badly in an oven. It is not surprising if Americans prefer meat, even raw. Let us hope that our countrymen will introduce a new industry, and will carry away in exchange a satisfactory remuneration. One sees windmills which transform the lawns into a Dutch land-scape, but they are not very successful here. M. Maurice Yvon, the son of the celebrated painter, has located over there an oriental landscape which commands attention: it is Tunis, with its minarets and crowded booths; it is Annam with its curved roofs. For the first time Christopher Columbus was right: the Redskins are next door to the Far East. Professor Putnam has put them all into this picturesque corner. Buffalo Bill is not at the celebration; alas! it would do him no good. But the Indian is there with his companion the "squaw," and the "papoose" hanging from the branches which form the tent or "tepee." Krupp and his 60-ton cannons are there also: the two extremes of civilization! Think of having exchanged this, the Indian, for that, the throat of steel which belches forth grape-shot and death! A long breakwater with a walk on top extends out into the lake and protects a peninsula where a convent of La Rabida in miniature contains the collection of souvenirs of the great navigator Christopher Columbus, in whose honor this festival of industry is being celebrated.

The Leather Pavilion which displays its elegant outlines be-tween the lagoon and the lake, is the work of a French architect, M. Alex. Sandier, whom the construction committee asked to come over from Paris in order to contribute to the embellish-ment of the buildings. The Dairy Exhibit and the Forestry Pavilion complete the east part of this section. Toward the west extend stables, stalls, and a hippodrome where the most perfect types of living races of animals will be exhibited. Half-blooded French trotters, Percherons, Boulonnais, are there in consider-able numbers, and will win new laurels to add to those which have been awarded them in all competitions. Our cattle were not admitted to American soil: American agriculture dreads the terrible pleuro-pneumonia which is causing such ravages, and rather than expose itself, it has imposed on foreign cattle conditions of quarantine that are so expensive and dangerous as to be unacceptable.

The long building extending over there at the west at the edge of the park, contains the barracks reserved for the French sailors who act as guards for the various sections and national collections.

Retracing our steps we go through the Machinery Building, not without glancing with surprise at the immense engines ready to set in motion the marvelous implements that man has made for himself. Without these engines, without steam, what would Chicago be? It is this power that has made an immense city out of what would still be today, perhaps, a town of a few thousand inhabitants. As in Paris, in the Galerie des Machines, we have here a rolling bridge which will pass above the splendid exhibit sent over from Creusot, and from which one will be able to see the coining stamp from Cail striking medals with the image of the discoverer of America. If the discoverer of Chicago, Robert de la Salle, were known in France, it would be a fine idea not to forget this modest hero, who paid with his life his ambition to serve and enlarge his country.

The Electricity and Mining Buildings have no outstanding characteristics that particularly attract attention: France occupies very large and well-situated places in them. Our beacons, our meteorological material, our telegraphy equipment, cannot but attract the crowds. The Transportation Building is not very well located; the main door, a great arch with neo-Byzantine lines, is almost hidden behind the Palace of Mines. The foundry products are numerous, and many of our countrymen such as Leopold Bonet and Bruneau, have left the imprint of their talent there. The Horticulture Building, constructed by Jenney, a pupil of our École Centrale, will shelter the French wines. People are so unaccustomed to this sort of drink in the United States that only a small wing was reserved for the industry which affords a living to millions of men not only in France, but in Spain, Portugal, Italy, and Austria. Here the grape vine is considered an ornamental plant, whereas the cultivation of grapes brings in millions in lands where they are raised.

The north wing of the Conservatory, the Children's Pavilion, (another work of Sandier next to it), and the Woman's Building, are surrounded by lawns which French horticulturists have ornamented and embellished. MM. de Vilmorin have already done enough to prove that in Chicago as elsewhere they have no rivalry to fear. At the east of the Children's Pavilion a bridge leads to the wooded isle, and beyond the Japanese village one comes to the opposite bank where the majestic Manufactures' Building stands.

The original plan had been to construct four long galleries with iron arches, around a rectangular court. But the Galerie des Machines at Paris was too renowned for the American engineers not to want to demonstrate that the great roof trusses of the École Militaire, which had won the prize of 100,000 francs, was mere child's play for them. Moreover space was already growing scarce, and it was convenient to make use of the inside court originally left open to the sky. It was accordingly resolved to construct 22 steel trusses which should each have a span of 116 meters, and that the ridge line of the roof should be 62 meters above ground. The Parisian gallery was beaten, for it could pass under the gallery at Chicago as the Arc de l'Étoile would pass under it if the corners of the Arc were taken off. This victory was bought at the expense of certain disadvantages. What effect would be produced by objects exhibited under this immense dome? Place an ordinary altar under the dome of Saint Peter's at Rome: what height would it have to have in order not to appear short and narrow? The "nave" at Chicago is so admirably proportioned that one does not suspect its size until one has tried to walk the length of it. It then seems endless. The bases of the trusses are wide and cut off the light, and since it is between them that it is necessary to put windows two meters ten long, a little higher than a man, the objects risk not being displayed to their entire advantage. Now in an exposition of objects the buildings should rather be made to put the objects in relief than to be put in relief by the objects.

The edifice covers 12 hectares and is costing 7 millions and a half of francs. An interesting problem to solve was to know how to group the competing nations. The systems of classification used at Paris might be studied: the curvilinear order of 1867, and the rectilinear order of 1878, each circle or each rectangle containing similar articles produced by the different nations, each sector or each "slice" containing all the collections of a certain country. The Latin civilizations could have grouped themselves beside the Anglo-Germanic, the Slavic civilization beside the Asiatic, these groupings exhibiting human genius in the forms that it assumes because of the old or new traditions, religion, education, or climate, that inspire it. It would also have been suitable to turn over each of the four main doors to one of the four great commercial nations of the globe—France, Germany, England, the United States—with the request to give to the decoration of these entrances a national character, which would have been not without a certain grandeur. The plan adopted was the following.

Struck with the fact that the American exhibitors were all trying to obtain space in the center of the structure, the General Director concluded that that must be the desirable location, the place of honor. He assigned to each of the four great nations one corner of this central area. The foreign commissions were given entire liberty to arrange their products as they chose. But from four commissions how could any unanimity be expected in regard to a uniform central decoration? The administration, despairing of any success, planned to erect at the center of the building a graceful steel dome, which should admirably fill the immense "nave" and show its great size. But the project was costly, and the foreign commissions had no funds to contribute. They were forced to content themselves with a tower that M. Sandier, to his great regret, had to substitute for the rotunda planned and prepared by him with the fine artistic taste that characterizes his talent.

The responsibility for the general decoration of the French section was given by the government to MM. Henri Motte and René Dubuisson. The section occupies a half of the principal entrance on the lake; it extends to the south a distance of 11 trusses, that is, 90 meters: from the east door to the center it is 110 meters. Thus it is 10,000 square meters on the ground floor and 4500 square meters on the second floor, that France occupies in this building alone. In ignorance of definite plans of the Exposition in respect to the central arrangement, the French architects had to locate the principal entrance on the central avenue, Columbian Avenue as it is called. The 20-meter door, arched and semicircular, has allegorical decorations in its half-dome. Outside the door are escutcheons, with the names of the great cities of France. Two pylons with trophies ornament either side of the door, and the cornices rest on Corinthian columns. The inclosure of the section is formed by very elegant crossbeams supported by caryatides placed sidewise. Above each pillar which joins two crossbeams rises a flag pole, at the top of which floats the oriflamme in the colors of France. The main entrance opens into a square room, the Gobelin Room, where are exhibited the products of the nation's manufacturing industries,—an admirable collection of Sèvres, and splendid tapestries decorating the panels. Leaving the Gobelin Room one approaches a double stairway which leads to the Lyons exposition in the upper gallery. The two branches of the stairs leave clear the passageway which leads to the door and to the Hall of Bronzes. It is there that Parisian art is preparing to captivate the attention of the American millionaire. A painted frieze decorates this room whose cornice rests on graceful caryatides. The Ceramics Room, next to the preceding one, is also well conceived in its classic simplicity. National pride aside, there is not the slightest doubt that this section is one of the most attractive in the whole Palace. Annexed to the section is a French restaurant which fell to the creator of the Café Américain, Peters, the founder of the Parisian restaurant of that name.

The shore of the lake, onto which our section opens, is one of the most charming promenades on the grounds: it is 100 kilometers from this shore to the opposite one in the state of Michigan, and 500 kilometers north to Mackinaw; such are the dimensions of this little fresh-water sea; and though situated 180 meters above the level of the Atlantic it is nevertheless 300 meters deep, a real abyss which has had its victims since the day when La Salle's "Griffon" went down to its eternal resting-place.

The Federal Government is exhibiting its public services in a building which rises at the north of the Manufactures' Building. Opposite, clear out in the lake, is a monitor built of bricks, with its armor plate imitated in painted plaster, which should give the people of the west an idea of the Naval forces of the Union. The straits of Lake Erie and of the St. Lawrence are too narrow to let a real battleship through, and furthermore the treaties with England forbid the presence of such vessels in the waters separating the United States from Canada. The Exposition is none the less interesting. Farther north and beyond a little stream is the Oyster House, designed by Sandier, then the Fisheries Pavilion, very original in its details: a Trocadéro Palace in miniature, whose friezes, capitals, and tympanums are decorated with motifs all of an aquatic nature. Vast aquariums contain interesting kinds of fish.

The last large palace located at the north is the Fine Arts Building. Classic as it is, it is declared the masterpiece of the Exposition: at the edge of a tranquil lagoon ten or twelve steps lead to a peristyle: four Ionic columns support a frieze surmounted by a triangular pediment. On either side of the portico extend galleries of exquisite simplicity and good taste. The portico leads to a rotunda surmounted by a dome. On top of the dome is a statue of Victory bestowing wreaths, a monumental work by Martiny. The caryatides and the sculptures of the Palace are also by Martiny and by a Parisian sculptor, M. Wagner, his co-worker. The picture gallery has often been seen in Athens, in Munich, and in all architecture classes. Indeed it is with this sketch that Besnard, a French architect, won the Prix de Rome in 1866. It produces nevertheless an excellent effect, and for an American who has not yet had either the time or the money to go to Europe, the surprise and the pleasure are equally great. Two annexes are situated at the sides of the palace on the west and the east: in them are placed all the works sent from France.

It is around the Fine Arts Building that the pavilions of the states are grouped. Each architect, guided by instructions or a special program thought above all of the work that he himself was going to produce, without considering at all the plans that his next neighbors might be making. Now the space allotted to this kind of construction was extremely limited. The result is some incoherence in the lines as a whole, even if it be true that all these pavilions are worthy of belonging to a great Exposition.

The French pavilion is the first one seen when one leaves the French annex of the Fine Arts Building, in the immediate vicinity of which it stands on the edge of the lake. It is the work of MM. Motte and Dubuisson. It is composed of two wings united by a semicircular colonnade. The north pavilion with tall Corinthian columns contains a reproduction of the Salon d'Apollon at the château of Versailles, where Franklin and M. de Vergennes signed the treaty of 1778 which recognized the independence of the United States: this was the first treaty that the young Nation had ever signed. In this reproduction of the room are exhibited all the souvenirs and the presents received by La Fayette at the time of his travels in the United States after the War of Independence. The south wing with Ionic columns contains the special exhibit of the city of Paris.

Back of the great hall are installed the offices of the French Commission who are responsible for seeing to the interests of our countrymen, taking care of the conservation of the collections, and making certain that the rules are observed.

Adjoining the French pavilion is the Russian one, an isba similar to the one displayed at Paris on the Rue des Nations. Ceylon has a display immediately to the south: that large island has devoted itself with more energy than prudence to the production of tea: it must have numerous markets, or incalculable economic distress will result. It has come here to conduct a campaign. An excellent place, incidentally, this region where the national beverages besides ice water and whisky, are tea and coffee. The German Building is a reproduction of a rich bourgeois dwelling of the middle ages; almost a million francs was spent on this construction whose existence is necessarily ephemeral. The English Building is an elegant cottage such as one sees everywhere at the seashore. Indeed it is placed right on the sand of the beach, where it is beaten by water and winds.

In walking up the broad avenue along the north of the Fine

Arts Building one passes in only a moment a succession of the most varied examples of American architecture. The State of Massachusetts presents a historic house; the State of New York affords itself the luxury of a pompous prefectorial or governmental establishment. Florida constructed an unusual fortress: a triangle of bastioned walls, some souvenir of local history. All these constructions represent great sums of money and when one reflects over the matter one does not see clearly either the usefulness or the advantage of them. The Exposition lacked land and money to erect a palace of liberal arts, and the requests of so many exhibitors were rejected because of lack of space for their contributions!

Money,—that is the most difficult thing to obtain in connection with an Exposition. It is notable that no enterprise of this kind ever ends in financial success. However the organizing group still hopes to receive dividends. They are relying for this largely on the concessions that they have granted, on a profit-sharing basis, in the section of Bazaars. The Midway Plaisance is a sort of Avenue de Neuilly, 1600 meters long by 80 or 100 meters wide. On both sides of the avenue lots were laid out and given over to certain enterprises supposedly remunerative. You cannot imagine the number of persons who count on making a magnificent fortune in the less than six months that a celebration of this kind lasts. From all corners of the world the requests poured in, from China and Russia, from Egypt and Annam, from Austria and British India. More than 8000 letters were addressed to the Exposition, and it was to the committee on ways and means that fell the difficult and painful task of choosing from among the 8000 requests the 30 or 40 enterprises which seemed to have real value, and to send out, politely if the petitioners were agreeable, or tersely if they were refractory, the 7960 refusals necessary.

The preferred procedure was not to give the concessions to the highest bidder, but to give out monopoly contracts at very high prices. They say that a tradesman pays 500,000 francs for the exclusive privilege of selling "peanuts," a sort of pistachio that is quite popular in Chicago. To keep children quiet people often buy them a little bag, not of candy but of toasted corn [popcorn]. It is detestable but it suffices to occupy the youngsters: 800,000 francs, it seems, for the monopoly on the sale of this article, the joy of parents and the tranquillity of children. Seltzer water, cigars, ices, and canes, were also the objects of exclusive concessions. The restaurants have a special organization. There is a central kitchen let to a restaurant owner of the city for a considerable sum; the other restaurants must buy their provisions there, and, in addition, they must pay the Exposition 25 per cent of their gross receipts. The right to sell the guide book was disposed of at 2 millions and a half, without privilege of selling advertising, but with the right to charge 25 francs a line additional that an exhibitor might want to add to the customary and allotted statement.

The principal attractions of the Midway Plaisance seem to be: M. Barre's hydraulic train, the same one that ran at the Esplanade des Invalides; the Tunisian and Algerian café of Sifico, a man from Algiers; the Dahomey village of M. Pène, a Bordelais; the restaurant of Mora, a Marseillais who fears nothing when it is a question of making money with simple ideas; and the captive balloon sent over from Paris. There are also a street in Cairo, a Persian harem, a German village, and an Irish market town. China has its corner and its tea-house, and Morocco has its mosque. There are many Indians and Eskimos; there are two panoramas: the Hawaiian volcano and the Alps around Berne; they are even building a model of Saint Peter's at Rome and one of the Eiffel Tower. As for a real tower 300 meters high, no one could be found who would undertake it in spite of a hundred plans proposed, so the offers of the chief of construction, de Lavallois, have not been accepted.

In all, from these various enterprises, from which the concessionaires hope to make fabulous sums, the Exposition intends to obtain a supplementary amount of 12 millions and a half of francs. It has already received 25 million francs from the stockholders, and 25 millions lent by the city of Chicago; it has obtained a loan, secured by the receipts, which should produce 25 millions. The national treasury, after long resistance, decided to grant a subvention of 12 millions and a half in special fifty-cent silver coins which they intend to sell at twice their face value; and finally, it is calculated that there will be more than 100,000 admissions a day, that is 20 millions for 180 days, or 50 millions of francs, an admission costing 2 francs 50. If all these expectations are realized and if several millions are made from the sale of the materials, the Exposition will find that it has spent 90 millions and received 170 millions. There will remain therefore 80 millions to pay back the secured loan, the sum borrowed from the city, and the stockholders,—a total of 75 millions,—leaving a balance of 5 millions to distribute in dividends at the rate of 20 per cent per share. But it is best to wait until accounts are settled before being carried away by too sudden hopes.

Dividends, shares, profits, all that seems very mercenary. Is there not, then, in the festival in preparation, any ideal to lift the mind out of the domain of business and tangible results? There is indeed, beside the sphere of material interests, the sphere of principles and progress. The responsibility for conducting the visitor to this region was given to Mrs. Palmer and Mr. C. C. Bonney.

Mrs. Palmer has as a task to accomplish the placing in evidence of all the means possible which can contribute to the civil and economic independence of woman. The Exposition has allowed her a million francs to show what has been done, what is being done, and what can be done, in order that the weak, delicate, and dependent being that woman has always been, may learn through tangible means to enter into full possession of herself, and how to escape the sufferings of life, through work, ingenuity, and intelligence. The constitution of the United States guarantees to everyone the right to pursue happiness; the Exposition is to show how woman is succeeding in making this pursuit effective. The funds once allotted, directions were immediately given for a building. The plans were drawn up by Miss Heyden, who is hardly more than twenty; the architectural decoration is intrusted to Miss Rideout, who is not even that old; the artist of the caryatides that support the cornice is Miss Yandell of Kentucky, who is twenty-two. The building is composed principally of a high central gallery, around which extend two stories of lower-ceilinged rooms. It had been planned at first to display there all the works produced by the hand of woman. But it was soon recognized that work has no sex, and that a general division was impossible. Besides, where there is rivalry, woman prefers to display her products with those of man, rather than in her own domain. The palace, then, will contain only a history of the work of woman—the dead have no choice—and collections showing the benevolent and charitable work of woman in the world.

Mr. C. C. Bonney also has the problem of penetrating into the realm of principles and ideas. He is organizing a great number of congresses for the advancement of the natural and social sciences: there are few subjects which will escape the proposed studies: religions, legislation, literatures, scientific problems and methods; all the thinkers, all the investigators, are called together at Chicago at certain dates, and asked to bring the products of their research or to indicate the different objectives to be considered and attained. The conferences are to take place in a special building being constructed on the "Lake Front," called the Institute. If the Institute is not ready the Auditorium Theater which holds as many as 5000 persons will be used for these academic meetings.

The opening of the Exposition is fixed for May 1, 1893. But the official opening of the buildings took place last October. The 12th of October had been chosen, but since New York City was celebrating its centennial on that day, it was necessary to wait until the distinguished persons attending that solemnity should have time to get to Chicago, and for this reason the opening was postponed until October 21, which is the real anniversary according to the Gregorian calendar which was introduced in the sixteenth century, that of the discovery. The legations had been invited, as well as the foreign commissions. The president of the United States was to be present. But death was hovering over the White House, and it was Mr. Morton who presided at the ceremony. The guests of honor, numbering more than five hundred, formed early in the morning an immense procession, filing past the National Guards sent from different states of the Union. At one o'clock the first landaus entered the Midway Plaisance, passed in front of the Woman's Building, and proceeded by way of the court of honor to the Manufactures' Building. More than a hundred thousand persons were waiting under the great arch. As soon as the diplomatic corps appeared on the platform which had been erected adjoining the French section, the crowd began to move like a rolling sea, handkerchiefs waving in air and shouts breaking out on all sides. A chorus of 5,000 persons and an orchestra of 500 were located in the back of the room. But the edifice was too big; neither the chorus nor the orchestra nor the orators could succeed in filling the hall with their sound waves. The program was nevertheless carried out line by line, until Cardinal Gibbons, assisted by the pontifical ablegate, Mgr. Satolli, had given the benediction to the edifice, as had been done at the beginning of the ceremony by a Protestant bishop from California.

These exercises will doubtless begin anew during the course of the coming summer.[3]

But after all, it will not be these ceremonies nor even the Exposition itself that will most surprise the foreigner who is enterprising enough to come as far as Chicago.

The most beautiful exhibition will be Chicago itself, its citizens, its business, its institutions, its progress. Those who come here will wonder how, in less than fifty years, that is, in less than a man's lifetime, it has been possible to transform a swamp,

---

[3] "Our readers know that the Exposition was opened May 1, in the presence of a great crowd, by the President of the United States, Mr. Cleveland. Among the numerous guests in the presidential party was noticed the Duke of Veragua, the last descendant of Christopher Columbus. The ceremony took place in the Administration Building where a great platform had been erected. It opened with prayer and the reading of a poem on Christopher Columbus written by a journalist, Mr. Croffut, and entitled 'The Prophecy.' Next the General Director read a report on the work completed, and thanked the foreign nations for their participation. Finally President Cleveland delivered a brief address which appeared in all the newspapers. In conclusion, at exactly noon, he pressed a button, and all the machines were immediately started, the fountains began to play, the bells rang, the flags of all the nations were run up at once on the buildings, while the cannons fired the national salute, and the chorus began to sing Haydn's 'Hallelujah.' According to witnesses it was a magnificent climax, and the crowd received it with great acclamation" (footnote in original).

producing only a sort of wild onion, into a powerful and flourishing city; by what means a bad soil, condemned to sterility, could transform itself into valuable land; by the aid of what implements these energetic people, who would be the pride of any nation, have been able to build this temple of labor and the riches that it contains. If the trip taught a useful lesson from which it were possible to benefit in connection with the great colonization that will be taking place in the next century, in newly-opened continents, it would have an inestimable value and would certainly leave no regrets.

When one leaves Chicago in the summer or autumn, the customary trip includes an excursion through a French country,— Canada. One could make by water, in reverse order, the trip made by the early explorers, going by way of Mackinaw, Detroit, Niagara, the Thousand Islands, and the rapids of the St. Lawrence. But time is precious today; consequently one contents himself with going by railroad either to Kingston or to Alexandria Bay, on Lake Ontario, and taking the boat to Montreal. From Montreal one takes a train to Lake Champlain and Lake George, the abode of the last of the Mohicans. One sees Saratoga, the Catskills, takes the boat down the Hudson, and finds again, at New York, the place of departure for returning to France.

MULJI DEVJI VEDANT[1]

BIOGRAPHICAL information regarding the author of this account could not be found. Undoubtedly, he was one of the many foreign visitors to the World's Fair whose impressions were chronicled particularly for his fellow-countrymen.

-»» «««-

THE WHITE CITY

To me the World's Fair presented a spectacle that exceeded all my expectations of grandeur. The majestic *White City* where poverty has no place to live, exercises over the mind such a charm, that its defects, like the dark spots of the sun, are invisible to the naked eye, owing to the great halo of lustre that pervades throughout. Look from the lake, from the tower, or from the flying trains, its attractiveness is the same. Poets evolve creations from their imagination, which can be enjoyed by the imagination alone. But here, the great poets of science and art created things which can be perceived by the senses and then dwelt upon by the imagination.

When I entered the Transportation Building by the golden gate I felt as if I were in a world of unmixed bliss. Of the multitude that meets the gaze on all sides, no one is sullen or sad.

Here we have all the implements of minimizing distance. The history of the progress of the art of locomotion is depicted by examples of carriages, ships, cycles, steam-engines, etc., etc., of different periods. The comfort and speed of the present conveyances, when compared with the slow motion and repulsive form of the wooden carts of more primitive ages, excites wonder at human skill and ingenuity. The Director General engine is reported to be capable of running nearly a hundred miles per hour.

[1] Mulji Devji Vedant, "A Brahmin's Impressions at the Chicago World's Fair," *Littell's Living Age*, CC (February 17, 1894), 435–41. Also in the *Asiatic Review*, N.S., XVII (January, 1894), 190–96. Reprinted by permission of the *Asiatic Review* and the *Living Age*.

The magnificent saloon cars and the state-rooms of the standard ships exceed in splendor the royal hall of an Oriental prince. But the objects which tend to increase the material happiness of human beings are not unaccompanied by others calculated to destroy human beings themselves and all their works in a twinkling. Steel armor plates and breech-loading guns of enormous sizes and powers stare at you with their ominous looks, and inform you that the present civilization has not been successful in abolishing the profession of free-booters, because instead of small associations we have large ones each of which consists of one nation or more. The innocent Siamese or the ignorant African, the red Indian or the passive Hindu, is driven to accept one of the two alternatives, either to give up the fruits of his labor or to end his existence, whenever lawless Might finds it pleasant to civilize its victims, under the shelter of the law that: "they have no rights who cannot successfully maintain them."

Next comes the building devoted to the subjects of mining and minerals; various useful and curious mineral products are exhibited in large quantities, as also machines and models. There is, in the gallery, an assay office where useful information is given to those interested in metallurgy. The Electric Building is a building of wonders. Here Edison, the great magician, produces sunlight at night with a slight turn of his wand; brings to you the voice of your friend several thousand miles away; conveys your autograph instantaneously to any distance; records speeches, songs, and musical notes to reproduce them at will; puts the air in motion; and supplies force, as well, to heavy machines. Electricity cures headache, carves glass, extracts iron as well as refines gold, signals the approach of a railway train, and does other manifold services to man.

The building devoted to manufacture is the greatest building in the world, and draws you irresistibly to itself. Here France has the most beautiful collection of goods of silk, wool and cotton, and furniture. Those who are familiar with Russia through such scanty reports as only appear in newspapers and books, are led to believe, when they find themselves surrounded by samples of her art and manufacturing industry, that she is by no means inferior to other countries. Germans have shown their love of music by the great variety of musical instruments. China, the France of Asia, has a pavilion splendidly decorated with her artistic goods, of which almost all have been sold, unlike the fate of other exhibits. Undoubtedly the "pigtails" surpass the pig-eaters in handicrafts. That India has been impoverished is manifest from the small yet nice exhibit in the gloomy verandah from which an Indian visitor cannot but avert the gaze in shame and dismay. Where, where is her ancient glory? We are "proud of the past, and lazy amidst ruins," though not "a wornout stock." By this mournful miniature she reproaches her sons for their narrow-mindedness, disunion, and impotence. She laments to see that, though under the rule of her enlightened, honest, just, and free sister, instead of respecting her common bond her sons slaughter one another at the instigation, direct or indirect, of some bloodthirsty Rakshasas.

In the Austrian pavilion there are charming glass-wares made in Bohemia. According to the narration of a Bohemian gentleman, the present emperor of Austria has not the loyal homage of the Bohemians, who would prefer to place themselves under Russia if they could do so.

Swiss wood-work is second to none but that of China.

The United States occupy a large portion of this building.

While our eyes are enjoying the sight of skilful works in gold, silver, copper, brass, iron, ivory, wood, silk, cotton, and wool, etc.; and the mind is absorbed in the happy reflection that man can produce such marvels out of rude materials, our attention is suddenly drawn towards a butcher's den by the shocking smell of the hides, carcasses, tails, feathers, etc., designated by the name of "furs." The barbarous tribes of America used to kill their fellow-beings to adorn themselves with human scalps. The more humane tribes of the world desist from killing man for the sake of utilizing any portion of his body. So also, amongst the flesh-eaters, less cultured societies "murder" lower animals for the sake of making ornaments and garments; and the better cultured, only for food. This desire of decorating themselves with skins and dead birds is a remnant of the barbarism of the ancient times; a remnant of which even the most barbarous communities ought to be ashamed in this era of science and art. Bentham and Spencer agree that "that depravity, which, after fleshing itself upon animals, presently demands human suffering to satiate its appetite" should be prevented by "making criminal gratuitous cruelties." The aborigines of America have no reason to give up their liking for ornaments of teeth of sharks, skins of animals, and of feathers, so long as their civilized conquerors do not show their superiority in this themselves. The most lamentable circumstance about this barbarism is that it is cherished by the fair sex, which should be the source of gentleness, purity, and kindness.

To mention the various educational exhibits would take up too much space. Americans deserve great credit for their institutions for the education of the American Indians. The members of the wild tribes not only receive free education but are supported entirely at the expense of the States. However blameworthy their past conduct towards the Indians may have been, the settlers evince a keen sympathy and compassion towards the departing race. When the secretary of the Institute was pointing out to me the change effected by education in Indian boys and girls, her eyes were beaming with internal joy. Their training, before extinction, includes practical lessons of self-government.

In America the Kindergarten system is prevalent in many elementary schools. Children are not forced to learn a fact, but their curiosity is artificially encouraged and satisfied by a sensible governess. America provides for the masses ample means of acquiring knowledge. In free and liberal education alone lies the safety of a real republic. It can never die or deteriorate so long as the citizens are kept alive to their duties. They will have no danger from within and none from without. What potentate would be so foolish as to conceive the idea of sacrificing money and time for the conquest of a people whose spirit recognizes no superior except the Almighty? The government that either positively or negatively excludes any class of its subjects from sharing in the benefits of education must be tyrannical, because it not only refuses to its subjects their "birth-right," but also reduces them to the level of beasts of burden and inanimate machines; lest they might cease to sacrifice men, women and children on the altar of its greed. Formerly, it is said, light came from the East; but now, as far as material civilization is concerned, the American Eagle has soared so high that both East and West may, with advantage, look up to it as the greatest propounder of the equality of man, and as the wisest distributor of pleasure and pain.

The Agricultural Building is stocked with the many products of the surface of this earth which supply the necessities of human existence; together with these are exhibited agricultural implements and machinery. Here it is made evident that, with the aid of science, we can produce any sort of cereal, plant, or vegetable on the poorest soil by employing the appropriate means.

The Machinery Hall gives uniform pleasure to all its visitors; for the giants that save time and labor are appreciated even by the dullest intellects. One pump there can raise ten million gallons of water per hour.

The Leather Building did not interest me much, although the riding-boots of the immortal soldier Napoleon Bonaparte were there.

The Forestry Building possesses a vast collection of different varieties of wood. A tree eight hundred and seventy-five years old, of fourteen feet in diameter, has been brought from California. The axe used by the Grand Old Man of Mid-Lothian in felling trees is more agreeable to view in this forest, than are the trophies from ravished Hind in the Tower of London.

To show the history of man and beast there is the Anthropological Building. The exhibitors of folk-lore verify the conclusions of the linguists as to the relationship of different families of the human race. That the Persians, Greeks, Romans, Hindus and other branches of the Aryan family, played the same games, worshipped similar deities, and had similar social customs is proved most convincingly. Yet the origin of man is left in obscurity. Here Darwin's theory is supported only by the skeletons of tailless monkeys.

The quaint utensils, door-posts with emblems of animals representing the families of the owner and his wife, ornaments, arms, tools, and dresses of American Indians are the most interesting articles on the main floor. Near the Anthropological Building are the ruins of Yukatan, from the structure of which, some have come to the conclusion that the inhabitants of America, prior to the settlement of the tribes that greeted Columbus on his landing, were more advanced in civilization than the tribes that are now becoming extinct.

The reproduction of the Convent de la Rabida where Columbus found his best friends, and passed most of his youth, is full of associations of the great navigator. His little fleet that worked wonders lies at anchor before the convent in the narrow inlet of the lake.

Krupp's Gun Exhibit well repays the trouble of a visit.

In the United States Government Building we see the Postal Department which is not unworthy of the Fair. It is the general post-office of the White City. Here are exhibited various modes of conveying mails: the old-time Rocky Mountain mail coach; the horseman; the cyclist; the sledge drawn by dogs; etc. There are kept innumerable stamps and coins of different years and different value. There are samples of lamps and models of lighthouses and marine signalling apparatus.

The Patent Office is replete with models of numerous inventions. In the War Department, you are shown how guns and cartridges are manufactured. There is the bronze cannon of Great Britain with inscriptions, "Made in 1759" and "Capitulation at Yorktown, 19th October, 1781."

To the east of the Government Building is the representation of a battleship, in which you see the storage of ammunition, the life of the crew, the manner of turning the big guns, and the rest of the equipage. You wonder how a big ship[2] like that could be brought in that lake which has no navigable communication with the sea!

[2] "This is the warship Illinois—really not a warship at all, for it was built up from the bottom of the lake and is fast aground. It is constructed of wood and canvas, the canvas guns and smokestacks are so cunningly contrived and mounted as to be indistinguishable from real man-o'-war appliances.—Ed."

The name of "Fisheries Building" explains itself.

Sculpture, painting, drawing, carving, engraving, are all collected in the art galleries to bewilder with wild admiration the hasty visitor who passes from scenes of the land to views of the sea; from rock to ruin; from woe to weal; mourning to music; morn to eve; sun to shade; spring to winter; youth to age; birth to death; from earth to heaven; and from many complex scenes to their opposite ones, which turn and twist the untutored traveller, till, "tired with all these, from these would he be gone" to find himself the same lonely man.

In the Woman's Building we do not see women of different sizes, colors, and form, like fishes in the Fisheries Building; but we see how far woman competes with man in manufactures and fine arts. In India woman generally shares with man the trouble and reward of any occupation consistent with her natural constitution; and in many cases the husband feels it degrading to his manliness to allow the wife to work out of doors. We look upon woman as part of man; because the wife is called *ardhänganä* (half-bodied) of the husband and every girl of age is a wife. The union of man and wife is not broken before the death of either. Woman's interests are so closely interwoven with man's, that the rise or fall of one is necessarily that of the other. Man must procure subsistence and provide against danger; and woman's duty is to manage the home. If anything is done by the husband it is done mostly for the welfare of the wife. However much husband and wife may be strangers to each other before marriage, they soon manage to make a world of their mystic affections in which every one else becomes an intruder. Though our women are almost illiterate, our home happiness is more enduring, more elevating, and more sincere, than what is found in England. In India woman rules man not by the threat of tearing asunder the ties which are sacred spiritually and beneficial materially; but she rules man with her tender tongue, appealing eye, and loving heart. It is easier for an Indian to oppose the armed legions of a tyrant, than to oppose the tyrant will of the wife who is classed among slaves by foreigners—who judge Indian life by their own limited experiences which, at best, are always superficial and confined to a few monstrosities such as may be found in any civilized community. I am sure that if Mahomedan and Hindu girls are well educated they can exercise a greater check on civil commotions, such as recently disturbed the peace of many towns, than mounted artillery. This being the status of woman in India, the Woman's Building seemed to me a great curiosity. Then naturally the question arises, "Why is woman totally separated from man in this Exposition?" In Europe and America there are thousands of women who *will not* marry and many more who *cannot*. Competition for husbands is as keen amongst Englishwomen, as for civil appointments amongst the educated Indians. In the poorer classes the wife marries dress and the husband "home;" in the well-to-do classes the husband marries wealth or influence or both, and the wife marries the prefix "Mrs." to show to her sisters that she has made a successful haul, of course with due regard to her position in "Society." It may be one in a hundred where heart marries heart. Marriage is a contract of sale of goods which are to be delivered by instalments for a valuable consideration to be paid from date to date. If there appears any "force, fraud, duress, or undue influence," at any moment, law makes the contract void on proof of such defect and compensates the injured party so far as is practicable. The principle that "sending a defamatory letter to a wife about her husband is a *publication*" serves to show the separation of husband and wife quite clearly. In such societies, it is, of course, necessary that woman should be able to support herself and to provide for decrepitude which steals upon an old maid sooner than upon an old bachelor. Here are, in this building, exhibits of her self-help. But these articles do not tend to prove that civilized woman can undertake works requiring great physical or mental force. Woman is an excellent nurse, lively painter, effective preacher, sweet musician, melodious singer, ingenious needlewoman, and, above all, a charming companion of man.

How natural it is to turn from the Woman's Building to the Children's Building! They have very wisely placed the child in the care of woman. Here the child learns in a small school; plays in the gymnasium; amuses itself with pretty toys and enjoys the society of his comrades.

Besides the above-mentioned buildings, there are buildings of the several States of America, each of a different style; of these California and Illinois are the most important. Buildings of France, Germany, Hindustan, Ceylon, Siam, Japan, Great Britain, Canada are also interesting features of the Great Exposition. A European is in charge of the Indian building. He is revered by the Mahomedan and Hindu attendants with greater awe than they would revere their Allah and Ishwára. In this building a large number of things are piled up, one upon another, like so many Indian passengers in an unsanitary ship plying between two Indian ports.

At night the Fairy Venice presents a marvellous spectacle, more especially near the Columbian Fountain. If you stand midway between the Fountain and the Administration Building, you see towards the east showers of pearls, diamonds, rubies and emeralds, of light, dark, and mixed colors, gushing forth from the two electric fountains; the search lights dancing here and there; gondolas and electric boats gliding slowly and silently over the dimpling waters of the canal whose banks are ablaze with light; towards the west, you see the dome of the Administration Building whereon bright stars hold their conference in set rows. The band plays merry tunes. Turn your eyes to whatever building you please, you see hosts of suns, moons, and satellites illuminating this model of an earthly heaven.

The exhibitors, guards, porters, and American visitors are very polite and obliging. In India when two persons meet, they generally talk about the health of themselves and their relatives; about rain and crops; and about private matters indiscriminately. But the favorite topic of an American is his constitution. He is proud of it and almost worships its founders. It is a constitution "to which," according to Mr. Bryce, "as by a law of fate, the rest of civilized mankind are forced to move, some with swifter others with slower, but all with unresting feet." May the American never be deprived of a single atom of his present constitution! In America national feeling is so much cultivated that many other sensibilities have been paralyzed. If you tell an American that Maiman Sing was cruelly insulted by a magistrate, or that a guard outraged a woman and escaped almost scot-free, he will pity neither the former victim nor the latter. But if you tell him that the viceroy deprived a large population of the right of trial by jury; that "the salt-tax, now about two thousand per cent, on the cost of production, operates as an oppressive *poll-tax;* or that nearly three hundred millions of the British subjects have no representation in Parliament, local or supreme, he will, first, distrust the statement; next, wonder how living and sentient beings can bear such a state of things; and lastly, "glare like a lordly lion." Even boys of ten and twelve know that "taxation without representation" is the greatest misfortune of a nation (or country). In the post-office department at Washington I saw tears in the eyes of a lady of about fifty, when she said, "I grieve to hear of an injustice to a country." If a government educates its subjects, secures the safety of their persons and property, builds roads and public institutions for their welfare, it performs, in an American's opinion, nothing more than part of its duty towards the governed. He thinks that a government ought to give the greatest possible happiness to the community, and that a good government deserves no gratitude but praise for having done its duty.

The World's Fair is a great achievement of modern civilization. It is the mart of the world; and the congress of all congresses. From the peaceful and contented behavior of the various nations and States that have made, on the Fair grounds, their common abode for a time, one is led to hope that a day may come when civilized communities will enlist themselves as members of an Universal Confederacy with an international tribunal like the Supreme Court of Appeal of the United States of America; and that nations will vie with each other, not in inventing means of wholesale murder and destruction, but in inventing and improving means of promoting the prosperity, health, wealth, and advancement of man. This hope seems Utopian. But, if we take into consideration the generally law-abiding disposition of civilized communities; the rapid modes of transmitting messages, men, and goods; the ease with which good sentiments supplant bad; the vast increase of resources of human happiness that have been opened within the last few years by the increase and spread of knowledge; the real extension of the principles of humanity under one form of religion or another; and the willing obedience of independent nations to the decisions of impartial arbitrators as shown in the Behring Sea dispute; the fulfilment of such a hope is by no means an absolute impossibility. Certainly it will be long before the traits of existing barbarism are extinct and when all the conditions will be favorable for the formation of the Grand Union. Till such time arrives the more World's Fairs we have the better. Before I conclude I beg to quote a few lines which will not be unsuitable with my general remarks.

"Thus she (Rome) did illustrate the truism, often repeated and nearly always forgotten, that the empire of the intellect is higher than the empire of the strong hand. Thus did she show, as she fell, what is not less worth remembering, that the acquisitions made in the course of human progress are always in jeopardy so long as there is any section of humanity cut off from the enjoyment of them" (History of Crime in England, Oven Pyke).

Mulji Devji Vedant

JAMES FULLARTON MUIRHEAD[1]

JAMES FULLARTON MUIRHEAD, author, was born in Glasgow, December 25, 1853, the son of John James Muirhead and Isabella Fullarton. His formal education was received at Craigmount School in Edinburgh and at Edinburgh University. For three years he was employed on the *Chamber's Encyclopaedia*, but at the expiration of this time he became associated with Karl Baedeker, and for more than thirty-five years Dr. Muirhead was editor of the English and American editions of Baedeker's *Handbook for Tourists*. The *Handbook to the United States*, as well as those for England, was compiled from personal visits and observations. By 1902 the American handbook had reached its third edition. Dr. Muirhead's association with Baedeker was severed at the outbreak of the World War, and since then he has given unofficial help to his brother Findlay in establishing the *Blue Guides*. In addition to the guidebooks and the *Land of Contrasts*, Dr. Muirhead has translated poetry and written articles for the *Encyclopaedia Britannica*.

Dr. Muirhead's first visit to the United States was in 1888. This was of short duration, however; and in 1890 he again visited the United States and spent three years here, traveling in almost every state of the Union and coming into contact with all classes of citizens. This visit was made primarily for the preparation of the Baedeker guidebook, but it also served as the basis for the *Land of Contrasts*. In 1894 he married Helen Quincy of Boston. In 1898 Dr. Muirhead made a third visit to the United States, and the changes which he found had taken place are incorporated in the footnotes of his book.

American women, children, sports, journalism, and scenery all received their due amount of attention. The book does not represent a hasty impression of the country but is based on several years of study and close observation.

CHICAGO, THE CITY OF CONTRASTS

Since 1893 Chicago ought never to be mentioned as Porkopolis without a simultaneous reference to the fact that it was also the creator of the White City, with its Court of Honour, perhaps the most flawless and fairy-like creation, on a large scale, of man's invention. We expected that America would produce the largest, most costly, and most gorgeous of all international exhibitions; but who expected that she would produce anything

[1] James Fullarton Muirhead, *America the Land of Contrasts* (3d ed.; New York: John Lane Co., 1898), pp. 205–8. Reprinted by permission of Dodd, Mead & Co., publishers.

351

so inexpressibly poetic, chaste, and restrained, such an absolutely refined and soul-satisfying picture, as the Court of Honour,
with its lagoon and gondolas, its white marble steps and balustrades, its varied yet harmonious buildings, its colonnaded vista
of the great lake, its impressive fountain, its fairy-like outlining
after dark by the gems of electricity, its spacious and well-modu-
lated proportions which made the largest crowd in it but an un-
obtrusive detail, its air of spontaneity and inevitableness which
suggested nature itself, rather than art? No other scene of man's
creation seemed to me so perfect as this Court of Honour.
Venice, Naples, Rome, Florence, Edinburgh, Athens, Constanti-
nople, each in its way is lovely indeed; but in each view of each
of these there is some jarring feature, something that we have to
ignore in order to thoroughly lose ourselves in the beauty of the
scene. The Court of Honour was practically blameless; the
aesthetic sense of the beholder was as fully and unreservedly
satisfied as in looking at a masterpiece of painting or sculpture,
and at the same time was soothed and elevated by a sense of
amplitude and grandeur such as no single work of art could produce. The glamour of old association that illumines Athens or
Venice was in a way compensated by our deep impression of the
pathetic transitoriness of the dream of beauty before us, and by
the revelation it afforded of the soul of a great nation. For it
will to all time remain impossibly ridiculous to speak of a country or a city as wholly given over to the worship of Mammon
which almost involuntarily gave birth to this ethereal emanation
of pure and uneconomic beauty.

Undoubtedly there are few things more dismal than the sunless cañons which in Chicago are called streets; and the luckless
being who is concerned there with retail trade is condemned to
pass the greatest part of his life in unrelieved ugliness. Things,
however, are rather better in the "office" quarter; and he who
is ready to admit that exigency of site gives some excuse for
"elevator architecture" will find a good deal to interest him in
its practice at Chicago. Indeed, no one can fail to wonder at
the marvellous skill of architectural engineering which can run
up a building of twenty stories, the walls of which are merely a

veneer or curtain. Few will cavil at the handsome and comfortable equipment of the best interiors; but given the necessity of their existence, the wide-minded lover of art will find something to reward his attention even in their exteriors. In many instances their architects have succeeded admirably in steering a middle course between the ornate style of a palace on the one hand and the packing case with windows on the other; and the observer might unreservedly admire the general effect were it not for the crick in his neck that reminds him most forcibly that he cannot get far enough away for a proper estimate of the proportions. Any city might feel proud to count amid its commercial architecture such features as the entrance of the Phenix Building, the office of the American Express Company, and the monumental Field Building, by Richardson,[2] with what Mr. Schuyler[3] calls its grim utilitarianism of expression; and the same praise might, perhaps, be extended to the Auditorium, the Owings Building, the Rookery, and some others. In non-commercial architecture Chicago may point with some pride to its City Hall, its University, its libraries, the admirable Chicago Club (the old Art Institute), and the new Art Institute on the verge of Lake Michigan. Of its churches the less said the better; their architecture, regarded as a studied insult to religion, would go far to justify the highly uncomplimentary epithet Mr. Stead applied to Chicago.

[2] Henry Hobson Richardson (September 29, 1838—April 27, 1886) was one of the leading architects in the United States. He designed Trinity Church, Boston; the Senate Chamber, room for the Court of Appeals, and the western staircase in the New York state capitol; Sever and Austin halls, Harvard University; and Marshall Field's in Chicago. Shortly before his death he was elected an honorary and corresponding member of the Royal Institute of British Architects. He was also a fellow of the American Institute of Architects, the American Academy of Arts and Sciences, and the Archaeological Institute of America.

[3] Eugene Schuyler (February 26, 1840—July 16, 1890), American author and diplomat. He was appointed United States consul to Moscow in 1866 and, while there, translated Turgeneff's *Fathers and Sons*. Later he traveled extensively in Europe and served as secretary to the legation at Leningrad (then St. Petersburg), consul-general at Rome, chargé d'affairs at Bucharest, and minister resident and consul-general to Roumania, Serbia, and Greece. He was a constant contributor to the *Nation* and other American and English periodicals. He wrote *American Diplomacy and the Furtherance of Commerce*. While serving as consul-general at Cairo, Egypt, his health failed. He died at Venice, July 16, 1890.

In some respects Chicago deserves the name City of Contrasts, just as the United States is the Land of Contrasts; and in no way is this more marked than in the difference between its business and its residential quarters. In the one—height, narrowness, noise, monotony, dirt, sordid squalor, pretentiousness; in the other—light, space, moderation, homelikeness. The houses in the Lake Shore Drive, the Michigan Boulevard, or the Drexel Boulevard are as varied in style as the brownstone mansions of New York are monotonous; they face on parks or are surrounded with gardens of their own; they are seldom ostentatiously large; they suggest comfort, but not offensive affluence; they make credible the possession of some individuality of taste on the part of their owners. The number of massive round openings, the strong rusticated masonry, the open loggie, the absence of mouldings, and the red-tiled roofs suggest to the cognoscenti that Mr. H. H. Richardson's spirit was the one which brooded most efficaciously over the domestic architecture of Chicago. The two houses I saw that were designed by Mr. Richardson himself are undoubtedly not so satisfactory as some of his public buildings, but they had at least the merit of interest and originality; some of the numerous imitations were by no means successful.

The parks of Chicago are both large and beautiful. They contain not a few very creditable pieces of sculpture, among which Mr. St. Gaudens' statue of Lincoln[4] is conspicuous as a wonderful triumph of artistic genius over unpromising material. The show of flowers in the parks is not easily paralleled in public domains elsewhere. Of these, rather than of its stockyards and its lightning rapidity in pig-sticking, will the visitor who wishes to think well of Chicago carry off a mental picture.

4 In Lincoln Park.

WILLIAM T. STEAD[1]

WILLIAM THOMAS STEAD (July 5, 1849—April 15, 1912), author, and founder of the British *Review of Reviews*, was the son of a Congregational minister. His formal education was received at Silcoates School, Wakefield, and at fourteen he was apprenticed to a merchant in Newcastle-on-Tyne. Early in life he began to write. In 1871 he was made editor of the *Northern Echo* at Darlington, remaining until 1880, when he left to become assistant editor of the *Pall Mall Gazette*. Three years later, a well-known journalist, he was promoted to the editorship. In 1890 he founded *Review of Reviews*, the periodical for which he is especially remembered. The next year he helped to organize the American *Review of Reviews*, and in 1894 he started the Australasian *Review of Reviews*. Several other magazines also originated through his genius for editing.

In the autumn of 1893 he visited America for the first time. Of the four months spent on this side of the Atlantic, most of the time was passed in Chicago, which in his opinion mirrored the whole United States. Religious upbringing and a desire for social uplift gripped him to such a degree that his attitudes reflect in no small measure their influence. Some years later as he surveyed his visit he declared:

"Looking back on the whole of my visit, I have every reason to be grateful and pleased with the use I was able to make of my time in the city of Chicago. Whether or not Chicago will ever become the ideal city of the world is for the future to say; certainly she, more than any other city, has the opportunity at her feet. She is not laden down by any *damnosa hereditas* of the blunders and crimes of the past; her citizens are full of a boundless élan, and full of faith in the destiny of their city. They have a position of unique prominence in the heart of the New World. They have the incentive of the aspiration of the World's Fair; they have at their head a young and capable chief magistrate, who has set himself against the worst evils which afflict city life in America. It seems to me that nowhere on the whole of the earth's surface, for one of my ideas and aspirations, could I have been more profitably employed than I was in Chicago in the winter of 1893–94."[2]

It had been Mr. Stead's intention to bring out a pamphlet setting forth impressions of his visit, but he finally incorporated them in a book of about five hundred pages entitled *If Christ Came to Chicago!* Almost all of the four

---

[1] William T. Stead, "My First Visit to America," *Review of Reviews* (English edition), IX (January–June, 1894), 414–17. Reprinted by permission of Review of Reviews Ltd., London.

[2] From an unpublished article by W. T. Stead quoted in Frederic Whyte, *The Life of W. T. Stead* (Boston: Houghton Mifflin Co., 1925), II, 52–53. Reprinted by permission of Houghton Mifflin Co.

months he was in America were spent in Chicago, for he believed that by staying in one place instead of traveling through the country he would gain more insight "into the present perils and future prospects of American institutions."

During his stay in Chicago he read no newspapers except those of that city. "I lived and breathed and had my being in Chicago, assimilating the atmosphere, conforming with the customs, and generally becoming acclimatised and naturalized with such rapidity as possible," he wrote. Both his son and he were urged to remain in the city and were assured that if they would only pledge themselves to vote the Democratic ticket they would be naturalized citizens of Chicago in time to vote at the April elections. They were denied this experience due to their departure—"an interesting object-lesson with the futility of the safeguards with which the Republic fences the palladium of citizenship."[3]

In 1898, Stead began lecturing on pacifism, and founded the weekly, *War against War*. During the Boer War, *Shall I Slay My Brother Boer?* created a sensation, and he began the publication of the weekly periodical, *Stop the War Committee*. Stead's books have the tone of a moral crusader for universal peace. His list of titles include *Truth about the Navy; Maiden Tribute of Modern Babylon* (for which he was imprisoned several months); *If Christ Came to Chicago!; The Labour War in the United States; A Study of Despairing Democracy, The United States of Europe;* and sundry pamphlets against war.

-»»·««-

THE WORLD'S FAIR

The day that I arrived in New York, Carter Harrison, the Mayor of Chicago, was assassinated by Prendergast, an event which cast a gloom over the ceremonies with which it had been intended to mark the close of the World's Fair. I arrived in Chicago on the morning of the last day on which the Fair was open. It was a day after the fair, in very truth, for it had been closed officially the day before, and I had but a few hours in which to ramble round the vast extent of the Exhibition buildings. They were, however, the most remarkable feature of that great show. All exhibitions, so far as exhibits go, are much the same: they resemble the contents of a great dry goods store mixed up with the contents of museums. What glimpses I did obtain of the exhibits at Chicago differed in no way from what I had seen at the Paris Exhibition; but the buildings—these indeed were altogether unique. Never before have I realised the effect which could be produced by architecture. The Court of Honour, with its palaces surrounding the great fountain, the slender columns

3 *Ibid.*, p. 417.

of the peristyle, now unhappily destroyed by fire, and the golden dome of the Administration Building, formed a picture the like of which the world has not seen before. They might have been hewn out of solid marble, these great palaces of staff, but it would have been impossible to have produced the delicacy of the moulding and the lightness of the tracery in any less plastic material than that which yielded such marvellous results in the hands of the architects of the World's Fair. . . . .

On the night of the 31st of October the great buildings were illuminated for the last time. The fountains did not impress me as being superior to those of the Paris Exhibition, but nothing that I have ever seen in Paris, in London, in St. Petersburg, or in Rome, could equal the effect produced by the illumination of these great white palaces that autumn night. Overhead stretched a cloudless sky, in which the stars gleamed faintly. Beneath the stars the lake lay dark and sombre, but on its shores gleamed and glowed in golden radiance the ivory city, beautiful as a poet's dream, silent as a city of the dead. It was more wonderful to have seen that city in the silence and solitude, with no one near except lonely sightseers fleeting like wandering ghosts across the electric lighted squares into the dark shadows of the projecting buildings, than to have seen it even on Chicago Day, when three-quarters of a million visitors crowded into Jackson Park, filling the Fair with a human exhibit more marvellous than the Exhibition itself. The few sightseers who had gathered to see the last of the Fair were for the most part congregated in the Midway Pleasance [sic], where the great wheel of Ferris was still making revolutions and the last revel of the season was rapidly drawing to a close. If a thing of beauty is a joy for ever, then that vision of the White City by night, silent and desolate, was well worth crossing the Atlantic to see.

DESTRUCTION OF WORLD'S FAIR BUILDINGS

With this impression strong in my mind, it was with dismay and indignation that I heard every one discussing the demolition of the buildings. The exhibits would of course be scattered to the four ends of the earth, but the buildings which formed the peculiar glory of the exhibition, why should they be destroyed? A fierce impatience seemed to have taken possession of the people of Chicago. They were tired of their toy and wished to be done with it. Now that the exhibition was over, why not pull down the buildings and restore Jackson Park to its primitive condition of a marshy swamp? They declared that its buildings, as beautiful as a dream, were as perishable as the fancies of the night. Most people professed to deplore the necessity, but all were agreed that it was inevitable. Doubting whether this was really the case, I went down to the exhibition and interviewed Mr. Graham,[4] the Director of Works, and several of the builders who had helped in the construction of the White City. I found, as I expected, that the prevalent belief as to the destructibility of the buildings was mistaken. I was assured by the best authorities that the buildings would last for ten or fifteen years if they were preserved merely as architectural monuments. To preserve them as buildings in which exhibits might be shown would cost a great deal of money, but merely to preserve the architectural effect, which was all that I cared for, would cost next to nothing. In fact, I was assured without any doubt that the architectural glories of the World's Fair, the one unique thing about the great Columbian Exposition, could be preserved for the miserable sum of £5,000 a year. The smaller buildings of course would come down, but the great edifices round the Court of Honour, and those which form the vista looking down from the Administration Building to the Art Palace, these could be preserved at a cost, so far as the architect was concerned, of 25,000 dols. a year. It seemed monstrous that a city which had subscribed five million dollars to put up the Fair, should grudge such a bagatelle to preserve for ten or twenty years its most characteristic feature. When the facts were set forth a great deal of discussion followed, and the buildings were ultimately handed over to the South Park Commissioners, who professed an intention to preserve them.

Unfortunately, however, this intention did not include a reso-

---

[4] Ernest R. Graham, chief assistant to Daniel H. Burnham, architect of the World's Fair.

lution to protect them from fire. When the buildings were handed over to the South Park Commissioners the public was once more admitted to its heritage, with the result that tramps made it their resting-place, and vandal multitudes laid their hands upon everything that was within reach, in order to provide themselves with relics of the Fair. After a time fire after fire broke out and created such devastation as to terribly impair the architectural splendour of the great monument. The peristyle was one of the first to go, then part of the Agricultural Building went, then part of the Illinois State Building, which nearly involved the destruction of the Art Palace, to the preservation of which as a permanent building Mr. Marshall Field had subscribed a million dollars, and which had been selected as the storehouse for the treasures bequeathed to the city by the exhibitors. How much of the White City will be left when the fire has done its worst I do not know, but it is a thousand pities that an architectural monument so splendid should have been left in the hands so careless as those of the South Park Commissioners. A trifling outlay and a comparatively small exercise of authority would have kept the place clear from intruders, and preserved at least until the next century a vision of beauty and of architectural glory the like of which cannot be seen elsewhere. But Chicago, great in executing enterprises which can be executed under the stress and strain of a strong stimulus, is not equally great in preserving and maintaining that which she has created. It is difficult to know whether most to admire the resolution and energy which created the White City or to deplore the fatuity which led such mediocrities as the South Park Commissioners to fool away by their negligence what should have been regarded as the heirloom of the continent, a priceless heritage which would reflect glory upon Chicago.

The greatest of all the buildings of the Fair—the greatest building with which mortal man ever enclosed space—was that dedicated to manufactures. Mr. Washington Porter[5] conceived

[5] Washington Porter (October 26, 1846—June 24, 1922) came to Chicago in 1869 and engaged in the fruit business. In this year he received the first carload of fruit to come to Chicago from California, and also brought the first full carload of bananas to Chicago from Panama. He was a member of the committee which waited on Congress to get the

the idea of transporting this immense structure of glass and iron from Jackson Park to the lake front. Chicago has an advantage over other cities in being able to extend its territories by filling in the shallow water on the edge of Lake Michigan. The whole of the front of the city stands upon reclaimed land, and there is a large stretch of shallow water enclosed by breakwaters, which it is proposed to partly fill in and to convert into a park. The Lake Front in Chicago is famous for having been rescued from the railway company by the decision of the Supreme Court, which was chiefly due to Mr. Harland,[6] who was one of the American arbitrators in the Behring Sea Arbitration. This space is at present untenanted excepting by the Art Institute, where the World's Congresses were held, and by a couple of armouries. It was upon this vacant space where it was proposed to establish the Manufactures Building as a People's Palace, and as a general rallying centre for all conventions, exhibitions, and for other public purposes. Chicago is singularly lacking in any such institutions. I was asked by the representative of the *Inter-Ocean* to describe the Paris Labour Exchange, the People's Palace, and the Polytechnic of London, and generally to suggest from Old World experience what might be done by way of filling up the blank in the social organism of the Western capital. It was in this way, without in the least anticipating it, that I was launched upon the work which kept me in Chicago for four months.

THE TRADE AND LABOR ASSEMBLY

It came about in this way. The *Inter-Ocean* published a long interview with me on Saturday, in which I set forth, as best I could the advantages which London and Paris derived from institutions of the kind which it was proposed to establish in Chicago. The next day the Trade and Labour Assembly, which meets every fortnight on a Sunday afternoon in the Bricklayers'

World's Fair at Chicago. He was a member of the committee for the reduction of expenses and of the ways and means committee of the Fair. He had hoped to preserve the Manufactures Building, but the fire which destroyed it stopped his plans.

[6] John Marshall Harlan.

Hall, was in session, and I was aked if I would go down and recommend the scheme to the representatives of labour. I demurred at first, but ultimately consented to go, thinking that possibly I might be able to say a word which might be useful. On my way down to the Bricklayers' Hall that afternoon I was warned not to say a word that would imply that there was anything religious about the scheme. "They do not," said my guide, "take any stock in the churches. Not five per cent of these men ever go to a place of worship. If you say anything about God or Christ or the Churches, you will be hissed off the platform. It will spoil everything if you give the boys an idea that you are approaching this thing from a religious point of view and by any desire to rope them in to the church." It was Sunday afternoon, and I did not care to address a meeting on a Sunday excepting from a religious point of view. However, I bided my time and watched to see if an opportunity presented itself. Mr. Pomeroy[7] was in the chair. He is one of the most remarkable and capable of all the labour leaders in America, and he possesses to an unequalled degree the gift of conducting and controlling the deliberations of a labour parliament. The Trade and Labour Assembly in Chicago is composed of representatives of some two or three hundred labour unions in the city. In the Assembly men and women sit in a free and easy fashion, smoking and talking while the discussion goes on, which covers a range wide enough to include almost any variety of opinion.

The proceedings were suspended in order that I might address the assembly. I was enthusiastically received, chiefly, as they said, because they believed that I had been in jail in a just and righteous cause. I spoke for a short time about the People's Palace and the Labour Exchange, and the proposed transferring of the Manufactures Building to the lake front, and then naturally passed on to describe the London County Council and its attitude to labour, and the relation of the labour party to politics and religion. After eulogising the work of John Burns and his colleagues, I urged them to go into politics and to use all the city and State machinery in order to realise their ideal. I then

[7] William C. Pomeroy, Illinois labor leader.

ventured to disregard the warning of my introducer and made the plunge. "I am told," I said, "that you do not take much stock in the churches." "Hear, hear!" said the men. "I do not ask you to take any stock in them if you do not think that they are worth while taking stock in, but you must be worse than idiots if from any prejudice on your part you refuse to accept the help of the churches in order to realise the objects which you have in view. It is with us the accepted formula that the indispensable condition of social progress and the amelioration of the condition of the mass of the people is to be found in a firm and fighting alliance between the Labour Unions on one side and the churches on the other. If you wish to win you must make allies, and your natural allies are the churches." My guide, who was sitting in the meeting, told me afterwards, he was momentarily expecting the meeting to loudly express its displeasure, but to his infinite astonishment "the boys stood it." From that moment the die was cast, and I could not turn back. I was committed to an agitation which in many respects was the most interesting, and I hope not the least useful, of any of those in which I have been engaged in a somewhat eventful life.

THE INTERESTING YEAR 1893

I arrived in Chicago at a very interesting time. The day on which we arrived the World's Fair closed, the day following I attended the funeral of Carter Harrison, the murdered mayor. During my stay in the city two elections were held—one, the regular November elections when Judge Gary who tried the Anarchists was re-elected as a protest against the action of Governor Altgeld in pardoning the Anarchists, and the other, a bye-election for mayor to fill the place of Mr. Carter Harrison. I was also present at the stormy scenes when the acting mayor was elected *pro tem.*, and witnessed the beginnings of a new administration which promises to be memorable in the history of America. . . . .

There were other than merely accidental circumstances which render Chicago peculiarly interesting. America is passing through the incipient stages of a civic revival. Many of her people are being awakened to the fact that the nation as a nation has forgotten God. Chicago, in a special degree, felt the impulse of this civic revival as one of the natural consequences of the World's Fair. Chicago had invited the foremost people of the older world, of Asia and of Europe, to visit the Columbian Exposition, and to attend the World's Congresses. There was therefore in the World's Congresses, over which Mr. C. C. Bonney presided with such loving care and such Catholic sympathy, a great pooling of the best thought of the best thinkers of the modern world. It was impossible that such a comparison of ideals and such an array of aspirations should have taken place in that city without leaving behind a strong impulse towards a higher civic life than that to which they had hitherto attained. There is about Chicago a magnificent *élan* which had been illustrated several times in the short history of the city. The rebuilding of the old city after the great fire and the construction of the White City for the World's Fair are but two among the many notable demonstrations of the spirit of the city. It was natural therefore that Chicago as the scene of the World's Fair should find itself on the crest of the civic revival.

THE ROMANCE OF CHICAGO

Chicago is naturally more interesting to me than any other city in the New World. One of the first articles I ever wrote about America in my early journalistic days was prompted by the great fire which lay the city in ashes, and the first Christmas story I ever wrote was called forth by the World's Fair. To all Englishmen, Chicago has more interest than any American city. It is the only city which has had anything romantic about its recent history. The building of the city, and still more its rebuilding, are one of the romances which light up the somewhat monotonous materialism of Modern America. Its surprising growth is one of the wonders of the nineteenth century. . . . .

From the point of view of the city builder Chicago holds a unique place. . . . . Her latest triumph has been the adaptation of iron to the work of building and the universal use of the elevator, which enables people to live nearer to the stars than mortals have ever done before with ease and comfort. These immense sky-scrapers of twenty and twenty-two stories are singularly lightly built. They are indeed little more than so many Eiffel Towers, enclosed in veneering of stone or terra-cotta, but standing four-square to all the winds that blow, and yielding less to the violence of the blizzard than the ordinary three-and four-storied houses. As Chicago is built on a marsh, there is no natural foundation on which to rest these huge edifices, and therefore it is necessary to build them on artificial foundations of railway iron and cement, spread on the ground some forty or sixty feet below the surface of the soil. From this iron and cement foundation a frame-work of steel is built as high as the building regulations of the City Council will permit. When the slender masts of steel are run up to the requisite height, they are fastened together by girders, and then the ingenious builder begins putting on his veneer of marble, brick, or stone. As each story is finished the outside casing rests upon the flange of the girder, so that there is nothing to hinder the work going on at each story at the same time. One of the first sights I saw in Chicago was the building of one of these sky-scrapers from the top downwards. The buildings when completed are sometimes as ugly as sin, and resemble nothing more than huge packing cases pierced with windows. In other cases, however—notably in the Woman's Temple and the Columbus Memorial Building —they have rather an attractive appearance. Under the roof of a single building are domiciled whole colonies of industrious human ants: lawyers, doctors, dentists, business men of every description, are all to be found next door to each other, and the elevators are continually flitting from the roof to the basement. The Masonic Temple, the tallest of the tall buildings of Chicago, requires the service of fifteen elevators, and even if the city regulations did not forbid the carrying of the buildings much higher, they would be limited by the fact that as they require two elevators for every three stories, if you were to carry the buildings much higher the whole of the space would be taken up with elevators, and none would be left for use as offices. The larger buildings are all heated throughout by radiators, which are regulated by electricity. Thermometers are fixed in every room, and the moment the temperature falls below a certain number of degrees the heat is turned on at the radiator and continues until the temperature is raised and the thermometer detaches the electrical arrangement and the heat is shut off. These radiators are in use night and day.

PART IV

FROM WORLD'S FAIR TO WORLD'S FAIR

INTRODUCTION

AS THE World's Fair came to a climactic close in the autumn of 1893, its receipts were said to total $14,117,-332 and an attendance of 27,539,531 persons, by far the most successful of international fairs, up to that time, judging by the amount of money taken in and by the number in attendance. Indeed, approximately three times as many people had entered the gates of "the White City" as had visited Philadelphia in 1876; and only Paris, in 1889, exceeded with both paid and free admissions the paid attendance at Chicago. As the curtain was rung down on what was universally agreed to be not only a large but a magnificent undertaking,[1] and the city was faced with a return to the normal avenues of life, Mayor Carter H. Harrison was assassinated by a disappointed office-seeker, leaving the city, now desolated of vast hordes of visitors, without the pilot of many years to guide in the solution of problems impending in a growing urbanization—an urbanization for which there had been little time for preparation. Although peopled by more than a million souls, Chicago still possessed many of the earmarks of the frontier town and rural community, a condition frequently causing comment by observers of that time (and even of today), whose point of view was not colored by daily contact. "As a society amalgamated into a settled ethnic or civic composite, Chicago cannot yet be described," declared one writer in the early nineties.

In that respect the city is still in the village state, in which every impulse asserts itself with utmost and sometimes crude freedom. Wealth and culture though generously prevalent cannot make society in a day. Like a choice edible, this product has to undergo the mixing, proportioning, selecting, and lapse of time akin to the slow oven, to form a consistent tissue. Chicago is now a

[1] See, for example, *Chicago Record*, Saturday, October 7, 1893, for the enthusiastic comments of a citizen of India and one of Norway.

thing of parts, energies, movements, devoid of combination. Her industrial, social, philanthropic, and artistic elements are all self-centered as yet,[2]

—a state said to persist for many years, a "stage of adolescence—an adolescence beautiful but dumb."[3]

To some, rapidity of growth and the cosmopolitan character of the residents offered an explanation of this so-called provincialism and lack of cohesion, held to be indigenous in Chicago's civic and social body. In 1890 the city's population of more than a million was spread over an area of 169.836 square miles, but ten years later boundaries were stretched to include 190.638 square miles, with a constantly and quickly growing populace.

Of all American cities, Chicago, by 1900, possessed the largest number of Poles, Swedes, Bohemians, Norwegians, Dutch, Danish, Croatians, Slovakians, Lithuanians, and Greeks. At that time as the second largest Bohemian, the third Norwegian, the third Swedish, the fourth Polish, and the fifth German city of all the world, she came to be to strangers "a veritable Babel of the age," a "miracle of paradox and incongruity."[4] Indeed, by the early years of the twentieth century, it still appeared "as if all the millions of human beings disembarking year by year upon the shores of the United States were unconsciously drawn to make this place their headquarters." For Chicago was "the land of promise to all malcontents and aimless emigrants." "More than half of its inhabitants are foreigners," said one visitor, "and there are whole quarters where nothing but German is spoken. Others are inhabited entirely by Slavs. Nowhere else has immigration assumed such huge proportions, and nowhere else does the immigration question so seriously affect the local administration and development."[5]

Into the fitful months which followed the close of the Columbian Exposition in this city of many races and divergent estate,

[2] Noble Canby, "Some Characteristics of Chicago," *Chautauquan*, XV (August, 1892), 610. Quoted by permission of *New Outlook* (holding editorial rights).

[3] R. L. Duffus, "Chicago: City of Superlatives," *New York Times Magazine*, February 23, 1930, p. 2.

[4] See the description by George Warrington Steevens, pp. 395–401.

[5] See the account by Count Vay de Vaya and Luskod, pp. 426–27.

crowded many and momentous problems. By no means the least were the necessities born of the financial distress of '93. Throughout the whole country bankruptcy and closures fell upon business enterprises. Labor was unsettled, and a floating population wandered into the city where the Fair but recently had been held. Added to the city's own jobless, these invaders (during the trying winter and spring of 1893 and '94), proved a cause of considerable anxiety to those charged with the maintenance of the law. Although Chicago probably suffered to a less degree than some other American cities, armies of unemployed tramped through the streets, hardy, determined and hungry, some joining forces with Coxey's "Commonwealth of Christ" in their march on Washington. Others remained to eke out a bare subsistence in a city burdened with multifarious problems of human misery, hunger, and poverty.

In the light of these trying financial conditions, many large business organizations felt justified in reducing the wages of those whom they employed. Among them was the Pullman Company, building and operating sleeping and parlor cars. Upon a wage reduction their employees, members of the American Railway Union, went on strike. When out a month, under the influence of Eugene V. Debs, organizer of the Union, the strikers sent emissaries to the officials of the Pullman Company, asking that the dispute be arbitrated. Meeting with a refusal, the employees gained recruits among railroad men in general, who refused to serve on trains equipped with Pullman cars. Seriously handicapped in performing their own work, the railroads decided to fight a condition for which they were not responsible and to man their trains with non-union workers. Disorder and dissension resulted. Railroad transportation, sadly handicapped and seriously crippled in carrying on its normal functions, appealed to the federal government. In the emergency thus created, President Cleveland held that there should be free passage of the mails; and, although federal troops usually enter a state upon the request of the governor, two thousand soldiers arrived in Chicago to guard the railroads, over the protest of Governor Altgeld, who asked their immediate withdrawal.

"Should the situation," said the Governor, "at any time get so serious that we cannot control it with the State forces, we will promptly ask for Federal assistance, but until such time I protest with all due deference against this uncalled for reflection upon our people, and again ask for immediate withdrawal of the troops."[6]

On July 8, 1894, with disorder mounting, since the contingent of troops sent seemed insufficient, President Cleveland issued a warning to the rioters that their resistance to authority would not be tolerated, and proceeded to gather a military force sufficient to deal with the situation. Before this manifestation of determination the rioters turned back and permitted trains to run as scheduled. By July 20 troops were withdrawn, and order again reigned.

As the difficulties attending labor disagreements gradually subsided, problems of local concern for the government pressed for consideration—problems accompanying at all times all aspects of urban change and development. Charges of graft and corruption were not unknown, public officials open to bribery were said frequently to be holders of the trust of the city's citizenry, until not only America but all Europe came to think of Chicago not for her cultivation of the arts, her expansive park system, her unusually beautiful skyline, and her magnificently now turbulent and now placid lake, her commercial achievements, and her exemplary citizenry, but for political corruption, gangsters, racketeers, notorious criminals, destruction of property, and bombings. In widely read press dispatches, periodical literature, and bulky tomes Chicago's darker side was heralded abroad. It shocked and interested the world to know from the pen of a reputable journalist that, in 1929, it was estimated "that sixty odd rackets are in fairly active operation," costing the people of Chicago "$136,000,000 per year" or "approximately $45 for every man, woman and child in the city."[7]   It

[6] *John Peter Altgeld Memorial* (Pamphlet), Sunday, April 20, 1902, p. 11. Reprint of Louis F. Post's "John Peter Altgeld," *Public*, March 22, 1902.

[7] John Gunther, "The High Cost of Hoodlums," *Harpers Magazine*, CLIX (October, 1929), 530–40.

came to be a common question for inquirers from abroad to ask Chicago citizens about bullet-proof vests and to be astonished when informed as to the relative safety of the greater number of those living within the confines of the city.

With American visitors commenting on crime as one of the conspicuous features of the city, it is not strange that foreign observers also noted breaking of the law as an outstanding characteristic of the metropolis near Lake Michigan. "Hands up! It is the classic command of the Western robber, as he enters, revolver in hand, his first business to make sure that you have not yours," said Paul Bourget, the French novelist writing of Chicago in the early nineties. "How many times has it been uttered in the suburbs of this city, the meeting-place of the adventurers of the two worlds? How many times will it yet be uttered?"[8]

Yet, contrary to the opinion of part of the world at large, crime was not permitted to run unheeded and unchecked. Among Chicago's chief executives and their assistants in enforcing the law were those whose efforts to emblazon the name of Chicago as a law-abiding city have been untiring and unfaltering. Early in the twentieth century Carter Harrison, the son of the World's Fair mayor, as the city's executive, instituted a cleanup of the city. Others followed, conspicuous among whom was William E. Dever. At all times the endeavors of those administrators directed toward observance of the law have been sustained by bodies of citizens organized to combat the elements of lawlessness. In the nineties, among others, a civic awakening begot the Civic Federation and the Municipal Voters' League. In 1902 the Civil Service Reform Association came into being to correct abuses in political offices. More latterly the Chicago Crime Commission and "the Secret Six" or the Citizens' Committee for the Prevention and Punishment of Crime have proved sources of offense to transgressors of the law and have set up obstacles which have proved barriers to the criminal element of the community.

In the meantime, the cost of government has mounted steadi-

[8] See description by Bourget, p. 385.

ly; and indebtedness had reached, by 1932, hitherto unknown proportions. In 1907, a total indebtedness of $84,449,874 met the taxpayers, with a per capita tax of $38.41. Fifteen years later it had reached $214,090,506, with a per capita apportionment of $75.85; and by 1928, the sum of $393,340,537 with a per capita tax of $138.24. But a condition of high governmental costs is not found in Chicago alone, for other cities are today burdened in the same manner, with Chicago's per capita tax by no means the highest in cities of over 500,000 population. Yet, of the cities of New York, Chicago, Philadelphia, Detroit, Boston, San Francisco, and Buffalo, the amount spent in Chicago before the war increased, by 1930, 339 per cent, exceeded only by San Francisco.

Recent defaults in interest on the city's debt, non-payment of municipal employees, and city bonds selling below par represent some of the tangled threads of the intricately woven pattern of Chicago's financial status in 1932. Discrimination in assessments, alleged as going hand-in-hand with political favor or disfavor, received a setback in the action of the state legislature in 1930 compelling Chicago tax-gatherers to make assessments public on property.

But if the shadows in the picture of governmental conduct seem more pronounced than the lighter shades, other sides of Chicago's urban development offer reassurance that "anything it unitedly wishes to do, it can and will do."[9] Although charged with being "self-centered and independent," Chicago is credited by nearly all visitors with possessing unbounded energy and industry,[10] youthful vigor, and an "indefatigable combativeness."[11]

In no realm of human endeavor did these qualities flower more abundantly than in the industrial expansion to which the

[9] Duffus, *loc. cit.*, p. 2.

[10] See, for example, Philip Gibbs, *People of Destiny; Americans as I Saw Them at Home and Abroad* (New York: Harper & Bros., 1920), pp. 61–62; Frederic Harrison, *Memories and Thoughts* (New York: Macmillan Co., 1906), p. 191.

[11] Paul Bourget, *Outre-Mer Impressions of America* (New York: Charles Scribner's Sons, 1895), p. 133; Duffus, *loc. cit.*, pp. 2, 18.

city early dedicated a part of her powers. In spite of the Panic of 1893, Chicago soon found herself the broker and middleman of the Central Valley, a position held undisputed in the succeeding four decades. The story of her industrial life reads like a page from the *Arabian Nights*. In less than one hundred years a frontier post became the leading commercial distributor of North America, outdistanced only by New York in volume of trade. Today Chicago is the greatest live-stock and meat packing center in the world, as well as having no peer in the grain market. As the largest of all railroad points, the city has assembled and distributed to all parts of the country the raw crops gathered from wide stretches of rich and productive farm land. In the processing of raw materials, such as woodworking, flour-milling, and tanning, Chicago assumes enviable rank. The year after the World's Fair, 168,549,000 bushels of grain were received in the city and 131,925,000 bushels shipped away. By 1900 grain receipts had reached 307,726,000 bushels, while 232,-268,000 were dispatched. By 1930, however, a general change in economic conditions had brought about a reduction of the grain trade to the figures of those of approximately the year following the Fair, but Chicago had taken long strides toward preeminence as a center of the iron and steel industry. The manufacturing of a variety of products in the metropolitan area has assumed considerable proportions, attaining in 1925, $4,688,-696,674, a sum equal to 7.47 per cent of all the manufactured goods in the whole country. In the brief span of twenty years following 1905, in wholesale trade alone, the volume of business trebled, climbing to $4,844,761,000.

A notable position in the field of finance, a natural concomitant of growth in commerce and industry, was reflected in Chicago's bank clearings, which, by 1911, reached $13,925,709,802. By 1928 these had been nearly trebled, to be diminished, through the forces of an economic crisis, the following two years by nearly ten billions.

To lay too great emphasis upon commercial and industrial prowess would merely serve to strengthen the opinion of some observers who failed to see, as others saw, the city's yearning for the spiritual. Travelers who were sensitive to it occasionally thought it a newborn aspiration in the hearts of the people instead of one as long-lived as the city herself. Like Bourget, they believe that "in earlier days they would talk to you of their packing-houses, with that artless pride which is one of the charms of great *parvenus*," but

they are now tired of having their detractors call them the inhabitants of Porkopolis. They find it a grievance that their city is always "identified," as they say here, with that brutal butchery, when it has among its publishing houses one of the vastest marts of books in the world, when its newspapers never let any incident of literature or art pass without investigating it, when it has founded a university at a cost of seven millions of dollars, when it has just gathered together representatives of all forms of belief, at its remarkable Parliament of Religions,—a phenomenon unique in the history of human idealism! Chicago aspires to be something more than the distributor of food. . . . . [12]

A comment subscribed to a little less than ten years later by Frederic Harrison, the English author, who felt that Chicago had been "somewhat unfairly condemned as devoted to nothing but Mammon and pork," an impression based chiefly on the fact that during his visit he heard "of nothing but the progress of education, university endowments, people's institutes, libraries, museums, art schools, workmen's model dwellings and farms, literary culture, and scientific foundations."

I saw there [said he] one of the best equipped and most vigorous art schools in America, one of the best Toynbee Hall settlements in the world, and perhaps the most rapidly developed university in existence. . . . . No city in the world can show such enormous endowments for educational, scientific, and charitable purposes lavished within ten years, and still unlimited in supply.[13]

Indicative of steadily expanding cultural aspirations has been the increase in numbers of teachers, actors, and showmen; artists, teachers of art, and sculptors; musicians and teachers of music; authors, editors, and reporters, by 30 per cent during the decade following 1920, although the population increased only 25 per cent. By 1930 Chicago had one school teacher for every 173 of the population, as against 192 as given in the Census of 1920; and corresponding increases in all other cultural vocations were recorded with the exception of musicians and teachers of

[12] Bourget, *op. cit.*, p. 121.

[13] Harrison, *op. cit.*, p. 190. Quoted by permission of The Macmillan Co., publishers.

music, who were one for every 430 persons in 1930 but in 1920 had been one for every 345 people. Mechanical musical devices, such as the radio, may have contributed to this condition, approximately five-eighths of all families in Chicago reporting to the Census Bureau in 1930 the possession of a radio.

Although the Symphony Orchestra, first made famous by Theodore Thomas, frequently suffers financial reverses, for years it has furnished Chicagoans with the best in music, and today, under the direction of Frederick Stock, carries on according to its traditional, high standard. In no less degree has opera afforded music-lovers seasons rich in the world's best vocal art.

Theater-lovers no longer hunger for the artistry of the stage which at one time was found only in the cities of the eastern seaboard, for within their own city have come the greatest stars of the stage: Mansfield, the Barrymores, Jefferson, Drew, Goodwin, Julia Marlowe, Grace George, Otis Skinner, Maude Adams, Hampden, Mrs. Fiske, and many others, where, according to the English actress Mrs. Patrick Campbell, artists are received with "warmth and enthusiasm."[14]

In the realm of literature the march forward has also been notable. The Columbian Exposition brought to the city a perspective of world-wide magnitude and afforded an emancipation which expressed itself in artistic literary productions with a cosmopolitan viewpoint. In the ten years following 1890 alone, seventy periodicals were born, and the next six years added forty-eight more. The field of American letters at the same time was enriched by Chicago writers, who include, among their numbers, Eugene Field, George Ade, Hamlin Garland, Henry B. Fuller, Finley Peter Dunne, William Vaughn Moody, Floyd Dell, Edna Ferber, Susan Glaspell, Robert Herrick, and Sherwood Anderson. Both the foreign language and native American press, through a wide circulation throughout the years, bore witness to an interest in current happenings. In this connection it should be observed that in 1929 the circulation of the foreign language press outstripped that of English publications, dailies

[14] Mrs. Patrick Campbell, *My Life and Some Letters* (London: Hutchinson & Co., 1922), p. 164.

in Polish, Yiddish, German, Swedish, Czech, Greek, and Italian serving the peoples of those racial extractions.

Clubs, churches, and schools have also shown the influences of expansion so evident in all other phases of life. Organizations of men and women for literary, social, and civic uplift have played a large part in the evolution of the city's human side. By 1926 the Roman Catholic Church embraced within that faith 837,623 members, and the Jewish denomination counted 325,000 adherents. The third largest church membership, the negro Baptists, reckoned 65,000 among their followers. The public school system in 1931 was said to cost Chicago taxpayers $101,418,641.75, betokening a growth in school offerings as well as in enrolment. Many private schools, likewise, open the avenues of education to others. In the same manner, numerous institutions of higher learning annually expend vast sums in research and teaching in efforts to widen the scope of human knowledge. The Art Institute, museums, the various libraries of the city, including the Public, John Crerar, Newberry, and the Chicago Historical, in addition to those directly connected with institutions of higher learning, lay at the feet of the people the treasures of the ages.

Especially of late, architectural achievements of no mean beauty have called forth the plaudits of visitors. With more land to build upon than New York, spaciousness and design have produced "incredible dreams in steel and stone."[15] In 1903, $37,447,175 was expended in the erection of 6,221 buildings. By 1926, the number had increased to 14,263, at a cost of $366,586,-400. The Merchandise Mart, completed in 1930 and said to be the world's largest building, challenges the eye of the visitor with its immensity. The Tribune Tower, the Wrigley Building, the Carbon and Carbide Building, and the Straus Building, a few among the representatives of architectural achievement since the World War, in the words of Edgar Lee Masters,

Skyscrapers, helmeted, stand sentinel
Amid the obscuring fumes of coal and coke.[16]

[15] Samuel Merwin, "Chicago, the American Paradox," *Saturday Evening Post*, CCII (October 26, 1929), 18.

[16] Edgar Lee Masters, "Chicago," in *Starved Rock* (New York: Macmillan Co., 1920), p. 49.

Indeed, no longer is Chicago's architecture a subject upon which there are many "who censure and very few who praise";[17] but, like Samuel Merwin, visiting the city in 1929, the observer today, in describing the architectural masterpieces of the past few years, falls into "a perfect bramble thicket of superlatives" in which are "fines" and "splendids" and "monumentals."[18]

In the promotion of projects for beautifying the city, utilizing resources already at hand and creating others, the Chicago Plan Commission has been the most effective force. Early in the twentieth century, Daniel H. Burnham, the World's Fair architect, conceived the plan which was to transform and reconstruct physical Chicago. At first it was taken up by the Merchants Club and the Commercial Club, and then as a municipal enterprise. In 1909, Mayor Fred A. Busse appointed three hundred fifty-three citizens, under the chairmanship of Charles H. Wacker, to evolve details and to educate Chicago's citizens as to the advantages of expending huge sums of the public monies in reconstructing the city. Streets have been widened, boulevards continued, bridges built, and the lake shore extended and beautified. Although not yet completed, its promise of fulfilment is so great that a visitor of 1929 declared: "I can raise no question —after a busy week among them, watching the great wheels go round—that Chicago will be, within ten to twenty years, our one greatly outstanding city."[19]

All this seems bigger and more permanent than the graft and corruption said to exist in the administration of this city's government, which, by 1930, had under its protection 3,376,438 people. By this time the Poles headed the list of alien groups, the Germans came second, followed by the Russians, Swedes, Irish, Bohemians or Czecho-Slovaks, Canadians, and English, making 70 per cent of the total white population, 4 per cent lower than that of Boston and 7 per cent behind New York. In the World War, however, regardless of a large foreign populace Chicago subscribed to the Liberty Loans with a generosity characteristic of the enthusiasm with which all activities were attacked.

[17] Canby, *loc. cit.*, p. 615.   [18] Merwin, *loc. cit.*, p. 118.   [19] *Ibid.*, p. 122.

From 11.7 per cent of the nation's offering in the First Loan to 14.7 per cent in the Victory Loan, Chicago gave from $357,-195,950 to $772,046,550. In all, by these means there were contributed to the war $3,293,183,450, besides the sum of $12,-000,000 given to the Young Men's Christian Association and similar organizations, and $15,000,000 to the Red Cross.

In 1932 plans were going forward designed to celebrate the achievements of a community which in 1833 had within its area less than 1 square mile and only a handful of settlers, but which today houses millions of inhabitants in the city proper of 210 miles. Due to hard-surfaced roads and the automobile, latterly small urban centers have developed where residences of the workers of the central part of the city have their habitat. Modern systems of transportation have likewise joined a vast, surrounding hinterland to Chicago through ties of a constantly expanding commercial and industrial dependence. Far larger than corporate Chicago is a Metropolitan Chicago, said to include a population of some 4,800,000 souls within a radius of approximately 4,800 square miles, encompassing 3 states, 15 counties, 204 cities, 165 townships, as well as other governmental agencies, which swell the total to 1,642.[20]

This, then, is, in brief outline, the story of what some travelers called in varying phrases the most American of cities, "a city of infinite possibilities,"[21] where "great magic had been at work,"[22] and whose motto is "I will." To one who sojourned awhile within the gates, the utterance of Daniel H. Burnham of over a quarter of a century ago epitomizes the spirit of this "paradox" of cities:

Make no little plans; they have no magic to stir men's blood, and probably themselves will not be realized. Make big plans. . . . . Remember that our sons and grandsons are going to do things that would stagger us. Let your watchword be order and your beacon beauty.[23]

[20] Charles E. Merriam, Spencer D. Parratt, and Albert Lepawsky, *The Government of the Metropolitan Region of Chicago* (Chicago: University of Chicago Press, 1933).

[21] Duffus, *loc. cit.*, p. 18.

[22] See Mary Borden's description, pp. 488–99.

[23] Merwin, *loc. cit.*, p. 122.

PAUL BOURGET[1]

P AUL BOURGET, French novelist and member of the French Academy, was born at Amiens, France, September 2, 1852, the son of a Russian father and an English mother. His early education took place at the Lyceum of Clermont-Ferrant, where his father was professor of mathematics. Later Bourget attended the College of Sainte Barbe, graduating with high honors in 1872.

He began his career as a journalist in 1873, and for the next ten years he contributed various articles to different French periodicals and published three volumes of poetry. In 1883 he brought out *Essais*, in which he showed rare ability and strength as a writer, according to the critics of the day. His first novel, *L'irréparable*, appeared in 1883, by which he was established as a well-known novelist. By travel, Mr. Bourget widened his outlook, and in 1894 he came to the United States. This trip was the source of *Outre-Mer Impressions of America*, in which he describes American society, American business, including capitalists and laborers, farmers, and cowboys. He surveys American education and recreation. His impressions he based upon visits throughout the North and the South.

-≫≫-≪≪-

A STRANGE AND UNREAL SCENE

It is two hundred and seventy feet high, and it crowns and dominates a chaotic cyclopean structure which connects a colossal hotel with a colossal theatre. One's first visit on arriving should be here, in order to get the strongest impression of the enormous city, lying black on the shore of its blue lake.

Last night, when the conductor called out the name of the station at which I was to leave the train, a frightful storm, such as one experiences nowhere but in America, was deluging the whole country with cataracts of water, and between the station and the hotel I could see nothing but the outlines of gigantic buildings hanging, as it were, from a dark sky streaked with lightning, and between them small wooden houses, so frail that it seemed as if the furious wind must scatter their ruins to the four quarters of the tempest-tossed city.

[1] Paul Bourget, *Outre-Mer Impressions of America* (New York: Charles Scribner's Sons, 1895), pp. 114–23, 126–28, 129–33. Reprinted by permission of Charles Scribner's Sons.

This morning the sky is clear, with a soft, warm clearness, washed clean by the rain. It brings out all the more strikingly the dark coloring of the city, as it is reflected back from the deeper azure of Lake Michigan, ploughed with steamboats like a sea. Far as the eye can reach Chicago stretches away, its flat roofs and its smoke—innumerable columns of whitey-gray smoke. They rise straight upward, then stoop to heap themselves into vapory capitals, and at last meet together in a dome above the endless avenues.

It needs but a few minutes for the eyes to become accustomed to the strange scene. Then you discern differences of height among these levels. Those of only six or seven stories seem to be the merest cottages, those of two stories are not to be distinguished from the pavement, while the "buildings" of fourteen, fifteen, twenty stories, uprise like the islands of the Cyclades as seen from the mountains of Negroponte.

A mighty murmur uprises from below like that of no other city. There is an incessant tinkle of locomotive bells, that seem to be sounding in advance the knell of those they are about to crush. They are everywhere, crossing the streets, following the lake shore, passing over the river which rolls its leaden waters under soot-colored bridges, meeting and crossing each other's tracks, pursuing and overtaking one another. Now you distinguish an elevated road, and there, beside the railways on the level of the street, you see other trains on the avenues, three or four cars long, but without locomotive. It is the cable system. And there are steamers lowering their yards and coming to anchor in the harbor.

Yes, the scene is strange even to unreality, when one reminds oneself that this Babel of industry grew out of a tiny frontier post,—Fort Dearborn. The Indians surprised it and massacred the garrison about 1812. I am not very far beyond my youth, and yet how many men have I known that were alive then, and how near that date is! In 1871, that is to say, later than the Franco-Prussian War, there was fire writhing around this very place where I am standing this bright morning. The irresistible devouring force of one of the most terrific conflagrations mentioned in history transformed this entire plain into a burning mass which still smoked after many days had passed.

"Where this tower now stands," said my Chicago guide, concluding the epos of that awful event, "you might have stood in a bed of ashes, with not a single house between the lake on your right hand and the river on your left."

I looked from one to the other, the river and the lake, as I heard these words. That month of October, 1871, was more than near to me; it seemed as if I could touch it, as if I were still in it. I could tell the names of the books that I was reading then, the articles that I was writing. I could remember how I spent almost every day. I realized with an almost physical accuracy the length of the years since that date,—twenty-two. How few hours that makes, after all! and I leaned again over the balustrade of the tower, gazing down upon this prodigy, stunned with the thought of what men have done!

Men! The word is hardly correct applied to this perplexing city. When you study it more in detail, its aspect reveals so little of the personal will, so little caprice and individuality, in its streets and buildings, that it seems like the work of some impersonal power, irresistible, unconscious, like a force of nature, in whose service man was merely a passive instrument.

This power is nothing else than that business fever which here throbs at will, with an unbridled violence like that of an uncontrollable element. It rushes along these streets, as once before the devouring flame of fire; it quivers, it makes itself visible with an intensity which lends something tragical to this city, and makes it seem like a poem to me.

When, from this overhanging tower, you have gazed down upon this immense volcano of industry and commerce, you go down to look more closely into the details of this exuberant life, this exhaustless stream of activity. You walk along the sidewalks of streets which bear marks of haste,—here flagstones, there asphalt, yonder a mere line of planks crossing a miry swamp. This want of continuity in road material is repeated in the buildings. At one moment you have nothing around you but "buildings." They scale the very heavens with their eighteen and twenty stories. The architect who built them, or rather, made them by machinery, gave up all thought of colonnades, mouldings, classical decorations. He ruthlessly accepted the speculator's inspired conditions,—to multiply as much as possible the value of the bit of earth at the base by multiplying the superimposed "offices."

One might think that such a problem would interest no one but an engineer. Nothing of the kind! The simple power of necessity is to a certain degree a principle of beauty; and these structures so plainly manifest this necessity that you feel a strange emotion in contemplating them. It is the first draught of a new sort of art,—an art of democracy made by the masses and for the masses, an art of science, where the invariability of natural laws gives to the most unbridled daring the calmness of geometrical figures. The portals of the basements, usually arched as if crushed beneath the weight of the mountain which they support, look like dens of a primitive race, continually receiving and pouring forth a stream of people. You lift your eyes and you feel that up there behind the perpendicular wall, with its innumerable windows, is a multitude coming and going,—crowding the offices that perforate these cliffs of brick and iron, dizzied with the speed of the elevators. You divine, you feel the hot breath of speculation quivering behind these windows. This it is which has fecundated these thousands of square feet of earth, in order that from them may spring up this appalling growth of business palaces, that hide the sun from you and almost shut out the light of day.

Close beside the preposterous, Babel-like building extends a shapeless bit of ground, undefined, bristling, green with a scanty turf, on which a lean cow is feeding. Then follows a succession of little wooden houses, hardly large enough for a single family. Next comes a Gothic church, transformed into a shop, with a sign in great metal characters. Then comes the red and pretentious ruin of some other building burned the other week. Vacant lots, shanties, churches, ruins,—speculation will sweep over it all to-morrow, this evening perhaps, and other "buildings" will spring up. But time is needed, and these people have none.

These two years past, instead of completing their half-finished city, they have been amusing themselves in building another over yonder, under pretext of their exhibition. It is entirely white, a dream city, with domes like those of Ravenna, colonnades like those at Rome, lagoons like Venice, a fair of the world like Paris.

They have succeeded, and now the most composite, the most cosmopolitan of human mixtures fill these suburban and elevated railways, these cable cars, coaches, carriages, which overflow upon these unfinished sidewalks before these wildly dissimilar houses. And as at Chicago, it seems that everything and everybody must be larger, more developed, stronger, so from block to block in the middle of these streets are posted, to maintain order, enormous mounted policemen, tall as Pomeranian grenadiers; gigantic human barriers against which break the seething eddies of this multitude. Most of them are Germans; their red faces are unformed as if hewn out with a hatchet, as if hastily blocked out, and their bullock-like necks and shoulders make a striking comment on divers facts of the daily papers, which continually tell of some "hands up" performed in the taverns, the gambling-houses, or simply in a carriage, or on the tramway.

"Hands up!" It is the classic command of the Western robber, as he enters, revolver in hand, his first business to make sure that you have not yours. How many times has it been uttered in the suburbs of this city, the meeting-place of the adventurers of the two worlds? How many times will it yet be uttered? But the spirit of adventure is also the spirit of enterprise, and if the size of the policemen of this surprising city attests the frequency of surprises attempted by these ruffians, it completes its complex physiognomy; different, surely, from every other since the foundation of the world, a mosaic of extreme civilization and almost barbarism, a savage existence only part discerned through the abruptness of this industrial creation. In short, it is Chicago, a miracle that would confound the dead of seventy years ago, if they were to return to earth and find themselves in this city, now the ninth in the world as to population, which when they were alive had not a single house.

THE TRAFFIC IN MEAT

One of the enormous branches of traffic of this city is in meat. The Chicago folk are a little ashamed of it. In earlier days they would talk to you of their packing-houses, with that artless pride which is one of the charms of great parvenus. It is the simplicity natural to an elemental strength, which knows itself strong and loves to exercise itself frankly. They are now tired of hearing their detractors call them the inhabitants of Porkopolis. They find it a grievance that their city is always "identified," as they say here, with that brutal butchery, when it has among its publishing houses one of the vastest marts of books in the world, when its newspapers never let any incident of literature or art pass without investigating it, when it has founded a university at a cost of seven millions of dollars, when it has just gathered together representatives of all forms of belief, at its remarkable Parliament of Religions,—a phenomenon unique in the history of human idealism! Chicago aspires to be something more than the distributor of food, although last year a single one of its firms cut up and distributed one million seven hundred and fifty thousand hogs, a million and twenty-five thousand beeves, and six hundred and twenty-five thousand sheep. Its enemies seek to crush it under figures like these, omitting to remember that Chicago of the abattoirs is also the Chicago of the "White City," the Chicago of a museum which is already incomparable, the Chicago which gave Lincoln to the United States.

On the other hand, these abattoirs furnish material most precious to the foreigner who desires to understand the spirit in which the Americans undertake their great enterprises. A slaughter-house capable of shipping in twelve months, to the four parts of this immense continent, three million, five hundred thousand dressed cattle is worth the trouble of investigating. Everywhere else the technical details are very difficult to grasp. They are less so here, the directors of these colossal manufactories of roast beef and hams having discovered that the best possible advertisement is to admit the public to witness their processes of working. They have made a visit to their establishments, if not attractive,—physical repulsion is too strong for that,—at least convenient and thorough. On condition of having your nerves wrung once for all, these are among the places where you shall best see how American ingenuity solves the problems of a prodigiously complicated organization.

I therefore did like other unprejudiced tourists, and visited the "stock yards" and the most celebrated among the "packing-houses," as they are called,—cutting-up houses, rather,—which is here in operation; the one, indeed, the statistics of whose operations I have but now quoted. This walk through that house of blood will always remain to me one of the most singular memories of my journey. I think, however, that I owe to it a better discernment of the characteristic features of an American business concern. If this is so, I shall have no reason to regret the painful experience.

To reach the "Union Stock Yards" the carriage crosses an immense section of the city, even more incoherent than those which border on the elegant Michigan Avenue. It stops before the railways, to permit the passage of trains running at full speed. It crosses bridges, which immediately after uprear themselves to permit the passage of boats. It passes by hotels which are palaces, and laborers' houses which are hovels. It skirts large plots of ground, where market-gardeners are cultivating cabbages amongst heaps of refuse, and others which bear nothing but advertisements. How shall I deny myself the pleasure of copying this one, among a hundred others:—

"Louis XIV was crowned King of France at the age of five years (1643). X——'s pepsin had been crowned with success as a remedy for indigestion before it had been publicly known a single year."

The advertising fields give place to more houses, more railways, under a sky black with clouds, or smoke,—one hardly knows which,—and on both sides of the road begin to appear fenced enclosures, where cattle are penned by the hundred. There are narrow lanes between the fence, with men on horseback riding up and down. These are the buyers, discussing prices with the "cowboys" of the West.

You have read stories of the "ranches." This adventurous prairie life has taken hold upon your imagination. Here you behold its heroes, in threadbare overcoats, slouch hats, and the inevitable collar and cuffs of the American. But for their boots, and their dexterity in guiding their horses by the knees you would take them for clerks. They are a proof, among many others, of the instinctive disdain of this realistic people for the picturesque in costume. That impression which I had in the park in New York, almost the first day, as of an immense store of ready-made clothes hurrying hither and thither, has never left me. And yet, nothing can be less "common," in the bad sense of the word, than Americans in general, and these Western cowboys in particular. Their bodies are too nervous, too lithe, under their cheap clothes; their countenances, especially, are too intent and too sharply outlined, too decided and too stern.

The carriage stops before a building which, in its massiveness and want of character, is like all other manufactories. My companions and I enter a court, a sort of alley, crowded with packing-boxes, carts, and people. A miniature railway passes along it, carrying packing-boxes to a waiting train, entirely composed of refrigerator cars, such as I saw so many of as I came to Chicago. Laborers were unloading these packing-boxes; others were coming and going, evidently intent upon their respective duties. There was no sign of administrative order, as we conceive it, in this establishment, which was yet so well ordered. But already one of the engineers had led us up a staircase, and we enter an immense hall, reeking with heavy moisture saturated with a strong acrid odor, which seems to seize you by the throat. We are in the department where the hogs are cut up. There are hundreds of men hard at work, whom we have not time so much as to look at. Our guide warns us to stand aside, and before us glides a file of porkers, disembowelled and hung by their hind feet from a rod, along which they slip toward a vaulted opening, where innumerable other such files await them. The rosy flesh, still ruddy with the life that but now animated them, gleams under the electric light that illuminates those depths. We go on, avoiding these strange encounters as best we may, and reach at last, with feet smeared in a sort of bloody mud, a platform whence we can see the initial act of all this labor, which now seems so confused, but which we shall shortly find so simple and easy to understand. . . . .

If there was nothing but killing to be seen in this manufacture of food, it would hardly be worth while to go through so many bloody scenes for the sake of verifying, in one of its lower exemplifications, what the philosopher Huxley somewhere magnificently calls "the gladiatorial theory of existence," the severe law that murder is necessary to life. But this is only a first impression, to experience before passing to a second, that of the rapidity and ingenuity of the cutting-up and packing of this prodigious quantity of perishable meat. I don't know who it was who sportively said that a pig that went to the abattoir at Chicago came out fifteen minutes later in the form of ham, sausages, large and small, hair oil, and binding for a Bible. It is a witty exaggeration, yet hardly overdone, of the rapid and minute labor which we had just seen bestowed upon the beasts killed before our eyes; and the subdividing of this work, its precision, simplicity, quick succession, succeeding in making us forget the necessary but intolerable brutality of the scenes we had been witnessing.

An immense hall is furnished with a succession of counters placed without much order, where each member of the animal is cut apart and utilized without the loss of a bone or a tendon. Here, with quick, automatic blow, which never misses, a man cuts off first the hams, then the feet, as fast as he can throw them into caldrons, which boil and smoke them before your eyes. Farther along, a hatchet, moved by machinery, is at work making sausage-meat, which tubes of all sizes will pour forth in rolls ready for the skins, that are all washed and prepared. The word "garlic," which I see written on a box in German, "Knoblauch," and the accompanying inscription, transports me to the time of the Franco-Prussian War, when each Prussian soldier carried in his sack just such provisions, which had come from this very place. These products of Chicagoan industry will be sent far enough beyond New York!

Elsewhere the head and jowl are cleaned, trimmed, and dressed, to figure in their natural form in the show windows of some American or European market. Elsewhere, again, enormous receptacles are being filled with suet which boils and bubbles, and having been cunningly mixed with a certain proportion of cream will be transformed into margarine, refined in an automatic beating machine of which we admired the artful simplicity.

"A workingman invented that," said our guide. "For that matter," he added, "almost all the machines that are used here were either made or improved by the workmen."

These words shed light for us upon all this vast workshop. We understood what these men require of a machine that for them prolongs, multiplies, perfects the acts of men. Once again we felt how much they have become refined in their processes of work, how they excel in combining with their personal effort the complication of machinery, and also how the least among them has a power of initiative, of direct vision and adjustment.

Seated again in our carriage, and rolling away over the irregular wooden pavement made of round sections of trees embedded at pleasure in the mud, we reflected upon what we had just seen. We tried to discern its intellectual significance, if we may use this word in reference to such an enterprise. And why not? We are all agreed that the first characteristic of this enterprise is the amplitude, or rather the stupendousness, of its conception. For an establishment like this to have, in a few years, brought up the budget of its employees to five million five hundred thousand dollars, that is, to more than twenty-seven millions of francs, its founders must have clearly perceived the possibilities of an enormous extension of business, and have no less clearly perceived, defined, and determined its practical features.

A colossal effort of imagination on the one hand, and, on the other, at the service of the imagination, a clear and carefully estimated understanding of the encompassing reality,—these are the two features everywhere stamped upon the unparalleled establishment which we have just visited. One of us pointed out another fact,—that the principal practical feature is the railway, reminding us that the locomotive has always been an implement of general utility in American hands. By it they revolutionized military art and created a full-panoplied modern warfare, such as the Germans were later to practice at our expense. . . . .

Our guide, who listens to our philosophizing without seeming much to disapprove, tells us that this very year, in order to elude a coalition of speculators in grain, which he explains to us, the head of the house which we have just visited was forced to erect in nineteen days, for the housing of his own wheat, a building three hundred feet square by a hundred high!

"Yes, in nineteen days, working night and day," he said, smiling; "but we Americans like 'hard work.' "

With this almost untranslatable word,—to one who has not heard it uttered here,—our visit ends. It sums it up and completes it with a terseness worthy of this people of much action and few phrases!

THE SUNDAY EDITION OF A NEWSPAPER

I visited in detail the building of one of the principal Chicago newspapers, just when they were printing the Sunday edition,— a trifling affair of twenty-four pages. I had seen in New York also on a Sunday evening, the making up of such a number,— that of the *Herald*. It had forty pages, and pictures! There was a matter of a hundred and fifty thousand copies to be sent out by the early morning trains. When the circulation reaches such figures as these, a newspaper is not merely a machine for moulding public opinion, of a power incalculable in a democratic country, it is also an inconceivably complicated business to carry on. Precisely because this business differs radically from that which the day before yesterday I was endeavoring to understand, I shall be the better able to judge whether the general features which I there discovered are to be found in all American enterprises. I can judge of that more easily here than in New York, the number of copies of the paper being somewhat less than in New York, and the process of shipping more convenient to follow.

It needed not five hundred steps in these offices to make evi-

dent to me the simultaneous play of those two mental tend-
encies which appeared to me so characteristic the other day,—
the enormous range of invention, and the constant, minute,
ever-watchful adoption of new means. The American journalist
does not propose to himself to reach this or that reader, but all
readers. He does not propose to publish articles of this or that
kind, but of all kinds. His purpose is to make his newspaper an
accurate mould of all that actually is, a sort of relief map, which
shall be an epitome, not of the day, but of the hour, the minute,
so all-embracing and complete that to-morrow a hundred thousand, two hundred thousand, a million persons shall have before
them at breakfast a compendious picture first of their own city,
next of their State, then of all the States of the Union, and
finally of Europe, Asia, Africa, and Australia. Nor does this
ambition content them; it is their will that these hundred thousand, two hundred thousand, million of readers shall find in
their favorite newspaper that which shall answer all questions of
every sort which they may put to themselves upon politics,
finance, religion, the arts, literature, sport, society, and the sciences. It is a daily encyclopedia, set to the key of the passing
moment, which is already past.

The meaning of this colossal project is shown naturally and in
every possible way in every part of the newspaper building.
Workmen and editors must be able to take their meals at any
hour, and without leaving the building. They have therefore
their own bar and restaurant. The printing of the pictures, so
dear to Americans, must not be delayed. The paper has its type
foundry, a regular smelting-shop, where the lead boils in the
coppers. The news must be gathered up to the last second, like
water in the desert, without losing a drop. The paper has its
own telegraph and telephone wires, by which it is in communication with the entire world. At the time of the last presidential
election, a number of Mr. Cleveland's partisans came together
here, in one of the editorial rooms which was shown me, and from
there they conversed with the candidate, himself in New York,
receiving his instructions and giving him information. And
what presses! Capable of turning off work which thirty years

ago would have required a force of how many hundreds of men! Two workmen are enough to-day.

I find here a press of the kind of which I saw a large size in the New York *Herald* building, which, they told me there, turned off seventy-thousand numbers in two hours. The enormous machine is going at full speed when I approach it. Its roar is so great that no voice can be heard beside it. It is a noise like the roar of Niagara, and the colossal strip of paper rapidly unrolling as it is drawn through the machine gives an effect as of falling water, or the eddying of liquid metal. You see a whiteness gliding by, bent and folded by the play of innumerable bars of steel, and at the other end a sort of mouth pouring forth newspapers of sixteen pages all ready for distribution. The machine has seized the paper, turned and returned it, printed it on both sides, cut it, folded it, and here is a portion of a colossal number which without undue haste a child joins with the other portions.

In presence of this formidable printing creature—it is the only expression that will serve my turn—I feel again, as in New York, a sensation as of a power which transcends the individual. This printing press is a multiplier of thought to an extent not measurable by any human arithmetic. There is a singular contrast between the extreme precision of its organs—as delicate and accurate as those of a watch—and that indefinite reach of mind projection which Americans accept as they accept all facts. To their mind amplitude calls for amplitude by a sequence which it is easy to follow in the history of journalism; having conceived the idea of a paper of enormous circulation, they invented machines which would produce copies enough, and, as their machines appeared to them capable of producing a large number of copies, their conception of circulation increased in parallel lines. There can be no doubt that in less than twenty years they will have found means of producing papers of which five hundred thousand copies a day will be sold, like our *Petit Journal*, only theirs will have sixteen, twenty-four, forty, sixty folio pages.

This is the practical aspect of the plant; there is another. In vain is a newspaper conceived of and managed as a matter of business—it is a business of a special kind. It must have a moral purpose, must take its stand for or against such a law, for or against such a person; it must have its own individuality. It cannot owe its individuality, as with us, to the personality of its editors, since its articles are not signed; nor even, as in England, to the style and manner of the articles. The "editorial," as they call the leaders, occupies too small a place in this enormous mass of printed paper. And yet each one of the great newspapers of New York, Chicago, or Boston, is a creation by itself, made in the image of him who edits it,—usually the proprietor. In the same way the president of a railway company is usually the principal stockholder.

Here, again, is a particular feature of large business enterprises in America and one which explains their vitality; a business is always the property of a man, the visible will of that man, his energy, as it were, incarnated and made evident. The formula which I just now used and emphasized very happily expresses this intimate relation between the man and his work. You will hear it currently said that Mr. So-and-so has long been "identified" with such a hotel, such a bank, or railway, or newspaper, and this identification is so complete that if, on passing in a street car before that hotel or bank, or railway station, or newspaper, you ask your neighbor about it, he will always reply to you with a proper name. From this it results that in all American enterprises there is an elasticity, a vitality, a continual "Forward!" and also an indefatigable combativeness.

GEORGE WARRINGTON STEEVENS[1]

G EORGE WARRINGTON STEEVENS, English journalist, born December 10, 1869, acquired his education at Oxford. After graduation he entered the field of journalism. His early training was received on the *National Observer*. Later he joined the editorial staff of the *Pall Mall Gazette*, and in 1896 that of the *Daily Mail*. At the time of his death, January 15, 1900, during the siege of Ladysmith, England lost one of her most promising young journalists. He had gained, in a comparatively short time, a fine reportorial reputation; and in addition to his American tour he also covered the Dreyfus trial and the South African War. His experiences as a special correspondent furnished him the materials for his books, the best known of which is *With Kitchener to Khartum*. His other books are *The Land of the Dollar*, *With the Conquering Turk*, and *The Tragedy of Dreyfus*.

Steevens came to the United Sates in the summer of 1896 to report the presidential campaign of that year. In the light of the political agitation regarding money going on at that time he appropriately called his book *The Land of the Dollar*. He traveled as far west as San Francisco and south to Wilmington, North Carolina. Everywhere he went he found the country obsessed with the question of gold and silver; and politicians using all available means to swing votes. He has penned a vivid picture of that summer—the mass meetings, the rallies, and the parades in Chicago, New York, and elsewhere.

-»» «««-

CHICAGO, THE AMAZING

Chicago, October 4

CHICAGO! Chicago, queen and guttersnipe of cities, cynosure and cesspool of the world! Not if I had a hundred tongues, every one shouting a different language in a different key, could I do justice to her splendid chaos. The most beautiful and the most squalid, girdled with a twofold zone of parks and slums; where the keen air from the lake and prairie is ever in the nostrils, and the stench of foul smoke is never out of the throat; the great port a thousand miles from the sea; the great mart which gathers up with one hand the corn and cattle of the West and deals out with the other the merchandise of the East; widely and gen-

[1] G. W. Steevens, *The Land of the Dollar* (New York: Dodd, Mead & Co., 1897), pp. 144-52. Reprinted by permission of Dodd, Mead & Co.

erously planned with streets of twenty miles, where it is not safe to walk at night; where women ride straddlewise, and millionaires dine at mid-day on the Sabbath; the chosen seat of public spirit and municipal boodle, of cut-throat commerce and munificent patronage of art; the most American of American cities, and yet the most mongrel; the second American city of the globe, the fifth German city, the third Swedish, the second Polish, the first and only veritable Babel of the age; all of which twenty-five years ago next Friday was a heap of smoking ashes. Where in all the world can words be found for this miracle of paradox and incongruity?

Go first up on to the tower of the Auditorium. In front, near three hundred feet below, lies Lake Michigan. There are lines of breakwater and a lighthouse inshore, where the water is grey and brown, but beyond and on either hand to the rim spreads the brilliant azure of deep water—the bosom of a lake which is also a sea shining in the transparent sunlight. White sails speckle its surface, and far out ocean-going steamers trail lazy streaks of smoke behind them. From the Lake blow winds now soft and life-giving like old wine, now so keen as to set every nerve and sinew on the stretch. Then turn round and look at Chicago. You might be on a central peak of the high Alps. All about you they rise, the mountains of building—not in the broken line of New York, but thick together, side by side, one behind the other. From this height the flat roofs of the ordinary buildings of four or five storeys are not distinguishable from the ground; planting their feet on these rise the serried ranks of the heaven-scaling peaks. You are almost surprised to see no snow on them: the steam that gushes perpetually from their chimneys, and floats and curls away on the lake breeze, might well be clouds with the summits rising above them to the sun. Height on height they stretch away on every side till they are lost in a cloud of murky smoke inland. These buildings are all iron-cored, and the masonry is only the shell that cases the rooms in them. They can even be built downward. You may see one of them with eight storeys of brick wall above, and then four of a vacant skeleton of girders below; the superstructure seems to be hanging in air. Broader and more massive than the tall buildings of New York, older also and dingier, they do not appear, like them, simply boxes of windows. Who would suppose that mere lumps of iron and bricks and mortar could be sublime? Yet these are sublime and almost awful. You have awakened, like Gulliver, in a land of giants—a land where the very houses are instinct with almost ferocious energy and force.

Then go out on the cable car or the electric car or the elevated railroad—Chicago has them all, and is installing new ones with feverish industry every day—to the parks and the boulevards. Along Lake Shore Drive you will find the homes of the great merchants, the makers of Chicago. Many of these are built in a style which is peculiarly Chicago's own, though the best examples of it are to be seen in the business centre of the city. It uses great blocks of rough-hewn granite, red or grey. Their massive weight is relieved by wide round arches for doors and windows, by porches and porticoes, loggias and galleries, over the whole face of the building from top to bottom. The effect is almost pre-historic in its massive simplicity, something like the cyclopean ruins of Mycenae or Tiryns. The great stones with the open arches and galleries make up a combination of solid strength and breeziness, admirably typical of the spirit of the place. On the other side of the Drive is the blue expanse of lake; in between, broad roads and ribbons of fresh grass. Yet here and there, among the castles of the magnates, you will come on a little one-storeyed wooden shanty, squatting many feet below the level of the road, paint and washed-out play-bills peeling off it, and the broken windows hanging in shreds. Then again will come a patch of empty scrubby waste, choked with rank weeds and rub-ble. It is the same thing with the carriages in which the million-aires and their families drive up and down after church on Sun-day. They are gorgeously built and magnificently horsed, only the coachman is humping his back or the footman is crossing his legs. These are trivialities, but not altogether insignificant. The desire to turn out in style is there, and the failure in a little thing betrays a carelessness of detail, an incapacity for order and proportion, which are of the essence of Chicago. Never was a better found vessel spoiled for a ha'porth of tar.

It will be well worth your while again to go South to Washington Park and Jackson Park, where the World's Fair was held. Chicago, straggling over a hundred and eighty-six square miles was rather a tract of houses than an organic city until somebody conceived the idea of coupling her up with a ring of parks connected by planted boulevards. The southern end of the system rests on the Lake at these two parks. Chicago believes that her parks are unsurpassed in the world, and certainly they will be prodigiously fine—when they are finished. Broad drives and winding alleys, ornamental trees, banks and beds of flowers and flowering shrubs, lakes and ornamental bridges, and turf that cools the eye under the fiercest noon—you bet your life Chicago's got 'em all. Also Chicago has the Art Building, which is the one remaining relic of the World's Fair, and surely as divinely proportioned an edifice as ever filled and satisfied the eye of man. And always beyond it is the Lake. Seeming in places almost to rise above the level of the land, it stretches along the whole western [sic] side, so that Chicago is perhaps the only one of the world's greatest cities that is really built along a sea-line. Sparkling under the sun by day, or black beneath a fretwork of stars by night, it is a perpetual reminder that there is that in nature even greater and more immeasurable than the activities of Chicago.

The Art Building aforesaid is now the Field Columbian Museum, having been endowed by a leading citizen of that name[2] with a cool million dollars. Other gifts, with dividends contributed by holders of exhibition stock, brought up the total to half as much again. Chicago has a University hard by,[3] which has come out westward, like Mahomet to the mountain, to spread the light among the twenty-five million souls that live within a morning's journey of Chicago. This University has not been in existence for quite five years; in that time it has received in benefactions from citizens of this place nearly twelve million dollars.

[2] Marshall Field.   [3] University of Chicago.

Think of it, depressed Oxford and Cambridge—a University endowed at the rate of half a million sterling a-year! Two other prominent Chicago men[4] found themselves in Paris a while ago, when a collection of pictures were being sold; promptly they bought up a hundred and eighty thousand dollars' worth for the gallery of their city. There is hardly a leading name in the business of the place but is to be found beneath a picture given or lent to this gallery. And mark that not only does the untutored millionaire buy pictures, but his untutored operative goes to look at them. It is the same impulse that leads school teachers of sixty to put in a course at the University during their summer vacation. Chicago is conscious that there is something in the world, some sense of form, of elegance, of refinement, that with all her corn and railways, her hogs and by-products and dollars, she lacks. She does not quite know what it is, but she is determined to have it, cost what it may. Mr. Phil D. Armour, the hog king, giving a picture to the gallery, and his slaughter-house man painfully spelling out the description of it on Sunday afternoon—there is something rather pathetic in this, and assuredly something very noble.

But there is another side to Chicago. There is the back side to her fifteen hundred million dollars of trade, her seventeen thousand vessels, and her network of ninety thousand miles of rail. Away from the towering offices, lying off from the smiling parks, is a vast wilderness of shabby houses—a larger and more desolate Whitechapel that can hardly have a parallel for sordid dreariness in the whole world. This is the home of labour, and of nothing else. The evening's vacancy brings relief from toil, the morning's toil relief from vacancy. Little shops compete frantically for what poor trade there is with tawdry advertisements. Street stretches beyond street of little houses, mostly wooden, begrimed with soot, rotting, falling to pieces. The pathways are of rickety and worm-eaten planks, such as we should not tolerate a day in London as a temporary gangway where a house is being built. Here the boarding is flush with the street; there it drops to it in a two-foot precipice, over which you might easily break

4 Philip D. Armour and B. P. Hutchinson.

your leg. The streets are quagmires of black mud, and no attempt is made to repair them. They are miserably lighted, and nobody thinks of illuminating them. The police force is so weak that men and women are held up and robbed almost nightly within the city limits; nobody thinks of strengthening it. Here and there is a pit or a dark cellar left wholly unguarded for the unwary foot-passenger to break his neck in. All these miles of unkempt slum and wilderness betray a disregard for human life which is more than half barbarous. If you come to your death by misadventure among these pitfalls, all the consolation your friends will get from Chicago is to be told that you ought to have taken better care of yourself. You were unfit; you did not survive. There is no more to be said about it.

The truth is that nobody in this rushing, struggling tumult has any time to look after what we have long ago come to think the bare decencies of civilisation. This man is in a hurry to work up his tallow, that man to ship his grain. Everybody is fighting to be rich, is then straining to be refined, and nobody can attend to making the city fit to live in. I have remarked several times before that America is everywhere still unfinished, and unless the character of the people modifies itself with time I do not believe it ever will be. They go half-way to build up civilisation in the desert, and then they are satisfied and rush forward to half-civilise some place further on. It is not that they are incapable of thoroughness, but that in certain things they do not feel the need of it. In Chicago there is added to this what looks like a fundamental incapacity for government. A little public interest and a small public rate would put everything right; both are wanting. Wealth every man will struggle for, and even elegance; good government is the business of nobody.

For if Chicago is the lodestone that attracts the enterprise and commercial talent of two hemispheres, it is also the sink into which drain their dregs. The hundred and twenty thousand Irish are not a wholesome element in municipal life. On the bleak west side there are streets of illiterate, turbulent Poles and Czechs, hardly able to speak a word of English. Out of this rude and undigested mass how could good government come? How could citizens combine to work out for themselves a common ideal of rational and ordered civic life? However, Chicago is now setting her house in order. It is thought a great step forward that there are now actually one-third of the members of the municipal body who can be relied upon to refuse a bribe. Some day Chicago will turn her savage energy to order and co-operation. Instead of a casual horde of jostling individuals she will become a city of citizens. She will learn that freedom does not consist solely in contempt for law. On the day she realises this she will become the greatest, as already she is the most amazing, community in the world.

-》》《《-

PRICE COLLIER[1]

PRICE COLLIER (May 25, 1860—November 3, 1913), American author, came of a wealthy and cultured family. His early education he acquired abroad at schools in Geneva and Leipzig, after which he returned to the United States and entered Harvard, graduating in 1882.

Although writing finally became his profession, Collier at first tried several other types of work. For nine years he was a minister of the Unitarian church, and during the Spanish-American War he served as a naval officer. In 1897, however, he published anonymously *America and the Americans from a French Point of View*. This venture proved so successful that hereafter he wrote, almost exclusively, books of travel, for his foreign education and voyages abroad gave him excellent insight into the attitude of European peoples toward America. So cleverly did he adopt the foreign point of view that book reviewers were unable to decide whether the author were American or French, many attributing the authorship to the latter. Among the things which he found to criticize and which caused him amusement were American official titles in secret societies, the social life of the East, especially of New York, women's clubs, and the American attitude toward wealth. Newspapers also received a share of unfavorable criticism. Collier held that editorials were artificial and that the papers did not train people to think but merely fed them news. He argued with those foreign observers who considered the American child poorly disciplined and badly behaved.

After the success of *America and the Americans*, Collier brought out *The West in the East from an American Point of View*, *England and the English from an American Point of View*, and *Germany and the Germans from an American Point of View*.

-》》《《-

A CITY OF PORK AND PLATO

I had about finished putting my journal in order to send it to my friend in New York, when I received, forwarded by him to my address, an extraordinary letter from Chicago. The letter ran about as follows: "My dear Monsieur X.: You will remember that we met in Chicago. My friend Y., of New York, tells me that you have consented to put some of your notes, taken while in America, in his hands for printing. If you

[1] [Price Collier] *America and the Americans from a French Point of View* (8th ed.; New York: Charles Scribner's Sons, 1897), pp. 253–65. Reprinted by permission of Charles Scribner's Sons.

say anything about the Windy City, you might mention my name, as you fellows say, just *en passant!*" Then there were several pages of personal flattery, and an offer to send me any facts I might want concerning the writer himself in particular, and about society in general in Chicago. This young gentleman surely deserves that I give his name here, but too many Americans have been kind to me to permit of my indulging malice toward even one of them knowingly.

I had not intended to describe Chicago, or Detroit, or Kansas City at any great length, though I paid short visits to all three. A casual tour about Chicago, with a Chicago gentleman and his wife, left a vague impression of slaughter-houses, cemeteries, parks, and lake-front. I was much impressed, too, by the strange combination of Pork and Plato there. My hostess attended twice a week a Plato club, and the winter before, so she told me, she had attended a similar class in Browning. Her husband, on the other hand, took me to see, as possibly the most interesting sight in the city, the slaughter-houses and stock-yards. I witnessed a procession of pigs becoming sausages at the rate of I have forgotten how many a minute. He laughed at her Plato, she laughed at his pigs. It seemed to me that the one was taken no more seriously than the other.

One-fifth of the total population of Illinois is made up of Germans and Irish, and in Chicago itself more than two-thirds of the population is foreign-born. This state of things would seem to offer ample food for study and reflection to the more serious-minded citizens.

With a self-proclaimed anarchist as Governor of their State,[2] and riots in Chicago only lately that required the federal troops to suppress them,[3] one would imagine that the study of Plato and Browning, and the net-work of clubs for which the city is notorious, for investigating kindergarten methods, for promoting the rights of women, for the study of pre-Raphaelite art, for the study of the history of Fiction, for collecting funds for excavations in Greece, for the study of the pre-Shakespearian

[2] Governor John P. Altgeld.   [3] The Pullman strike of 1894.

dramatists, and many more topics equally unrelated to the real problems of the city, were not to the point.

Be it said, to my shame, that never before at a dinner have I conversed with a lady on the subject of Plato. I believe Plato kept but a meagre place in his republic for women. It would, no doubt, surprise him, as much as it surprised me, to visit this city, the name of which hitherto had been made familiar to me by seeing it on tins of meat, to find himself served up with the soup at his first dinner-party.

One charm, at least, about the intellectual life in America is its unexpectedness. People here in Chicago are not trammelled by centuries of training and precedent. We Europeans begin with the alphabet, go on to simple words of one syllable, then on from primer to reader, and begin our national classics with La Fontaine, and so on through a regularly graded intellectual training, step by step. But here in Chicago a lady, who talked glibly of Plato, surprised me by saying that she did not know an English poet named Peacock, and thought I was joking when I told her that his full name was Thomas Love Peacock.

The only sustained bit of English prose that has come out of Chicago, so my novelist friend told me, is a little book, half fiction, half reminiscence, of Italian life. I asked this same lady, therefore, if she had read "The Chevalier of Pensieri-Vani," and she had never heard of the book.[4] Here is another illustration—alas! that there are so many—of the superficial, short-and-easy methods here. Culture! Yes, culture is the word they use.

I know men and women in France, in Russia, in Italy, who speak and read half a dozen languages, who have travelled over all Europe and much of the East, who know and have learned much from distinguished people all over the world, who have gone through the hard continental school and university training, and who do not dream that anyone thinks them men and women of pre-eminent culture.

But here, God bless you! these women who only just know how to write their notes of invitation and their letters properly, talk of culture! It reminds me of Boston, of Concord again, and

4 Henry B. Fuller's *The Chevalier of Pensieri-Vani,* published in 1891.

of Plymouth, where, as here, the side-issues of life, the fringe, the beads, the ornaments of the intellectual life are worn tricked out on the cheap and shabby stuff of an utterly inadequate preliminary mental drill.

One young man I met here, a professor in the university,[5] who turned out to be a distinguished Greek scholar and the editor of an erudite book on the American Constitution. I confided to him my impressions of the superficiality of much of this learning and reading and studying by short-and-easy methods, but he was too much the gentle scholar himself to chide others, though I learnt later that he has written of this flimsy pretentiousness of the intellectual life in unmeasured terms. All this study and reading are not bad; it is the choice of subjects and the assumption that when one has a little superficial knowledge of the great classics, one is therefore an equal of those who have endured the drill and training of years of academic life, which is mischievous.

These are a young people in a hurry, and they often mistake haste for swiftness. There is an intellectual ocean of difference between knowing things, and knowing about them. The chief value of knowledge is the training gained in its pursuit. The Chicago method consists in a kind of conviction of knowledge, akin to the mystic's conviction of righteousness, or the Calvinist's conviction of sin, and they are all three equally harmless and equally useless.

Chicago is the metropolis of the great middle West, an enormous territory of vast promise, and is now a city of a million inhabitants. As a witty gentleman in New York said to me, they have municipalized the prairies. It is a rough and raw civilization, and it is a fatal blunder to attempt to put fine French furniture-polish on rough boards before they have been planed and smoothed to receive it.

It is said by anthropological students who have investigated the subject that certain barbarous races are weakened and finally exterminated by civilization. It is said, too, that minds accustomed to training and to study can bear training as minds of

[5] Professor Paul Shorey, of the Greek Department of the University of Chicago, co-translator of Von Holst, *The Constitutional and Political History of the United States.*

less cultured ancestry cannot. Sometimes I think that the enormous increase of wealth, of opportunity, of luxury, in such a community, say, as Chicago, have for the moment weakened that fortunate growth of the men and women to whom they have come in the largest proportion.

For reasons unnecessary to mention here, I was obliged to spend a day and two nights some hundreds of miles from Chicago, in a rough little village. I met there the genuine unwashed, unabashed, unaffected American in all his glory. At a certain so-called "grocery-store," whither I went in the evening to find a notary, I spent some two hours. During those two hours I heard some of the shrewdest talk I had heard during my entire stay in America. . . . .

As for me, when I returned to Chicago from my visit to the prairies, it seemed to me that there was more chance for Chicago than I had thought, when I first saw that in this socialistic foreign population many of the people I met were pretending to be serious about Browning, Plato, and the pre-Raphaelite poets.

Somehow *dilettanteism* in Chicago seems out of place. It is a little too much as though the coachman should turn round on the box to tell you what Ruskin says about sunsets, or the laundress turn from the tub to chat about the chemistry of soap-bubbles. Not that a coachman may not enjoy a sunset, and a laundress wonder about the iridescence of a soap-bubble, but for the time being their thoughts should be of other things.

Pork, not Plato, has made Chicago, and Chicago people have not arrived at a stage of civilization yet where they can with propriety or advantage change their allegiance.

One other feature of American life attracted my attention first in Chicago, though I found that it was common in the clubs in all parts of America.

We were sitting, some half a dozen of us, in the club, when another member appeared on the scene. He called a servant, said to him, "Take the orders!" and then turning to us all, said: "What'll ye have, gentlemen?" Thus this young man had his one drink, with his bill multiplied by six or seven. This practice is almost universal. It is done in New York as it is done here, and at Kansas City, and everywhere else I have been. "Take the orders!" and "What'll ye have?" might well be emblazoned on the club-crests like "*Ich Dien*," or "*Non sans droict*." They illustrate the hospitable tendency of the people, and the everywhere-prevailing dislike of solitariness.

It is of no consequence on these occasions that the inviter is not acquainted with the invitees. He includes them all in his generous embrace. He invites you to partake of potables first, and makes your acquaintance afterward. This custom leads to an unnecessary multiplication of potations, perhaps, but is an easy and gracious way of introducing one's self, or of re-introducing one's self to new-found company.

This cheerful, all-embracing "What'll ye have?" sounds in my ears now, when I am so many thousand miles away, and I smile involuntarily as I think of the happy-go-lucky, prosperous, and genial young heirs of a mighty nation's wealth, to all of whom I would gladly say, as so many of them have said to me: "What'll ye have?"

-》》《《-

WILLIAM ARCHER[1]

WILLIAM ARCHER (September 23, 1856—December 27, 1924), author of *The Green Goddess*, was born in Perth, Scotland, and educated at Edinburgh University. Early in life he considered a career in law but soon gave this up for journalistic work. From 1884 to 1905 he served as dramatic critic of the *World*, and later for the *Tribune*, the *Nation*, and the *Star*. In addition to *America To-Day*, Archer has written on Ibsen, minor modern poets, India, Nietzsche's philosophy, and Woodrow Wilson's place in history. He traveled much during his life, first visiting the United States in 1877.

At the close of the Spanish-American War he revisited America. His observations show clearly his admiration for this country, particularly for her progressiveness and prosperity. He was among those desiring to cement close and amicable relations between the British and American peoples, to which end he directed his resources. Among others, he looked forward to the day when American schools would desert what, to him, seemed a prejudiced view to Anglo-American relations. Unlike some foreign observers he did not condemn American literary effort, but remarked: "Let the purists who sneer at 'Americanisms' think for one moment how much poorer the English language would be today if North America had become a French or a Spanish instead of an English continent."

According to the Preface of *America To-Day*, it was Archer's purpose, in visiting the United States, to study the American stage; but he found many other things to engage his interest. His observations, covering only eight weeks, he admits may be somewhat superficial; but in that time he gained a thorough liking and high regard for things American.

-》》《《-

CHICAGO—ITS SPLENDOR AND SQUALOR

When I was in America twenty-two years ago, Chicago was the city that interested me least. Coming straight from San Francisco—which, in the eyes of a youthful student of Bret Harte, seemed the fitting metropolis of one of the great realms of romance—I saw in Chicago the negation of all that had charmed me on the Pacific slope. It was a flat and grimy abode of mere commerce, a rectilinear Glasgow; and to an Edinburgh

---

[1] William Archer, *America To-Day* (London: William Heinemann, 1900), pp. 87–98. Reprinted by permission of William Heinemann, Ltd.

408

man, or rather boy, no comparison could appear more damaging. How different is the impression produced by the Chicago of to-day! In 1877 the city was extensive enough, indeed, and handsome to boot, in a commonplace, cast-iron fashion. It was a chequer-board of Queen Victoria Streets. To-day its area is appalling, its architecture grandiose. It is the young giant among the cities of the earth, and it stands but on the threshold of its destiny. It embraces in its unimaginable amplitude every extreme of splendour and squalor. Walking in Dearborn Street or Adams Street of a cloudy afternoon, you think yourself in a frowning and fuliginous city of Dis, piled up by superhuman and apparently sinister powers. Cycling round the boulevards of a sunny morning, you rejoice in the airy and spacious greenery of the Garden City. Driving along the Lake Shore to Lincoln Park in the flush of sunset, you wonder that the dwellers in this street of palaces should trouble their heads about Naples or Venice, when they have before their very windows the innumerable laughter, the evershifting opalescence, of their fascinating inland sea. Plunging in the electric cars through the river subway, and emerging in the West Side, you realise that the slums of Chicago, if not quite so tightly packed as those of New York or London, are no whit behind them in the other essentials of civilised barbarism. Chicago, more than any other city of my acquaintance, suggests that antique conception of the underworld which placed Elysium and Tartarus not only on the same plane, but, so to speak, round the corner from each other.

As the elephant (or rather the megatherium) to the giraffe, so is the colossal business block of Chicago to the sky-scraper of New York. There is a proportion and dignity in the mammoth buildings of Chicago which is lacking in most of those which form the jagged sky-line of Manhattan Island. For one reason or another—no doubt some difference in the system of land tenure is at the root of the matter—the Chicago architect has usually a larger plot of ground to operate on than his New York colleague, and can consequently give his building breadth and depth as well as height. Before the lanky giants of the Eastern metropolis, one has generally to hold one's aesthetic judgment in abeyance. They are not precisely ugly, but still less, as a rule, can they be called beautiful. They are simply astounding manifestations of human energy and heaven-storming audacity. They stand outside the pale of aesthetics, like the Eiffel Tower or the Forth Bridge. But in Chicago proportion goes along with mere height, and many of the business houses are, if not beautiful, at least aesthetically impressive—for instance, the grim fortalice of Marshall, Field & Company, the Masonic Temple, the Women's Temperance Temple (a structure with a touch of real beauty), and such vast cities within the city as the Great Northern Building and the Monadnock Block. The last-named edifice alone is said to have a daily population of 6000. A city ordinance now limits the height of buildings to ten storeys; but even that is a respectable allowance. Moreover, it is found that where giant constructions cluster too close together, they (literally) stand in each other's light, and the middle storeys do not let. Thus the heaven-storming era is probably over; but there is all the more reason to feel assured that the business centre of Chicago will ere long be not only grandiose but architecturally dignified and satisfactory. A growing thirst for beauty has come upon the city, and architects are earnestly studying how to assuage it. In magnificence of internal decoration, Chicago can already challenge the world: for instance, in the white marble vestibule and corridors of The Rookery, and the noble hall of the Illinois Trust Bank.

At the same time, no account of the city scenery of Chicago is complete without the admission that the gorges and canyons of its central district are exceedingly draughty, smoky, and dusty. Even in these radiant spring days, it fully acts up to its reputation as the Windy City. This peculiarity renders it probably the most convenient place in the world for the establishment of a Suicide Club on the Stevensonian model. With your eyes peppered with dust, with your ears full of the clatter of the Elevated Road, and with the prairie breezes playfully buffeting you and waltzing with you by turns, as they eddy through the ravines of Madison, Monroe, or Adams Street, you take your life in your hand when you attempt the crossing of State Street, with its endless stream of rattling wagons and clanging trolley-cars. New York does not for a moment compare with Chicago in the roar and bustle and bewilderment of its street life. This remark will probably be resented in New York, but it expresses the settled conviction of an impartial pedestrian, who has spent a considerable portion of his life during the past few weeks in "negotiating" the crossings of both cities.

On the other hand, I observe no eagerness on the part of New York to contest the supremacy of Chicago in the matter of smoke. In this respect the eastern metropolis is to the western as Mont Blanc to Vesuvius. The smoke of Chicago has a peculiar and aggressive individuality, due, I imagine, to the natural clearness of the atmosphere. It does not seem, like the London smoke, to permeate and blend with the air. It does not overhang the streets in a uniform canopy, but sweeps across and about them in gusts and swirls, now dropping and now lifting again its grimy curtain. You will often see the vista of a gorge-like street so choked with a seeming thundercloud that you feel sure a storm is just about to burst upon the city, until you look up at the zenith and find it smiling and serene. Again and again a sudden swirl of smoke across the street (like that which swept across Fifth Avenue when the Windsor Hotel burst into flames) has led me to prick up my ears for a cry of "Fire!" But Chicago is not so easily alarmed. It is accustomed to having its airs from heaven blurred by these blasts from hell. I know few spectacles more curious than that which awaits you when you have shot up in the express elevator to the top of the Auditorium tower—on the one hand, the blue and laughing lake, on the other, the city belching volumes of smoke from its thousand throats, as though a vaster Sheffield or Wolverhampton had been transported by magic to the shores of the Mediterranean Sea. What a wonderful city Chicago will be when the commandment is honestly enforced which declares, "Thou shalt consume thine own smoke!"

What a wonderful city Chicago will be! That is the ever-recurring burden of one's cogitations. For Chicago is awake, and intelligently awake, to her destinies; so much one perceives even in the reiterated complaints that she is asleep. Discontent is the condition of progress, and Chicago is not in the slightest danger of relapsing into a condition of inert self-complacency. Her sons love her, but they chasten her. They are never tired of urging her on, sometimes (it must be owned) with most unfilial objurgations; and she, a quite unwearied Titan, is bracing up her sinews for the great task of the coming century. I have given myself a rendezvous in Chicago for 1925, when air-ships will no doubt make the transit easy for my septuagenarian frame. Nowhere in the world, I am sure, does the "to be continued in our next" interest take hold on one with such a compulsive grip.

Culture is pouring into Chicago as rapidly as pork or grain, and Chicago is insatiate in asking for more. In going over the Public Library (a not quite satisfactory building, though with some beautiful details) I was most of all impressed by the army of iron-bound boxes which are perpetually speeding to and fro between the library itself and no fewer than fifty-seven distributing stations scattered throughout the city. "I thought the number was forty-eight," said a friend who accompanied me. "So it was last year," said the librarian. "We have set up nine more stations during the interval." The Chicago Library boasts (no doubt justly) that it circulates more books than any similar institution in the world. Take, again, the University of Chicago: seven years ago (or, say, at the outside ten) it had no existence, and its site was a dismal swamp; to-day, it is a handsome and populous centre of literary and scientific culture. Observe, too, that it is by no means an oasis in the desert, but is thoroughly in touch with the civic life around it. For instance, it actively participates in the admirable work done by the Hull House Settlement in South Halsted Street, and in the vigorous and widespreading University Extension movement.

At the present moment Chicago is not a little resentful of the sharp admonitions addressed to her by two of her aforesaid loving but exacting children. One, Professor Charles Zueblin,[2] has

[2] Charles Zueblin, professor of sociology, was born in Pendleton, Indiana, May 4, 1866. He attended the public schools of Philadelphia, and his college work was done at the University of Pennsylvania; his graduate work at Northwestern, Yale, and Leipzig universities. In 1892 he became an instructor at the University of Chicago, and attained full professorial rank in 1902. His death occurred September 15, 1924.

been telling her that "in the arrogance of youth she has failed to realize that instead of being one of the progressive cities of the world, she has been one of the reckless, improvident, and shiftless cities." Professor Zueblin is not content (for example) with her magnificent girdle of parks and boulevards, but calls for smaller parks and breathing spaces in the heart of her most crowded districts. He further maintains that her great new sewage canal is a gigantically costly blunder; and indeed one cannot but sympathise with the citizens of St. Louis in inquiring by what right Chicago converts the Mississippi into her main sewer. But if Professor Zueblin chastises Chicago with whips, Mr. Henry B. Fuller,[3] it would seem, lashes her with scorpions. Mr. Fuller is one of the leading novelists of the city—for Chicago, be it known, had a flourishing and characteristic literature of her own long before Mr. Dooley sprang into fame. The author of *The Cliff-Dwellers* is alleged to have said that the Anglo-Saxon race was incapable of art, and that in this respect Chicago was pre-eminently Anglo-Saxon. "Alleged," I say, for reports of lectures in the American papers are always to be taken with caution, and are very often as fanciful as Dr. Johnson's reports of the debates in Parliament. The reporter is not generally a shorthand writer. He jots down as much as he conveniently can of the lecturer's remarks, and pieces them out from imagination. Thus, I am not at all sure what Mr. Fuller really said; but there is no doubt whatever of the indignation kindled by his diatribe. Deny her artistic capacities and sensibilities, and you touch Chicago in her tenderest point. Moreover, Mr. Fuller's onslaught encouraged several other like-minded critics to back him up, so that the city has been writhing under the scourges of her epigrammatists. I have before me a letter to one of the evening papers, written in a tone of academic sarcasm which proves that even the supercilious and "donnish" element is not lacking in Chicago culture. "I know a number of artists," says the writer,

[3] Henry Blake Fuller, author, was born in Chicago, January 9, 1857. His work was varied in style, ranging from editorials in the *Chicago Record-Herald* to poetry in *Lines Long and Short* (1917). Among his other works are: *The Chevalier of Pensieri-Vani* (1891); *The Puppet Booth* (1896), dramatic sketches; *From the Other Side* (1896), short stories; and *On the Stairs* (1918). He died July 28, 1929.

"who came to Chicago, and after staying here for a while, went away and achieved much success in New York, London, and Paris. The appreciation they received here gave them the impetus to go elsewhere, and thus brought them fame and fortune." Whatever foundation there may be for these jibes, they are in themselves a sufficient evidence that Chicago is alive to her opportunities and responsibilities. She is, in her own vernacular, "making culture hum." Mr. Fuller, I understand, reproached her with her stockyards—an injustice which even Mr. Bernard Shaw would scarcely have committed. Is it the fault of Chicago that the world is carnivorous? Was not "Nature red in tooth and claw" several aeons before Chicago was thought of? I do not understand that any unnecessary cruelty is practised in the stockyards; and apart from that, I fail to see that systematic slaughter of animals for food is any more disgusting than sporadic butchery. But of the stockyards I can speak only from hearsay. I shall not go to see them. If I have any spare time, I shall rather spend it in a second visit to St. Gaudens's magnificent and magnificently placed statue of Abraham Lincoln, surely one of the great works of art of the century, and one of the few entirely worthy monuments ever erected to a national hero.

Postscript.—The above-mentioned Hull House Settlement in South Halsted Street, under the direction of Miss Jane Addams, is probably the most famous institution of its kind in America; but it is only one of many. There is no more encouraging feature in American life than the zeal, energy, and high and liberal intelligence with which social service of this sort is being carried on in all the great cities. This is a line of activity on which England and America are advancing hand in hand, and however much one may deplore the necessity for such work, one cannot but see in the common impulse which prompts and directs it a symptom of the deep-seated unity of the two peoples. Nothing I saw in America impressed me more than the thorough practicality as well as the untiring devotion which was apparent in the work carried on by Miss Addams in Chicago and Miss Lillian D. Wald in Henry Street, New York. And in both Settlements I recognized the same atmosphere of culture, the same spirit of plain living, hard working, and high thinking, that characterises the best of our kindred institutions in England.

A lady connected with the University of Chicago, who is also a worker at the Hull House Settlement, told me a touching little story which illustrates at once the need for such work in Chicago, and the unexpected response with which it sometimes meets. She had been talking about the beauties of nature to a group of women from the slums, and at the end of her address one of her hearers said, "I ain't never been outside of Chicago, but I know it's true what the lady says. There's two vacant lots near our place, an' when the spring comes, the colours of them—they fair makes you hold your breath. An' then there's the trees on the Avenoo. An' then there's *all* the sky." On another occasion the same lady met with an "unexpected response" of a different order. She was showing a boy from the slums some photographs of Italian pictures, when they came upon a Virgin and Child. "Ah," said the boy at once, "that's Jesus an' His Mother: I allus knows *them* when I sees 'em." "Yes," said Miss R——, "there is a purity and grandeur of expression about them, isn't there ———" " 'Tain't that," interrupted the boy, "it's the rims round their heads as gives 'em away!"

Apart from the Settlements, there are many energetically-conducted societies in America for the social and political enlightenment of the masses. I have before me, for instance, a little bundle of most excellent leaflets issued by the League for Social Service of New York. They deal with such subjects as *The Duties of American Citizenship, The Value of a Vote, The Duty of Public Spirit, The Co-operative City,* &c. They include an admirable abstract in twenty-four pages of *Laws Concerning the Welfare of Every Citizen of New York,* and the same Society issues similar abstracts of the laws of other States. They have a large and well-equipped lecture organisation, and they issue excellent practical *Suggestions for Conferences and Courses of Study.* The problem to be grappled with by this Society and others working on similar lines is no doubt one of immense difficulty. It is nothing less than the education in citizenship of the most heterogeneous, polyglot, and in some respects ignorant and degraded population ever assembled in a single city since the days of Imperial Rome. The spread of political enlightenment in New York and other cities cannot possibly be very rapid; but no effort is being spared to accelerate it. I sometimes wonder whether the obvious necessity for political education in America may not, in the long run, prove a marked advantage to her, as compared, for instance, with England. Dissatisfaction, as I have said above, is the condition of progress. We are apt to assume that every Briton is born a good citizen; and in the lethargy begotten of that assumption, it may very well happen that we let the Americans outstrip us in the march of enlightenment.

MONSIGNOR COUNT VAY DE VAYA AND LUSKOD[1]

MONSIGNOR COUNT PETER DE VAYA AND LUSKOD was born in Hungary in 1864 of a cultured and wealthy Magyar family. Little is known of his early education; but when he made his first visit to the United States, he was already a dignitary in the Roman Catholic church.

The Count came to America several times—his accommodations varying from the luxury of the "Kaiser Wilhelm der Grosse" in 1890 to the squalor of an emigrant ship in 1906. As chaplain of the latter, he recorded his impressions of conditions on the ship in the *Living Age*, January, 1907. The article deals also with the causes for Hungarian emigration to America and the position his people assumed in the New World.

De Vaya's *The Inner Life of the United States* is a philosophical study of the nation. In it he comments on the economic status of immigrants; makes observations on the production of cotton, sugar, and grain; and notes the contrast between the condition of the agricultural and industrial laborer.

In all his travels in America, the position of women, their importance in the home, their opportunities for education, and their economic endeavors impressed him particularly. He found the American educational system worthy of approval, American suffrage in its lack of uniformity in the different states a cause of concern, and a growing spirit of imperialism in the government contrary to the principles of the Monroe Doctrine. However, the influence of America in molding the world's history he held to be considerable, increasing in power as the years passed.

Among the cities he visited, Philadelphia, Washington, and Boston pleased him. The last, with its museums and libraries, he called the "Athens" of the United States. To him Pittsburgh was a "City of Dreadful Night," and New York he condemned for affectations and mannerisms. He came to Chicago in 1905.

-»» «-

INDUSTRY AND STRIKES

The huge railway station of Chicago was in charge of the police. To every passenger—and there were not a few—I counted at least one stalwart guardian of the peace. The large square in front of the station also swarmed with policemen; I even saw

[1] Monsignor Count Vay de Vaya and Luskod, *The Inner Life of the United States* (London: John Murray, 1908), pp. 159–61, 167–70, 172–85. Reprinted by permission of John Murray; also by permission of E. P. Dutton & Co., Inc., New York (American publishers).

some seated on the boxes of the waiting carriages. There was a strike in the town. That great workshop of the United States had once again suspended operations, and all the enormous vitality usually absorbed by the factories and foundries had suddenly broken loose. Like the waters overflowing the banks of a swollen river, so these seething, surging masses of disorganised humanity flooded the town. On my way from the station I saw many sad and evil sights. Workmen and police officers were constantly in conflict, and street fights, regular battles, raged in all directions. The strikers harangued the workmen, urging them to join their ranks, and those who attempted to continue their work were knocked down and mobbed by the infuriated populace. Factories and stores were ransacked by parties of unemployed. Howls and shrieks mingled with the lugubrious sounds of rifle and pistol shots.

Such was Chicago on the day of my arrival. As by chance, it was given me to see this huge mechanism of human labour, unique of its kind, in disorder and confusion. The spectacle was sensational and cruel, such as only the United States are capable of producing. In a few days matters improved, the outbreak was suppressed, the blazing volcano of human passion had spent its force. The daily routine of work was resumed, millions of hands once again seized their tools, and outward peace was restored. . . . .

Chicago may be called the city of labour and strikes. Everybody works, great and small, rich and poor, all with the same marvellous intensity. Its favourable situation, in the centre of the country, and within easy access of all the high-roads of communication, makes this town one of the greatest agricultural and industrial markets of the world; and Chicago may in truth be regarded as the commercial capital of the United States. The business done from day to day amounts to several million dollars. Factories and foundries of every description abound in the far-extending suburbs. There are establishments where some 10,000 persons find employment, as, for instance, at the Pullman works, where the celebrated railway carriages are made. The Illinois Steel Factory and many other industrial undertakings are towns in themselves, the population being composed of the workmen and their families, recruited from all parts of the world.

I had come to open the first church erected by workmen who had emigrated from my own country. The little wooden structure stands on the Pullman road in South Chicago, about 20 miles distant from the centre of the town. At present it is surrounded by maize-and corn-fields, is, in fact, in the heart of the country, but I was told that in a few years these would all be converted into rows of palatial residences. At Chicago anything is possible, and I have not the slightest doubt that this forecast will come true. Meanwhile, these suburban establishments offered me an excellent opportunity of making myself acquainted with the industrial world, of seeing how things are made and produced, and of learning something about the workers themselves. The rapid development of industry in the United States is one of the most striking phenomena of our time, and if we consider that all this great commercial activity has practically arisen within the last fifty years, it becomes a subject well worthy of our interest. . . . .

It was on a hot morning in the month of June that my amiable host, the Rev. Father S——, one of the most distinguished orators of the United States and a direct descendant of the great general and popular hero of that name, undertook to pilot me through the labyrinth of the slaughter-houses. To give some idea of the enormous extent of these abattoirs, it will be sufficient to mention that they cover close upon 250 acres of ground. The alleys and passages intersecting this area measure over 75 miles, and the railway net on the premises is approximated at a length of 300 miles of line. It is a town, or rather a world in itself, peopled by the workmen, butchers and pig-killers—a dismal community in truth. . . . . It is true that these famous stockyards of Chicago, so often criticised and described, present one of the most sorrowful phases of modern industry but they also show the successful substitution of machinery for manual labour, and a hitherto unrivalled utilisation of the residue. "Nothing is wasted," would be an appropriate motto to place over the packing-houses. Nothing is wasted, neither material nor labour nor time. . . . .

I have purposely not entered into a more detailed description of the stockyards. No doubt there is much that is objectionable in the manipulation of the abattoirs; they have their evil sides, and voices are raised more and more vehemently against the abuses practised there. Perhaps only the most advantageous side of the business was shown to me, or perhaps the house of Swift, which is the one I visited, is a model establishment. To me it certainly appeared perfect in every detail. The building which contains the offices of the directors and clerks, and where all the business is transacted, might fitly be styled a "Palace of Administration," and is a model of comfort and cleanliness. The offices are tastefully furnished, and have that air of elegance which characterises every American house of business, but is here almost carried to excess. It is a fine iron building, with large windows, and provided with all the latest improvements. The pinewood furniture, the writing machines and telephone boxes, all are arranged on the most approved principles to satisfy the requirements of this growing trade; and to give an idea of the luxury of the establishment it will suffice to mention that by the aid of refrigerators the temperature is always kept at 64° F. The air of the offices is mechanically purified, and by some ingenious contrivance the smells from the slaughter-houses are intercepted so that they cannot penetrate to these precincts.

The directors of this unique establishment entertained me at luncheon in the large dining-room, situated over these palatial offices, which is also kept at a low temperature and artificially aired. This imposing hall is furnished with little tables where the employés can get a good dinner at a very low figure. Adjoining the dining-hall is a smoking-room, provided with books and newspapers, where the business of the day can be discussed over a cup of black coffee. This is the *ne plus ultra* of comfort, and thoroughly in keeping with the American conception of the "Office," where the men spend the greater portion of their life. . . . .

Another day I was invited to visit one of the stores. These

huge establishments are from twelve to fifteen stories high, and contain every possible article of trade, from matches and boot-laces, to the most exquisite art treasures and priceless gems. Anything, indeed, can be purchased there, even to real estate and country houses. They are "Bon Marchés" and "Whiteleys" on a larger and, if possible, more complete scale, more daring and perhaps more fantastic in their display.

The house I was invited to visit was that of Marshall Field & Co., of almost historical renown, because its growth and success is so intimately connected with that of the city itself. . . . . I viewed all the various departments with interest, and also went into the adjoining warehouse. This has all the appearance of a fortress. It is situated on the banks of the river, and the goods are transported from there by boats to the shop. This is indeed a wonderful establishment. One might wander through it from morning to night without coming to the end of it, without ex-hausting its hoards, without having seen, in fact, one-thou-sandth part of all the marvellous confections with which the wealth and fashion of Chicago is pleased to adorn itself. But what impressed me far beyond all the delights of this fairy show, was the person of the originator, the man round whom all this machinery moves—Mr. Field, since the liquidation of the firm, sole proprietor of the concern.

The young clerk who was showing me round, and who told me the history of the establishment, came to a sudden stop as we turned a corner, and pointing to a kind of little office, or rather box, with glass partitions, in which a white-haired gentleman was sitting at his desk, he whispered: "The master!" There was a catch in his voice as of fear at the mention of the power upon whom his earthly existence depended. Mr. Field was then about seventy years old. His hair was quite white and his face had a tired expression, the result of a life of toil and struggle. My con-ductor explained that "the master" was always in that place, the first to arrive and the last to leave the premises. Seated in his glass cage, like a spider in his web, he held the threads and concentrated the movements of the whole of this gigantic busi-ness. "It is hard work to make millions," the pleasant young merchant remarked, "but it is harder still to keep them." In this land of ever keener growing competition, once relax the hold, and failure is imminent. Respite is synonymous with being swallowed up by legions of competitors. Incessant activity, unflagging zeal, alone can dominate the market, and self-sacrifice is the first condition to insure success.

Suddenly a muffled sound coming from the other end of the building interrupted our conversation. The police were at once on the spot, but the strikers came rushing in from the street and attacked the men who had remained at their work, such as the drivers of the carts and waggons, and the carters carrying out the goods. The noise came nearer. Uproarious vociferations were now distinctly audible, the howls of a delirious crowd mingled with the moans of the wounded and the dull sound of blows. The reason of this tumult was the same as always—a clamour for a small increase of wages. It was but a fresh outburst of that inveterate hatred existing between labourer and capitalist which from day to day is becoming more pronounced. All the sad and bloody scenes which I had witnessed since my arrival in the town were to me so many manifest confirmations of the growing feeling of hostility of the poor towards the rich, and long after I had left that palace of gold and gewgaws, the angry voices of the malcontents sounded in my ears like the refrain of a sordid fanfare. . . . .

As my thoughts went back to that glass cage, and the white-haired man toiling at his books from morning till night, I could not help asking myself: Who is more to be pitied, the men who have failed to secure a rise in their wages, or the millionaire who spends his life shut up in a cage? . . .

EDUCATIONAL AND RELIGIOUS INSTITUTIONS

During my stay at Chicago I visited most of the public institutions of which the city is justly proud, such as the City Hall and County Court House, which building occupies an entire square, and has been erected at a cost of $5,000,000; the famous Auditorium, comprising a large hotel and a theatre to hold 5,000 people, the construction of which is estimated at $3,000,000. In

America one is expected to know or to ask the cost of every-thing, and no sooner do we stop to admire a thing, no matter whether it be great or small, than some one volunteers to tell us its value in current coin.

The Public Library and the Chicago Art Institute are un-doubtedly among the handsomest buildings of the city. The lat-ter, erected by A. Coolidge, is a classic structure, admirably situated on a greensward on the borders of Lake Michigan. The interior is artistically decorated and well lighted, and contains many beautiful paintings of the modern schools. The great con-temporary masters, such as Millet, Troyon, Corot, Deraille, Munkacsy, Meissonier, Courbet, Rosa Bonheur, Makart, Isa-bay, Gerôme, and De Neuville, are represented by excellent canvases.

The Library is also richly decorated. It contains nearly 300,-000 volumes, but there is room for double that number. The ex-terior of the building is almost severe in its simplicity, but the interior is fitted up in precious marbles, and ornamented with carvings and bronzes. What struck me more than these institu-tions themselves, however, was the public which frequents both. Humble people they were, mostly of the working classes, wear-ing their dusty working clothes. Any spare moments they seem gladly to devote to the improvement of their mind; and so, by learning a little from day to day, they acquire a fund of knowl-edge which enables them to rise some day to positions of emi-nence. Thus it is that the men of talent, recruited from office or factory, so often surprise us by the extent of their learning.

The Newbury [sic] Library is another noteworthy institution, founded in memory of a wealthy citizen who bequeathed $3,000,000 for that purpose. It contains 200,000 volumes. An-other inhabitant of Chicago, Mr. J. Crerar,[2] left $2,000,000 to be

[2] John Crerar was born in New York City in 1857. He came to Chicago in 1862 in the employ of the railway supply firm of Jessup and Company. The manager of the Chicago branch was J. McGregor Adams, with whom Crerar later formed a partnership. In his own business Crerar acquired a large fortune, and during his life he gave freely to charity. He died October 19, 1889, and in his will he left a sum for the founding of the John Crerar Library. In order not to duplicate the work being done by Newberry and other libraries, the trustees have confined themselves largely to collecting scientific works.

spent in the erection of a library in the southern and poorest quarter of the town. The Chicago Historical Society is among the oldest educational establishments of the city, and contains numerous reminiscences of the time of its foundation. Then there is the famous University, covering an area of 24 acres.[3] The four faculties—arts, science, commere, and politics—together with the houses of the students and the lecture halls, are expected, when completed, to occupy forty buildings. At present only half this number is finished, and even now the cost of construction, including the Cobb Hall, the Chemical Laboratory and the Museum, surpasses $5,000,000. The schools are all built on an expensive scale, and on the most modern principles.

Besides the University, the schools and other establishments of a purely educational character, Chicago possesses two very interesting institutions, for the moral elevation of the most neglected and poorest inhabitants. One of these was founded by the Armour family, and includes an asylum for deserted children, a kindergarten, a free dispensary, library, etc. I was also deeply impressed by the arrangements of Hull House, which is administered by ladies of high culture, and is intended to form a centre for the promotion of intellectual pursuits among the working population of the neighbourhood, and for the material assistance of the deserving poor amongst them. Besides a kindergarten and a preparatory school, it contains a museum, and lays itself out for social entertainments, lectures, concerts, theatricals, all with the object of keeping the people from the street, and of helping them to raise themselves to a higher moral and intellectual standard. How far either of these establishments fulfils the expectations of their originators it is difficult to determine, only as far as the school of arts and crafts goes, its beneficial influence is becoming daily more apparent. But even where the result is not so visible, the fact that the experiment has been made is commendable in itself, and affords another proof that this comparatively new city, which possesses no traditions to support its prestige, recognizes the necessity of elevating its children to the highest possible standard, apart from all monetary considerations.

[3] University of Chicago.

Thanks to almost universal patronage, the number of Catholic establishments of education are increasing, for parents of different denomination often send their children to the schools of that community. To name a few, we would specify the great St. Xavier College, and the schools of the Paulist Fathers, the Young Ladies' Pensionate of the Sisters of Lorette and of the Sacred Heart. All these are model establishments, owing their great popularity in the first place to the serious instruction given there, and also to the exceptional care bestowed upon the development of the moral qualities of the scholars. One of the pleasantest boarding establishments is situated in Lincoln Park, surrounded by green fields and shady shrubberies. We could almost fancy ourselves in the middle of the country.

PARKS AND RECREATION

Indeed, strange as it may seem, Chicago, the town of factories and furnaces, possesses public parks and recreation grounds covering an area of 2,230 acres, giving walks to an extent of 66 miles. Jackson and Washington parks cover 523 acres; Douglas Park, 180, Garfield Park, 186, and Humbert[4] Park, 200 acres. All these grounds are well wooded, and dotted over with restaurants and places of amusement. The famous Lakeshore Drive, leading to Lincoln Park, is the promenade of the wealthy. It is a long boulevard, giving an unlimited view over the silvery surface of the lake. On the shore the mansions of the millionaires form an uninterrupted line of sumptuous dwellings. They are of different sizes and styles: some imitate the Italian villa, some the glorified cottage of Anglo-Saxon origin. Others, again, affect the style of the French *château*, or of the crenellated, turreted Tudor castle. All these are attempts to create something impressive, and if not always a success from an aesthetic point of view—for even if built in the most perfect style, both *château* and castle are out of place on a modern boulevard, and cannot be admired—these mansions have at least the advantage of insuring privacy—a rare commodity in the States.

4 Humboldt Park.

FOREIGNERS IN CHICAGO

However, it is not an absolute necessity to be a millionaire to permit oneself the luxury of a private home in Chicago. The chief ambition of every citizen seems to be to build himself a house standing in its own grounds, and so the town grows in extent at a prodigious rate. There are rows of houses, such as Western Avenue, measuring from end to end over 20 miles. And there are suburbs, as, for instance, the Pullman settlement, which are almost towns in themselves, the inhabitants being composed of all nationalities, the agglomerated sweepings of the four quarters of the globe. Chicago, with its 3,000,000 inhabitants, is one of the largest metropolises from a cosmopolitan point of view. It is a veritable babel of languages. It would seem as if all the millions of human beings disembarking year by year upon the shores of the United States were unconsciously drawn to make this place their headquarters. Chicago is the land of promise to all malcontents and aimless emigrants. More than half of its inhabitants are foreigners, and there are whole quarters where nothing but German is spoken. Others are inhabited entirely by Slavs. Nowhere else has immigration assumed such huge proportions, and nowhere else does the immigration question so seriously affect the local administration and development. For naturally among this mass of fortune-seekers, carried westward on the waves of destiny, there are many undesirable elements, and it is not sufficient to provide for their material sustenance, they have also to be raised to a higher moral and spiritual level.

THE INAUGURATION OF A CHURCH

The reason of my visit to Chicago this time was, as already said, to inaugurate the little Catholic church, erected by the immigrants recently arrived from the shores of the Danube and the Tisza. I had left the United States some time previously, and when the amiable invitation of my compatriots reached me, I was in the extreme north of Canada, on the shores of the Atlantic; I had just been visiting a colony of Hungarian artisans working in the iron foundries of Sidney (Nova Scotia). Although it was a long way back to Chicago, I willingly undertook the tedious journey—occupying three days and three nights—in order to comply with the complimentary request. On arriving at Chicago I found that the place of my destination was rather difficult to get at, and a good way off, being situated in the southernmost suburb of the town. First I had to travel by rail up to a certain point, then by the overhead railroad, and finally by street car. We went right through the city, past sumptuous palaces and warehouses, through labyrinths of modest streets, until at last I found myself democratically seated in an ordinary street car, which carried me away into what seemed the heart of the country. To right and left stretched endless fields of maize, and with the exception of a few tall chimneys on the horizon, the scene before me appeared in its primeval verdure, one immense expanse of untilled loneliness. No streets, no houses!— "But all that will come by and by," I was told, and on my next visit I should see this rural landscape transformed into blocks of houses and streets, just like all the rest of the town.

At a little distance among the marshy pasture land I detected the small wooden structure. From its roof waved the American and Hungarian flags, stars and stripes and the tricolour (red, white and green) harmoniously blending together. "That is the church, and the school is underneath," some one proudly volunteered. A humble edifice truly, but speaking of much sacrifice and labour. These simple folk have built it with their hardearned savings, for the glory of God and the religious education of their children.

More than half the population of Chicago are foreigners. The German and Austrian contingent alone is nearly 1,000,000 strong. The Slav lands under Austrian dominion are also largely represented, while Poles and Bohemians, including the southern Slavs, amount to 300,000 souls. There are over 200,000 Italians, and the Hungarians proper, not included in other categories, must be estimated at nearly 15,000 new arrivals within the last few years. These latter are chiefly employed as butchers in the slaughter-houses, and as blacksmiths and carpenters in the Pullman establishment. It was at the expense of these people that the little church was built which now met my view. It stands like a beacon amid the surrounding marshes; it is the nucleus of a new suburb, which will spring up around it, and will certainly be no less important a part of the metropolis than the others which have arisen at 16 miles from the centre of the town. It is a first step towards progress, another foundation stone of civilisation and culture.

The workmen and their families awaited me at the entrance of the building. For the greater part they were still dressed in their simple costume "from over the sea," and their whole demeanour showed that they had not long since arrived in these parts. Set adrift in that great city, without knowing the language, without friends, or any one to advise them, these poor folks are at the mercy of chance. And, in addition to all the other difficulties and problems which the municipal authorities have to face, we can well understand that this question of dealing with the foreign population of inferior civilisation is one of the greatest and hardest to solve. They have not only to be fed, they have also to be protected and educated. The church and the school are their only safeguards. As long as the people will go to church and are willing to have their children brought up on religious principles there is nothing to fear. As long as they recognise their duty towards God they will also recognise and fulfil their duty towards their neighbour.

The inauguration of that humble little church and its simple worshippers has left an indelible impression upon me. It was one of those never-to-be-forgotten scenes which, in spite of their apparent unimportance, form a page in the annals of history. This small beginning, representing the accumulated savings of those hardy workmen, is the centre of new efforts and new struggles. Let us hope these may lead here to as successful an issue as they have done in other parts of the town. Let us hope that its inhabitants may one day be as prosperous and wealthy as their fellow-citizens in older Chicago. Above all, let us hope that the little church may grow into a cathedral, and its elementary school into a great scientific establishment. And although in the past the place has so often been shaken by strikes and tumults, let us hope that henceforth faith and culture may ensure peace and prosperity to this marvellous city.

EDWARD HUNGERFORD[1]

EDWARD HUNGERFORD, born in Dexter, New York, December 21, 1875, has had a varied career as an American business man, journalist, and writer of novels. At twenty-one he began work as a reporter for the Rochester *Herald*, and two years later joined the staff of the New York *Sun*. Next he assumed the editorship of the Glen Falls *Times*. In 1912 he left journalism to become advertising manager of the Wells-Fargo Express Company, a position which he held for six years. In the meantime railroads had become a subject for Hungerford's pen, and in 1911 he published *The Modern Railroad*. Since then he has brought out other works on railroads and directed the Fair of the Iron Horse, held in Baltimore, October, 1927. He has also written a few novels, among which is *Gertrude*.

It is perhaps appropriate that a man of letters, also interested in the railroads of the nation, should write a book on the chief cities of the land, each of importance to some particular railroad line. *The Personality of American Cities* is a series of impressions by an American who has visited at least once each place mentioned. To each city he has given a picturesque name. "The Old French Lady by the Riverbank" is New Orleans; "The Gateway to the Southwest," St. Louis; "The City of the Little Squares," San Antonio; and "The American Paris," Denver. No section of the country is neglected, and there are descriptions of Seattle and Portland as well as the Mississippi Valley and eastern towns. These sketches were first published separately in several magazines, but in 1913 were gathered together and published in book form as *The Personality of American Cities*.

In his book the author is not particularly interested in plumbing the depths of American mental processes. Rather, he seeks only to depict the matchless energy of the industrial centers and to proclaim the increasing material prosperity of the land. He hastens to add, however, that America is not all materialism. He found even Chicago stressing another side of life, building a famous system of parks. As an explanation of such characteristics, Hungerford points out that America is still young and has many years of growth before her, and, therefore, one should not be impatient.

⇶ ⇷

CHICAGO AND THE CHICAGOANS[2]

Early in the morning the city by the lake is astir. Before the first long scouting rays of earliest sunlight are thrusting them-

[1] Edward Hungerford, *The Personality of American Cities* (New York: McBride, Nast & Co., 1913), pp. 198–211. Reprinted by permission of Robert M. McBride & Co., New York.

[2] Title as in the original.

selves over the barren reaches of Michigan—state and lake—
Chicago is in action. The nervous little suburban trains are
reaching into her heart from South, from North and from West.
The long trains of elevated cars are slipping along their alley-
routes, skirting behind long rows of the dirty colorless houses of
the most monotonous city on earth, threading themselves
around the loop—receiving passengers, discharging passengers
before dawn has fully come upon the town. The windows of the
tedious, almost endless rows of houses flash into light and life,
the trolley cars in the broad streets come at shorter intervals, in
whole companies, brigades, regiments—a mighty army of trucks
and wagons begin to send up a great wave of noise and of clatter
from the shrieking highways and byways of the city.

The traveler coming to the city from the east and by night
finds it indeed a mighty affair. For an hour and a half before his
train arrives at the terminal station, he is making his way
through Chicago environs—coming from dull flat monotonies of
sand and brush and pine into Gary—with its newness and its
bigness proclaimed upon its very face so that even he who flits
through at fifty miles an hour may read both—jolting over main
line railroads that cross and recross at every conceivable angle,
snapping up through Hammond and Kensington and Grand
Crossing—to the right and to the left long vistas with the ungainly, picturesque outlines of steel mills with upturned rows of
smoking stacks, of gas-holders, and of packing-houses, the vistas
suddenly closed off by long trails of travel-worn freight-cars,
through which the traveler's train finds its way with a mighty
clattering and reverberating of noisy echoes. This is Chicago—
Chicago spreading itself over miles of absolutely flat shore-land
at almost the extreme southern tip of Lake Michigan—Chicago
proudly proclaiming herself as the business and the transportation metropolis of the land, disdaining such mere seaport places
as New York or Boston or Baltimore or San Francisco—Chicago with the most wretched approaches on her main lines of travel
of any great city of the world.

If you come to her on at least one of the great railroads that
link her with the Atlantic seaboard, you will get a glimpse of her

one redeeming natural feature, for five or six miles before your train comes to a final grinding stop at the main terminal—the blue waters of the lake. This railroad spun its way many years ago on the very edge of the lake—much to the present-day grief of the town. It gives no grief to the incoming traveler—to turn from the sordid streets, the quick glimpses of rows of pretentious but fearfully dirty and uninteresting houses—to the great open space to the east of Chicago—nature's assurance of fresh air and light and health to one of the really vast cluster-holds of mankind. To him the lake is in relief—even in splendid contrast to the noise, the dirt, the streets darkened and narrowed by the over-shouldering constructions of man. From the intricate and the confusing, to the simplicity of open water—no wonder then that Chicago has finally come to appreciate her lake, that she seizes upon her remaining free water-front like a hungry and ill-fed child, that she builds great hotels and office buildings where their windows may look—not upon the town, stretching itself to the horizon on the prairie, but upon the lake, with its tranquillity and its beauty, the infinite majesty of a great, silent open place.

In the terminal stations of the city you first begin to divine the real character of the city. You see it, a great crucible into which the people of all nations and all corners of one of the greatest of the nations are being poured. Pressing her nose against the glass of a window that looks down into surpassingly busy streets, overshadowed by the ungainly bulk of an elevated railroad, is the bent figure of a hatless peasant woman from the south of Europe—seeing her America for the first time and almost shrinking from the glass in a mixture of fear and of amazement. Next to her is a sleek, well-groomed man who may be from the East—from an Atlantic seaport city, but do not be too sure of that, for he may have his home over on Michigan avenue and think that "New York is a pretty town but not in it with Chicago." You never can tell in the most American and most cosmopolitan of American cities. At a third window is a man who has come from South Dakota. He has a big ranch up in that wonderful state. You know that because last night he sat beside you on a bench in the dingy, busy office of the old Palmer House and told you of Chicago as he saw it.

"I've a farm up in the South Dakota," he told you, in brief. "This is my first time East." You started in a bit of surprise at that, for it had always occurred to you that Chicago was West, that you, born New Yorker, were reaching into the real West whenever you crossed to the far side of Main street, in Buffalo. You looked at the ranchman, feeling that he was joking, and then you took a second look into his tired eyes and knew that you were talking to no humorist.

"The first real big town that I ever ran into," he said, in his simple way, "was Sioux City, and I set up and took a little notice on it. It seemed mighty big, but that was five years ago, and four years ago I took my stock down to Cudahy in Omaha —and there *was* a town. You could walk half a day in Omaha and never come to cattle country. Just houses and houses and houses—an' you begin to wonder where they find the folks to fill them. This year I come here with the beef for the first time— an' you could put Omaha in this town and never know the difference."

After that you confessed, with much pride, that you lived in New York city, and you began. You knew the number of miles of subway from the Bronx over to Brooklyn, and the number of stories in the Woolworth building, all those things, and when you caught your breath, the stockman asked you if Tom Sharkey really had a saloon in your town, and was Steve Brodie still alive, and did New York folks like to go down to the Statue of Liberty on pleasant Sunday afternoons. You answered those questions and then you told the stockman more—of London, made of dozens of Omahas, where the United States was but a pleasant and withal a somewhat uncertain dream, of Paris the beautiful, and of Berlin the awfully clean. When you were done, you went with the stockman to eat in a basement—that is the Chicago idea of distinction in restaurants—and he took you to a lively show afterwards.

Now you never would have wandered into a Broadway hotel lobby and made the acquaintance of a perfect stranger, dined with him and spent the evening with him—no, not even if you were a Chicagoan and fearfully lonely in New York. It is the Chicago that gets into a New Yorker's veins when he comes within her expanded limits, it is the unseen aura of the West that creeps as far east as the south tip of Lake Michigan. It made you acknowledge with hearty appreciation the "good mornings" of each man as he filed into the washroom of the sleeping car in the early morning. You never say "good morning" to strangers in the sleeping cars going from New York over to Boston. For that is the East and that is different.

A Chicago man sits back in the regal comfort of a leather-padded office chair and tells you between hurried bites of the lunch that has been placed upon his desk, of the real town that is sprawled along the Lake Michigan shore.

"Don't know as you particularly care for horse-food," he apologizes, between mouthfuls, "but that's the cult in this neck-o'-woods nowadays."

"The cult?" you inquire, as he plunges more deeply in his bran-mash.

"Precisely," he nods. "We're living in cults out here now. We've got Boston beaten to culture."

He shoves back the remnant of his "health food" luncheon with an expression that surely says that he wishes it was steak, smothered with onions and flanked by an ample-girthed staff of vegetables, and faces you—you New Yorker—with determination to set your path straight.

"Along in the prehistoric ages—which in Chicago means about the time of the World's Fair—we were trying to live up to anything and everything, but particularly the ambition to be the overwhelmingest biggest town in creation, and to make your old New York look like an annexed seaport. We had no cults, no woman's societies, nothing except a lot of men making money hand over fist, killing hogs, and building cars and selling stuff at retail by catalogues. We were not aesthetic and we didn't particularly care. We liked plain shows as long as the girls in them weren't plain, and we had a motto that a big lady carried around on a shield. The motto was 'I will,' and translated it meant to the bottom of the sea with New York or St. Louis or any other upstart town that tried to live on the same side of the earth as Chicago. We were going to have two million population inside of two years and—"

He dives again into his cultish lunch and after a moment resumes:

"The big lady has lost her job and we've thrown the shield—motto and all—into the lake. We're trying to forget the motto and that's why we've got the cult habit. We're class and we're close on the heels of you New Yorkers—only last winter they began to pass the French pastry around on a tray at my club. We learn quickly and then go you one better. We've finally given Jane Addams the recognition and the support that she should have had a dozen years ago. We're strong and we're sincere for culture—the university to the south of us has had some funny cracks but that is all history. Together with the one to the north of us, they are finally institutions—and Chicago respects them as such.

"Take opera. We used to think it was a fad to hear good music, and only the society folks went to hear it—so that the opera fairly starved to death when it came out here. Now they are falling over one another to get into the Auditorium, and our opera company is not only an institution but you New Yorkers would give your very hearts to have it in your own big opera house."

"You'll build an opera house out here then," you venture, "the biggest—."

He interrupts.

"Not necessarily the biggest," he corrects, "but as fine as the very best."

The talk changes. You are frankly interested in the cults. You have heard of how one is working in the public schools, how the school children of Chicago work in classrooms with the windows wide open, and you ask him about it.

"It must be fine for the children?" you finally venture.

"It is," he says. "My daughter teaches in a school down Englewood way, and she says that it is fine for the children—

but hell on the teachers. They weren't trained to it in the beginning."

You are beginning to understand Chicago. A half an hour ago you could not have understood how a man like this—head of a giant corporation employing half a hundred thousand workmen, a man with three or four big houses, a stable full of automobiles, a man of vast resources and influences would have his daughter teaching in a public school. You are beginning to understand the man—the man who is typical of Chicago. You come to know him the more clearly as he tells you of the city that he really loves. He tells you how Sorolla "caught on" over at the Institute—although more recently the Cubists rather dimmed the brilliance of the Spaniard's reception—and how the people who go to the Chicago libraries are reading less fiction and more solid literature all the while. Then—of a sudden, for he realizes that he must be back again into the grind and the routine of his work—he turns to you and says:

"And yesterday we had the big girl and the motto. It was hardly more than yesterday that we thought that population counted, that acreage was a factor in the consummation of a great city."

So you see that Chicago is only America, not boastful, not arrogant, but strong in her convictions, strong in her sincerity, strong in her poise between right and power together, and not merely power without right. A city set in the heart of America must certainly take strong American tone, no matter how many foreigners New York's great gateway may pour into her ample lap in the course of a single twelvemonth. Chicago has taken that dominating tone upon herself.

She is a great city. Her policemen wear star-shaped badges after the fashion of country constables in rural drama, and her citizens call the trolleys that run after midnight "owl cars," but she is a great city none the less for these things. Her small shops along Michigan avenue have the smartness of Paris or of Vienna, the greatest of her department stores[3] is one of the greatest department stores in all the land, which means in the whole

3 Marshall Field and Company.

world. It is softly carpeted, floor upon floor, and the best of Chicago delights to lunch upon one of its upper floors. Chicago likes to go high for its meals or else, as we have already intimated, down into basements. The reason for this last may be that one of the world's greatest *restauranteurs*,[4] who had his start in the city by Lake Michigan, has always had his place below the sidewalk level on a busy corner of the city.

The city is fearfully busy at all of its downtown corners. New Yorkers shudder at Thirty-fourth street and Broadway. Inside the Chicago loop are several dozen Thirty-fourth streets and Broadways. There you have it—the Chicago loop, designed to afford magnificent relief to the town and in effect having tightly drawn a belt about its waist. The loop is a belt-line terminal, slightly less than a mile in diameter, designed to serve the elevated railroads that stretch their caterpillar-like structures over three directions of the widespread town. Within it are the theaters, the hotels, the department stores, the retail district, and the wholesale and the railroad terminals. Just without it is an arid belt and then somewhere to the north, the west and south, the great residential districts. So it is a mistake. For, with the exception of a little way along Michigan avenue to the south, the loop has acted against the growth of the city, has kept it tightly girdled within itself.

"Within the loop," is a meaningful phrase in Chicago. It means congestion in every form and the very worst forms to the fore. It means that what was originally intended to be an adequate terminal to the various elevated railroads has become a transportation abomination and a matter of local contempt. For you cannot exaggerate the condition that it has created. It is fearful on ordinary days, and when you come to extraordinary days, like the memorable summer when the Knights Templar held their triennial conclave there, the newspaper print "boxed" summaries of the persons killed and injured by congestion conditions "within the loop." . . . .

It is no laughing matter to folks who have to thread it. Trolley cars, automobiles, taxicabs, the long lumbering 'buses that

4 Charles Rector.

remind one of the photographs of Broadway, New York, a quarter of a century ago or more, entangle themselves with one another and with unfortunate pedestrians and still no one comes forward with practical relief. The 'buses are peculiarly Chicago institutions. For long years they have been taking passengers from one railroad station to another. A considerable part of Western America has been ferried across the city by Lake Michigan, in these institutions. For Chicago, with the wisdom of nearly seventy-five years of growth, has steadily refused to accept the union station idea. St. Louis has a union station— and bitterly regrets it. Modern big towns are scorning the idea of a union station; in fact, Buffalo has just rejected the scheme for herself. For a union station, no matter how big or how pretentious it may be architecturally, will reduce a city to way-station dimensions. . . . .

In Chicago . . . . four-fifths of the through passengers have to be carried in the omnibuses from one of the big railroad stations to another. They know that in advance, and they generally arrange to stop over there for at least a night. This means business for the hotels, large and small. It also means business for the retail stores and the theaters. And it is one of the ways that Chicago preserves her metropolitanism.

And yet with all of that metropolitanism—there is a spirit in Chicago that distinctly breathes the smaller town, a spirit that might seem foreign to the most important city that we have between the two oceans. It is the spirit of Madison, or Ottumwa, or Jackson, perhaps a little flavor still surviving of the not long-distant days when Chicago was merely a town. You may or may not know that in the days before her terrific fire she was called "the Garden City." The catalpa trees that shaded her chief business streets had a wide fame, and older prints show the Cook County Court House standing in lawnplats. In those days Chicago folk knew one another and, to a decent extent, one another's business. In these days, much of that town feeling remains. You sit in the great tomb-like halls of the Union League, or in the more modern University Club, perhaps up in that wonderful bungalow which the Cliff-Dwellers have erected upon the roof of Orchestra Hall, and you hear all of the small talk of the town. Smith has finally got that franchise, although he will pay mighty well for it; Jones is going to put another fourteen-story addition to his store. Wilkins has bought a yacht that is going to clean up everything on the lake, and then head straight for laurels on the Atlantic seaboard. You would have the same thing in a smaller western town, expressed in proportionate dimensions. After all, the circle of men who accomplish the real things in the real Chicago is wonderfully small. But the things that they accomplish are very large, indeed.

They will take you out to see some of these big things—that department store, without an equal outside of New York or Philadelphia at least, and where Chicago dearly loves to lunch; a mail order house which actually boasts that six acres of forest timber are cleared each day to furnish the paper for its catalogue, of which a mere six million copies are issued annually; they will point out in the distance the stacks and smoke clouds of South Chicago and will tell you in tens of thousands of dollars, the details of the steel industry; take you, of course, to the stockyards and there tell you of the horrible slaughter that goes forward there at all hours of the day and far into the night. Perhaps they will show you some of the Chicago things that are great in another sense—Hull House and the McCormick Open Air School, for instance. And they will be sure to show you the park system.

A good many folk, Eastern and Western, do not give Chicago credit for the remarkable park system that she has builded up within recent years. These larger parks, with their connecting boulevards, make an entire circuit around the back of the town, and the city is making a distinct effort to wrest the control of the water-front from the railroad that has skirted it for many years, so that she may make all this park land, too—in connection with her ambitious city plan. She has accomplished a distinct start already in the water-front plan along her retail shop and hotel district—from Twelfth street north to the river. The railroad tracks formerly ran along the edge of the lake all that distance. Now they are almost a third of a mile inland; the city has reclaimed some hundreds of acres from the more shallow part of Lake Michigan and has in Grant Park a pleasure-ground quite as centrally located as Boston's famous Common. It is still far from complete. While the broad strip between Michigan avenue and the depressed railroad tracks is wonderfully trim and green, and the Art Institute standing within it so grimy that one might easily mistake it for old age, the "made ground" to the east of the tracks is still barren. But Chicago is making good use of it. The boys and young men come out of the office-buildings in the noon recess to play baseball there, the police drill and parade upon it to their heart's content, it is gaining fame as a site for military encampments and aviation meets.

Chicago makes good use of all her parks. You look a long way within them before you find the "Keep off the Grass" signs. And on Saturday afternoons in midsummer you will find the park lawns thronged with picnic parties—hundreds and even thousands of them—bringing their lunches out from the tighter sections of the town and eating them in shade and comfort and the cooling breezes off Lake Michigan. For Chicago regards the lake as hardly more than an annex to her park system, even today when the question of lake-front rights is not entirely settled with the railroad. On pleasant summer days, her residents go bathing in the lake by the thousands, and if they live within half a dozen blocks of the shore they will go and come in their bathing suits, with perhaps a light coat or bath-robe thrown over them. A man from New York might be shocked to see a Chicago man in a bathing suit riding a motor cycle down an important residence street—without the semblance of coat or robe; but that is Chicago, and Chicago seems to think nothing of it. She wonders if a man from Boston might not be embarrassed to see a coatless, vestless, collarless, suspendered man driving a four-thousand-dollar electric car through Michigan avenue.

Chicago is fast changing, however, in these respects. She is growing more truly metropolitan each twelve-month—less like an overgrown country town. It was only a moment ago that we sat in the office of the manufacturer, and he told us of the Chicago of yesterday, of the big girl who had "I will" emblazoned upon her shield. There is a Chicago of tomorrow, and a hint of its glory has been spread upon the walls of a single great gallery of the Art Institute, in the concrete form of splendid plans and perspectives. The Chicago of tomorrow is to be different; it is to forget the disadvantages of a lack of contour and reap those of a magnificent shore front. In the Chicago of tomorrow the railroads will not hold mile after mile of lake-edge for themselves, the elevated trains will cease to have a merry-go-round on the loop, the arid belt between downtown and uptown will have disappeared, great railroad terminal stations and public buildings built in architectural plan and relation to one another are to arise, her splendid park and boulevard system is to be vastly multiplied.

Chicago looks hungrily forward to her tomorrow. She is never discouraged with her today, but with true American spirit, she anticipates the future. The present generation cares little for itself, it can tolerate the loop and its abominations, the *hodgepodge* of the queer and the *nouveau* that distinguishes the city by the lake in the present year of grace. But the oncoming generations! There is the rub. The oncoming generations are to have all that the wisdom and the wealth of today can possibly dedicate to them. There, then, is your Chicago spirit, the dominating inspiration that rises above the housetops of rows of monotonous, dun-colored houses and surveys the sprawling, disorderly town, and proclaims it triumphant over its outer self.

JULIAN STREET[1]

JULIAN STREET, author, was born in Chicago, April 12, 1879. He was educated in the Chicago public schools and at Ridley College Preparatory, St. Catharines, Ontario. In 1899 he began work as a reporter on the *Mail and Express* (New York), and the following year became its dramatic critic. His literary production includes children's stories, novels, and plays. In 1925 he won the O. Henry Short Story Prize.

Street, now a resident of New York City, has traveled extensively and has preserved his impressions in a number of books written in a whimsical and entertaining style—*The Need of Change* (1909); *Paris à la Carte* (1911); *Ship-Bored* (1911); *Mysterious Japan* (1921); and *Abroad at Home* (1914). In *Abroad at Home* he essays to reflect his reactions gained in travel through his native country. His tour of America was neither business trip nor vacation, but one without purpose except "traveling." He visited Detroit and the Ford factory; the celery and breakfast-food towns of Kalamazoo and Battle Creek; Chicago, with her Marshall Field's, the *Tribune*, and the stockyards. He saw "somnolent St. Louis," and studied journalism in Kansas. Pike's Peak, Salt Lake City, and San Francisco also made up part of the itinerary. Wherever he went he talked to porters, restaurant cashiers, and people in all stations of life, interested in finding what the "other half" thinks.

The result of his tour was an unusual description of the nation by one of her own sons. The account of Chicago is of particular interest since it is written by a native of the city who returned after a few years and saw such phenomenal changes that he hardly recognized the scenes of his childhood.

-》》-《《-

CHICAGO'S INDIVIDUALITY

Imagine a young demigod, product of a union between Rodin's "Thinker" and the Wingèd Victory of Samothrace, and you will have my symbol of Chicago.

Chicago is stupefying. It knows no rules, and I know none by which to judge it. It stands apart from all the cities in the world, isolated by its own individuality, an Olympian freak, a fable, an allegory, an incomprehensible phenomenon, a prodigious paradox in which youth and maturity, brute strength and soaring spirit, are harmoniously confused.

[1] Julian Street, *Abroad at Home* (New York: Century Co., 1914), pp. 139–40, 141–46, 147–58, 160, 164–70, 181–93. Reprinted by permission of Century Co.

Call Chicago mighty, monstrous, multifarious, vital, lusty, stupendous, indomitable, intense, unnatural, aspiring, puissant, preposterous, transcendent—call it what you like—throw the dictionary at it! It is all that you can do, except to shoot it with statistics. And even the statistics of Chicago are not deadly, as most statistics are.

First, you must realize that Chicago stands fourth in population among the cities of the world, and second among those of the Western Hemisphere. Next you must realize that there are people still alive who were alive when Chicago did not exist, even as a fort in a swamp at the mouth of the Chicago River— the river from which, by the way, the city took its name, and which in turn took its own name from an Indian word meaning "skunk."

I do not claim that there are many people still alive who were alive when Chicago wasn't there at all, or that such people are feeling very active, or that they remember much about it, for in 102 years a man forgets a lot of little things. Nevertheless, there *are* living men older than Chicago. . . . .

One knows in advance what a visitor from Europe will say about New York, just as one knows what an American humorist will say about Europe. But one never knows what any visitor will say about Chicago. I have heard people damn Chicago— "up hill and down" I was about to say, but I withdraw that, for the highest hill I remember in Chicago is that ungainly little bump, on the lake front, which is surmounted by Saint Gaudens' statue of General Logan.

As I was saying, I have heard people rave against Chicago and about it. Being itself a city of extremes, it seems to draw extremes of feeling and expression from outsiders. For instance, Canon Hannay, who writes novels and plays under the name of George A. Birmingham, was quoted, at the time of his recent visit to this country, as saying: "In a little while Chicago will be a world center of literature, music, and art. British writers will be more anxious for her verdict than for that of London. The music of the future will be hammered out on the shores of Lake Michigan. The Paris Salon will be a second-rate affair."

Remembering that the Canon is an Irishman and a humorist —which is tautology—we may perhaps discount his statement a little bit for blarney and a little more for fun. His "prophecy" about the Salon seems to stamp the interview with waggery, for certainly it is not hard to prophesy what is already true—and, as everybody ought to know by now, the Salon has for years been second-rate.

The Chicago Art Institute has by all odds the most important art collection I visited upon my travels. The pictures are varied and interesting, and American painters are well represented. The presence in the institute of a good deal of that rather "tight" and "sugary" painting which came to Chicago at the time of the World's Fair, is to be regretted—a fact which is, I have no doubt, quite as well known to those in charge of the museum as to anybody else. But as I remarked in a previous chapter, most museums are hampered, in their early days, by the gifts of their rich friends. It takes a strong museum indeed to risk offending a rich man by kicking out bad paintings which he offers. Even the Metropolitan Museum of Art in New York has not always been so brave as to do that.

"Who's Who" (which, by the way, is published in Chicago) mentions perhaps a score of Chicago painters and sculptors, among the former Lawton S. Parker and Oliver Dennett Grover, and among the latter Lorado Taft.[2]

There are, however, many others, not in "Who's Who," who attempt to paint—enough of them to give a fairly large and very mediocre exhibition which I saw. One thing is, however, certain: the Art Institute has not the deserted look of most other art museums one visits. It is used. This may be partly account-

[2] Lawton S. Parker, portrait-painter, was born in Fairfield, Michigan, August 7, 1868. In 1903 he served as president of the Chicago Academy of Fine Arts. In 1913 he received the gold medal of the Salon, Paris, the first American to receive this honor.

Oliver Dennett Grover, painter, was born in Earlville, Illinois, in 1861. He received his education at the University of Chicago and various foreign schools. He died February 14, 1927.

Lorado Taft, sculptor, was born in Elmwood, Illinois, in 1860. He studied art in Paris. He is an instructor at the Chicago Art Institute. Several notable pieces, among which are the "Black Hawk" statue, the "Spirit of the Great Lakes," and the "Fountain of Time," are among the results of his labors.

ed for by its admirable location at the center of the city—a location more accessible than that of any other museum I think of, in the country. But whatever the reason, as you watch the crowds, you realize more than ever that Chicago is alive to everything—even to art.

Years ago Chicago was musical enough to support the late Theodore Thomas and his orchestra—one of the most distinguished organizations of the kind ever assembled in this country. Thomas did great things for Chicago, musically. He started her, and she kept on. Besides innumerable and varied concerts which occur throughout the season, the city is one of four in the country strong enough to support a first-rate grand opera company of its own.

About twenty-five musicians of one sort and another are credited to Chicago by "Who's Who," the most distinguished of them, perhaps, being Fannie Bloomfield Zeisler,[3] the concert pianist. But it is the writers of Chicago who come out strongest in the fat red volume, among followers of the arts. With sinking heart I counted about seventy of these, and I may be merely revealing my own ignorance when I add that the names of a good two-thirds of them were new to me. But this is dangerous ground. Without further comment let me say that among the seventy I found such names as Robert Herrick, Henry B. Fuller, Hamlin Garland, Emerson Hough, Henry Kitchell Webster, Maud Radford Warren, Opie Read, and Clara Louise Burnham—a hatful of them which you may sort and classify according to your taste.

Canon Hannay said he felt at home in Chicago. So did Arnold Bennett. Canon Hannay said Chicago reminded him of Belfast. Arnold Bennett said Chicago reminded him of the "Five Towns," made famous in his novels. Even Baedeker breaks away from his usual nonpartizan attitude long enough to say with what, for Baedeker, is nothing less than an outburst of passion: "Great injustice is done to Chicago by those who rep-

[3] Fannie Bloomfield Zeisler was born in Bielitz, Austrian Silesia, July 16, 1863. She came to Chicago when she was two years old. She studied chiefly with Leschetizky at Vienna. She died in Chicago, August 20, 1927.

resent it as wholly given over to the worship of Mammon, as it compares favorably with a great many American cities in the efforts it has made to beautify itself by the creation of parks and boulevards and in its encouragement of education and the liberal arts."

Baedeker is quite right about that. He might also have added that the "Windy City" is not so windy as New York, and that the old legend, now almost forgotten, to the effect that Chicago girls have big feet is equally untrue. There is still some wind in Chicago; thanks to it and to the present mode in dress, I was able to assure myself quite definitely upon the size of Chicago feet. I not only saw them upon the streets; I saw them also at dances: twinkling, slippered feet as small as any in the land; and, again owing to the present mode, I saw not only pretty feet, but also— However, I am digressing. That is enough about feet. I fear I have already let them run away with me.

A friend of mine who visited Chicago for the first time, a year ago, came back appreciative of her wonders, but declaring her provincial.

"Why do you say provincial?" I asked.

"Because you can't pick up a taxi in the street," he said.

And it is true. I was chagrined at his discovery—not so much because of its truth, however, as because it was the discovery of a New Yorker. I always defend Chicago against New Yorkers, for I love the place, partly for itself and partly because I was born and spent my boyhood there.

I know a great many other ex-Chicagoans who now live in New York, as I do, and I have noticed with amusement that the side we take depends upon the society in which we are. If we are with Chicagoans, we defend New York; if with New Yorkers, we defend Chicago. We are like those people in the circus who stand upon the backs of two horses at once. Only among ourselves do we go in for candor. . . . .

Necessarily, when the adherents of two cities start an argument, they are confined to concrete points. They talk about opera and theatres and buildings and hotels and stores, and seldom touch upon such subtle things as city spirit. For spirit is a hard thing to deal with and a harder thing to prove. Yet "greatness knows itself." Chicago unquestionably knows that it is great, and that its greatness is of the spirit. But the Chicagoan, debating in favor of his city, is unable to "get that over," and is therefore obliged to fall back upon two last, invariable defenses: the department store of Marshall Field & Co. and the Blackstone Hotel.

The Blackstone, he will tell you, with an eye lit by fanatical belief, is positively the finest hotel in the whole United States. Mention the Ritz, the Plaza, the St. Regis, the Biltmore, or any other hotel to him, and it makes no difference; the Blackstone is the best. As to Marshall Field's, he is no less positive: It is not merely the largest but also the very finest store in the whole world.

I have never stopped at any of those hotels with which the New Yorker would attempt to defeat the Blackstone. But I have stopped at the Blackstone, and it is undeniably a very good hotel. One of the most agreeable things about it is the air of willing service which one senses in its staff. It is an excellent manager who can instill into his servants that spirit which causes them to seem to be eternally on tiptoe—not for a tip but for a chance to serve. Further, the Blackstone occupies a position, with regard to the fashionable life of Chicago, which is not paralleled by any single hotel in New York. Socially it is pre-eminently the place.

General dancing in such public restaurants as Rector's—the original Rector's is in Chicago, you know—and in the dining rooms of some hotels, was started in Chicago, but was soon stopped by municipal regulation. Since that time other schemes have been devised. Dances are held regularly in the ballrooms of most of the hotels, but are managed as clubs or semi-private gatherings. This arrangement has its advantages. It would have its advantages, indeed, if it did nothing more than put the brakes on the dancing craze—as any one can testify who has seen his friends offering up their business and their brains as a sacrifice to Terpsichore. But that is not what I started to say.

The advantage of the system which was in vogue at the Black-stone, when I was there, is that, to get into the ballroom people must be known; wherefore ladies who still have doubts as to the propriety of dancing in a public restaurant need not, and do not, hesitate to go there and dance to their toes' content.

MARSHALL FIELD'S AND THE CHICAGO TRIBUNE

Of course we visited Marshall Field's.

The very obliging gentleman who showed us about the inconceivably enormous buildings, rushing from floor to floor, poking in and out through mysterious, baffling doors and passageways, now in the public part of the store where goods are sold, now behind the scenes where they are made—this gentleman seemed to have the whole place in his head—almost as great a feat as knowing the whole world by heart.

"How much time can you spare?" he asked as we set out from the top floor, where he had shown us a huge recreation room, gymnasium, and dining room, all for the use of the employees.

"How long should it take?"

"It can be done in two hours," he said, "if we keep moving all the time."

"All right," I said—and we did keep moving. Through great rooms full of trunks, of brass beds, through vast galleries of furniture, through restaurants, grilles, afternoon tea rooms, rooms full of curtains and coverings and cushions and corsets and waists and hats and carpets and rugs and linoleum and lamps and toys and stationery and silver, and Heaven only knows what else, over miles and miles of pleasant, soft, green carpet, I trotted along beside the amazing man who not only knew the way, but seemed even to know the clerks. Part of the time I tried to look about me at the phantasmagoria of things with which civilization has encumbered the human race; part of the time I listened to our cicerone; part of the time I walked blindly, scribbling notes, while my companion guided my steps.

Here are some of the notes:

Ten thousand employees in retail store—Choral society, two hundred members, made up of sales-people—Twelve baseball teams in retail store; twelve in wholesale; play during season, and, finally, for championship cup, on "Marshall Field Day"— Lectures on various topics, fabrics, etc., for employees, also for outsiders: women's clubs, etc.—Employees' lunch: soup, meat, vegetables, etc., sixteen cents—Largest retail custom dressmaking business in the country—Largest business in ready-made apparel—Largest retail millinery business—Largest retail shoe business—Largest branch of Chicago public library (for employees)—Largest postal sub-station in Chicago—Largest— largest—largest!

Now and then when something interested me particularly we would pause and catch our breath. Once we stopped for two or three minutes in a fine schoolroom, where some stock-boys and stock-girls were having a lesson in fractions—"to fit them for better positions." Again we paused in a children's playroom, where mothers left their youngsters while they went to do their shopping, and where certain youngsters, thus deposited, were having a gorgeous time, sliding down things, and running around other things, and crawling over and under still other things. Still again we paused at the telephone switchboard—a switchboard large enough to take care of the entire business of a city of the size of Springfield, the capital of Illinois. And still again we paused at the postal sub-station, where fifty to sixty thousand dollars' worth of stamps are sold in a year, and which does as great a postal business, in the holiday season, as the whole city of Milwaukee does at the same period.

At one time we would be walking through a great shirt factory, set off in one corner of that endless building, all unknown to the shoppers who never get behind the scenes; then we would pop out again into the dressed-up part of the store, just as one goes from the kitchen and the pantry of a house into the formality of dining room and drawing room. And as we appeared thus, and our guide was recognized as the assistant manager of all that kingdom, with its population of ten thousand, saleswomen would rise suddenly from seats, little gossiping groups would disperse quickly, and floor men, who had been talking with saleswomen, would begin to occupy themselves with other matters. I remember coming upon a "silence room" for saleswomen—a large, dark, quiet chamber, in which was an attendant; also a saleswoman who was restlessly resting by rocking herself in a chair. And as we moved through the store we kept taking off our hats as we went behind the scenes, and putting them on as we emerged into the public parts. Never before had I realized how much of a department store is a world unseen by shoppers. At one point, in that hidden world, a vast number of women were sewing upon dresses. I had hardly time to look upon this picture when, rushing through a little door, in pursuit of my active guide, I found myself in a maze of glass, and long-piled carpets, and mahogany, and electric light, and pretty frocks, disposed about on forms. Also disposed about were many "perfect thirty-sixes," with piles of taffy-colored hair, doing the "débutante slouch" in their trim black costumes, so slinky and alluring. Here I had a strong impulse to halt, to pause and examine the carpets and woodwork, and one thing and another. But no! Our guardian had a professional pride in getting us through the store within two hours, according to his promise. I would gladly have allowed him an extra ten minutes if I could have spent it in that place, but on we went—my companion and I dragging behind a little and looking backward at the Lorelei—I remember that, because I ran into a man and knocked my hat off.

At last we came to the information bureau, and as there was a particularly attractive young person behind the desk, it occurred to me that this would be a fine time to get a little information.

"I wonder if I can stump that sinuous sibyl," I said.

"Try it," said our conductor.

So I went over to her and asked: "How large is this store, please?"

"You mean the building?"

"Yes."

"There is fifty acres of floor space under this roof," she said. "There are sixteen floors: Thirteen stories rising two hundred and fifty-eight feet above the street, and three basements, extending forty-three and a half feet below. The building takes up one entire block. The new building devoted exclusively to men's goods is just across Washington Street. That building is—"

"Thank you very much," I said. "That's all I want to know about that. Can you tell me the population of Chicago?"

"Two million three hundred and eighty-eight thousand five hundred," she said glibly, showing me her pretty teeth.

Then I racked my brains for a difficult question.

"Now," I said, "will you please tell me where Charles Towne was born?"

"Do you mean Charles A. Towne, the lawyer; Charles Wayland Towne, the author; or Charles Hanson Towne, the poet?" she demanded.

I managed to say that I meant the poet Towne.

"He was born in Louisville, Kentucky," she informed me sweetly. She even gave me the date of his birth, too, but as the poet is a friend of mine, I will suppress that.

"Is that all?" she inquired presently, seeing that I was merely gazing at her.

"Yes, you adorable creature." The first word of that sentence is all that I really uttered. I only thought the rest.

"Very well," she replied, shutting the book in which she had looked up the Townes.

"Thanks very much," I said.

"Don't mention it," said she—and went about her business in a way that sent me about mine.

Aside from its vastness and the variety of its activities, two things about Marshall Field's store interested me particularly. One is the attitude maintained by the company with regard to claims made in the advertising of "sales." When there is a "sale" at Field's comparisons of values are not made. It may be said that certain articles are cheap at the price at which they are being offered, but it is never put in the form: "Was $5. Now $2.50." Field's does not believe in that.

"We take the position," an official explained to me, "that things are worth what they will bring. For instance, if some manufacturer has made too many overcoats, and we are able to get them at a bargain, or there is a mild winter and overcoats do not sell well, we may place on sale a lot of coats which were meant to be sold at $40, but which we are willing to sell at $22.50. In such a case we never advertise 'Worth $40.' We just point out that these are exceptionally good coats for the money. And, when we say that, it is invariably true. This advertising is not so sensational as it could be made, of course, but we think that in the long run it teaches people to rely upon us."

Another thing which interested me in Field's was the appearance of the saleswomen. They do not look like New York saleswomen. In the aggregate they look happier, simpler, and more natural. I saw no women behind the counters there who had the haughty, indifferent bearing, the nose-in-the-air, to which the New York shopper is accustomed. Among these women, no less than among the rich, the Chicago spirit seemed to show itself. It is everywhere, that spirit. I admit that, perhaps, it does not go with omnipresent taxicabs. I admit that there are more effete cities than Chicago. The East is full of them. But that any city in the country has more sterling simplicity, greater freedom from sham and affectation among all classes, more vigorous cultivation, or more well-bred wealth, I respectfully beg to doubt.

No, I have *not* forgotten Boston and Philadelphia.

In an earlier chapter I told of a man I met upon a train, who, though he lived in Buffalo, had never seen Niagara Falls. In Chicago it occurred to me that, though I had worked on a newspaper, I had never stood as an observer and watched a newspaper "go through." So, one Saturday night after sitting around the city room of the Chicago "Tribune"—which is one of the world's great newspapers—and talking with a group of men as interesting as any men I ever found together, I was placed in charge of James Durkin, the world's most eminent office boy, who forthwith took me to the nether regions of the "Tribune" Building.

With its floor of big steel plates, its towering presses, vast and incomprehensible, and its grimy men in overalls, the pressroom struck me as resembling nothing so much as the engine room of an ocean liner.

The color presses were already roaring, shedding streams of

printed paper like swift waterfalls, down which shot an endless chain of Mona Lisas—for the Mona Lisa took the whole front page of the "Tribune" colored supplement that week. At the bottom, where the "folder" put the central creases in them, the paper torrents narrowed to a disappearing point, giving the illusion of a subterranean river, vanishing beneath the floor. But the river didn't vanish. It was caught, and measured, and folded, and cut, and counted by machinery, as swift, as eye-defying, as a moving picture; machinery which miraculously converted a cataract into prim piles of Sunday newspapers, which were, in turn, gathered up and rushed away to the mailing room—whither, presently, we followed.

In the mailing room I made the acquaintance of a machine with which, if it had not been so busy, I should have liked to shake hands, and sit down somewhere for a quiet chat. For it was a machine possessed of the Chicago spirit: modest, business-like, effective, and highly intelligent. I did not interrupt it, but watched it at its work. And this is what it did: It took Sunday papers, one by one, from a great pile which was handed to it every now and then, folded them neatly, wrapped them in manila paper, sealed them up with mucilage, squeezed them, so that the seal would hold, addressed them to out-of-town subscribers and dropped them into a mail sack. There was a man who hovered about, acting as a sort of valet to this highly capable machine, but all he had to do was to bring it more newspapers from time to time, and to take away the mail bags when they were full, or when the machine had finished with all the subscribers in one town, and began on another. Nor did it fail to serve notice of each such change. Every time it started in on a new town it dipped its thumb in some red ink, and made a dab on the wrapper of the first paper, so that its valet—poor human thing—would know enough to furnish a new mail bag. I noted the name to which one red-dabbed paper was addressed: *E. J. Henry, Bosco, Wis.*, and I wondered if Mr. Henry had ever wondered what made that florid mark. . . . .

Up-stairs, on the roof of the "Tribune" Building, in a kind of deck-house, is a club, made up of members of the staff, and here, through the courtesy of some of the editors, my companion and I were invited to have supper. When I had eaten my fill, I had a happy thought. Here, at my mercy, were a lot of men who were engaged in the business of sending out reporters to molest the world for interviews. I decided to turn the tables and, then and there, interview them—all of them. And I did it. And they took it very well.

I had heard that the "Column"—that sometimes, if not always, humorous newspaper department, which now abounds throughout the country, threatening to become a pestilence—originated with the "Tribune." I asked about that, and in return received, from several sources, the history of "Columns," as recollected by these men.

Probably the first regular humorous column in the country—certainly the first to attract any considerable attention,—was conducted for the "Tribune" by Henry Ten Eyck White, familiarly known as "Butch" White. It started about 1885, under the heading, "Lakeside Musings." After running this column for some five years, White gave it up, and it was taken over, under the same heading, by Eugene Field, who made it even better known than it had been before. . . . .

SKYSCRAPERS AND THE STOCKYARDS

It is rather widely known, I think, that Chicago built the first steel-frame skyscraper—the Tacoma Building[4]—but I do not believe that the world knows that Kohlsaat's in Chicago was the first quick-lunch place of its kind, or that the first "free lunch" in the country was established, many years since, in the basement saloon at the corner of State and Madison Streets. Considering the skyscrapers and quick lunches and free lunches that there are to-day, it is hard to realize that there ever was a first one anywhere. But the origin of things which have become national institutions, as these things have, seems to me to be worth recording here. It may be added that the loyal Chicagoan who told of these things seemed to be prouder of the "free lunch" and the quick lunch than of the skyscraper.

[4] There was some dispute as to whether the Tacoma Building or the Home Insurance Building was the first skyscraper.

Of two things I mentioned to him he was not proud at all. One was the famous pair of First Ward aldermen who have attained a national fame under their nicknames, "Hinky Dink" and "Bathhouse John." The other was the stockyards.

"Why is it," he asked in a bored and irritated tone, "that every one who comes out here has to go to the stockyards?"

"Are you aware," I returned, "that half the bank clearings of Chicago are traceable to the stockyards?"

He answered with a noncommittal grunt.

His was not the attitude of the Detroit man who wants you to know that Detroit does something more than make automobiles, or of the Grand Rapids man who says: "We make lots of things here besides furniture." He was really ashamed of the stockyards, as a man may, perhaps, be ashamed of the fact that his father made his money in some business with a smell to it. And because he felt so deeply on the subject, I had the half idea of not touching on the stockyards in this chapter.

However, the news that my companion and myself were there to "do" Chicago was printed in the papers, and presently the stockyards began to call us up. It didn't even ask if we were coming. It just asked *when*. And as I hesitated, it settled the whole matter then and there by saying it would call for us in its motor car, at once.

I may say at the outset that, to quote the phrase of Mr. Freer of Detroit,[5] the stockyards "has no esthetic value." It is a place of mud, and railroad tracks, and cattle cars, and cattle pens, and overhead runways, and great ugly brick buildings, and men on ponies, and raucous grunts, and squeals, and smells—a place which causes the heart to sink with a sickening heaviness.

Our first call was at the Welfare Building, where we were shown some of the things which are being done to benefit employees of the packing houses. It was noon-time. The enormous lunch room was well occupied. A girl was playing ragtime at a piano on a platform. The room was clean and airy. The women wore aprons and white caps. A good lunch cost six cents. There

[5] Charles Lang Freer, the great art collector, Detroit railway and manufacturing magnate.

were iron lockers in the locker room—lockers such as one sees in an athletic club. There were marble shower baths for the men and for the women. There were two manicures who did nothing but see to the hands of the women working in the plant. There were notices of classes in housekeeping, cooking, washing, house furnishing, the preparation of food for the sick—signs printed in English, Russian, Slovak, Polish, Bohemian, Hungarian, Lithuanian, German, Norwegian, Swedish, Croatian, Italian, and Greek. Obviously, the company was doing things to help these people. Obviously it was proud of what it was doing. Obviously I should have rejoiced, saying to myself: "See how these poor, ignorant foreigners who come over here to our beautiful and somewhat free country are being elevated!" But all I could think of was: "What a horrible place the stockyards is! How I loathe it here!"

On the North Side of Chicago there is an old and exclusive club, dating from before the days of motor cars, which is known as the Saddle and Cycle Club. The lunch club for the various packing-house officials, at the stockyards, has a name bearing perhaps some satirical relation to that of the other club. It is called the Saddle and Sirloin Club, and in that club I ate a piece of sirloin the memory of which will always remain with me as something sacred.

After lunching and visiting the offices of a packing company where, we were told, an average daily business of $1,300,000 is done—and the place looks it—we visited the Stockyards Inn, which is really an astonishing establishment. The astonishing quality about it is that it is a thing of beauty which has grown up in a place as far removed from beauty as any that I ever looked upon outside a mining camp. A charming, low, half-timbered building, the Inn is like something at Stratford-on-Avon; and by some freak of chance the man who runs it has a taste for the antique in furniture and chinaware. Inside it is almost like a fine old country house—pleasant cretonnes, grate fires, old Chippendale chairs, mahogany tables, grandfather's clocks, pewter, and luster ware. All this for cattlemen who bring their flocks and herds into the yards! The only thing to spoil it is the all-pervasive smell of animals.

From there we went to the place of death. . . . .

The progress of the pig is swift—if the transition from pig to pork may be termed "progress." The carcass travels presently through boiling water and emerges pink and clean. And as it goes along upon its trolley, it passes one man after another, each with an active knife, until, thirty minutes later, when it has undergone the government inspection, it is headless and in halves—mere meat, which looks as though it never could have been alive.

From the slaughter-house we passed through the smoke-house, where ham and bacon were smoking over hardwood fires in rows of ovens big as blocks of houses. Then through the pickling room with its enormous hogsheads, giving the appearance of a monkish wine cellar. Then through the curing room with its countless piles of dry salt pork, neatly arranged like giant bricks.

The enthusiastic gentleman who escorted us kept pointing out the beauties of the way this work was done: the cleanliness, the system by which the rooms are washed with steam, the gigantic scale of all the operations. I heard, I noticed, I agreed. But all the time my mind was full of thoughts of dying pigs. Indeed, I had forgotten for the moment that other animals are also killed to feed carnivorous man. However, I was reminded of that, presently, when we came upon another building, consecrated to the conversion of life into veal and beef.

The steers meet death in little pens. It descends upon them unexpectedly from above, dealt out by a man with a sledge, who cracks them between the horns with a sound like that of a wood-man's ax upon a tree. The creatures quiver and quickly crumple.

It is swift. In half a minute the false bottom of the pen turns up and rolls them out upon the floor, inert as bags of meal. Only after death do these cattle find their way to an elevated trolley line, like that used for the pigs. And, as with the pigs, they move along speedily; shortly they are to be seen in the beef cooler, where they hang in tremendous rows, forming strange vistas—a forest of dead meat. . . . .

CITY PLANNING

In city planning, as in other things, Chicago has thought and plotted on an Olympian scale, and it is characteristic of Chicago that her plan for her own beautification should be so much greater than the plan of any other city in the country, as to make comparisons unkind. For that reason I have eliminated Chicago from consideration, when discussing the various group plans, park and boulevard systems, and "civic centers," upon which other American cities are at work.

The Chicago plan is, indeed, too immense a thing to be properly dealt with here. It is comparable with nothing less than the Haussman plan for Paris, and it is being carried forward, through the years, with the same foresight, the same patience and the same indomitable aspiration. Indeed, I think greater patience has been required in Chicago, for the French people were in sympathy with beauty at a time when the broad meaning of the word was actually not understood in this country. Here it has been necessary to educate the masses, to cultivate their city pride, and to direct that pride into creative channels. It is hardly too much to say that the minds of American city-dwellers (and half our race inhabits cities) have had to be remade, in order to prepare them to receive such plans as the Chicago plan.

The World's Columbian Exposition, at Chicago, exerted a greater influence upon the United States than any other fair has ever exerted upon a country. It came at a critical moment in our esthetic history—a moment when the sense of beauty of form and color, which had hitherto been dormant in Americans, was ready to be aroused.

Fortunately for us, the Chicago Fair was worthy of the opportunity; and that it was worthy of the opportunity was due to the late Daniel Hudson Burnham, the distinguished architect, who was director of works for the Exposition. In the perspective of the twenty-one years which have passed since the Chicago Fair, the figure of Mr. Burnham, and the importance of the work done by him, grows larger. When the history of the American Renaissance comes to be written, Daniel H. Burnham and the men by whom he was surrounded at the time the Chicago Fair was being made, will be listed among the founders of the movement.

The Fair awoke the American sense of beauty. And before its course was run, a group of Chicago business men, some of whom were directors of the exposition, determined to have a plan for the entire city which should so far as possible reflect the lessons of the Fair in the arrangement of streets, parks and plazas, and the grouping of buildings.

After the Fair, the Chicago Commercial Club commissioned Mr. Burnham to proceed to re-plan the city. Eight years were consumed in this work. The best architects available were called in consultation. After having spent more than $200,000, the Commercial Club presented the plant to the city, together with an elaborate report.

To carry out the plan, the Chicago City Council, in 1909, created a Plan Commission, composed of more than 300 men, representing every element of citizenship under the permanent chairmanship of Mr. Charles H. Wacker,[6] who had previously been most active in the work. Under Mr. Wacker's direction, and with the aid of continued subscriptions from the Commercial Club, the work of the Commission has gone on steadily, and vast improvements have already been made.

The plan itself has to do entirely with the physical rearrangement of the city. It is designed to relieve congestion, facilitate traffic, and safeguard health.

Instead of routing out the Illinois Central Railroad which disfigures the lake front of the whole South Side, the plan provides for the making of a parkway half a mile wide and five miles long, beyond the tracks, where the lake now is. This parkway will extend from Grant Park, at the center of the city, all the way to

[6] Charles H. Wacker (August 29, 1856—October 31, 1929) was educated at Lake Forest Academy, Stuttgart, and Geneva. In 1880 he and his father founded the malt firm later known as the Birk Brewing and Malting Co. Of this firm he was president until 1901. He was director of the Ways and Means Committee of the World's Columbian Exposition, and from 1909 to 1927 he was chairman of the Chicago Plan Commission. He also served as director of the Chicago Council of Social Agencies, and was interested in the Red Cross, Civic Music Association, the Art Institute, and the establishment of the forest preserves.

Jackson Park, where the World's Fair grounds were. Arrangements have also been made for immense forest areas, to encircle the city outside its limits, occupying somewhat the relation to it that the Bois de Boulogne and the Bois de Vincennes do to Paris. New parks are also to be created within the city.

It is impossible to go into further details here as to these parks, but it should be said that, when the lake front parkway system, above mentioned, is completed, practically the whole front of Chicago along Lake Michigan will be occupied by parks and lagoons, and that Chicago expects—and not without reason —to have the finest waterfront of any city in the world.

Michigan Avenue, the city's superb central street which already bears very heavy traffic, now has a width of 130 feet at the heart of the city, excepting to the north, near the river, where it becomes a narrow, squalid street, for all that it is the principal highway between the North and South Sides. This portion of the street is not only to be widened, but will be made into a two-level thoroughfare, (the lower level for heavy vehicles, and the upper for light) crossing the river on a double-deck bridge.

It is a notorious fact that the business and shopping district of Chicago is at present strangled by the elevated railroad loop, which bounds the center of the city, and it is essential for the welfare of the city that this area be extended and made more spacious. The City Plan provides for a "quadrangle" to cover three square miles at the heart of Chicago, to be bounded on the east by Michigan Avenue, on the north by Chicago Avenue, on the west by Halsted Street, and on the south by Twelfth Street. When this work is done these streets will have been turned into wide boulevards, and other streets, running through the quadrangle, will also have been widened and improved, principal among these being Congress Street, which though not at present cut through, will ultimately form a great central artery, leading back from the lake, through the center of the quadrangle, forming the axis of the plan, and centering on a "civic center," which is to be built at the junction of Congress and Halsted Streets and from which diagonal streets will radiate in all directions.

Nor does the plan end here. A complete system of exterior

roadways will some day encircle the city; the water front along the river will be improved and new bridges built; also two outer harbors will be developed.

By an agreement with the city, no major public work of any description is inaugurated until the Plan Commission has passed upon its harmonious relationship with the general scheme. The Commission further considers the comprehensive development of the city's steam railway and street transportation systems; very recently it successfully opposed a railroad union depot project which was inimical to the Plan of Chicago, and it has generally succeeded in persuading the railroads to work in harmony with the plan, when making immediate improvements.

One of the most interesting and intelligently conducted departments under the Commission has to do with the education of the people of Chicago with regard to the Plan. A great deal of money and energy has been expended in this work, with the result that city-wide misapprehension concerning the Plan has given place to city-wide comprehension. Lectures are given before schools and clubs with the idea of teaching Chicago what the plan is, why it is needed, and what great European cities have accomplished in similar directions. Books on the subject have been published and widely circulated, and one of these, "Wacker's Manual," has been adopted as a textbook by the Chicago Public Schools, with the idea of fitting the coming generations to carry on the work.

If the plan as it stands at present has been accomplished within a long lifetime, Chicago will have maintained her reputation for swift action. Two or three lifetimes would be time enough in any other city. However, Chicago desires the fulfillment of the prophecy she has on paper. Work is going on, and the extent to which it will go on in future depends entirely upon the ability of the city to finance Plan projects. And when a thing depends upon the ability of the city of Chicago, it depends upon a very solid and a very splendid thing. . . . .

SIR ARTHUR E. SHIPLEY[1]

SIR ARTHUR E. SHIPLEY, scientist and educator, was born March 10, 1861, at Datchet, Buckshire, and died September 22, 1927. He was educated at Christ's College, and at the age of twenty-six was commissioned by the Colonial Office to investigate plant disease in the Bermudas. He was a member of the Council of the Senate; vice-president of the Linnean Society; chairman of the governing body of the West Indian Agricultural College; foreign member of the American Association of Economic Entomologists and of the Helminthological Society of Washington; and vice-chancellor of Cambridge University. His work gained for him high standing in science; and for his achievements he was accorded the honorary degrees of D.Sc. from Princeton, LL.D. from the University of Michigan, and M.Sc. from Drexel Institute of Philadelphia. Shipley visited the United States as early as 1886, and in 1918 he came as a member of the British University Mission invited to visit American universities by the Council of Defense at Washington.

For more than sixty days the Mission traveled, covering thousands of miles and seeing so many universities that Shipley confessed that, although he had lived some years in the States, he now leaned toward the belief that all the American cities had universities and all the citizens were professors. The universities he found well equipped and accomplishing much in the way of research. His tour included the universities of Johns Hopkins, Princeton, Yale, Harvard, Boston College, Michigan, Northwestern, Chicago, Illinois, Wisconsin, Minnesota, Texas, Washington, Transylvania, Tulane, Iowa State College, and several Canadian colleges. Besides reflecting his reactions to university cities, his *The Voyage of a Vice-Chancellor* mirrors his opinion of American democracy, hospitality, dinners, and other phases of American life.

UNIVERSITIES AND ARMISTICE DAY

We arrived in Chicago in a deluge of rain and saw what remained of the celebration.[2] We were soon housed in the luxurious and comfortable University Club and "so to bed."

[1] Arthur Everett Shipley, *The Voyage of a Vice-Chancellor* (Cambridge: University Press, 1919), pp. 83-85, 87-92. Reprinted by permission of Cambridge University Press.

[2] The celebration on November 7, 1918, when word was received that the Germans had asked for an armistice.

Friday, November 8th

We spent to-day at the University of Chicago. This is one of the youngest, one of the most original of the United States Universities. Youth accounts for much of this originality, President Harper[3]—he was President of Chicago when first I visited it—accounted for more. Youth is also responsible for the fact that though at other centers there may be single edifices more stately and more beautiful than any at Chicago, it is, as regards its buildings, one of the most complete and most uniform of all American Universities. Like the Unities of the Drama, as expounded by Mr. Curdle to Nicholas Nickleby, it combines "a completeness—a kind of universal dovetailedness with regard to place and time—a sort of general oneness, if I may be allowed to use so strong an expression."

The President of the University[4] is away in Persia, and it is interesting to note that *en route* he went chasing all the way from London up to Scapa Flow to ask the Admiral of the Grand Fleet[5] and his wife, *née* Marshall Field, to sign a legal document empowering the University to purchase a small alley-way which somehow stood in the way of the extension of the already ample University campus. In his absence we were hospitably entertained by his wife and the acting President.

We had a helpful conference during the afternoon with the Faculty in the Ida Noyes Building, the home of the lady students, but it is not fair to expect a lot of newcomers to confer in a room decorated, as this was, with the most charming of modern frescoes. We couldn't help looking at all the graceful and gorgeous young creatures depicted in them and we were, I fear, more interested in them than in the exchange of Professors and Students. Why can't we exchange frescoes? Later we dined in the Hall of the same institution and all made speeches. . . . .

[3] William Rainey Harper, first president of the University of Chicago, was born July 26, 1856. He graduated from Muskingum College in 1870; received his Ph.D. from Yale in 1875 and a D.D. from Colby in 1891. From 1879 to 1886 he was professor of Hebrew at the Baptist Union Theological Seminary in Chicago. From 1886 to 1891 he was professor of Semitic languages at Yale. In the latter year he became president of the University of Chicago, and remained in that office until his death, June 10, 1906.

[4] Dr. Harry Pratt Judson.   [5] Admiral David Beatty.

Sunday, November 10th

We went a long drive along the North Shore and then visited the Academy of Fine Art. Among many priceless possessions is a whole room filled with Monets!

Monday, November 11th.

"Peace hath murdered Sleep."

Hardly had we dozed off than we were awakened at 2 A.M. by a most infernal din. "Peace," as they will call an armistice, seemed to have been declared again. We were naturally sceptical, but being sceptical in bed whilst a million and a half were credulous outside doesn't bring sleep.

The noise was overwhelming. All that night and all next day and most of the next night, the hooters hooted, the whistles whistled, the syrens syrened, brass utensils brayed, tin-trumpets trumpetted, the people yelled, the motors rushed about with tin-can accompaniments, boys banged bones, grown-up men frantically beat iron telegraph posts with crow-bars; every conceivable instrument was beaten, brayed, or blown, but the hooters were the worst. They seemed to have an uncanny quality about them and as they moaned and boomed and shrieked they seemed to come into your room and you felt as though you could touch them. The parading people were excited, but good-natured and friendly. An elderly divine who took part in these nocturnal celebrations told us next morning that quite respectable ladies had put feathers down his neck; he added that after a time "one got quite used to it."

In the morning this noise increased. Thousands of lorries and motors pervaded the city packed with children and women, the latter by now beginning to look like Sisters of Mercy after a bump-supper. A peculiar manifestation of the enthusiasm of the people was the casting forth from every window innumerable scraps of paper—I believe the Telephone Directories suffered most—which blackened the skies and whitened the ground. It cost the City of New York $85,000 to clear up their paper litter after their dress-rehearsal last Thursday!

To-day we visited the North Western University. Like many others, it has certain of its Departments in the City, such as the Medical, the Commercial, the Dental, and the Legal. We had time only to visit the last two and found them well equipped and well staffed. There is even in the last-named a replica of a Law Court, and here the students try cases. I don't know whether I am more afraid of dentists or of lawyers; I suppose one is a physical and the other a moral fear, but I was glad to find myself on the way to Evanston, some twelve miles north of Chicago, where the main buildings of the North Western State University[6] are situate. Our progress was impeded by parades; all the schools, all the organized Societies paraded and all made as much noise as they could. Finally, however, we arrived at the Campus, beautifully placed on the shores of the lake. We found here the same freshness of view, and belief in the future, the same numerous staff and adequate equipment that we had found elsewhere; but there seems always some novel and original feature in each new institution we visit, and at the North Western University we found a large building entirely devoted to Oratory.[7] Any future Mission to this country, before embarking on its career of speeches, might well take a short course of Oratory at Evanston. After a comforting lunch at the charming University Club, which was somewhat prolonged by all of us making speeches, we returned to Chicago.

We dined this evening with the Association of the Presidents of State Universities. I was so tired that, like the late Lord Hartington, I nearly fell asleep during my own speech and I could not help dozing off again and again during those of my colleagues. Each time I lost consciousness I had a strange nightmare and it recurred again and again. I dreamed that I had heard it all before. . . . .   ·

Tuesday, November 12th

The members of the University Club where we were lodged, whose hospitality is boundless, gave us a sumptuous lunch in

[6] Northwestern University.   [7] Cumnock School of Speech.

their great dining-room which is a replica of Crosby Hall seen under a magnifying lens. The speeches were few, but good.

In the afternoon we attended a meeting of the Presidents of State Universities and amongst other good things heard a masterly and witty address from the President of Berkeley University.[8]

[8] Benjamin Ide Wheeler, president of the University of California at Berkeley, California, was born July 15, 1854. He graduated from Brown University in 1875, and received his Ph.D. from the University of Heidelberg in 1885. He taught at the universities of Brown, Harvard, and Cornell, and in 1899 accepted the presidency of the University of California, serving until 1919 when he became President Emeritus. He died May 3, 1927.

WALTER LIONEL GEORGE[1]

W ALTER LIONEL GEORGE, author, was born of British parents in Paris, March 20, 1882, and educated in Paris and Germany. He became well known as a special correspondent for various papers in France, Belgium, and Spain, and as a contributor to many London periodicals. During the World War he served in the French army. Although he died at the age of forty-four, at the time of his death he had published a large number of books, dealing with various political and economic problems, the modern woman, and fiction, as well as writing a biography of Anatole France.

During his brief lifetime, George traveled extensively including a six months' visit to the United States in 1920. The result of this voyage was *Hail Columbia!* a book in which he frankly avows a liking for America gained even before his trip to this country. "I came to America," said he, "interested only in subsidiary fashion in scenery, business, and politics; I had to take notice of these, but primarily I came over to meet the Americans, to try to understand them, and to take on the easy task of liking them."

In New England he was disappointed, but he liked the Yankee farmer. In the Middle West he found what he called the "true America," a comment frequently made by visitors from all parts of the world. He was, with other commentators, impressed with American vitality; and our court and prison systems received praise from him. In short, he found "America is a great country for a young man to get born in." But American restlessness and pride he held undesirable qualities. He thought the American home was too bare and too new, and he disliked American children. George disagreed with the opinion of many visitors as to the high place of women in America, insisting that women in the United States were forced to surrender their intellectual interests. In spite of uncomplimentary remarks, however, he is not unfriendly nor caustic in his pictures.

He died January 30, 1926.

-»»-«««-

A CITY WITHOUT PEACE

There is no peace in Chicago. In Chicago the past and the future give birth to an unruly being that angrily shakes the fetters of one tradition as it creates another which it throws away as it goes, like a snake which wearies of its skin and sloughs it off for

[1] W. L. George, *Hail Columbia!* (London: Chapman & Hall, Ltd., 1923), pp. 46–47, 49–51, 53–57, 60–61, 71–72; American edition (New York: Harper & Bros., 1921), pp. 37–38, 40–43, 45–48, 49–50, 54–55, 66–67. Reprinted by kind permission of Mrs. W. L. George.

a new one. It is a city of terror and light, untamed and un̲
wearied. It has harnessed a white-hot energy to beginnings;
upon its roofs it erects cities; it has torn the vitals of its streets
for railway cuttings, set up porticoes as promises of colonnades.
Grim is the heart within, and hot as molten metal. The city
writhes in its narrow communications, as the head of Medusa
among its tangled hair. Its suburbs lie like disjointed members,
deprived of easy transit to the body: the suburban stores forbid
it; they fear for their custom, and the politicians tumble and
crawl, in graft, threat, and proclamation, over the great body
that heaves, angry and chafed, yet negligent of what is not its
daily labor, like a dray horse with bent head that shakes the
tenacious flies. Here is room for lust and its repression, none for
listlessness; here is everlasting struggle, no mild aspiration to
peace. There is no peace in Chicago. . . . .

In eight months, in Chicago, three thousand automobiles were
stolen. Such a fact gives one an idea of the magnitude of the
commercial activities of that city. I do not mean that automobile stealing has yet become a national industry, though it is going strong, but if automobiles can be stolen at the rate of forty-
five hundred per annum, many scores of thousands must be
making Chicago into the city of noise which it is. My first impression of Chicago was indeed noise. For nothing had I seen
the traffic in Piccadilly Circus and on Boulevard Montmartre.
I had still to realize the impact upon the human ear of two lines
of trolley cars running over cobbles, on wheels that are never
oiled; this, combined with several hundreds of motor vehicles
with their throttles open; this combined with a double line of
elevated railways whose couplings are never oiled; and this combined with a policeman who acts as master of the revels by
means of a whistle! What a whistle! A steam whistle? A steam
policeman? In Chicago you never can tell. It was magnificent.
I had a sense that here was something animal and untamed,
something (as Carl Sandburg might put it) sanguinary and husky. Here no hint of leisure, nor of mercy, for mercy is a draft on
time and life—in Chicago there is no time for life.

This immense crowd that burrowed among the raging traffic

wanted to get somewhere; it wanted that with an intensity, with a singleness of object, which I did not discover in Fifth Avenue. As I stood dazed, while the orange-sided taxicabs flitted past me, I began to understand the Chicago that says, "I want," and at the same time says, "I will." The policeman with his whistle at once taught me something; in London the policeman puts up a languid hand and is obeyed; in New York he puts out a white-gloved hand, remarks, "Go back," and is often obeyed; in Chicago he needs a whistle as a word of command, to control a people who will not obey. Chicago is a city which must be dominated, as if it were a magnificent and savage animal that plunges and rears.

It is not for nothing that the predominating color of Chicago is orange. It is as if the city, in its taxicabs, in its shop fronts, in the wrappings of its parcels, chose the color of flame that goes with the smoky black of its factories. It is not for nothing that it has repelled the geometric street arrangement of New York and substituted therefor great ways with names that a stranger must learn if he can. As a rule he fails. His brain does not work properly. He is in a crowd city, and if he has business there, he tells himself, "If I weaken I shan't last long."

The psychology of Chicago is deeply colored with self-love. It harbors blinding pride, the pride of the man who can do things, and has no use for the man who can't. Almost every educated person in Chicago will call his city crude, perhaps even vulgar, but the end of the sentence exhibits love and pride. Pride is the essence of his feeling; the inhabitant of Chicago seems to find in his city an immense, unruly child, something that bellows, breaks windows, says unsuitable things . . . . but grows, grows magnificently, secretly grows in dominating charm of eternal adolescence, the charm of eternal desire. . . . . And, at Chicago, I was interested by a big business building opposite my hotel, when I noticed that at nine o'clock in the evening many of the offices were still tenanted. I began to watch that building. At nine o'clock work was going on in thirty-eight offices; at 10:15 P.M. there was energy still in ten; at 11:35 P.M. three offices were preparing to break into the next day. I don't know what happened next, for I went to bed; I am not from Chicago.

MASS AND SPACE

In Chicago work is dramatic; its spirit is impressive; I cannot ignore a picture postcard I bought there; it bears merely these words, "Experience is a dead loss if you can't sell it for more than it cost you." A variation of an immortal truth . . . . which may shock some gentle soul. Well, it doesn't shock me. I like the extremism of it, just as I like the massive place where this sentiment circulates. I like Chicago, I like the colossal lines of its point of view, its religion of utility, its gospel of fitness, just as I like its streets, its attempt on South Michigan Boulevard to force even the lakeside into straight lines. You will find this heavy power in a store like Marshall Field's, a commercial city within a commercial city, a place so vast that one would welcome as a guide through its labyrinth a thread woven by Arachne. This mystic thread of the mythological spider—does Marshall Field stock it? Probably.

You have the same feeling in Washington Park, in the vast space which suggests that America always has plenty of land, even enough for its pleasure grounds. To an outsider Chicago seems too big for mankind, but mankind in Chicago does not appear worried by that fact. Indeed, it enjoys size; it likes the enormous whiteness of the monument to Time,[2] in Washington Park; it finds its great university[3] worthy of itself; it is typical of Chicago's faith in its own future that, in one part of that university, it called a certain space a quadrangle when only two sides of it were built.

The Middle West can afford to trust a future of which the present is merely the vestibule. I like to think of the time to come when the ledges between the Lakes have been dredged out and when the fleets of the world will come sailing up the St. Lawrence, through the Lakes, and moor opposite the Congress Hotel, there to unload the spices of India and the caviar of the Black Sea. Mass and space; that, to me, defines the Middle

---

[2] Made by Lorado Taft.   [3] University of Chicago.

West. Consider the Continental and Commercial Security Company's Building. It is a bank in Chicago, and conducts its activities in a hall that looks like a railway station. The building exhibits all the splendid dryness of line of American architecture; its pillars rise up contemptuous to an obscure heaven. Indeed, the Continental and Commercial Security Company is housed in a work of art made more estimable by being also a work of perfect utility. . . . .

ARMOUR'S PACKING PLANT

But these altitudes are by the way, though they are to a certain extent indications of spirit. It is in the manufacturing plants of America that human vigor expresses itself best. I have seen a number of them, dealing in steel, flour, timber, but in a way Armour's is most remarkable. Armour's is remarkable not so much because it has divided the operations of labor as far as human ingenuity can go, but because of the material on which it works. To watch an animal from the pen to the tin is an extraordinary experience. You see it killed; it falls; a conveyor carries it away. It is flayed while you wait. It disappears. Then, suddenly, it is an open carcass; it passes the veterinary; in a few seconds it is cut up, and hurriedly you follow the dwindling carcass that is no longer an ox, but fragments of meat; you see the meat shredded; in another room the manicured girls are filling the shreds into tins, and the tin is closed and labeled. The thing that astounds is the quiet officialdom of this murder. It is as if nothing had happened. Death is so swift, the evidence of tragedy so soon gone, that one feels no shock that flesh loses its character. Cattle are being handled like brass, so swiftly that life becomes merely a raw material. That is Chicago. A superior force, which is called organized industry, has cut up the cattle on a traveling belt and carried them away. For a moment I have a vision of Chicago carried away on its own traveling belt. Carried away . . . where to? . . . .

The great plants of the Middle West seem to me to sublimate human intelligence and to promise a time when mankind will be free from sweat; the curse of Adam may yet be lifted by Chicago.

In so doing the Middle West is doing something else; it is creating beauty. I say this, realizing the contempt that may fall upon this opinion from academic quarters. There is beauty elsewhere than in lace; there is a rugged beauty, and there is a beauty of supreme utility. These great factories are worthy exponents of the forgotten William Morris; there everything is useful, and it is not excessive to say that everything is beautiful because everything is strong. Naturally the strong are not also the subtle; with strength goes a certain crudity of expression and of thought. . . . .

CHICAGO'S "BOOSTING"

The Middle West, by the fact of its novelty, shows its "seamy side"; the dust of ages, which has filled the seams of Paris and London town, has not had time to make for the West a glossy surface. And so the East, with three hundred years behind it, is more acutely conscious of Chicago than the foreigner can be. Certainly from the Eastern point of view, Chicago is what you might call difficult. I can understand that a banking family in Manhattan, harking back to bankers of New Amsterdam, dislikes the unashamed boosting which Chicago indulges in. Do not attack me because I say "boosting"; it is Chicago's own word. At the top of every page of one of the Chicago newspapers you will find every day a different legend. Here are two, which I extract, collected during my stay in Chicago: "Why Chicago is great: Chicago has more than twenty thousand manufacturing plants." Here is another: "Be a Chicago booster to your friends in other cities." Well, yes, it is a little difficult; it crows over the fallen; there is nothing delicate about it. But Chicago never was delicate; no more was any man at arms. Chicago is the man at arms of modern industry; that has to be remembered when you criticize it at work or at leisure. It has a passion for fact; a passion for realities malleable as cement before they are applied to industry, hard as cement in the end. Chicago is prouder than Boston, because it is surer of itself. It has built its castle upon the future—for Chicago a secure foundation. That is why there is no peace in Chicago, and why, if ever Chicago attains peace, it will be the nefarious peace of a termination.

Indeed, the whole Middle West is Chicagoan; it is conscious of itself, more conscious than any other part of America. Its local feeling is intense. . . . .

ATTITUDE TOWARD THE ARTS

The Middle West respects the arts. In Europe the arts are the scullions of the idle and the rich. In the Middle West they seem to be ignored by a great many busy people, but they do somehow earn their respect. There are large circles which specialize in the arts, whose appreciation sometimes takes unexpected forms. For instance, at a large tea party in Chicago, some fragments from a novel of mine were read aloud. It was very embarrassing. It was something that could never have happened in Europe. Europeans would have felt as self-conscious about it as I. But when I recovered from my embarrassment I understood that here was honest appreciation; here was a real liking for the words that were being read. It is this genuineness that in the Middle West appeals to one all the time. In places culture attains singularity. There is in Chicago a curious, decadent little club, with orange couches, gray-green walls, and orange curtains decorated with black lace; the yellow walls are flowered in black. Here are crystal and dancing and an aspiration to Paris or Vienna. That is a new Middle West, no longer the Middle West of the lecture club, but a Middle West which has digested its conquests and is developing into sophistication.

HAROLD SPENDER[1]

E HAROLD SPENDER, author, journalist, and lecturer, was born at Bath, June 22, 1864. As his father was a physician and his mother a novelist, Spender's education was of a high order. At Bath College he was Head Boy for 1882–83. He took his Master of Arts degree at Oxford, and sometime later was elected fellow of the Royal Geographical Society. In 1887 he obtained a place on the staff of the *Echo* and started on his journalistic career. Two years later he was appointed lecturer for the Oxford University Extension Delegacy, a post he retained until 1892, when he returned again to journalism as a member of the staff of the *Pall Mall Gazette*. He then worked in turn for the *Westminster Gazette, Daily Chronicle, Manchester Guardian,* and *Daily News.* Throughout the period of the World War he devoted his full time to sponsoring war savings, to volunteering, and to other war activities. Besides numerous short stories and magazine articles, Spender has published books consistently from 1893, when he brought out the *Story of the Home Rule Session,* to the year before his death, when he wrote *The Cauldron of Europe.*

In the winter of 1920–21 he came to the United States, with four other Britons, at the invitation of the American "Mayflower" Council. His impressions of America, as published in *A Briton in America,* were originally set forth in a series of letters written from this side of the Atlantic and published at the time in the *Daily Telegraph.* The book, however, has several additional letters, and all have been revised.

Of America in general he has much to say: "We saw a nation immensely wealthy. . . . . We blinked at the glare of New York. . . . . Business America —the grave, diligent, ardent America of commerce—now resumes the mundane march. . . . . A nation impassioned for new ideas and yet anchored to her own creeds. . . . . We found a people certainly much brighter and happier than the shadowed folk of Europe. . . . . " Spender attempted to be impartial in his appraisal of the United States. He tried to "steer a way between the Scylla of prejudice and the Charybdis of flattery." In a large measure he has succeeded. Flattery, however, outweighs his criticism, but this might be expected, as he came with a definite purpose to help cement the friendship between the two great English-speaking nations.

Spender died April 15, 1926.

[1] Harold Spender, *A Briton in America* (London: William Heinemann, 1921), pp. 51–55. Reprinted by permission of William Heinemann, Ltd.

A HOTEL, A RESTAURANT, AND NEWSPAPERS

Chicago, *Nov.* 16. [1920]

We reached Chicago this morning in a heavy snowstorm, and found the great city as dark as London under fog conditions. Coasting along the shore of Lake Michigan before we reached the city we almost seemed to be moving along the shore of a sea, so big were the waves which broke along that coast.

We took off our baggage from a great trolley at the station and carried it with us on a taxi to the La Salle Hotel. Arrived there, we found the great hall packed with men standing in queues waiting for rooms. There is a Convention going on in Chicago—there seems always a Convention everywhere on this Continent—and we hear that all the hotels are crowded. But this crowding of hotels is now a common phenomenon of American life. For America has its housing problem as well as Europe, and it is due to the same cause—the cessation of building operations for the last two years of the war. There was nothing for it but that we should sit in the hall writing our letters and diaries, waiting till a room was free.

It is easy to do this sort of thing in America. The hotels are public places, and all the world seems to resort to them. The "Lounge" of the La Salle was like the lobby of the House of Commons on a day of political crisis. Everyone seemed to stand; and everyone seemed to talk at the top of his voice. There was a great sense of hustle and exhilaration, combined with an immense sense of discomfort for wearied travellers.

During the morning we visited one of the great Y.M.C.A. buildings, with their wonderful profusion of facilities for the young life of America—libraries, reading-rooms, lecture-rooms, gymnasia—and we learned that there are eight similar buildings in Chicago. The superintendent of this particular building told us that the working of Prohibition was proving an immense boon to the young life of the city.

"It takes away a great temptation," he said, "and the result is that they have more money for books and classes!"

He was quite enthusiastic about it.

We lunched at one of those wonderful food shops which are christened with the beautiful name of "Child's." They are everywhere, full of a profusion of cheap, good food, an immense boon to the workers of this great city. We fell into conversation with a lady civil servant in the municipal service who was lunching there. She gave us a curious account of the mingled enterprise and graft of the Chicago civic functions. These two sides of life—graft and enterprise—seem to be strangely intertwined in the public life of America. It seems due to that perpetual change of public servants which still goes on under the system of "spoils to the victors." I am disappointed to find that Civil Service Reform has made so little progress in America.

Then we wandered about the town for a while and realised the tremendous contrast between Chicago and New York. In New York the traffic goes like clockwork. There is not a better regulated city in the world. But in Chicago it seems all confusion. In this part of the city one obtains a fearful impression of chaos and disorder in the noisy, tumultuous vortices of traffic between high buildings which tend to shut out light and air. This old part of Chicago is like a city of Ratcliffe Highways, though Chicago's noble parks go far to redeem the city as a whole.

During the last twenty-four hours I have been visited by the Editor of the *Chicago Daily News*,[2] and I have paid a call on the Editor of the *Chicago Tribune*.[3] I have also bought and read the Hearst papers, and a strange paper called the *Chicago Republican*, representing the views of Mayor Thompson, who now rules Chicago. These Chicago papers reflect a political atmosphere quite different from that of New York. They are more remote from Europe, and it now seems to be their vogue to avoid with all possible care any expression of friendliness toward Europe—and especially towards Great Britain. The view of the *Chicago Republican* is that America made her greatest mistake when she came into the war. The view of all these Chicago papers seems to be that Europe is an effete, corrupt continent, containing little of interest to so progressive a community as Chicago.

The American newspapers, of course, are grouped in zones,

[2] Victor F. Lawson.   [3] Robert R. McCormick.

and the Chicago zone is very different from the New York zone. There is no national Press in the United States at all corresponding to our London Press. The country is too vast. But unhappily, the nearest thing to a national Press is the Hearst Press, which runs right across America and publishes a newspaper in almost every great city with syndicated articles. Thus the Hearst Press is almost the only approach to a national Press.

Perhaps the most ominous thing between Great Britain and the United States is the virulent and sustained hostility to Great Britain of the whole of this gigantic Hearst combine.

A LECTURE AT NORTHWESTERN UNIVERSITY

This evening, however, we have obtained a better impression of this vast community of nearly three million human beings. I was fixed to speak at the North-Western University, twelve miles out of Chicago. The train took us through the suburbs out to Evanston—a pleasant township of broad roads and handsome, spacious, detached villas. There I dined with a distinguished company of politicians, professors and journalists, and after dinner I lectured in the University Theatre on the Pilgrim Fathers, illustrated by Newton's slides.

At the end of the lecture the audience remained seated. I was rather surprised at this, and not altogether pleased, as I had done my work and imagined that I deserved some rest. But the chairman then rose and explained to me that though they were very pleased to hear about the Pilgrim Fathers they were not content to let me go at that. Having before them a visitor from Europe they wanted to hear something about that troubled continent, of which the papers now told them far too little. They also wanted to hear about Ireland. In fact, they wanted something "real and actual."

I told them that I had made a vow on board ship that I would not talk politics in America. But they only laughed, and as it seemed clear that they had no intention of leaving until they were gratified, I had to make them another speech, this time on the events of the day. It seemed rather perilous, as I did not pretend to admire the present foreign policy of the United

States. Nor in regard to Ireland did I affect to believe that the American attitude is altogether helpful. I suggested that Ireland, being a common trouble to both nations, might, in the end, bring us together. That seemed such an original and surprising idea it filled them with enthusiasm. For the Americans love a new idea, almost as much as we dislike one.

The upshot was that we all parted good friends. We got back to Chicago very late tonight, but on the whole thoroughly pleased and satisfied with our first adventure into American politics.

WALDO FRANK[1]

WALDO DAVID FRANK, American author, was born in Long Branch, New Jersey, August 25, 1889. He received both his baccalaureate and Master's degrees at Yale, where he was elected to Phi Beta Kappa. The author of novels, a contributor to the New York *Evening Post* and the *New York Times*, one of the founders and editors of the *Seven Arts*, and American correspondent of *La nouvelle revue française*, Frank's literary activities have been far-flung and varied. In addition, he has served as contributing editor to the *New Republic* and *New Masses*, and has written short stories which have appeared in sundry "Best Short Story" collections.

Our America, from which extracts are reproduced here, was written at the request of Gaston Gallimard, director of the publishing house of *La nouvelle revue française*, and Jacques Copeau, of the Théâtre du Vieux, organizations representing Young France. The purpose of the book is to apprise the French of America and her institutions as seen by an American.

-->>> <<<--

THE SOUL OF CHICAGO

Surely no other American city lives so close to its earth. You must think of prairie. Beyond the flatness of Lake Michigan another flatness. A thousand miles of it, rising with incalculable leisure to the sudden climax of the Rocky Mountains. This is the prairie. Rich black earth spread like the sky. The Mississippi and his legion of waters make it fecund. Nations of Indians called it their world and their mother. Buffalo roamed over it like the winds. And then the white man. Buffalo and Indians vanished. But the loam of the plains was ready like a wanton woman. Here was a race who would plant endless wheat and corn, a race of insatiate desire. The prairie would have fruit to dower and dominion the world. Here at last was a race of lovers to satisfy a prairie.

The train flows over the flat land. Green farms, the warm, brown lurch of country roads wither away. Here is a sooty sky hanging forever lower. The sun is a red ball retreating. The

[1] Waldo Frank, *Our America* (New York: Liveright, Inc., 1919), pp. 117-24, 147. Reprinted by permission of Mr. Waldo Frank and Liveright, Inc.

478

heave of the prairie lies palpable still to the grimed horizons. But on it, a thick deposit: grey, drab, dry—litter of broken steel, clutter of timber, heapings of brick. The sky is a stain: the air is streaked with runnings of grease and smoke. Blanketing the prairie, this fall of filth, like black snow—a storm that does not stop. . . . . The train glides farther in toward the storm's center. Chimneys stand over the world, and belch blackness upon it. There is no sky now. Above the bosom of the prairie, the spread of iron and wooden refuse takes on form. It huddles into rows: it rises and stampedes and points like a lay of metal splinters over a magnet. This chaos is polarized. Energy makes it rigid and direct. Behold the roads without eyes wrench into line; straighten and parallel. The endless litter of wood is standing up into wooden shanties. The endless shanties of wood assemble to streets. Iron and smoke and brick converge and are mills and yards. The shallow streets mount like long waves into a sea of habitations. And all this tide is thick above the prairie. Dirt, drab houses, dominant chimneys. A sky of soot under the earth of flaming ovens. Rising into a black crescendo as the train cuts underneath high buildings, shrieking freight-cars, to a halt. But on all sides still, with vast flanks spreading and breathing and inviting, the unburied prairie. . . . .

Chicago is a symbol. A splendid one, not subtle and hidden away but brutal like itself, and naked clear. A symbol that speaks in the facts of its life. An open city. On the east, the fresh Michigan sea. Prairie everywhere else. Let it spread free like the dirty winds that tear it to bits. Even the Lake makes contribution of its mud. Widens the shores. Even the Lake— and all else to what measure!—gives of its depths to fatten Chicago.

You have come in on a train. Everywhere trains come into Chicago. In the moneyed precincts by the Lake, in the endless wooden miles of the poor West Side, in the industrial hells to the South. A vast flat city, cut to bits by tracks of steel. A lacerated city. A city destroyed by the iron flails that beat it into being.

There is no peace in the Chicago streets. But there are freight-cars.

A mile of avenue. Low houses, soiled and blind, with garish fronts for shops, facing a clanging gutter. And then, the trolley lurches with gnashing wheel and there is a freight-yard. Myriad tracks, burdened with unloading box-cars, along which the engines scatter their black message over the city. A dim place at day with its soot and grime and the dust of the plains shedding from its iron conduits. And at night an inferno: red flame and black shadow and the loom of masses sliding on tracks through the torn city.

With the long steel thrusts of its railways, all America mangles Chicago: and by the channels of its thrusts pours produce, pours wealth, pours of its life, and makes Chicago. Freight-cars block streets, engine smoke blinds windows. Even water comes in upon the open city. Two rivers curl about the town like sleepy pythons. High boats from the Lake stand also above the houses. Like the roads of steel, the river-roads play havoc with the streets: cut them open, choke traffic. Masses of men black the fenders of a draw-bridge while three fat tugs laze by, piled up with onions and manure. By the river as by the tracks, the streets have their shapes and their meaning.

Warehouses stand sheer from the waters, where boats can moor and time be saved. And on the houses' other side, the frenzy of shops and merchantmen, selling the stuff of the ships. Factories make their way close to the train-yards. The cars run their coal and their ore to the ovens' mouth. Such are the masters, hewing the city to their imperious needs. Houses where men dwell merely are shoved away, out of sight, into off-hand pools where neither rail nor river runs. For these are the true blood-conduits of Chicago. By them, the life is quickest, life's meaning clearest. Factory and mill, standing insatiate over the train-yards and the rivers, speak for the city which they have gathered about them.

In the South Side, in what has become the heart of Chicago, stretch the stinking miles of stock-yards. Dante would have recognized this world. A sunken city of blood. Black buildings loom over narrow, muddy paths where the sun cannot dry the slime. Fantastic chutes and passageways twist again the sky, leading into the shadow of muffled houses. Muffled sounds disappear against the reeking walls. Men move about with bloody hands and the whites of their eyes gleaming. Beyond, the pens of the cattle. Miles of them also. A prostrate, charted world for the towering hell. Cut through by steel-rails and snorting locomotives. And on the other side, the pens of the men and women who slay the cattle and who, in turn, are consumed.

Less regular, these pens of men. Streets? Scarcely. Rather alleys that limp through puddles and broken gutters to other alleys—or into refuse piles— or into walls. Low, sodden houses of wood. Windows tight shut in summer, in order to keep out the thickest of the stench. Acid-eaten, soot-stained houses, soaked with all the floating excrement of the meat-mills. In them at night, Slav and Magyar and Croat who dreamed of a Promised Land. And at day, children playing in the filth of the streets, waiting to grow up, waiting to join their parents.

On the one side, trains pour in the cattle and the hogs. On the other, trains pour in the men and the women. Cattle and hogs from the West. Women and men from the East. Between, stockaded off by the dripping walls, the slaughter-houses stand mysterious, and throb to their ceaseless profit. High buildings over a sunken world, knitted together by elevated rails and secret compacts. Knitted into a sort of hierarchy whose sort of power is manifest about them. But over all, and joining all, over the meat and the men and the feudal masters, is something else. The spirit of the place—perhaps its soul: an indescribable stench. It is composed of mangled meat, crushed bones, blood soaking the floors, corroding the steel, and sweat. A stench that is warm and thick, and that is stubborn. A stench somehow sorrowful and pregnant, as if the sweat of men joined with the guts of beasts brought forth a new drear life. And when the wind is from the south, this stench is wafted out to the entire city.

. . . .

Chicago is the dream of the industrial god. Chaos incarnate.

The miracle of Chicago is that it is also something else. The miracle of Chicago is that this stew of steel and smoke should be inhabited by men and women.

)king upon Chicago, you might see no miracle. Here is a sticky smudge on the face of the prairie. Alive it must be with maggots and with midges. Makers of soot: eaters of soot: dwellers in iron. Not men and women. So the observer might have it. The poet has only his dream. . . . .

Go into the Chicago streets. The elevated trains make greater noise, the street cars are more brutal tangents of commotion, than in the Eastern cities. The murky coating over the sky shuts in the fever of life, raises it to a higher, stifled power. But though the city reaches up in stone, or flattens to an unending desert of wood dwellings, there is an unbridled force about, that is not these things.

The Chicagoan is alive. He is not cowed: he is not refined away: there is a part of him still which the Machine has not sucked nor the black air blighted. The Chicagoan walks with swift step through the harshness of his city. But his feet are somehow planted on the prairie. His feet have not forgotten the feel of the rich loam: nor the greenness which comes forth from it.

Do not talk to the Chicagoan! He will talk business. He will talk size. He will talk ugly. He will boast of the steel-straight-jacket which has not yet quite girthed him. He will compare his mills and railroads with the cash of New York. He does not know what he is saying. He does not know that he is still alive. He is like a young free man, with happy gait, aping the authoritative stiffness of his Papa. This life in him is all unuttered: and he is pouring it fast into a mould that must destroy it. Only the hell in which he somehow has survived speaks and knows its meaning. He gives his life to the furtherance of that death. He rushes like a poet through the streets. But it is to serve the Mills.

Therefore, if Chicago is the city of Hope, the reason is that there, Despair has simply not yet altogether won. Chicago is still fluent, still chaotic. In the black industrial cloak are still interstices of light.

New York has *set*. New York is so perfectly Industrialism's flower, that no flower is left. Industrial disorder has its order.

Industrial anarchy has its law. New York is clutched in them. But in Chicago, the chaos is still chaos. The material is still raw, and therefore pregnant. In many ways, this turbulent city represents to-day what New York was years ago. It is unkempt, uncouth, ceremonious and callous. It has little inkling of Metropolitan behaviour. It is not organized. It lacks co-ordination. It is not altogether and irrevocably pledged. New York was once like this, but with a difference. Thirty years ago, Industrialism was still hale and absolute in its blighting sway. It held New York in a grip that no other force contested, no vision in America could swerve. New York was doomed. To-day, Chicago moves in the same course, is driven by the same control. But during these thirty years Industrialism has grown weaker, Puritanism paler. They have proved their failure to supply the loves and the desires of already one non-pioneering generation. A new Order raises its rebel head and looks about for itself. A new vision disputes the encompassing blindness.

Another thirty years like the thirty that have passed, and the Miracle would live no more in the Chicago streets. It would be dead. The prairie would be buried under the smoke and the steel and the stench. The men who walk would not feel the loam beneath their feet: the touch of creative life would be gone from their blood. They would be altogether bound by the dead world they gave their lives to build. But another thirty years like the thirty that have passed—? . . . .

Such then, the miracle of Chicago. The industrial Despair is still loose enough and weak in the Middle-West so that such truths as these could push up into some sort of light. These spirits are facts. They cannot be ignored. And cannot be destroyed. They create values out of the American chaos. They show that men may still meet their city and their prairie, and have life of them. With them, new gods come out of the corn: and shoulder their way across the iron streets.

SIR CHARLES CHEERS WAKEFIELD[1]

SIR CHARLES CHEERS WAKEFIELD, author and philanthropist, was born in 1859, the son of John Wakefield and Mary Cheers. In 1908 he was created Knight, and in 1919 Commander of the Order of the British Empire. He is also a member of the Order of the Legion of Honour, Order of the Crown (Belgium), Order of Leopold (Belgium), Order of St. Sava (Serbia), Order of the White Lion (Czechoslovakia). Colgate University conferred upon 'him the degree of LL.D.

Sir Charles has held several political offices, such as alderman of London, justice of the peace for London and Kent, and lord mayor of London. Many organized charities have enlisted his support, and he has been president of the royal hospitals of Bridewell and Bethlem, of the Mental After-care Association, of the London branch of the League of Mercy, and has been interested in the National Children's Home and Orphanage.

In 1922 Sir Charles headed the British Sulgrave Commission, which presented statues of Burke, Pitt, and Bryce to the cities of Washington, Pittsburgh, and New York. Upon returning home, he published *America To-day and To-morrow*, which is, in part, the record of the Sulgrave Commission, and as such received favorable attention at the hands of the reviewers. The book describes the various cities and scenes Sir Charles saw in America, but the author also endeavors to analyze our national characteristics and to discover the future path of this country. He was favorably impressed with America, and he believed that she would lend assistance in solving European problems.

Other of Sir Charles' books are *Future Trade in the Far East* (1896) and *On Leaving School and the Choice of a Career*. Throughout all of his works there runs a current of idealism which is well shown in *America To-day and To-morrow*.

-⫸⫷-

THE TUMULTUOUS MAGNIFICENCE OF CHICAGO

Chicago is a city of tumultuous magnificence. It has slums and overcrowded areas that are probably worse than anything we have in London, although not worse than can be found in other of our urban centres. It is at the heart of a densely industrial (and industrious) area, and in its vast and various population there are much squalor, racial and economic friction, and unhealthy conditions. But with it all, Chicago is a great city,

[1] Sir Charles Cheers Wakefield, *America To-day and To-morrow* (London: Hodder & Stoughton, 1924), pp. 191–95. Reprinted by kind permission of Lord Wakefield.

and it is time the world acknowledged its claims to greatness. Although its population within the last decade has increased by about twenty-five per cent. (it is now nearly up to the three million mark), during the same period Chicago has made immense progress in the provision of amenities. The lakeside is adorned by beautiful buildings, and the boulevard system has been adopted and is being developed with great energy. Land is being reclaimed from Lake Michigan, and will eventually be one more of Chicago's network of parks and open spaces. New and splendid roads are being cut, bordered by new villas. Nor are the arts neglected. Has not Chicago the unique Marshall Field Museum, a building whose imposing size and classic marbled beauty would glorify any city?

Chicago, as I have said, struck us as a city of "tumultuous magnificence." It has all the qualities that entitle it to be admitted into the select circle of the world's titanic cities that are great in imaginative grasp of the possibilities of their situation and their corporate wealth as well as in numbers. It is a thousand pities that more Englishmen do not travel in America. Such legendary tales as that Chicago is a city of skyscrapers, slaughtered pigs, and little else notable save only size and noise —such legendary tales would vanish like smoke before the wind. We should learn to understand—and to admire.

Chicago took us warmly to its heart. The Association of Commerce gave us luncheon, and evinced in its oratory sincere sympathy with the objects of our mission. We found that the business world of Chicago was fully alive to the disadvantages of a too complete isolation, and that study of the situation in Europe was constant and discerning. We were shown a pamphlet entitled "What shall our Foreign Policy be?" which had been written by a special committee for the Chicago Association of Commerce and published in April 1922. It was a brief, concise, and fair-minded study of present-day world-problems as they affect the economic position of the United States, and although, in a foreword, it was stated that the memorandum was intended solely to provoke thought and discussion, it was clear that the trend of thought was very much towards a realisation that the world is an economic unit, and that dislocation in one part affects the others. A straightforward, unsentimental document such as this, with no apparent leanings towards any but strictly self-interested conclusions, and issued under the authority of some of America's leading business builders, must carry very great weight with public opinion in America. As an indication of the direction in which even pre-occupation with their own problems, as affected by foreign affairs, is leading such shrewd minds, it is clearly most significant. . . . .

Mr. Spender[2] and myself were speakers at the Chicago Sunday Evening Club, which seemed to be the American equivalent of our Brotherhood movement, being "organized to maintain a service of Christian inspiration and fellowship in the business centre of Chicago, and to promote the moral and religious welfare of the city." I noticed that the "box-holders" announced for the season included most of the leading concerns in the city, such as Swift & Co., the Quaker Oats Co., the National City Bank, and the Northern Trust Company.

It was an enormous audience, numbering over three thousand, I was informed. We did our best to put our case before them, and all our points seemed to go "home," judging by the generous applause that punctuated our remarks. Mr. Spender's vivid metaphor that "the sun cannot set in Europe without throwing a shadow on America" appealed to them, as did his humorous reference to the British debt to America (then very much a burning question), when he remarked that an Englishman never owes any debts except to his tailor, so that they in America might be sure we should pay! Indeed if only the temper of public meetings could be taken as a reliable index to public opinion as a whole, we should have judged from our reception by these good citizens of Chicago that American help in restoring Europe was a foregone conclusion. Certainly there would be no dissentient voices to be heard, and our addresses must, I am sure, have led to an awakening of interest in Europe's troubled life.

[2] E. Harold Spender.

While in Chicago we were made honorary members of the Union Club, where we made many friends for ourselves and our work. On the Sunday morning we set out with our hosts for an automobile tour of the outskirts of the city and some of its miles of parks, being given tea at the Country Club, and dinner at the Blackstone Hotel.

-»»-«««-

MARY BORDEN[1]

MARY BORDEN, novelist, was born in Chicago, 1886, the daughter of William Borden, and educated at Vassar. Shortly after the outbreak of the World War, she went to France, where she equipped and directed Mobile Hospital from 1915 to 1918. For her many war services she was decorated with the Legion of Honor and made a member of the French Red Cross. In 1918 she married an English army officer, Brigadier-General E. L. Spears, and since that time has resided in England save for one visit to the United States in 1930.

After her marriage, Miss Borden turned to literary work. At first she published her works under the pseudonym of Bridget Maclagan; but as success came her way she permitted her real name to appear on the title-page of her novels, which have been popular sellers and favorably received by reviewers. These include *Jane—Our Stranger, Three Pilgrims and a Tinker, The Romantic Woman, Jericho Sands, Four O'Clock, Flamingo, Jehovah's Day*, and *The Forbidden Zone*. In addition, Miss Borden has found time to contribute to various magazines sundry articles on British and American manners and customs.

The reactions of her visit to the United States, after an absence of twelve years, she chronicled, in the case of Chicago, in the accompanying article.

-»»-«««-

THE SOUP KITCHEN OF A GANGSTER

I did not see Al Capone, in spite of the fact that when I told them in Paris and London and New York I was going back to Chicago, my native city, they had all immediately said that I should. It was the inevitable response, though the tone varied. Sometimes scornfully, sometimes slyly, maliciously, sometimes enviously they said, "Oh! You'll see Al Capone." I didn't. I saw only his soup kitchen. But it was through no fault of my own, for I am a sufficiently typical daughter of my great, roaring, bumptious town to feel that it needs from me no apology; that as long as all American cities are going in for gangs and rackets, and all the American world, including congressmen, senators, wet and dry judges, policemen and parsons, are buy-

[1] Mary Borden, "Chicago Revisited," *Harpers Magazine*, CLXII (April, 1931), 541–47. Reprinted by kind permission of Mary Borden.

ing whisky, it need not be particularly ashamed of having produced the Ace of Bootleggers, Al the Scarface.

No. I saw the soup kitchen because it was there for all to see
with "Free Soup, Coffee, and Doughnuts for the Unemployed"
printed in large letters over its grimy doorway, and I didn't see
Al Capone because he was invisible. Wanted by the police on
the charge of being a public enemy, he was not, when I arrived,
granting audiences to sightseers. Al is discreet if Chicago is not.
He is more difficult of access than the Pope. But not from shame
does he hide. No one is ashamed of anything in Chicago; everything is moving too quickly; everyone is too specialized, and it is
all too much fun. Each one, whether crook or politician or expert gunman, architect or banker or broker, is too good of his
kind to be conscious of anything less positive and less exhilarat-
ing than his own power. The city itself is like that, too big, too
busy, too powerful, and in too much of a hurry to have any
negative emotions. There's a lot of room in Chicago. There's
the whole prairie to spread over in three directions, but there's
no room for doubt or hesitancy. Everything about the big,
blustering place is positive and superlative. I should as soon
think of apologizing for Henry VIII or Lorenzo de Medici.

Chicago the notorious, the talk of the world, laughs at
its critics. To quote from Carl Sandburg: "laughing the
stormy, husky, brawling laughter of youth; half naked; sweat-
ing, proud pork butcher; tool maker, stacker of wheat, player
with railroads and freight handler to the nation." Go there, as
I did. Get out of your train and drive up Michigan Avenue. I
defy you not to respond to the excitement in the air, not to feel
the drumming pulse of the great dynamo beating in your own
veins, not to throw your hat to the sky and shout.

Beautiful! How beautiful it is as you whirl northward past
the Tribune Tower, cross the river, and make for the Lake
Shore Drive. Palaces rise on your left, the lake shimmers on
your right. On you go, fast, so fast. You can drive all day and
not come to the end of it. The circuit of Chicago parks forms a
system of boulevards measuring a hundred miles, and the lake is
ninety miles across, and the prairie to the west stretches out to

the Rockies, and these establish the standards of measurement. Space. The City of Great Spaces. Everything is wide and open. Wide streets, wide parks, wide slums, wide open tracts of the underworld, blatantly spread out for all to see.

Chicago is gorgeous and it is awful. Seen from a high window near the lake shore, it is too beautiful to be credible, for its architects have made exquisite use of the space offered them, and the lovely towers of skyscrapers rise into the early morning sunlight, strange, pale rose-tinted clusters of spires with the blue waters of Lake Michigan gleaming between them, or burn white at night, translucent as alabaster against the sky. But if, leaving Michigan Avenue or the Lake Shore Drive behind you, you drive west along one of those wide streets that have no bending nor ending for twenty-five miles, you will pass through a vast scene of desolate ugliness, impossible to match in any slum in Europe. And I think what makes the slums of Chicago more dreadful than any others is that they are so flimsy, so shallow, so open, and so bleak. I saw no crowded buildings, no deep, cozy pockets of shadow, no warm, crumbling, tumble-down houses. Instead, there are thousands upon thousands of new, shabby, square wooden boxes, no more solid than packing cases, perched on the hard ground. They look as if the icy wind would blow them away, and round them, between them, are vacant lots, ragged patches of prairie littered with scrap-iron, stones, and garbage. "No place to hide in here," I muttered to myself and I realized that to be a bank robber, a gunman, or the driver of a contraband truckload of whisky one would have to be quick and always on the move in Chicago.

The bread line outside Al Capone's soup kitchen stretched down one of these bleak, windswept streets past Police Headquarters. I had been there, turning the leaves of what they call the Death Book, most dreadful of all souvenir albums in the world. And there was undoubtedly a connection between the two lots of men, those who stood shivering outside the soup kitchen and those who, enclosed in the covers of the police album, lay sprawled on the bare boards of matchbox rooms or crouched in the corners of taxis with their heads bashed in. For

Al Capone is an ambidextrous giant, who kills with one hand and feeds with the other.

I had seen other sights that day and had met other notable, if less picturesque citizens. I had seen the University and had met its boyish President,[2] the youngest university president in the world, and I had met, too, the Chinese Mayor, polished representative of one of the world's oldest races, and then, in the Arab quarter, dingiest and dreariest slum of all I visited, I had come upon a great aristocrat, also a member of a very old and civilized nation. He was sitting in the back of his little shop, behind piles of cheap rugs and cheaper embroideries, smoking an Eastern water pipe, and he rose as we came in and bowed to us with the easy dignity of a very noble lord and engaged us in grave conversation.

"Have you ever seen a pipe like this one?" he asked me, smiling gently as one would smile at a child.

"Oh! yes," I answered. "I have seen many in Damascus and in Palestine."

His face changed at that. His face was somber and deeply lined. Now it lighted up.

"You have been in Damascus and Palestine?" he cried softly.

"Yes. I spent a month in Palestine," I answered; and then again, in that soft, urgent longing voice he said, "Perhaps; it is just possible that you have been to a village named ———" and he gave me its name. "It is not far from the Sea of Galilee. I have not been there for thirty years and it is my home," and then he waited with his lips parted over his strong white teeth and his eyes fixed on my face.

But I had not been to his village and I could not lie to him. I longed to and to a lesser man I should have, but with him it was impossible. And so I said, "No," and watched the shadow of disappointment fall on his pale, brown face and then, presently, when we had talked a little of his country, I asked him if he had

[2] Robert M. Hutchins of the University of Chicago.

ever heard of Lawrence of Arabia, and at that suddenly his eyes filled with tears.

"Know Lawrence of Arabia? But he is the friend of my people. We have called him King, and indeed he deserves the title, for he would have done everything for our country had it not been. . . . . " He checked himself. He looked at the man beside me who had been presented to him as a British general and smiled his apologies. "The British Government," he said lightly in the way a consummate man of the world would if he wanted to dismiss a difficult topic of conversation, "the British Government is in a very awkward position between the Arabs and the Jews in Palestine," and he smiled again.

He accompanied us to the door. "I have been in Chicago for thirty years," he regretted. He bowed over my hand, and we went out into the street, the long, awful street of gimcrack buildings and vacant lots and heaps of scrap-iron, and I looked again at the faces of the passers-by, and they looked ugly, vacant, idiotic, bestial, just as they had looked in the Death Book.

THE FOUR HUNDRED

I went to a dinner dance that same evening and, haunted still by the pages of the Death Book and the face of the exiled Arab, I met a lovely member of Chicago's four hundred who spoke to me with tears in her eyes of Capone. I was already getting rather sick of the Scarface, but this suddenly made me feel quite ill, this sentimentality frightened me. I had heard, of course, of the Capone fans—he had more adorers, so I'd been told, than any movie star—but I had not expected the friends of my childhood to be numbered among them. That the hungry and ragged army of unemployed waiting in the street to partake of his bounty should, with a catch of the throat, mumble the maudlin words, "Good-hearted Al" seemed natural enough; but that the petted and pampered daughters of Chicago's old families should be moved to tears by the spectacular display of the bootlegger's big heart was startling. It seemed to indicate a creeping civic paralysis, the spread of some moral intoxication or fever that, like the effects of certain drugs, will produce in time a complete immunity from the sensation of horror or disgust or fear; that will eventually distort the five senses themselves, rendering fetid odors agreeable to the most sensitive nostril and nauseous tastes palatable to the most delicate palate.

But what was the drug, if drug it was, that was penetrating the nervous system of my brawny, lusty, native city? Perhaps I was wrong. Perhaps I was foolish to be frightened. Perhaps this, too, didn't matter. Certainly I had seen no signs of paralysis in the living body of the city. The town didn't seem to care for any of us, that was all. It had apparently no time to waste on its gangsters or its old families. Probably neither element was important. It was moving so fast that it would sweep them along or sweep them away, and the pretty sentimentalist would be one of those who assuredly would not be remembered.

I looked about me. Would any of this lot survive? We were on the roof of a hotel downtown, a hundred of us, and the party represented the younger set of a very small knot of people known as Chicago Society. Such pretty, delicate girls, such nice, boyish men! Champagne was flowing and a jazz band was playing and everyone was happy as children are happy at a party. But weren't we dancing high up in the sky, above stored dynamite? I asked myself. For again my nerves were jumping. To get to the roof we had walked through the seething, smoke-laden lobby of the hotel; and I suppose that the crowd of men who eyed us over their large cigars, their hats pushed back onto the backs of their heads, as we stepped past in satin slippers and ermine coats, represented as tough a crowd of crook politicians and crook business men as any you could find in the world. Just the usual hard-boiled American gang of grafters, gamblers, bootleggers, vice merchants, police superintendents, friends of theirs, shyster lawyers, and political bums that manage most American towns and traffic, much to their financial advantage, in crime. Suppose that crowd downstairs hadn't chosen to let us have our party? Suppose they decided not to let these attractive people have any parties any more? Suppose they told them to clear out of the town altogether? Weren't they helpless? Wouldn't they quickly disappear? What could they do about it? Fight? Well, why didn't they fight, then? Why wait? What actually were they doing in regard to the governing of this town of theirs? Nothing. And what were they waiting for? I had been waiting twenty years to see some of them take a hand in city or in national politics. Not one of them had done so. They were too nice, too honest, too decent, and too busy making money. That last was, after all, the point. They didn't have to bother yet. The town might be corrupt. It was so prosperous that it could afford any amount of corruption. True, I had opened my London paper one morning to find that Chicago had gone bankrupt. That evidently had meant nothing of any vital consequence to the people who lived in it. Its City Corporation would have to go bankrupt half a dozen times, I gathered, before its decent citizens would touch its indecent management of the city's finances.

THE CHICAGO MELTING-POT

I thought of London. Then I gave up thinking of London. It was no good, I realized, thinking of London in Chicago. One got nowhere. One only grew bewildered. Nothing that mattered to us in London mattered here, and nothing that mattered here mattered in London. "But London, too, after all," I said to myself, "is a big place. Chicago isn't the only city in the world that has a Chinatown, and an Italian population as big as Pisa and half a million Jews. What of Whitechapel and the London Docks? Isn't the Jew's market foreign enough in all conscience? Yes, but it doesn't matter. No one notices them. No one bothers about them except the police who keep them in order, and the deaconesses and other sweet old maids who run settlements among them down there in the East End. But Chicago's Little Sicily and its Little Mexico and its Black Belt, where half a million negroes, vice ridden, dope ridden, booze ridden, sprawl and laze and die of tuberculosis, not to mention the Germans and the Swedes and the Russians and the Greeks and the Irish—that's different; all that mixture is dangerous. Why?" I didn't quite know and I had no time to find out, to get to the bottom of anything, but I think that it is because it is all so new. It's a new mixture, a boiling, explosive mixture that hasn't had time to simmer down or settle down. As yet few of these people speak English and few think of themselves as Americans any more than does my Arab friend, and to none has such an idea as civic responsibility ever occurred. Lawless? Of course they are. Each community, including the gangsters, has its own laws. Why should they respect the common law of the land? They know nothing about it. They come from old countries, bringing old racial habits, customs, and superstitions and they've squatted here, have set up their tents and their temples, and have taken the law into their own hands. One hears, applied to the racketeers, the phrase, "A government, within a government," but my impression is that there are as many governments in Chicago as there are nationalities, and that these preserve what order there is in the city, and that there is no higher or central authority. The Chinese Guildhall with its Buddhist temple and its Mayor and its Council Chamber where the Tong meets in judgment, is only one example. Each race is organized, each is separate, each is antagonistic to all the others, and the racketeers invade them all, crashing with armored cars and machine guns through the frontiers that are marked by railway bridges and tramlines.

And the white men, the natives who've spoken English for three generations or even two, are so few. One is reminded of a new sort of topsy-turvy colony, a place the exact opposite of Bombay for instance, or Singapore. If you can imagine that the white men were in Singapore first and that the influx of Malays flowed in on top of them, you'll get a little the feeling I had at moments in Chicago.

It would be natural in such circumstances that the original inhabitants should be somewhat isolated and rather helpless, and natural, too, that within their small circle they should keep rigidly to their own customs and develop within their citadel a mode of life increasingly exotic, fastidious, and stiff in direct proportion to the growing hooliganism and immorality outside; and that is just what the old families of Chicago are doing.

They are living in a small world of their own, surrounded by a turbulent torrent of primitive life.

CHICAGO, THE CITY OF MAGIC

It is very pleasant inside the walls of this social citadel and very luxurious and very quiet. The streets are quiet, and the people are quiet and gentle. All the subtle amenities of life are to be found there. You might imagine at one of its dinner tables that you were in Paris, in London, or better still, in the Chicago you knew as a child. You could almost imagine that you were safe. You would forget, and all your companions would conspire to make you forget, the wild, cold darkness outside. For it is dark, that darkness (the facts are black; let us have no nonsense on that score). But every now and then, at a bridge table or a dinner table, I would think of that immense black track of desolation cut into squares by black streets that stretched endlessly out across the prairie, with strange specters looming above it, the specters of gangland. And sometimes, sipping champagne from a lovely goblet, I would see on the wall beyond the lighted candles of this pretty dinner table, the giant menacing shadow of this thing.

But Lake Michigan during those November days looked just like the Mediterranean, so soft and blue and smooth in the bright sunlight, and people were sitting out in the sun on benches just as they do at Cannes or Nice. I stood there, one day, looking across the shining water, but I was not thinking of the Riviera. Nor did I see in my mind's eye the silly, trivial architecture of those French hotels, casinos, and villas. I saw quite another city, a city that no longer existed anywhere on the earth, the town of Chicago that I'd been born in and that had vanished as if by magic.

Magic. That was and is the word to describe my true impression of the visit. Great magic had been at work here since I had been a child by this lake shore and had gone away to live in an older, safer country—beautiful, impressive, and terrifying magic. Genii had risen out of the lake and ogres out of the prairie land. They had woven monstrous spells above this spot where

I stood, and the earth had opened, and towers of steel had spurted into the air like geysers, like fountains, and great blocks of marble had gone hurtling through space and had been planted in stone gardens and clustered, tapering groves of stone, and a great energy had poured through the bodies of these stones, galvanizing them into life. Obviously the magic wasn't finished. It had only just begun, but one could see what it was going to be and, seeing, one had that special, curious sense of being convinced at last of the impossible. I had grown old, you see, in London and resigned to a humdrum reality. I had learned to believe that there was nothing new under the sun and I had lost interest in fairy tales, did not believe any more, as Americans do, in miracles and had given up hoping for a big shock of surprise. Now I'd got it. Chicago had given me the surprise of my life. And as I stood listening, trying to catch again the echo of the sound of my far-away childhood, I heard the city shouting in my ear.

"Hello!" it shouted. "Hi, there! You who've come back from London. You thought the world was tired, didn't you? You thought men would never do anything grand and awful again, didn't you? Thought they'd not got the guts to cheek the Gods any more or the nerve to build a city with Gates of Pearls? Why, say, sister, those Pearly Gates you read about as a kid, they're nothing to what this town's going to show you, and pretty quick, too. You just shut your eyes again and count three and turn around, and you'll see something that'll make the New Jerusalem seem like No Man's Land."

I didn't want to listen just then to this boastful voice. I was listening for another, and I didn't want to look about me at the astounding proof that the boasting was warranted. I was looking for another place that was gone. Memory was strong that day. I was a child again, standing in my nursery window, looking out across the lake. It was my birthday, and we were going on a picnic. The brake that my Father drove, with its pair of shining chestnuts, was waiting at the front door, and presently a dozen of us would pile into it with our picnic baskets and drive out through Lincoln Park to Edgewater, where we would find violets in the woods. Edgewater. But I had just been through Edgewater, and there were no woods there any more. Great apartment buildings and hotels loomed gigantic where the trees had been. There was scarcely a blade of green anywhere to be seen. I rubbed my eyes. The brake with its lovely horses was gone. It would be of no use now. One couldn't drive a pair of horses eighty miles on a spring afternoon to hunt for violets. I turned, frightened, my back to the lake. The charming gray-stone house I'd been born in was still there and there was my nursery window; but immense towers of stone loomed behind it, seemed to bend over it as I looked, seemed about to fall on it and crush it. Soon that would happen. Soon it, too, would be gone. Chicago was on the move. It had no use for old and pleasant houses or for old and gentle things or for gentle, indolent people. It would sweep them all away. If I closed my eyes, as it told me to do, and turned around and looked again, the few remaining landmarks would be gone.

What did it matter? It didn't matter. Chicago laughed at me as I stood there. Let London and Paris preserve their old, lovely stones, old streets, old monuments, old customs. They'd nothing better to do, nothing new to offer. Chicago had something new, and I saw that it had. I didn't know what it would be. I could not see how order was to be brought forth out of this disorder, or how all these warring tribes were to be welded together into a homogeneous civic body, or what type of man was going to emerge. I did not know what his ethics would be—Mexican, Chinese, Arab, or Semitic; I could not comprehend, in advance, his mentality. But I saw the shape of the city. I saw it forming against the sky; had caught sight of it in the very process of being molded. Indeed, I seemed to see it that day moving, twisting, growing, being shaped before my eyes as if it were inspired clay being handled by a giant sculptor. And I knew that the strange creature that would emerge would be America.

I stared fascinated. I stared with a growing excitement. I forgot the city of my childhood and I forgot London, the city of my adoption, and when at last I went away, I was conscious of only one desire, to come back again so that I could see again what was happening in this astounding place. I wanted to be in it. I wanted to share in the drama. "And, after all," I said to myself as I got on the train for New York, and I repeated it a week later when I sailed for Southampton, "I've a right to it, for I was born here."

And that, finally, I declare bluntly, is the feeling I brought away from my visit. Gangsters and bootleggers and racketeers don't matter to me; I'm glad I was born in that town.

GILBERT K. CHESTERTON[1]

GILBERT K. CHESTERTON, author, was born at Campden Hill, Kensington, 1874. He began his literary career reviewing books on art for the *Bookman* and then for the *Speaker*, and since then he has contributed to the *Daily News, Pall Mall Gazette, Bystander*, and to other periodicals.

In 1922 Chesterton visited the United States and published his impressions in *What I Saw in America*. He found the United States a strange and paradoxical place, attractive and not repulsive. In his opinion the American citizen was energetic, impulsive, and possessed of a childlike curiosity. The Americans, he wrote, were more free from cynicism than any people in the world. He called New York a new city, a characteristic he applied to all American cities. He noted that streets were constantly torn up to be paved anew; buildings were erected only to be torn down and larger ones built in their places. To him American cities always had a new appearance.

In his writings Chesterton professes an admiration for the American business man. He considers him not a materialist but an idealist; the dollar his idol because it is a symbol of success and not of enjoyment.

In 1930–31 Chesterton again visited the United States, remaining here almost four months. At the end of this sojourn he wrote a light, whimsical article for the *New York Times*, from which the following extracts are taken. He found the United States as he found it nine years before—a land of paradoxes. He believes the American has been "bullied" into being a "bully." "There is nothing the matter with Americans," he writes, "except their ideals. The real American is all right; it is the ideal American who is all wrong. It is the code and conception of life imposed from above, much more than the merely human faults and weaknesses working up from below."

-≫≪-

THE GUNMAN AND THE RACKETEER

When we say that this is the age of the machine, that our present peace, progress and universal happiness are due to our all being servants of the machine, we sometimes tend to overlook the quiet and even bashful presence of the machine gun. But the machine gun has been overcoming its shyness of late, and has been persuaded to figure in a field where it was never seen before.

[1] G. K. Chesterton, "Mr. Chesterton Looks Us Over," *New York Times Magazine*, February 1, 1931, pp. 2, 20. Reprinted by kind permission of Mr. Chesterton.

In one sense, of course, the machine gun is, like many modern things, so familiar as to be almost old-fashioned. Governments have long used it, of course, against barbarians so brutal and ignorant as not instantly to surrender their own mines or oil fields to the foreign millionaires who govern most of the governments. So an early poem of Mr. Belloc summed up forever the moral qualities that make for world mastery and the really essential virtues of a conquering race:

> *Whatever happens, we have got*
> *The Maxim gun and they have not.*

But an entirely new development has appeared in America, and especially in Chicago. It consists of the organized use of machine guns by the ordinary criminal classes. The millionaires, of course, were not members of the criminal classes; they were only criminals without the redeeming weakness of class consciousness. But it really does mark rather an interesting phase in history: that Bill Sikes, the coarse and common burglar of our boyhood dream, is no longer defending himself with a pistol but with a park of artillery.

I do not mean to be at all Pharisaic about Chicago. It has many beauties, including the fine fastidiousness and good taste to assassinate nobody except assassins. Criminal society in Chicago seems to be extraordinarily exclusive; and it is impossible for any mere journalist or traveler to penetrate into the best circles or receive an invitation or "to be taken for a ride" (a hospitable formula for death) by the true leaders of fashion. While I was in Chicago a very distinguished individual had the misfortune to be murdered, being caught between the fire of two machine guns and falling with a ton of lead in him. But as I gather that the same gentleman had himself murdered no less than thirty-four persons in exactly the same way, it was impossible to feel that any advantage had been taken of his innocence and youth, or that he had been lured into a game of which the rules had not been explained to him.

It is not every town in the world that has this strict segregation and close corporation of crime. Rather as the art-for-art's sake school used to maintain that only artists should criticize artists, so these refined gunmen feel that only murderers are competent to condemn murderers. I wish there were a similar rule, in other towns, by which only cheats should be cheated, only swindlers should be swindled, and only usurers should be ruined and sold up, as there is in this elegant conception that only killers should be killed. . . . .

I ought to add here, however, that quite lately, I believe within the last few years, there has been a new violation of this virginal isolation of the artists in crime; a new method called racketeering. It seems, for some mysterious reason, to be applied especially to beauty parlors, which are now very nearly the national industry of America. A gentlemanly stranger enters the shop and asks the shopkeeper whether he wishes his business to succeed. The shopkeeper replies that such was indeed his purpose, paradoxical as it may seem, in opening the shop. The stranger then says, "You will leave so many thousand dollars on the counter this afternoon," and disappears. If the shopkeeper neglects this advice his shop is blown up.

It seems simple. I cannot quite understand why it is not done everywhere, if it can be done anywhere. But anyhow, it is another step outside the self-contained society of mutual murder, and as such regrettable. A member of the F. F. C. K., or First Families of Chicago Killers, should not stoop to associate with people who run beauty parlors. As a mere matter of romance and sentiment, I should be relieved if most of the beauty parlors were blown up; but I draw the line when there are people inside them. Perhaps people are blown up in the very act of being beautified. It would lend a new and impressive meaning to face-lifting.

But this is a parenthesis. What I wished to note as significant and ominous about the murderer and his machine gun is this: It is a commonplace that each of us, coming into the world, sees as a tableau what is in fact a drama. He sees the procession standing still; or it moves so slowly that he can hardly believe it has been moving. The young cannot imagine a world without motors; I can remember it, but I cannot imagine a world without railways. Yet I have met old men who could remember a world without railways. Similarly, I have met very old men who could remember a world without policemen.

That universal and equal pressure of police organization everywhere, the loneliest village policeman in instant touch with Scotland Yard—all that is a comparatively recent thing. It is not so long ago that Bow Street runners in top-hats ran in vain after successful highwaymen on horseback; and so back to time when bands of robbers could hold some natural stronghold like that of the Doones or the MacGregors. At other times a robber baron would hold the king's castle against the king; and command companies of bows and spears equipped like the royal army. In other words, the criminal classes were often armed and organized like the police.

Perhaps, after all, it has been but a moment of time in which we have seen poor Bill Sikes reduced to a shabby bludgeon, or a pistol he had to hide in his pocket. Perhaps it is only for a flash that we behold the Victorian vision of the omnipotent policeman. In the advanced, inventive, scientifically equipped and eminently post-Victorian city of Chicago the criminal class is quite as advanced, inventive and scientifically equipped as the government, if not more so. If our modern society is breaking up, may it not break up into big organizations having all the armament and apparatus of independent nations; so that it would be no longer possible to say which was originally the lawful government and which the criminal revolt? God knows there are criminals enough in both of them.

That is the significance of the criminal with the machine gun: that he has already become a statesman; and can deal not in murder but in massacre.

MORRIS MARKEY[1]

MR. MORRIS MARKEY was born in Alexandria, Virginia, January 1, 1899. His education was in the public schools of Richmond. At age of twenty he started his career in newspaper work and since then has contributed to the *Atlanta Journal* and more latterly the *New York World*. In addition, articles from his pen have appeared in the *New Yorker*, the *Atlantic Monthly*, *McCall's*, and other periodicals. A novel, *The Band Plays Dixie*, appeared in 1927.

The impressions of Mr. Markey which appear on the following pages are those which he gained in a visit to Chicago during 1932. At this time he was touring the United States to discover what his countrymen were like. In this tour he embraced sixteen thousand miles of territory and interviewed many citizens of the United States. His reactions to his travels he has chronicled in a series of articles which appeared in *McCall's* during the spring of 1932. Later, these were incorporated and expanded in a volume entitled *This Country of Yours*, published by Little, Brown and Company in Boston, in which he discusses "The Iron Empire," "The Urgent City," "The Prairies," "The Frontier," "The Pacific Rim," "The South," "The East," and "New York."

-»» «««-

CHICAGO'S DRAMATIC APPROACH

From the level prairie the way led into a maze of suburban industry: crooked, ill-paved streets lined with bleak houses and thick with the murk of factory vapors. But presently it broke suddenly from the ugly welter and gave into a broad parkway. Off to the right, now, the waters of the lake were very blue in the late sunshine. A few drifts of snow were laid cleanly against the hedges and the dark evergreens. The wind sang, and it was a cold wind, but it had a tonic quality. There was a long drive down the curving road of this parkway. The ugly factory suburb was forgotten. And the trees and the water, the distant gleam of the dying sun, the wind and the emptiness of the earth made cities seem very far away. Then, without the least warning, a long reach opened ahead and the towers of Chicago were lifting against the sky like towers in a dream.

[1] Morris Markey, "Land of the Pilgrims' Pride, The Urgent City," *McCall's*, LIX (March, 1932), 12–13, 56, 62, 67. Reprinted by kind permission of Mr. Morris Markey.

The approach was like that—dramatic. And the sense of some planned drama increased by even stages until I was in the heart of the city. I stopped the automobile at the end of Michigan Avenue—where the bridge crosses the Chicago River—and got out and looked around. Darkness had fallen, and a million electric bulbs were glowing from the towers. The streets were a confusion of jammed motor traffic and people who ran headlong in all directions. Each of the million lights struck down to make a trembling reflection in the black river, and the superb peaks of the lofty towers were piled in close, hard outline against the black sky.

The thing was explosive in its effect upon the eye—more the fabulous projection of a city than a city itself. New York and London, Paris and Berlin and Vienna suddenly became old-fashioned in the memory. This was like a monstrous theatrical spectacle, when the curtain first goes up and you are a little dazed and you say, "But heavens! It's more stunning than the real thing!" I felt as if the fireworks would commence at any instant, with rockets soaring and terrible detonations shaking the air, and that a flaming screen a mile high would begin to spell in red and white and blue: "Chicago—World's Greatest City."

No such thing happened, of course. The people were straining to get home. The police were blowing their whistles. One of them came up to me and asked whether I knew that I was blocking traffic. I apologized, and spent an hour fighting my way through the crush to the biggest hotel on earth.

I was to learn, during the next few days, that this physical aspect of Chicago—the sheer combination of buildings and streets and parks and bridges—is in very many respects its most fascinating element. For ten or fifteen years nearly all of the communal energy has been spent upon this very thing—upon a complete rearrangement of the sticks and stones, the steel and the concrete and the earth itself—upon, indeed, the manufacture of a new city out of an old one. Surely the undertaking is one of the most remarkable in the world. And even if the problems of government and crime, of education and the nurturing of the humanities, have lain in abeyance while the city builders labored at their task, the result is still a thing to stir a good deal of awe.

CIVIC PRIDE

Just after the World's Fair, civic pride was high in Chicago. It stung, particularly, a few rich men, and these decided that they must have the finest city on the globe. They formed a City Plan Commission and gave it money to employ engineers. And although this commission has never had any authority except that of a general public enthusiasm, its edicts have been obeyed as explicitly as Napoleon's were when he commanded Baron Haussmann to rebuild Paris. Through shifting administrations and the worst city government on earth, the work has progressed. "How?" I asked. The answer was a wink. "Remember—there is always big graft in letting such huge contracts for improvements."

The Plan Commission began by saying that a billion dollars' worth of real estate along the lake front should have no buildings upon it, and now the lake front is a continuous and magnificent park. It meant tearing down a few houses, and putting land where there had been no land and covering a sunken railroad track with green lawn, but it was done. With a ruthless cutting down of homes and factories, a ruthless wiping out of streets and alleys, they have built two boulevard systems that belt the town. The inner boulevard has a circumference of thirty miles, and the outer is more than a hundred miles long. Along these boulevards, which widen here and there to become parks, there are lagoons with artificial bathing beaches and with anchorage for small boats. Every mile or so there is a golf course— more than a hundred within the city. And beyond the outer boulevard miles of wooded lands have been purchased. These lands are called the City Forest Preserve.

Buildings have been destroyed merely because they were ugly, and others built merely because they would fill the vacant space handsomely.

The work is not completed yet, of course, and even the most

competent guide is likely to be a little baffled as he leads you through the new city emerging from the old.

"Why, now," said my own guide, "I certainly did not know they had this job done. The last time I was through this street it was just an alley." It had become a fine thoroughfare with handsome light towers, and the change had been accomplished by the simple expedient of cutting twenty feet from the front of every house on both sides of the street.

He showed me Wacker Drive. It seems that a Mr. Wacker felt there should be a more efficient connection between Jackson Boulevard and Michigan Avenue. So with all his energy and most of his money he tore out the whole commission merchant district along the river, moved the willing merchants somewhere else, and built a new street with three traffic levels to suit his notion. This most pretentious of all streets runs directly over the spot where a few worried pioneers once built a blockhouse in the wilderness and called it Fort Dearborn.

The rush of building, of converting a haphazard old city into a stunning new one, is not the private hobby of a few people. The waitress in the restaurant will ask whether you've taken a drive around the outer boulevard. "Finest in the world," she will say, with forthright conviction. More than a dozen people, observing the New York license plate on my car, wanted to know whether Chicago was not far more splendid than Manhattan. Even if I had thought the contrary, I would not have dared to say so. There was an urgency in their pride, a deep personal belief in the magnificence of their town. It was a thing they lived by, for it comforted and stimulated them.

Together with this new and quite exciting beauty another thing has gripped the imagination of the people of Chicago. And that is size—the elemental quality of bulk and stature. I rode about in an automobile with a machinery salesman and his wife, and their feeling was all for the immensities.

"In two more generations," the man said, with certainty, "we'll have fifty million people here. It's bound to come. Our transportation and our natural location at the key spot of the country will do it. Look at that building—the Merchandise

Mart. It's the largest man-made structure in the world. Actually! And remember this: Chicago is already the greatest wholesale lumber market in the world. Chicago is the greatest market in the world for leather and hides. Chicago distributes more automobiles than any other city. No city raises or ships more flowers than Chicago. . . . . "

I interrupted him with a confession that his facts were impressive, and then I asked: "Why does this seem so important to you? Why do you care, either of you, whether Chicago is a big city or a little one? Why do you get such a kick out of it?"

He looked at me as if I had asked him, "Why do you breathe?"

"Why, man!" he exclaimed, "that's progress. You're interested in progress, aren't you? Chicago's destined to be the most important city in the world. If energy and ambition count, we'll do it."

I am quite convinced that two million people living in that city feel precisely the same way. Their town is genuinely a part of their religion, their fundamental belief. I must have talked to two or three hundred people there. They were in all planes of society. From Paul Romano (I shall tell you about him) to the dignified matrons of the Gold Coast, they all managed to express in one way or another a profound excitement over living in Chicago, and an even profounder ambition for seeing it the Colossus of all the world's cities. It was an intimate and satisfying experience for them, simply to be a citizen of such a place.

SOME CHICAGO CITIZENRY

I suppose it was a little ridiculous for me to call on Mr. Romano. Yet somehow, when in Chicago, it seems proper to make the acquaintance of at least one gangster, and an obliging newspaper reporter said it would be very simple. The reporter had engaged to show me a little of the city's night life, and we began with a glass of beer. That, however, was not so simple. Despite the tales of the bootleg kings, beer isn't just around the corner in Chicago.

"We'll have to drive out a way," the reporter said—and he

was a police reporter who had worked there a long time. "There isn't a place in the Loop we can get into. Oh, I guess there are ten or twelve speakeasies downtown, but they're well hidden. Most of them are swell joints, hooked up with gambling, and nobody but the rich boys and the professional gamblers ever goes there."

We drove for about a mile and came up before a grubby-looking house with heavy curtains at the windows. They let us in, after the reporter had gone to considerable lengths to prove his identity. And in a gloomy room, with somebody plunking at a piano, we sat for half an hour over our beer. It was not very pleasant. That simply was not the way to enjoy a glass of beer. Presently we were on our way.

The reporter drove from Jimmy's to Police Headquarters. We saw the radio room, where messages were being sent out— ten every minute—to cruising cars equipped with receiving sets. The announcer's voice went in a steady monotone:

"Report from Division Four. Three young men in Buick coupe held up and robbed filling station at 2117 Hillis Avenue. Shot proprietor. Escaped in direction Jackson Boulevard. Two wore light felt hats and one wore cap."

We saw prisoners coming in, a steady stream of them, black and white and yellow and brown, and we chatted with a Lieutenant of Detectives.

"It's the gals," he said. "More crooks are made by greedy gals than all the rest of it put together. The gals go to the movies and see some handsome egg get away with murder and buy his dame a fur coat, and they say: 'I want me a smart guy like that. I want some excitement and a fur coat.' And the boys are saps. They fall for it. The girls know, too, if we finally grab the boys, the photographers from the papers will be around to get pictures: 'Beautiful Blonde Sweetheart of Gangster.' They eat it up."

An automobile, armed with three machine guns, drove up and three weary detectives got out. They reported ill luck in the chase after the holdup gang.

"But," said the Lieutenant, after nodding dismissal to them, "you ought not spend your time in Chicago on crime. Everybody's sick of hearing about that. Why don't you write something about all the parks we've got, and the way the kids can go out and play in the woods? I had my kids out there last Sunday. . . ."

He launched into the marvels of Chicago, and we left him. The reporter said that we would go now to see Romano. "Paul is sort of hiding out," he said. "One of his crowd killed a man four or five days ago down in Gary."

We rode endlessly through the streets, and walked up two flights of steps in a small apartment house, and a dark girl in a blue dress opened the door for us. Paul was glad to see his friend the reporter. He sat in a blue plush armchair in a small living room that was crowded with furniture. There was a huge colored photograph of Paul over the buffet and a very expensive radio was going softly. Paul was about twenty-five, thin and dark, with hands full of nervous vitality.

"New York, eh?" he asked. "Well, I was in New York once. That is a tame town." He poured three drinks in absurd Czecho-Slovakian goblets, and we drank to each other's health.

I said, "Tell me, Paul—how does it feel to kill a man?"

He looked up with a gleam in his eye and began a slow gesture, as if he were going into some elaborate explanation. But then he stopped, with a quick glance at the girl who sat quietly in the corner and laughed. "No—no," he said. "I would not know about that." He laughed again, and the reporter and I laughed heartily with him.

We sat for a long time. Very little of the talk was about gangs and the rackets, and most of it was about the women he had known. Occasionally, when he grew exceptionally tender at some memory, the girl would move her hands a little in her lap and drop her gaze. She never spoke.

It was tame. Paul was tame. He wanted to talk about night clubs, and that was boring, but he talked about them nevertheless. "You know," he said, "New York night clubs haven't got the class. Chicago, now, they have the class." He wanted to show me places that were better and bigger than anything anywhere in the world, but before we could make a definite engagement the telephone rang.

Paul answered it, and exclaimed sharply, and told us he would have to go. He hurried down the steps without saying goodbye to us or to the girl, and we heard his car start off very rapidly.

"He's scared," the reporter said on the way down. "These fellows stay scared most of the time."

The visitor to Chicago has an acute consciousness of men like Paul Romano moving beneath the surface of the city's life—and women like Maria. In the valley, which is a wide and shallow depression falling away from the very middle of the city, there are hordes of people and long streets of mean houses. The visitor is aware of swirling human conflicts going on in the valley, of harsh scrambling for a crumb of the city's wealth, and a muted hubbub of devious schemes in the shadows of the finest skyscrapers in the world. But this does not impinge very much upon the thoughts of the honest citizens. They are all working too furiously.

A CITY OF URGENCY AND OF FURIOUS ENDEAVOR

The whole of Chicago seems organized for toil, a breathless outpouring of energy with all goals obscured in the clamor of labor for its own sake. The noise of the hive is in the air. In the World's Largest Dance Hall, two thousand couples keep time to continuous music with a fierce concentration, and in the slaughter houses the faces of the pig-stickers make a study in absorption. The quarter million of Negroes huddled in South Chicago have shaken off their Southern carelessness. You hear little laughter from them, and they have caught the hurrying stride. To where? They do not know.

Amid such preoccupation with immediate tasks there is little wonder that government is ignored, that the drones of the hive likewise are ignored and left to work out their own unhappy destinies.

Even in such a place, for example, as the Institute of Fine Arts there is the same hypnotic concentration upon the job at hand. It is a most excellent institution and boasts more students than any place of its sort in the world. From the remote farms of the Middle West, from the factories and from the stockyards, the youth that is touched with a gleam of talent comes to learn. A young instructor, who was born in a tiny house far down the Mississippi, led me into one of his classes where a hundred young men and women were working from a nude. Every one of the hundred was going fiercely at his work, handling brush and pencil with a terrible haste, as if life itself depended upon what happened in the next ten minutes.

The instructor said: "About half of them are here because it is the fashionable thing to do, but they work just as hard as the rest. Of the others, the majority are studying to be commercial artists. But there are quite a few who are going in for fine art. They have plenty of talent. They have tremendous ambition. It's almost certain that two or three will be good artists.

"But," he said, "the most interesting thing to me is the changing attitude of the people toward talent in the family. A few years ago the boy in this part of the world who liked to paint or draw was a sissy. There was something wrong with him, and he had to make his little pictures on the sly. The notion of spending money to develop his gift was just ridiculous. But nowadays we have the most unexpected people in the world bringing their youngsters to us and telling us to make artists out of them—and in a hurry. They're always in a hurry."

I watched the pencils and the brushes flying, and I could believe that.

This same urgency, this same acute devotion to the job in hand, is instantly noticeable in the colleges also. The University of Chicago is quite an impressive place. In the thirty years of its existence it has grown to be an important institution of learning. The standards of scholarship are very high, and it is one of the few universities in the nation that maintains an almost complete indifference toward the absurd glamour of athletic prestige. But still there is no faint suggestion of quiet in its precincts, of studious retirement in contemplation of the world's learning.

A professor told me: "The men who study here are not interested in the amenities of the life that lies ahead of them. They

have no concern with understanding the rich variety and resource of the human spirit. There goes a boy who majors in economics. Very well. He simply wants to know all the economics
there is to know, in the shortest possible time. He is in a rush to
learn the things that are written in the books, and to leave here,
and to apply that learning to the next specific job he has to
tackle. Heaven help him on the day he sits back and begins to
wonder what he has been working for."

Such a one I did encounter a few evenings later—a man who
had worked with uninquiring fury for the best part of a lifetime
and had just begun to wonder why. We sat, at first, in the parlor of the small suburban house that he rented. Then a tall
young fellow called to see the daughter of my acquaintance, and
we moved upstairs to leave them alone.

I already knew something about the man: Forty-five or
thereabouts. Graduate of an obscure college. Mechanical
draftsman in the employ of one big firm for the past twenty
years. A pleasant wife, devoted and marvelously thrifty. A son
working his way through some technical school. This pretty
daughter downstairs, who was in love.

He was terribly anxious to talk—to almost anybody—in the
hope of clarifying his own confused thoughts. He was worried.
Not about his job, because he knew he had that forever, but
about the disposal of the rest of his life.

"I was ambitious when I came out and got married," he
said. "I had it all planned to be president of the company some
day. But now I know I never will be. I've worked for years
with a lot of vague plans in my head for the future—dreaming
about the time when my ship would come in and all these little
problems of dimes and dollars automatically solved. And now
I've begun to realize that the ship just isn't coming in at all. I'm
a mechanical draftsman, and not a very exceptional one at that.

"Now here's what I'm wondering. Do I want to plug out the
rest of my life earning that two-fifty a month and trying to make
it seem more? Do I want to chuck all those day dreams, and admit I'm just what I am, and give up the ambitions—just plod it
out to the finish? Or do I want to do something about it?

"There is something I can do. I came off a farm down state to begin with. And there are still sixty or seventy acres lying around that belong to me. Why not pull out, and go back there, and raise enough to keep myself comfortable? Quit plugging, day in and day out, at a job that doesn't satisfy me, and just get out on the land again?"

He puffed at his cigar and fell into a brown study. When he moved again, it was to make a gesture in the direction of the parlor downstairs. "I'm hopeful of that," he said. "He seems a nice kind of boy, and his prospects are good enough. If he likes the girl well enough to marry her, I won't have that to worry about any more. I'll be pretty free again—more free than I've been since the day that son of mine was born.

"I've been struggling so long," he went on after a moment, "that I hardly remember what I was struggling for. Wealth? I'm not so sure. Just success, I suppose, and I never stopped to think what I meant by success. I've worked so steadily that I can't sit down at night any more and read a book. Forgotten how to do that sort of thing. Maybe it would be nice to sit on that patch of ground and get to living again—just quietly and peacefully—and quit bothering about dollars, about the raise in pay I ought to have."

I told him that this seemed an extraordinarily sensible idea. He knew that the work on a farm would be hard, but he was sure it would have a lift to it, and a satisfaction that the drudgery at the office did not provide. He became quite enthusiastic in his contained way, pointing out things he could do: the little crops he would raise, and the chickens, and a cow or two. But then, toward the last, he shook his head.

"You can't just go away from Chicago," he said a little mournfully. "We've been excited over Chicago for so long, my wife and I, that we'd feel lost without it. We've talked so much about the growth, and the crowds, and the future of the city. It's part of us. I'm so used to going down town in the rush, and talking big plans at the office—new buildings and new machines and important developments. I would miss it, and get lonely. And I've forgotten how to amuse myself when I'm lonely."

He was interrupted by a burst of laughter from the parlor downstairs, laughter that was full of gayety and a fine confidence.

"I guess," he said, "I'll have to get mine out of watching this new generation come along—what they do with the city and with their lives."

So much for the millions: those ambitious ones caught in the ecstasy of struggle, pounding their way toward a career—the first career that occurs to them.

I went also to the country house of an old Chicago family. It was on the shore of Lake Geneva, and it was a fine, unpretentious house set in grounds that were quietly beautiful. A considerable number of guests were there, and they were quite thoroughly civilized people by any standard that you might call up. They were filled, all of them, with an intense belief in Chicago as the germinating point for a culture that will be genuinely American. They think of Chicago as the seat of a nationalism that will engage itself with the embellishment of existence: the creation of art and literature and music that will give to American life a coherent identity and a distinction.

This was not simply a matter of enthusiastic theory with them. Among them were two women who had written novels of the first quality—the wives of rich men they were, the conductor of a symphony orchestra, and a native sculptor. Also, they were able to produce a fresh example to support their feeling. He was a young composer and he was quite honestly of the people. His father held some little city job and his mother was a seamstress, but Chicago, in some fashion, had nourished his gift for music.

He had brought his opera with him. It was a new opera and it sounded very good as two or three of them sketched it out on the piano. It was very pleasant to see all of these people listening so seriously and full of such a fine faith that the ennobling arts are beginning to flower among them.

An elderly man—he had made a great deal of money out of leather—began murmuring to me:

"That is interesting, but to me the writing of things, the creation of them, is not the most important. Let me tell you. . . .

"These people in this part of the world have been living in the factory districts and on the farms—they have been working in the shops and offices, planning to get rich and buy all the things they need to make them happy. That was all they thought about: get rich and buy those lovely things. Now it is beginning to dawn on them that they might never get rich after all. They will never be able to buy the things—which would not make them happy anyway, of course. So they might begin to think.

"I believe they will. They might even begin to see that the things to make a man happy don't cost very much money. Such things just have to be learned, not bought. That pictures are good to look at and music is good to hear and books are good to read.

"These people around here will be the first to learn. They have the vitality. Do you see? Their sons are already painting the pictures and making the music and the books. The creative instinct always comes first—out of the ground, out of nowhere. Then comes the art of enjoyment. It is a more difficult thing to learn, and so it comes more slowly. Just now, it is having its struggle with the cheap things—cheap movies and cheap literature and cheap music. But they will learn better, and learn quickly."

But here is the odd thing. Presently this man got hastily to his feet and looked at his watch. Others, too, were looking at their watches, and there was a great hurrying to leave. Everybody had to go somewhere and get to work. Not bread-and-butter work, mind you, for all of these people were distinguished for their possession of great fortunes. They had to get away to committees and planning boards. The women too— both of the women novelists had half a dozen enterprises besides the writing of novels and the management of their households.

I made the natural inquiries and discovered that there is no genuine leisure class in Chicago. Work has become so habitual to them that even with wealth won they have to keep on working—and they keep their sons and daughters working too. The men busy themselves with speeches and the rebuilding of Chicago and the new World's Fair that is coming and the making of more money. The women tend the poor and search out talent that should be encouraged and run baby clinics—all with a furious energy.

From the meanest to the highest in Chicago there is no repose. And I think it is the spot on which they live, the enormous excitement of the city itself that makes this true. Millions have gathered there. They have already made Chicago the capital of the Iron Empire and a dozen other empires besides. They are intoxicated with the rush of their growth. They are determined to make of Chicago the world's largest city, the world's most beautiful city, the world's richest city, the world's most cultured city. There is not much doubt that it will dominate the stream of American civilization. But the high pitch of its vitality, the unchanging tension of its thrust, will remain a little exhausting to the visitor from less favored regions.

LIST OF TRAVELERS' ACCOUNTS

AMPÈRE, J. J. *Promenade en Amérique: États-Unis, Cuba, Mexique.* 2 vols. Paris: Michel Lévy Frères, 1860. Translated by Irene Bassett.

ANONYMOUS. "A Visit to the States," Article XXIX, *Times* (London), October 21, 1887.

ANONYMOUS. "A Visit to the States," Article XXX, *Times* (London), October 24, 1887.

ANONYMOUS. "Chicago in 1856," *Putnam's Monthly Magazine,* VII (June, 1856), 606–13.

ARCHER, WILLIAM. *America To-Day.* London: William Heinemann, 1900.

[BISHOP, ISABELLA LUCY (BIRD)]. *The Englishwoman in America.* London: John Murray, 1856.

BORDEN, MARY. "Chicago Revisited," *Harpers Magazine,* CLXII (April, 1931), 541–47.

BOURGET, PAUL. *Outre-Mer Impressions of America.* New York: Charles Scribner's Sons, 1894.

BREMER, FREDRIKA. *The Homes of the New World.* 2 vols. New York: Harper & Bros., 1853.

BRUWAERT, M. E. "Chicago et l'Exposition Universelle Colombienne," *Le tour du monde,* LXV (1893), 291–304. Translated by Irene Bassett.

BUCKINGHAM, J. S. *The Eastern and Western States of America.* 3 vols. London: Fisher, Son, & Co., [n.d.].

BUTLER, CHARLES. To Chicago Historical Society, December 17, 1881. *Autograph Letters,* Vol. XXXI, Chicago Historical Society, Chicago.

CHESTERTON, G. K. "Mr. Chesterton Looks Us Over," *New York Times Magazine,* February 1, 1931, pp. 1–2, 20.

[COLLIER, PRICE]. *America and the Americans from a French Point of View.* 8th ed.; New York: Charles Scribner's Sons, 1897.

FERGUSON, WILLIAM. *America by River and Rail.* London: James Nisbet & Co., 1856.

FRANK, WALDO. *Our America.* New York: Liveright, Inc., 1919.

FREAR, ALEXANDER. "Chicago. The Full Story of the Great Fire. Narrative of an Eye Witness," *New York World,* October 15, 1871.

FULLER, S. M. *Summer on the Lakes in 1843.* New York: Charles C. Little & James Brown, 1844.

GEORGE, W. L. *Hail Columbia!* London: Chapman & Hall, Ltd., 1923.

GIACOSA, GUISEPPE. "Chicago and Her Italian Colony," *Nuova Antologia,* CXXVIII (March, 1893), 15–33.

HARDY, LADY DUFFUS. *Through Cities and Prairie Lands.* New York: R. Worthington, 1881.

HOFFMAN, CHARLES FENNO. *A Winter in the Far West.* 1st ed.; 2 vols. London: Richard Bentley, 1835.

HUNGERFORD, EDWARD. *The Personality of American Cities.* New York: McBride, Nast & Co., 1913.

JEVNE, CHRISTIAN H. "An Immigrant in Chicago, 1864," The Norwegian-American Historical Association, *Studies and Records* (Northfield, 1928), III, 67–72. Translated by Brynjolf J. Hovde.

KEATING, WILLIAM H. *Narrative of an Expedition to the Source of St. Peter's River.* 2 vols. London: George B. Whittaker, 1825.

KIPLING, RUDYARD. *From Sea to Sea: Letters of Travel,* Part II. New York: Charles Scribner's Sons, 1906.

LATROBE, CHARLES JOSEPH. *The Rambler in North America.* 2d ed.; 2 vols. London: R. B. Seeley & W. Burnside, 1836.

LENG, JOHN. *America in 1876.* Dundee: Dundee Advertiser Office, 1877.

MARKEY, MORRIS. "Land of the Pilgrims' Pride, The Urgent City," *McCall's,* LIX (March, 1932), 12–13, 56, 62, 67.

MARQUETTE, FATHER JACQUES. In REUBEN GOLD THWAITES (ed.), *The Jesuit Relations and Allied Documents,* LIX, 173–83. 73 vols. Cleveland: Burrows Bros. Co., 1896–1901.

MARTINEAU, HARRIET. *Society in America.* 3 vols. London: Saunders & Otley, 1837.

MUIRHEAD, JAMES FULLARTON. *America, the Land of Contrasts.* 3d ed.; New York: John Lane Co., 1898.

PECKHAM, E. L. "My Journey Out West," *Journal of American History,* XVII (3d quarter, No. 3, 1923), 225–35.

PEYTON, JOHN LEWIS. *Over the Alleghanies and across the Prairies: Personal Recollections of the Far West One and Twenty Years Ago* [1848]. 2d ed.; London: Simpkin, Marshall & Co., 1870.

RALPH, JULIAN. *Our Great West.* New York: Harper & Bros., 1893.

ROUSIERS, PAUL DE. *American Life.* Paris: Firmin-Didot & Co., 1892. Translated by A. J. Herbertson.

RUSSELL, WILLIAM HOWARD. *My Diary North and South.* Boston: T. O. H. P. Burnham, 1863.

ST. COSME, JOHN FRANCIS BUISSON DE. In JOHN GILMARY SHEA (ed.), *Early Voyages up and down the Mississippi by Cavelier, St. Cosme, Le Sueur, Gravier, and Guignas.* Albany: Joel Munsell, 1861.

SHIPLEY, ARTHUR EVERETT. *The Voyage of a Vice-Chancellor.* Cambridge: University Press, 1919.

SHIRREFF, PATRICK. *A Tour through North America; Together with a Comprehensive View of the Canadas and United States as Adapted for Agricultural Emigration.* Edinburgh: Oliver & Boyd, 1835.

SPENDER, HAROLD. *A Briton in America.* London: William Heinemann, 1921.

STEAD, WILLIAM T. "My First Visit to America," *Review of Reviews* (English ed.), IX (January–June, 1894), 410–17.

STEEVENS, G. W. *The Land of the Dollar.* New York: Dodd, Mead & Co., 1897.

STORROW, SAMUEL A. "The North-West in 1817," in Wisconsin State Historical Society, *Collections,* VI (1869–72), 154–87.

STREET, JULIAN. *Abroad at Home.* New York: Century Co., 1914.

TIPTON, JOHN. Journal in MS, Tipton Collection, Indiana State Library, Indianapolis.

VAYA, PETER, COUNT VAY DE VAYA AND LUSKOD, Apostolic Proto Notary. *The Inner Life of the United States.* London: John Murray, 1908.

VEDANT, MULJI DEVJI. "A Brahmin's Impressions at the Chicago World's Fair," *Littell's Living Age*, CC (February 17, 1894), 435–41.

WAKEFIELD, SIR CHARLES CHEERS. *America To-day and To-morrow.* London: Hodder & Stoughton, 1924.

ZINCKE, F. BARHAM. *Last Winter in the United States.* London: John Murray, 1868.

MISCELLANEOUS CITATIONS

ANDREAS, A. T. *History of Chicago.* 3 vols. Chicago: A. T. Andreas Co., 1886.

ARMSTRONG, MOSES K. *The Early Empire Builders of the Great West.* St. Paul: E. W. Porter, 1901.

BEECHER, HENRY WARD. *Eyes and Ears.* Boston: Ticknor & Fields, 1862.

BRITISH PUBLIC RECORD OFFICE. *Calendar of State Papers, America and West Indies, 1700.* London, 1910.

CAMPBELL, MRS. PATRICK. *My Life and Some Letters.* London: Hutchinson & Co., 1922.

CANBY, NOBLE. "Some Characteristics of Chicago," *Chautauquan,* XV (August, 1892), 610–17.

Chicago Daily Tribune, January 1, 1863.

Chicago Record, October 7, 1893.

COX, ISAAC JOSLIN (ed.). *The Journeys of Réné Robert Cavelier Sieur de La Salle as Related by His Faithful Lieutenant, Henri de Tonty* . . . . ("The Trail Makers," JOHN BACH MACMASTER, consulting ed.). 2 vols. New York: A. S. Barnes & Co., 1905.

CURTISS, DANIEL S. *Western Portraiture and Emigrant's Guide.* New York: J. H. Colton, 1852.

DICEY, EDWARD. *Six Months in the Federal States.* 2 vols. London: Macmillan Co., 1863.

Documents Relative to the Colonial History of the State of New York Procured in Holland, England and France, Vol. IX. E. B. O'CALLAGHAN, ed., and JOHN ROMEYN BRODHEAD, agent. Albany: Weed, Parsons & Co., 1855.

DUFFUS, R. L. "Chicago: City of Superlatives," *New York Times Magazine,* February 23, 1930, pp. 1–2, 18.

FAITHFULL, EMILY. *Three Visits to America.* Edinburgh: David Douglas, 1884.

FONDA, JOHN H. "Early Reminiscences of Wisconsin," Wisconsin State Historical Society, *Collections,* V (1867–69), 216–17.

FOSTER, LILLIAN. *Way-Side Glimpses.* New York: Rudd & Carleton, 1860.

GARRAGHAN, GILBERT G., S.J. *The Catholic Church in Chicago, 1673–1871.* Chicago: Loyola University Press, 1921.

GIBBS, PHILIP. *People of Destiny; Americans as I Saw Them at Home and Abroad.* New York: Harper & Bros., 1920.

GUNTHER, JOHN. "The High Cost of Hoodlums," *Harpers Magazine,* CLIX (October, 1929), 530–40.

HARDY, ARTHUR SHERBURNE. "Last Impressions," *Cosmopolitan,* XVI (December, 1893), 195–200.

HARRISON, FREDERIC. *Memories and Thoughts.* New York: Macmillan Co., 1906.

521

HUBBARD, GURDON SALTONSTALL. *The Autobiography of Gurdon Saltonstall Hubbard*. Chicago: Lakeside Press, 1911.

HYDE, JAMES NEVINS. *Early Medical Chicago* ("Fergus Historical Series," No. 11). Chicago: Fergus Printing Co., 1879.

KELLOGG, LOUISE PHELPS (ed.). *Early Narratives of the Northwest*. New York: Charles Scribner's Sons, 1917.

KELLOGG, LOUISE PHELPS. *The French Régime in Wisconsin and the Northwest*. Madison: State Historical Society of Wisconsin, 1925.

[KIRKLAND, MRS. C. M.]. "Illinois in Spring-time: With a Look at Chicago," *Atlantic Monthly*, II (September, 1858), 486–88.

MASSIE, JAMES WILLIAM. *America: The Origin of Her Present Conflict, Her Prospect for the Slave, and Her Claim for Anti-Slavery Sympathy*. London: John Snow, 1864.

MASTERS, EDGAR LEE. "Chicago," in *Starved Rock*. New York: Macmillan Co., 1920, p. 49.

MERENESS, NEWTON D. (ed.). *Travels in the American Colonies*. New York: Macmillan Co., 1916.

MERRIAM, CHARLES E.; PARRATT, SPENCER D.; and LEPAWSKY, ALBERT. *The Government of the Metropolitan Region of Chicago*. Chicago: University of Chicago Press, 1932.

MERWIN, SAMUEL. "Chicago, The American Paradox," *Saturday Evening Post*, CCII (October 26, 1929), 8–10, 118–22.

O'RELL, MAX. *Jonathan and His Continent*. (*Rambles through American Society*). New York: Cassell & Co., 1889. Translated by Mme. Paul Blouët.

PARTON, JAMES. "Chicago," *Atlantic Monthly*, XIX (March, 1867), 325–45.

PETO, SIR MORTON, BART. *The Resources and Prospects of America Ascertained during a Visit to the States in the Autumn of 1865*. New York: Alexander Strahan, 1866.

PORTEOUS, ARCHIBALD. *A Scamper through Some Cities of America*. Glasgow: David Bryce & Son, 1890.

POST, LOUIS F. "John Peter Altgeld," *Public*, March 22, 1902.

QUAIFE, MILO M. *Chicago and the Old Northwest, 1673–1835*. Chicago: University of Chicago Press, 1913.

RAUMER, FRIEDRICH VON. *America and the American People*. New York: J. and H. G. Langley, 1846.

REYNOLDS, JOHN. *Sketches of the Country on the Northern Route from Belleville, Illinois to the City of New York, and Back by the Ohio Valley*. Belleville: J. A. Willis, 1854.

SCHOOLCRAFT, HENRY R. *Narrative Journal of Travels through the Northwestern Regions of the United States*. Albany: E. and E. Hosford, 1821.

SHEAHAN, J. W. "Chicago," *Scribner's Monthly*, X (September, 1875), 529–51.

STECK, FRANCIS BORGIA. *The Jolliet-Marquette Expedition, 1673* (The Catholic University of America, "Studies in American Church History," Vol. VI). Washington, D.C.: Catholic University of America, 1927.

STEVENS, WAYNE EDSON. *The Northwest Fur Trade, 1763–1800* (University of Illinois, "Studies in the Social Sciences," Vol. XIV, No. 3). Urbana: University of Illinois Press, 1928.

STIRLING, JAMES. *Letters from the Slave States*. London: John W. Barker & Son, 1857.

TROLLOPE, ANTHONY. *North America*. New York: Harper & Bros., 1862.

WEED, THURLOW. "Report of the River and Harbor Convention," *Albany Evening Journal*, July 14, 1847. Reprinted in ROBERT FERGUS (comp.), *Chicago River-and-Harbor Convention. An Account of Its Origin and Proceedings by William Mosley Hall, John Wentworth, Horace Greeley, Samuel Lisle Smith, Thurlow Weed* .... ("Fergus Historical Series," No. 18). Chicago: Fergus Printing Co., 1882, pp. 147–74.

WENTWORTH, JOHN. *Early Chicago—Fort Dearborn. An Address Delivered at the Unveiling of the Memorial Tablet To Mark the Site of the Block-House, on Saturday Afternoon, May 21st, 1881* .... ("Fergus Historical Series," No. 16). Chicago: Fergus Printing Co., 1881.

WISCONSIN STATE HISTORICAL SOCIETY. *Collections*. Madison, 1855—.

INDEX

INDEX

527

Jesuits: obtain Edict of 1696, 4; seek control of western country, 4

Jevne, Carl, 176

Jevne, Christian H.: biographical sketch, 176; impressions of, 176–81

Jevne, Hans, 176, 179

Jevne, Otto, 176, 178, 179

Jevne and Almini, fresco painters, 176, 179, 181

Jewett, Charles, succeeded by Alexander Wolcott, 29 (n. 4)

Jews, churches of, 378. *See also* Population

John Crerar Library, *see* Crerar Library, John

Jolliet, Louis, crosses Chicago Portage, 3

Jouett, Charles, *see* Jewett, Charles

Judd, N. B., 107

Judson, Dr. Harry Pratt, president of the University of Chicago, 462, 462 (n. 4)

Juneau, Solomon, trading post at Milwaukee, 7

Kaskaskia: location, 4 (n. 2); Marquette given cordial reception at, 4

Keating, Baron John, father of William H. Keating, 31

Keating, William H.: biographical sketch, 31; impressions of, 32–39

Keeling, Reverend R. J., 186

Kenna, Michael, 454

Kew Gardens, 225

Kimball, Dr., *see* Kimberly, Dr. E. S.

Kimberly, Dr. Edmund S., spoken of as Dr. Kimball, 43

Kinzie, Ellen Marion: first white child born in Chicago, 29 (n. 4); wife of Alexander Wolcott, 29 (n. 4)

Kinzie, James: biographical sketch, 44 (n. 13); builds Green Tree Tavern, 42; mentioned, 44

Kinzie, John: cabin found by G. S. Hubbard, 7; escapes to Detroit, 6; evacuation of Fort Dearborn and, 6; returns to Chicago after War of 1812, 6

Kinzie, John H.: biographical sketch, 44 (n. 13); illustrates Indian life, 85–86;

mentioned, 44, 47, 128; Miss Fourlegs and, 129

Kinzie, Mrs. John H., captivity of mother of, 128–29

Kinzie, Robert A.: biographical sketch, 44 (n. 13); illustrates Indian life, 85–86; mention of, 44; offers to sell land, 49

Kipling, Rudyard: biographical sketch, 250; impressions of, 250–61

Knights of Labor, 216

Knowles, Cloyes and Company, 176, 178

Kohlsaat's Restaurant, origin of quick-lunch, 453

Labor: Buckingham on, 89; De Vaya on, 417–18; Giacosa on, 283–84; Stead on, 360–62; Street on, 454–55; strikes, 215–16, 371–72, 417–18; at Union Stockyards, 454–55

Lake House: Buckingham on, 88, 89; used for religious services, 86

Lake Michigan: Ampère on, 135; Ferguson on, 149–50; Fuller on, 96–98; Giacosa on, 276; Leng on, 222; Marquette observes tides, 16; Steevens on, 396, 398; transportation on, 92–93; Zincke on, 182–83.

Lake Shore Drive, 425, 489

"Lakeside Musings," 453

Land: drainage of, 100, 107–9, 233; sale and speculation of, 10, 50–52, 66, 83–84, 92, 102–4, 153, 164–65, 167; school lands, 137. *See also* Real estate

Largilliers, Jacques, Jesuit *donné* of Marquette, 13, 14, 15

La Salle Hotel, 474

La Salle, Robert: crosses Chicago Portage, 3 (n. 1); makes Chicago a post in western trade, 4

La Toupine: biographical sketch, 14 (n. 3); notified of Marquette's presence at Chicago, 14

Latrobe, Charles Joseph: biographical sketch, 54–55; impressions of, 55–64

Law and Order League, 213

Lawson, Victor F., 475 (n. 2)

Lawyers, *see* Professions